The Cook's Bible

THE
Cook's Bible

THE BEST OF AMERICAN HOME COOKING

~

Christopher Kimball

LITTLE, BROWN AND COMPANY

New York   Boston   London

Little, Brown and Company
Hachette Book Group
1290 Avenue of the Americas, New York, NY 10104
littlebrown.com

Originally published in hardcover by Little, Brown and Company, October 1996
First Little, Brown paperback edition, May 2015

Little, Brown and Company is a division of Hachette Book Group, Inc. The Little, Brown name and logo are trademarks of Hachette Book Group, Inc.

The publisher is not responsible for websites (or their content) that are not owned by the publisher.

The Hachette Speakers Bureau provides a wide range of authors for speaking events. To find out more, go to hachettespeakersbureau.com or call (866) 376-6591.

Illustration on page 238 by Elaine Sears. Illustrations on pages 240–241 by Nenad Jakesevic. All other illustrations by Harry Davis.

The author is grateful for permission to include the following previously copyrighted material:
Recipe for Molasses Cookies reprinted by permission of Rosemarie Brophy.
Recipe for Spicy Buttermilk Fried Chicken from the East Coast Grill reprinted by permission of Chris Schlesinger and John Willoughby.
Recipe for Creamy Avocado Dressing with Tofu reprinted by permission of Laurel Vukovic.

Library of Congress Cataloging-in-Publication Data

Kimball, Christopher.
    The cook's bible : the best of American home cooking / Christopher
Kimball.
        p.   cm.
    Includes index.
    ISBN 978-0-316-49371-0 (hc) / 978-0-316-73570-4 (pb)
    1. Cookery.   I. Title.
TX651.K56   1996
641.5—dc20   95-48467

10 9 8 7 6 5 4 3 2

RRD-W

Printed in the United States of America

For Adrienne

*Good home cooking demands the hospitality
of a farmer, the curiosity of a scientist, the
affection of a mother, the hands of an artist,
and the enthusiasm of a child.*

Contents

~

Acknowledgments

~

First and foremost, this book would not have been possible without the tireless efforts of my wife, Adrienne, who spent countless hours over many years testing recipes and editing copy. She contributed not only her time and expertise but her affection and support. I also owe a great debt to my culinary mentor, Malvina Kinard, whose generous energy and enthusiasm for cooking and people have left me richer in both knowledge and friendship. Marion Cunningham, the quintessential American home cook and author of the revised *Fannie Farmer Cookbook,* has been an ardent supporter and comrade-in-arms when it comes to inspiring the rank and file of America's home kitchens. God bless her common sense and zeal.

I also owe a great debt to the folks at *Cook's Illustrated,* especially Pam Anderson, our food editor, who shares my passion for American home cooking. I am grateful for the advice and support of Mark Bittman, whose knowledge of book publishing and fish cookery has been invaluable; Doc Willoughby, along with his coauthor and friend Chris Schlesinger, for their help with the grilling chapter; Jack Bishop for his knowledge of kitchen equipment; and Adam Reid for researching cookware. Many thanks as well to Shirley Corriher, whose knowledge of food science is limitless; Gordon Hamersley, whose dexterity with a chef's knife is duly recorded in these pages; Jack Ubaldi, who taught me everything I know

about meat; Harold McGee, whose classic tome *On Food and Cooking* has been crucial to my understanding of food chemistry; Roger Berkowitz from Legal Sea Foods, who generously supplied oysters on 24 hours' notice; and Lonnie Van Wagner, owner of Lonnie's Meating Place in Manchester, Vermont, who taught me the ins and outs of ribs and shanks. Many test cooks were enlisted in this task along the way, including Anne Tuomey, Paula Boles, Ann Flanagan, Kris Ehrsam, Pat Henry, and Eva Katz. A special thanks to each of them, especially to Eva, whose contribution to these pages was substantial. Also a sincere thanks to friends and neighbors from Connecticut, Vermont, and Boston who cheerfully endured endless tastings.

I thank my agent, Angela Miller, not only for her superb skill at navigating the perilous waters of New York publishing but for her wit and good humor. My editor, Jennifer Josephy at Little, Brown, has been not only supportive but insightful and a most welcome partner on this project. Peggy Leith Anderson, my copy editor, did yeoman's work and significantly improved the manuscript. My illustrator, Harry Davis, worked tirelessly for most of one summer on the 200 illustrations herein, making sense of oyster shucking and chicken boning. A special thanks also to my photographer, Jim Thomas, who in just two days of work shot hundreds of step-by-step photos for Harry's reference.

I owe a great deal as well to James Beard,

who, but a casual acquaintance, gave of his time and wisdom in assisting me with the launch of *Cook's Magazine* nearly twenty years ago. When I asked him to define American cookery, he said, "It is what your neighbors are making for dinner." That is the essence of this book and my philosophy of food. Also many thanks to Julia Child, whose enthusiasm and support for any well-meaning culinary endeavor is legendary.

Finally, this book is in remembrance of Marie Briggs, the baker in our small Vermont town, who taught me that there is more to cooking than just food. Her tiny kitchen in the yellow farmhouse was a place of hard work, frugality, and most of all, fellowship and commitment to others. She is sorely missed.

Introduction

~

Home cooking and gourmet cooking have little in common. One is about family and neighborhood, the other is about dinner parties and international travel. One is about thrift, the other is about indulgence. One is a reflection of who we are as Americans, the other is about who we pretend to be.

While looking over my 1941 seventh edition of the *Boston Cooking School Cookbook,* it became clear to me that American cooking has been a bit of both. Macédoine of Vegetables à La Poulette makes an odd marriage with Cape Cod Blueberry Grunt. Perhaps Fannie Merritt Farmer, the book's author, and her readers counted on cooks and maids to help out in the kitchen, making more elaborate culinary adventures practical. In this day and age, however, most of us have more in common with early New England settlers than with a wealthy Boston family of the late 1890s in terms of support staff and disposable income. Americans exactly one century later (the first edition was published in 1896) need a practical guide to modern home cooking, which is perhaps a bit more sensible, less inclined to borrow wholesale from the French and English, and certainly more likely to present the full, natural flavors of ingredients, thereby producing a healthier cuisine. But this is no health cookbook. Flavor still reigns supreme in these pages, although wholesome foods properly prepared and consumed in moderation are certainly nourishing for both body and soul.

My own culinary education began in the late 1950s. I spent summers in a very small town (population 180) in southern Vermont, earning 75 cents an hour working for Junior Bentley, the local dairy farmer. I pitched hay, helped milk his small herd, and did odd jobs like birthing calves and mending electric fences. Every day at noon, the farmers gathered at the home of Marie Briggs, the town baker and cook, who set out an impressive spread of meat, gravy, potatoes, homemade biscuits, fresh milk from the barn, apple or lemon meringue pie, and the occasional vegetable. Marie could cook — she made the best anadama bread and molasses cookies I have ever eaten — but she hardly had a lick of cookware. She also didn't have running water — the sink featured a hand pump connected to a well — and a lot of the baking was done on an old soot-black woodstove.

For Marie, there wasn't anything fancy about home cooking. Nothing was for show and everything had a purpose. Farmhands had to be fed, bread had to be baked and sold, and food had to be put by for the winter. Today using locally grown food is a "trend," but for Marie this was merely being practical. The milk came from the Holstein out back, raspberries and blackberries were picked in July and August for cobblers, and the meat was raised in the upper pasture beyond the sugarhouse.

Midday dinners at that yellow farmhouse taught me something else about home cooking. When we cook, we bring family and friends together through hard work, planning, and sharing of our bounty. Home cooking is an intimate act, one that builds community when shared with those outside the family. It exemplifies the timeless Yankee traditions of thrift, sharing, humility, and generosity. Home cooking isn't just about the food, it's about the process. A homemade meal touches the spirit in a manner never equaled by a dinner at the best four-star restaurant.

My interest in cooking came to life in 1979, the year I founded *Cook's Magazine.* I was attending a small cooking school in Connecticut at the time, and I noted that the other students were more interested in learning the techniques of good cooking than in the specifics of individual recipes. With a strong conviction that other food publications were not addressing the why's and how's of home cooking, plus a business plan and a few intrepid investors, I launched the charter issue of *Cook's* in January 1980. During the next ten years, I founded the annual Who's Who of Cooking in America awards (now part of the James Beard awards), and the magazine grew to 225,000 circulation from a launch issue of only 25,000.

In 1990, a few months after I had left *Cook's Magazine,* it was sold to *Gourmet* magazine and ceased publication. Two years later, still convinced that home cooks wanted a magazine devoted to practical home cooking, I relaunched the magazine as *Cook's Illustrated,* with a policy of accepting no advertising. I wanted to focus on the kitchen, an impossible editorial mission when confronted with advertisers who were selling a lifestyle that had little to do with roasting chicken, making pot roast, or rolling out pie dough. This policy has also given us the freedom to review and rate cookware, foods, cookbooks, and wine without prejudice. Today, *Cook's Illustrated* has surpassed the circulation of the original *Cook's Magazine* and continues to grow rapidly. We receive more

than fifty letters per week from good home cooks around America who, like ourselves, find home cooking to be a great deal more than a hobby; it's an intimate part of our everyday lives.

This book is therefore a practical marriage of real home cooking with the culinary knowledge and skills necessary to produce honest, from-scratch food quickly and well. It takes the form of an investigation into the mysteries of how things work in the kitchen, with the twists and turns of any good detective story. This is not a collection of my favorite home-style recipes, it's a passionate pursuit of the best way to make a pot roast or the easiest, most dependable method of shucking an oyster. Almost nothing is taken for granted. Of course, the "best" way of doing anything includes elements of subjectivity, but the testing process is edifying and invigorating nonetheless. It also means that most of the recipes should be "pretty fair," the most sincere form of praise I have ever received from a Vermonter.

My wife, Adrienne, and I have three children: two daughters, Whitney and Caroline, and a son, Charles, born last year. We split our time between our farm in Vermont, in the same town I grew up in, and Boston, where *Cook's Illustrated* has its offices. The yellow farmhouse still stands near the town line, and as I drive by, my memory captures a scent of molasses and yeast, of warm baking powder biscuits and fresh, frothy milk, and the vision of Marie Briggs in her sensible square-heeled shoes, hair in a bun, with thick black-framed glasses, standing over the kitchen table, cutting out rounds of buttermilk spice doughnuts. I also remember the farmhands who developed a taste for burned cookies; the good specimens were always bagged and sold at the local country store.

Now that Marie is gone, I've taken up the baking. I make her spice doughnuts for coffee hour at the Methodist church, which stands by the cornfield on the banks of the

Green River. Most of all, Adrienne and I spend time cooking with the kids, giving them a good dose of rolling pie dough, kneading bread, and cutting cookies. We lure them with the magic of the kitchen in the hopes that they will take away with them memories of Dad's deep-dish apple pie and Mom's butter-dipped Parker House rolls. We are betting that the pies and rolls will stand the test of time because our family made them together.

Many years from now, we hope to have our grandchildren spend time at the farm, stirring batter for a lemon chiffon cake or clipping sprigs of basil just before the first frost. And after they've gone back home, we'll sit in front of the fire with memories of small voices ringing out, "Let me do it!" And we will realize, at last, that as we were giving our own children memories, they were giving us something more important: the gift of a home filled with many generations, warmed with the blessing of tiny hands sharing hard work and good food. It is to this shared vision that Adrienne and I dedicate this book.

Boston, 1996

The Cook's Bible

What You Need to Know About Kosher Salt

Most of the recipes in this cookbook call for kosher salt rather than regular table salt. I prefer kosher salt because I use a small box to hold salt for cooking, and kosher salt has large, fluffy grains that don't clump and are easy to pick up with the fingers. Another advantage of these large irregular grains is that they stick well to foods.

Anyone who has used kosher salt knows that it is less salty than table salt, not when compared by weight, but by volume. Two ounces of kosher salt measures ⅓ cup (a little over 5 tablespoons) in volume, whereas the same weight of table salt measures slightly over 3 tablespoons. (I weighed ⅓ cup of each and found that kosher salt weighed 2 ounces and table salt weighed 3.2 ounces.) The fine, miniature pellets of table salt fit together tightly, whereas the big, fluffy flakes of kosher salt leave lots of air spaces.

If you don't have kosher salt on hand, simply use table salt, BUT USE ABOUT ⅔ OF THE AMOUNT CALLED FOR IN THE RECIPE. (If the recipe lists 1 tablespoon of kosher salt — 3 teaspoons — simply use 2 teaspoons of table salt.) No matter which kind of salt you

Salt Box: Any small box will do nicely to hold kosher salt for cooking. Wooden boxes are often available at cookware stores, as are salt boxes decorated with Dutch designs. An antique store that carries kitchenware will almost always have a suitable container. (The box in the illustration is an antique from the 1930s.) A salt box is a must for every home cook because it makes salt readily accessible — a container of salt with a pour spout is difficult to work with.

use, I strongly recommend that you get into the habit of using a salt box. It is much easier to scoop a teaspoonful from a box of salt than to measure it from a pour spout.

~ 1 ~

What to Buy for the Kitchen

Are bread machines worth $250? Is a $20 Revere saucepan as good as the $80 All-Clad model? Here are some kitchen tests and shopping lists to help you decide.

~

A few well-worn tools in experienced hands are preferable to the latest electronic gadgets. I don't need an electric steamer when I can throw a steaming basket into any old pot; I don't bother getting out the food processor when I want to dice one onion or chop a couple of carrots. Yet I use an electric knife sharpener (I have never mastered the traditional whetstone method), I let my standing mixer knead all of my dough these days, and I've even fallen into the habit of mincing my garlic and ginger in a mini–food processor, the only two tasks it seems able to handle well (forget breadcrumbs, parsley, nuts, and onions). I even cook all of my rice in an electric cooker, my most-used and highest-rated kitchen appliance. And I sometimes use a fancy electric ice cream machine that replaced the old White Mountain freezer we used when I was a kid — I sort of miss the noise, the rock salt, and the ice cubes, but it's a lot easier to plug in the newer model and walk away.

Like most people, I have romantic notions about food. I like to think that most home cooks still knead bread dough by hand and chop onions with a battered chef's knife. The old Yankee in me believes that life shouldn't be too easy — real satisfaction comes only from accomplishing difficult tasks. But New Englanders are nothing if not practical, cobbling together whatever works best, regardless of whether it's new or old. Perhaps a bread machine or a pasta maker isn't all that out of place — Ben Franklin would have been proud to invent either of them — and they are gadgets that fit right in with hand-cranked corn strippers, early Rube Goldberg stationary hay balers, horse-powered oat threshers, and my favorite, dog-powered washing machines (power was supplied by a dog walking on a treadmill — you could tell it was wash day because dogs were scarce).

So, like everyone else's, my kitchen is a marriage of old and new, a functional mix of the latest gadgetry and primitive tools. I have tested most of the items discussed in this chapter in my own kitchen, using two rules of thumb: Is it worth the money, and is it better than whatever it replaced? The answers will depend on your pocketbook and your skill as a cook, but I hope that you will find my comments and test results useful when deciding what to buy and what to forgo.

A few notes about the testing. For the three most important kitchen utensils — knives, skillets, and saucepans — I tested a variety of brands in an effort to tell you exactly which manufacturer has the best product. For other categories, I have tested at least one model and have also provided a rundown of the available models with current prices.

MAJOR APPLIANCES: STOVES AND OVENS

GAS VERSUS ELECTRIC STOVETOPS

For stovetop cooking, gas is simply the better choice, even if you have to use bottled rather than natural gas (bottled gas doesn't burn as hot as natural gas). When immediate change of temperature is important, gas performs well, whereas electric is slow to adjust. Also review the BTU (British Thermal Unit) output of the burners. Stovetops with low outputs, under 10,000 BTUs (most consumer ranges run from 7,000 to 10,000), will do a poor job of keeping a sauté or stir-fry hot when a lot of food is added. However, Magic Chef makes a range with two 12,000-BTU burners and two 9,200-BTU burners. Also available are consumer models of professional gas stoves with burners that produce 15,000 BTUs each, although the restaurant models put out up to 40,000 BTUs.

Conventional wisdom says that an electric range boils water more quickly than a gas range does. I set out to test this and found it not to be true. Starting with 2 cups of water at 75°F, I discovered the following:

KITCHEN TEST	
Elapsed Time to Boil Water	
Gas Versus Electric Stove	
Gas stovetop	5 minutes, 40 seconds
Electric stovetop with cold coils	7 minutes, 45 seconds
Electric stovetop with hot coils	4 minutes, 30 seconds

Electric ranges may be better at maintaining a very low heat, although I find it difficult to maintain a consistent temperature with electric models.

If you do purchase a gas stovetop, there are two important optional features to consider: sealed burners and electronic controls. The former make it somewhat easier to keep the stovetop clean (the area under the gas burner is sealed, which prevents food from spilling through), and the latter are not much of a convenience — dial controls work just fine. The difference in price between a basic stove and one with both these features is about $200. I would buy the basic model.

GAS VERSUS ELECTRIC OVENS

Many cooks claim that electric ovens are better than gas ovens, as they maintain a steadier temperature and adjust more rapidly to changes of temperature (when you open the oven door, for example). However, I find gas ovens to be preferable. Exposed electric ovens generate very intense heat in the immediate vicinity of the heating elements; as a result, I find gas heat to be more even and more gentle. Also, if you like to fling ice cubes into your oven when baking bread (to create steam), this is not advisable with an electric oven because you could burn out the element.

Be sure that a new oven is properly calibrated. I once cooked a Christmas dinner in a new oven and found, when the buttermilk pie wasn't done after an hour of baking, that the setting was more than 75° off. Use an oven thermometer to check the settings.

SHOULD YOU PURCHASE A PROFESSIONAL STOVE?

Professional gas stoves, although they provide a lot of horsepower, are usually not worth the money (up to $5,800) for the home cook. Older models were poorly insulated and required additional insulation or space between the stove and cabinetry or walls. (This is not the case with the models listed in the table — the new models are designed for zero clearance.) The gas lines in the burners get clogged easily. Large griddles,

The models below are designed for zero clearance — they can be placed against walls or cabinetry. If a stove uses pilot lights instead of electronic ignition, ask how much gas it will consume per month. I find that grills and griddles are usually best purchased separately — the grills on these stoves are too small for most jobs and the griddles are less efficient and practical than an inexpensive electric model. Finally, look at the burner design. Some burners have an inner and outer ring for even heating or have a star-shape burner, which I think is an advantage. Models are listed in order of price. (Note: Model names, numbers, and prices are subject to constant change and are provided only as a basis for comparison.)

Maker and Model	Burner Design	Dimensions (Inches)	BTU Output	Features	Price
Viking VGSC305	Stainless; round	29⅞W 24¹⁵⁄₁₆D 35⅞–37⅞H	15,000 max.; 1,000 min.	Switchable convection/ conventional oven; infrared broiler; 4 burners, adjustable height; oven door window	$2,800
Fivestar TF280-W	Stainless; round	30W 24D 36H	14,000 max.; 400 min.	Convection oven; gas or electric broiler; 4 burners; oven door window	$2,500
Thermador CGRG304	Cast iron; sealed	29⅞W 26¹³⁄₁₆D 35½–37½ H	15,000 max.; 350 min.	Convection oven; infrared broiler; 4 burners; adjustable height; oven door window	$2,399
Dynasty DGR30-4	Stainless; round	30W 29½D 36H	15,000 max.; 1,000 min.	Conventional oven; infrared broiler; 4 burners	$2,150
Garland IR30	Cast iron; star shape	30W 29D 34½–36H	14,500 max.; 1,000 min.	Infrared broiler; 4 burners	$1,900

WHAT TO BUY: The only real reason to purchase a professional stove is BTUs — heat output. However, some home stoves also have respectable output, Magic Chef being one model, and at a fraction of the cost. If you can't live without a professional stove, I would go with a basic model and wait to find it on sale. After all, a stove is not rocket science, it's just a box that gets hot with a few burners on top. I have the Viking model listed above. For more information, call Garland at 717-636-1000 ext. 253; Fivestar at 800-251-7485; Viking at 601-455-1200; Thermador at 213-562-1133; and Dynasty at 213-728-5700.

a feature of many of these stoves, are impractical for home use — they take 10 minutes or so to heat up properly, expending a great deal of energy for a few eggs or pancakes. Besides, a good electric griddle does the job better (they heat more evenly than most gas griddles) and for a fraction of the price. Also, the pilot lights for restaurant-size burners throw off a good deal of heat, plus they burn a fair amount of gas (many newer models use electronic ignition rather than pilot lights). Although I have four- and six-burner stoves, I find that four burners is plenty.

That being said, the big advantage is that you get major-league horsepower with the burners, about 15,000 BTUs each. If you like to stir-fry or do a lot of very high-heat sautéing, this is important. A professional-quality gas stove will cost $2,200–$3,500 for a 30-inch stove and $4,600–$5,800 for a 36-inch model.

MICROWAVE OVENS

Do you want to spend $200 on an appliance that boils water, cooks bacon, and melts chocolate? Well, that's about the size of it. In Chapter 2, I outline the results of 30 kitchen tests to determine exactly what a microwave oven is good for. Here is a quick summary:

- The time savings are minimal. A few minutes one way or the other just don't make a whole lot of difference. I have also found that some of these "time-saving" recipes were actually more time-consuming. In *Bread in Half the Time,* authors Linda West Eckhardt and D. Butts suggest using the microwave to proof bread before baking. This did shorten rising time but resulted in a madcap series of carefully timed procedures that kept me busy for an hour.

- The microwave almost never does a better job than a conventional oven. I can steam vegetables, poach fruit, and cook fish just fine with a regular stove.

- Timing is critical. In conventional baking, for example, cooks go out of their way to extend the time window during which food is perfectly cooked. A custard sauce, for instance, is cooked at low temperatures in order to maximize the time during which it sets properly but does not curdle. The microwave, however, shortens cooking time and therefore food can become overcooked in seconds.

- Irregular foods are irregularly cooked. If you've ever tried to bake an odd-shaped potato or defrost a chicken in a microwave, you know what I mean. Many foods will cook at different rates depending on how many are cooked at the same time.

All of this leads to the conclusion that a conventional oven is easier, more forgiving,

and better at producing flavor. So why bother? Well, like an old-fashioned Yankee farmer, home cooks will find a use for just about anything, even if it is a use the inventor had not intended. And, it turns out, the microwave oven is very good at certain highly specific tasks, such as softening butter, melting chocolate, reheating leftovers, making polenta, and cooking bacon. If you feel compelled to own one, purchase a basic model and use it as a kitchen tool, not as a cooking device. Select a fairly small model (1 cubic foot is fine), forget the options, and go for price.

Price Ranges and Wattages for Microwave Ovens

In the last ten years, microwaves have become increasingly economical. Here is how the wattage and interior capacity of microwave ovens affect current pricing:

Interior Capacity	Power Range	Price Range
0.5–0.8 cubic feet	525–799 watts	$99–$169
0.9–1.2 cubic feet	800–899 watts	$179–$229
1.3–1.6 cubic feet	900–1100 watts	$229–$279

INDUCTION STOVETOPS

Many people feel that induction stovetops are the wave of the future because they are very safe and can deliver a lot of heat very quickly (they are not yet a major presence in the consumer market and therefore I have not listed models and prices). Here is how they work. The cooking surface of an induction stove is perfectly flat — no burners or heating elements. Underneath is a high-frequency electromagnetic wave inducer, which reacts with the magnetic material in your pan. The molecules in the pan are agitated, capturing energy from the magnetic waves. (If you take a piece of metal, stick two electrodes on either side, and then run a current through it, the metal will heat up — this is a similar effect.) This is a very safe method of cooking, since the stovetop itself

SHOPPING FOR MICROWAVE OVENS

Here's my survey of what's available in stores these days. Microwave ovens are kitchen tools rather than cooking devices, and therefore a purchasing decision may be based on price and appearance rather than features or power. Models are listed in order of price. (Note: Model names, numbers, and prices are subject to constant change and are provided only as a basis for comparison.)

Maker and Model	Power	Capacity (Cubic Feet)	Dimensions (Inches)	Features	Price
Sharp R4A95	900 watts	1.2	21 5/8W 17D 12 1/4H	Snack, breakfast, reheat, compuDefrost, compuCook settings; plus-1-minute key; child lock safety door; turntable; 4-stage cooking	$219
Tappan SMS107T1B1	1,000 watts	1.0	22 3/4W 13 1/8D 12 3/8H	10 power levels; auto defrost; plus-1-minute key; turntable; popcorn key; 6-stage memory; 4-stage cooking	$199
Whirlpool MG309OXAQ	850 watts	0.9	21 3/4W 15 3/4D 13 1/4H	3-in-1 cooking action; auto defrost; auto cook; 1,200-watt grilling element; plus-1-minute key; popcorn key; turntable; crispness settings	$199
Panasonic NN-6503A	900 watts	1.2	21 7/8W 16 3/4D 12H	5 power levels; auto defrost, reheat, and cooling; 3-stage memory; popcorn and potato keys; child lock safety door; Spanish/English/French display; turntable	$199
General Electric JES1224T	900 watts	1.2	21 3/4W 16 1/2D 12H	10 power levels; express cook, dual-time cook; auto defrost; auto reheat; popcorn key; turntable	$179
Sanyo EM804ET	900 watts	1.2	22W 18D 12 1/4H	3-stage programmable cooking; quick-set feature; hold/warm feature; auto reheat; auto defrost; vegetable and frozen dinner keys; child lock safety door; turntable	$169
Samsung MW6330T	900 watts	1.1	21 5/8W 16D 13 1/16H	Popcorn, potato, bacon, pizza, frozen dinner auto settings; auto defrost; auto reheat; plus-1-minute key; child lock safety door; turntable	$159
Goldstar MultiWave MA1172MW	1,000 watts	1.1	20 1/4W 15 1/4D 12H	10 power levels; popcorn, pizza, potato, vegetable, frozen dinner keys; auto defrost; auto reheat; child lock safety door; turntable	$159
Admiral 8571	900 watts	1.2	Not listed	10 power levels; automatic custom-cook calculates time and power for 5 frequently cooked foods; 10 cooking levels; custom defrost; popcorn, soup, beverage settings; turntable	$149

WHAT TO BUY: I purchased the Tappan, and at $199, it was a good buy. It's also large enough to handle an 8-cup glass bowl, which is the outer limit of required capacity.

gets warm but won't cause burns. If a pot overflows, the food simply spills onto an easy-to-clean surface. It is also extraordinarily cost-effective, running at an 80 percent efficiency rate, compared with 60 percent for electric and 35 percent for gas cooking. In a restaurant kitchen, this is a big plus. Boiling water for 20 pounds of pasta costs $3.30 with an induction unit, $6 with electric heat, and $11 with a gas stovetop. Although I am a primitive at heart and prefer to see flames licking at the bottom of my pan, this technology bears watching.

POTS AND PANS

Of all the cookware decisions, selecting just the right pots and pans is the most difficult. Although there are only three basic types of pots and pans — skillets, saucepans, and large pots — they come in a variety of mod-els and utilize many different materials, including copper, anodized aluminum, non-stick surfaces, stainless steel with a copper or aluminum core, porcelain over steel, and basic cast iron. To make matters more complicated, each manufacturer produces a very different product. Revere has a "copper" bottom that is nothing more than a paper-thin layer of copper over stainless steel, whereas a company such as Bourgeat makes a serious copper pot, one that is solid, thick, and will cost more than $200.

Which Is the Best Material for Pots and Pans?

Pots and pans need to conduct heat fast. You know what I mean if you have ever tried to sear meat for a stew or sauté chicken breasts in a poor-quality pan. As soon as the meat hits the hot metal, the pan loses heat and the meat stews rather than sautés. You also want

COOKWARE CHOICES: THE SEVEN BASIC TYPES AND THEIR USES		
Here is a summary of the basic cookware choices, including price ranges for a 10-inch skillet.		
Type	Comments	Price Range
Copper	Great conductor of heat; heavy-duty; very expensive; best for saucepans	$80–$250
Stainless steel shell with aluminum or copper core	The aluminum core is a good conductor, but steel is not; very durable but can be expensive	$40–$100
Anodized aluminum	Solid aluminum with an anodized surface that is hard and scratch-resistant; good conductor of heat; good for a Dutch oven	$40–$80
Nonstick	Top-of-the-line brands are excellent; a must buy for skillets; I recommend Calphalon or All-Clad	$25–$85
Enamel over steel	Porcelain enamel finish over carbon steel; not a great conductor of heat; food sticks easily; poor choice overall	$40–$80
Enameled cast iron	Good, even heating, but food easily sticks to the enameled surface; very heavy and therefore cumbersome	$30–$80
Cast iron	When properly seasoned, an inexpensive, heavy-duty choice; must be maintained properly	$10–$20

a pan that distributes heat evenly over the whole cooking surface; this means a nice thick bottom to a saucepan or skillet. Thin-gauge pans heat up quickly, but they heat very unevenly. To test the effects of pan gauge, I tried heating butter in two pans side by side. One was a heavy-gauge skillet and the other was a less-expensive, lighter model. The butter in the cheap skillet burned quickly, and the pan displayed an obvious hot spot in the middle. The expensive pan melted the butter without burning and without hot spots. Even for a simple recipe such as french toast, uniform cooking is crucial.

To solve the heat-transfer problem, you obviously need a material that is highly conductive. Copper is clearly the best choice in this category. Aluminum is next best, and stainless steel is dead last. That's why many stainless steel pans have an inner core of either copper or aluminum. But you also want some heft to a pot or pan, for uniform heat distribution. Go to the store, pick up several pots, and feel their weight. All things being equal, choose the heavier model. Thinner pans, by the way, can warp over time. The center of the bottom can become higher (and in some cases, lower) than the sides; this is disastrous, as oil or butter will run to the perimeter, leaving the center area high, dry, and hot, a perfect recipe for scorching your Wednesday-night chicken cutlets. I have this problem with two pans — one a stew pot and one a large Dutch oven — both manufactured by Commercial Aluminum Cookware. I called the customer service department and was told that this warping is due to drastic temperature changes. Her example was cooking pasta. If you empty the hot pasta water into the sink and then rinse the pot with cold water, the bottom may warp. I consider this to be a serious liability, as I frequently subject my cookware to this kind of dramatic temperature change.

That being said, you really have a handful

COOKING TIP

Seasoning Cast Iron Cookware

To season a cast iron skillet, most cookbooks instruct you to oil it and then bake at 350°F for 1 hour. This does not develop the type of deep nonstick finish you really need. The following technique is adapted from the one used by Barbara Tropp, who is an expert on wok cooking and author of *The China Moon Cookbook*. Place the skillet on top of the stove and turn heat to high. Tear off three wads of paper towels (two or three sheets each) and place near the stove with a bottle of vegetable oil. After about 5 minutes, when the skillet is very hot (the inside rim of the pan should also be really hot), drizzle about 2 tablespoons of oil on one of the wads and rub the inside of the skillet, including the sides. The oil will smoke. Use the second and third wads of paper towel to immediately wipe off any excess oil, pressing down hard to burnish the surface. Be careful—the pan will be *very* hot. It would be best to wear an oven mitt to do this. Remove pan from heat and let cool for 30 minutes. Repeat this three times. (It does not have to be done all on one day.)

After each use, immediately wipe the skillet clean with a soap-free sponge. Place back on the burner (which has been turned off) to dry while you eat. Repeat the initial seasoning process (giving the pan only one coating) after each use until the pan is thoroughly seasoned and has a deep, lustrous finish, usually a half-dozen or so times.

of basic choices. If you were born with a trust fund and you have a scullery maid to do the polishing, purchase copper. I have the same copper pans I bought in 1980. (I don't have a trust fund, but I do buy cookware at wholesale prices.) They are indestructible, react quickly to changes in temperature, and conduct heat evenly without hot spots. Their only drawbacks are that they need occasional cleaning and they are not nonstick. Copper also needs to be relined every several years, a drawback that I feel is marginal. (You should not cook in an unlined copper pot, because it reacts chemically with acids such as vinegar and wine, and copper itself is potentially toxic. This is why copper pots are lined with tin or silver.) The average home cook can go ten years or more without relining copper cookware. I have a 2-quart copper saucepan that has been in constant use for fifteen years and has yet to need relining.

For most home cooks, a solid copper pot is simply too expensive. Lucky for all of us, there are plenty of more reasonable alternatives. For less money you can buy heavy-duty stainless steel cookware with a core of copper or aluminum. I have a set of stainless steel Bourgeat pans from France that are in perfect shape after eight years of constant use. Many manufacturers use an outer shell of stainless steel because it is easy to clean and does not react with foods. However, stainless steel is a lousy conductor of heat, hence the internal sandwich of a superior conductor, either copper or aluminum, the latter being about half as good as the former.

A third choice, and a very popular one these days, is anodized aluminum cookware, which is made by Calphalon and All-Clad, among others. (Be sure not to purchase untreated aluminum pans. They can react to acidic foods — tomatoes, for example — discolor, and can affect flavor as well. Aluminum is also thought to be dangerous when ingested — there is some evidence to suggest that there may be a link between aluminum and Alzheimer's disease. One study of Alzheimer's patients showed an unusually high concentration of aluminum, although no link was established between cookware use and the disease.) Unlike the early Teflon cookware, these new brands don't apply a coating — the aluminum itself undergoes an electrochemical process that alters the surface of the pot or pan, creating a thick oxide film as an outer shell. This process, called anodization, involves dipping a metal in an electrolytic bath charged with an electric current. In the case of anodized cookware, the aluminum reacts with the acid and the molecular composition of the outer layer of the metal is changed. What most cooks don't realize is that this chemical process only penetrates to a depth of 25–30 microns (a micron is one-thousandth of a millimeter). This means that some aluminum will still leach out into the food and that there will still be some reaction with acidic foods, although at much smaller levels. (Don't store acidic foods in anodized cookware and don't run anodized cookware through a dishwasher.) The good news is that this process makes the aluminum harder than stainless steel. Note, however, that although the surface is smoother and harder it is not nonstick. Anodized aluminum cookware is often referred to as "low-stick" because it has better "release" characteristics than untreated aluminum pans — in other words, it has a smoother surface that food is less likely to stick to.

To produce a truly nonstick surface, cookware manufacturers use a substance called PTFE (a fluoropolymer), which is bonded to the aluminum through a series of applications. How and how much of this polymer is applied as well as the nature of the underlying pan determines the differences among nonstick pans. The only drawback with this type of surface is that its volatilization point (the temperature at which it changes into a cloud of noxious gas) is 250°C (around 480°F), which is possible to achieve on a home stovetop. Therefore, do not leave an empty nonstick pan over high heat for any length of time. I find that these pans are best for omelet and sauté pans and unnecessary for stockpots, Dutch ovens, or saucepans. Later in this chapter, I rate the different models of nonstick sauté pans I have tested.

Some manufacturers make carbon steel pans coated with porcelain enamel. I have tested these pans and find they have two drawbacks. First, steel is not an even conductor of heat nor is it as good a conductor as copper or aluminum. Second, the porcelain coating is as far from a nonstick surface as you can get. In my experience, porcelain is a far cry from the new anodized aluminum surfaces. If you have ever scorched a porcelain-

Nonstick Skillets

To test nonstick quality, 1 egg beaten with 1 teaspoon water was added to preheated pan, allowed to sit for 1 minute, then removed with a spatula. Pans are listed in order of preference based upon their performance as a nonstick cooking surface. Price ranges are for 10-inch skillets.

Brand	Comments	Price Range
Calphalon	Excellent performance; the clear winner. Egg did not stick and the texture of its bottom surface was natural and pleasing. Heavy, high-quality construction.	$58–$63
All-Clad	Egg did not stick, but its bottom texture was not quite as good as the one made in the Calphalon. The pan itself is not as heavy-duty as the Calphalon model and the cooking surface is a bit rougher — the Calphalon by comparison is very smooth.	$80–$84
Circulon	Bottom interior of pan has indented circular rings. Egg did not stick, although its bottom surface was shiny and unappetizing.	$57–$60
Farberware	Egg stuck to the pan and its bottom emerged with a shiny, vinyl-like sheen.	$72
Scanpan	The egg stuck to the pan; its bottom was very smooth and unappealing.	$50–$54

WHAT TO BUY: The All-Clad and the Calphalon are close, but the Calphalon wins out. The Calphalon is the heaviest pan of the lot and the nonstick surface is slightly better. I tried sautéing soft-shell crabs in both the Calphalon and Farberware pans and found that when using the same level of heat, the Farberware pan burned the butter quickly while the Calphalon model produced a nice, even heat without burning.

coated pan, you know what I mean. Cleaning it is like trying to get dried egg yolk off a dinner plate — it just won't budge. I'll take copper, stainless steel with an aluminum core, or anodized aluminum cookware any day over these models. I would consider them, however, for a covered baking dish, where a nonstick surface is not necessary and the weight is a plus, not a drawback.

Enameled cast iron pans have the same drawbacks as the carbon steel models, but since iron is a better conductor than steel, they provide a more even heating surface. The cast iron makes this type of cookware extremely heavy. This eliminates hot spots on the cooking surface, a possibility with lighter-gauge pans, but makes them a bit cumbersome to move around the kitchen.

The last and least expensive type of cookware you can purchase is cast iron. I love these pans because they are cheap and if well seasoned are good nonstick surfaces. They hold heat well and distribute it evenly. However, most home cooks have neither the knowledge nor the patience to maintain them properly. As a result, they are discarded in frustration. Keep in mind that an iron skillet weighs in at 4–5 pounds, which can be a drawback for some cooks. However, the price — try $10 for a 9-inch skillet — is very attractive.

SKILLETS

Skillets come in two basic shapes. One has straight sides and the other has sloping sides. After a lot of investigation and numerous phone calls, I have found that there is no consensus on nomenclature. That is, I had always thought that a skillet had straight sides and a sauté pan had sloping sides. Nope, it just ain't so — nobody agrees on which is which. So, for my purposes, they are both skillets.

Straight sides are best for pan-frying or any operation that requires liquids or large quantities. Sloping sides are best for sautéing because they allow the cook to slide a spatula into the pan under the food. You'll need to purchase two sizes: a 9- or 10-inch nonstick skillet is great for omelets, and a 12- or 14-inch skillet is a must for stir-fries, fried chicken, sauces, and larger sautés. The latter does not necessarily have to have a nonstick surface (if you like to stir-fry, however, this is a big plus), but it should be heavy and a good conductor of heat.

I carried out a quick test using five of the top-selling brands of nonstick sauté pans. I preheated each pan over medium heat for 2 minutes and then, using no fat whatsoever, poured 1 beaten egg mixed with ½ teaspoon of water into the pan. I let the egg sit for 1 minute and then used a spatula to test whether the egg had stuck to the cooking surface. The Kitchen Test chart on page 11 shows the results.

SAUCEPANS

These simple round pans with either straight or sloping sides come in many sizes, from 2 cups to 4 quarts. Purchase two saucepans: 2-quart and 3-quart capacity. The 1-quart size is optional. A pouring lip or rim adequate in size for the capacity of the saucepan is a plus. (Bourgeat makes pans with a curled lip around the perimeter, which makes pouring easier.) Also, look for pans that have stay-cool handles. Manufacturers use a poor heat conductor such as stainless steel or wood for the handle and/or make the handle hollow. It is a blessing

---

SHOPPING FOR STOCKPOTS

The prices below are for an 8-quart stockpot unless otherwise noted. Stockpots come in many different sizes, from 6 to 20 quarts. Prices may vary and are often discounted. I have added a price-per-pound column to give you some indication of value. Although stockpots are primarily for heating liquids, you might as well get the thickest-gauge pot for the money in the event you wish to use it for sautéing. (I sometimes use a stockpot for making large quantities of stew.) Models are listed in order of price.

Brand	Material	Weight	Price	Price per Pound
Bourgeat (12-quart)	Heavy-duty stainless steel	8 lb.	$156	$19.50
All-Clad LTD	Stainless steel with an aluminum core	5 lb.	$149	$29.80
Calphalon	Nonstick anodized aluminum	6 lb.	$120	$20
Le Creuset	Enameled steel	5 lb.	$75	$15
Reston-Lloyd (8½-quart)	Enameled steel	4 lb.	$43	$10.75
Progressive	Stainless steel	1½ lb.	$22	$14.67
General Housewares (7-quart)	Graniteware II, ceramic on steel	1 lb.	$12.50	$12.50

WHAT TO BUY: Stockpots are made to heat larger quantities of liquids and therefore construction and heat conductivity are not that important. On a cost-per-pound basis, the Reston-Lloyd is the best buy and it weighs a decent 4 pounds. Save your money for the skillet and saucepans.

Saucepans

Each pan was filled with 3 cups of water at 50°F and then brought to a full boil uncovered. The heat was turned off and then the temperature of the water was measured after 30 minutes to determine how well the pan retained heat. I also checked the handles at the point of boiling to see if an oven mitt would be required to move the pan. I also melted 1 tablespoon of butter in each pan and then added a heaping tablespoon of diced onion. A pan that burned the butter quickly on medium heat was listed as fast. A pan that took a long time to heat up was listed as slow. Note that prices fluctuate wildly, with pans usually selling at 10–30 percent below the manufacturer's suggested retail. The All-Clad Master Chef, for example, is listed by the manufacturer at $80, yet I found it at retail for $57. Models are listed in order of price. (Note: Model names and prices are subject to constant change and are provided only as a basis for comparison.)

Model: Description	Capacity	Weight	Temp. After 30 Minutes	Handle	Sauté Speed	Price
Revere: stainless steel, copper-coated bottom, plastic handle, stainless lid	2 quarts	1⅜ lb.	101°F	Cool	Very fast	$30
Calphalon stainless: aluminum core, rolled steel handle, glass lid	2½ quarts	2⅓ lb.	94°F	Hot	Fast	$52
All-Clad Master Chef: stainless steel, aluminum core, stainless handle, stainless lid	2 quarts	2⅓ lb.	106°F	Cool	Perfect	$57–$80
All-Clad LTD: stainless interior, aluminum core, anodized exterior, stainless handle, stainless lid	2 quarts	2¼ lb.	105°F	Cool	Perfect	$70–$105
Chantal: enamel-coated carbon steel, stainless handle, glass lid	2 quarts	2 lb.	108°F	Warm	Very fast	$80
Calphalon nonstick: solid aluminum, rolled steel handle, glass lid	2½ quarts	2¾ lb.	95°F	Hot	Slow	$86–$93
Le Creuset nonstick: cast aluminum, plastic handle, glass lid	2 quarts	1¾ lb.	100°F	Cool	Slow	$100
Le Creuset cast iron: enamel finish, wood handle, cast iron lid	2 quarts	4 lb.	100°F	Cool	Fast	$115
All-Clad Cop-R-Chef: stainless interior, aluminum core, copper exterior, stainless handle, copper/stainless lid	2 quarts	2⅓ lb.	105°F	Cool	Perfect	$154
Bourgeat Jacques Pepin series: stainless steel, aluminum core, stainless handle, stainless lid	1½ quarts	2 lb.	115°F	Hot	Perfect	$193–$248

WHAT TO BUY: If you are willing to spring for a serious saucepan, go for the All-Clad Master Chef saucepan. The handles are truly "stay-cool," the pot is heavy-duty, and all of the pots in the line are relatively small in diameter, which is good for maintaining heat. On sale at $57, it is a terrific bargain. I also recommend the Bourgeat and the Calphalon stainless with the aluminum core. I don't recommend a 2-quart saucepan that weighs under 2 pounds — you need the heft for a constant, even heat. Stay away from Revere and the Chantal line of cookware, as they are both poor for sautéing foods — they get very hot very quickly and do not maintain a nice steady heat. They would be fine, however, for heating liquids.

not to have to use a pot holder or oven mitt. In this regard, All-Clad was the clear winner. Their handles were literally cold after boiling 3 cups of cold water. The Calphalon handles, by contrast, were warm enough that you would want to use a pot holder.

LARGE POTS

First, you will need an 8- or 12-quart stockpot even if you never make stock. A large stockpot is essential for boiling pasta, making large quantities of soup, cooking lobsters, steaming shellfish, and so on. Second, you need a Dutch oven, which is a large (usually 4-quart) pot with handles and a lid. It looks like a short stockpot. It doubles as a skillet and is perfect for dishes that require both stovetop and oven cooking. I suggest purchasing a model 12 inches in diameter, as this will accommodate a whole cut-up chicken, 4 large chops, and other foods that often do not fit into a 10-inch model.

KNIVES

The choice of a knife is very personal and depends on the size of your hand, as handle designs vary tremendously. That being said, I always look for a heavy knife. Some 8-inch chef's knives weigh in at 10 ounces; others weigh only 6 ounces. That's quite a difference. By the way, a chef's knife is a chopping knife and has an indented handle so that your knuckles do not hit the work surface as you chop. I also prefer a 10-inch chef's knife to an 8-inch, although many professionals prefer the smaller knife. I find that the extra 2 inches gives me a lot more horsepower when chopping a pile of onions or cutting through potatoes or carrots. You are going to need a 3- or 4-inch paring knife (a 2½-inch model is also very useful), an 8- or 10-inch chef's knife, a 5- or 6-inch boning knife (this has a narrow blade for precision cutting of meat), and a serrated knife for bread, which should have a stiff blade for ease of cutting

crusty loaves. A long slicing knife is also handy for carving meat, although a chef's knife will do fine in a pinch.

In addition to choosing a style of knife, you must also consider the type of metal used for the blade. All knives are made of steel, which is a mixture of iron (about 80 percent) and other elements (20 percent). Carbon steel, which was invented thousands of years ago, has been the metal of choice for most kitchen knives until recently. It is easy to sharpen, but it corrodes easily and will stain quickly when in contact with acids such as citrus fruits. If chromium or nickel is added to iron, a stainless or high-carbon steel blade is created. Stainless steel looks great and is not subject to corrosion, but it is very hard (hardness is measured on the Rockwell scale — most chef's knives register around 55 on this scale and most sharpening steels about 65) and is therefore very difficult to sharpen at home. High-carbon steel is the best choice, because it is easy to sharpen and also more resistant to corrosion than a regular carbon steel blade. Superstainless alloy

---

SCIENCE OF COOKING

The Rockwell Scale

The Rockwell scale is a test for measuring the hardness of materials. There are two methods used: one uses a steel ball and the other uses a conical diamond with a spherical tip. The item to be tested, a knife in this case, is placed in a machine. Either the steel ball or diamond is forced into the test material and then the depth of the indent is measured. The deeper the indentation, the softer the material, and the *smaller* the number. If a steel ball is used, the scale runs from 0 to 130, the latter being the hardest. If the diamond is used, the scale runs from 0 to 100. The steel ball measurement is prefaced by the letter *B* (e.g., Rockwell B80), and the diamond system is prefaced by the letter *C* (e.g., Rockwell C80). A knife with a higher Rockwell number than another is therefore harder. Harder knives, such as stainless steel, keep their edge longer but are more difficult to sharpen.

8-Inch Chef's Knives

For this test, I chopped onions and carrots and also minced parsley. Although I tested 8-inch knives, I recommend that you purchase a 10-inch model — the larger blade facilitates chopping and cutting, especially when cutting up chicken or preparing large quantities of vegetables. Knives are listed in order of preference. All knives tested were high-carbon steel and had plastic handles without rivets.

Brand	Comments
Wusthof Grand Prix	A precision instrument with a well-designed handle (which is slightly textured for a good grip). The blade is curved at the tip, which is good for the rocking motion used in chopping large quantities. Using this knife is like driving a Mercedes. Weight: 10 ounces. $80.
Henckels	A very well-balanced knife although a bit of a lightweight at only 8 ounces compared with the Wusthof and Chef's Choice models. The Wusthof is clearly the superior knife, but I would purchase the Henckels over the Chef's Choice because the overall balance is better. Weight: 8 ounces. $85.
Chef's Choice	Very heavy blade, but I don't like the handle. It's too thin even for me, and I do not have large hands. The narrow handle feels unwieldy with such a solid blade (the handle is about 20 percent thinner than the Wusthof model's). However, high-quality construction throughout. If they changed the handle, I would give this knife top marks. Weight: 10 ounces. $85.
Commercial Sabatier	Very good knife, but the balance between handle and blade could be better. However, this is a serious and well-made knife. Weight: 8.5 ounces. $85.
Herschner Victorinox	Although the handle design is fine, this knife weighs only 7 ounces, well under the 10 ounces for the top-of-the-line knives. The handle feels a bit light in comparison to the blade. Weight: 7 ounces. $24.
Bio Curve	This contender is a bantamweight at only 6 ounces. Not a bad design, but not a serious knife. Weight: 6 ounces. $20.

WHAT TO BUY: The Wusthof Grand Prix is a clear winner, weighing in at 10 ounces, with great balance and a great handle. The Henckels is also top quality but is a bit of a lightweight at 8 ounces. The Chef's Choice is an excellent knife, but I found the handle to be a bit narrow in comparison to the heavy-duty blade. Be sure to heft any knife before purchasing it—every hand and every cook is different. It's tempting to spend only $20 on a chef's knife, but over the years, the investment in a top-of-the-line knife is worth every penny.

steel produces a beautiful knife blade, but this alloy is so hard that a home cook will never be able to sharpen it.

There is a lot of controversy among knife manufacturers regarding construction techniques. Most would say that a forged blade — the knife is made from one piece of steel that is heated and then shaped with a mechanical hammer — is better than knives made from sheets of steel that are stamped into knives, the theory being that stamped knives are thinner than their forged cousins. Most knife experts would also claim that a full tang — the tang is the part of the blade that extends into the handle — is important for control and balance. However, some well-respected knife manufacturers, Henckels, for example, make the blade, the bolster (the part of the knife between the handle and the blade), and the tang out of different types of steel and then weld them together, the argument being that each piece benefits from a different metal. My conclusion is that this is a theoretical argument among competing manufacturers, with little relevance to the home cook. A knife should be solid, heavy, and well balanced, and should have a handle that suits your hand, full tang or not.

Chefs and manufacturers also argue about what material is best for the handle — wood or molded plastic. I tend to prefer the plastic because it makes for a firmer, more certain grip. However, this is not a make-or-break issue. Others fight about whether the handle should be riveted to the tang. Experts prefer rivets, but this is, in my opinion, merely splitting hairs. To help sort out which knife to buy, I tested six different chef's knives to give you my comments (see page 15), which should be a good starting point for your own shopping trip. Keep in mind that everyone has a different grip, and what feels right in my hand may feel uncomfortable in yours.

CUTTING BOARDS

You also need to consider the cutting surface. For years, everyone in the culinary world thought that wood cutting boards easily harbored germs whereas plastic cutting boards were safer. However, a study at the University of Wisconsin disputed that result, finding that bacteria are more likely to survive on plastic than on wood. In either case, be sure to wash thoroughly any board you use

immediately after cutting meat or fish, and wash all your boards in an occasional weak solution of bleach to kill bacteria (salt and vinegar also work well). I use plastic because wood does not stand up to hot water over a long period of time, plastic cutting boards are usually thinner and easier to store, and finally, bleaching wood cutting boards makes them very unattractive over time.

ELECTRIC KNIFE SHARPENERS

You have four choices when it comes to sharpening knives. The classic choice is a traditional whetstone or a diamond-impregnated stone — the surface looks like a honeycomb. I tried both of these for years and could never get the hang of it. The knife must be held at exactly the right angle to the surface, you need to move the blade across and down the surface of the stone simultaneously, and you need to be patient. Graduates of the Culinary Institute of America master it, but for years I had a large inventory of semisharp knives. About ten years ago, the Chef's Choice knife sharpener was invented; this is your second — and in my opinion, best — choice. It is an electric sharpener that uses magnets to hold the blade at the proper angle as you draw it through the grinding

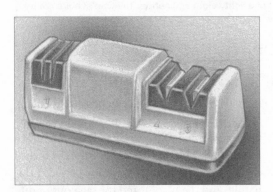

Electric Knife Sharpener: The Chef's Choice knife sharpener was the first electric model that really worked. This model has three levels of sharpening: the far left slots are used for a major regrinding; the middle slot is used for regular sharpening; and the far right slot is used for tuning up the blade each time you use the knife. This model costs about $80. A less expensive model has only two slots.

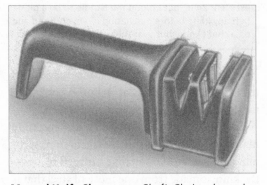

Manual Knife Sharpener: Chef's Choice also makes an inexpensive nonelectric model. In tests, I have found this model difficult to use and recommend the more expensive electric sharpener.

There are sharpening stones, sharpening steels, manual knife sharpeners, and electric models. The stone is impossible for nonprofessionals to use. The steel only aligns a knife edge — it provides a minor tune-up for a blade, not a serious sharpening. The electric models are best, the Chef's Choice taking high honors as the first (it was introduced in 1986) electric knife sharpener that really worked. Manual sharpeners are less expensive alternatives to the electric models but do only a mediocre job. Models are listed in order of price. (Note: Model names, numbers, and prices are subject to constant change and are provided only as a basis for comparison.)

	Maker and Model	Features	Price
Electric Sharpeners	Chef's Choice Diamond Hone 110	3 bevels, 3 stages, including "presharpening"	$79
	Sabatier	2 stages	$68 ($49 on sale)
	Chef's Choice Diamond Hone 310	2 bevels, 2 stages	$50
	Oster Cutting Edge	1 stage; "floating grinding action"	$23
Manual Sharpeners	Chef's Choice Diamond Hone 450	2 bevels; 2 stages	$29
	Henckels TwinSharp Combo	2 stages; similar to Chef's Choice Model 450	$24
	Wusthof Ceramic	2 stages, one for resharpening and the other for fine honing; ceramic wheels; wood handle	$24
Sharpening Rods	Diamond Vee	2 diamond rods set in a solid base; hand guard	$32
	Chicago Cutlery Always Sharp	2 sharpening rods set in a hand-held tool	$19
Sharpening Stones	Diamond	Coarse or fine finish; wood storage box; 6-in., 8-in., and 12-in. lengths	$41 (6 in.) $67 (8 in.) $104 (12 in.)
	King, Norton, Razor's Edge	Some models used dry, others with oil	$15–$20

WHAT TO BUY: If you have $80 to spend, buy the Chef's Choice 110 and be done with it. This sharpener has three grinding bevels: one for a major sharpening every few months, one for a more modest monthly sharpening, and one that tunes up the knife edge, replacing the function of a sharpening steel. The Model 310 is less expensive but has only two bevels; I find that all three are necessary. When used properly, an inexpensive sharpening stone works well and you can save yourself up to $60. However, most home cooks find them difficult to use.

mechanism, one trough for each side of the knife. There are three types of grinds: one for a major regrinding of the blade, which is used about once per year; one for a serious resharpening, which is used every couple of months; and one for toning up the knife edge almost every time you use it, performing the same task as a sharpening steel. This is a must-buy kitchen gadget, but be prepared to spend up to $80. (However, you don't need to buy a sharpening steel if you have a Chef's Choice, a savings of $25 or so.) The third choice is the manual knife sharpener — the model I tested was also made by Chef's Choice. I found two problems: it only has one grind (the electric model has three), and maintaining the proper angle is not always easy — the knife must be pressed up evenly against two rollers. The last choice is a sharpening steel, a long wandlike implement, but contrary to what most home cooks believe, this device does not actually sharpen, it simply aligns the knife's edge — a quick tune-up in between sharpenings. You will have to invest well over $100 in knives, so protect your investment and purchase the electric sharpener.

SMALL KITCHEN APPLIANCES

FOOD PROCESSORS

Food processors are a must buy for every serious home cook. I don't use mine every day, but I can't live without it for making pie dough or mayonnaise, kneading bread dough in 60 seconds, pureeing soups, and chopping chocolate and nuts. I don't use it for mincing or chopping small quantities of anything — a sharp knife is faster and easier. If you have ever grated onions in a food processor, for example, you've noticed a lot of liquid in the bottom of the bowl. Hand dicing preserves the moisture in foods. The processor, on the other hand, is very rough and forces juices out of the shredded bits.

Buy the heaviest, most durable food processor you can find. This comes in handy when chopping chocolate or nuts, grating Parmesan cheese, or kneading bread. How do you tell if a food processor is heavy-duty? Just pick it up. It should be heavy (the Cuisinart weighs about 14 pounds; the Braun weighs only 9 pounds). If you never intend to do any of the tasks above, you can get away with a lesser model such as a Braun ($100) or Panasonic ($85). The Braun may cost half as much but it also weighs much less. The cheaper models, therefore, are no bargain. If you pay less, you also get an inferior machine.

You may ask why you need such a serious piece of equipment. In tests of food processors done at *Cook's Magazine* many years ago, I watched the economy models run around the counters like dogs off their leashes while attempting to chop chocolate. You may also wish to knead bread dough in a food processor (see page 337). A mediocre machine will start to act like a lawnmower in a dense patch of weeds — it will slow down, wheeze, and burn out if you are not careful. My advice is to spend the extra money and

(see page 337)

COOKING TIP

The plunger of a food processor should have a small hole in it for slowly dripping oil into an emulsion, great for salad dressings or mayonnaise. After the emulsion is formed, remove the plunger and pour the rest of the oil in a steady stream through the food chute with the machine on.

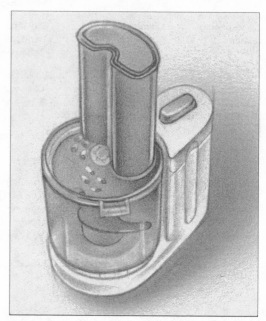

Mini–Food Processor: The mini–food processor is good for mincing garlic and fresh ginger, although I did not find it particularly valuable for most other kitchen tasks. The model shown here, the Black & Decker HMP-30, is a good value, although this is definitely an optional piece of kitchen equipment.

Only purchase a food processor that weighs over 10 pounds. You'll need the horsepower and the bulk when chopping chocolate or kneading bread dough. Models are listed in order of price. (Note: Model names, numbers, and prices are subject to constant change and are provided only as a basis for comparison.)

Maker and Model	Weight	Motor	Features	Price
Cuisinart Professional 14 Food Prep Center DLC-7	15 lb.	800 watts	14-cup capacity; 2 blades; 3 disks; whisk	$299
Cuisinart Custom 11 DLC-8M	13 lb.	750 watts	11-cup capacity; 2 blades; 3 disks	$200
Rival Select FP505W	8 lb.	500 watts	4-cup-capacity bowl; high-speed blender drive with 4-cup blender bowl; variable speed control; pulse feature; Sabatier blade; 2 slice/shred disks; spatula; dough hook; beater; whisk	$199
KitchenAid Classic Food Processor KPF600	15 lb.	No rating	11-cup capacity; Sabatier cutting blade and dough blade; 3 disks; minibowl and blade; pulse feature	$179–$199
KitchenAid Classic Food Processor KPF500	15 lb.	No rating	9-cup capacity; Sabatier cutting blade and dough blade; 3 disks; minibowl and blade; pulse feature	$179–$199
Braun Multipractic 280 UK 280	9 lb.	460 watts	4-cup liquid/6½-cup dry capacity; 5 blades and disks; whisk; adjustable cutting; variable speed	$149
Regal La Machine II	10 lb.	300 watts	10-cup-capacity bowl; 1 reversible slice/shred disk; 1 reversible chop/mix blade; pulse feature	$79
Black & Decker Power Pro Food Processor FP 1000	6 lb.	200 watts	4- and 6-cup-capacity bowls; 12 speeds; digital timer; auto shutoff; 1 blade; 1 reversible disk	$79

WHAT TO BUY: Either of the KitchenAid or Cuisinart models should be the first choice of any home cook. I have used the Cuisinart for years but recently purchased the KitchenAid because it is extraordinarily quiet and offers a mini-workbowl that allows one to chop very small quantities, such as a few cloves of garlic. Both the Cuisinart and KitchenAid are terrific for chopping chocolate or kneading bread dough, the two most demanding food processor tasks.

The Mini–Food Processor

I used the Black & Decker Handy Shortcut Micro-Processor Model HMP-30 for all of the tests.

Test	Results	Recommendation
Mince single clove of garlic	Perfect minced garlic in 7 seconds	Worth the price of the machine for this one application
Mince 1-inch piece of ginger, peeled	Almost perfect minced ginger in 15 seconds — pieces not completely uniform	Much easier than mincing by hand
Chop ½ cup walnuts	Texture from fine to coarse; some nuts left on top of grater	Not recommended — easier and better when chopped by hand
Chop small onion, peeled and quartered	Good job, but onion is not diced; it is sliced into thin slivers	Prefer chopping by hand to get a nice square dice
Grate Parmesan cheese	Took about 30 seconds and cheese had texture of millet; small pearls instead of a truly grated cheese	Much better to simply grate with a flat grater or a Mouli grater
Mince parsley	Can handle leaves but not stems	The stems of Italian flat-leaf parsley have lots of flavor, and therefore I would mince by hand; parsley is easy to mince by hand
Crumb 1 cup three-day-old bread	Texture varied from coarse to fine; machine slowed down considerably	Better to use a regular food processor with a larger motor

get one that can handle heavy-duty tasks — you'll be glad you did.

MINI–FOOD PROCESSORS

These machines first appeared in the mid-1980s and were designed to chop small amounts of food that would otherwise slip under the blades of a larger machine — 1 or 2 cloves of garlic or a small bunch of parsley. They have a capacity of 2½–3 cups. Some models have feed tubes and special features such as a slicing/shredding disk (one side shreds, the other slices). They cost from $35 to $50. I prefer to use a well-sharpened chef's knife for most of my mincing and chopping and therefore did not own one. However, in research for this book, I went out and purchased the Black & Decker Handy Shortcut Micro-Processor Model HMP-30. I tested it out on the applications that are most difficult to do either by hand or with a full-size food processor.

Based on my testing, I found that these machines are excellent at mincing small quantities of ginger and garlic, two of the most tedious food-preparation tasks. It is worth the price of the machine if you do a fair amount of the above, although this is certainly an optional purchase. The other recommendations listed in the manual — chopping and slicing carrots, celery, potatoes, and squash — are usually required in large enough quantities to use a regular food processor. A good sharp chef's knife can do the job in just seconds for smaller quantities. A few other considerations:

■ I would purchase a small-capacity mini-food processor. Some models have capacities of up to 6 and 7 cups, too large to handle 1 or 2 cloves of garlic.

■ You cannot dice with these machines. Instead they tend to cut vegetables such as onions into thin shreds. I find that this

I have only listed models with smaller capacities. Some "mini" food processors handle 6–7 cups, which is too large to mince 1 or 2 cloves of garlic. Models are listed in order of price. (Note: Model names, numbers, and prices are subject to constant change and are provided only as a basis for comparison.)

Maker and Model	Weight	Power	Features	Price
Sunbeam/Oskar 4817	4 lb.	500 watts	3-cup capacity; stainless steel blade; 2 disks; feed tube attachment; salad chute attachment	$45
Black & Decker Handy Shortcut Micro Processor HMP-30	4 lb.	120 watts	3-cup bowl; slice/shred disk; blade, feed tube	$35
Cuisinart Mini-Prep Processor DLC-1	4 lb.	250 watts	2½-cup capacity; reversible sharp/blunt blade; high and low speeds	$35
Krups Mini-Pro Processor 708	2 lb.	240 watts	2½-cup capacity; 1 blade; 1 speed	$25
Black & Decker Handy Chopper HC 2000	1.5 lb.	60 watts	1½-cup capacity; removable blade; 1 speed	$25
Rival Select Mini-Chopper CH 100	4 lb.	70 watts	1½-cup capacity; removable blade; oil droplet hole in lid; pulse control plus	$25
Toastmaster Chopster Model 1111	4 lb.	45 watts	1-cup capacity; removable blade; 1 speed	$20

WHAT TO BUY: The only thing these machines are good for is mincing garlic and ginger, but the price differential between the bottom of the line and the top is small. You can live without this appliance, but if you do want one, go for the Black & Decker HMP-30 or the Cuisinart DLC-1. They are only $10 more than the less expensive models.

produces a tougher end product than a good, square dice. Machine dicing also extracts too much liquid from a vegetable.

■ The motors in these machines are not sufficient to handle any heavy-duty work. Even 1 cup of three-day-old bread slowed down the Black & Decker model I tested.

■ They are quick and easy to clean, since the bowl and cutting blade are tiny. They also won't take up much room on a drainboard.

■ If you have the KitchenAid food processor with the small bowl attachment, a mini–food processor is unnecessary.

STANDING MIXERS

If you are just planning on beating cake batter and whipping egg whites, you can make do with a hand-held mixer, but if you plan on kneading bread dough or creaming butter, you'll need a solid standing mixer. I prefer models that have a head that tilts up and away from the bowl (the 4½-quart KitchenAid) over stationary-head mixers with a bowl that is raised and lowered (the 5-quart KitchenAid). The tilt-up head makes the addition of ingredients and removal of attachments easier. I suggest a minimum bowl capacity of 4 quarts, the size required

If you don't make bread or bake cakes very often, a hand-held electric mixer is a cheaper alternative to a standing mixer. Kneading bread dough and creaming butter, however, require a heavy-duty appliance. Don't go for the "food preparation" models — you'll probably never use the attachments. Pay attention to the weight of each model, as this is an excellent indication of quality (note that the Braun goes for over $300 and weighs only 15 pounds, compared with the $199 KitchenAid at 24 pounds). Models are listed in order of price. (Note: Model names, numbers, and prices are subject to constant change and are provided only as a basis for comparison.)

Maker and Model	Weight	Power	Features	Price
Braun Food Preparation Center K1200	15 lb.	600 watts	Variable speeds; 4 disks for shred, slice, grate, and julienne; 4½-quart dry-capacity dough bowl; 2¾-quart dry-capacity food processor bowl; 1-cup dry-capacity small bowl	$299–$350
KitchenAid KSM90	25 lb.	300 watts	4½-quart bowl; 10 speeds; planetary action of beater; locking bowl; flat beater; dough hook; wire whip; tilt-up mixer head	$250–$299
KitchenAid KSM5	30 lb.	325 watts	5-quart bowl; 10 speeds; planetary action of beater; locking bowl; flat beater; dough hook; wire whip; bowl can be raised and lowered, mixer head is stationary	$250–$299
Rival Select KM210	19 lb.	600 watts	5-quart bowl; variable speeds with pulse; high-speed drive; spatula; whisk; beaters; dough hook; bowl cover with feed tube	$250
KitchenAid K45SS	24 lb.	250 watts	4½-quart bowl; 10 speeds; planetary action of beater; locking bowl; flat beater; dough hook; wire whip; tilt-up mixer head	$199
Oster 2743-5	16 lb.	450 watts	1½- and 4-quart glass bowls; 12 speeds; 2 beaters; 2 dough hooks; salad maker with slicer, shredder, french fry cutter; adjustable turntable; blender attachment	$189
Sunbeam Mixmaster 01401/2355	11 lb.	210 watts	1½- and 4-quart glass bowls; 12 speeds; dough hook; auto adjust speed and power	$100
Krups Power Mix Plus	4 lb.	220 watts	3½-quart rotating bowl; 3 speeds; dough hook; beaters; arm oscillates or remains stationary; detachable power unit for hand mixing	$80

WHAT TO BUY: Weighing in at a solid 25 pounds, the KitchenAid KSM90 is the best money can buy (look for it at discount outlets and you'll save some money), and it will last forever. I prefer the smaller model because the head tilts up and away from the bowl, which makes the addition of ingredients easy. The larger model has a bowl that is lifted up into the beaters—the head itself is stationary.

for making a large batch of bread dough. However, a 5-quart bowl is a bit large for whipping a couple of egg whites. Forget about attachments other than the whisk, the dough hook, and perhaps the mixing paddle. The shredder, slicer, and french fry cutter attachments will end up in the bottom of a drawer. KitchenAid makes the best machine in the category. It's worth the money for a serious home cook.

PRESSURE COOKERS

A new generation of pressure cookers has come onto the market. These are substantially safer than your grandmother's model — most of them have two or three steam-release safety valves — and the pots themselves are of a higher quality, usually made from stainless steel with a sandwich of aluminum in the bottom for superior heat conductivity. They are also more accurate — a pressure indicator rises up from the top of the cover when the pressure is at the right level. (Older models were less precise; it was difficult to gauge when the steam was at the correct pressure.) After speaking to a few pressure cooker experts, I chose the 5-liter-capacity Kuhn Rikon, which requires a minimum of liquid to create pressure and is very heavy-duty, good for sautéing or browning. A small valve on top of the cooker starts to rise as the pressure builds. You can cook foods at half-pressure — this is indicated by a red ring that appears as the valve lifts — or at high pressure, indicated by a second ring, which comes into view once the valve is fully vertical. Most recipes call for cooking under high pressure.

Pressure cookers offer two advantages, claim their devotees. They are fast — food cooks much more quickly under pressure — and they render tough meats moist and tender. The second point was of great interest, as I had performed dozens of tests with pot roasts in order to find the best cooking method. I purchased a 3½-pound chuck roast

and it cooked in just 60 minutes. It did lose weight during cooking, but the meat was fall-apart tender and succulent. This was the best pot roast I had ever made.

Excited by this success, I decided to make an entire dinner in the pressure cooker. I started at 3:30 on a Saturday afternoon with a ricotta cheesecake that was steamed in a small springform pan wrapped in aluminum foil (20 minutes under high pressure). I then made a tagine (a Moroccan lamb stew with prunes, lemons, and spices), which was done in 12 minutes. A vegetable stock followed (10 minutes). I finished up with a simple risotto, which took 6 minutes under high pressure followed by 5 minutes of cooking and stirring on the stovetop. I was finished in just 2½ hours, and the dishes were excellent. The cheesecake was light and moist although slightly undercooked in the center, the lamb was succulent, the vegetable stock was quick and easy, and the risotto was the best I have ever made and, at 10 minutes of cooking, was by far the fastest. Since that meal, I have also prepared grains and dried beans (a pressure cooker is an excellent tool for quickly preparing any legume) and three different soups, all of which came out well.

The only drawback to pressure cookers is your inability to check the food as it cooks. You can't shove an instant-read thermometer into a pot roast or look at the top of a cheesecake to see if it has set properly. In fact, it takes 10–15 minutes for the pressure to subside once the heat is turned off, and until the pressure is lowered, there is no way to open the cooker. (As a safety feature, steam pressure makes it impossible to turn the top to the open position.) There is a manual steam-release valve, but this takes about 3 minutes. If the food is not properly cooked, the pot needs to be heated a second time to resume cooking. This is not critical for stew or for chicken stock, but it does make a difference with cheesecake (mine was slightly undercooked) or a large pot roast (what if

Unlike old-fashioned models, the new pressure cookers have plenty of safety features, including gaskets that will allow steam to escape in an emergency. They also have gauges that indicate when the cooker is at the proper temperature. Note that prices vary considerably depending on the retailer. Models are listed in order of price. (Note: Model names, numbers, and prices are subject to constant change and are provided only as a basis for comparison.)

Maker and Model	Weight	Capacity	Features	Price
Kuhn Rikon 3047	8 lb.	7 liters	Stainless steel with aluminum sandwich; rack; 1 handle	$200
Kuhn Rikon 3046	5 lb.	5 liters	Stainless steel with aluminum sandwich; rack; 1 handle	$190
Farberware C8806	5 lb.	6 quarts	Stainless steel; steamer basket; pressure adjuster switch; 2 handles	$150
Kuhn Rikon 3051	5 lb.	2 liters	Stainless steel with aluminum sandwich; 1 handle	$135–$170
Preferred Stock 42106	6 lb.	10 quarts	Stainless steel with copper sandwich; steamer basket; rack; 2 handles	$130
Fagor Multirapid	5½ lb.	4 quarts	Stainless steel with aluminum sandwich; pressure adjuster switch on handle; steamer basket; 2 handles; attachable timer	$100–$129
Preferred Stock 42108	5 lb.	8 quarts	Stainless steel with copper sandwich; steamer basket; rack; 2 handles	$100
Preferred Stock 42106	4 lb.	6 quarts	Stainless steel with copper sandwich; steamer basket; rack; 2 handles	$85
T-Fal Safe2	4 lb.	6 liters	Stainless steel; rack; 2 handles	$65–$70
Presto 01360	4 lb.	6 quarts	Stainless steel; rack; 1 handle	$60–$90
Presto 01340	3½ lb.	4 quarts	Stainless steel; rack; 1 handle	$50
Mirro Speed/Health Cooker	4 lb.	6 quarts	Aluminum; 2 handles	$40
Mirro Speed/Health Cooker	3 lb.	4 quarts	Aluminum; 1 handle	$28–$35

WHAT TO BUY: I strongly suggest purchasing a model with a minimum capacity of 5 quarts, which is essential when cooking a pot roast, a good amount of stock, or enough soup for two or three days. I also recommend a model with a sandwich in the bottom of either aluminum or copper. This is helpful when sautéing foods before pressure cooking. Check for a rack, which is useful when cooking a pot roast or steaming a cheesecake or pudding (the food needs to be up off the bottom of the pan). Be sure that the model you buy is a newer model; older models did not have many safety features and it was difficult to tell when the cooker was at the right pressure. I have the Kuhn Ricon 5-liter cooker; although it is very expensive, it works like a charm and is considered the Cadillac of the industry. The only drawback to the Kuhn Ricon models is that they have only one handle, a problem when carrying a 5- or 6-liter cooker filled with stock or stew.

you have a 4-pound roast instead of a 3-pounder?).

A related problem is that foods cannot be added during cooking, which is a drawback when making a stew, for example. The carrots will come out overcooked by the time the meat is ready. However, quick-cooking or precooked ingredients can be added to the pot once the basic dish is done and the pressure is released. If you are finicky about texture, simply steam ingredients such as carrots or potatoes separately and then add them to the stew or soup when the meat is ready. On the whole, however, the time savings are dramatic and pressure cooking is a superior method for preparing tough cuts of meat.

PASTA MACHINES

Electric pasta makers first appeared in the mid-1980s, then faded in popularity; they have now returned with a vengeance, becoming one of the top-selling kitchen items in the last two years. Flour and eggs are added to the mixing bowl and the machine kneads the dough and then extrudes it through a variety of disks that make everything from capellini to macaroni to bucato. Manufacturers claim that they also can be used for pasta, pizza, pretzels, breadsticks, and won ton wrappers.

It should be stated that I am biased against making my own dried pasta at home — linguine, spaghetti, fettuccine — and even the Italians usually purchase this sort of pasta at a store. I have two reasons. First, commercial pasta manufacturers have improved the quality of their product in the last ten years to the point that I rated Ronzoni number one in a blind taste test. The pasta had a lively, nutty flavor and good tooth. I find that fresh pasta is often flabby and lacking in bite and also lacking in flavor when made with simple all-purpose flour. A commercial pasta operation has access to a much wider range of flours, which provide better texture and flavor than all-purpose. That being said, I do

make homemade ravioli because this dish makes excellent use of leftovers. I also find that homemade ravioli is a great improvement on the commercial brands, which have rather tasteless fillings in gummy dough. However, I use a hand-operated Atlas pasta machine for this operation (see Chapter 17 for instructions), and it works just fine.

Nevertheless, I borrowed the Simac Pasta-Matic MX 700 for a test, just to see if it was worth the investment (the Simac is supposed to be the best machine on the market). The machine consists of a sizable, counter-hogging housing into which one inserts a plastic mixing bowl that contains a combination kneading paddle–mixing blade. This unit is covered with a clear plastic lid with an intake hole for adding the eggs or water. At the bottom of the machine, in the front, is the extruder onto which one screws any one of 24 different disks that shape the pasta as it is forced out of the hole by a rotary screw. I began with the basic recipe, which is 1 pound (about 3¼ cups) of flour and about 4 large eggs. Simac gives you a small plastic measuring box for the eggs (or water) which has fill lines for ½ pound and 1 pound of pasta. The flour is placed in the bowl and then the eggs are added with the machine on. I noted that the liquid intake hole on the cover is in fact too small for the yolk of a large egg — I had to break two of the yolks to get them to slide through. The machine kneads for 5 minutes and then the dough is checked and more liquid or flour is added if necessary to get the right texture. The machine is kept running for an additional 5 minutes or until the dough is properly kneaded. In my test, the dough kept pushing up against the plastic lid, which causes the machine to shut off. This happened a dozen times. The manual suggests pushing it back down (I tried this, but it simply happened again in a few seconds) or removing some of the dough and then adding it later. This didn't seem to make much sense, as the

The following models are electric except for the Atlas model at the bottom of the chart. Prices are often discounted as much as 20 percent. Note that most machines have plastic rather than metal extrusion disks. Metal is preferred. Models are listed in order of price. (Note: Model names, numbers, and prices are subject to constant change and are provided only as a basis for comparison.)

Maker and Model	Capacity	Power	Features	Price
Cuisinart DPM-3	3 lb.	225 watts	5 metal disks; 6 shapes plus breadsticks; see-through cover	$350
Simac PastaMatic MX 700	1½ lb.	270 watts	8 metal disks with machine, 16 others available	$229
Creative Technologies Pasta Express X-2000	1½ lb.	155 watts	Plastic disks; 11 shapes; auto shutoff; built-in blower/dryer	$225
Popeil Pasta Maker PM 400	5 lb.	385 watts	Plastic disks; 24 shapes; built-in dryer and cutter; 3 amp motor	$225
Vitantonio Pasta Perfetto 900	1 lb.	200 watts	Plastic disks; 8 shapes	$200
Maverick MP M6468	1½ lb.	180 watts	Plastic disks; 11 shapes; auto reset; dryer	$150
Waring Primo Pasta PS201	1½ lb.	250 watts	Plastic disks; 10 shapes	$110
Rival Pasta Chef PM 1000	1 lb.	235 watts	Plastic disks; 10 shapes	$100
Atlas Manual 150	—	—	Makes sheets, linguine, and spaghetti	$45

WHAT TO BUY: Save some money and purchase the Atlas manual model for $45. It makes great ravioli, about the only thing worth doing with one of these contraptions. It's also easy to clean up and will take less time than the electronic models. This is one electric appliance you can live without.

dough that was removed would not be properly kneaded.

To extrude pasta, the proper disk is placed over the extrusion hole (I used the small fettuccine disk) and the dough is then forced out into the desired shape. This worked fine. I placed the pasta in an airtight plastic bag and then refrigerated it for about an hour until I was ready to cook it. (This was recommended in the manual, although I find refrigerating pasta dough to be a tricky business — it quickly deteriorates into a gummy mass. It is much better to freeze or dry fresh pasta dough.) The fresh pasta cooked quickly — in 2–4 minutes — but the results were mediocre at best. There was no tooth to the pasta and a few of the strands stuck together. I'd rather eat Ronzoni. I did go back and retest with a semolina flour mix, designed specifically for an electric pasta machine. The results were better but still not as good as store-bought dried pasta. One could dry homemade pasta, but that would contradict the notion of an electric machine — easy, last-minute pasta.

The big surprise was cleaning up. Although the process up to this point was easy and moderately quick (about 45 minutes total — the extrusion process is very slow), I realized that I now had seven separate items to clean, some of them rather nasty. The lid, the kneading paddle, the bowl, and the measuring cup were easy, but the disk, the plastic ring nut that holds the disk to the machine, and the interior of the machine once the bowl was removed were no picnic. The disk had little bits of dough caught in the holes, somehow dough had gotten underneath the bowl and turned to liquid from the heat of the machine, and the ring nut had dough jammed into its threads. At $229, this is an aggravation I can live without.

The best alternative is the hand-cranked Atlas manual, which costs about $45. First, the dough is kneaded in a food processor, which takes less than a minute. This works better and faster than a $200 pasta machine. Then you crank the dough through the rollers (the Atlas is really a mini–clothes wringer), starting with the thickest setting, working your way down to the thinner sheets. This process further kneads the dough and takes just a few minutes. The result is long sheets of pasta dough that can then be used for ravioli or cut into simple flat pastas such as fettuccine, using the rotary cutters on the machine. The other alternative is to roll out pasta dough by hand. I did this once and found it nearly impossible to get dough of uniform thickness. Leave this to the experts. Atlas also sells a ravioli attachment, which automatically parcels out dollops of filling between two sheets of dough. Don't bother with it — it's more difficult than doing it by hand, plus the cleanup is time-consuming. The simplest method for making ravioli is to use a mold, a simple metal form that quickly transforms two sheets of fresh dough and filling into individual raviolis.

For most home cooks, neither an electric machine nor the Atlas is worth the trouble — I suggest buying store-bought pasta and leaving it at that. If you are partial to ravioli, however, the Atlas is a good investment and will last forever.

ICE CREAM MAKERS

Ice cream makers vary from the $60 freezer model (Donvier Premier) to the $500 electric version (Simac Il Gelataio Magnum). The freezer models have a canister filled with a super-coolant that is prechilled, slipped into the outer case, and then used to chill the ice cream ingredients. Either a hand crank or an electric-powered paddle is used for stirring during the freezing process. The Simac electric model works much like a small air conditioner. The machine cools down the workbowl, the ingredients are added, and then the ice cream is constantly mixed with an electric-driven paddle.

Electric models make superior ice cream. The size of the crystals is a function of both the temperature at which the ice cream is frozen as well as the churning action. The expensive refrigerated models keep the ingredients colder than freezer models and the constant motion of the electric paddle is su-

---

KITCHEN TEST

My Neighbors' Freezer Temperatures

Check your freezer temperature before you go shopping for an ice cream maker. Whether you're making ice cream or not, your home freezer should register between –4° and +2°F. Unfortunately, my freezer registered only 14°F, which is not cold enough for ice cream machines that use a freezer container. In fact, I did a little survey of my neighbors and here is what I found:

Type of Freezer	Temperature
Amana	4°F
General Electric	4°F
General Electric	6°F
Whirlpool	5°F
General Electric	3°F

There are three basic types of ice cream machines. The most basic model requires prefreezing the removable inner shell, adding the ingredients to it, and then hand-cranking every few minutes. Some manufacturers add a motor to do the cranking — these models are 60–70 percent more expensive. Finally, the fully electric models — the machines include minifreezers built in — are quite expensive, running in the $400 range. Check your freezer temperature before you purchase one of the first two models. Models are listed in order of price. (Note: Model names, numbers, and prices are subject to constant change and are provided only as a basis for comparison.)

Maker and Model	Capacity	Features	Price
Simac Il Gelataio Magnum	1 quart	Totally electric ice cream maker with timer	$499
Vitantonio Gelato Pro 880	1 quart	Totally electric ice cream maker like the Simac; 150-watt motor	$399
Vitantonio Gelato Modo II 875	1 quart	Electric motor for mixing, but container needs to be prefrozen	$80
Donvier Premier	1 quart	Must freeze container, churn ice cream manually	$60
Krups La Glacière	1 quart	Electric motor for mixing, but container needs to be prefrozen	$60
Waring FDM 810	1 quart	Electric motor for mixing, but container needs to be prefrozen; auto-off	$60
Simac Gelataio SC	1¼ quarts	Canister design with electric motor attachment	$59–$99
Oster 4746	2 quarts	Ice cubes and rock salt used to chill canister	$50
Rival 8550	5 quarts	Ice cubes and rock salt used to chill canister; electric motor	$50

WHAT TO BUY: For the price, the Waring is the best bet. However, any of the freezer models with an electric motor for churning are fine. If you have too much money and too much counter space, go for the $400-plus fully electric models — they really work and produce superior ice cream.

perior to the occasional motion of a hand-cranked machine. The Simac also produces ice cream that can be eaten immediately — ice cream from the freezer models requires additional time in the freezer before serving. If you buy one of the cheaper models, be sure that your freezer has sufficient room to hold the container that must be prechilled. Unless you make a great deal of ice cream and sorbets (and have lots of extra counter space),

an inexpensive freezer model with an electric motor for churning is your best bet.

But don't buy any freezer model without checking your freezer temperature first. According to the manufacturer's instructions, the Donvier requires 0°F; otherwise it simply won't work (and didn't when I tried it with my freezer). To check on this, I called Peter Browne, the CEO of Donvier. He stuck to the party line — the freezer must be at 0°F for the canister to work properly. Since a crowded freezer may not reach this temperature and since none of my neighbors had a freezer this cold (see Kitchen Test), I suspect that models that require chilling the inner bowl in advance may not work as well as promised. However, I did test the Donvier in a freezer that maintained 3°–4° and found that if the custard base was properly chilled (I let it sit in the refrigerator overnight), it worked fine. Before purchasing one of these models, however, it is a good idea to check your freezer temperature in advance. If your freezer runs above 5°F, the canister-style ice cream machine is not for you.

IMMERSION BLENDERS

Immersion blenders look like large electric toothbrushes and are just about as useful. Other kitchen appliances you probably already own — the food processor and the blender come to mind — can handle the

---

SHOPPING FOR IMMERSION BLENDERS

These blenders are often found on sale. The Cuisinart was advertised at $49 (list price $70), the Braun MR 380 was selling for $39 on sale (list price $50), and the Braun M 880 was discounted to $39 (list price $80). Models are listed in order of price. (Note: Model names, numbers, and prices are subject to constant change and are provided only as a basis for comparison.)

Maker and Model	Power	Features	Price
Braun Multi-Mix Hand-Held Food Prep M 880	220 watts	Hand mixer, kneader, blender, chopper; 3 speeds plus pulse	$80
Cuisinart CSB-1C	150 watts	Blades for whipping, blending, and chopping; 16-oz. plastic container; 24-oz. stainless container; varispeed control; wall mount	$70
Braun Hand Blender & Chopper MR 380	160 watts	Chopping attachment; whipping disk; beaker; wall mount	$50
Black & Decker 9220	230 watts	Mix, chop, and whisk attachments; 2 speeds; wall mount	$40
Waring HHB75-1	No rating	2 speeds; opaque beaker	$36
Rival 951 W	100 watts	2 speeds; opaque beaker	$31
Moulinex Turbo 071	150 watts	Whipping attachment; pureeing blade; clear beaker with sieve; wall mount	$30
Hamilton Beach 59700	80 watts	No special attachments	$25
Salton MX 2	150 watts	No special attachments	$15

WHAT TO BUY: I find that the attachments are not worthwhile and would therefore purchase a stripped-down model at about half the price of the deluxe. The Cuisinart and the Braun would be good buys if found on sale for under $50. The Moulinex at $30 would be a best buy.

same tasks targeted for the immersion blender. I've had one sitting on my kitchen counter for over a year; I have used it twice. But they are not totally without redeeming qualities. I purchased the Cuisinart model for testing and found that it was good for pureeing soups in the pot (without removing the contents to a food processor) and could take salad dressing ingredients and whip them into a thick, frothy frenzy in just seconds. Chefs use them to whip up quick sauces of chicken stock, olive oil, and seasonings — these little machines can force just about anything into an emulsion. I'd put immersion blenders in the same category as mini–food processors, pasta machines, and "food preparation centers" — save your money for a good chef's knife or heavy-duty standing mixer.

ELECTRIC FRYERS

There are two kinds of frying: deep-frying and skillet-frying. You can fry just about anything in a skillet or Dutch oven with an inch of oil or less, including a cut-up chicken. However, a deep fryer is handy when you want to fry large quantities of small ingredients. Most fryers come with a wire basket, which makes removal of the fried foods convenient, and they also come with a lid, which reduces both odors and spattering (the T-Fal has a removable charcoal filter, which does reduce odors substantially). The most important issue, however, is oil temperature. With an electric fryer, temperature control is supposed to be automatic, eliminating the problem of constantly checking oil temperature and adjusting the heat.

In my tests, however, I found that many

SHOPPING FOR ELECTRIC DEEP FRYERS

If you are frying small quantities of foods or fry foods infrequently, use a $10 cast iron skillet and fry in 1 inch of oil or less. If you do a lot of frying, you may wish to consider one of the fryers below. Models are listed in order of price. (Note: Model names, numbers, and prices are subject to constant change and are provided only as a basis for comparison.)

Maker and Model	Power	Features	Price
DeLonghi D-20	1,500 watts	300°–375°F settings; view panel; rotating basket; 4-cup oil capacity	$200 ($169 on sale)
DeLonghi D-4W	1,500 watts	300°–375°F settings; view panel; 8–10-cup oil capacity	$125 ($99 on sale)
Kenwood (Rival Select) DF 370	1,500 watts	300°–375°F settings; clear top; basket; 8-cup oil capacity	$100
Presto GranPappy	1,500 watts	Auto-temp (no thermostat); no basket; no cover; 6-cup oil capacity	$35
Dazey Chef's Pot DCP-6	1,400 watts	0°–400°F settings; no viewing panel; no cover; 7½-cup oil capacity	$30–$40

WHAT TO BUY: The DeLonghi is the best bet model although very pricey—save money by purchasing the 8-cup model on sale for $99. The smaller-capacity model is more expensive because it has a rotating basket, which requires about half as much oil. I use a T-Fal (Model 8215M), which costs about $80 and fries as well as the DeLonghi. However, I could not find it in stores and therefore have not listed it. The next choice is the Kenwood. I would not purchase a deep fryer with no top, which leaves out the Presto and the Dazey.

electric fryers have a big problem, which is that they are incapable of maintaining the proper temperature. That is, once the food is added, the recover time — the time it takes for the oil to come back up to 370°F, the proper temperature for deep-frying — is often too long. The electric coils don't deliver enough horsepower to get the oil back up to speed (the DeLonghi and T-Fal models had short recover times). This is why shallow-frying in a skillet makes a lot of sense; you can keep the oil at the proper temperature without much trouble. By the way, if the oil temperature drops too rapidly for too long, your fried chicken or french fries will become soggy and the food will soak up the oil. In frying, oil temperature is everything.

In addition to short recover time, a good fryer has a viewing panel so that you can check on the progress of your fried foods

Electric Deep Fryer: Models such as this one (T-Fal) fry foods in relative safety, as the top is closed during cooking. Other features include a filter to reduce odors, a basket that lowers automatically into the hot oil, and variable temperature settings. Although most models have windows to allow you to see the food as it cooks, steam from frying usually makes viewing difficult if not impossible. Look for a model that has a manual "windshield wiper" to clear away steam from the viewing window.

Oils for Deep-Frying

The smoking point of oils is not an issue for deep-frying. Any of the oils available in your supermarket will not start smoking until 450°F or so, well above the 360°–370°F recommended for frying. (Peanut oil, which is often touted as having a high smoking point, starts smoking at only 440°F, 70° sooner than safflower oil, and 35° before corn oil.) For health reasons, I suggest canola oil. I discard oil after using it twice for frying, not the four or five times often recommended in other cookbooks. Be sure to strain used oil through a coffee filter before storing.

without opening the top. But a viewing panel without a wiper blade is useless, as condensation will fog up the window in short order, much like a steamy bathroom mirror. Some models, by the way, do not have a lid and this is a disadvantage — a lid is safer, decreasing the likelihood of splattered hot oil. Also check for safety. Will your hand be in the way of escaping steam when opening the top? How hot does the exterior of the fryer get? (Very hot in all the models I tested.) How about the temperature of the handle?

In my tests of deep fryers, I kept asking myself, "Is this worth the trouble?" Although the DeLonghi and T-Fal models are well designed and easy to use, cleanup is a real problem. The oil needs to be filtered for reuse or thrown out (name a quick and easy way to dispose of old frying oil). The unit often requires some disassembly before cleaning (to clean the T-Fal, the charcoal filter, the cover gasket, and the steam sponge all need to be taken off before rinsing). Since electric models cannot be immersed in water for cleaning, they need to be wiped clean, which takes more than one handful of paper towels. The top-of-the-line machines do work, but a large cast iron skillet (under $20) also does the job, especially for infrequent fryers. If, however, you are a frequent fryer, the DeLonghi and T-Fal (if you can find it) are worth the money. If not, stick with the skillet.

ELECTRIC STEAMERS

Let's be frank. You can go to any cookware shop in North America and buy a $7 leaf steaming basket that will fit into just about any good-size pot. Pour a half-inch of water in the bottom of the pot, bring it to a simmer, add the vegetables, cover, and you're done in less than 15 minutes from start to finish. So who needs to spend $50 on another appliance that you have no room for?

Well, I bought the Dazey Pasta Primo Plus, which cooks pasta and also steams vegetables and rice, to find the answer. Basically, this is a metal pot with a heating coil underneath plus a timer. Using one of these for cooking pasta is like reading *Newsweek* online — it's more expensive and a bit more difficult. Instead of simply pouring out hot water and pasta into a colander, the pasta must be lifted out in the strainer basket, which is more cumbersome, especially if the electric cooker is not stationed next to the sink. One needs an extra appliance for this? The vegetable steaming test was more successful. Pour 2 cups of water into the steamer, add the vegetables to the steaming basket, cover, and turn the timer to the correct setting as shown in the chart that comes with the machine. (The time required includes the time it takes to bring the water to a boil). I tried cauliflower florets and it worked fine. Unfortunately, the timer did not ring when it was done. I also wondered if you could let your vegetables sit a few minutes after cooking, so

I taste-tested the cauliflower after leaving it in the basket for an extra 10 minutes (after the machine had turned itself off) and it was overcooked. Unlike a rice cooker, which turns itself off automatically and can hold rice for at least half an hour with no change in texture, these steamers offer little in the way of added convenience. You can also steam rice in these machines, but a rice cooker is by far the better tool for this task and costs only about $30. I also found that after a bit of use, the nonstick coating started to flake off, which prompted serious health concerns. Whatever the nonstick coating is made from, I know that I don't want to eat it.

SHOPPING FOR NONELECTRIC VEGETABLE STEAMERS

If you plan on steaming regularly, purchase a large-diameter steamer. A double-compartment steamer is also useful for cooking two foods at once. If you rarely steam foods, the collapsible steamer basket is fine and cheap.

Maker	Type	Comments	Price
Various	Collapsible steamer basket	Fits into a large saucepan or stockpot. Hard to remove vegetables.	$2.50–$8.00
Various	Bamboo steamer	Only works with a wok. Woks can rust if used for boiling water. Inconvenient to store due to size.	About $3 per basket
Various	Steamer insert	Made from either stainless steel or aluminum. Expensive. Fits inside standard-size pots.	$35 for 2–3 quarts; up to $85 for 12-quart model
Various	Steamer ensemble	Some models also come with a pasta insert. Made of stainless steel or nonstick aluminum.	$20–$60; 2- to 8-quart capacity
Demeyere-Silvinox	Steamer ensemble	Belgian steamer with a huge pot and 2 very large steamer compartments. Rubber gaskets between stackable sections keep steam contained. Can steam a chicken and a large quantity of vegetables at one time. Available through Zabar's in New York City (212-787-2000—they will ship). The Rolls-Royce of steamers.	$139
AMC	Steamer ensemble	Heavy-gauge oval steamer that is 13 inches long. Can handle a large fish. Pot doubles as a roasting pan.	$149
Bridge	Steamer ensemble	Stainless steel; 2 steamer inserts; 8 inches in diameter. Available through Bridge Kitchenware in New York City (212-688-4220).	$200

WHAT TO BUY: If you are serious about steaming, you need a large steamer. You can buy a large insert, a large ensemble piece, or one of the more expensive models, the Demeyere-Silvinox or the AMC. A large steamer allows you to cook an entire meal at once without overcrowding the vegetables (vegetables piled in more than one layer will not cook evenly). I own the Demeyere-Silvinox and recommend it, despite the high price tag, to anyone who intends to steam at least once per week. Steamers are also good for keeping foods warm and for reheating foods.

STOVETOP STEAMERS

If you want to steam vegetables but don't want an electric steamer, you have four choices: a collapsible steamer basket, a bamboo steamer, an insert that fits an existing pot, or a stovetop steamer set that includes a pot for the water and one or two steaming baskets with a top. I have kitchen-tested most everything and find that size is crucial. It is important to have the vegetables in a single layer for even cooking. I also found that a steamer with stackable compartments is a plus — you can steam asparagus and potatoes at the same time, for example. Collapsible steamer baskets are cheap but often difficult to remove from a pot of steaming water (the models with screw-on posts are best).

ELECTRIC RICE COOKERS

This is one of my favorite kitchen appliances. They prepare any type of rice automatically. Just place the ingredients in the pot, plug it in, and come back when it's done (the machine switches from a cooking mode to a warming mode when the rice reaches the proper temperature). Rice cookers will also keep rice hot after it is cooked or reheat rice, and most models can be used for steaming vegetables (a small tray fits into the bottom of the cooker to hold vegetables). Larger models cost up to $100, although most models are about $50. I use the National Rice O Mat, which comes in two sizes. The smaller size (about $30) can handle up to 4 cups of uncooked rice, the larger up to 8 cups (about $50). I have both models and find that the 8-cup model is lousy for small quantities. When only 2 cups of rice are cooked in an 8-cup cooker, for example, too much of the cooked rice will end up on or near the bottom, where it becomes glutinous and waxy due to the nonstick cooking surface. As a result, you want to match the size of your cooker to the amount of rice you usually cook.

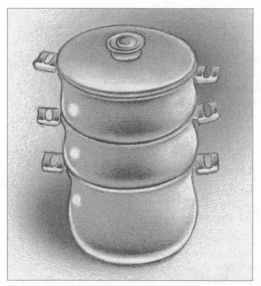

Two-Tiered Steamer: Two-tiered steamers come in all shapes and sizes. This model is Belgian and can handle a whole chicken in each tier. The pot, minus the steaming trays, can also be used as a stockpot or for boiling pasta. This particular model, the Demeyere-Silvinox, has rubber gaskets between tiers, which provide a perfect seal. This steamer is available through Zabar's in New York City.

Electric Rice Cooker: This is a must-have kitchen appliance. It cooks perfect rice every time and also keeps it warm after cooking. Purchase the smallest model that suits your needs. Large models do only a mediocre job at cooking small amounts of rice. The model shown is made by National. Most rice cookers cost between $30 and $50.

Most rice cookers also claim to be vegetable steamers. After some testing, I found that this is not the case. It is difficult to get the vegetables out of the cooker. (The small perforated steaming tray that sits on the bottom of the rice cooker has a tiny wire handle that makes removing it while still hot nearly impossible. You have to dump the contents into a colander, a dangerous task with a very hot cooking bowl and steaming vegetables.) I also prefer to steam in a wider pot so that the vegetables do not have to be more than one layer deep. Most home cooks will purchase a 4-cup rice cooker, which is a bit small for steaming.

One great benefit of these machines is that they not only make rice automatically, but they also hold it well in the "steaming" mode (simply a low-heat setting) once the rice is cooked. In some models, the rice is actually better if held 5–10 minutes in the steaming mode after cooking — it needs the extra time to fully cook. Cleaning is also a breeze — rice cookers have a nonstick cooking surface that washes up in seconds.

Bread Machines

Cook's Magazine first tested electric bread machines in the mid-1980s. At that time I felt that they made decent supermarket bread, a little cakey and without much chew. Since then, the machines have been improved, yet the availability of good commercial bread has also increased. I borrowed a Zojirushi Home Bakery (Model BBCC-S15) to find out if an electric bread machine was really worth the money.

Here's how they work. The bread is made in a removable rectangular baking pan (some machines have round pans), which is fitted with a removable kneading blade at the bottom. The liquid ingredients are added first, then the flour, then the yeast is sprinkled on top. The pan is inserted into the machine, the top closed, and then you press start. That's it. The bread is ready about 4 hours later.

Rice cookers work much better than vegetable steamers that also cook rice. Their biggest asset is that they can hold rice a long time after cooking without loss of texture. Rice cookers are not easy to find. Williams-Sonoma usually carries the National brand. A Chinese or Japanese market, however, carries lots of models. Models are listed in order of price. (Note: Model names, numbers, and prices are subject to constant change and are provided only as a basis for comparison.)

Maker and Model	Cooked Rice Capacity	Price
Oster 3811-20	24 cups	$59
Zojirushi NAZC 06	3 cups	$50
Sanyo EC 23	10 cups	$40
Rival 4310	11 cups	$38
Hitachi RD 4053	5 cups	$35
National SRW10FN	8 cups	$35
Salton RA 10	10 cups	$29

WHAT TO BUY: I prefer a smaller-capacity model. Large models do a poor job of cooking small amounts of rice. Be sure that the bowl is nonstick.

You can use the built-in timer to start your bread during the middle of the night (only if you use powdered milk so it doesn't spoil). The machine also has special settings for quick baking (using rapid-rise yeast), raisin bread (the machine beeps when it is time to add the raisins), French bread (less kneading and more rising time), and a dough setting that allows you to remove the dough after the first rise, at which point you shape it and let it rise a second time (outside the machine) before baking in a conventional oven. The manufacturers claim that you can also make quick breads, cakes, and jams with this unit, although I stuck to a basic white bread for my tests. After all, why make a cake that is shaped like a loaf of bread?

My first time out, the bread did not rise properly, which was probably due to my using a very high-protein flour that requires more liquid than a supermarket-variety bread flour. I tried it a second time with regular bread flour and the dough rose better, but the top end was still not properly inflated. I fiddled with the recipe and came up with a good basic white bread that is dependable (see Chapter 37). However, I find that handmade bread is more foolproof than the machine variety. Besides being limited to a basic sandwich loaf, these machines are finicky —

you may need to adjust your master recipe for a particular machine to get the results you want. Based on my experience with the Zojirushi, which does have an excellent instruction manual, the recipes that accompany these machines often leave a lot to be desired. I suggest that you purchase Lora Brody's *Bread Machine Baking* (Morrow, 1993).

I also tried some of the optional settings on the Zojirushi, with mixed results. I tried making "French" bread, and what I ended up with was a basic white loaf with a harder, thicker crust similar to zwieback biscuits. The interior was still soft and cakelike. This is about as French as french toast. I then

SHOPPING FOR BREAD MACHINES			
Some of these machines are heavily discounted. I have seen discounts of up to 27 percent. Shop carefully for a bread machine; you could save a lot of money. Models are listed in order of price. (Note: Model names, numbers, and prices are subject to constant change and are provided only as a basis for comparison.)			
Maker and Model	**Loaf Size/Shape**	**Features**	**Price**
Zojirushi Home Bakery BBCC-S15A	1½-lb. loaf; square	3 crust-color settings; 4 bread modes; memory storage for custom recipes; programmable timer; dough setting; power interrupt; cooling fan; viewing window	$339
American Harvest Bread Classic II BC-2000	Two 1½-lb. loaves; square	4 crust-color settings; 5 bread modes; 24-hour programmable timer; fruit/nut addition beeper; cast aluminum loaf pans; front loading; viewing window; bakes 2 loaves at once	$334
Regal Automatic Bread Maker K6773	1½-lb. loaf; square	2 crust-color settings; 4 bread modes; rapid-bake setting; dough setting; no viewing window	$330
Hitachi Breadmaster HB-B301	1½-lb. loaf; square	3 crust-color settings; 3 bread modes; rapid-bake setting; cake and jam settings; 13-hour programmable timer; dough setting; power interrupt; cooling fan; viewing window	$299
Pillsbury Automatic Bread and Dough Maker 1020	2-lb. loaf; square	3 crust-color settings; 7 bread modes; 3-stage fermentation; 13-hour programmable timer; nonstick loaf pan; viewing window	$249
Panasonic Automatic Bread Bakery SD BT 56 P	10½-oz. loaf; square	3 bread modes; rapid-bake setting; 13-hour programmable timer; nonstick loaf pan; yeast dispenser; no viewing window	$249

spoke to Lora Brody, who told me the dirty little secret about bread machines. They are great for proofing and rising the dough but lousy for actually baking bread. In other words, I was really testing a $300 proofing box! With that tip in mind, I set out on a new batch of tests. I started with a basic white bread recipe. I baked one loaf entirely in the machine and I used the machine as a proofing box for the other, actually baking the bread in the oven. The machine-baked loaf had a subpar crust and cakelike chew; the oven-baked loaf was quite good by comparison, with a thin, pleasant crust and the solid but tender chew one associates with American bread. I can live without these machines, but if you do use one, I suggest doing the baking in an oven. Bread machines are convenient for kneading and rising dough. (They can also be used just for kneading.)

WHAT EVERY KITCHEN SHOULD HAVE

The items discussed below are essential for any good home cook. I have noted specific brand or other specifications where appropriate. For more detailed buying information about specific kitchen appliances and certain cookware items, see the preceding text and charts.

Maker and Model	Loaf Size/Shape	Features	Price
Black & Decker All-in-One Automatic Bread Maker B1500	1½-lb. loaf; square	6 bread modes; 13-hour programmable timer; dough setting	$199
Williams-Sonoma Bread Baker	1½-lb. loaf; square	3 bread cycles; 13-hour programmable timer; nonstick pan; viewing window	$199
Oster Deluxe Bread and Dough Maker 4811	1- or 1½-lb. loaf; square	4 bread modes; rapid-bake setting; 13-hour programmable timer; fruit/nut addition beeper; cast aluminum pan; cooling fan; viewing window	$184
Breadman TR 500	1½-lb. loaf; square	3 crust-color settings; 3 bread cycles; nonstick pan and paddle; viewing window	$180
Sunbeam Automatic Bread Maker 4810	1-lb. loaf; square	4 bread modes; rapid-bake setting; 13-hour programmable timer; fruit/nut addition beeper; cast aluminum pan; cooling fan; viewing window	$149
Welbilt Bread Machine ABM 2200	1-lb. loaf; round	2 crust-color settings; dough setting; start and stop buttons only; no viewing window	$149

WHAT TO BUY: You have to make a decision early on about a bread machine. If you are going to use it as a proofing box — the bread will be baked in an oven — then you can save some money and buy a less expensive model (most models listed above have a "dough setting," which will stop the machine after the first rise). If you are actually going to bake bread in the machine itself, the two most expensive machines are probably the best. When purchasing a bread machine, check out the shape of the bread pan (I dislike cylindrical loaves) and take a close look at the special cycles, useful for adding ingredients such as raisins. The Oster and the Sunbeam are the same machines except that the Oster can handle a 1½-pound loaf, whereas the Sunbeam only makes a 1-pound loaf.

Bread machines vary in the size of the bread pan. Some have 8-cup pans and others have 12-cup. However, both sizes often claim to make a 1½-pound loaf. If you are having trouble with your bread machine, try adjusting the amount of ingredients. If the loaf inflates and then collapses, increase the recipe. If it overflows the pan, cut back. By using the machine just for kneading, however, you will find capacity no longer a problem.

Pots and Pans

Dutch Oven: This is the most important piece of cookware you'll purchase, as it doubles as a container for roasts, braises, pot roasts, stews, soups, and so forth. You'll need a 12-inch-diameter pot, a must for cooking a cut-up chicken, for braising, or for frying. All-Clad and Calphalon are the top choices.

Omelet Pan, Nonstick: The best size is 8 inches. This is the inside diameter of the bottom of the pan, not including the sides. Calphalon is the top choice, followed by All-Clad.

Roasting Pan: This is essential for everything from the Thanksgiving turkey to roasted vegetables. Make sure that either a cake rack or a roasting rack will fit inside it. Be wary of a roasting pan that is either too light or too heavy. Don't forget that you will need to heat a roasting pan on top of the stove from time to time (when making a gravy, for example), and a lightweight pan will have hot spots and not conduct heat properly. A very heavy pan is also a problem — I have an enameled cast iron pan that is very hard to handle, especially when filled with a large piece of meat. A nonstick surface is optional.

Roasting Rack: A must for any roast, a roasting rack will keep the meat up off the bottom of the pan; this promotes even cooking and also keeps the roast from stewing in the accumulated juices. I prefer a rack with sides that are slightly angled, not the V-shaped racks, which press hard into the side of the bird or roast, sometimes sticking to the skin or meat.

Saucepans: Purchase a 2- and a 3-quart saucepan made from stainless steel with an interior core of aluminum or copper. All-Clad is the top in this category. Bourgeat also makes great saucepans. Both brands are expensive.

Skillet, Nonstick: You'll need a 12-inch pan with sloping sides, which is a serious investment but worth it. This is a must for stir-fries. Purchase Calphalon or All-Clad.

Stockpot: Purchase a 12-quart pot (an 8-quart stockpot is too small). You can save some money here and buy a less expensive model, as they are for boiling or simmering liquids. Just about any pot will do.

Items for Baking

Baking Sheet: The most important aspect of a baking sheet is its thickness — it should be heavy-duty. The new nonstick surfaces are fine, although I prefer to use parchment paper on a baking sheet for cookies. I just slide the parchment (and cookies) off onto a cooling rack and then slide on a new batch of cookie dough.

Cake Pans: I find that 9-inch round pans are better than 8-inch; the latter make a narrow high-rise of a cake. These don't have to be fancy pans, as you should line the bottom of a cake pan with parchment paper prior to baking. In fact, you can purchase precut rounds of parchment for either 8-inch or 9-inch pans — 25 rounds will cost about $4. Look for a cake pan with removable bottom and high sides, about 3 inches. Instead of baking separate layers, one cake is prepared and then sliced into either two or three rounds. This yields perfectly flat cake layers for filling. (You can also purchase two pans with lower — 1½-inch — sides if you prefer. You'll need to increase baking time about 20 percent and reduce oven temperature 25°F if using one higher pan instead of two shorter ones.)

Cake Rack: Make sure that it is large enough to handle two 9-inch cakes. If you do not have a roasting rack, get a cake rack that fits inside your roasting pan so it can serve double duty.

Casseroles: Although a soufflé dish works fine in a pinch, a couple of all-purpose casserole dishes come in handy—a 2-quart and a 3-quart are good sizes. Make sure that they come with lids, although aluminum foil makes a good impromptu cover.

Loaf Pan: This is the classic 8½ × 4½ × 2½ pan. If you line the bottom of a loaf pan with parchment paper, you don't need a nonstick surface. Purchase two so you can bake two loaves of bread at one time.

Muffin Tin: This is one place where nonstick pans really pay off. I use two pans frequently, as I need more than 12 muffins for weekend guests.

Pie Plate: A glass pie plate is best. It conducts heat well and will crisp up the pastry crust. I like a 9-inch-diameter pie plate and also prefer a deep-dish pie.

Plastic Flour Bucket: If you do much baking at all, a plastic container with tight-fitting lid is essential. A 6-quart bucket will run you about $5. Don't use containers that have small openings, and make sure that it can hold at least 5 pounds of flour, preferably 10. Glass flour containers are not large enough,

are too heavy, and the openings are too narrow.

Soufflé Dish: The 1½-quart size is best suited for most soufflés — I find that the 2-quart dish is too large. A soufflé dish can also be used for baking stuffing at Thanksgiving or for any number of other baked dishes.

Tart Pan: You will need a tart pan for a simple quiche or for a variation on an American pie. (You can use a basic American pie dough and fit it into a tart pan — it's a more elegant presentation.) Purchase a 9-inch-diameter pan (the large sizes are too big for most recipes, and the filling will cook too quickly). Purchase a tart pan with removable bottom.

BASIC KITCHEN TOOLS

Chopping Surface: I use the standard polyethylene chopping board. The cut marks don't show and it is relatively thin, which makes it easy to store. You should thoroughly clean your cutting board once a month with a mixture of bleach and water and be especially vigilant about washing the board after cutting meat or fish. Vinegar and kosher (coarse) salt are also recommended for cleaning. (Using a plastic scrubber, clean the cutting board with 1 teaspoon vinegar and 1 tablespoon kosher salt.) I suggest a cutting board with gutters to hold juices, because you are sure to cut up a roast chicken or carve meat on it.

Colander and Sieve: The classic large colander is necessary for draining pasta and cooked vegetables. Make sure that the legs are sturdy and solidly attached to the body — I have three colanders, two of which are short at least one leg. Most newer models have a round base, which is the preferred design. I would invest $20 in an 8-quart stainless steel colander, large enough to handle most any task. Beware of the high-priced models. I have seen a major national brand with a 5-quart nonstick colander advertised at $87! I would buy two sieves — a small wire-mesh sieve for straining citrus juices, et cetera, and a larger one for stocks, soups, and custards. The larger sieve should not be shaped like a basket — it should have a long handle and very fine holes. A sieve can also be used to sift flour.

Corkscrew: The waiter's variety is the cheapest and best alternative (it looks like a little Swiss army knife with a corkscrew and a small blade). If you are a klutz when it comes to opening wine bottles, purchase a Screwpull ($19) — anybody can use it successfully.

Grater: I use a flat grater, not the box graters found in most kitchens, for grating orange peel, cheese, and other simple tasks. It is easy to store and easy to clean (cleaning the inside of a box grater is very hard). To grate a small amount of cheese for individual servings, a simple flat hand-held grater with a handle is best, although it can be dangerous — my hand has slipped more than once, with unpleasant consequences. The Mouli handcrank drum grater is the safest and perhaps easiest method — there are 4 different grater drums, from coarse to fine. However, they are not easy to clean and over time the drums can bend.

Instant-Read Thermometer. You can't live without one. These are small thermometers with tiny dials (some newer models have large dials) that will register temperature within 10 seconds. You really can't cook a chicken or a roast without one, or bake a loaf of bread for that matter (just stick it into the bottom of the loaf — breads are done when cooked to 190°–208°F, depending on the type of bread). You can also purchase a digital instant-read thermometer, which is wonderful but which also costs as much as my first car, about $65. Stick to the old-fashioned model. It costs about $10.

Juicer: The old-fashioned one-piece glass juicers are best. The newer models with a screw-on plastic top break easily.

Kitchen Scale: You can purchase either a manual scale ($25 and less) or an electronic scale ($50 and up). The former is fine for gross measurements but is only accurate to within an ounce or so. The latter is better for precise measurements, which is important when measuring flour and other ingredients for baking. Electronic scales are also easy to reset to zero (called "taring"), handy when measuring a group of items in succession so that they do not have to be weighed individually. The bowl should be able to accommodate 8 apples and the scale measure up to 10 pounds. If purchasing a manual scale, look closely at the lines for ounces. If they are too close together, it will be difficult to take precise measurements.

Kitchen Shears: Very few home cooks have a good pair of shears. They are essential for cutting up or butterflying a chicken (shears are the tool of choice for removing the backbone), cutting fish into pieces for stock, or trimming off the last wing joint from a turkey before roasting. Fiskars makes a terrific pair of shears that will cut through anything for only $9. Henckels also makes kitchen shears, but they cost $25. Go with the Fiskars.

Knives: You'll need a 3- or 4-inch paring knife (a 2½-inch model is optional but very useful), a 10-inch chef's knife, a bread (serrated) knife, and a boning knife (see Chapter 3 for more information). A slicing knife is optional (you can use the chef's knife to slice meat). Wusthof, Henckels, and Chef's Choice are the best knives on the market. I prefer the Wusthof Grand Prix line.

Measuring Cups and Spoons: Purchase a 2-cup and a 4-cup glass measuring cup, two sets of metal measuring spoons, and two sets of metal dry measuring cups (¼ cup, ⅓ cup, ½ cup, and 1 cup). Neither the spoons nor cups should be plastic — the handles of the cups will break off and the cups themselves can crack over time. Measuring spoons should be made from a heavy-duty metal. The thinner models can bend over time, making them inaccurate. Two sets are essential so that you can find the right size when you need it.

Metal Dough Scraper: Very few home cooks own one of these, but everyone needs one. It consists of a broad, short, stiff metal blade attached to a handle. It is indispensable for scraping dough off a counter, moving chopped vegetables, or cleaning up a work surface. I use it to lift rolled pie dough onto a rolling pin before either flipping it over or transferring the dough to a pie pan. Dough scrapers come in two sizes. The smaller ones are $5.95 and the larger ones are $7.95. You can purchase them with wood or polyethylene handles.

Metal Pancake Turner: It is important that the leading edge be very thin to slip neatly under a pancake or fish fillet. Some spatulas have a thick, blunt end, which I find awkward.

Metal Spatula: This is a 6–8-inch-long metal blade with a rounded end used for frosting a cake.

Mixing Bowls: Three sizes are best: a small one, a medium-size one for most kitchen tasks such as waffle or cake batters, and a huge bowl for large quantities of bread dough or for big salads. I find it easier to mix ingredients in oversize bowls.

Oven Thermometer: Don't assume that your oven is properly calibrated. Go out and buy an inexpensive oven thermometer and check the settings at least once a year. You may find that your oven is off by 25 degrees or more, which can seriously alter cooking times. An oven thermometer is also useful for a slow-cook barbecue. Just put it on the grill to make sure that the cooking temperature does not rise much above 200°F.

Pepper Grinder: I have tried most models of grinders and have come to appreciate the advantages of a large wooden Peugeot grinder. (The small model starts at $29.95 and the giant size is $44.95 — I find the $34.95 model the best value and a good size for home cooks.) Small grinders are difficult to use, delivering a jerky and uneven grind. The one-handed grinders are clever. They work and are easy to fill. But for a nice, easy grind, go with an oversize model (it will also hold more peppercorns, a big advantage).

Rolling Pin: I have a personal preference for a tapered rolling pin (the ends are thinner than the middle and the pin is relatively small in diameter — it is perfect for rolling out rounds of dough as for a pie crust). I also find that I have better control over the dough with a small-diameter pin. If you can't find a tapered pin, purchase the smallest-diameter pin you can find. Stay away from chunky rolling pins with separate handles — a good rolling pin is just one piece of wood. By the way, don't ever wash an unvarnished rolling pin — it will make the wood stick to the dough over time. Simply wipe off with a kitchen towel after use.

Rubber Spatulas: You need at least two of them: one medium-size for most jobs and a very large one for dealing with large quantities. I prefer a blade that is somewhat flexible.

Salad Spinner: Be sure to purchase a salad spinner with an outer bowl that does *not* have slots for draining the excess water, so that it can be converted into a mini–washing machine for lettuce and greens. Simply fill the outer bowl three-quarters full with water, place the inner bowl with the lettuce into it, and then, using your hands, swish the lettuce around to clean. Lift out the inner bowl, pour the water from the outer bowl, replace the inner bowl, and then use the spinner to dry the lettuce. Avoid models with pull-strings — they will break. The Triumph salad spinner is a good solid design and costs about $15.

Salt Box: Very few home cooks have a salt box, but everyone needs one. First, always use kosher salt — it is coarser and easier to handle. (Contrary to popular belief, there is no difference in flavor between kosher, sea, and regular table salt). Keep it in a small box; I prefer a covered model. The box makes the salt instantly accessible to either your hand or a measuring spoon. However, it is very difficult to find a salt box these days in kitchen shops, although almost any small box with a lid will do nicely.

Shellfish Shuckers: The best tool for opening oysters is a short, squat screwdriver with a stubby end. It works right into the hinge and is easily twisted to open the shell. A traditional oyster/clam knife is also necessary to cut the oyster or clam from the inside of the top shell. An old paring knife is a bit dangerous but will open almost any clam because the blade is very thin. It can be worked between the shells of the most stubborn clam. Be sure to wear thick work gloves on one hand while shucking, or use a folded-up kitchen towel to hold the oyster or clam.

Steamer: The cheapest steaming mechanism is a collapsible basket steamer that costs about $7, but if you do much steaming, you'll need something more expensive. A stackable two-tier steamer is best; this can be purchased as a set with a pot or as an insert for standard-size pots. Forget electric steam-

ers — they just take up counter space. If you want the top-of-the-line steamer, purchase the Demeyere-Silvinox or the AMC and be prepared to shell out over $100.

Swivel Peeler: There are two types of peelers: the traditional swivel peeler and the fixed-blade peeler. To use the former, the peeler is pushed away from the body; the fixed-blade peeler is drawn toward the body. I prefer the swivel blade because it is quicker.

Timer: Go buy a three-way timer so that three separate events can be handled at once (e.g., the pasta water, the sauce, and the dessert). Don't buy a tiny timer — they are hard to read, and the buttons are so small that they are hard to use when your hands are greasy. I prefer the West Bend Model 40033, which has a clock, will display three separate countdowns simultaneously, will tell you how much time has elapsed since the timer went off, and can also measure total elapsed time, important when you are trying to test a recipe. The drawback is that these timers are expensive. Expect to pay up to $35. By the way, I have also used spring-driven timers and have found them to be inaccurate, which is okay for a soup but disastrous for a cake.

Wire Whisk: Don't buy those large balloon whisks that kitchen stores still have in stock (these were used for whipping egg whites before everyone took to electric mixers). You will need one relatively small, flexible whisk for mixing together dry ingredients or for whisking a few whole eggs. Don't purchase a very stiff, rigid whisk — they are difficult to use.

Wooden Spoons: I keep three spoons around my kitchen. One of them is not really a spoon — it has a flat end like a small pancake turner. This is very good for scraping up food from the bottom of a pan, useful when you are making a risotto or a stir-fry.

Miscellaneous Items: Any reasonably serious home cook will also need scissors, a pastry brush, string for trussing roasts, two aprons, four kitchen towels, a pair of metal tongs, a wooden ruler (useful when measuring dough for dinner rolls, et cetera), a ladle, plastic wrap, plastic storage bags, aluminum foil, wax paper, toothpicks, a biscuit cutter (in a pinch you can use the mouth of a small glass or the top of a small jar), cheesecloth (for straining stock and other liquids), parchment paper, and a large metal serving spoon.

ELECTRIC APPLIANCES

Electric Griddle: Vitantonio makes the best model. The heating element is embedded in the unit, not simply placed underneath it, which results in a very evenly heated cooking surface. This is the only way to cook pancakes or a large quantity of bacon.

Heavy-Duty Food Processor: The new KitchenAid is the best model on the market and comes with a minibowl insert, great for small quantities. You can't live without one, especially for making any sort of dough, from piecrust to bread to biscuits. See page 18.

Knife Sharpener: Purchase the top-of-the-line Chef's Choice sharpener (about $80) and don't bother with a sharpening steel or whetstone. See page 16.

Standing Mixer. This is a must for beating eggs and sugar, making certain breads, whipping egg whites, and so on. The KitchenAid is the top of the line. Expect to spend around $250 for the 4½-quart model. You can make do with a hand-held mixer if you don't do a lot of baking.

Waffle Iron: One manufacturer makes a clearly superior waffle iron — Vitantonio. They embed the heating element within the metal, creating a wonderful even heat that stays at temperature. Waffles in the Vitantonio iron will cook in about 2 minutes — other models I tested take up to 5 minutes. The green light on most waffle irons is like the red light on a bank security camera — it doesn't mean a thing. The light on the Vitantonio, which, by the way, also has accurate temperature settings, works perfectly. When the light goes on, the waffle is really done.

NONESSENTIAL COOKWARE

Here are some items that you can live without but may wish to invest in over time. Some of them, such as a springform pan, have very particular uses (a springform pan is handy when baking cheesecakes), and you may wish to hold off buying them until you come across a recipe that demands a piece of cookware you don't have.

Double Boiler: I almost never use one, although I have two. I find that a good heavy-bottomed saucepan over very low heat works just fine. You just have to pay attention and keep stirring.

Food Mill: Since the invention of the food processor, most American home cooks do not own a food mill, a device that is used for pureeing soft foods. However, a food processor is heavy-handed and easily liquefies foods rather than pureeing them, which robs the fruit or vegetable of its natural texture. I have an Acea food mill, which costs about $25 and is available through Williams-Sonoma. It looks like a small colander or saucepan. A crank handle run through a horizontal brace attaches to a blade that revolves to force the food through a perforated disk. (Some models such as the Acea have interchangeable disks with holes of different sizes.) You can also use a chinois (a heavy-duty conical strainer) for pureeing, but the food mill is easier and a good chinois is more expensive. This is not a necessary kitchen tool if you have a food processor, but if you enjoy pureed foods, you'll notice a big difference in texture.

Ice Cream Maker: I find that I rarely use my ice cream machine, but they are great for making fruit sorbets. Buy an inexpensive model that has a removable lining that must be prefrozen and an electric motor to churn the ingredients as they freeze. See page 27.

Jelly Roll Pan: This is a baking sheet with sides, used for making flat thin cakes for jelly rolls or for baking cornbread, for example, in a thin sheet to use as an appetizer. The lightweight models can warp in a high-heat oven, which is a disaster — the batter will not cook evenly. The basic models run about $12, and nonstick versions are about $25.

Pasta Machine: If you plan on making homemade ravioli, purchase the Atlas manual machine for $45 (see page 27). Otherwise, don't bother with a pasta machine at all. Buy your dried pasta at the store — it's better than homemade.

Peel: This is the large, long-handled spatula used by bread and pizza makers to get bread in and out of an oven safely. I have both a wooden and a metal peel and find no difference between them.

Pizza Stone: It is best to bake a pizza directly on a hot surface rather than place the dough on a pizza pan and then insert the cold pan into a hot oven. You can purchase one-piece pizza stones that are large enough for a 14-inch pizza — they cost about $25. Or you can go to a tile store and get a few unglazed Mexican tiles or even use ceramic tiles. Some cooks claim that leaving a pizza stone in the oven all the time creates a more evenly heated baking environment. I'm skeptical about this, but pizza stones really do make better pizza and bread.

Ramekins: These are individual baking cups used mostly for desserts such as custards. I find it easier to prepare most of these dishes in one larger container, such as a soufflé dish. However, you will need to purchase a set if you plan on making crème brûlée. I prefer the 8-ounce size (about $5 each — they are inexplicably expensive).

Small Saucepan: These are good for melting butter, for heating small quantities of maple syrup, or for steeping a few crushed cloves of garlic in a small quantity of olive oil. When you are dealing with a cup or less of liquid, a 2-quart saucepan is just too big.

Springform Pan: These are very useful when baking a cheesecake (getting a cheesecake out of a cake pan is difficult) — a springform pan just unbuckles and the sides are easily removed. These are useful pans but optional and cost about $8. The standard size is 10 inches in diameter.

Tube Cake Pan: This is necessary for an angel food or chiffon cake, although other cake recipes call for one occasionally. Never grease the inside of a tube pan when baking an angel food cake — in order to rise properly, the cake needs to hold itself up by the sides of the pan, which would provide no purchase if greased. A Bundt pan is optional but is occasionally called for in a recipe. The standard-size tube pan measures 9½ inches in diameter across the top.

Miscellaneous: Here are a few items that are entirely optional but that I find helpful: a pastry bag and tips for cake decorating, a jar opener (I have a "Gilhoolie," a metal gadget that will open any jar in just seconds), a candy thermometer (I use it about once a year, but you'll need one for cooking a sugar syrup or for frying), a potato masher, a pair of needlenose pliers for removing fish bones, a meat pounder (you can use a small, heavy skillet instead), a small vegetable brush (these are good for cleaning mushrooms), a corn stripper (indispensable for removing kernels from an ear and for milking corn, tasks required when making a corn chowder, soup, or fritters), and a scoon (a small kidney-shaped piece of plastic which is great for scooping out batter and other foods from bowls).

BASIC FOODSTUFFS
A good cook will keep a well-stocked pantry and a few essential items in the refrigerator. Be sure to purchase very small quantities of dried herbs and replace them once a year. I find that spices will last longer, although two years should be the outer limit for storage. For most recipes, fresh herbs are infinitely better than dried, although dried herbs are important as a backup. By the way, fresh herbs should be used toward the end of cooking, unlike dried herbs, which can be added early on. Triple the quantity of dried herbs called for in a recipe when using fresh, although this rule is made to be broken. The amount depends heavily on the type and quality of the herb in question.

Baking Goods: Unbleached and cake flours, bread flour, cornmeal, cornstarch, baking powder, baking soda, yeast, cocoa, unsweetened and semisweet chocolate.

Canned Goods: Four cans (28 ounces) tomatoes, 4 cans chicken stock, 2 cans beef stock, 2 cans white beans for emergencies.

Condiments: Apricot jam for baking, Dijon mustard, ketchup, capers, anchovies (anchovies are an excellent flavor enhancer for stews, soups, and sauces), mayonnaise.

Dairy Products: One quart milk, one dozen eggs, buttermilk, a chunk of Parmesan, one pint heavy cream.

Dried Spices and Herbs: Whole black peppercorns, cayenne pepper, ground cinnamon, ground cloves, ground coriander, ground cumin, curry powder, ground ginger, kosher or sea salt, dry mustard, nutmeg (whole), oregano, hot red pepper flakes, rosemary, tarragon, thyme.

Flavorings: Almond extract, vanilla extract, unsweetened cocoa, Tabasco, good-quality soy sauce, orange-flavored liqueur, brandy, sherry. Do not use "cooking" brandy or sherry. Use the same quality liquor that you would serve to guests. If you wouldn't drink it, don't cook with it.

Fresh Herbs: Italian (flat-leaf) parsley (flat parsley has more flavor than curly parsley). Other fresh herbs should be purchased only when needed or grown year-round on a windowsill.

Fruit: Two lemons, one orange.

Legumes: Dried lentils and one other basic bean (any white bean will do, such as Great Northern beans or navy beans) for soups.

Nuts: Shelled pecans, walnuts, almonds.

Oils and Vinegars: High-quality extra virgin olive oil (a small bottle for dressings and drizzling), good-quality olive oil, large bottle vegetable oil for frying (I use canola oil since it is the healthiest oil on the market), red wine vinegar, white wine vinegar, balsamic vinegar. Toasted sesame oil (different from regular sesame oil) is optional but is wonderful for stir-fries and Asian marinades.

Shortening: Unsalted butter (use a butter that is low in water content, such as Land O'Lakes), Crisco (should be kept refrigerated for use in pie pastry).

Sweeteners: White, light brown, and confectioner's sugars, corn and maple syrups, molasses, honey.

Vegetables: Four medium onions, one head garlic, carrots, celery, potatoes.

Miscellaneous: White and/or brown rice, spaghetti, linguine, lasagna, small pasta for soups.

Should a Good Cook Use a Microwave Oven?

Is a microwave oven only good for cooking bacon and melting chocolate? After trying more than two dozen much-touted microwave tricks, techniques, and recipes, I found a few welcome surprises but remain convinced that this is a technology still in search of a sensible application.

~

Cooking started millennia ago over open fires. It then moved inside into fireplaces and eventually to wood-stoves, gas stoves, electric stoves, and now the microwave oven. At each step along the way, there were legions of vocal detractors, claiming, for example, that cooking in a woodstove just wasn't as good as roasting over a wood fire. And it is quite true that after two centuries of progress, we have dramatically reduced the flavor of our food in order to gain convenience. A marinated and spit-roasted chicken is quite a different culinary experience from a bird zapped in a microwave oven.

Although I have a strong allegiance to the past, there is no question that sacrificing quality to convenience makes some sense. I use an electric knife sharpener, a standing mixer, and my food processor all the time. But since the promise of the microwave oven is a marriage between speed and convenience, the issue is just how fast and convenient this machine really is. After performing more than 30 tests in a microwave, from pot roast to melting chocolate, I can state with some assurance that this machine is very in-convenient for preparing most recipes but has a few food preparation tricks that it does quite well.

WHAT IS CONVENIENCE?

There are many things about a microwave oven that are truly inconvenient. For starters, to check on cooking, you have to take the food out of the oven to see into the pie plate, soufflé dish, or 8-cup measuring glass. Compared to stovetop cooking, where you can add ingredients, stir foods, or check on cooking with no problem, the microwave is terribly awkward. Also, most containers get quite hot in a microwave — this was a revelation to me in the tests — because as the food heats up it transfers heat to the cooking vessel. It is irritating if not outright danger-ous to remove a piping hot 2-quart soufflé dish from an oven with marginal clearance around the baking dish.

This is all part and parcel of the biggest drawback of microwave cooking. It is the most finicky method of cooking ever in-vented. Try baking 3 potatoes following the recipe for 1 and see what happens. The size and type of oven, the amount of food, the weight of the food, the type of container, and so on all affect the outcome, much more so than in a conventional oven. In addition, cooking times in a microwave are often measured in seconds, not minutes, which greatly reduces the window between undercooked and overcooked. Adjusting recipes in terms of serving size is problematic as well, since this may affect cooking times in unforeseen ways. It can also be difficult to, say, double a recipe in a microwave. I once followed a recipe for coarsecut Irish oatmeal that worked fairly well for 1 serving and then realized that I couldn't make it for 4 because the oatmeal would bubble up out of the container into the oven. In all my years of cooking, I never had more outright failures than when using the microwave.

I am also nonplussed by the notion of "faster" when it refers only to time in the oven. First of all, many of these recipes aren't faster at all. I made black-eyed peas, which took over 3 hours, and fish and vegetables really don't cook up any faster than by most traditional methods (fish can be roasted or braised in 10 minutes or less, and most vegetables take just a few minutes to steam). The biggest drawback, one that the microwave oven's adherents won't tell you about, is that you have to keep moving food in and out of it. You cook on high for 2 minutes, take it out, add something, cook for 10 minutes at 80 percent power, take it out, stir, let it rest, put it back, et cetera. Although the total oven time may be less, so what? It's not easier. I'd rather leave a roast in the oven for 2 hours unattended than muck about with a series of precision maneuvers. And, to top it off, I find that most microwave recipes are woefully inaccurate in terms of timing because of the large number of variables that affect cooking speed.

BUT DOES IT TASTE BETTER?

I keep hearing microwave devotees say, "But it does a great job of cooking vegetables."

Or, "I love fish cooked in a microwave." Well, I'll take steamed vegetables (or better yet, roasted vegetables) any day over the microwave variety, which take on an unpleasant texture unless cooked absolutely perfectly. I did make a good swordfish steak in a microwave, although I can do much better by browning the steak first on top of the stove, adding some rice wine vinegar, soy sauce, scallions, and the like, and then popping it covered in a high oven for 8 minutes. I find that microwaved food just doesn't have much flavor. Deep down it is an antiseptic cooking method that adds nothing to the food in question. Other than bacon, which does taste great when cooked in a microwave, there is nothing I would not prefer to cook by steaming, boiling, roasting, baking, or grilling.

THE MICROWAVE AS KITCHEN TOOL

Now we come to the only area where microwaves can add value. Although the microwave oven is lousy at defrosting any irregularly shaped foods such as chicken, it does a reasonably good job of reheating rice, and I would use it to soften butter in a pinch, although leaving a stick out at room temperature does a better, more even job. I was disappointed when I defrosted bagels before toasting — they became a bit soggy and can be toasted when frozen anyway. However, the microwave oven does a fantastic job of melting chocolate, which otherwise takes about 15 minutes in a 250° oven. It is also very good at heating maple syrup in just 60 seconds. I was also astonished to find that a decent polenta can be made in about 10 minutes in the microwave, a big time savings over the stovetop method, which takes a good half hour or more. Of course, the microwave is quite good at heating up leftovers and baby formula, as well as boiling water for coffee or tea. But for real cooking, forget it. This is one kitchen tool with very limited application.

KITCHEN TESTS

Here are the results of my tests, with specific recipes included where appropriate. I used recipes and techniques from the top microwave cookbooks.

CHICKEN

Cooking Chicken Cutlets: These are boneless chicken breasts that have been butterflied so they are relatively thin and of an even thickness. I placed them in a glass pie plate, covered them with plastic wrap, and cooked on high for 2 minutes. They were cooked through and were relatively tender. Of course, I could sauté them quickly in just a bit of oil in a nonstick skillet or broil them, but this method was fine. I would not recommend this technique for a regular boneless chicken breast because the meat varies dramatically in thickness. The thinner portions will become tough and overcooked.

Defrosting Chicken: I tried using the 30 percent power setting, defrosting for 4 minutes and then resting for another 5. I repeated this four times, turning the bird once during every power cycle. The result was a chicken that was frozen solid on the inside, slightly cooked at the tips of the drumsticks, and defrosted on the outside. I had to constantly fiddle with it during the 36 minutes of defrosting — turning the bird, resetting the timer, et cetera. I don't know how long it would take to extract that frozen packet of giblets out of the cavity, but I didn't have the patience to find out. By that time, the drumsticks would probably be cooked. (Microwave cookbooks tell you to put small pieces of aluminum foil on the ends of the legs and the wings. Come on, the microwave

oven is supposed to make life easier!) How about putting a frozen chicken in the refrigerator overnight? Works fine for me.

Poaching Chicken Breasts: In a glass pie plate, the breasts were poached with ½ cup chicken stock for 8 minutes on high. They were tasteless and the texture was wet and unpleasant. Roasting, frying, or sautéing are superior methods.

FISH

Filet of Sole: I melted 1 tablespoon butter in a glass pie plate, added 2 tablespoons stock and 1 tablespoon white wine. I placed the fish in the plate, covered the plate with plastic wrap, and cooked for 2 minutes at full power. The fish was overcooked, with an unpleasant, soft texture. Sole needs to be pan sautéed or fried for texture. Sole is very fragile and requires perfect timing.

Swordfish Steak: I placed a half-pound steak in a glass pie plate on top of 3 tomato slices and some cilantro. I drizzled some olive oil and lemon juice on top with salt and pepper, covered the dish with plastic wrap, and microwaved it at full power for 3½ minutes. I removed the dish and punched two holes in the plastic wrap and let it sit for 2 minutes. The steak was excellent. There was lots of juice from the tomatoes and the fish was perfectly cooked.

DEFROSTING, HEATING, SOFTENING, AND MELTING

Defrosting Bagels: I wrapped a frozen bagel in a sheet of paper towel and zapped it on high for 30 seconds. It defrosted, but the texture was terrible — damp and spongy. Since a frozen bagel can be toasted directly, without defrosting, there is no point in defrosting it first. However, if you wish to serve a bagel untoasted, I recommend that you either use a toaster that has a defrost setting or simply let the frozen bagel thaw at room temperature.

By the way, frozen bagels can be cut in half with a good bread knife.

Heating Maple Syrup: Sixty seconds on high, with the syrup in a small pitcher, works fine. This is much easier than using the stovetop, as maple syrup boils over easily when heated. Do not fill the pitcher more than ¾ full.

Heating Frozen Soup: I started with 3½ pounds of frozen soup in a plastic container with the lid off. I defrosted at full power for 12 minutes. At that point, about ⅓ of the soup was liquid; the rest was frozen solid. This did not seem any faster than simply throwing it in a pot over low heat. What's the point?

Softening Brown Sugar: I placed 1 cup brown sugar in a glass dish, added a slice of apple, wrapped it, and used the high setting for about 40 seconds. This was faster than the traditional oven method (place in a covered baking pan with a small container of water and heat at 200°F for 20 minutes). After softening, the sugar must be placed in an airtight bag or it will become hard again rather quickly.

Softening Butter: This worked pretty well. It took just over 1 minute on 30 percent power. However, to get the inside really soft, some of the outer layer melted, which is not ideal for creaming butter for a cake, for example. Still, it took me about 90 minutes to soften a stick of butter at room temperature. I prefer the old-fashioned method but would use a microwave in a pinch.

Softening Cream Cheese: I put an unwrapped refrigerated package of cream cheese in a large glass measuring cup and cooked at 50 percent power for about 75 seconds. The cheese touching the bowl melted while the interior was still fairly stiff.

It's better to soften cream cheese at room temperature.

Softening Dried Fruit: Place dried fruit — I used apricots that had been sitting in my pantry for about a year — on a plate, sprinkle with water, and then cover with plastic wrap. Heat on high for about 30 seconds, a little more for very dry fruit. This worked pretty well, although I noticed that some pieces were softer than others. This is also easy to do on top of the stove and doesn't take much time. I would stick to the stovetop method, which produces more even results.

Melting Butter: I cut half a stick of butter into 4 pieces, 1 tablespoon each, placed them in a glass measuring cup, and covered the top with a paper napkin. The butter was melted after about 90 seconds on high. However, it sputtered and splattered, soaking the top of the paper towel and covering the inside of the cup. It's just as easy and less messy to simply melt butter on top of the stove.

Melting Chocolate: Okay, this is the "killer application." Melt chocolate uncovered in a glass bowl or measuring cup at 50 percent power for 4 minutes, stirring after 2 minutes. I can get the same result in a 250°F oven in about 15 minutes, but this was quicker and easier.

Melting Crystallized Honey: I removed the top from a medium jar of honey and zapped it on high for about 40 seconds. This worked very well and is a whole lot easier than using a hot-water bath.

MEAT
Bacon: I tried cooking 4 slices of medium-cut bacon on a triple thickness of paper towels for 3 minutes (45 seconds per slice). They were a little undercooked, so I extended the time an extra 30 seconds and then let them rest for 5 minutes after cooking. Perfecto!

Crisp and not greasy. This beats broiling or pan-frying any day.

Pot Roast: This was really a braised brisket. First, the recipe called for 2¼ pounds of brisket, which really doesn't fit into a 2-quart soufflé dish unless it is rolled into a roast, which I did. I then cooked on high for 35 minutes covered. The meat was already at 165°F internally, and it was supposed to need another 25 minutes! The meat was incredibly tough (although brisket does have a lot of flavor). The microwave really ruined the meat. It did make a decent sauce, but nothing like a sauce made in a slow oven. Forget it!

RICE AND GRAINS

Millet: I placed 2 tablespoons butter in a deep Pyrex pie dish and melted for 2 minutes

---

KITCHEN TEST

What to Do with a Microwave Oven

Here are eight things that a microwave oven does best.

Test	Technique	Results
Defrost and cook bacon	Defrost by heating unwrapped package on high for 15–30 seconds; cook 6 slices on high on a triple bed of paper towels, 45 seconds to 1 minute per slice; let stand 5 minutes after microwaving	Excellent bacon without the grease. Bacon does splatter, however, when cooking.
Soften butter	Defrost at 30 percent power.	This took a little over 1 minute with good results, although some of the butter actually melted. This technique is not recommended to soften butter for creaming.
Melt chocolate	Place ½ pound of chocolate in a glass bowl or measuring cup. Melt uncovered at 50 percent power for 3–4 minutes; stir after 2 minutes.	This is the killer application. Great results and truly faster than the traditional method.
Melt crystallized honey	Place jar without lid on high for 30–45 seconds. If jar is large, repeat.	Excellent use for microwave.
Cook polenta	In a casserole, combine 1 cup cornmeal with 3½ cups water, 1 tablespoon olive oil, and 1 teaspoon salt. Cover and cook on high for 9–12 minutes, stirring after 5 minutes.	Very good polenta and fast.
Soften brown sugar	Place 1 cup of hard brown sugar in a glass dish with a slice of bread or apple. Cover with wrap and heat on high for 30–60 seconds.	Works well and is much faster than the oven method.
Warm pancake syrup	Heat on high in serving pitcher for 60 seconds.	Nothing could be easier.
Cook swordfish steak	In a glass pie plate, place steak on a bed of tomatoes and fresh herbs such as basil or cilantro. Drizzle with olive oil, lemon juice, salt, and pepper. Cook covered with plastic wrap for 3½ minutes on high. Prick holes in plastic and let sit out of oven for 2 minutes.	Perfectly cooked swordfish steak. Cooks in just 5 minutes.

at 100 percent. I added 1 cup millet and stirred and then added 2 cups broth on top. It was cooked for 10 minutes uncovered on high. The millet was tough, not properly cooked. The microwave dried out the grains like baked tapioca pearls.

Polenta: I placed 1 cup cornmeal, 3½ cups water, 1 tablespoon olive oil, and 1 teaspoon kosher salt in a soufflé dish, covered it with plastic wrap, and cooked on high for 5 minutes. I then stirred the mixture, recovered it, and cooked it on high for an additional 3 minutes. To my surprise, the polenta was lump free, creamy, and quite good. (For a half recipe, combine ½ cup cornmeal with 1¾ cups water, 1 teaspoon olive oil, and ½ teaspoon kosher salt in an 8-cup Pyrex measuring cup. Cover with plastic wrap and heat at 60 percent power for 4 minutes. Stir and cook an additional 4 minutes at the same power setting. Stir and serve.) This beats the lengthy double boiler method, which takes 1½ hours and requires stirring every 10 minutes. This was a dark horse application for the microwave, but it was a hands-down winner. I'll never make polenta on the stovetop again. One note of caution. Polenta will continue to cook after removal and a creamy, loose polenta will turn into a thick porridge in about 30 minutes. By the way, microwave polenta is great as a hot breakfast cereal served with maple syrup and butter.

Rice Pilaf: I melted 3 tablespoons unsalted butter in a 2-quart soufflé dish for 4 minutes on high. I then added 1 cup white basmati rice, stirred, and cooked another 4 minutes on high. Next I added 1½ cups chicken stock, covered, and cooked on high for 13 minutes. The rice was horrible — tough and chewy, with a bad taste from the browning of the butter and stock. The butter burns after a few minutes. This was the worst rice I have ever eaten (and one of the worst microwave recipes I have ever tested). Although I could

have retested this recipe after making some adjustments, I can cook a very good rice pilaf in about the same amount of time (21 minutes) on top of the stove. The stovetop method is virtually foolproof, and therefore the microwave method, which is finicky and no quicker, gets a thumbs down.

Reheating Cooked Rice: This can be a problem when cooking conventionally, although I have found steaming to be an easy method. Still, you need to have a steamer. I placed 4 cups of precooked rice in a baking dish, covered it with plastic wrap, and heated it for 5 minutes on high. The rice was heated through, although a bit moist and sticky. Considering the alternatives, this is a good use of the microwave.

Risotto: I melted oil and butter in a deepdish glass pie plate for 2 minutes on high and then added ½ cup chopped onions and cooked them on high for 4 minutes. One cup arborio rice was stirred into the butter and onions and cooked for another 4 minutes on high, at which point some of the onions had burned. I then added 3 cups stock and cooked for 9 minutes on high. I stirred the mixture and then returned the rice to the oven on high for another 9 minutes. I was using canned stock, which turned very dark during this process. The rice itself tasted like Rice-a-Roni — dark and leathery instead of creamy and rich. Anyone who thinks that this is anything like real risotto probably thinks chow mein is authentic Chinese fare. As with the pilaf test, I did not make this recipe a second time, since it required 28 minutes of cooking and produced dismal results. Even if I could make the recipe work, the stovetop method is easier (there is no stopping and starting) and the results are excellent. For cooks with a pressure cooker, wonderful risotto can be made in less than 10 minutes. I suggest you purchase *Cooking Under Pressure* by Lorna

Sass, which includes a terrific risotto recipe.

VEGETABLES

Acorn Squash: I cut 1 squash in half, scooped out the seeds, trimmed the bottoms so that they would sit flat, and then wrapped them in plastic wrap. They cooked on high for 6 minutes and were cooked through. I didn't care much for the flavor — this is steamed squash instead of baked squash. Also, the outer rind was cooked through, which I found unpleasant. I prefer oven baking for acorn squash.

Artichokes: I tried wrapping an artichoke in plastic after trimming it, and then cooking on high for 10 minutes. It was like a dried-up locust — all the water had been sucked out, leaving behind a featherweight husk. I tried it a second time and the results were okay, but not as good as the recipe on page 75.

Black-Eyed Peas: I followed a recipe from a well-known microwave cookbook. It took over 3 hours to prepare these beans in seven separate steps, including four stints in the microwave. The plastic wrap burst twice, the beans were overcooked long before the end of the cooking time, and they were half as good as beans prepared in a nice slow oven. The traditional method is so simple. Soak the beans overnight and then cook them on top of the stove for 20 minutes. You're done. No microwave oven. No four-step process. No plastic wrap. No 3 hours of cooking.

Broccoli: I cut the florets from one stalk, leaving behind the woody stems, and trimmed the stalk as demonstrated on page 66. I placed the broccoli in a small dish covered with plastic wrap and cooked it for 3 minutes on high. It was terribly overcooked. I tried again and this time I cooked it for only 1 minute. It was about right. Most microwave cookbooks suggest cooking broccoli for 4 minutes. Although large quantities may take longer, I suggest you start with 1 minute and work your way up. I prefer to steam my vegetables because timing is less crucial. If you are off by 15 seconds in a microwave, vegetables can end up overcooked.

Carrots: I used ½ pound of peeled baby carrots (they are sold already peeled in large plastic bags) with 1½ teaspoons sugar and 1 tablespoon butter. I cooked them on high for 8 minutes covered, then pierced the plastic wrap and let them sit for 1 minute. They were badly overcooked, with the texture of cheese puffs. I tried it again for only 3 minutes and they were still a bit overcooked. This is not a forgiving preparation method.

Mixed Vegetables: On a serving plate, I placed broccoli florets on the outside and red peppers on the inside, the theory being that slower-cooking vegetables such as peppers should be on the inside, with faster-cooking specimens around the perimeter. The plate was covered with plastic wrap and cooked briefly at full power. The flowers of the florets were a bit dried out and I noticed that the vegetables continued cooking after being removed from the oven. Unlike steaming, microwaving tends to dry out vegetables and the cooking times must be very precise.

Potatoes: I pricked a large baking potato with a fork and cooked it on high for 5 minutes. It was cooked throughout, but the skin was limp and soft. If you like potato skin, forget it. If you are baking the potato to use as a thickener in a sauce, for example, this is a good technique. By the way, I also tried this with a red waxy potato, not usually used for baking. It sputtered and sizzled because of the higher water content but cooked up just fine.

~ 3 ~

How to Use Knives

Yes, you do need to spend $80 on a high-quality chef's knife.

~

I f you ever invited me over for dinner, I would take a moment to slip into your kitchen and rustle through the kitchen drawers looking for the knives. Although this is hardly good manners (it may actually be an obsession), I usually find one or two stainless steel knives, not one good high-carbon steel chef's knife, and, of course, all the knives are so dull they would have trouble cutting through a head of cabbage. I also find that most home cooks own a sharpening steel but no sharpener — not a whetstone or electric device in sight. This happens in even the best of kitchens, where the residents have invested in the finest marble, the most expensive stoves, and top-of-the-line handmade kitchen cabinetry. I am confronted with this problem every year when I am asked to carve the Thanksgiving dinner at my in-laws'. They present me with a knife that can barely cut butter and a sharpening steel, and then they stand around waiting for some miracle of precision carving. It's like performing brain surgery with a pickax. This is why chefs have their own tool boxes full of knives and a whetstone — and why I now take my own carving knife to my in-laws'. You simply cannot cook without a sharp knife.

SIX BASIC CUTTING TOOLS

There are six basic kitchen tools you need to use for cutting: a chef's knife, a paring knife, a boning knife, a serrated knife, a peeler, and a good pair of kitchen shears. A chef's knife, an 8- or 10-inch knife with a recessed handle, is a cook's most important cutting tool. Although it is a large knife, it can handle everything from slicing mushrooms to cutting through bone. A quick glance at a chef's knife tells the story. The part of the blade closest to the handle, the heel, is very wide and heavy, whereas the point is narrow and pointed. Each part of the blade — the heel, the point, and the portion in between — is used for a different purpose. The point is used for delicate slicing, the heel is used for heavy-duty jobs (cutting through chicken bones, cutting hard vegetables such as carrots or turnips), and the middle part of the blade is used for most everything else. The bolster is the portion of the knife between the blade and the handle.

There are basic grips for holding a chef's knife. If you require a lot of control over the blade for precision cutting, move your hand up toward the blade, placing your thumb on

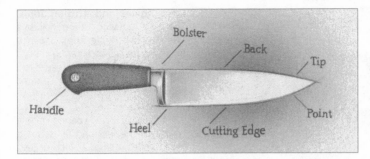

Anatomy of a Chef's Knife: A chef's knife has a recessed handle, which makes chopping possible. Otherwise, the cook's knuckles would strike the work surface. The most common sizes of chef's knives are 6-inch, 8-inch, 10-inch, and 12-inch. If you intend to buy only one such knife, purchase the 10-inch size.

one side of the blade and your forefinger on the other. This is a good grip for slicing a tomato or onion. For mincing herbs or vegetables, move your hand back off the blade and onto the handle, with your thumb and forefinger resting on the bolster of the knife. When chopping, the hand not holding the knife should be placed flat along the top edge of the blade and then used to help guide the blade.

The paring knife comes in a variety of sizes, from a 4-inch blade down to my favorite size, the 1½-inch blade. These knives are used for peeling, trimming, coring peppers, trimming artichokes, and so on. For most applications, the hand should be moved up well onto the blade for maximum control. I find the smaller sizes most useful, as I can use a chef's knife or a boning knife for most other tasks. The boning knife is 5 or 6 inches long and has a thin blade that is good for trimming meat and poultry or filleting fish. Most home cooks will rarely use a boning knife, because these days cooks do very little boning. If you are watching your budget, you could hold off on this purchase. A serrated knife is used for cutting bread and should have a stiff blade. A vegetable peeler should have a simple swivel blade — I prefer this design to either the rigid blade peelers or the French peelers that look like small slingshots. A good pair of kitchen shears is very important. For under $10 you can purchase Fiskars shears, which work just fine (more expensive models run around $30). A pair of needlenose pliers is

also handy, for removing the pin bones from certain types of fish.

KNIFE TECHNIQUES

Most home cooks are not skilled at basic knife techniques: chopping, dicing, mincing, slicing, segmenting, and so forth. In my experience, fewer than 5 percent of cooks can properly and quickly chop an onion or mince garlic, hence the popularity of the food processor. But once you learn the basics, you'll find that a good knife is often a lot faster than an appliance. In fact, I tested that proposition by timing a professional chef (Gordon Hamersley from Hamersley's Bistro in Boston) when performing basic dicing and mincing tasks. Chef Hamersley's times made

---

KITCHEN TEST

How Fast Can a Chef Dice an Onion?

A professional chef, Gordon Hamersley, wielding a chef's knife was timed dicing an onion, chopping two carrots, and mincing parsley, garlic, and shallots.

Technique	Time
Dice 2 onions	45 seconds
Dice 2 carrots	60 seconds
Mince 1 bunch parsley	50 seconds
Mince 2 cloves garlic	35 seconds
Mince 2 shallots	32 seconds

---

it clear that a properly used knife is quick and efficient for small jobs, especially considering the advantage in terms of cleanup. A

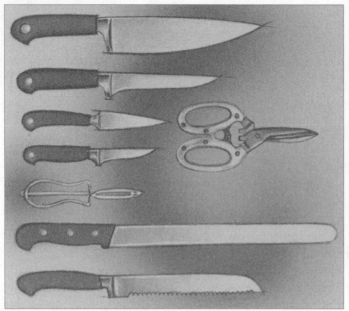

Basic Knives and Kitchen Tools: The basic tools for cutting include a 10-inch chef's knife (top), a 6-inch boning knife, a 3-inch paring knife, a 2½-inch paring knife, a vegetable peeler, a slicing knife, a serrated knife, and poultry shears. If you wish to invest less money, start with just a 10-inch chef's knife, a paring knife, a vegetable peeler, and a serrated bread knife. A small (2-inch or less) paring knife is very helpful for precision tasks such as coring peppers, and poultry shears are wonderful for removing the backbone from a chicken for butterflying. The larger paring knife is best for larger tasks such as peeling apples. Needlenose pliers are also useful for removing the small pin bones that are present in salmon and other fish.

food processor is time-consuming to wash and takes up a lot of room in a drainboard or dishwasher.

BASIC CUTS AND TERMS

This cookbook and most others use instructions such as mince, dice, cube, and chop. Each instruction has a specific meaning. The finest cut of all is minced — the food is chopped into the smallest possible pieces. Garlic and fresh herbs are most often minced. If the food is cut into cubes, there are a variety of terms that apply. A very small cube — ⅛ inch square or less — is referred to as a brunoise by chefs. For the rest of us, however, this is just a fine dice. A medium dice is about ¼ inch square, and a large dice is over ½ inch square. Onions are most often diced, as are other vegetables such as carrots, celery, and potatoes. Many cookbooks refer to the julienne, which is a small matchstick cut, a leftover from haute cuisine fine for a four-star restaurant but silly for a home cook. You'll see no reference to julienned foods in this book, because they are too

much trouble. Unlike mincing, which is an extremely fine cut, and dicing, which is really cubing, chopping is a simple, relatively coarse cut for which the shape and relative size of the pieces is not that important. Foods can be finely or coarsely chopped. For a stew, for example, I would coarsely chop onions, not mince or dice them. For a risotto, however, I might finely chop the onions, because the other recipe ingredients are small and a large piece of onion would be out of place.

HOW TO USE A SHARPENING STEEL

If you do not own a good electric knife sharpener such as the Chef's Choice (see page 16), you'll need to tune up the edge of the knife frequently with a sharpening steel. A steel is a thin, round, slightly tapered length of steel with a handle. It is used to smooth out any rough spots in the edge of a knife and to realign its molecules as well. (Many steels are magnetized and manufacturers claim that this assists in molecule realignment, although this sounds a bit far-fetched to me.) There is one thing a sharpening steel does not do, though, and this is sharpen! Only a true sharpener (a whetstone, for example) can handle this properly. I do, however, suggest using the sharpening steel (or the Chef's Choice electric sharpener) every time you use a knife.

The safest and easiest method for using a sharpening steel is to place the point of the steel on a work surface with the handle standing straight up. If the counter is slippery, dampen a kitchen towel and place it underneath the tip of the steel. Hold the handle of the steel with your left hand (assuming you're right-handed) and with the right hand hold the knife blade at a 20-degree angle to the steel, as though you are going to shave thin strips off the length of the steel. Start with the heel of the blade (the part closest to the handle) against the steel. As you move the edge of the knife down the steel, slowly pull the knife toward you so that only the point of the blade is touching the steel when the blade arrives at the work surface. Contrary to popular belief, only light pressure should be applied — this is not a grinding action but a light, quick pass with the knife. You should hear a clear ring as you work, not a grinding noise. If you hear the latter, you are applying too much pressure. Pass the knife blade five times on each side of the steel (alternate from one side to the other). Once you become more proficient, you can hold the sharpening steel across and about a foot away from your body with the handle mid-chest and the tip at the height of your right shoulder. With your thumb and forefinger moved well up onto the blade, hold the knife vertically, tip pointing up. Start with the heel of the blade against the tip of the steel and move the knife toward the handle of the sharpening steel while pulling downward. As the knife reaches the handle, only the point of the knife should still be making contact with the steel. Do this on the other side of the steel and repeat four additional times.

Holding a Chef's Knife for Precision Cutting: The hand should be high up on the handle, with the forefinger draped over the top of the blade and the thumb exerting pressure from the other side. This provides control for precision cutting and chopping.

Holding a Chef's Knife for Chopping: The thumb and forefinger rest on the bolster, the section between the blade and the handle.

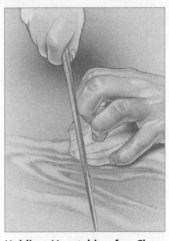

Holding Vegetables for Chopping: The hand not holding the knife should hold vegetables in a clawlike grip, with the large finger joints pointing toward the side of the knife. The knife blade should brush against the joints, with the fingertips curled away safely underneath.

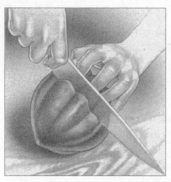

Heavy-Duty Cutting: The heel of the knife is best for heavy-duty jobs such as cutting an acorn squash in half.

Light Cutting: For relatively delicate foods such as a tomato, start with the tip of the knife leading the way.

Now push downward and forward, slicing through the tomato.

Quick Chopping: Position the knife tip on the cutting surface, holding the knife handle high in the chopping position and placing the other hand on top of the blade near the end. Make rapid chopping motions, moving the knife in an arc while the hand on top of the blade applies gentle pressure to provide guidance and keep the knife tip in contact with the cutting board. After each pass, mound the food into a pile and repeat.

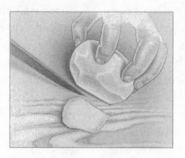

Preparing Vegetables for Cutting: Most vegetables need to be trimmed to provide a flat surface for stability while cutting. For round or oblong objects — an onion, potato, or turnip, for example — simply slice off a small piece from one side.

For long objects such as a carrot, it often helps to cut them in half lengthwise before chopping, although this depends on the type of cut you require.

Peeling a Garlic Clove: Place the broad, flat side of the knife over a clove and strike the blade with your fist or the heel of your hand. The clove will now separate easily from the outer skin. You can also hit the garlic clove gently but firmly with a small rock.

Mashing Garlic: Peeled garlic cloves can be mashed by using the end of the knife, pressing the heel of your palm to crush the clove under the slightly flexed flat side of the blade. A sprinkling of coarse salt on the clove will make this process easier.

Smear the clove under the blade, spreading it out over the work surface. Scrape it back together and repeat until clove liquefies.

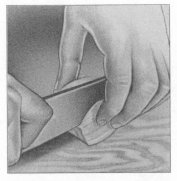

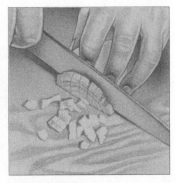

Dicing an Onion: Cut the onion in half lengthwise and then peel it. (It is much easier to peel an onion after it is cut in half.) With the flat, cut portion down, make a series of horizontal cuts parallel to the work surface. The distance between these cuts will determine the size of the dice. To keep the onion in one piece during dicing, do not cut all the way through the root end.

Now make a series of lengthwise vertical cuts. When dicing an onion, some chefs will use the tip of the knife for these cuts, starting the cut short of the root end. This leaves the tough root end intact, which holds the onion together during chopping.

Now make a series of cuts perpendicular to the last cuts. Repeat with the other half.

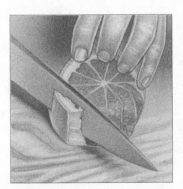

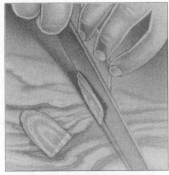

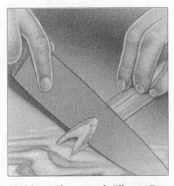

Peeling Large Round Fruits and Vegetables: Oranges, grapefruits, rutabagas, and some hard squashes, such as butternut, should be peeled in this manner. Start by trimming off the top and bottom. Then make a series of downward cuts, following the contour of the fruit or vegetable. Be careful not to cut too deeply.

Cutting on the Bias: This technique is often used when preparing vegetables for a stir-fry. Hold the knife at a slight angle to the length of the vegetable when cutting.

Making Elongated Slices: Turn the knife so that it makes a shallow, elongated cut through the vegetable.

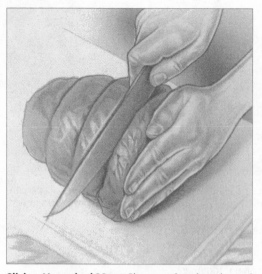

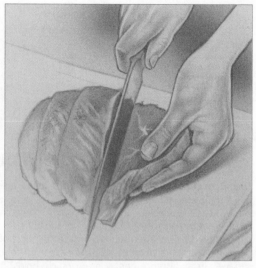

Slicing Uncooked Meat: Place one hand on the end of the meat and pull the knife toward you through the meat with the handle higher than the tip.

Repeat, pulling the sliced section away from the meat with your thumb and forefinger.

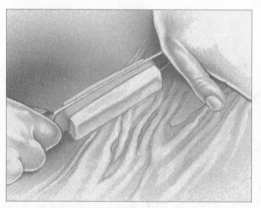

Chopping Butter for Pastry: Butter should be cut into small pieces before being worked into flour for pie dough, biscuits, or pastry. Start by cutting a stick in half lengthwise. Turn the stick onto its side and make a second lengthwise cut.

Now cut across the stick. Each slice will come apart into four pieces.

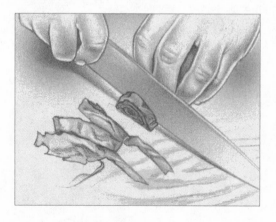

Preparing a Chiffonade: Roll up the leaves (spinach, cabbage, et cetera) and then cut into strips. (A chiffonade is thin strips of leafy greens or herbs.)

I rarely use a paring knife, because I find that a chef's knife does most jobs rather well, including peeling, when your thumb and forefinger are moved up onto the sides of the blade. However, there are a few delicate tasks that do require a smaller knife.

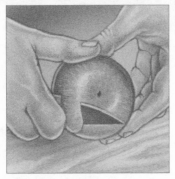

How to Peel: Place your thumb on the fruit or vegetable and move the blade toward you.

Scraping Vanilla from a Bean: Cut the bean in half lengthwise and scrape out the vanilla with the sharp edge of the knife.

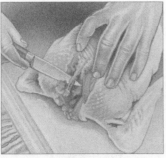

Removing the Wishbone Before Roasting Poultry: This makes carving the breast meat easier. Start by cutting underneath both sides of the wishbone to free it from the flesh.

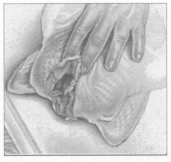

Cut through the bottom of the wishbone to free the ends. The wishbone will still be attached at the top.

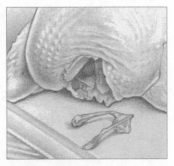

Holding the wishbone close to the top, twist and pull until it comes free.

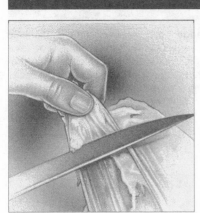

Trimming Fat: With a very sharp boning knife, start to cut away excess fat. Now pull the fat up and away with your free hand while cutting with the boning knife.

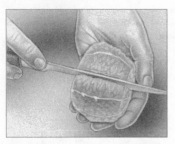  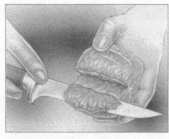

Segmenting an Orange or Grapefruit: Start by peeling the fruit as shown on page 59. Hold the fruit in one hand. Make a cut parallel to one of the membranes, moving the knife toward the center of the fruit.

When you reach the center, flip the knife away from the center of the fruit, pushing the blade edge up against the next membrane.

Continue cutting outward, sliding out the segment as you work.

THE SERRATED KNIFE

 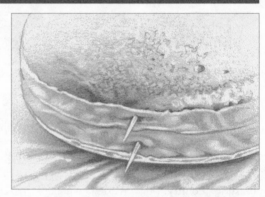

Cutting Cake Layers: Start by making a slight cut all the way around the cake at the height at which you wish to cut it. Now make the actual cut, using a gentle sawing motion, following the line that you marked.

Mark the position of the layers with toothpicks so that the cake can be properly reassembled after it is filled.

THE VEGETABLE PEELER

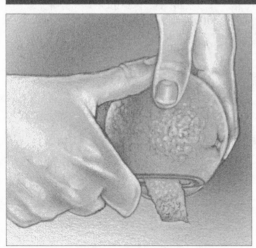

Zesting an Orange: Many recipes call for grated orange peel. I find that zested and then minced peel provides a brighter, cleaner flavor. (Grating orange peel releases fragrant oils, which results in a loss of flavor.) Pull the peeler toward you, removing just the outer skin, leaving behind the bitter white pith. Now the peel, or zest, can be minced with a chef's knife.

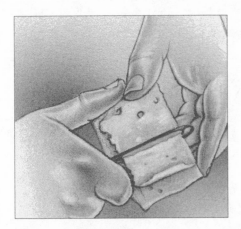

Shaving Parmesan: Use a vegetable peeler to shave off thin slices of Parmesan or other hard cheese.

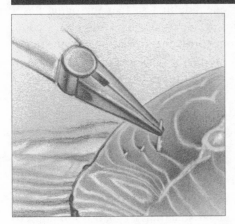

Removing Pin Bones: Salmon steaks have small pin bones sticking up through the flesh. To remove them, simply extract them with needlenose pliers.

~ 4 ~

An Illustrated Guide to Quick Fruit and Vegetable Preparation

How do you cut up a mango without mangling it? How do you perfectly dice a tomato, leaving behind the seeds and juice? Here's a short course in quickly prepping fruits and vegetables.

~

The best way to test someone's culinary skills is to ask them to dice an onion. Some people remove half the onion along with the skin. Others spend 10 minutes carefully mincing as if they were neurosurgeons. Still others violently hack away, leaving large pieces and small, a Freddy Krueger approach to vegetable preparation. This chapter is about how to do it right and do it fast.

There are a few basic rules that make all of this easier. First, for many tasks, it's best to create a flat surface by either cutting the item in half or trimming off one side. Otherwise, the vegetable or fruit can slip easily, and that can cause a serious accident. To slice an onion, for example, remove a shallow slice from one side first so that the onion has a stable surface to sit on as you cut. Second, get your cutting hand right up over the top of the knife blade. This gives you lots of control. Otherwise, it's like trying to eat with a fork held at the very end of the handle. Third, the knife has to be absolutely sharp. Dicing an onion is nearly impossible with a dull knife. Finally, don't be too fussy. My wife, Adrienne, an excellent cook, takes pains to perfectly dice an onion or mince a clove of garlic. My diced onion looks ragged by comparison, but I can do 5 onions to her 1. Your home kitchen is not Lutèce — nobody will be measuring the evenness of your dice.

APPLE

To slice an apple for a tart or pie, peel and then remove the core with an apple corer. Cut in half and then slice each half into thick (for a pie) or thin (for a tart) pieces.

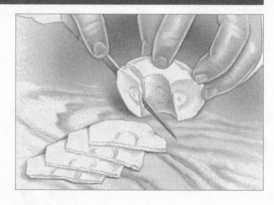

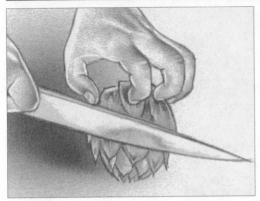

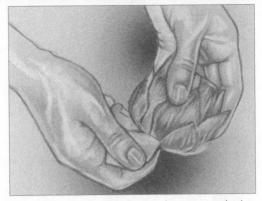

To trim an artichoke for cooking whole, cut off the stem. Now cut off about one-third of the top of the artichoke with a large chef's knife.

Pull off the tough outer leaves that are attached to the bottom of the choke.

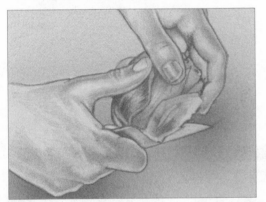

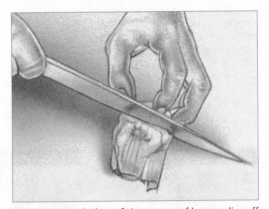

To prepare an artichoke bottom, trim off all leaves with a very sharp paring knife, starting at the bottom.

When you reach the soft inner core of leaves, slice off the bottom.

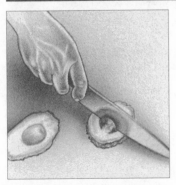

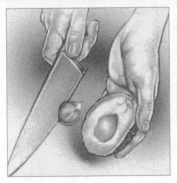

To remove an avocado pit, cut avocado in half lengthwise, twist the two halves apart, and place the half with the pit on a flat work surface. Using the edge of a large chef's knife, make a quick downward stroke into the pit.

Hold the avocado half in one hand and remove the pit, still attached to the knife, with the other.

To peel an avocado, make four lengthwise cuts, dividing the skin into quarters. Do not cut through into the flesh. Now peel off the four strips of skin.

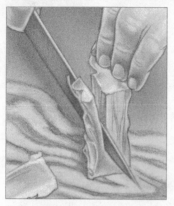

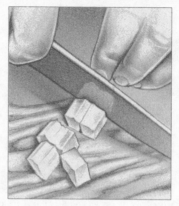

To separate the florets and prepare the stalk, start by removing the stalk in one piece. If the stalk is long, cut it in half crosswise before trimming. Cut away about ⅛ inch of the outer layer of the stalk by placing one end of the stalk on the work surface and slicing downward with a chef's knife.

Cut the stalk in half lengthwise and then cut into bite-size pieces.

Cut off the florets by placing the head upside down and trimming with a chef's knife. Cut close to the florets, leaving behind the small woody stems. Do not leave tough-looking stems attached to the florets unless you want to peel them.

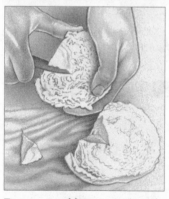

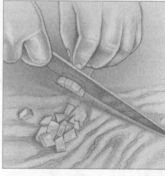

To core a cabbage, cut the cabbage in half and then make V-shaped cuts on either side of the core and remove it. Cabbages can also be quartered, and then the core is trimmed away from each piece.

To dice a carrot, cut the carrot in half lengthwise. With the flat side down, make a series of lengthwise cuts in the carrot half. Space the cuts according to the desired size of the dice.

Cut across the carrot for a quick, even dice. (Use this same technique for chopping celery.)

CAULIFLOWER

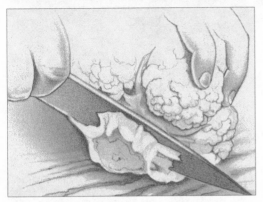

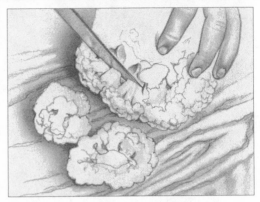

To remove the florets, start by cutting the stem very close to the head.

Next, cut off the florets from the stem.

CHILI PEPPER

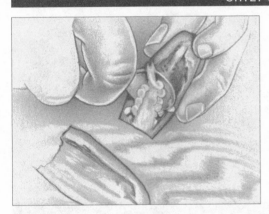

To seed a chili pepper, cut in half and remove the seeds and white pith with a metal ½-teaspoon measuring spoon.

CUCUMBER

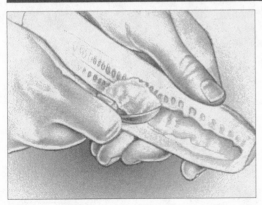

To slice a cucumber, cut the cucumber in half lengthwise. Remove the seeds by using a metal 1-teaspoon measuring spoon (or a melon ball cutter).

Now place the two halves side by side and cut with a chef's knife.

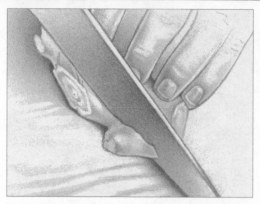

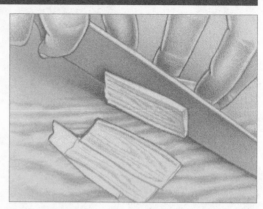

To peel ginger, cut the root into uniform pieces and then remove the outer skin with a vegetable peeler.

To dice ginger, cut the peeled root lengthwise into thin slices.

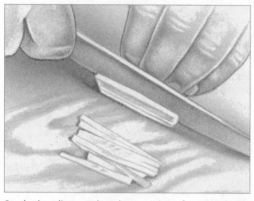

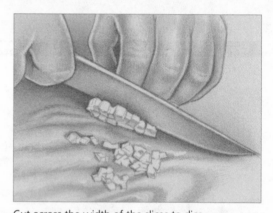

Stack the slices and make a series of even, closely spaced, lengthwise cuts.

Cut across the width of the slices to dice.

To stem greens, stack a few leaves and then make cuts on either side of the tough stems to remove.

An alternate method is to hold the stem and then hack away the leafy green with a sharp knife.

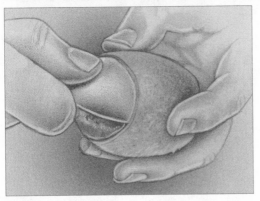

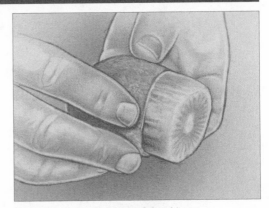

To peel kiwi, slice off the ends and then use a spoon to separate the flesh from the skin.

Simply push the flesh out of the skin.

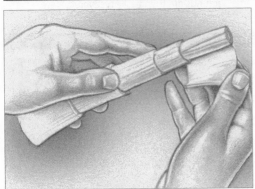

To prepare leeks for chopping, cut off the root end and the tough, dark green leaves. Using a paring knife, cut away the dark green outer layers of the leek, moving up toward the top of the leek as you work. The leek will be tapered when you are done. Cut the leek in half lengthwise and then rinse under running water before chopping. This method provides the maximum amount of usable leek. (Alternatively, if you wish to use only the white part of the leek, begin by simply cutting off the root end and all the green end; cut the leek in half lengthwise, rinse, and chop.)

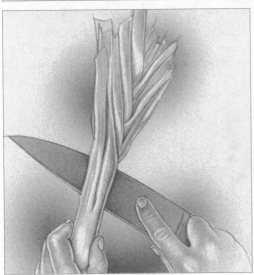

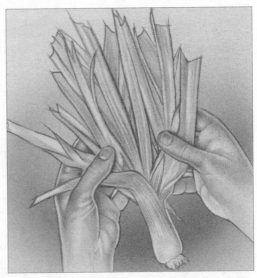

To rinse a whole leek, make two slits through the length of the leek, starting about 2 inches from the root end.

The interior of the leek is now exposed and can be rinsed in cold water to clean.

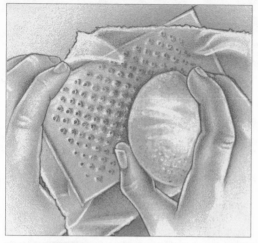

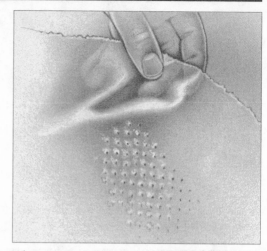

To grate lemon peel, place wax paper or parchment paper over the grater.

When you are done grating, lift off the paper and the small gratings are then easily recovered.

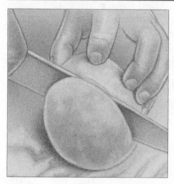

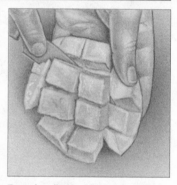

To remove the flesh, cut off a slice from each side of the mango, cutting as close to the broad, flat pit as possible.

Make a crosshatch pattern in each slice, cutting to but not through the skin.

Turn the slice inside out so that the pieces stand up and separate. Cut these pieces off the skin.

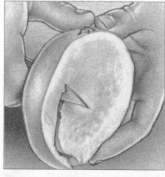

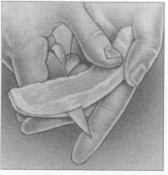

With the remaining mango, use a paring knife to trim away the outer flesh from around the pit.

Cut away the skin and cut fruit into pieces.

To pit olives, place on a work surface and then mash lightly by hitting the side of a large chef's knife with the heel of your hand.

The pits are now easily removed.

 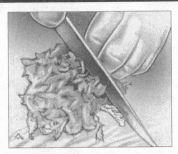

To mince parsley, bend sprigs into a U.

Mince with a chef's knife, being sure to hold your fingers in the ``claw'' position.

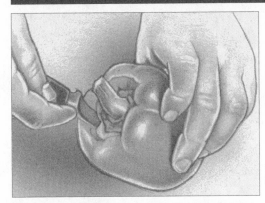

To seed a pepper, use a paring knife to cut a hole in the top of the pepper.

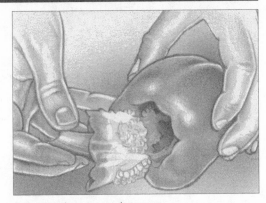

Pull away the stem and core.

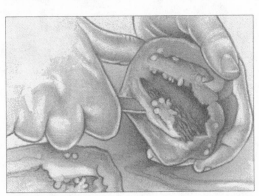

Cut the pepper in half and cut away any remaining white membrane and seeds.

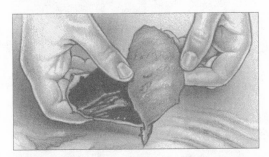

To peel a pepper, seed the pepper and then place the halves skin up in a roasting pan. Roast at 500°F for 15–20 minutes, or place under a broiler until skin blackens. Place pepper in a double plastic bag and close with a twist-tie. Let sit for 10 minutes and then remove skin by hand.

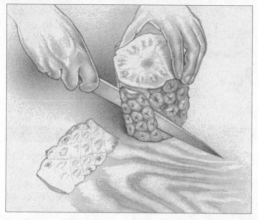

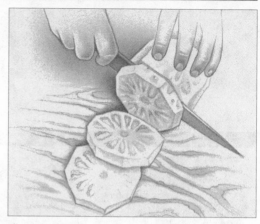

To slice a pineapple, cut off both ends. Using a very sharp chef's knife, cut downward to remove the peel.

Slice into rounds.

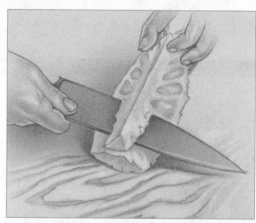

To prepare pineapple for individual servings, slice the pineapple in half with a large chef's knife. Cut each half again into quarters.

Cut off the bottom end, leaving the crown intact, and then cut away the core.

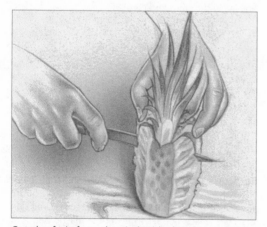

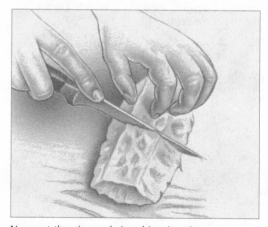

Cut the fruit from the rind with the pineapple in a standing position.

Now cut the pineapple into bite-size pieces.

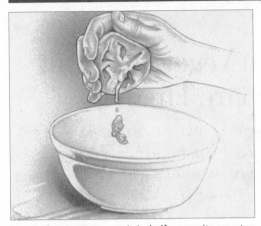

To seed a tomato, cut it in half across its equator. Holding the tomato half firmly above a bowl, give it a quick, downward jerk and a slight squeeze to force the seeds out.

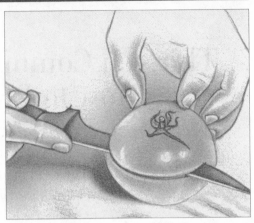

To dice a tomato, cut across the tomato, about an inch down from the top, stopping the cut ⅜ inch from the side.

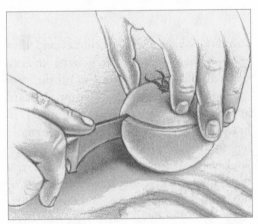

Now turn the knife downward, cutting parallel to and ⅜ inch in from the side of the tomato.

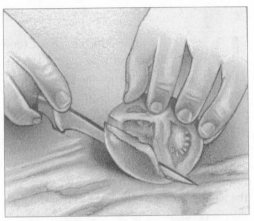

Cut off the remaining sides of the tomato, leaving behind the seeds and core.

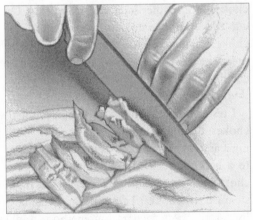

Now cut the flesh into strips.

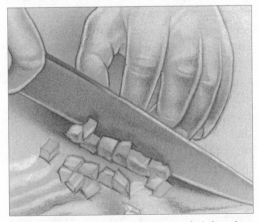

Put the strips together and cut across their length to dice.

~ 5 ~

Thirteen Common Vegetables and How to Prepare Them

Vegetable cookery is full of rules, some of which are true (don't trim beets before roasting), some of which are outdated (boil corn for 8 minutes), and some of which are just plain silly (cut an X in the bottom of broccoli stalks before cooking). Here's what works.

~

Perhaps the most difficult type of food to prepare at home is vegetables. Although fresh-from-the-garden varieties are usually full of flavor, supermarket vegetables are often lackluster, having been bred for shipping, not eating, or having been trucked thousands of miles to your store. There is no comparison between a just-picked carrot, rich with flavor and snap, and the bag of wooden tubers for sale in the produce section.

For most top-notch vegetables, steaming is my cooking method of choice. It's simple, fast, and preserves colors and flavors. Many root vegetables, especially supermarket varieties, are best roasted, which caramelizes natural sugars, thereby enhancing taste. Dull supermarket vegetables usually need a flavor enhancer, and that is why sautéing, stir-frying, and baking are favorite methods, as these methods lend themselves to the addition of other ingredients.

ARTICHOKES

Purchase artichokes that are green, with leaves fully closed. To prepare them for steaming whole, wash artichokes and then trim off the top third with a large knife (a serrated knife works well). Cut off the stem so that it is flush with the bottom. Discard any tough outer leaves. If you prefer to braise or sauté an artichoke, start by removing the tough dark green leaves, working your way around the artichoke until you reach the tender, yellow leaves. Trim off the top of the remaining leaves and the tough areas around the base. Cut off the stem end and trim away the tougher fibers around the stem. At this point, you can cook the artichoke whole, either steaming or braising. Or, cut the artichoke in half and remove the choke, the inedible pod that sits on top of the meaty heart. The remaining artichoke can be cut into wedges, quickly steamed, and then, if you like, sautéed.

I tested three methods for preparing artichokes: boiling, steaming, and braising. Boiling has two drawbacks: bringing the water to a boil takes a long time, and boiled artichokes are inferior in texture and flavor to steamed artichokes. I found that braising is by far the best preparation method, and I have included a recipe below.

Master Recipe for Steamed Artichokes

The size of the artichokes will affect the cooking time by up to 70 percent. Make sure that they are thoroughly cooked — there is nothing worse than half-cooked artichokes. I don't bother rubbing the trimmed artichokes with lemon juice, as many cookbooks recommend. I can live with a little discoloration.

4 artichokes, prepared for steaming (see above)

Prepare a steaming basket or bring 1 inch of water to a simmer in a pot large enough to hold the artichokes. Place artichokes in pot, stem end up. Cover pot and steam for about 40 minutes for mature whole artichokes, less for smaller or baby artichokes or wedges. Artichokes are done when the stem end is tender when pierced with the tip of a knife.

Serves 4

Artichokes Braised in Chicken Stock with Capers

The chicken stock, butter, and capers in this simple preparation impart a subtle but welcome flavor to a vegetable that, in my opinion, can use a little lift. As a bonus, the braising liquid can be served as a lighter, more interesting, and healthier dipping sauce than the usual melted butter and lemon juice.

4 large artichokes, stems removed and top third trimmed off
1 tablespoon butter
2 tablespoons capers
2 cups chicken stock

1. Add 1 inch of water to a large pot and bring to a boil. Add the prepared artichokes and cover, reducing heat to maintain a simmer. Cook for 20 minutes.

2. Remove artichokes and discard cooking liquid. Add butter to pan over medium-high heat. When foam subsides, add capers and sauté for 30 seconds. Add chicken stock and bring to a simmer. Add artichokes, cover, and braise for an additional 20 minutes or until tender.

3. Serve artichokes with stock on the side for dipping. (For a stronger dipping sauce, boil stock mixture until reduced by ⅓).

Serves 4

Fried Artichokes with Salt and Parmesan

This recipe violates all of my rules about home cooking. The recipe, at least the original on which my copy is based, is from Reed Hearon, chef at Lulu's in San Francisco, which violates my first rule — never make chef recipes at home. Second, it calls for a "baby" vegetable, which is absolutely banned from my cooking repertoire (what's wrong with "adult" vegetables?). Finally, it calls for frying, which makes a mess and leaves one with all that hot oil to clean up. That being said, this is my favorite appetizer. Thin slices of Parmesan are made for fried artichokes, and you can get down an awful lot of beer in the process as well. Baby artichokes do not have a developed choke, so it does not have to be removed. Just pull away the tougher outer leaves, chop off the top ½ inch or so, and quarter them. If you can't find baby artichokes, you can use quartered artichoke hearts with the choke removed but with a few of the really tiny, pale yellow leaves still attached to the heart. Forget the outer leaves — it's like chewing on vinyl. A 10-inch iron skillet can fry up 4 baby artichokes at one time.

8 baby artichokes
Canola oil for frying
4 cloves garlic, peeled and lightly crushed
Salt to taste
3 ounces Parmesan, thinly sliced into large pieces

1. Trim off the stem at the base of each artichoke and pull off the tougher outer leaves. Cut ½ inch off the top and then quarter.

2. Heat ¾ inch of oil in a 10- or 12-inch skillet or Dutch oven until it reaches 330°F. Add the garlic cloves and the artichoke pieces and fry for 2 minutes. Remove the garlic as soon as it starts to turn dark brown and discard. Remove the artichoke pieces to a double thickness of paper towel and let drain for at least 10 minutes or until almost ready to serve.

3. Heat oil to 360°F and fry artichokes a second time for an additional 2 minutes or until nicely browned. Drain on paper towels for 1 minute. Flip onto fresh paper towels and salt to taste. Serve on a platter topped with slices of Parmesan.

Serves 4–6

ASPARAGUS

Asparagus should be washed, snapped to re-move the tough stem ends, and the remaining stem ends peeled with a vegetable peeler if the stems are thick and tough. Thin spears do not require peeling. (If you hate to peel asparagus, just snap the spears in half and cook only the tips. This is affordable at the height of the season, but not recommended the rest of the year.) Some cookbooks recommend soaking asparagus to remove any dirt that has accumulated under the scales. I don't find this to be a problem and just give them a quick rinse under running water. For each single serving as a side dish, I use 4–5 thick spears, 6–8 medium spears, or 10–12 of the pencil-thin spears available in early spring.

I tested five methods of preparation: steaming, braising, roasting, grilling, and stir-frying. Steamed asparagus is wonderful — bright in color with good bite and flavor. Braised asparagus is easy to overcook and absorbs too much liquid. Both grilled and roasted asparagus come out crisp-cooked and surprisingly tasty. Stir-fried asparagus with plenty of fresh basil is my favorite preparation.

Master Recipe for Steamed Asparagus

Asparagus comes in different thicknesses. The thin "pencil" asparagus that arrives early in the season cooks in just 2 or 3 minutes. Thicker-stalked asparagus requires longer cooking — up to 6 minutes — and the ends of the stalks must be peeled as well. Properly steamed asparagus should neither be crunchy nor soft.

> 1 pound asparagus, washed, ends snapped
> Salt and freshly ground black pepper to taste

If using a steaming basket, bring 1 inch of water to a boil in a large pot. If you do not have any steaming equipment, bring ⅛ inch of water to a boil in the bottom of a large pot. Add the asparagus, cover the pot, and steam over medium heat for 3–5 minutes, depending on the size of the asparagus. To test, simply remove one spear, wait a few seconds until cooled, and then bite into the large, snapped end. It should be firm but not crispy. Drain and sprinkle with salt and freshly ground black pepper to taste.

Serves 4 as a side dish

Master Recipe for Roasted Asparagus

This is an unusual preparation method but is easy and heightens the vegetable's flavor. Roast asparagus is best served immediately, as it tends to soften after cooking.

> 1 pound asparagus, washed, ends snapped
> Olive oil
> Salt and freshly ground black pepper to taste

Heat the oven to 400°F. Place prepared asparagus in a shallow roasting pan and brush with olive oil. Sprinkle with salt to taste. Cook for 10 minutes. Add freshly ground black pepper to taste and serve.

Serves 4 as a side dish

Asparagus with Ginger-Citrus Dressing

The combination of ginger and citrus goes well with fresh asparagus. You can use almost any vinaigrette with steamed asparagus.

1 pound asparagus, washed
1 tablespoon minced fresh ginger
½ teaspoon minced orange peel
2 tablespoons orange juice
2 teaspoons white wine vinegar
¼ teaspoon soy sauce
¼ teaspoon kosher salt
¼ teaspoon freshly ground black pepper
3 tablespoons olive oil

1. Snap off the tough ends of asparagus.

2. Whisk together the ginger, orange peel, orange juice, vinegar, soy sauce, salt, and pepper. Whisk in the olive oil slowly to form an emulsion. Let sit for 1 hour.

3. Bring ⅛ inch of water to a boil in a large sauté pan. Add the asparagus, cover, and steam over low heat until stalks are bright green, crisp, and tender, 4–6 minutes. Place asparagus on a serving platter and dress with vinaigrette to taste.

Serves 4

Asparagus with Olive Oil, Balsamic Vinegar, and Parmesan

This recipe was suggested to me by the editor of this book, Jennifer Josephy. She also suggests using blue cheese instead of Parmesan for a simple variation.

1 pound asparagus, washed, ends snapped
3 tablespoons olive oil
2 teaspoons balsamic vinegar
1 teaspoon red wine vinegar
2 ounces Parmesan, grated

Steam or grill asparagus (see Chapter 33 for grilling instructions). Whisk together olive oil and vinegars. Top asparagus with vinaigrette and grated Parmesan.

Serves 4

Stir-Fried Asparagus with Ginger, Garlic, and Basil

Basil, asparagus, and ginger may appear to be an odd combination, but there is no better way to prepare this vegetable. Use a large nonstick skillet instead of a wok and be sure to get the pan plenty hot before starting the stir-fry (see Chapter 35 for more information). If you do not have a nonstick pan, you will need to use additional oil, up to twice the amount called for below.

2 tablespoons good-quality soy sauce
1 tablespoon dry sherry
1 tablespoon water or chicken stock
1 tablespoon canola oil
1½ pounds asparagus, washed, ends snapped, and cut into small pieces
2 teaspoons minced garlic
2 teaspoons minced fresh ginger
½ cup minced fresh basil
1 tablespoon chopped scallions
½ teaspoon sugar

1. Combine the soy sauce, sherry, and water and set aside. Place a large (at least 12-inch) skillet over high heat for 4 minutes. Add 2 teaspoons canola oil and heat for 1 minute or until the oil just starts to smoke. Add the asparagus and stir-fry for about 2 minutes or until barely tender. Clear the center of the pan, add the garlic and ginger and 1 teaspoon of oil, and sauté for 10 seconds. Remove pan from heat and stir the ingredients to combine.

2. Place pan back on heat, stir in the soy sauce mixture, and cook for 30 seconds. Add the basil, scallions, and sugar and cook and stir for another 30 seconds.

Serves 4–6

BEETS

Beets should be firm (some supermarket beets are old and flabby), though they can be plenty dirty. The tops, if attached, should be fresh-looking and bright green. For cooking beets whole, just trim off all but 1 inch of the tops and most of the root end — don't actually remove or puncture the skin — and scrub thoroughly. I've roasted, steamed, and boiled beets and found that the first is by far the best method, especially when followed by a quick sauté with butter and seasonings.

Master Recipe for Roasted Beets

The easiest way to remove the skins after roasting is to rub them vigorously with a wad of paper towels. I have also tried using kitchen towels, which work fine but end up deeply stained. You can also peel the roasted beets with a small sharp paring knife, although you will have to wait a bit for the beets to cool.

8 large beets, about 2¼ inches in diameter

Heat oven to 400°F. Cut away tops, leaving 1 inch of stalk. Leave root end intact. Wash beets gently. Put beets in one layer in a roasting pan and cover tightly. Roast for 45–50 minutes or until beets are easily pierced with a sharp thin knife. Let cool for 10 minutes. Remove skins by rubbing beets one at a time with paper towels. Remove tops and root end. (To serve, cut into ¼-inch slices, toss with butter, and season liberally with salt and pepper. If beets have cooled before serving, place slices in a nonstick skillet and toss with butter to coat, cooking until beets are warmed through. Season with salt and pepper.)

Beets Glazed with Butter and Vinegar

This is my favorite preparation for beets. I prefer to use raspberry vinegar, which imparts a beautiful glaze to the beets and also provides a sweet and sour flavor. Don't be shy with the freshly ground pepper just before serving.

16 small beets or 8 large beets, roasted and skinned according to master recipe
⅔ cup chicken stock
½ cup raspberry vinegar
3 tablespoons unsalted butter
Salt and freshly ground black pepper to taste

If using large beets, cut into quarters. In a large sauté pan, combine stock, vinegar, and butter and bring to a simmer. Lower heat and simmer until slightly thickened, about 5 minutes. Add the beets and simmer for about 8 minutes, rolling the beets in the sauce. Add salt and plenty of freshly ground black pepper to taste.
Serves 6–8

Roasted Gingered Beets with Orange

Although roasted beets can be finished in a quick sauté with butter and almost any type of flavoring or seasoning, I find that the combination of ginger and orange makes a wonderful marriage with the deep but startling flavor of beets. This recipe is best served with meat (especially pork) or poultry. Do not serve with any other sweet dishes.

2 tablespoons unsalted butter
1 tablespoon minced fresh ginger
1 teaspoon grated orange peel
2 tablespoons orange juice
2 teaspoons sugar
6–8 large beets, roasted according to master recipe and quartered
Salt and freshly ground black pepper to taste

Melt butter in a skillet over medium heat. Add ginger and sauté for 20 seconds. Add next 3 ingredients and cook for 30 seconds. Add beets and cook for 5 minutes, tossing frequently. Add salt and liberal amounts of freshly ground black pepper to taste.
Serves 4–6

Red Flannel Pancake

The classic version of this dish is a real hash made with cubed potatoes and beets. This is more of a beet-potato pancake, which is called a roesti. *If you are not partial to bacon fat, omit it and substitute an equal amount of butter. Canola oil can be substituted for the butter, but the pancake will be less flavorful and will also not brown as well. Be sure to use a nonstick skillet for this recipe, otherwise the pancake will stick. This is one occasion when the grater attachment for a food processor comes in handy.*

2 slices bacon
½ pound beets, peeled, grated, and patted dry with paper towels
1 pound all-purpose potatoes, grated, and patted dry with paper towels
1 medium onion, peeled and chopped
2 tablespoons minced scallions
Salt and freshly ground black pepper to taste
2 tablespoons unsalted butter

1. Fry the bacon in a large nonstick skillet with sloping sides. Remove bacon when it is crisp, drain on paper towel, and crumble into a large bowl. Drain off all but 2 teaspoons of bacon fat.

2. Add beets, potatoes, onions, and scallions to the bowl with the bacon and stir to combine. Add salt and freshly ground pepper to taste.

3. Melt the butter in the skillet over medium heat. When melted, press the beet-potato mixture into the pan and cook for about 15 minutes.

4. Use a spatula to free the hash from the bottom of the pan. Flip hash onto a large plate and then return it to the skillet, bottom side up. Cook another 10–15 minutes or until the bottom is browned and crusty.

Serves 4

BROCCOLI

Remove broccoli florets from the small stalks before cooking. Otherwise, the stalks will have to be peeled, which is tedious. The large stem should be peeled with a paring knife — remove about a ⅛-inch layer of the outer skin — and cut lengthwise in half and then across the width into ½-inch pieces. Cut florets into manageable clusters. Place stem pieces then florets in ½ inch of boiling water (or place in a steaming basket) and cover. Cook for 5–6 minutes or until just tender. Never cook broccoli for more than 7 minutes — the color and texture both begin to deteriorate. Steam broccoli for only 3½ minutes covered, 4 minutes uncovered, if you plan to sauté or stir-fry it to finish.

In searching for the best way to prepare broccoli, I tested seven common procedures: presoaking in water (no difference); presoaking with sugar and salt (sweeter but not more flavorful); presoaking in acidulated water (no difference); cutting an X in the base of the stems and stalk without peeling (no difference); adding stale bread to the cooking liquid to reduce the broccoli odor (wet bread with undiminished broccoli odor); boiling with the pot covered versus uncovered (it takes about 1 minute longer uncovered; the old wives' tale about allowing "gases to escape" is just that); and tying broccoli together and standing it up in boiling water (just try getting a bunch of broccoli to stand up straight!). None of these variations were improvements.

A few other testing notes. I stored broccoli for 24 hours in a loosely closed bag, in a perforated bag, in a tight-closed bag, and exposed. The first two methods are fine, but the latter two are not recommended. The tightly

---

SCIENCE OF COOKING

I investigated why broccoli deteriorates rapidly after 7 minutes of cooking and found that this is due to two distinct actions: heat and acid. As broccoli is cooked (heated), the chlorophyll begins to break down, resulting in a change of color and texture. In addition, all vegetables contain acids that leach out during cooking. This acid environment, water and/or steam, also contributes to the breakdown of the chlorophyll structure. None of this is an issue, however, if broccoli is not cooked past 7 minutes.

closed bag creates too much moisture and imparts a musty smell. The exposed broccoli stems quickly became rubbery.

Master Recipe for Steamed Broccoli

The florets and stalk are cooked simultaneously with two different methods. The thicker pieces of stalk will be boiled in the ½ inch of water, yet many of the florets will be steamed, thus cooked a bit more slowly, as they sit above the water.

> 2 pounds broccoli
> ½ teaspoon kosher salt

Wash broccoli. Remove florets from stalks and separate into manageable bunches. Remove ⅛ inch outer skin from large stalks; cut peeled stalks in half lengthwise and then into ½-inch pieces. Bring ½ inch salted water to a boil in a large, wide-bottomed pan with lid. Add stem pieces and then florets and cover. Reduce heat to maintain a slow boil. Cook for 5–6 minutes or until stalk pieces and stems are just tender. Drain.

Serves 4

Master Recipe for Blanched Broccoli

I recommend blanching for any recipe in which broccoli is cooked twice — a sauté, for example. For stir-fries, I simply cut the broccoli into very small pieces to avoid double cooking.

> 3 quarts water
> 1½ teaspoons kosher salt
> 2 pounds broccoli

Bring the water and salt to a boil in a large pot. Add cleaned and trimmed stems and florets (see Master Recipe for Steamed Broccoli). Cook covered for 3½ minutes or uncovered for 4 minutes. Drain and refresh under cold water. The broccoli is now ready for further cooking.

Serves 4

Broccoli with Cumin and Red Wine

This is a version of an old Roman recipe. It sounds unusual, but the cumin and red wine work nicely with the flavor of broccoli.

> 2 pounds broccoli, steamed according to master recipe
> 1 teaspoon ground cumin
> ¼ cup red wine
> ¼ cup olive oil
>   Salt to taste

Drain steamed broccoli and place in a large bowl. Combine remaining ingredients and pour over broccoli. Toss and serve.

Serves 4

Broccoli with Anchovy Sauce

When heated in oil, anchovies dissolve and take on a muted flavor. Small quantities of minced anchovies are also wonderful as a flavoring for sautéed onions to be used in soups or stews.

> 1½ pounds broccoli, steamed according to master recipe
> 1 small red onion, peeled and thinly sliced
> ½ cup high-quality olive oil
> 4 anchovies, minced
> 1 tablespoon Dijon mustard
> 2 tablespoons white wine vinegar
>   Freshly ground black pepper to taste

Place drained broccoli in a large bowl and toss with onion. Heat olive oil in a small pan over low heat. Add anchovies and cook about 5 minutes or until they dissolve. Whisk together the heated oil mixture with the mustard and vinegar. Pour over broccoli and season with freshly ground black pepper to taste.

Serves 4

Choose cabbage that is firm, feels heavy for its size, and has no limp leaves. There are five varieties of cabbage available in most supermarkets: green, red, Savoy, Napa, and bok choy. The first four are head cabbages, that is, they grow in round compact heads, although Napa is more cylindrical in shape. Bok choy looks like a huge head of celery with large green flat leaves. The recipes below are for green, red, and Savoy cabbages only.

I don't bother washing cabbage before cooking; I simply remove any tough or withered outer leaves. There are three techniques for coring cabbages: use a paring knife to cut a conical piece out of the bottom; quarter the head and then cut out the tough inner part of the core from each piece; or cut the cabbage in half and remove the core from each piece with two cuts in the form of a V (see page 66). Most recipes call for cutting cabbage into strips. To do this, start by cutting the cabbage in half and then removing the core. With the cut side down, cut lengthwise into strips with a chef's knife. To cut cabbage into pieces, first cut it into strips and then bunch the strips together and cut across them. Some cooks prepare cabbages in wedges (they usually steam them). Simply quarter and core the cabbage and then cut each quarter in half. Cookbooks often suggest that these wedges be tied with string to keep them intact — I find this to be a waste of time for the home cook. Leaving just a little of the core intact usually keeps the wedges from falling apart. Steam for about 6 minutes or until done. Cabbage can also be braised by cooking covered over low heat with chicken stock and vinegar (see recipe below). Toss cabbage for salads with a little vinegar to set color (2 tablespoons per head of cabbage).

Steamed cabbage needs to be tossed with a dressing. A simple vinaigrette will work well, but I find that an Asian vinaigrette, using fresh grated ginger and soy sauce, is also appealing.

1 head green, red, or Savoy cabbage, cored
   and cut into wedges or strips

Place prepared cabbage in a steamer or on a rack in a large pot. Steam for about 6 minutes (strips will take less time than wedges). Toss while still warm with a vinaigrette.

Serves 4–6

Braised Cabbage with Toasted Caraway Seeds

This is also good with rice wine vinegar. Make sure that the caraway seeds are fresh for a burst of flavor. This recipe is good with either pork or duck.

1 tablespoon caraway seeds
2 tablespoons butter
1 small onion, peeled and diced
2 small Savoy cabbages, core removed and cut
   into strips
½ cup chicken stock
¼ cup white wine vinegar
   Salt and freshly ground black pepper

1. Place caraway seeds in a nonstick skillet over medium-low heat and toast about 5 minutes, stirring frequently. Remove from heat and set aside.

2. Melt the butter in the skillet over medium heat. Add the onion, cabbage strips, and chicken stock and cook covered for about 12 minutes or until tender. Stir in the vinegar and caraway seeds and season with salt and freshly ground pepper.

Serves 8 as a side dish

Simple Cabbage Soup

Simply follow the Master Recipe for Vegetable Soup (page 133), substituting 2 pounds of cabbages for the vegetables. You can also substitute only 1 pound of cabbage for 1 pound of vegetables, choosing any vegetables you like for the other pound. Or try the Vegetable Soup with Beans (page 134), substituting 1 pound of cabbage for the vegetables.

CARROTS

Carrots should not be rubbery, nor should they have large cracks. I don't find much difference between carrots sold in plastic bags and those sold in bunches with their tops still intact. Little prebagged baby carrots are often light on flavor. Carrots should be peeled if large (young carrots should just be washed). A quick, easy way to prepare carrots is to cut into pieces ¼ inch thick, then boil or steam until barely tender, 3–4 minutes. Finish them in a sauté pan with butter or oil, vinegar, and a fresh herb such as oregano. A flavored oil or vinegar may be used for variation.

Carrots with Oregano and Vinegar

This recipe is based on carote in scapece from Marcella Hazan. I use balsamic vinegar and water in place of regular wine vinegar and have increased the amount of sugar to give the carrots more of a glaze. I also prefer to steam rather than boil my carrots.

- 2 tablespoons olive oil
- 3 large cloves garlic, peeled and halved
- 2 pounds carrots, peeled, cut into ¼-inch rounds, and steamed until al dente
- ¼ cup balsamic vinegar
- ⅓ cup water
- 1 tablespoon sugar
- 1 teaspoon kosher salt

- ⅛ teaspoon cayenne
- ¼ teaspoon dried oregano or 1 teaspoon fresh

Heat oil in a large sauté pan over medium-high heat. Add garlic and cook until golden, about 2 minutes. Remove garlic and discard. Add carrots and toss until heated through, about 2 minutes. Add remaining ingredients and cook over medium-high heat for about 5 minutes or until liquid is reduced to a glaze.
Serves 8

Baked Carrots with Maple Syrup and Nutmeg

Make sure that the carrots are thoroughly cooked. Carrots, like apples, are unpleasant and rubbery when only semicooked. Baking time will vary depending on the size and age of the carrots.

- 2 pounds carrots
- 1 tablespoon olive oil
- ⅛ teaspoon ground nutmeg
  Salt and freshly ground black pepper to taste
- ¼ cup chicken stock
- 3 tablespoons maple syrup
- 1 tablespoon butter
- 1 tablespoon cider vinegar

1. Heat oven to 400°F. Trim and peel carrots. Cut each carrot in half lengthwise and then into 2-inch pieces. (Very thick carrots can be quartered lengthwise.) Toss with olive oil, nutmeg, and salt and freshly ground pepper to taste. Place in a small roasting pan or baking dish.

2. Heat the remaining ingredients in a small saucepan until butter melts, and pour over carrots. Cover dish with lid or aluminum foil and bake for 30 minutes. Uncover and bake for an additional 45 minutes or until tender when pierced with a fork.
Serves 6–8

CAULIFLOWER

Look for cauliflower that is creamy white with no off colors, including yellow patches or black spots. The leaves should still be bright and fresh-looking. Although cauliflower can be steamed whole, most recipes call for cooking florets. To remove the florets, trim away the leaves and then cut away individual florets, leaving the stalks still attached to the main stem. You can also cook the stem. Trim away all small stems and about ⅛ inch of the outer skin and then slice the stem into thin pieces. For a stir-fry, cauliflower should be cut into very small pieces so that it does not have to be precooked. A whole head of cauliflower can be steamed in about 12 minutes — florets can be steamed for 4 minutes and then sautéed in oil with garlic or other ingredients. Cauliflower also makes a good base for soups, which are quite good when spiced with ground cardamom. Many cookbooks claim that cauliflower should not be salted before cooking as this will adversely affect its color. I tested this and found it not to be true.

Stir-Fried Cauliflower with Nutmeg and Cardamom

This is a basic stir-fry but with the addition of two unusual ingredients: nutmeg and cardamom.

Sauce
2 tablespoons good-quality soy sauce
1 tablespoon dry sherry
1 tablespoon chicken stock
⅛ teaspoon ground nutmeg
¼ teaspoon ground cardamom
½ teaspoon sugar

For the stir-fry
1 tablespoon plus ½ teaspoon canola or peanut oil
1 head cauliflower, cleaned, trimmed, and cut into small pieces
1 tablespoon minced fresh ginger

1. Mix together sauce ingredients and set aside.

2. Heat a 12- or 14-inch nonstick skillet over high heat for 4 minutes (the pan should be so hot that you can hold your outstretched palm 1 inch above its surface for no more than 3 seconds); add 1 tablespoon oil and rotate skillet so that the bottom is evenly coated. Let oil heat for about 1 minute or until it just starts to shimmer and smoke. Add cauliflower to the pan and stir-fry for about 4 minutes or until just tender. Clear the center of the pan and add the ginger. Drizzle with ½ teaspoon of oil. Mash ginger into pan with the back of a spatula. Cook for 10 seconds. Remove pan from heat and stir ginger into cauliflower for 20 seconds.

3. Return pan to heat, stir in sauce, and stir-fry 1 minute to coat all ingredients. Serve immediately with rice for a simple vegetarian meal, or use as a side dish.

Serves 4

Cauliflower Stew with Capers, Olives, and Anchovies

This simple stew takes about 30 minutes to cook and is full of flavor from the anchovies, olives, and capers.

2 slices bacon
1 tablespoon olive oil
1 medium onion, peeled and chopped
2 anchovy fillets, chopped
1 head cauliflower, washed and cut into florets
1 tomato, seeded and coarsely chopped, or ½ cup chopped canned tomato
1 tablespoon capers
¼ cup imported black olives, pitted and chopped
¼ pound green beans, ends snapped, cut into 1-inch pieces
1 cup chicken stock
Salt and freshly ground black pepper to taste

1. Fry the bacon in a large pot or skillet with straight sides. Remove bacon and all but 1 tablespoon of bacon fat. Reserve bacon for another use. Add the olive oil and onion and sauté over medium heat for 3 minutes. Add the anchovies and sauté for 2 minutes. Add the cauliflower, increase heat to medium high, and cook for 4 minutes, stirring occasionally.

2. Add tomato, capers, olives, green beans, and stock. Bring to a boil, then simmer covered until beans are cooked, about 12 minutes. Add salt and freshly ground pepper to taste.

Serves 4

CORN

Corn can be cooked from 2 to 8 minutes, depending on the type of corn and how fresh it is. There are basically three types of corn. According to Betty Fussell in *The Story of Corn,* basic "sweet" corn is 5–10 percent sugar, "sugar-enhanced" corn is 15–18 percent, and "supersweet" is 25–30 percent. The newer supersweet varieties have colorful names, including Kandy Korn, Sugar Buns, Sweet Desire, Kiss and Tell, and Peaches and Cream. These new varieties can hold their sugar content for up to 2 weeks, unlike old-fashioned corn, which converts the sugar to starch within hours, even minutes, of picking.

Betty Fussell suggests a mere 30-second dip in boiling water for just-picked supersweets, so I decided to run my own test. I put 7 ears of corn (store-bought supersweets out of season) in boiling water and took 1 ear out every minute. The 4- and 5-minute ears were best; the former had a slight edge, although it is hard to be precise because the sweetness and freshness of the ears may vary. When I tested locally grown, fresh-picked corn, I found that 2 minutes was best. (Good locally grown corn, despite the new hybrids, is always better than supermarket corn.) Ba-

sic sweet corn, however, needs 6–8 minutes to soften the kernels. My advice is to boil fresh corn for 2 minutes and then taste-test it; boil supermarket corn for 4 minutes before tasting. Corn can also be steamed, although I cannot taste a difference between steamed and boiled corn.

To remove the kernels, cut the husked ear in half crosswise (so that you have a flat surface for the half-ear to stand on as you work) and then cut down along the outside with a large, sharp chef's knife. A useful device is a "corn stripper," which both removes kernels and/or milks them (see page 45). You can also use a "Kernel Kutter," a toothed metal ring with handles which slides down the outside of an ear of corn, quickly stripping off the kernels. I have one and it works like a charm. (For big jobs, drive a nail through the center of a small board and then impale the ear of corn on it to hold it stationary while you work.) Kernel Kutter Inc. can be reached by calling 815-943-1510 or by writing to P.O. Box 98, Harvard, IL 60033.

Boiled Corn

I used to prefer my corn steamed until I did a blind tasting of boiled versus steamed and couldn't tell the difference. Now I just boil it. A fresh-picked, locally grown supersweet ear will cook in just 2 minutes in boiling water; an out-of-season standard ear of sweet corn can take 8 minutes to soften up the kernels. If you purchase corn at a store, be sure to find out what type of corn it is: sweet, sugar-enhanced, or supersweet.

8 ears corn, shucked

Bring a large pot of water to boil. Boil fresh-picked supersweet corn for 2 minutes and supermarket supersweets for 4 minutes. Regular supermarket sweet corn, unless it is grown locally, is not worth eating.

Simple Corn Chowder

There are more recipes for corn chowder than there are types of corn, but this is the simplest and therefore the best version I know of. Use 2 cups of chicken stock and 2 cups of water if using a salty canned stock. This is one recipe in which a homemade chicken stock will make all the difference.

- 2 slices bacon
- 2 onions, peeled and diced
- 2 teaspoons minced garlic
- 1 quart chicken stock, preferably home made
- 2 cups corn kernels
- 2 cups diced potatoes
- 2 cups milk
- ½ teaspoon minced fresh thyme
- Salt and freshly ground black pepper to taste
- Dash of hot pepper sauce, optional

Fry the bacon in a large pot. Remove bacon and all but 1 tablespoon of bacon fat. Reserve bacon for another use. Add the onions and sauté over medium heat for 4 minutes. Add the garlic and sauté for 2 minutes. Add the next 5 ingredients, bring to a boil, and then simmer for about 30 minutes or until potatoes are cooked. Add salt, freshly ground black pepper, and hot pepper sauce to taste.

Serves 4 as a main course

Whitney's Buttermilk Corn Fritters

My daughter Whitney does not like fresh corn but she loves these corn fritters. We have them for breakfast in August on our farm in Vermont when we have an abundance of corn. I like to make fairly large fritters (3 tablespoons of batter each), but you can make fritters with just 1 or 2 tablespoons. Reduce the frying time if using smaller quantities. Don't make fritters larger than 3 tablespoons, as they will not cook properly in the center.

- 1 tablespoon sugar
- 1 teaspoon baking powder
- ½ teaspoon baking soda
- ½ cup cornmeal
- 1 cup all-purpose flour
- ⅛ teaspoon ground nutmeg
- ⅞ cup buttermilk
- 2 tablespoons butter, melted
- 2 eggs
- 1 cup fresh or frozen corn kernels (one ear's worth)
- Oil for frying
- Maple syrup

1. Whisk together the first 6 ingredients in a large bowl. Stir together the buttermilk, butter, and eggs and add to the bowl in a thin steady stream, using a rubber spatula to gently fold together the batter. While still rough and unmixed, add the corn kernels and fold together. The batter may still be a bit lumpy and have streaks of flour.

2. Heat ½ inch of oil in a large skillet or pot until a small bit of batter dropped into the oil causes bubbling and foaming (the oil should be at about 370°F). Use a ¼-cup measuring cup, filled ¾ full, to drop batter into the oil. Don't crowd the skillet. Fry until golden brown, about 2 minutes per side. Drain on paper towels and let sit for about 5 minutes, as the fritters will continue cooking (they should be wet in the middle when removed from the oil). Serve hot with maple syrup. Let oil come back up to temperature between batches.

Serves 4

Roasted Corn Relish

Corn can be "roasted" right in a hot skillet, much as you would toast grains or spices. A nonstick skillet is recommended.

- 1 cup corn kernels
- ½ cup diced onion
- 1 teaspoon minced jalapeño pepper
- 1 cup seeded and diced tomato

½ cup seeded and diced red bell pepper
1 tablespoon lime juice
1 tablespoon high-quality olive oil
1 tablespoon minced cilantro
1 tablespoon minced flat-leaf parsley
Salt and freshly ground black pepper to
taste

Heat a nonstick skillet for 3 minutes over high heat. Add the corn kernels and sauté, shaking the pan frequently, for about 6 minutes. Combine with remaining ingredients and serve.

Makes about 2½ cups

EGGPLANT

From large to tiny, from fat to thin — eggplants come in many sizes and shapes. There are two main varieties: Italian, which are plump and purple or white, and Japanese, which are long and slender and come in purple or white as well. Japanese varieties are often less acid and bitter than the Italian kind. One medium Italian eggplant weighs about the same as 4–5 Japanese eggplants — about 1¼ pounds. Many cooks swear that male eggplant is better than female (supposedly, female eggplants have a larger indentation on the bottom — it looks like a belly button — than the male variety), the reason being that the males have fewer, if any, seeds. After publishing this tip in *Cook's Illustrated*, we were overwhelmed by letters from scientists claiming that this difference is an old wives' tale. The rule is simple. Regardless of sex, young, less developed eggplants are always best, as they have fewer bitter seeds.

The problem with eggplant is its high water content, which, if not reduced, causes eggplant slices to become mushy and unappealing when cooked. To solve this problem, eggplant should be cut into thick strips (skin left on), placed in a colander, and then salted — use about 2 tablespoons of salt per medium eggplant. Be sure to salt eggplant

strips on all sides. Let stand for 2 hours, rinse, place between layers of paper towels, and then use a rolling pin to squeeze out remaining moisture (leave the eggplant between layers of paper towels for this step). Now the eggplant will also be less likely to absorb oil when sautéed. Eggplant can also be cooked into a puree with sugar and spices and served as a side dish.

Master Recipe for Sautéed Eggplant

The trick to good sautéed eggplant is to salt, rinse, drain, and then press it before cooking so that it does not absorb too much of the oil, becoming soggy. My wife, Adrienne, discovered that a rolling pin is the perfect tool for squeezing moisture out of salted and rinsed eggplant slices. I also recommend that you use a nonstick skillet, which will dramatically reduce the amount of oil required for sautéing.

1 medium Italian eggplant (about 1¼ pounds)
or 4–5 Japanese eggplants
2 tablespoons kosher salt
1 tablespoon olive oil
Salt and freshly ground black pepper to
taste

1. Remove stem end and green cap from eggplant(s). Cut eggplant (skin left on) into rounds ½ inch thick. If using Japanese eggplants, cut ½-inch-thick slices on the bias (the pieces will be oval, not round). Toss pieces in a large bowl with 2 tablespoons kosher salt. Remove pieces from bowl and layer in a large colander. Place colander over bowl to catch drippings.

2. Let eggplant pieces stand for 2 hours, rinse, place between layers of paper towels, and then use a rolling pin to squeeze out remaining moisture. (Leave the eggplant between the paper towels for this step.)

3. Heat a large nonstick skillet with half the oil. Sauté the eggplant in two batches, using the remaining oil for the second batch. (Tongs work well for moving eggplant pieces.) The eggplant should be cooked until nicely browned, about 4–5 minutes per side. Season to taste with freshly ground black pepper and kosher salt.

Each eggplant yields 10–15 slices

Master Recipe for Roasted Eggplant

I like roasting eggplant because it produces a cleaner, less oily texture than sautéing. Roasted eggplant is very good in sandwiches (see recipe below).

1 medium Italian eggplant (about 1¼ pounds) or 4–5 Japanese eggplants
2 tablespoons kosher salt
1 tablespoon olive oil
Salt to taste

1. Follow steps 1 and 2 of the Master Recipe for Sautéed Eggplant.
2. Heat oven to 400°F. Oil a baking sheet with the olive oil. Lay eggplant slices flat on the baking sheet, sprinkle with salt to taste, and roast for 35–40 minutes for Italian eggplant and 30 minutes for Japanese. Turn eggplant slices halfway through cooking.

Roasted Eggplant Sandwiches with Onions and Tomatoes

Ingredients for double recipe of Master Recipe for Roasted Eggplant
¼ cup olive oil
3 large onions (about 1 pound), peeled and sliced into ¼-inch rings
6–8 plum tomatoes (about 1¼ pounds), cored and sliced in half lengthwise
Salt and freshly ground black pepper to taste
1 tablespoon dried oregano or 3 tablespoons minced fresh
1 large loaf country bread, sliced and toasted
Fresh goat cheese, optional

1. Prepare roasted eggplant as directed in master recipe above. Set aside.
2. Heat oven to 400°F. Brush two roasting pans or heavy-gauge jelly roll pans with 2 tablespoons olive oil each. Place onions in one pan and the tomatoes, cut side up, in the other. Sprinkle with salt, pepper, and oregano. Place pans in oven. Toss onions after 15 minutes and remove from oven after 30 minutes or when they are soft and slightly caramelized. The tomatoes require a total cooking time of 1 hour.
3. Assemble sandwiches. Add optional goat cheese.

Makes 6 sandwiches

Roasted Eggplant Caviar

There are many recipes for eggplant dips and spreads, but I find that roasting the eggplant first makes all the difference. Serve this "caviar" on hot slices of toasted bread as an appetizer.

1 head garlic, roasted (see page 105)
2 medium eggplants, roasted (see Master Recipe for Roasted Eggplant)
1 teaspoon kosher salt
1 tablespoon fresh thyme leaves
1 tablespoon Dijon mustard
1 tablespoon lemon juice
1 egg yolk
⅔ cup high-quality olive oil
Freshly ground black pepper to taste

Squeeze the roasted garlic from its skin and place with roasted eggplant in the bowl of a food processor. Add the salt and fresh thyme. Process until smooth. Add the mustard, lemon juice, and egg yolk and turn on machine. With the machine running, add the oil in a thin stream. Add plenty of freshly ground pepper to taste. Serve on small slices of hot toasted bread.

Note: If you are concerned about the safety of consuming uncooked eggs, omit the egg yolk from this recipe.

Makes 2¾ cups

GREEN BEANS

The best green beans are small, without spots or withered ends. Avoid those that are large, with overdeveloped seeds. Before cooking, trim off the ends with a knife or snap them off. (I find that a large chef's knife speeds up this operation considerably — just line up the ends so that you cut half a dozen beans at once.) Green beans are best lightly steamed and then quickly sautéed with olive oil and garlic or other flavorings. See Chapter 7, "Steaming Vegetables," for more information. They can also be simmered with chopped tomatoes and cumin as they are in Greece, or cooked for an hour or more as they are often prepared in Italy. I suggest steaming 4–5 minutes, as indicated in the chart on page 99.

Warm Salad of Green Beans and New Potatoes

In late July, I dig up new potatoes from the garden and also have an ample supply of green beans. Together, they make one of the best and simplest meals you can have in the summer. I often serve this dish for dinner with toasted country bread and plenty of slightly chilled white wine.

  1 pound new potatoes, scrubbed and cut into quarters
  1 pound green beans, washed, trimmed, and cut into bite-size pieces
  ½ cup All-Purpose Vegetable Salad Dressing (page 120)
  ¼ cup minced flat-leaf parsley
    Salt and freshly ground black pepper to taste

Steam the potatoes until barely tender, about 10 minutes. Add the green beans and steam for an additional 5–6 minutes or until just tender. Remove to a bowl, toss with dressing and parsley. Add salt and freshly ground black pepper to taste. Serve immediately.

Serves 4

Sautéed Green Beans with Lemon and Walnuts

Pecans or walnuts are a traditional garnish for green beans. The lemon adds an extra kick of flavor.

  1 pound green beans, washed and trimmed
  3 tablespoons butter
  3 teaspoons grated lemon rind
  2 teaspoons lemon juice
  ½ cup chicken stock
  ¼ cup coarsely chopped walnuts

Steam beans until barely tender and still crisp, about 3 minutes. In a sauté pan, boil the butter, lemon rind, lemon juice, and chicken stock over medium-high heat for 2 minutes. Add the beans and simmer until beans are cooked through, about 2 minutes more. Toss with walnuts and serve.

Serves 4

GREENS

Greens, which include kale, collard greens, mustard greens, broccoli rabe, or other tough greens such as turnip greens, should be brightly colored and have fresh, crisp leaves with no wilting. (Spinach, beet greens, and chard are more tender and are therefore prepared differently.) Greens need to be stemmed and coarsely chopped and then boiled for about 5 minutes before further cooking. Then the wet greens are sautéed in olive oil and garlic in a covered pan for about 5 minutes more. You can also add ¼ cup of chicken stock to the sauté pan if you prefer your greens soft and tender.

Master Recipe for Greens

This is a two-step cooking process, as greens are bitter and tough. The precooking removes some of the bitterness and helps to soften the leaves.

After boiling, I braise greens in a small amount of liquid, usually chicken stock. This recipe is best for collard greens, kale, mustard greens, and broccoli rabe.

2 pounds greens (kale, mustard greens, collard greens, broccoli rabe), stems removed, coarsely chopped
¼ cup olive oil
¼ cup chicken stock
Salt and freshly ground black pepper to taste

1. Cook greens in a large pot of boiling salted water for 5 minutes. Rinse under cold water and drain. Place in a kitchen towel and squeeze dry.

2. Heat oil in large saucepan over medium heat. Add greens, turn up heat, and sauté for 2 minutes. Add chicken stock and bring to a simmer. Lower heat to maintain simmer and cover. Cook for about 5 minutes or until greens are tender.

Serves 4

Greens Sautéed with Garlic and Anchovy

You may add 2 cups of cooked white beans to this dish along with the greens during the last 5 minutes of cooking. The beans are a nice counterpoint to the sharp flavor of the greens.

2 pounds greens (kale, mustard greens, collard greens), stems removed, coarsely chopped
¼ cup olive oil
2 teaspoons minced garlic
1 anchovy, minced
¼ cup chicken stock
2 cups cooked white beans, optional
1 teaspoon white wine vinegar, optional
Salt and freshly ground black pepper to taste

1. Cook greens in boiling salted water for 5 minutes. Rinse under cold water and drain. Place in a kitchen towel and squeeze dry.

2. Heat oil in large sauté pan over medium heat and cook garlic for 1 minute. Add anchovy and cook for an additional minute. Add greens, turn up heat, and sauté for 2 minutes. Add chicken stock and bring to a simmer. Add optional beans. Lower heat to maintain simmer and cover. Cook for about 5 minutes or until greens are tender. Add optional vinegar and salt and freshly ground pepper to taste.

Serves 4–6

PEAS

Fresh peas should be firm and not wrinkled. Remove a pea from its pod before buying — it should be fresh, crisp, and moist. The best peas are the small ones, which are light and delicate. Beware of the large, mealy peas that often find their way into supermarkets. Purchase about ½ pound of unshelled peas per person. Given the fact that fresh peas are not available for much of the year, many of us resort to frozen peas for most of our cooking. This is one vegetable that is worth growing if you have a garden.

Master Recipe for Fresh Peas

Nothing is better or simpler than cooked fresh peas. I like the addition of mint, although this is optional. If using canned chicken stock, replace ¼ cup of the stock with water.

2 pounds peas, unshelled
2 tablespoons unsalted butter
½ cup chicken stock
Salt to taste
2 teaspoons minced fresh mint, optional

Shell peas. Add butter and chicken stock to a saucepan and melt butter over medium heat. Add peas, reduce heat to low, and simmer until cooked, about 5 minutes. Add salt to taste and toss with optional mint.

Serves 4

Pasta with Peas and Prosciutto

This is a simple weeknight meal in which the oil is infused with the flavor of garlic. Use this same technique in other recipes in which you want the subtle aroma of garlic instead of a strong garlic flavor.

¼ cup high-quality olive oil
4 cloves garlic, peeled and lightly crushed
1 pound dried pasta such as spaghetti
1 package (10 ounces) frozen peas, cooked according to Master Recipe for Fresh Peas
¼ pound prosciutto, sliced paper-thin and cut into ½-inch squares
2 tablespoons minced flat-leaf parsley
Salt and freshly ground black pepper to taste
Freshly grated Parmesan, optional

1. Heat a large pot of salted water. Meanwhile, heat the olive oil in a small saucepan and when hot, add the garlic (the oil should bubble and froth). Turn off heat and let garlic steep for at least 10 minutes. Remove and discard garlic.

2. Cook pasta in the salted water until done. Drain and place back in pot. Toss with infused oil and add remaining ingredients, including plenty of salt and freshly ground black pepper to taste. This dish may be served with freshly grated Parmesan.

Serves 4

SPINACH

Spinach is easily prepared and cooked. To stem, simply grab a bunch of leaves, roughly align the stems, and then trim with a chef's knife. I do not remove the entire stem, just woody or deteriorated sections. Do not bother trimming each leaf individually — you'll be at it all night. To clean, follow the cleaning instructions for salad greens on page 123. To precook spinach, simply place washed, drained leaves into a hot, deep skillet or pot, cover, and cook for about 2 minutes. The water will turn into steam, cooking the leaves. To use spinach as a filling (for ravioli, for example), steam the leaves per the instructions above and then chop. Next, place chopped spinach in a kitchen towel and twist hard to remove excess moisture. Follow these same directions when cooking Swiss chard. Many cooks warn against salting spinach until the end of cooking; otherwise, they say, the leaves will turn black. I tested this with my master recipe below and found no truth in this statement. The spinach cooks so quickly that salting has no effect whatever on color.

Master Recipe for Steamed Spinach

This recipe requires no oil for cooking. Just make sure that the spinach is quite wet, which will result in plenty of steam in the hot sauté pan.

2 pounds spinach, trimmed and washed (see above)

Preheat a large, deep skillet or pot over medium heat for about 2 minutes. Add the wet prepared spinach and cover. Cook for about 2 minutes, stirring 2–3 times.

Serves 4–6

Spinach with Garlic and Nutmeg

This is a very simple preparation and can be varied to create lots of other dishes. For an Asian version, replace 1 tablespoon of olive oil with 1 tablespoon of toasted sesame oil and proceed with recipe. After 1 minute of cooking, add 1 tablespoon of soy sauce and 1 teaspoon of white wine vinegar or rice vinegar. Cook for an additional minute.

2 tablespoons olive oil
3 large cloves garlic, peeled and halved

2 pounds fresh spinach, trimmed and washed
½ teaspoon grated nutmeg
  Salt and freshly ground black pepper

1. Heat the oil in a large skillet over medium-high heat. When hot, add the garlic cloves and sauté until they turn dark brown, about 3 minutes. Remove and discard garlic.

2. Add spinach, cover, and cook for 2 minutes, stirring occasionally. Season with nutmeg, add salt and pepper to taste, and serve.

Serves 4–6

Spinach Sautéed with Garlic and Pine Nuts

Follow instructions for Spinach with Garlic and Nutmeg, but substitute ⅓ cup toasted pine nuts for the nutmeg.

~ 6 ~

Potatoes Explained

There are two basic types of potatoes, starchy and waxy,
and each has its own uses.

~

There are five common varieties of potatoes found in most grocery stores: russet, Idaho, Maine, red, and all-purpose potatoes. The first two are "mealy" potatoes; they are best baked or mashed because they have a nice light texture. In fact, these potatoes are high in starch, which, when heated, expands. The fluffy texture you find in a good baked potato is created by starch cells separating from one another. Maine and red potatoes are waxier in texture and are best either boiled or steamed. They have a high moisture content, low starch content, and thin skins. These potatoes are best for potato salads because they hold their texture nicely and, unlike a mealy potato, they will not absorb an excess of salad dressing. I find all-purpose potatoes to be ill-suited to both baking and mashing — they are not light and fluffy enough for baking — and they are not waxy enough for a good potato salad. Instead, use a specific variety for a specific purpose. There are also sweet potatoes, which are light-colored and fairly dry in texture, as well as yams, which have a deep orange color and a moister consistency.

THE POTATO TESTS

I tested cooking times for each of the four basic varieties of supermarket potatoes (I left out all-purpose) for baking, steaming, and boiling and found that baking times do vary between the high-starch and waxy potatoes although boiling and steaming times were the same. Keep in mind that these times will vary depending on the size of the potato or the size of the pieces being cooked. I had always heard that baking potatoes should never be cooked in aluminum foil, but having had success with roasting vegetables, including potatoes, in a roasting pan that was covered with foil for half the cooking time, I decided to test this theory. I discovered that wrapping a potato in aluminum foil for the first 25 minutes of baking produces a moist, tender interior, while the skin has plenty of time to crisp up nicely during the last 35 minutes. I never coat a baking potato with oil or butter prior to or during cooking — that simply softens the skin. Pricking a potato with a fork before baking is often recommended in cookbooks (to let the steam escape while baking) but is totally unnecessary unless baking a sweet potato or yam, which is moister and develops more steam.

Baked Potatoes

Heat oven to 350°F. Wrap individual russet or Idaho potatoes in aluminum foil and bake for 25 minutes. Unwrap and bake an additional 35 minutes or until done.

Boiled Potatoes

Wash Maine or red potatoes and slice them into 2-inch pieces (peeling is optional). Place in plenty of boiling salted water (use 2 quarts water for 4 potatoes, and 2 teaspoons kosher salt per quart of water) and boil uncovered for 18 minutes. Check after 15 minutes with a fork. When tender, drain, place back in empty pot, cover, and let sit for 5 minutes. Potatoes can also be boiled whole — allow 25–30 minutes.

Steamed Potatoes

Wash Maine or red potatoes and cut them into 2-inch pieces (peeling is optional). Place

on a rack above boiling water, cover, and steam for 20 minutes or until done. New potatoes or small red potatoes can be steamed whole in about 12 minutes.

French-Fried Potatoes

This is a two-step cooking method. The potatoes are fried first at 340°F and then again at 370°F. Why two different temperatures? Well, if you were to cook a thick french fry at just the higher temperature, the outside would brown before the inside was properly cooked. By starting at the lower temperature, the inside cooks properly (the starch granules gelatinize; the french fries should be limp at this stage) and then, after cooling to room temperature, the french fry is cooked again at 370°F to brown the exterior, a process that also adds flavor. This provides the optimum crisp exterior with a moist, soft interior. A metal frying basket or an electric deep-fat fryer with a basket is useful but not essential. You can easily remove the fries with a slotted spoon.

    4 large russet or Idaho potatoes
      Peanut oil for frying
      Salt to taste

1. Scrub and peel the potatoes. Cut them into strips ¼–⅓ inch square. If not using right away, cover with cold water.

2. Pour oil in a large saucepan or pot to a depth of 3 inches, or use an electric deep fryer. Heat oil to 340°F — use a thermometer to check temperature. Pat potato strips dry with paper towels. When oil is hot, fry potatoes for 5 minutes, until soft but not browned. Cook in batches to avoid overcrowding the pan. Remove fries to paper towels to drain.

3. When ready to finish cooking, heat oil to 375°F and fry for about 2 minutes or until brown. Remove to paper towels for draining. Sprinkle with salt to taste.

Serves 4

SCIENCE OF COOKING

Cooking Methods and Nutrition

There are two factors at work in the loss of vitamin C in potato cookery. The problem is that vitamin C will break down when in the presence of oxygen. To preserve the nutritional value of a potato, therefore, one would steam it rather than boil it, or boil it whole rather than in pieces. (The objective is to expose the surface of the potato to the least amount of water, which, of course, contains lots of oxygen.) The second concern is cooking time. Enzymes in the potato will start to break down the vitamin during a prolonged time in a hot environment. This is why baking a potato — a relatively slow process — results in more vitamin C loss than steaming or even boiling. So, solely from a nutritional point of view, steaming is the best method, followed by boiling whole, boiling in pieces, and then baking.

Potato Chips

You can deep-fry potato chips in a deep saucepan or an electric deep fryer. You can also fry them in just ½ inch of oil in a large skillet, although this is messier. The potatoes can be sliced very thin for a crispy potato chip or sliced thicker for a meatier chip. I use peanut oil, instead of corn or canola oil, for frying since it significantly enhances the flavor. Be liberal with the salt.

> 4 russet or Idaho potatoes, scrubbed (peeling optional)
> Peanut oil for frying
> Salt to taste

1. Slice potatoes thinly crosswise and soak in cold water for 20 minutes. Remove from water and dry with paper towels.

2. Heat oil in a deep saucepan or iron skillet to 370°F. Place some of the slices in the oil (don't crowd the pan) and fry until nicely browned. Turn halfway through cooking. Drain chips on paper towels and sprinkle liberally with salt. Bring oil back up to temperature between batches.

Serves 4

Sweet Potato Chips

Follow the recipe for Potato Chips but substitute sweet potatoes. Just before frying, I like to dip the sweet potato slices in milk followed by flour to which I have added a pinch of salt and a good dose of cayenne pepper. These make great eat-in-the-kitchen appetizers.

Roasted Potato Fans with Rosemary

You can add quartered onions at the beginning of cooking, or peeled garlic cloves when you remove the aluminum foil. This preparation is based on a recipe found in Roger Vergé's Vegetables in the French Style.

> 4 russet or Idaho potatoes, scrubbed and peeled

Cooking Times for the Four Most Common Varieties of Potato

Russet and Idaho potatoes are recommended for baking. Maine and red potatoes are recommended for steaming or boiling. Medium-size potatoes were baked at 350°F using the method described below. Potatoes were quartered for steaming and boiling.

Potato	Baking	Steaming	Boiling
Russet	60 minutes	20 minutes	18 minutes
Idaho	60 minutes	20 minutes	18 minutes
Maine	50 minutes	20 minutes	18 minutes
Red	50 minutes	20 minutes	18 minutes

The Best Way to Bake a Potato

I had always been told that wrapping potatoes in aluminum foil produced a soft skin, which I find undesirable in a baked potato. However, I tested baking potatoes for the first 25 minutes in foil, removing it, and then completing the baking. All potatoes were baked for 1 hour.

Technique	Results
350°F; wrapped in foil 1 hour	Moist and creamy interior, soft skin
350°F; in foil 25 minutes, then unwrapped	Crispy skin, moist interior; best method
375°F; in foil 25 minutes, then unwrapped	Interior not quite as creamy as 350°F
400°F; in foil 25 minutes, then unwrapped	Interior not quite as creamy as 350°F

> 1 large branch fresh rosemary
> ¼ cup olive oil
> Salt to taste

1. Heat oven to 450°F. Cut potatoes in half lengthwise. Place flat side down in a roasting pan and make a series of cuts, ¼ inch apart, across the width. Don't cut all the way through the potato. Place 2 fresh rosemary leaves in each of the cuts.

2. Baste potatoes with oil. Cover pan with aluminum foil and roast for 30 minutes. Remove foil and roast another 30 minutes or until easily pierced with a fork. Serve with plenty of salt.

Serves 4

Mashed Potatoes

Never use a food processor for mashing potatoes. This will liquefy them, resulting in a glue-like consistency. Buy an old-fashioned potato masher and work the potatoes as little as possible, or use a potato ricer. I prefer mashed potatoes that are chunky and not overprocessed. The best potatoes for mashing are Idaho or russet.

    3 pounds russet or Idaho potatoes, scrubbed
    1 tablespoon plus ½ teaspoon kosher salt
    5 tablespoons butter, softened
    1 cup buttermilk or milk, room temperature
      Salt and freshly ground black pepper to
      taste

1. Fill a large pot or stockpot ⅔ full of water. Bring to a boil. Peel potatoes, cut into quarters, and place in a bowl of cold water to avoid discoloration. To stockpot add 1 tablespoon kosher salt (or to taste) and potatoes and cook covered until tender, about 20 minutes. This will depend on the size if the potatoes and the size of the pot.

2. When potatoes are cooked, drain and mash with a potato masher or fork to desired consistency. Do not use a food processor or electric mixer. Place potatoes back into the drained, still-warm stockpot. Cut butter into pieces and add to potatoes along with buttermilk. Mash until potato mixture is thoroughly combined. If the butter doesn't melt, place the pot over very low heat. Season to taste with salt and freshly ground pepper.

Serves 6

Creamy Garlic Potatoes

This recipe uses an important technique — extracting the flavor of garlic by simmering whole cloves in a liquid (milk). In this recipe, the garlic cloves are also used in the final dish for extra flavor. Try simmering garlic cloves with olive oil, then using the flavored oil on pasta or in a salad dressing. Be careful not to let the garlic burn.

    2 pounds russet or Idaho potatoes, scrubbed
      and quartered (peeling optional)
    8 cloves garlic, peeled
    ¾ cup milk
    4 tablespoons butter
    1 cup heavy cream
      Salt and freshly ground black pepper to
      taste
    ½ cup minced flat-leaf parsley

1. Boil the quartered potatoes uncovered in a large pot of unsalted water until tender, about 20 minutes. Drain.

2. Put garlic cloves, milk, butter, and cream into a medium saucepan. Bring to a boil and simmer uncovered until garlic is tender, about 15 minutes.

3. Combine all ingredients except salt, pepper, and parsley in a large bowl and mash with an old-fashioned potato masher. Do not use a food processor or electric mixer.

4. Season with salt and pepper to taste. Add minced parsley and serve.

Serves 4

Charcoal-Roasted Potatoes

It's best to place the potatoes around the perimeter of a pile of coals rather than right in the middle of them. Otherwise, the butter will drip out easily, causing flare-ups. You need a good hot fire for this recipe.

    4 large russet or Idaho potatoes
    2 cloves garlic, peeled and minced
    1 tablespoon minced flat-leaf parsley
    6 tablespoons unsalted butter, softened
    ½ teaspoon kosher salt
      Freshly ground black pepper

1. Scrub the potatoes and cut into ½-inch slices without cutting all the way through.

2. Using a fork, combine the garlic and parsley with the butter, salt, and freshly ground black pepper in a small bowl. Mash until smooth and well combined.

3. Place each potato in a small sheet of aluminum foil and add a bit of butter mixture between the slices. Reassemble potatoes and wrap in heavy-duty foil.

4. Nestle wrapped potatoes in the hot coals and roast about 1 hour. To test for doneness, remove 1 potato from coals, open foil package. Potato is done when easily pierced with a fork.

Serves 4

Cider Sweet Potatoes with Cinnamon and Allspice

Apples go well with most root vegetables, especially sweet potatoes. Be sure to use juicy, firm baking apples such as Macoun, Cortland, or Northern Spy. Do not use a Delicious or McIntosh apple.

 5 medium sweet potatoes
 1 cup apple cider or unfiltered apple juice
 ¼ cup dark brown sugar
 2 tablespoons granulated sugar
 1 teaspoon ground cinnamon
 ½ teaspoon ground allspice
 ¼ teaspoon ground ginger
 4 tablespoons butter
 3 medium cooking apples, peeled, cored, and cut into ¼-inch-thick slices
 Salt to taste

1. Scrub sweet potatoes. Bake in a 375° oven until tender (up to 1 hour, depending on size). Keep oven on.

2. Heat cider in a saucepan almost to a boil. When sweet potatoes are cool enough to handle, peel them and slice into ½-inch-thick slices. Combine the sugars and the spices in a small dish.

3. Use 1–2 teaspoons of the butter to grease a casserole large enough to hold the apples and sweet potatoes. Layer in the pota-

toes and apples, dot each layer with some of the remaining butter, and sprinkle with sugar mixture and salt to taste. Before adding butter and sugar to the final layer, pour heated cider over entire casserole. Add butter and sugar to top layer. Bake for 40 minutes at 375°F.

Serves 8

Sweet Potatoes with Cinnamon and Ginger

I found this recipe in Ginger East to West, *by Bruce Cost, a well-known expert on Asian cooking who owns the restaurant Ginger Island in Berkeley, California. The original recipe is Moroccan — Bruce found it in* Moroccan Cooking, *by Lafita Bennanni Smire.*

 2 pounds sweet potatoes, peeled and cut into eighths
 1 teaspoon kosher salt
 Freshly ground black pepper
 1 tablespoon minced fresh ginger
 4 tablespoons butter
 1 tablespoon olive oil
 ½ teaspoon ground cinnamon
 ¼ teaspoon ground allspice
 ½ cup brown sugar

Place all ingredients in a saucepan. Over medium heat, cook until butter melts. Turn heat to low and cover. Simmer for 20 minutes, stirring occasionally.

Serves 6–8

Potato Salad with Tarragon and Chives

I prefer new potatoes for this recipe because they hold their texture nicely and have a fresh, earthy flavor. You can add steamed green beans or asparagus to this salad. Potato salads should be served at room temperature.

 2 pounds waxy or new potatoes
 3 tablespoons white wine vinegar
 ½ teaspoon kosher salt

2 teaspoons Dijon mustard
6 tablespoons high-quality olive oil
1 tablespoon minced chives
1 tablespoon minced tarragon
1 tablespoon minced flat-leaf parsley
   Freshly ground black pepper to taste

Wash potatoes. Steam or boil until done (about 20 minutes — this will vary depending upon the size of the potato). Cut into ¼-inch-thick slices. Whisk together the vinegar, salt, and mustard, then add the olive oil in a thin drizzle, whisking constantly. Pour over warm potatoes in a large bowl and toss. Just before serving add herbs and freshly ground black pepper to taste.

Serves 4–6

German Potato Salad

I find that a German potato salad tastes better if the vinegar is heated before mixing into the potatoes, and therefore I add it to the skillet when the onions have been cooked. It is important to drain off all but 1 tablespoon of the bacon fat; otherwise the salad will be greasy.

2 pounds waxy or new potatoes
4 slices bacon
2 tablespoons olive oil
1 cup diced onion
4 tablespoons cider vinegar
1 tablespoon dry sherry
½ teaspoon kosher salt
3 tablespoons minced flat-leaf parsley
1 tablespoon minced chives

1. Wash potatoes and steam or boil until just done (about 20 minutes — cooking time will vary depending on size of potato). Fry bacon in a skillet and remove to paper towels.

2. Pour off all but 1 tablespoon of fat and add olive oil; place skillet over medium heat. When oil is hot, add onion and sauté for 5 minutes, stirring occasionally. Add vinegar and sherry and cook, stirring, for 30 seconds. Remove from heat.

3. Cut potatoes into ¼-inch-thick slices and place in a large bowl. Add onion mixture and toss. Crumble bacon and add to potatoes along with salt and herbs. Toss and serve.

Serves 4–6

~ 7 ~

Steaming Vegetables

Do you need special equipment to steam vegetables?
Is steaming really better than boiling?

~

Many years ago I traveled to Florence and spent a morning sitting in on a cooking class run by Giuliano Bugialli, who was constantly interrupted by a woman in the front row who seemed more favorably inclined to Chinese cuisine than *fusilli alla rustica*. As the morning was drawing to a close, she interrupted one last time, expounding on the virtues of al dente vegetables. Unable to contain himself any longer, Giuliano banged his fists down on the counter and shouted, "In Italy, madam, we cook our food."

I freely admit to more than passing irritation with undercooked vegetables, especially when they are palmed off as "al dente" or "steamed," euphemisms that do nothing to hide the rubbery texture of half-cooked carrots or green beans. Steaming is not about undercooking. You can do that in boiling water. It is about delicately cooking foods so that their bright, fresh flavors come to the fore, unmasked and undiminished by heavy-handed preparation methods.

HOW LONG SHOULD VEGETABLES BE STEAMED?

Steaming is not an exact science. The size and age of a vegetable will affect cooking time. Stacked vegetables will steam more slowly than those set out all in one layer. In fact, steaming times can vary quite a lot based on the preferences of the cook. After establishing cooking times for the vegetables in this chapter, I turned over my results to a test cook for confirmation. She came back with remarkably shorter times across the board because she prefers her vegetables on the crunchy side. That is why I reconstructed the timing chart to show two sets of times: one for an "al dente" texture and one for a fully cooked vegetable. The good news is, however, that you can slightly under- or overcook steamed vegetables without a culinary disaster.

During my testing, I discovered that I prefer to roast most root vegetables. Their natural sweetness is enhanced through high-heat cooking. However, I do steam new potatoes and then toss them with a little butter, chopped parsley, salt, and pepper. Their delicate flavor is enhanced by gentle cooking. I also found that vegetables can be steamed ahead of time, rinsed under cold water to stop the cooking, and then set aside until needed. They are best stored in the steaming basket in which they are cooked and then quickly reheated in the steamer.

Once they are steamed, the easiest way to

Steaming Times for Common Vegetables

The size and age of vegetables affects cooking times. These times are therefore approximate. The foods are added once the water is brought to a boil.

Vegetable	Al Dente	Fully Cooked
Asparagus	5 minutes	6 minutes
Beets (5–6 ounces each)	30 minutes	35 minutes
Broccoli	4½ minutes	6 minutes
Brussels sprouts	7½ minutes	11 minutes
Butternut squash	Not applicable	13 minutes
Carrots	6 minutes	8 minutes
Cauliflower florets	4 minutes	6 minutes
Fresh peas	Not applicable	2 minutes
Green beans	4 minutes	5 minutes
Leeks	Not applicable	6 minutes
New potatoes	Not applicable	12 minutes
Yams and sweet potatoes	Not applicable	15 minutes
Zucchini and summer squash	5 minutes	7 minutes

How to Prepare Vegetables for Steaming

Asparagus: Snap off tough ends.

Beets: Leave beets whole, peel them, and remove and discard the tops and root end.

Broccoli: Detach florets from large stalk; peel stalk, cut in half lengthwise and then into 2-inch pieces

Brussels sprouts: Peel away tough outer layers and remove long stems.

Butternut squash: Peel and cut into 1½-inch cubes.

Carrots: Peel and cut in half lengthwise, then cut into 2-inch lengths.

Cauliflower: Break into florets.

Fresh peas: Remove from pod.

Green beans: Remove ends.

Leeks: Remove and discard tough outer layers; cut in half lengthwise, rinse under cold water, and then cut into 2-inch lengths.

New potatoes: Do not peel, just clean and quarter them.

Yams and sweet potatoes: Peel and cut into 2-inch pieces.

Zucchini and summer squash: Leave skin on and cut into ¼-inch slices.

serve vegetables is to toss them in a simple vinaigrette. Some cooks will sauté steamed vegetables with butter or cream, but I find this at odds with the notion of steaming. Why muddy the bright, clean flavors of steamed fresh vegetables with fat? Fresh herbs are preferred over dried.

WHAT TO DO IF YOU DON'T HAVE A STEAMER

The simplest way to steam vegetables without a steamer is to place a small amount of water (¼ inch or less) in the bottom of a pot and then add the vegetables and cover. This is fine for quick-steaming vegetables that take just a few minutes, such as green beans or asparagus. If you are steaming more than one vegetable, place the slower-cooking vegetable at the bottom of the pan. You can also use a cake rack. Simply place it at the bottom of a large, not-too-deep pot (if the rack does not have high enough feet, make a platform for it — see below). The disadvantage here is that a cake rack has no handle, unlike a steamer basket with a handle. If the cake rack is not substantially smaller in diameter than the pot, it will be hard to remove, especially when hot (the rack should be a good 2 inches smaller in diameter).

You can create a platform out of tuna fish cans (both ends removed), custard cups, canning jar rings, or metal trivets to support a plate or wire rack. If you use a plate, make sure that it is small enough so that you will be able to get it out when it's hot. It is very easy to slip in a plate that is slightly smaller in diameter than the pot, but just try getting it out when the vegetables are done! This is particularly important when you are steaming fish — you do want to remove the whole plate because you want to save the extruded juices and the plate also doubles as a serving platter. Finally, a small metal colander works well as a steamer basket if you have a large enough pot to place it in.

Steamed Vegetables Lightly Dressed

A delicious way to prepare steamed vegetables is to dress them with a simple vinaigrette. Try any of the salad dressings listed in Chapter 10. I suggest a basic vinaigrette made with lemon juice (substitute lemon juice for ⅓ of the vinegar called for in the recipe). Add the vinaigrette just before serving.

1 pound steamed vegetables
¼ cup of vinaigrette (see Chapter 10)

Toss steamed vegetables with vinaigrette just before serving.

Serves 4 as a side dish

Master Recipe for Puree of Steamed Vegetables

This recipe is based on information found in Cuisine à la Vapeur, *which was translated and tested by a* Cook's Magazine *alumna, Stephanie Lyness. I was fascinated by the use of starchy potatoes or rice as a thickener for a vegetable puree. It is vastly preferable to the use of cream or crème fraîche, which so often ruins French vegetable cookery. This book is a must for anyone interested in the art of steaming (*Cuisine à la Vapeur: The Art of Cooking with Steam, *by Jacques Manière). The recipe works best with root vegetables. Beets and rice make a wonderful combination.*

1 pound root vegetable such as beets, parsnips, or sweet potatoes
½ pound high-starch potato such as Idaho, or ½ cup cooked white rice
1 cup hot chicken stock or milk
½ cup grated Parmesan cheese, optional
1 tablespoon high-quality olive oil
Salt and freshly ground black pepper to taste

Prepare and steam the vegetable (and potato, if using). Place vegetable, excluding the potato, in the bowl of a food processor and process until almost smooth. Add the potato or cooked rice and pulse a few times until chopped but not smooth. Add half the stock or milk and pulse. If necessary for a smooth puree, add more of the stock or milk and pulse (this will depend on the vegetable and personal preference). Add the cheese, olive oil, and salt and freshly ground black pepper to taste. Pulse to combine.

Serves 4 as a small side dish

Master Recipe for Steamed Vegetable Soup

This is similar to the Master Recipe for Puree of Steamed Vegetables. Just add more liquid for a thinner, more soupy consistency. Use any vegeta-

bles on hand — *this is an easy way to clean out the vegetable bin once a week. For fresh herbs, thyme and basil work well. Mint goes well with many green vegetables, such as peas or green beans. Tarragon and marjoram should be tried in smaller quantities (start with 1 teaspoon). See if you like their flavors before adding too much. Rosemary works well with root vegetables but is too strong for less hearty offerings.*

1½ pounds assorted vegetables
1 high-starch potato such as Idaho
3 cups hot chicken stock
1 tablespoon minced fresh herbs
2 tablespoons high-quality olive oil or cream, optional
    Salt and freshly ground black pepper to taste

Prepare and steam the vegetables and potato. Place vegetables, excluding the potato, in the bowl of a food processor and process until smooth. Add the hot chicken stock and process until smooth. Add the potato and pulse a few times until chopped but not pureed. Add the herbs, the optional olive oil or cream, and salt and freshly ground black pepper to taste. Process until smooth.

Serves 4

Master Recipe for Steamed Vegetable Sauce

I'm always looking for a healthy sauce, and steamed vegetables pureed with potato and/or yogurt fit the bill. You will have to experiment a bit with this sauce, as it does not go with everything. I like it best with fish and chicken; I prefer a lighter, stock-based sauce with red meat. I do not recommend mixing vegetables; it's best to use just one variety to maintain a simple, clean flavor. To prepare spinach, parsley, or watercress for steaming, remove woody stems and wash thoroughly.

3 cloves garlic, peeled and lightly crushed
1 medium onion, peeled, ends removed, and quartered
1 pound vegetable (such as carrots, spinach, parsley, watercress, or broccoli), prepared for steaming
1 small starchy potato such as Idaho, peeled and cut into quarters
2 cups hot chicken broth
⅓ cup plain yogurt, optional
2 tablespoons minced chives
    Salt and freshly ground black pepper to taste

Steam the garlic, onion, vegetable, and potato together for 20 minutes. Puree in the bowl of a food processor. With the machine running, add the hot chicken broth until the vegetables have the proper consistency. Add the optional yogurt, chives, and salt and freshly ground black pepper to taste. Puree until smooth.

Makes about 1 quart

Green Beans with Ginger and Toasted Sesame Oil

These beans are similar to those served in a Chinese restaurant. You may mince the ginger instead of grating it. A mini–food processor is terrific at mincing ginger. You can also mince ginger with a sharp chef's knife.

1 pound green beans (about 4 cups), ends trimmed
2 teaspoons toasted (Oriental) sesame oil
1 tablespoon peanut oil
2 cloves garlic, peeled and minced
2 teaspoons grated fresh ginger
⅛ teaspoon red pepper flakes (or more to taste)
½ tablespoon soy sauce
2 tablespoons water

1. Steam beans until barely cooked, approximately 3 minutes. Beans should still be crunchy. Drain beans and reserve.

2. In a sauté pan, add the sesame and peanut oils, garlic, and ginger over medium-high heat. When sizzling, reduce heat to medium-low and sauté until garlic turns light brown. Do not overcook. Add the red pepper flakes, green beans, soy sauce, and water. Cook over medium-high heat for 3 minutes, stirring once per minute, until the water evaporates.

Serves 4

Pecan Yellow Squash

A full-flavored olive oil is recommended here, such as Olio Santo Extra Virgin or Tipico Calabrese Extra Virgin. Colavita is also an excellent choice and is widely available. Toast pecans on a baking sheet in a 350°F oven for 6–8 minutes.

½ cup pecans, toasted
½ teaspoon kosher salt
⅛ teaspoon grated nutmeg
2 teaspoons white wine vinegar
2 tablespoons extra virgin olive oil
   Salt and freshly ground black pepper to taste
6 fresh basil leaves, sliced into strips lengthwise
2 medium yellow squash, cut into ¼-inch slices

1. Grind pecans in a food processor, blender, or coffee grinder. Add kosher salt and nutmeg and mix. In a small bowl, whisk together the vinegar, olive oil, and salt and pepper. Toss the basil leaves with the oil mixture.

2. Steam squash, covered, in a steamer basket set over lightly salted boiling water until just tender, about 6 minutes. Transfer squash to a large bowl. Spoon oil-basil mixture over it, sprinkle with a pinch of salt, and toss gently until coated evenly. Arrange squash on a platter and sprinkle with pecan mixture.

Serves 4

Steamed Beets with Dill and Onion

In this dish, the beets are diced before cooking. This reduces cooking time and makes for an evenly-cooked dish. Try different varieties of vinegar with this recipe — beets can handle assertive flavors.

1 tablespoon extra virgin olive oil
1 medium onion, peeled and finely diced
8 small to medium beets (about 1½ pounds), peeled, cut into ½-inch dice
1 cup chicken stock
1½ tablespoons raspberry vinegar (or red wine vinegar)
1 tablespoon minced fresh dill
   Salt and freshly ground black pepper to taste

1. Heat oil in a sauté pan with cover. Add onion and cook over medium-high heat until soft, about 5 minutes. Add beets and sauté for 3 minutes. Add chicken stock and additional water, if necessary, to cover the bottom of the pan to a depth of ¼ inch. Cover and cook over low heat until beets are just tender, about 15 minutes.

2. When the beets are barely tender, remove cover, turn heat to medium-high, and sauté until liquid evaporates, 4–5 minutes. Add the vinegar and dill and cook over medium-high heat for 1 minute, stirring to coat. Add plenty of salt and freshly ground pepper to taste. Remove from pan with a slotted spoon and serve.

Serves 4

Broccoli with Sesame-Ginger Vinaigrette

In this Oriental preparation the toasted sesame oil adds depth to the flavor. Fresh ginger is essential to this dish.

Vinaigrette
2 tablespoons lemon juice
1 teaspoon minced fresh ginger
1 teaspoon soy sauce
1 teaspoon toasted (Oriental) sesame oil

Broccoli
1 bunch broccoli
2 tablespoons olive oil

1 tablespoon toasted (Oriental) sesame oil
2 cloves garlic, peeled and minced
1 teaspoon sesame seeds
  Salt and freshly ground black pepper to
  taste

1. Prepare the vinaigrette by whisking together lemon juice, ginger, soy sauce, and toasted sesame oil.

2. With a chef's knife, cut away broccoli florets from the small stalks and stem. Trim off ⅛ inch of the outer layer of the stem, cut stem in half lengthwise, and then cut into bite-size pieces. Steam broccoli for 5 minutes. Drain.

3. Heat olive and sesame oils in a skillet over medium heat. Sauté the garlic for 1 minute — *do* let garlic brown. Add the broccoli and a pinch of salt and sauté briefly until evenly coated with oil.

4. Remove broccoli to a serving bowl. Whisk vinaigrette again, pour over broccoli, and toss to coat. Sprinkle with sesame seeds, add salt and freshly ground pepper to taste, and serve warm.

Serves 6

~ 8 ~

How to Roast Vegetables

Roasting caramelizes the natural sugars in root vegetables, making them sweeter and more flavorful. The trick is a hot oven and covering the vegetables for half the cooking time.

~

My mother's garden in the northwest corner of Connecticut is planted mostly with low-maintenance root vegetables, primarily beets, parsnips, potatoes, turnips, and carrots. She has a root cellar with a thermostatically controlled window (when it gets too hot in the basement, the window opens to let in the cold air), and she packs her vegetables in garbage bags filled with peat moss to keep them fresh. The beets last just until Christmas (she precooks and freezes most of them), but the carrots hold until June, and the sprouted potatoes go back into the ground as starters in May. Every time our family visits, we of course dine on root vegetables either steamed, boiled, microwaved, or roasted. Having already eaten more than one lifetime's worth of tubers, I can attest to the alchemy of roasting, a process that transforms a potentially dull parsnip or potato into something complex, aromatic, and suggestively sweet. The high heat is the active agent in the process. It intensifies flavors and caramelizes sugars to make the simple complex, the bland rich and satisfying.

THE TECHNIQUES OF ROASTING

Potatoes, carrots, turnips, or sweet potatoes are cut into pieces, drizzled with oil, sprinkled with salt and herbs, and then cooked in a hot oven for about 45 minutes. When I set out to discover the best technique I focused on two issues: oven temperature and whether the pan should be covered. The tests proved that covering and then uncovering the vegetables was the best approach and that a more moderate roasting temperature was optimum; higher temperatures burned the exterior and dried out the interior.

ROASTING TIPS

The best vegetable for roasting is potatoes with their skin on. The skin browns nicely and gets crispy. The inside, if cooked thoroughly, becomes light and fluffy. If you can stand a bit of fat, try cooking 4 pieces of bacon first and then using 2 tablespoons of the rendered fat plus 1 tablespoon of olive oil to

How to Roast Root Vegetables

Covering root vegetables during roasting prevents the interior from drying out, but the texture and flavor suffer a bit. The oven temperature was tested at three levels: 400°, 450°, and 500°F.

Oven Temperature	Technique	Results
400°F	30 minutes covered, 15 minutes uncovered	Tender, creamy, nicely browned
	45 minutes uncovered	Dry inside
450°F	20 minutes covered, 20 minutes uncovered	Best results; better flavor than at 400°F
	40 minutes uncovered	Very dry
500°F	20 minutes covered, 10 minutes uncovered	Burned on outside
	30 minutes uncovered	Dry and burned

dress the potatoes before cooking. When the potatoes are done, crumble the reserved bacon over them and serve. Do not hesitate to add lots of salt to roasted root vegetables. They need it. I also prefer a strong fresh herb such as rosemary (especially for potatoes) to pick up the flavor of this dish. Fresh thyme, although a more modest herb than rosemary, also works well.

Roasted Root Vegetables

This dish is substantially better if fresh herbs are used rather than dried. You can also add peeled cloves of garlic to roasted vegetables during the last 15 minutes of cooking.

- 2 pounds root vegetables (potatoes, carrots, sweet potatoes, turnips, or a combination), washed and cut into 1¼-inch pieces
- 1 large onion, peeled and cut into wedges
- 3 tablespoons olive oil
- 1 teaspoon dried herbs *or* 1 tablespoon minced fresh
  Salt and freshly ground black pepper to taste

1. Heat oven to 450°F. Place vegetables and onion in a roasting pan large enough to hold them in one layer. Toss with oil. Cover tightly with aluminum foil.

2. Place in oven. After 20 minutes, uncover pan and toss vegetables. Cook uncovered 10 minutes and toss again, then cook a final 10 minutes or until vegetables are crisp outside and fully cooked inside. Add herbs, salt to taste, and a few grindings of black pepper and serve.

Serves 4

Roasted Carrots

Prepare 2 pounds carrots as for Roasted Root Vegetables, adding 2 teaspoons of balsamic vinegar to the olive oil and using 1 tablespoon of fresh oregano or 1 teaspoon dried.

Roasted Garlic

This is a simple recipe that produces a garlic that is relatively mild and is excellent as a spread, as an ingredient in a vinaigrette, or used to coat meat or fish. Some cooks poach a head of garlic in milk before roasting to produce a milder flavor. I find that this is not worth the extra time and effort.

- 1 head garlic
- 1 teaspoon olive oil

Heat oven to 350°F. Remove loose, papery outer layer of skin. Cut a half-inch off the top of the garlic head. Place garlic in a square of aluminum foil and drizzle with the oil. Close the foil tightly, place package in oven, and cook for about 1 hour. Remove from oven. When pressed, the roasted garlic cloves will emerge from the top of the head.

New Potatoes with Rosemary and Garlic

These potatoes can be served with a roast, at a picnic, or even as an appetizer or first course tossed with roasted red peppers and Greek olives.

2 pounds new potatoes, scrubbed, eyes removed, and rinsed
6 cloves garlic, peeled and minced
½ cup dry white wine
2 tablespoons lemon juice
2 tablespoons soy sauce
2 tablespoons extra virgin olive oil
1 tablespoon dried rosemary *or* 2 tablespoons fresh
Salt and freshly ground black pepper to taste

Heat oven to 450°F. Bite-size potatoes can be left whole — larger potatoes should be sliced in half. Place potatoes in a large roasting pan. Whisk together remaining ingredients in a small bowl. Pour rosemary-garlic mixture over potatoes and toss. Turn potatoes cut side down, cover roasting pan with foil, and bake for 20 minutes. Remove cover and toss potatoes again. Bake for 10 minutes and toss again; bake another 10 minutes or until potatoes can be easily pierced with a fork. Toss with plenty of salt and freshly ground black pepper. Serve either hot or at room temperature.

Serves 8–10

~ 9 ~

Salsas, Relishes, and Chutneys

Cut-up fruit and/or vegetables mixed with vinegar plus herbs or spices — that's the basis for these quick and easy accompaniments for meat, fish, or poultry.

~

Calvin Coolidge was known for his dry, almost vitriolic wit, and Coolidge stories are still told by old-timers in our small town in Vermont. One of my favorite anecdotes was told to me by Charlie Bentley, the town's last farmer. Coolidge, asked if he had lived in his hometown all his life, didn't miss a beat and quickly shot back, "Not yet."

When I come across a new food trend, I always ask myself what Coolidge might have said about it. I think that he would have had a few words — he was always to the point — about the incredible popularity of the term "salsa." After all, it just means sauce or relish, and yet the term now has tremendous marketing cachet due to the wild popularity of Mexican, Tex-Mex, and other highly spiced cuisines. It's nothing fancy, just some cut-up fruit or vegetables, almost always served with vinegar or fruit juice. If you add sugar and cook it, you'll probably call it a chutney (though some chutneys are served raw). I am not sure that anyone could tell you the difference between salsa and a relish — they are really the same thing — except that these days, many salsas tend to be tropical, using mangoes, papayas, lime juice,

and plenty of hot chilis. (In classic American cooking, most relishes were cooked and then canned, a practical means of preserving large quantities of fresh vegetables. Today, however, most relishes are prepared fresh in small quantities and consumed immediately.) Of course, an old-fashioned American relish used the ingredients on hand, which included none of the above. No matter what you call them, these accompaniments are good, they are easy to make, and they are fresh and brightly flavored, a far cry from the "sauces"

COOKING TIP

Toasting Spices

As my friend and the coauthor of *Salsas, Sambals, Chutneys & Chowchows* Doc Willoughby often points out, toasting whole seeds, then grinding them yourself, is vastly preferable to using ground spices from a bottle. It's simple. Throw the seeds in a preheated sauté pan and toast about 3 minutes over medium heat, shaking constantly. Now grind the seeds in a spice grinder. You'll have twice the flavor and a much brighter, more complex aroma. Ground untoasted spices tend to have a dull, one-dimensional flavor without the complex highlights.

---

of French cuisine. But I'd feel better if we just called them relishes.

Master Recipe for Fruit Salsa

This is a do-it-yourself recipe for a fruit relish/ salsa. If you do not like the taste of cilantro, use basil or flat-leaf parsley. You can use lime or lemon juice, red or white wine vinegar, or include or exclude chopped olives. To crush the pepper-corns, put them in a plastic bag, place on a work surface or cutting board, and crush with the bot-tom of a small, heavy saucepan. See page 70 for information on cutting up a mango. This salsa is excellent with grilled fish and poultry.

3 cups ripe peaches, mangoes, or nectarines, peeled and cut into ½-inch cubes
¼ cup lime or lemon juice
2 tablespoons red or white wine vinegar
¼ cup good-quality olive oil
½ cup diced onion
¼ cup chopped cilantro, basil, or flat-leaf parsley
½ cup imported black olives, pitted and chopped, optional
1 tablespoon cored, seeded, and diced fresh chili pepper, optional
Salt and freshly crushed black pepper to taste

Combine all ingredients and let marinate in the refrigerator for 1 hour. For a smoother flavor, pulse once or twice in the workbowl of a food processor before marinating.

Makes 5 cups

Basic Vegetable Salsa

Salsa is nothing more than a raw vegetable sauce, usually containing tomatoes, peppers, cucum-bers, and onion. It can be used as a dip with tor-tilla chips, with a cold meat salad, in tortillas, or as a condiment with a variety of main courses. It's especially good with chicken, pork, and fish. If you want more heat, add one or two finely diced chili peppers. Be sure to add plenty of salt and freshly ground black pepper.

5 tomatoes, seeded and diced
1 red bell pepper, seeded and diced
1 cucumber, peeled, seeded, and diced
¼ cup diced onion
3 cloves garlic, peeled and minced
2 tablespoons minced flat-leaf parsley
2 tablespoons minced cilantro
2 tablespoons lime juice
6 drops Tabasco or to taste
3 tablespoons red wine vinegar
Salt and freshly ground pepper to taste

Combine all ingredients and marinate at room temperature for at least 1 hour. Adjust seasonings.

Makes about 5 cups

Classic Tomato-Basil Salsa

There are hundreds of variations on this salsa, but they all require good fresh tomatoes and fresh, flavorful basil. This salsa can be used as a dip or with fish.

½ cup basil leaves, tightly packed
2 cups seeded and diced tomatoes
¼ cup diced onion
1 clove garlic, peeled and minced
2 teaspoons red wine vinegar
1 teaspoon balsamic vinegar
2 tablespoons plus 1 teaspoon extra virgin olive oil
Pinch sugar
½ teaspoon kosher salt
Freshly ground black pepper to taste

Stack the basil leaves and roll up. Cut into thin strips. Combine all ingredients and let sit at room temperature for 1 hour before serving.

Makes 3 cups

Oven-Roasted Tomato Salsa with Olives, Garlic, and Anchovies

This is similar to an Italian puttanesca *sauce with tomatoes, anchovies, garlic, and olives. I use it with chicken and fish, although you can also use a small amount as a sauce for pasta.*

4 tomatoes, cut in half and seeded
¼ teaspoon kosher salt
¼ cup high-quality olive oil
2 anchovies, minced
4 cloves garlic, peeled and lightly crushed
1 tablespoon capers
¼ cup imported black olives, pitted and chopped
1 tablespoon red wine vinegar

Sprinkle the tomatoes with salt and then roast cut side up in a 250° oven for 2 hours. Heat olive oil in a small saucepan. Add the anchovies and the garlic cloves and cook over low heat for 5 minutes. Remove from heat and let steep for 10 minutes. Combine all ingredients.

Makes 4–5 cups

Black Bean Salsa with Olives

This is a simple winter salsa good with meat and fish. Be sure to use imported black olives such as Kalamata or niçoise.

¼ cup olive oil
3 cloves garlic, peeled and lightly crushed
1 cup cooked black beans
1 cup coarsely chopped onion
¼ cup lime juice
3 tablespoons white wine vinegar
¼ cup imported black olives, pitted and chopped
1 jalapeño pepper, seeded and diced

Heat olive oil in small saucepan over medium heat. When hot, add crushed garlic and cook over low heat for 6–7 minutes or until lightly browned. Remove from heat and let steep 10 minutes. Discard garlic cloves and mix oil with remaining ingredients. Let sit at room temperature for at least 1 hour.

Makes 3 cups

Grilled Corn Salsa

Grilled corn (make sure that you are using a supersweet variety for maximum flavor) is incredibly sweet and flavorful, and grilled onions lose their pungency and take on a rich, sweet flavor. This is my favorite summer salsa recipe.

1 red bell pepper, stemmed, seeded, and cut into eighths
1 onion, peeled and cut into thick rounds
 Olive oil for tossing
 Salt for sprinkling
3 ears corn, silked and husked
¼ cup cider vinegar
2 tablespoons high-quality olive oil
½ teaspoon kosher salt
¼ cup chopped flat-leaf parsley
 Freshly ground black pepper to taste

Toss the red pepper and onion with olive oil and a sprinkling of salt. Grill the corn (4 minutes), the red pepper (3 minutes), and the onion (4 minutes), over a hot fire. Chop the pepper and onion. Cut off corn kernels with a large knife. Toss vegetables together in a bowl. Add remaining ingredients and toss to combine.

Makes about 4 cups

Avocado Salsa with Corn and Red Pepper

To remove the pit from an avocado, strike it with the edge of a large chef's knife. With the pit firmly attached to the blade, move the knife to loosen and remove the pit while holding on to the avocado with the other hand. The skin of the avocado is easily removed if cut into quarters first. See page 65 for step-by-step illustrations. This salsa is particularly good with roast or grilled chicken.

¼ cup high-quality olive oil
4 cloves garlic, peeled and crushed
1 tablespoon cumin seeds
3 ears corn, silked and husked
1 red bell pepper, seeded and diced
½ cup diced onion
2 avocados, cut into large dice
2 teaspoons red wine vinegar
¼ cup lime juice
¼ cup chopped flat-leaf parsley
2 tablespoons chopped fresh oregano or thyme
   Salt and freshly ground black pepper to taste

Heat the oil over medium heat until hot. Add the crushed garlic cloves and cook over low heat for 6–7 minutes or until cloves turn light brown. Remove from heat and let steep 10 minutes. Discard cloves. Toast cumin seeds in a heated skillet for 3 minutes, shaking constantly. Grind in an electric spice or coffee grinder. Place corn under broiler and, turning the corn frequently, cook until it has small dark brown spots. Remove kernels with a large chef's knife. Combine all ingredients in a bowl, tossing gently but thoroughly.

Makes about 6 cups

Pear Relish

This relish is simple to make and very elegant. It is quite sweet, and I like it best with pork, although it would also work with a turkey or ham around the holidays. Carefully dice the pears so that the pieces are even. You should use firm pears, as very ripe pears do not hold up well to cooking.

¼ cup brown sugar
½ cup water
6 firm pears, peeled, cored, and diced
¼ teaspoon ground allspice
½ teaspoon ground cinnamon
¼ teaspoon ground cloves
½ teaspoon balsamic vinegar

Dissolve the brown sugar in the water over low heat in a medium saucepan. Add remaining ingredients to the saucepan and bring to a simmer. Cook 5–10 minutes, until pears are cooked but still firm. Remove from heat and cool.

Makes 5–6 cups

Tomato Relish

This recipe yields lots of leftover liquid that makes a good salad dressing, ideal for a spinach salad, for example. To seed a cucumber, peel it, cut it in half lengthwise, and, using a teaspoon-size measuring spoon, scoop out the seeds. A metal measuring spoon has sharp, thin sides, ideal for cutting through the flesh of a cucumber.

Relish
1 medium red onion, peeled and diced
3 large tomatoes, seeded and diced
1 red bell pepper, seeded and diced
1 green bell pepper, seeded and diced
1 cucumber, peeled, seeded, and diced
1 rib celery, diced
3 teaspoons seeded and minced mild chilis
2 tablespoons minced flat-leaf parsley

Dressing
2 cloves garlic, peeled and minced
2 teaspoons lemon juice
¼ cup balsamic vinegar
½ cup olive oil
2 teaspoons Dijon mustard
¼ teaspoon kosher salt
¼ teaspoon sugar

Combine all relish ingredients in a bowl. Whisk together dressing ingredients and pour over the relish. Let marinate for at least 1 hour. This salsa can be pulsed two or three times in the workbowl of a food processor to thicken.

Makes 6–7 cups

Ginger-Onion Chutney with Molasses

This recipe is a lot better if you can find whole cardamom and coriander seeds. Cardamom seeds are often sold in their pods; the tiny black seeds must be removed from the pods before sautéing. Toast the seeds by placing in a sauté pan for a few minutes over medium heat, shaking the pan frequently. Process in an electric spice grinder. This chutney is good with pork, ham, or lamb.

2 tablespoons olive oil
2 cups minced onion
1 tablespoon minced garlic
¼ teaspoon ground cardamom
¼ teaspoon ground coriander
2 tablespoons minced ginger
2 tablespoons molasses
2 tablespoons orange juice
2 tablespoons white wine vinegar

Place olive oil and onions in a large skillet and cook over medium heat about 12–15 minutes, stirring occasionally, until onions are very soft and rich brown. Stir in garlic and spices and cook for 2 minutes. Add remaining ingredients and cook an additional 5 minutes, stirring occasionally. Cool before serving.

Makes about 2½ cups

Grilled Pineapple Salsa

If you don't have a charcoal or gas grill handy, pineapple can be run under the broiler or dry-sautéed in a nonstick pan over medium-low heat for 6 minutes per side. This salsa is best served with grilled fish.

1 ripe pineapple, peeled and cut into ¼-inch-thick slices
2 tablespoons chopped cilantro
1 tablespoon white wine vinegar
1 tablespoon lime juice
2 tablespoons orange juice
1 tablespoon olive oil
1 teaspoon seeded and minced Anaheim (mild) chili
½ teaspoon kosher salt

Grill pineapple slices until browned on both sides. Cut into bite-size pieces. Combine with remaining ingredients. Serve immediately.

Makes about 6 cups

Dried Fruit Chutney

This recipe is based on one found in Salsas, Sambals, Chutneys & Chowchows, *by Chris Schlesinger and John Willoughby. I use dried fruits instead of fresh and suggest that you include 1 cup of dried apricots for flavor plus 1 cup of another dried fruit. I also sweat the onions over low heat to bring out their sweet, rich flavor. Serve with pork or lamb.*

1 teaspoon whole cumin seeds
2 tablespoons olive oil
1 cup coarsely chopped onion
2 cups dried fruit (peaches, pears, apricots, and/or apples)
¼ cup light brown sugar
¼ cup raisins
½ teaspoon kosher salt
1 tablespoon molasses
½ teaspoon ground coriander
¼ cup cider vinegar
¼ cup lemon juice
1 teaspoon chopped fresh mint

1. Place cumin seeds in a skillet over medium heat and toast for 3 minutes, shaking pan constantly. Remove and grind in an electric spice or coffee grinder.

2. Heat the olive oil in a medium saucepan. When hot, add the onions and cook, covered, over low heat for 15 minutes. Add ⅓ cup water and the 2 cups dried fruit, increase heat to medium, and cook, stirring occasionally, for 2 minutes. Add the remaining ingredients except the last 3 and cook uncovered over low heat for 45 minutes. Stir occasionally and add more water if necessary to prevent sticking. Remove from heat and stir in vinegar, lemon juice, and chopped mint. Let cool before serving.

Makes about 4 cups

The Secrets of Salad Dressings

What is the proper ratio of oil to vinegar? Can citrus juice be substituted in equal amounts for vinegar? Does an immersion blender make a better dressing?

~

I find that most home cooks, myself included, are a bit intimidated by salad dressings. These homemade blends are often either too acidic or too bitter, and the standard recipe directions — "whisk in oil drop by drop until an emulsion starts to form" — imply some form of temperamental alchemy that might go awry. After some investigation, however, I discovered that a good salad dressing is a simple matter indeed.

SELECTING AN OIL

A high-quality olive oil is the only real choice for a good salad. A poor-quality oil is greasy and without flavor; a good extra virgin oil, however, is fruity, clean to the palate, and has a soft, melting texture. The difference lies in how olive oils are made. For high-quality oils, the olives are pressed, which produces oil and water. (Low-quality oils are extracted using chemical solvents or heat.) The water is removed and the resulting olive oil requires no additional refining other than filtering. This pressing can be done with a mechanical press, which is still used in many places to produce extra virgin oils, or with more sophisticated machines that extract the oil through centrifugal force. The true test of an olive oil is acidity. An extra virgin oil must have an acidity of less than 1 percent. These oils have bright, fruity flavors and are often an emerald green, although color is not necessarily an indication of quality. Oils with high acidity, however, require refining, which draws out much of the flavor. Extra virgin oil is often added back to these oils after processing to restore some of the lost color and flavor. Other factors also affect the quality of the oil, including the ripeness of the olives when picked and how they were harvested (by hand or by machine, the former being preferable). Extra virgin oil (the oil made from the first cold pressing of the olives, which is very low in acidity) is preferable to oils made from subsequent pressings, which are labeled, in descending order of quality, extra fine, fine, or just plain virgin. My favorite brand of extra virgin oil is I Tattoli; it can be ordered from the Todaro Brothers in New York (212-532-0633). It is expensive — about $30 per liter — but since I use it only for drizzling and dressings, not cooking, one bottle, if stored properly, will last many months. If you are limited to purchasing an olive oil at the supermarket, I suggest the Filippo Berio brand extra virgin, which is widely available.

What Is the Best Olive Oil for a Salad Dressing?

I purchased thirteen different olive oils, including extra virgin and extra light varieties, and rated them based on the results of a blind tasting. A few oils had a strong olive flavor; many oils were flat and tasteless; and some were unpleasantly oily, almost industrial in flavor. Although the quality of olive oils may change from season to season and therefore it may be difficult to judge specific brands from year to year, all of the extra virgin oils placed higher than other varieties. This tasting also showed that extra light olive oils have an unpleasant oily texture and are flavorless. Avoid them at all costs. Also note that after eighteen months, olive oil will start to turn rancid even if held in an unopened bottle. Therefore, purchase olive oil at stores with high turnover. Brands are listed in order of preference, although the first five oils were roughly equal in ratings. (The sixth oil, Da Vinci extra virgin, was rated first by one participant because of its strong olive taste; others felt it was overpowering.) Note that price has little to do with quality. All brands were Italian except Italica, which is a Spanish olive oil. The last-place extra virgin oil, Colavita, had a harsh back-of-the-throat aftertaste that I find unpleasant, but which is characteristic of some Italian growing regions. It did have, however, a fresh olive flavor.

Brand	Type	Price per Ounce	Comments
Aprilia	Extra virgin	$ .31	Fresh, young, clean flavor
Filippo Berio	Extra virgin	$ .46	Smooth olive flavor
De Cecco	Extra virgin	$ .38	Good hint of olives; fruity
Costa d'Oro	Extra virgin	$ .29	Strong olive flavor
Olio Santo	Extra virgin	$ .67	Niçoise-style flavor
Da Vinci	Extra virgin	$ .80	Excellent olive flavor; a bit sour
Williams-Sonoma	Extra virgin	$ .35	Smooth, but very mild olive flavor
Le Fasce	Extra virgin	$ .35	Light with a hint of citrus
Colavita	Extra virgin	$ .32	Harsh back-of-the-throat aftertaste
Da Vinci	Regular	$ .35	Complete lack of olive flavor
Da Vinci	Extra light	$ .35	Bland; flavorless
Colavita	Regular	$ .47	Very light; little olive flavor
Italica	Regular	$ .31	Very light; little olive flavor
Filippo Berio	Extra light	$ .37	No flavor; flat and oily

There are two other types of oils you should be aware of. A good walnut oil, available in specialty stores, is often called for in salads because of its rich flavor. For an Asian flavor, substitute a small amount of Oriental-style toasted sesame oil for the olive oil called for in the recipe (regular sesame oil is pressed from the raw sesame seed — the nut-colored toasted sesame oil is pressed from toasted seeds).

SELECTING A VINEGAR

The proper vinegar is almost as important as selecting a good-quality olive oil. You have five good choices: white wine vinegar, red wine vinegar, sherry vinegar, balsamic vinegar, and rice wine vinegar. In general, red wine vinegar is a better all-round vinegar for salad dressings, since its flavor works well with a wide variety of ingredients. In addition, I find red wine vinegars less harsh than their white counterparts. Sherry vinegar is also a good choice; it's a bit milder and more complex than either a basic red or white wine vinegar. Balsamic vinegar is too concentrated and too sweet for my taste. I do not recommend it for dressing greens, although it can be used, along with red wine vinegar, for heartier fare such as a meat salad. (White balsamic vinegar, however, is mild and an excellent choice for salad greens. Balsamic vinegar is made by boiling down the concentrated juices of white grapes. High-quality balsamic vinegars are aged ten years or more and are very expensive — over $50 for a small bottle. The mass-market varieties are substantially inferior in quality but are relatively inexpensive.) Finally, rice wine vinegar is on the mild side and a good substitute for red or white wine vinegar if a good-quality brand is not available. One can also purchase flavored vinegars, but I find the herbal varieties (thyme, tarragon, rosemary, et cetera) both bitter and too acidic, since many manufacturers use an inferior-quality vinegar in these preparations. The one exception is raspberry vinegar, which I do find useful, especially with beets. Other commercially available vinegars include champagne vinegar and cider vinegar. The former is expensive, and the latter is not recommended for salad dressings due to its strong flavor. Do not use distilled white vinegar in a salad dressing, as it contributes little flavor. You can also use lemon or lime juice, although they should be used judiciously and added to one of the less pungent vinegars as part of a dressing.

CAN YOU DRESS A SALAD WITHOUT MAKING AN EMULSION?

What if you simply dressed a salad without doing any whisking? In fact, this works reasonably well for a simple dressing. Pour a little oil around a large salad bowl. Add the greens and toss with the oil and taste. Now splash on some vinegar, a little salt, and some fresh herbs. Toss. Taste again and adjust ingredients accordingly. I often use this method, especially for a quick midweek salad, but making a proper dressing, especially for more complicated recipes, does have its advantages. First, you can measure the ingredients more accurately. Second, seasonings can be properly distributed throughout the emul-

sion, providing more consistent flavor. Finally, a proper salad dressing is smoother. The vinegar is suspended in the surrounding oil, providing a more complex, more delicate flavor without any sharp notes of acidity. Since whisking together a dressing takes less than a minute, this is the preferred method. (The method above works best with high-quality oil and vinegar. Lower-quality ingredients benefit more from whisking, since the emulsion ameliorates their worst qualities, hiding the acidity of the vinegar, for example, behind the tongue-coating richness of the olive oil.)

SALAD DRESSING BASICS

WHAT IS THE BEST RATIO OF OIL TO VINEGAR?

My wife and I once had lunch at Le Petit Plat, a small bistro in Paris, and I ordered a salad of artichoke hearts and haricots verts. The dressing did not have a hint of harsh acidity. It was mild yet complex, easy on the tongue, yet with enough backbone to stand up to the salad ingredients. Of course, I assumed that it was simply a matter of using the best olive oil and vinegar, but when I mentioned this experience to Ed Behr, a Vermont resident and editor of *The Art of Eating*, he asked me what proportion of oil to vinegar I normally used. I told him 3 to 1. He suggested that I had probably experienced a vinaigrette with a much higher proportion of oil, so I went into the kitchen to test.

Using a good-quality red wine vinegar, I made six different vinaigrettes, starting at a ratio of 2½ to 1, increasing to 5 to 1. Although I had thought that 3 to 1 was the proper ratio, I found that 4½ tablespoons of oil to 1 tablespoon of vinegar was best. The resulting vinaigrette was mild — it had no harsh tang or bitterness — yet the creaminess of the olive oil did contain a pleasant counterpoint of acidity.

To determine whether different vinegars require different ratios of olive oil, I performed a taste test and discovered that a rice wine vinegar is best with only a 3-to-1 ratio of oil to vinegar, yet a low-quality white wine vinegar needs a full 5-to-1 proportion to temper its harsh bite. I also discovered that it is virtually impossible to make a good vinaigrette with a cheap supermarket vinegar, that red wine vinegars are better than white wine vinegars (more flavor), and that white balsamic vinegar is my number-one choice for flavor and balance.

How to Create an Emulsion

Most dressing recipes call for whisking in the oil drop by drop until an emulsion starts to form. This is how I performed my tests to determine the proper ratio of oil to vinegar. This method was a bit tedious, so I pulled out my immersion blender and found that when the same ingredients were all placed into the mixing container and then blended on the low setting for 15 seconds, the result was remarkably different. The vinaigrette was lemony in color, foamy, and full of air. It

also had a softer, more subtle flavor, which I found unappealing — the rich flavors of oil and vinegar were dulled — and it was much too thick for a simple salad dressing. The good news was that the emulsion did not break down even after 20 minutes of sitting on the counter. You can achieve a similar result, working with larger quantities, by placing the vinaigrette ingredients in the bowl of a food processor (use a mini-processor if making a small amount) and processing until

Salad Dressing Chemistry 101

Salad dressings are simple emulsions, although an emulsion is quite complicated from a scientific point of view. Simply put, an emulsion is a combination of two ingredients that usually do not mix: oil and water, for example. If droplets of either oil or water are suspended in the other, then an emulsion is formed. (Although most of us think of an emulsion as oil suspended in water, a stick of butter, another example of emulsion, is water suspended in fat.) In making salad dressings, there are three ways this can happen. First, you can use an emulsifier such as egg yolk. Egg yolk (and prepared mustard) contains chemicals that have a unique property. One end is attracted to oil and the other is attracted to water. The droplets of oil are coated in such a way that they are prevented from merging and are kept in suspense in the water. The second technique for creating an emulsion is to use powders — powdered sugar, paprika, dry mustard — which will coat the droplets of oil, helping them to form an emulsion with the water. However, this sort of emulsion is inferior in strength to an emulsion created by the first method. The third way is the use of mechanical action, whisking, which forces the oil into suspension, but without an emulsifier this is only temporary. The oil slowly comes out of suspension and reforms into a mass. An immersion or regular blender, however, is so powerful that it can break the oil into very fine droplets that will stay suspended for some time. The thickness of an emulsion is determined in large part by how much oil is being suspended in how much water. A mayonnaise is very thick because in addition to the use of egg yolks as an emulsifier, a large amount of oil is being forced into a few tablespoons of liquid (vinegar and lemon juice).

an emulsion forms. This method is recommended only for times when a long-lasting emulsion is necessary, such as for a buffet.

However, none of these tests left me with a simple method for producing an emulsion. I decided to test placing all the ingredients together at the outset and whisking, instead of adding the olive oil to the vinegar drop by drop. To my surprise, this worked fine; the emulsion was established in just 15 seconds. With a relatively high proportion of oil to vinegar, the emulsion is easy to produce. When left standing on the counter, the vinaigrette started to thin after 5 minutes but was still in good shape 15 minutes later. Not only was the 4½-to-1 ratio better for taste, it also made the emulsion easier to produce.

OTHER DRESSING INGREDIENTS
For thicker, longer-lasting emulsions, you can add either mustard or egg yolk. I found that ½ teaspoon of prepared mustard to 1 tablespoon of vinegar was best, and a mere ¼ teaspoon of egg yolk per tablespoon of vinegar did the job. Salt is crucial to a good vinaigrette — use ¼ teaspoon of kosher salt and whisk it into the vinegar to dissolve before adding the olive oil. Garlic is problematic. A diced clove of garlic will produce too much bite for a simple salad dressing (although 1 diced garlic clove works fine if an assertive dressing is called for). It's best to crush 1 clove, add it to the ingredients in a small bowl, whisk them into a vinaigrette, and then let stand at room temperature for a half hour or more. Just before serving, remove and discard the clove and whisk the dressing again to reform the emulsion. A quicker method of adding garlic flavor is to rub the inside of the salad bowl with a clove that has been peeled and cut in half. Lemon or lime juice can also be used, but substitute them for no more than ⅓ of the vinegar. Any small amount of fresh herb can be whisked into the ingredients.

SALAD DRESSING LITE
Mustard- or egg yolk–based vinaigrettes can be a bit thick and overpowering. With a salad of delicate greens, I often prefer a thinner, lighter-tasting dressing, and I have found that adding 2 teaspoons of water to the Master Recipe for Vinaigrette provides gentler flavor. (Adding water also makes sense when using a very strong vinegar.) I tried using boiling water to see if it would be better than tap water at binding the emulsion, but I did not find this to make any difference.

HOMEMADE FLAVORED OILS AND VINEGARS

Flavored oils and vinegars are easy to make at home and are much less expensive than the commercial varieties. A garlic oil, for example, is not only a nice change of pace for a salad dressing, but can also be used in a stir-fry or marinade. You can also start out with a good-quality oil or vinegar, something commercial producers don't always do.

I tested making my own flavored oils at home and found that oil temperature had a big impact on flavor and that the optimum temperature varied depending on the flavoring ingredient. Homemade flavored oils should not be stored for more than 2 months.

I also experimented with flavored vinegars. I made three different variations, using raspberries, crushed garlic, and crushed black peppercorns as the base flavorings, along with fresh herbs and a few hot peppers for some kick. The boiling vinegar was poured over the ingredients, allowed to steep for 1 week, and then strained and bottled. All three were easy, excellent, and a lot cheaper than store-bought. You can use distilled white vinegar, although a decent white wine vinegar is vastly preferable.

The Effect of Oil Temperature on Flavored Oils

I started with three different oil temperatures: room temperature, 130°F, and 350°F. The proper temperature for extracting the best flavor varied depending on the flavoring ingredient — 350°F for chili peppers and 130°F for toasted pecans and crushed garlic cloves.

Ingredient	Oil at 72°F	Oil at 130°F	Oil at 350°F
Chili peppers	Mild, little flavor	Slightly peppery	Toasty, peppery flavor; lots of heat
Toasted pecans	Mild, little flavor	Great burst of flavor; clear winner	Nutty flavor, but not as good as 130°F
Garlic cloves	Mild, good for a mild salad dressing	Good aroma, intense flavor	Cloudy appearance; milder than 130°F

Master Recipe for Flavored Oil

It's easy to make your own flavored oil. After much testing, I have found that toasted nuts, chili peppers, and garlic are the best and most useful flavorings. Fresh herbs do not work very well — they are best used in vinegars. To toast nuts, place them on a baking sheet in a 350° oven for 8–10 minutes.

4 cups extra virgin olive oil

Flavorings (choose 1)
2 cups toasted pecans or walnuts OR
10 cloves garlic, crushed, OR
¼ cup chopped chili peppers

1. For the nuts or garlic, heat the olive oil to 130°F. If using the chili peppers, heat the oil to 350°F. Pour over the flavoring ingredient.

2. Let sit for 1 week in a sealed glass container in a cool, dark place. Strain through cheesecloth and keep in a closed container in a cool, dark place.

Makes about 4 cups flavored oil

Master Recipe for Flavored Vinegar

Some of the flavoring ingredients can be combined, such as the jalapeño peppers, the garlic, and the black pepper.

4 cups white wine vinegar

Flavorings (choose 1 or more)
2 cups raspberries OR
10 cloves garlic, crushed, OR
2 tablespoons black peppercorns, crushed, OR
2 cups fresh herbs OR
4 jalapeño peppers, quartered

Bring vinegar to a boil and pour over flavoring ingredients. Let steep for 7 days. Strain through cheesecloth and store in a closed container in a cool, dark place.

Makes about 4 cups flavored vinegar

Master Recipe for Vinaigrette

This is a basic dressing for use with salad greens. One teaspoon of lemon or lime juice may be substituted for 1 teaspoon of vinegar. For a balsamic vinaigrette, substitute 1 teaspoon of balsamic vinegar for 1 teaspoon of red wine vinegar. Dried herbs are not a good substitute for fresh herbs. For more specific ratios of oil to vinegar, see chart on next page.

¼ teaspoon kosher salt
1 tablespoon red or white wine vinegar
Freshly ground black pepper to taste
4½ tablespoons olive oil
1 clove garlic, peeled and lightly crushed, optional
½ teaspoon Dijon mustard, optional
½ teaspoon minced fresh tarragon, basil, marjoram, or parsley, optional

Whisk together the salt and vinegar in a small bowl. Add remaining ingredients and whisk together for 15 seconds or until an emulsion forms (the mixture thickens and is uniform in texture and color). If using garlic, let dressing sit for at least 15 minutes and then remove crushed clove before serving.

Makes enough to dress a green salad for 6–8

Light Vinaigrette

If you use mustard in the basic recipe, a lighter version is easily created by adding 2 teaspoons of water and then whisking the ingredients together. If you do not use the optional mustard, the dressing will not benefit from the addition of water.

Master Recipe for Mayonnaise

The plastic plunger of many food processors has a small hole at the bottom. This is designed for drizzling oil into an emulsion. Just insert the plunger and pour in the oil. Turn on the machine and the oil will be added at the proper rate. Once the emulsion forms, you can remove the

---

KITCHEN TEST

Do Different Vinegars Require Different Ratios of Olive Oil?

I taste-tested ten different vinegars in a simple 3-to-1 emulsion with extra virgin olive oil. I then increased the amount of olive oil as needed until I felt that the vinegar and oil were balanced. Although I suggest a 4½-to-1 ratio of oil to vinegar for the average high-acidity supermarket vinegar, I found that different types and brands of vinegars require different amounts of olive oil for a balanced emulsion. The surprise entry in this taste test was the white balsamic vinegar, which won hands down. Its flavor, unlike that of regular balsamic vinegar, is more subtle, with a hint of sweetness. The majority of these vinegars are available in supermarkets.

Maker/Type	Price	Size	Acidity	Ratio (Oil to Vinegar)	Comments
Monari Federzoni White Wine Vinegar	$2.39	500 ml	7%	5 to 1	Little flavor; not worth using
Spectrum Natural Brown Rice Vinegar	$2.89	375 ml	4.5%	3 to 1	Not much flavor; mild
Heinz Distilled White Vinegar	$ .93	473 ml	5%	4 to 1	Oily and bland; insipid flat taste
Monari Federzoni Red Wine Vinegar	$2.39	500 ml	7%	4 to 1	Decent flavor; better than white wine vinegars
Dal Raccatto Chianti Vinegar	$4.70	500 ml	7%	5 to 1	Good flavor but on the strong side
Champ's Champagne Vinegar	$6.00	500 ml	7%	4 to 1	Not much flavor; bland
Chicama Vineyards Herbal White Vinegar	$4.00	375 ml	NA	4 to 1	Unpleasant strong flavor; harsh
De Soto Sherry Vinegar	$8.00	375 ml	6.5%	5 to 1	Strong and harsh
Alesso White Balsamic Vinegar	$3.50	250 ml	6%	4 to 1	Outstanding flavor; subtly sweet and full-flavored
Monari Federzoni Balsamic Vinegar	$3.79	500 ml	6%	5 to 1	Good flavor but too assertive for salad greens

MAYONNAISE QUANTITY CHART						
Oil	Egg Yolks	Mustard	Vinegar	Lemon Juice	Kosher Salt	Approx. Yield
1½ cups	2	½ tsp.	2 tsp.	1 tbsp.	½ tsp.	2 cups
2 cups	3	½ tsp.	1 tbsp.	2 tbsp.	¾ tsp.	2½ cups
2½ cups	4	1 tsp.	4 tsp.	3 tbsp.	1 tsp.	3¼ cups

plunger and pour the rest of the oil directly into the bowl at a faster rate. If you substitute olive oil for ½ cup of the vegetable oil, you will produce a slightly thinner mayonnaise, although olive oil does have a strong flavor. Refer to the chart below for making different quantities of mayonnaise. You can also add herbs to a mayonnaise (see Herb Mayonnaise, right).

> 1 tablespoon lemon juice
> 2 egg yolks
> ½ teaspoon Dijon mustard
> ½ teaspoon kosher salt
>   Freshly ground black pepper
> 2 teaspoons white wine vinegar
> 1½ cups vegetable oil

Add all ingredients except oil to the bowl of a food processor and pulse until well blended. With the machine on, drizzle the first ¼ cup of oil very slowly into mixture until emulsion starts to form (or place ½ cup oil into the plunger, which will drip oil into the mixture through a small hole in its bottom). With the machine still running, add the rest of the oil more quickly.

Makes about 2 cups

Watercress Mayonnaise

Add 1 cup of watercress leaves that have been washed, dried, and stemmed to the bowl of a food processor along with the lemon juice called for in the master recipe. Process until smooth, about 30 seconds. Now proceed with the master recipe.

Makes approximately 2½ cups

Herb Mayonnaise

This recipe flavors the oil by steeping it with a clove of crushed garlic. This is a good technique if you prefer a subtle hint of garlic to the harsher flavor of raw garlic used in most salad dressings. You can substitute shallots or chili peppers for the garlic if you like.

> Ingredients for Master Recipe for Mayonnaise (see at left)
> 1 clove garlic, peeled and lightly crushed
> 2 tablespoons flat-leaf parsley
> 1 tablespoon fresh basil, tarragon, or other herb

1. Before making Master Recipe for Mayonnaise, heat ½ cup of the oil called for in the recipe in a small saucepan. When very hot, add the crushed clove of garlic and turn off heat. Let steep for 10 minutes. Allow oil to cool to room temperature. Remove garlic.

2. Proceed with master recipe, processing the herbs in the food processor along with the other ingredients, and using the ½ cup of garlic oil prepared in step 1 as part of the oil called for.

Makes approximately 2 cups

All-Purpose Vegetable Salad Dressing

This is an excellent dressing for a vegetable salad. You may add a bit of sugar or honey, especially if the vegetables are a little bland. This is an easy dressing to make, as the mustard facilitates the creation of an emulsion. If you do not have marjoram and tarragon, try substituting summer savory or oregano. For a less garlicky dressing, lightly crush the 2 garlic cloves, let them stand in the completed dressing for at least 30 minutes, remove them, and then whisk the ingredients a second time just before serving.

- ½ teaspoon kosher salt
- ¼ cup red wine vinegar
- 1 tablespoon lemon juice
- 2 cloves garlic, peeled and finely minced with herbs below
- ½ teaspoon minced fresh marjoram or a pinch dried
- ½ teaspoon minced fresh tarragon or a pinch dried
- 1 tablespoon Dijon mustard
  Freshly ground black pepper
- 1 cup olive oil

Place the first 3 ingredients in a small bowl and whisk to dissolve salt. Add remaining ingredients and whisk until an emulsion forms (the mixture thickens and is uniform in texture and color), about 15 seconds.

Makes 1⅓ cups dressing

Tomato, Caper, and Olive Dressing

This full-flavored dressing can be used with an assertive salad, a vegetable salad, or even with pasta. For pasta, steam fresh garden vegetables, toss with this dressing, and then serve over hot pasta.

- 1 teaspoon Dijon mustard
- 1 clove garlic, peeled and minced
- 3 tablespoons red wine vinegar
- ½ cup plus 2 tablespoons extra virgin olive oil
- 1 medium tomato, seeded and finely chopped
- 2 teaspoons capers
- 2 teaspoons finely chopped imported black olives
- 1 tablespoon minced fresh basil
  Salt and freshly ground black pepper to taste

Whisk together the first 3 ingredients. Slowly add the olive oil and whisk until an emulsion forms. Lightly whisk in the remaining ingredients. Add salt and pepper to taste. Allow to sit for 1 hour at room temperature to marinate.

Makes about 1½ cups

Ginger-Carrot Dressing

This dressing will overwhelm a plate of delicate mixed greens. It is best used when the salad greens are sturdy and bland or with vegetables.

- 1 medium carrot, peeled and cut into 4 pieces
- ½ teaspoon ground ginger
- 1 tablespoon toasted (Oriental) sesame oil
- 2 tablespoons white wine vinegar
- ½ teaspoon soy sauce
- ¼ cup olive oil

Place all ingredients except olive oil in the workbowl of a food processor. Process until well blended. Add olive oil slowly with machine running. Process until dressing is smooth and well mixed.

Makes about 1 cup

Creamy Avocado Dressing with Tofu

There are many different kinds of tofu. Be sure to buy tofu that is labeled "soft," as a harder tofu will give this dressing a dry, grainy texture. Tofu and miso are available at health food stores and many supermarkets. Tofu is a form of cottage cheese made from soybeans which is then pressed into cakes, with varying consistencies depending on the process. Miso is a naturally fermented soybean-and-grain puree that is aged up to 3 years. Some varieties are light-colored, others are dark. It is usually used in soups and broths and has a rich, yeasty taste. This recipe was given to me by Laurel Vukovic, a caterer and expert on whole food cookery. This dressing is thick and is best used as a mayonnaise. The tofu must be simmered briefly in order to soften it for use in a salad dressing.

- ⅓ pound fresh soft tofu
- 1 ripe avocado, peeled and pitted

2 cloves garlic, peeled and finely minced
2 tablespoons diced onion
2 tablespoons lemon juice
¼ cup minced flat-leaf parsley
2 tablespoons brown rice vinegar
¼ cup extra virgin olive oil
¼ cup light miso
½ cup water
   Salt and freshly ground black pepper to taste

Drop tofu into boiling water to cover, simmer for 1 minute, turn off heat, and let rest for 5 minutes. Cool tofu in a cold-water bath and drain. Combine all ingredients except salt and pepper in a blender or food processor. Blend until smooth. Add salt and freshly ground black pepper to taste.

Makes about 3 cups

Sesame Salad Dressing

This is another "healthy" but rich salad dressing. Use this dressing with vegetables — its strong flavor will overpower lettuce. Toast the sesame seeds in a nonstick skillet over medium heat for 3–5 minutes, shaking frequently.

⅓ pound fresh soft tofu
1 clove garlic, peeled and finely minced
¼ cup regular sesame oil (not toasted)
3 tablespoons cider vinegar
¼ cup water
3 tablespoons white miso
1 tablespoon honey
1½ tablespoons toasted sesame seeds
2 tablespoons minced flat-leaf parsley
   Salt and freshly ground black pepper to taste

Drop tofu into boiling water to cover, simmer for 1 minute, turn off heat, and let rest for 5 minutes. Cool tofu in a cold-water bath. Drain. Combine all ingredients except sesame seeds, parsley, and salt and pepper in a blender or food processor. Process until smooth. Mix in seeds and parsley. Add salt and freshly ground pepper to taste.

Makes about 2 cups

Tomato-Basil Blender Dressing

This recipe was inspired by Chris Balcer, chef at The Prince and the Pauper in Woodstock, Vermont. Just throw the ingredients into a blender or food processor, turn on the juice, and you're done. Don't make this dressing unless you have fresh summer tomatoes. If you like, you can skin the tomato, but I find this step time-consuming and unnecessary.

1 medium tomato, seeded
¼ cup fresh basil leaves, packed
2 tablespoons white wine vinegar
½ cup olive oil
½ teaspoon sugar
¼ teaspoon kosher salt
1 teaspoon Dijon mustard
   Freshly ground black pepper to taste

Place all ingredients in a blender or food processor and mix until smooth.

Makes about 1½ cups

Olive Vinaigrette

Don't try this recipe with canned California olives — they have almost no flavor. If you do not have an electric appliance to do the blending, simply chop the olives by hand, make the vinaigrette (see instructions on page 118), and then add the olives.

¼ cup imported black olives, pitted
1 clove garlic, peeled and minced
1 teaspoon fresh thyme or ¼ teaspoon dried
2 tablespoons red wine vinegar
½ cup high-quality olive oil
   Freshly ground black pepper to taste

Combine all ingredients in a blender or small food processor, or in the beaker of an immersion blender, and process until smooth and an emulsion forms.

Makes about 1 cup

~ 11 ~

How to Build a Salad

Here's how to build better salads with meat, seafood, nuts, cheese, olives, fruit, rice, and vegetables.

~

I grew up around southern cooks, and the closest I ever got to a fresh green salad was celery stalks and radishes served on a glass tray. In those days, we mostly cooked our salads, making them from ingredients such as black-eyed peas, collard greens, and ham hocks. A "fresh" salad was usually made with Jell-O, fruit, or the occasional head of iceberg lettuce (or all three together). Although the revolution in American cooking has had its share of disasters ("blackened" filet of sole rates high on my list), American salads have been transformed from virtually inedible to extraordinary.

SALAD FUNDAMENTALS

THE SECRET OF QUICKLY WASHING GREENS

I have witnessed many cooks stand by the sink for half an hour, washing greens one leaf at a time under running water. Here's a real time-saver.

On a cutting board, use a chef's knife to cut the greens into bite-size pieces, removing tough stalks and wilted leaves. (This method works best with sturdy greens such as romaine. Delicate salad greens should be torn into pieces by hand.) Place the cut greens into

the slotted inner bowl of a salad spinner and immerse the bowl and greens in a sinkful of cold water. Agitate the greens with your hand to clean them, then remove the bowl from the water and allow greens to drain while you drain the sink. If the greens were especially dirty or sandy to begin with, fill the sink with fresh water and wash a second time.

If you have a salad spinner with an outer housing that can hold water, you can fill that with water instead of filling the sink. (This is why I recommend that you purchase a salad spinner with a solid outer housing, not one with holes or slits.) In this case, place the inner housing with cut-up greens in the outer shell, fill it with water, then agitate and drain as above.

Once the greens are washed and drained, place the slotted bowl of greens into the (empty) outer shell of the spinner and spin until dry. An entire head of lettuce (or two) can be cleaned and dried in about 90 seconds.

GREENS AND TEMPERATURE

How many times have you been to the fanciest restaurant in town while on vacation and been served a salad on a plate that hovered just above the freezing point? Salad greens (and the plate they are served on) should be slightly cool. If you wish to store prepared greens in the refrigerator (a good idea if you are not serving them immediately), allow at least 10 minutes at room temperature before serving. I tested resting times for lettuce and found that 30 minutes is the maximum amount of time that lettuce can be held at room temperature. After that, the leaves become limp and lose their bite. Also be careful of frigid refrigerators. If they are too cold, greens will wilt.

DRESSING A SALAD

There are two ways to dress a salad. The first method is quite simple. Pour a small amount of olive oil around the sides of a wooden salad bowl, add the lettuce and herbs and toss. Now add the vinegar and a pinch of salt and toss again. Instant salad. The other method, used for more complex dressings, is to make a vinaigrette (see Chapter 10) and then pour it over the salad and toss. The first method is best when using very high-quality olive oil and vinegar. A vinaigrette, however, has the advantage of softening vinegar's acidity, which is a big advantage if you are using supermarket-quality brands. Vinaigrettes are also preferred for more complex dressings — the emulsion caused by whisking marries different flavors to create a more subtle, complex taste.

You should be frugal with your dressing. Underdress rather than overdress. Salad dressing should be subtle, a quiet counterpoint to the flavor of the greens. Start by using about half the dressing you think you'll need, toss, and then taste. Add further amounts in small increments until the salad is properly dressed. Never dress a salad until you are ready to serve, and only dress the amount of greens that will be served immediately. To test salad dressings, dip a small piece of lettuce into the dressing and then taste.

HOW TO TOSS A SALAD

I was once given an exquisite black salad bowl made from ebony, with matching silver-trimmed utensils. Unfortunately, I only used it once because it was too small. I could never properly toss the greens. My advice is to go out and buy the biggest, most colossal salad bowl you can find. The bowl needs to be at least twice, preferably three times the volume of the greens. This will make tossing a salad a pleasure, not an exercise in containment.

THE BASIC GREEN SALAD

A basic green salad should be simple, with a light splash of dressing and without a profusion of ingredients. For most salads, I prefer to use a variety of greens. I often use romaine as a base, but other greens that work well are Boston, Bibb, red sail, and oak leaf lettuces. For flavor, I add smaller amounts of other greens, including watercress (peppery), arugula (bitter and spicy), radicchio (colorful, bitter, and often rubbery), and endive (bitter and crunchy). Other greens you may wish to consider are mâche (also known as lamb's lettuce and corn salad, mâche is delicate and very mild-flavored and can be served on its own or combined with a very mild lettuce such as Bibb or Boston lettuce) and curly endive (also called frisée), which is frizzy, peppery, and slightly bitter. Escarole is similar to curly endive but has more bite and flatter leaves. Salad greens can also be braised — cooked in a covered pot with a small amount of liquid — and grilled. I use romaine for both techniques (see recipe page 305).

INGREDIENTS THAT WORK WELL WITH SALADS

I don't care for the American "kitchen sink" salads with a mishmash of carrot peels, cucumbers, radishes, et cetera. I do find that one or two simple garnishes or additions can make a green salad special. The simplest and best of these is a small slice of Gorgonzola or other strongly flavored cheese such as Bleu d'Auvergne, Roquefort, or Stilton. Fresh goat cheese can also be a good addition. I add blue or harder cheeses to the side of the plate; a fresh goat cheese I would place in the middle of the greens. Toasted nuts — walnuts, pecans, or pine nuts — add both texture and flavor. Roasted pears are easy but very special; I serve a half pear for each guest. Garlicky croutons and black imported olives are two additional items that work well. I often combine two or more of these ingredients.

MEAT, BEAN, VEGETABLE, RICE, AND FRUIT SALADS

Deborah Madison, a well-known vegetarian cook and cookbook author, once said that a salad is anything with vinegar on it. I agree. You can make a salad with hot grilled or fried chicken, with cold sliced beef, with any legume (dried bean), with most fruits, and with any assortment of vegetables. Here are a few tips when improvising your own salads.

- First, beans and especially rice soak up vinaigrette rapidly. Some recipes call for dressing these salads ahead of time so that the ingredients marinate and develop flavor. That's fine, but be sure to add a splash of vinegar just before serving to punch up the flavor.

- When using fruit, peppery or slightly bitter greens (arugula is usually my first choice) are best as a counterpoint to the fruit's sweet flavor. Fruit salads also benefit from a vinaigrette made with a complementary citrus juice (lemon, lime, or

---

BUILDING A BETTER SALAD

All sorts of ingredients can go into a salad. Here are the basic categories of ingredients with many, but by no means all, of the possibilities listed.

Building-Block Ingredients

Basic greens	Romaine, Boston, Bibb, red sail, oak leaf, spinach, cabbage
Poultry	Fried or grilled boneless chicken strips, leftover roast chicken, sliced duck breast
Seafood	Grilled or broiled tuna or swordfish, shrimp, lobster
Rice	Long-grain white or brown rice, basmati rice
Meat	Grilled steak, leg of lamb thinly sliced, London broil, boiled or country ham
Fruit	Orange, grapefruit, mango, papaya, roasted pear, apple
Vegetables	Fennel, carrot, tomato, celery, cucumber
Salad cheeses	Gruyère, white cheddar, mozzarella

Accent Ingredients

Accent greens	Arugula, watercress, radicchio, endive, mâche, curly endive, escarole
Nuts	Toasted pecans, walnuts, or pine nuts
Accent cheeses	Gorgonzola, Bleu d'Auvergne, Roquefort, Stilton, Parmesan (shaved or grated)
Miscellaneous	Imported olives, garlic croutons
Dressing	Basic vinaigrette, citrus juice vinaigrette, cheese vinaigrette (creamy or with bits of cheese), vegetable vinaigrette (carrot, tomato, chili pepper)

orange). But you need to be careful. I suggest replacing no more than half of the vinegar called for in the recipe with citrus juice. This is especially true of lemon and lime juice, which are overpowering and quite sour if used in quantity.

- Think about texture as well. Apple, celery, toasted nuts, and croutons all add crunch, which is important.

- Don't ever put anything sweet into a salad using seafood. (I once served a mango-lobster salad. The guests separated the main ingredients into two quite separate piles and then proceeded to eat the mango first, pausing to let the taste fade, and then tucked into the lobster. The combination was deadly.)

- If serving a meat or poultry salad, dress the greens lightly and then top the meat with a drizzle of vinaigrette.

Master Recipe for Green Salad

The easiest way to dress a salad is not to make an emulsion at all. This is a simple dressing and works best with perfectly fresh delicate greens and with the highest-quality olive oil and vinegar. (Do not try this recipe with cheap supermarket brands.) Try to use as little oil as possible. Just coat the lettuce with a fine breath of oil.

Mixed salad greens for 4
2½ tablespoons extra virgin olive oil
1 teaspoon minced fresh herbs or ¼ teaspoon dried
2 teaspoons high-quality white or red wine vinegar, unflavored
Pinch salt

1. Tear greens into bite-size pieces, discarding tough or rotten pieces. Or use a chef's knife to rough-cut the greens (this works best with tougher greens such as romaine). Wash greens (see instructions earlier in this chapter) and dry in a salad spinner.
2. Pour olive oil around the inside of a large salad bowl. Add greens and herbs. Toss with your hands or a wooden fork and spoon. Add vinegar and salt and toss again. Taste. Add additional oil, vinegar, herbs, or salt as needed.

Serves 4

Green Salad with Pecans or Walnuts

Follow the master recipe but add 1 cup of oven-toasted pecan or walnut pieces (toast on a baking sheet in a 350°F oven for about 8 minutes — check after 5 minutes). You can also use one of the basic vinaigrettes from the preceding chapter.

Green Salad with Gorgonzola

Follow the master recipe and serve with a slice of Gorgonzola or other blue cheese on the side.

Green Salad with Roasted Pears

This is an impressive salad — it's standard fare on many tony restaurant menus — and it's a snap. The only trick is selecting the pears. They should give just a little when pressed gently. A properly ripe pear will be sweet and full of flavor when roasted but not watery and soft. This salad is also very good when served with toasted walnut pieces and Gorgonzola.

2 pears, ripe but firm
  Olive oil for brushing pears before roasting
  Salad greens for 4, washed and dried
  Master Recipe for Vinaigrette (see page 118), made with white wine vinegar

Heat oven to 400°F. Cut 2 pears into quarters and remove cores with a paring knife. Brush with a little olive oil and roast for about 30 minutes or until tender and flavorful. Dress salad greens and top each serving with 2 pear quarters.

Serves 4

Chicken Caesar Salad

This is an excellent summer lunch served on a patio or deck. Make sure that the ingredients are top quality. The romaine should be crisp, the bread should be a good toothy French or Italian loaf, and the Parmesan should have a coarse, nutty bite. A light white wine — a Sancerre or Vouvray — would go well here, cooled but not chilled.

Salad
2 heads romaine lettuce
2 whole chicken breasts, boned and skinned
8 slices French bread
1 tablespoon olive oil
 Salt and freshly ground black pepper to taste

Dressing
Double recipe of Master Recipe for Vinaigrette
 (page 118), made with red wine vinegar;
 substitute 2 teaspoons balsamic vinegar for
 2 teaspoons red wine vinegar
4 flat anchovies, drained and chopped
1 egg
1 clove garlic, peeled and minced
2 teaspoons Worcestershire
6 tablespoons grated Parmesan

1. Tear romaine leaves into medium-size pieces, wash, and dry. Heat a grill or broiler. Bring a small saucepan of water to a simmer. Wash chicken and pat dry.

2. To make croutons, toast the bread and then cut into ½-inch cubes.

3. Brush chicken with olive oil and then sprinkle with salt and pepper. Broil or grill until cooked — the cooking time will vary depending upon the thickness of the breasts (about 8 minutes in all). Set aside.

4. If you have not already done so, make the vinaigrette, substituting balsamic vinegar as indicated. Place chopped anchovies (you can use more to taste if you like) in a large salad bowl. Bring the saucepan of simmering water to a boil and cook the egg for 45 seconds. Break the egg into the salad bowl. Add the garlic, Worcestershire, and ¼ cup of the vinaigrette. Whisk ingredients until blended. Add lettuce to the bowl and toss with dress-ing. Sprinkle with grated cheese and crou-tons and toss.

5. Arrange salad on individual plates. Slice chicken into ½-inch strips and lay them across the top of each serving. Drizzle with an additional ¼ cup of dressing.

Serves 6

Mozzarella-Tomato Salad

This is as simple a summer recipe as you can find. The tomatoes must be bursting with flavor and the basil must be fresh. By the way, many varieties of basil these days have a wonderful perfume but no flavor. Be sure to taste a leaf before purchasing. For a less garlicky dressing, crush, don't mince, the garlic clove, and let stand in the whisked dressing for 30 minutes. Remove garlic and whisk ingredients a second time before serving.

2 teaspoons balsamic vinegar
1 tablespoon minced fresh basil
1 small clove garlic, peeled and minced
¼ teaspoon kosher salt
¼ cup olive oil
4 tomatoes, sliced into ¼-inch thickness
½ pound fresh mozzarella, sliced into ¼-inch
 thickness
 Freshly ground black pepper to taste
12 whole basil leaves for garnish, optional

1. Combine the vinegar, the minced basil, the garlic, and the salt in a small bowl. Whisk together. Add the oil and whisk for 15 seconds or until an emulsion forms.

2. Arrange the tomato and cheese slices on a plate in an overlapping row or circle. Drizzle with the dressing. Add a few grind-ings of fresh black pepper to top. Garnish with whole basil leaves if you like.

Serves 4–6

Winter Red Cabbage Salad with Bacon

Make sure to use fresh goat cheese — it should have the texture of a dry cottage cheese. It should not be dry and semihard. Fresh goat cheese is not as strong as crottins (small rounds) of aged goat cheese. A blue cheese also works well.

½ head red cabbage, cored and shredded
6 slices bacon

Dressing
2 medium cloves garlic, peeled and minced
¼ cup red wine vinegar
½ teaspoon kosher salt
  Freshly ground black pepper to taste
½ cup olive oil
5 ounces fresh goat cheese

1. Place cabbage in a large salad bowl.

2. Sauté the bacon until browned and drain the bacon slices on paper towels. Transfer 1 tablespoon of the fat to a small bowl and discard the rest.

3. Add the garlic and vinegar to the reserved bacon fat. Add the salt and a few grindings of black pepper. Whisk in the olive oil until the mixture forms an emulsion.

4. Place the dressing in a small saucepan and warm over low heat. Crumble the bacon over the cabbage and then top with the warm dressing. Toss and then transfer salad to individual plates. Crumble fresh goat cheese over each serving.

Serves 4

Fried Chicken Salad with Capers and Tarragon

If you cannot find sweet onions (Vidalia or Walla Walla) use a smaller amount of very thinly sliced red onion. This recipe can be used as a template for other meat salads. Try using thinly sliced grilled steak or chunks of grilled tuna or sword-fish. You could also use thin slices of London broil.

2 heads Boston lettuce
2 whole chicken breasts, boned and skinned
½ cup all-purpose flour
¼ teaspoon cayenne
  Salt and freshly ground black pepper to taste

⅓ cup milk
½ cup olive or peanut oil
2 teaspoons minced fresh tarragon
1 shallot, peeled and finely minced
¼ cup Master Recipe for Vinaigrette (see page 118), made with white wine vinegar
1 tablespoon capers, drained
1 sweet onion, peeled and cut into very thin rounds

1. Tear lettuce into bite-size pieces, wash, and dry. Place in a large salad bowl. Cut chicken into ½-inch-wide strips. In a plastic bag, mix flour with cayenne, ½ teaspoon salt, and a few grindings of black pepper. Place milk in a shallow bowl.

2. In a large frying pan or skillet, heat the oil over medium-high heat. Dip chicken strips (only as many strips as will fit without crowding into the skillet) in milk and then toss in flour mixture. When oil reaches 375°F (if you do not have a thermometer, you can check the temperature by dropping a small piece of dredged chicken into the oil — it should bubble and froth), fry strips in oil, turning once. Cooking time will be about 5 minutes. Repeat until all strips are fried, allowing oil to return to temperature between batches. Drain chicken on paper towels.

3. Add the tarragon and shallot to the vinaigrette and whisk. Toss lettuce with 2 tablespoons of vinaigrette. Arrange lettuce on plates and place fried chicken strips on top of leaves. Add capers and onion slices and then drizzle extra dressing over all.

Serves 4

Chicken-Endive Salad with Apple and Gruyère

This is my favorite luncheon salad. It reminds me of Waldorf salad, the classic American mixture of apples, lettuce, nuts, and cheese. Save the chicken broth; it can be frozen and used later in soups. The assembly of the salad is quick, but you will need to boil the chicken ahead of time and allow it time to cool before dicing. If you can't find Gruyère, use Jarlsberg cheese.

1 whole chicken, about 3 pounds
½ cup raisins
3 heads Belgian endive, cut into bite-size pieces
¾ pound Gruyère cheese, diced into ½-inch pieces
1 small red onion, peeled and minced
3 ribs celery, cut into medium dice
Juice of 1 lemon
2 medium tart apples, peeled, cored, cut into cubes, and sprinkled with the lemon juice
Double recipe of Master Recipe for Vinaigrette (page 118), made with white wine vinegar and prepared mustard
Lettuce for serving, optional

1. Place the whole chicken in a large pot, add water to cover by 1 inch, and bring water to a boil. Reduce heat to a simmer and cook until done, about 20 minutes. Remove from pot, allow to cool. Remove skin and bones, and cube meat. Reserve chicken broth for another use.

2. Toss chicken together with next 7 ingredients (raisins through apples) and add ½ cup dressing, or to taste (reserve remaining vinaigrette for another use). Serve over a bed of lettuce, if desired.

Serves 6–8

Almond Basmati Rice Salad

Basmati rice is used primarily in Indian and Middle Eastern cooking. It has a stronger flavor than white rice, full and nutty. Basmati is usually aged (up to 1 year) to provide more flavor. You can also buy brown basmati rice. Pecans or walnuts can be substituted for the almonds in this recipe. Rice salads can be served with cold meats or in combination with other more substantial salads.

Salad
½ cup whole almonds
Mixed salad greens for 4 servings

2 cups cooked brown basmati rice (see Chapter 13)
½ cup diced red bell pepper
¼ cup diced mild onion
½ cup chopped fennel or celery

Dressing
¼ cup balsamic vinegar
½ teaspoon kosher salt
2 tablespoons minced fresh basil
¼ cup extra virgin olive oil

1. Heat oven to 425°F and toast almonds, about 3 minutes. Cool and chop. Wash and dry salad greens.

2. Make the dressing in a small bowl, adding the vinegar, salt, and basil and then whisking in olive oil drop by drop until an emulsion starts to form. Continue whisking, adding olive oil in a thin stream until well blended.

5. Combine all salad ingredients except greens and toss with dressing. Serve on bed of mixed greens.

Serves 4

Orange-and-Fennel Salad

This is a good salad for the dead of winter when you crave something light and refreshing.

3 tablespoons orange juice
2 tablespoons lemon juice
2 tablespoons white wine vinegar
Salt and freshly ground black pepper to taste
1 cup high-quality olive oil
1 fennel bulb, trimmed and cut into ¼-inch strips
4 medium seedless oranges, peeled and sliced into rounds

Whisk together the orange juice, lemon juice, and vinegar with a little salt and freshly ground black pepper. Slowly drizzle in the olive oil, whisking constantly. Once an emulsion forms, the oil may be poured in more quickly. Arrange the fennel and orange slices on individual plates and drizzle with dressing.

Serves 6

Cucumber Salad with Onions and Balsamic Vinegar

This salad is also very good made with sweet onions such as Vidalias or Walla Wallas in place of the red onion (in this case, use 2 onions instead of 1). If you don't have balsamic vinegar, use red wine vinegar.

    4 medium cucumbers
    1 medium red onion, thinly sliced
    1 medium tomato, seeded and diced
    ½ cup olive oil
    1 tablespoon red wine vinegar
    1 tablespoon balsamic vinegar
    ½ teaspoon kosher salt
       Freshly ground black pepper to taste

Peel the cucumbers and cut them in half lengthwise. Scoop out the seeds using a metal teaspoon. Cut into ¼-inch-thick slices. Combine all ingredients and let sit at room temperature for 1 hour before serving.

Serves 6

Mangoes with Olives and Arugula

This recipe started, on the suggestion of a Boston chef, as a lobster and mango salad with arugula. I quickly dropped the lobster — fruit and seafood are a tough combination — and added olives. The three flavors (salty olives, sweet mangoes, and spicy arugula) work well together.

    2 ripe mangoes
    ½ cup Kalamata or niçoise olives, pitted and
       coarsely chopped
       Arugula for 4 servings, cleaned
    ½ Master Recipe for Vinaigrette (see page 118)

Cut the flesh of the mangoes into cubes (see page 70). Toss the olives and arugula

with dressing to taste in a large bowl. Place on plates and add the cubes of mango.

Serves 4

Barbecued Duck with Grilled Corn and Onions

This sounds like a recipe from a fancy Los Angeles restaurant rather than one designed for home cooks, but it's actually pretty easy to do and it is also the best recipe in this chapter. I stumbled across the combination after a morning of recipe testing. I happened to have all three ingredients already cooked and simply threw them together. It was the best lunch I had that summer. Although the duck takes about 3 hours, it requires little work. Just check the grill every hour. Corn and onions are grilled in only 4 minutes.

    1 duck, rinsed inside and out and dried with
       paper towels
    ¼ cup Barbecue Rub for Poultry (see page
       308)
    4 ears corn, shucked and silked
    2 large onions, peeled and sliced into ½-inch-
       thick rounds
       Olive oil and kosher salt for tossing
    1 head romaine lettuce
       Master Recipe for Vinaigrette (see page 118)

1. Coat the duck with barbecue rub and slow-barbecue according to the directions in Chapter 33. When the duck is done, add coals to the fire. When the fire is very hot, grill the corn, turning frequently, until ears are covered with dark brown spots (about 4 minutes). Brush onion slices with olive oil and sprinkle with salt. Grill for 2 minutes per side.

2. Remove duck meat from bone (leave skin on) and cut into bite-size pieces. Remove corn kernels with a large chef's knife. Coarsely chop the grilled onions. Chop romaine into bite-size pieces, wash, and dry.

3. Combine all ingredients and toss with vinaigrette to taste. Serve warm.

Serves 4

~ 12 ~

Improvising Soups

*With just five master recipes, you can improvise hundreds of soups,
using whatever is on hand.*

~

A good homemade soup shouldn't be too finicky or high-class. It should be easy to make, endlessly variable, and flexible enough to taste good even when overcooked or underseasoned. For purposes of this chapter, I have excluded cold soups and fruit soups. Cold soups are fairly limited in application and tend to be recipe specific. Fruit soups, in my opinion, are the ultimate culinary horror, too sweet for a soup course and too unimaginative for a good dessert. I prefer my fruit fresh, poached, or baked — not pureed and chilled.

The four types of soups that are best suited for home cooking are consommés, vegetable soups, cream soups, and bean soups. Consommés are the easiest of all soups — nothing more than stock with a smattering of other ingredients — and are also light, healthy, and clean to the palate. Vegetable soups have the most range. The master recipe in this chapter can be used to make thousands of different soups using almost any vegetable or combination, plus variations with beans, pasta, and leftover meats. Cream soups are, for the most part, variations on a basic vegetable soup with the addition of cream to provide a silky, richer texture. Bean soups are much like vegetable soups, substituting beans for the vegetables.

CONSOMMÉS

Unfortunately, consommés are the progeny of haute cuisine, calling for a perfectly clear stock and all sorts of ingenious but irritating little garnishes such as carved mushrooms. Or a French chef may float a quenelle (a poached dumpling) or two in the broth. However, when viewed from the perspective of a home cook, a consommé is nothing more than heated broth. Nothing could be simpler.

Traditionally, a consommé was made by using broth or stock and then adding ingredients such as ground meat and vegetables, as well as egg whites and shells to clarify the liquid. (A leafy vegetable such as parsley is also crucial to clarification, as the "flotsam" will stick to it.) In essence, the chef was making a double broth, starting with stock instead of cold water. To simplify this process, I often start with a stock and then reduce it by about a third without adding further ingredients. However, in a blind tasting, I discovered that the double broth is significantly better, hence my master recipe provides both options.

The strength of a consommé for the home cook is that it is a great last-minute soup and you can add almost anything to it, making it well suited for the improvised lunch or dinner. Here are just a few of the items that can be added: pasta, raw shrimp, shredded greens, diced or julienned vegetables, cooked rice, raw chicken, broccoli or cauliflower florets, fresh peas, chopped tomatoes, asparagus tips, sliced mushrooms.

Master Recipe for Consommé

You can either reduce homemade chicken or beef stock or make a double stock, using the optional ingredients listed below. In a blind tasting, I found that the double stock was vastly preferable. Never use a canned stock for consommé; it will be too salty, and commercial brands are of insufficient quality to serve as consommé.

Basic Recipe

2 quarts homemade chicken or beef stock
2 egg whites and 2 eggshells
¼ cup coarsely chopped flat-leaf parsley
½ teaspoon kosher salt
¼ teaspoon freshly ground black pepper

Optional Ingredients

½ pound chopped lean beef
1 cup coarsely chopped leeks
½ cup coarsely chopped carrots
½ cup chopped tomato
1 teaspoon cognac, rum, or dry sherry, optional

Bring all ingredients to a simmer, stirring constantly, about 10 minutes. The liquid will turn cloudy and a foamy crust will form. Simmer for 1 hour over low heat. Turn off heat and let sit for 15 minutes. Break open the top crust and ladle out consommé into a cheesecloth-lined strainer. Adjust seasonings.
Makes 5–6 cups

Vegetable Consommé

Almost any fresh vegetable may be used for this recipe; just make sure that it is cut into very small pieces for quick cooking. Do not substitute dried herbs for fresh.

1 quart homemade consommé
1 cup vegetables, diced, shredded, or julienned (carrots, peas, celery, cauliflower, beans, spinach, tomatoes, etc.)
2 tablespoons thinly sliced scallions
1 tablespoon minced fresh herbs (summer savory, basil, parsley, or chives)
Salt and freshly ground black pepper to taste
1 teaspoon cognac, rum, or dry sherry, optional

Place consommé in a saucepan, bring to a boil, and add the slower-cooking vegetables (carrots, peas, celery, cauliflower, beans). Simmer for about 4 minutes. Now add the last-minute vegetables (spinach, tomatoes, and so forth), scallions, and fresh herbs and cook for 2 minutes. Add salt and freshly ground black pepper to taste. Add optional liquor.
Makes 4 small first-course servings

Consommé of Celery

Celery has a unique bouquet that melds well with butter and chicken stock. This is a very easy soup to make and elegant enough for a dinner party.

5 tablespoons butter
4 cups minced celery
1 quart chicken stock
2 teaspoons cognac, rum, or dry sherry, optional
Salt and freshly ground black pepper to taste

In a large saucepan, melt the butter over low heat and then add the celery. Cover and cook for 15 minutes without browning the celery. Add the chicken stock, bring to a simmer, and cook uncovered an additional 30 minutes. Strain through a sieve lined with a quadruple thickness of cheesecloth. Add optional cognac and salt and pepper to taste.
Serves 4

Consommé of Leeks, Chicken, and Potatoes

The chicken and vegetables need to be cut into small pieces so that they will cook quickly in the hot chicken stock. Traditionally, these ingredients would have been julienned (cut into small matchsticks), but I think this is more trouble than it's worth. I just finely chop the vegetables and cut the chicken into thin slices.

1 quart homemade consommé
½ cup finely chopped leeks
½ cup finely diced potatoes
2 cups uncooked chicken, cut into very thin slices (about 1 pound boneless, skinless breast)
1 tablespoon minced parsley
Salt and freshly ground black pepper to taste

Bring the consommé to a simmer. Add the leeks and potatoes and cook until tender, about 5 minutes (this will depend on how finely you chopped the vegetables). Add the chicken and cook until just done, 1–2 minutes. Serve with a sprinkling of parsley. Add salt and freshly ground black pepper to taste.

Serves 4

VEGETABLE SOUPS

There are four basic ingredients in any vegetable soup: a basic flavoring such as bacon, onion, or garlic; vegetables; liquid (usually chicken, beef, or vegetable stock); and herbs and/or spices. The first ingredient is sautéed to bring out flavor. Onions are cooked about 8 minutes. Garlic for 2 minutes or less (if garlic burns it will ruin a recipe). You can use butter or oil or a mixture for the sautéing; adding oil to butter reduces the chances the butter will brown too quickly or burn. If you use bacon, just pour off all but about 2 teaspoons of fat, add a little olive oil, and then sauté the onion or garlic. Then the vegetables are added

and quickly sautéed to bring out their flavor, about 10 minutes. The chicken, beef, or vegetable stock is added next. Homemade stock is vastly superior to any commercial product (see Chapter 31 for recipes). Wine and water are two additional liquid ingredients that can be used. I suggest that most commercial stocks be watered down 50 percent before using unless they are low in sodium.

Total cooking time should be about 1 hour. You can also add beans or leftover meats. Once the soup is cooked, you can puree a portion of the solid ingredients (not including any meat) in a food processor or food mill and then add this back to the soup to thicken it. I prefer chunky textures, and therefore only puree a portion of the solids. You can also add, just before serving, cream or sour cream for richness. If bacon was used early in the recipe, it can be crumbled and sprinkled on top of individual servings. Another excellent addition is Pesto — a combination of basil leaves, oil, salt, nuts, and Parmesan cheese (see page 167). One heaping teaspoon of Pesto is enough for each serving.

Thick crusty bread (see page 333) makes a good accompaniment to homemade soups. You can also toast a piece of bread and then rub it with half a clove of peeled garlic. Place the toast in the bottom of the bowl, then top with soup. A splash of extra virgin olive oil is an excellent last-minute addition to a bowl of homemade vegetable soup.

Master Recipe for Vegetable Soup

If you prefer a chunky texture, puree only 1 or 2 cups of the vegetables (see step 6). Experiment with this recipe by using different vegetables, or combinations, trying different herbs and spices, or adding wine for part of the liquid. Since soup tastes better the second day, it's best to make a lot of soup at one time. If you like pasta in your soup, cook it separately and add it to the individual serving bowls. Otherwise, the pasta will swell overnight in the soup, reducing the amount of liquid and becoming soft and mushy. Use a combination of root vegetables, not just one variety. Turnips and parsnips can be overpowering on their own and are best combined with potatoes.

2 slices bacon
2 tablespoons olive oil
1 large onion, peeled and coarsely chopped
3 cloves garlic, peeled and minced
1½ pounds root vegetables such as potatoes, sweet potatoes, carrots, turnips, or parsnips, scrubbed, peeled, and coarsely chopped
6 cups homemade chicken broth or low-sodium canned chicken broth
1 teaspoon dried herbs or 1 tablespoon minced fresh (thyme and basil are the most frequently used herbs for vegetable soups)
Pinch of sugar
Salt and freshly ground black pepper to taste
½ pound vegetables such as corn kernels, green beans, or squash, coarsely chopped
½ pound spinach, Swiss chard, or kale, stems removed and coarsely chopped, optional
Sour cream, heavy cream, or yogurt to taste, optional
Freshly grated Parmesan cheese, optional

1. Sauté bacon in a large soup pot and when cooked, remove from pan and pour off all but 1 tablespoon of fat. Drain bacon slices on paper towel; reserve for another use, or crumble over individual servings of soup.

2. Add olive oil to pan and heat over medium-high heat for 2 minutes. Add onion and sauté over medium heat until softened, about 8 minutes. Add garlic and cook 2 minutes. Do not let the garlic burn.

3. Add root vegetables and sauté 10 minutes. Add more oil if necessary to keep vegetables from sticking.

4. Add chicken stock and herbs, if using dried.

5. Bring to a boil, cover, and simmer for 15 minutes. Add a pinch of sugar and salt and pepper to taste.

6. Add additional vegetables, cover, and continue to simmer until vegetables are just cooked through (5–10 minutes). Remove half the vegetables and place in a food processor. (If you prefer a chunky soup, you can skip this step.) Using a series of short bursts, puree mixture. Return pureed vegetables to pot. Add herbs, if using fresh, and optional spinach, chard, or kale and cook for 10 minutes.

7. Stir in a few tablespoons of sour cream, heavy cream, or yogurt, if you like (up to ¼ cup). Sprinkle individual servings with crumbled bacon and freshly grated Parmesan cheese if desired. Serve with thick slices of crusty peasant bread or French bread slightly toasted.

Serves 6

Vegetable Soup with Pasta

Cook macaroni (⅓ cup dried pasta per serving) or other small pasta separately and add to individual serving bowls. Ladle soup on top. Pasta that sits overnight in a liquid will swell and become unappetizing.

Vegetable Soup with Pesto

Add a heaping teaspoon of Pesto (see page 167) to each individual serving. Stir into soup.

Vegetable Soup with Tomatoes

Add half a 28-ounce can of crushed tomatoes to the soup after adding the chicken broth (step 4). If you use canned whole tomatoes, drain and coarsely chop before adding.

Vegetable Soup with Beans

Precook 1 cup of dried beans (see Chapter 14). Reduce root vegetables in master recipe to ½ pound. Add cooked beans along with fresh herbs, about 10 minutes before serving (step 6). Chopped fresh sage leaves or fresh rosemary go well with bean soup.

Vegetable Soup with Meat

Follow directions for the master recipe or the bean soup variation above. When the master recipe calls for adding liquid (step 4), also add 1 pound of cooked meat, cut into bite-size pieces. Try not to include any of the meat in the portion of vegetables being pureed in step 6.

CREAM SOUPS

There are three basic types of cream soups: bisques, vegetable purees, and then cream soups that use either a velouté (a classic French combination of butter, flour, and stock) or egg yolks and cream for thickening. For most home cooks, vegetable purees are the most practical, and I offer a Master Recipe for "Cream of" Soup below. I have also included a Master Recipe for Bisque. Cream soups based on a velouté or egg yolks are, in my opinion, too rich and therefore I have not included them.

Instead of using heavy cream in cream soups, you can substitute yogurt, using ½ cup yogurt in place of a full cup of cream. You can also try substituting ½ cup sour cream. I often use ½ cup cream and ⅓ cup sour cream to replace a full cup of cream.

Master Recipe for Bisque

This recipe is equally good with lobster, crab, or shrimp, the last being most practical for a home cook. For the lobster and shrimp, use the shells only, saving the meat to use as a garnish or reserving it for another recipe. For the crab, use the meat and the shell (after cleaning). Bisques require a garnish to add some interest to what would otherwise be a rather bland dish in terms of texture. The possibilities include meat (lobster, crab, or shrimp), toasted country bread rubbed with a split garlic clove and then cut into croutons, or lightly steamed vegetables such as asparagus tips or fresh peas. Be sure to puree the bisque in batches, as too much hot liquid in a food processor will leak.

2 tablespoons olive oil
2 tablespoons butter
1 cup chopped onion
2 cloves garlic, peeled and lightly crushed
½ cup chopped carrots
1 cup chopped celery
1 bay leaf
1 teaspoon minced fresh thyme or ½ teaspoon dried
1 tablespoon black peppercorns tied with cheesecloth
 Shells from 1 pound of shrimp *or* 3 lobster carcasses (meat removed), cut into pieces *or* ¾ pound crabs, cleaned and chopped into pieces
¼ cup all-purpose flour
½ cup dry sherry or cognac
1 cup white wine
2 cups chicken stock or broth
3 cups chopped tomatoes
3 cups water
3 sprigs flat-leaf parsley
½ cup long-grain white rice, uncooked
1 cup heavy cream
 Salt and freshly ground black pepper to taste
 Garnish (see notes under recipe title)

1. Heat the oil and butter in a large skillet and add the next 7 ingredients (onions through black peppercorns). Cover and cook over low heat for about 15 minutes — do not let vegetables brown.

2. Add the shrimp or lobster shells or crabs and sprinkle with flour. Stir for 2 minutes over medium heat. Add ⅓ cup of the cognac or sherry (the rest will be used at the end of the recipe) and the next 5 ingredients (wine through parsley) and bring mixture to a boil. Add the rice and simmer covered for 20 minutes. Remove from heat and then pour into a colander set over a large bowl. Remove the shells, the peppercorns, and the bay leaf from the colander and then pour the remaining solids into the soup. Place the soup in batches in a food processor and puree.

3. Reheat the bisque and add the cream.

Add salt and pepper to taste. Add the remaining cognac or sherry and bring almost to a boil. Serve with garnish.

Serves 6–8

Master Recipe for "Cream of" Soup

This recipe can be used for any "cream of" soup, such as cream of tomato or cream of asparagus. I have lightened this recipe a bit, but feel free to cut back on the cream if you prefer a less luxurious, silky texture in favor of either health considerations or a fresher, stronger vegetable flavor. The vegetables listed below are, in my opinion, best suited for a cream soup. The fresh herbs must be chosen based on the vegetable(s) selected. Mint goes well with fresh peas. Thyme works well with potatoes. Chervil is good with tomatoes.

    2   tablespoons butter
    1   tablespoon olive oil
    1   medium onion, peeled and chopped
    1   cup chopped leeks (white part only)
    1½ pounds cleaned and trimmed vegetables
        such as asparagus, fresh peas, parsnips,
        leeks, carrots, artichoke bottoms,
        potatoes, sweet potatoes, tomatoes, etc.
        (larger vegetables should be coarsely
        chopped)
    ½   teaspoon sugar
    3–4 cups chicken stock or broth
    1   tablespoon minced fresh herb(s) (basil,
        tarragon, chervil, thyme, mint, or
        marjoram)
    ¾   cup heavy cream
        Salt and freshly ground black pepper to
        taste
    ¼   cup minced flat-leaf parsley, for garnish

1. Heat the butter and olive oil in a large pot. Add the onion and leeks and cook covered over low heat for 15 minutes — do not let onion and leeks brown.

2. Add the vegetables, sugar, and 3 cups chicken stock, bring to a simmer, and cook until the vegetables are just tender (the amount of time required will depend on the

vegetable). Add the fresh herbs and cook for 5 minutes. Transfer the soup in batches to a food processor and puree.

3. Return the soup to the cooking pot, stir in the cream, and reheat almost to the boiling point. If soup is too thick, add more chicken stock. Add salt and pepper to taste. Garnish with parsley.

Serves 4

No Cream Cream Soup

Substitute ¾ cup cooked and pureed rice or potato for the heavy cream.

Cream of Roasted Tomato Soup

Cut 1½ pounds of tomatoes in half and seed. Place skin side up on a foil-lined baking sheet and broil for 10–15 minutes, turning once after the skin has blackened. Let cool and peel off charred skin. Proceed with master recipe, using the roasted tomatoes as the 1½ pounds vegetables called for. If you prefer a lighter, more flavorful soup, try adding just ¼ cup of heavy cream instead of the ¾ cup called for in the master recipe.

Cream of Pea Soup with Mint

Follow master recipe, using 2 tablespoons of minced fresh mint for the herb and increasing sugar to 1 teaspoon.

Cream of Parsnip Soup with Ginger

Add 1 teaspoon minced ginger and a dash of ground turmeric to the onions and leeks. Use ¾ pound of parsnips and ¾ pound of potatoes for vegetables. Replace 2 cups of the chicken stock with water.

BEAN SOUPS

These soups are quite similar to vegetable soups. Aromatics such as onions, garlic, and celery are sautéed and then other vegetables and beans are added. I use the cooking liquid from the beans (which consists of water and chicken stock for flavor) as the base for the soup. Refer to Chapter 14 for information on cooking dried beans.

Master Recipe for Bean Soup

The ham bones or ham hocks are optional, although they do add lots of flavor as well as bits of meat. However, a good smoky bacon will help to remedy this problem. If you do use a ham bone, simmer the soup for a good 2 hours (up to 3–4 hours if you have the time) to extract the full flavor of the bone.

½ pound dried beans (black, Great Northern, navy, red, chickpeas, etc.)
1½ quarts water
1 quart chicken stock
4 slices bacon (the smokier the better)
2 tablespoons olive oil
1 tablespoon butter
2 medium onions, peeled and chopped
3 garlic cloves, peeled and crushed
1 rib celery, chopped
1 leek (white part only), cleaned and chopped
1 bay leaf
2 teaspoons salt
Ham bone or 2 ham hocks, optional
¼ cup dry sherry
Freshly ground black pepper to taste

1. Wash the beans and soak overnight in cold water. Drain and cook in 1½ quarts of fresh water and 1 quart of chicken stock per the chart on page 151. Reserve beans and liquid.

2. Cook the bacon in a skillet and drain the strips on paper towels. Remove all but 1 tablespoon of bacon fat from the skillet and then add the olive oil and butter. Over medium heat, cook until foam subsides and then add onion, garlic, celery, and leek, and cook, stirring frequently, for about 8 minutes or until lightly browned. Add 2 cups of liquid from the beans and stir. Bring to a boil. Pour this mixture into the pot with the beans and add bay leaf, salt, and optional ham bone. Simmer for 1 hour.

3. Remove the bay leaf and bones, if any. Pour soup through a large sieve or colander over a large bowl. Puree the solids with some of the liquid in a food processor (do this in batches) or pass through a food mill. Return pureed solids to the pot with the liquid and stir to combine. Add the sherry, reheat soup, and add freshly ground black pepper to taste. Crumble bacon and sprinkle on individual servings.

Serves 4–6

~ 13 ~

Cooking Perfect Rice

Rice can be cooked in a skillet, in a saucepan, with lots of water, with a little bit of water, in a rice cooker, in an oven, boiled, or even steamed. Here are the best cooking methods for each type of rice.

~

Rice cookery is a bit like marriage. What starts off as a rather simple concept develops into something quite complex, replete with unexpected developments and pleasant surprises. Like most Americans, I learned to cook rice off the back of a box of Uncle Ben's. Years later I discovered that rice could also be baked in a covered loaf pan. Then I found a recipe for cooking rice in a large skillet, not a saucepan. Another cookbook suggested cooking rice with half as much liquid as usually called for. I finally ended up with an electric rice cooker, which did everything automatically, including holding the rice after cooking. Once I had mastered basic long-grain white rice, I discovered brown, basmati, Wehani, jasmine, pecan, and short-grain rice and things became exponentially confusing.

RICE FACTS

Rice is more than a grain. It is the staple food product for over two-thirds of the world's population. It is a symbol of fertility, prosperity, and abundance in many cultures. Rice also has a spiritual dimension — Chinese children often refer to rice kernels as "little Buddhas." Although rice is the fourth most rapidly growing commodity product in America, our annual per capita consumption is only 25 pounds, whereas other cultures consume up to 400 pounds per year per capita. More than 90 percent of the rice consumed in this country is domestic. (Rice labeled "Japanese" in a store, for example, does not refer to the country of origin — it simply describes the type of rice. Japan consumes all of its own production.) The key rice-producing states are Arkansas, California, Florida, Louisiana, Mississippi, Missouri, and Texas.

There are endless varieties of rice — over 40,000, to be exact. However, this chapter focuses on a few widely available varieties, most long-grain. I have intentionally excluded medium-grain rices, which are not often prepared at home (they are mostly used by commercial processors such as cereal companies), but I have included recipes for short-grain rices: one for risotto, which is made from arborio rice, one for plain short-grain white rice, and one for stovetop rice pudding.

I have a strong personal preference for either brown or aromatic rices rather than white, which I find lacking in character — flavorless and without bite. Although brown rice may bring to mind the sticky, overcooked mush served in the early days of the health food movement, in fact a long-grain brown rice can be perfectly light and delicate, even as it presents a toothier texture and fuller flavor than either white or aromatic rices. Before I discuss my research on cooking rice, however, here is what you need to know about the different varieties and processing methods.

WHAT'S THE DIFFERENCE BETWEEN WHITE AND BROWN RICE?

All rice starts with an outer hull, or husk, which protects the layers of bran, which in turn protect the inner portion of the kernel, the endosperm. The first step in the milling process is to remove the outer hull. At this point, the rice is termed "brown" rice. Further milling strips away the layers of bran and part of the endosperm, resulting in what we refer to today as "white" rice. Brown rice has more flavor, texture, and nutrients than white rice and takes twice as long to cook as white rice (about 40 minutes as opposed to 20 minutes). White rice has had the bran layer and germ removed and has also been polished, resulting in a food with less nutritional value, although new research suggests that some of the nutrients present in brown rice are not easily digestible and therefore are not absorbed by the body. "Converted" rice has been partially cooked before the bran and germ are removed, forcing some of the nutrients into the core of each kernel. The primary advantage of converted rice is that the grains remain whole, smooth, and separate even when the cooked rice is held for long periods on a restaurant steam table.

As it is less processed, one would assume that brown rice would also be less costly. However, a superior type of rice must be used to provide uniform color — the hull and bran colors of rice vary from pale gold to rust. In addition, the machine used to process brown rice is usually the same machine used to process white rice but it is run at about ⅓ the speed to ensure that the bran layer is not stripped away during processing.

WHAT'S THE DIFFERENCE BETWEEN LONG-GRAIN AND SHORT-GRAIN RICE?

There are three basic types of rice in terms of length: short, medium, and long. Short rice is the type served in Chinese restaurants — it is sticky and ideal for use with chopsticks, with sushi, in puddings, in paella, or cooked as risotto (arborio rice, an Italian short-grain variety, is used for risotto). The longer varieties are more popular in Western cultures, as they are less starchy and therefore fluffier when cooked. Medium-length rices are more similar to short-grain than long-grain in terms of cooking properties and may be used as a substitute, although this chapter omits them because they are not widely available. Short- and long-grain rices are never interchangeable. There is very little difference in nutritional value among the different grain lengths. Long-grain rice kernels are 3–5 times longer than they are wide; a kernel of short-grain rice is less than twice as long as its width.

SCIENCE OF COOKING

Why Is Short-Grain Rice Sticky?

Rice is mostly starch, and all starches, including wheat starch, tapioca, arrowroot, and cornstarch, contain both amylose and amylopectin. The ratio between these two elements is the primary determinant of stickiness in rice. (It is also the key factor in thickening power; that's why some root starches are better at thickening a fruit pie than others — see Chapter 42.) Amylose, which produces a less sticky rice, occurs in a higher percentage in long-grain rice than short-grain. Conversely, amylopectin is more dominant in the short-grain varieties. Amylopectin increases the water absorption capacity of starch; short-grain rice can absorb almost three times more water than long-grain, and is therefore stickier. Stickiness is also a function of other characteristics, including protein — a higher-protein rice generally produces a firmer, less sticky grain. Protein content is affected by the strain of rice and also by where it is grown.

There are many different kinds of rice now available in health food stores and super-markets. Some of these newer varieties are termed "aromatic" because of their nutty aroma and taste. This aroma is due to a higher concentration of a compound that is present in all rices.

Basmati: This rice is used in Indian and Middle Eastern cooking. It has a stronger flavor than white rice, with a full, nutty taste. Basmati is usually aged (up to two years) to provide more flavor and also to make the grains cook up fluffy and separate. Some Indian cooks will even set aside a canister of rice to be used on the occasion of their daughter's wedding more than twenty years away. Aged rices will absorb more liquid since they are drier, and therefore many cooks recommend that basmati rice should be soaked briefly before cooking. I found during testing, however, that basmati actually absorbed less liquid than long-grain brown rice, so soaking is not necessary. You can also buy brown (whole) basmati rice, although most varieties sold in this country are milled much like white rice. A kernel of basmati rice is long and slender and expands in length rather than width when cooked.

Jasmine: Jasmine rice is softer than basic long-grain varieties and is grown both domestically and in Thailand (the latter is usually referred to as Thai jasmine). It is less fragrant than basmati. Jasmine rice was originally developed in the Philippines and has a silky texture when uncooked which is derived from the water milling process used to produce it.

Wehani: This reddish-colored rice has a great deal of flavor and can be found at health food stores. It is named after the Lundberg brothers (Wendell, Eldon, Homer, Albert, and Harlan), who have a booming business growing, packaging, and selling rice. It is wonderful for special meals, as it looks bright and festive. It is more difficult to prepare than regular white and brown rice. In my experience, it goes from undercooked to overcooked rather quickly. Like many specialty rices, it tends to cook up a little on the sticky side.

Texmati: This is the American version of basmati, a hybrid of aromatic rice and regular long-grain varieties. It is available in both a white and a brown rice. Like basmati, it has a pleasant nutty flavor.

Black Japonica: This is an ancient Japanese variety that is somewhat bitter and also relatively difficult to cook — it tends to become sticky when cooked. Black japonica is just one of the "black" rices, which are actually deep purple inside. It is a medium-grain rice.

Arborio: These are short, fat grains that are used for risotto, an Italian rice dish cooked slowly on top of the stove with lots of liquid (see page 144 for recipe).

Wild Rice: Wild rice is not a rice but the seed of an aquatic grass. Traditionally, it was harvested by hand around lakes in the upper Midwest. Today, most wild rice comes from California, where it is raised in paddies and harvested mechanically. It is fermented for a week or two to develop its distinctive nutty flavor and is then heated to promote browning. Wild rice contains more protein than ordinary rice.

SEVEN BASIC COOKING METHODS

There are seven methods for cooking rice: the basic stovetop method, skillet cooking, boiling, baking, boiling then baking, boiling then steaming, and in an electric rice cooker. I tested each method using both long-grain brown and white rice, with the following results:

Basic Stovetop Method: In this method, the rice is simmered in a covered pot on top of the stove for about 20 minutes. I tried this with the usual formula of 2 cups water to 1 cup long-grain white rice and found the results to be mediocre. I then discovered a recipe in *Trucs of the Trade* (edited by Frank Ball and Arlene Feltman) that called for sautéing 1 cup rice in 2 teaspoons hot olive oil for 1 minute, simmering for 10 minutes covered in 1 cup of water, and then removing the pan from the heat to stand for an additional 15 minutes. This made separate, fluffy grains, but many kernels were undercooked, which resulted in an unpleasant, toothy crunch. By increasing the water to 1½ cups and the cooking time to 15 minutes instead of 10, all of the rice was properly cooked while attaining the proper texture. See Master Recipe for Long-Grain White Rice, page 142.

Skillet Rice: Noted rice expert Marie Simmons cooks her rice this way. Long-grain white rice is cooked uncovered in a 10-inch skillet for 5 minutes (using 2 cups water per cup of rice) and then covered and cooked an additional 15–20 minutes or until done. I prefer the stovetop method above for white rice, although this is a close second. I would not use this method for brown rice.

Boiling: When boiled in a large amount of water, I found, brown rice tastes a bit waterlogged even after being properly drained and is a bit stickier than when made by the boil/steam method below. Brown rice takes about 35 minutes and white rice was done in just under 20 minutes. White rice fared better under this method, but the stovetop method, as modified (see above), is still the preferred preparation method for white rice.

Baking: This is a good method but takes about 55 minutes at 350°F for brown rice and 20–30 minutes for white rice. The ingredients are brought to a simmer in an ovenproof saucepan, then the pan is covered tightly and placed in the oven for the entire cooking time. This is a convenient method for rice dishes with lots of extra ingredients (peppers, celery, et cetera) but does not yield the best results.

Boil Then Bake: The rice was boiled on top of the stove for 10 minutes and then baked covered at 350°F until done. The results were fine, although I did feel that some of the grains were a little rubbery. The extra effort did not appear to be worthwhile.

Boil Then Steam: This is a method reported by Jack Bishop from *Cook's Illustrated*. I found it an excellent means of preparation for brown rices. The rice was boiled uncovered (average boiling time, 30 minutes), then drained, returned to the pot, and steamed for 5 minutes. However, the white rices did not fare as well. They soften quickly during boiling and the steaming is just an added nuisance. The only problem with this method is that it is a two-step cooking process. When I described the method to Marie Simmons, the author of *Rice: The Amazing Grain*, she was astonished, exclaiming, "You are only cooking rice!"

Electric Rice Cooker: This is by far the easiest method. The water and rice are placed in the cooking container, the top is put on, and the machine plugged in. It makes perfect rice every time. Once the rice is properly cooked (the cooking time will vary depending on how much rice is placed in the machine), it is gently steamed until you need it. It holds well for about 20 minutes. After that time, the bottom of the rice becomes rubbery due to the nonstick surface of the cooker. The electric cooker works well with both brown and

How Much Water Is the "Right" Amount When Using an Electric Rice Cooker?

This test was based on using 1 cup of rice prepared in an automatic rice cooker. The rice is white unless otherwise indicated. These quantities are for rice cookers only, not for other methods.

Type of Rice	Water Quantity
Long-grain white	1¾ cups
Short-grain white	1¾ cups
Jasmine	2 cups
Basmati	2 cups
Wehani	2½ cups
Texmati	2 cups
Long-grain brown	2¼ cups
Short-grain brown	2¼ cups
Wild rice	2¼ cups

One useful outcome of this test was finding that *you can control the final texture by varying the amount of water.* That is, if you prefer a very firm, separate grain, simply use less water. If you prefer a softer, stickier rice, increase the water. Use the chart above as a starting point and then experiment on your own. Just view with skepticism the typical 2-to-1 formula found in most cookbooks — use your own palate as a guide.

white rices, although I have not had good luck cooking some specialty rices — Wehani in particular — with this device.

COOKING TIPS

■ Don't stir rice while cooking. This breaks the outer covering of the grains and produces a stickier, starchier rice.

■ Be sure to add salt at the beginning of the cooking process. Use ½ teaspoon of kosher salt per cup of rice.

■ You don't need to wash your rice before cooking. Washing is probably a leftover tradition from cultures in which the rice was dirty and needed a good wash before cooking to remove dirt and insects. In my tests, I found that washed rice was not only starchier and stickier when cooked, it was also undercooked in the center of the grain. Perhaps rinsing contributes additional water to the recipe, thus producing a stickier rice, but I could not explain why the rice required longer cooking time. Washing may also remove some of the nutrients. If you do wash your rice, you will require less cooking liquid and unless you make an adjustment, your rice will end up on the sticky side.

Master Recipe for Long-Grain White Rice (Modified Stovetop Method)

For years, I used the basic stovetop recipe found on the back of the box, but when testing recipes for cooking kasha, I became interested in the notion of sautéing rice with a bit of oil and then cooking with less water. This recipe uses only 1½ cups of water to 1 cup of rice, ½ cup less water than is usually called for, and it makes great rice. Also note that the rice has to sit for at least 10 minutes after cooking. This time is needed to finish the cooking and to let the grains "set" so they do not become sticky. If you are using commercial chicken stock, you will not need to add salt. Be sure to use a low-sodium brand.

> 2 teaspoons olive oil
> 1 cup long-grain white rice
> 1½ cups water or chicken stock
> ½ teaspoon kosher salt

1. Heat oil over medium heat in a medium saucepan and add rice. Stir for 1 minute. Add water and bring to a boil. Reduce heat to low, cover, and simmer for 15 minutes. Check after 3–4 minutes to make sure the water is at a slow simmer, not at a rapid boil.

2. Remove from heat and let stand covered for 10 minutes. Fluff with a fork and serve.

Serves 4

Master Recipe for Short-Grain White Rice

Short-grain rice is good with stir-fries, since it is stickier than long-grain varieties and therefore holds together better. It can easily be picked up with chopsticks.

- 1½ cups water or a combination of chicken stock and water
- ¼ teaspoon kosher salt
- 1 cup short-grain white rice

Place water and salt in a medium saucepan and bring to a boil. Add rice, reduce heat to a low simmer, cover, and cook for 15 minutes. Remove from heat and let stand covered for 10 minutes. Serve.

Serves 2–4

Master Recipe for Skillet Rice

Marie Simmons, author of Rice: The Amazing Grain, *gave me this tip for cooking rice. She cooks it in a large skillet uncovered for 5 minutes. Then she covers the pan and simmers for an additional 15–20 minutes. When I tested this method, I found the rice nicely cooked, not sticky or wet.*

- 1 cup long-grain white rice
- 2 cups water
- ½ teaspoon kosher salt

Place rice and water in a 10-inch skillet and simmer uncovered for 5 minutes. Cover and continue to simmer over very low heat for 15–20 minutes more.

Serves 4

Master Recipe for Baked Rice

This method is simple, as it requires no adjustment of stovetop heat. I only use it if I wish to make a rice casserole with celery, peppers, and other ingredients. If your saucepan is not oven-proof, the hot ingredients can be transferred to a loaf pan and covered with aluminum foil.

- 1 cup long-grain white or brown rice
- 2 cups water or 1 cup canned low-sodium chicken stock plus 1 cup water
- ½ cup chopped celery and/or bell pepper
- ¼ teaspoon cayenne pepper
- 2 tablespoons butter, optional
- ½ teaspoon kosher salt

1. Place all ingredients in an ovenproof saucepan with a lid and bring to a boil. Remove from heat and cover. Do not stir.

2. Bake in a 350°F oven for 25 minutes for white rice or about 55 minutes for brown rice.

Serves 4

Master Recipe for Rice Cooker Rice

For any variety of long-grain rice (including aromatic rices such as basmati and Wehani), use the recipe below. The recipe can be doubled or tripled. Refer to the chart in this chapter for the proper amount of water.

- 1 cup rice
  Water (see chart on page 142 for quantity)
- ½ teaspoon kosher salt

Place all ingredients in rice bowl of rice cooker. Cover and turn machine on. Machine will shut off when done, in 20–40 minutes.

Serves 4

Master Recipe for Rice Pilaf

To make a pilaf, rice is briefly sautéed in oil or butter (aromatics — onion or garlic — and perhaps some spices are often added). The sautéed rice is then cooked in the traditional method — liquid is added to the pan and the rice is cooked at a low simmer. You can also add vegetables such as peppers, celery, and mushrooms to the sauté. The first step of this recipe can be followed and then you can transfer all the ingredients to an electric rice cooker to finish the cooking.

    2 tablespoons olive oil
    1 medium onion, peeled and diced
    2 large cloves garlic, peeled and minced
    2 cups long-grain white rice
    2 cups chicken stock
    1 cup water

1. In a saucepan, heat olive oil over medium-high heat until hot. Add onion, reduce heat to medium, and sauté for 5 minutes. Add garlic and sauté for 2 minutes, being careful not to let garlic turn dark. Add rice and cook for 30 seconds, stirring gently.

2. Add stock and water, bring liquid to a simmer, cover, and cook for 15 minutes. Remove from heat and let stand covered for 10 minutes. If the chicken stock is unsalted, add 1 teaspoon of kosher salt along with the water.

Serves 8

Oriental Variation

Add 1 teaspoon toasted sesame oil to the olive oil and add 2 teaspoons soy sauce to the stock and water.

Master Recipe for Risotto

To improvise with this recipe, you can use two different types of ingredients. One type can stand a good deal of cooking, vegetables, for example. Sauté these ingredients for a few minutes in the pan after the onion has been cooked in the oil; then proceed with the recipe. Some ingredients cannot stand a half hour or so of cooking; add these at the end. However, they should be precooked separately beforehand. Seafood — shrimp, for example — would be precooked, then added at the end of cooking.

    4 cups homemade chicken or beef broth (or 1
      can commercial broth mixed with enough
      water to make 4 cups)
    3 tablespoons olive oil
    1 small onion, peeled and minced
    2 cups arborio rice

    1 cup dry white or red wine
    1 cup freshly grated high-quality Parmesan
      cheese
    1 tablespoon butter
      Salt and freshly ground black pepper to
      taste

1. Place broth (or broth and water) in a saucepan and heat to a simmer.

2. In a large saucepan or deep-sided skillet, heat the olive oil and onion over medium-high heat. Sauté for 5 minutes, stirring frequently. Add rice and stir for 3 minutes to coat.

3. Add 3 cups broth to rice and bring mixture to a boil. Reduce heat until liquid simmers slowly, stirring occasionally. When almost all of the liquid has been absorbed, add ½ cup wine. Adjust heat to maintain an even simmer. Continue cooking and adding liquid in ½-cup increments until all of the wine and most of the broth has been added. Test rice. It should be tender but still firm in the center. You may end up adding less liquid than called for.

4. Add cheese, butter, and salt and freshly ground pepper to taste. Serve.

Makes 4 main-course servings or 8 first-course servings

Master Recipe for Brown Rice (*Boil Then Steam Method*)

This recipe works for any length of brown rice (short, medium, or long). Brown rice, since it is less processed than white rice, takes about twice as long to cook. The only problem with this recipe, although it produces terrific rice, is that it requires two cooking techniques plus a steamer basket that can be inserted into the cooking pot. The easiest method for preparing rice is the electric rice cooker.

    6 cups water
    1 cup brown rice
    2 teaspoons olive oil or butter
    ½ teaspoon kosher salt

1. Bring water to a boil in a large pot. Stir in rice, oil or butter, and salt. Simmer uncovered until rice is almost tender, about 30 minutes.

2. Drain rice into a steamer basket that will fit inside the pot. Pour about 1 inch of boiling water in the pot and return it to heat. Place basket of rice in pot; cover and steam until tender, 5–10 minutes.

Serves 4

Master Recipe for Wild Rice

The boiling method used in this recipe is similar to the method I use for cooking many grains. Be sure to let the cooked rice rest undisturbed in a colander before fluffing with a fork. This will produce less sticky, more separate grains.

 1 cup wild rice
 4 cups water
 ½ teaspoon kosher salt

Place rice in a pot and add plenty of water. Swish rice gently with hands. Drain and repeat until water runs clear. Return rice to pot with the 4 cups of water. Bring to a boil and then reduce to a very low simmer. Cover and cook for about 50 minutes. Drain rice and let it sit in a colander or strainer for 10 minutes undisturbed. Fluff with a fork and serve.

Serves 6

Variations on Master Rice Recipes

The following variations are based on recipes using 1 cup of uncooked long-grain white or brown rice.

Rice with Parmesan

Add ¼ cup grated Parmesan cheese to hot, just-cooked rice.

Rice with Toasted Nuts

Toast ¼ cup coarsely chopped pecans or walnuts in a 350°F oven for 8 minutes. Sauté for 2 minutes in 1 tablespoon butter. Stir into hot, freshly cooked rice.

Rice with Chives and Sesame Oil

Heat 1 teaspoon olive oil mixed with 1 teaspoon toasted (Oriental) sesame oil in a small skillet. Add 2 tablespoons minced fresh chives and sauté for 1 minute. Add to hot, just-cooked rice.

Rice with Aromatic Spices

Add ¼ teaspoon ground cinnamon, ¼ teaspoon ground coriander, ⅛ teaspoon ground cloves, and ⅛ teaspoon ground cardamom to rice before cooking.

Rice with Hot Pepper

Add 2 tablespoons finely chopped celery, 2 tablespoons finely chopped red bell peppers, and one small jalapeño pepper, cored, seeded, and finely chopped, to rice before cooking.

Rice with Toasted Cumin

Toasted cumin seeds make a wonderful addition — use ½ teaspoon, adding them to the rice before cooking. To toast, place them in a heated skillet and shake the pan frequently for 3 minutes or until a thin wisp of smoke appears.

Rice with Spinach and Onion

Some cooks stir extra ingredients such as greens into the rice during the cooking process. I find that it's best to leave the rice undisturbed during cooking (to avoid making the rice starchy) and therefore combine all ingredients after the rice is cooked. The anchovy is optional but does add flavor and complexity. The rice should be just-cooked and still warm.

 1 tablespoon olive oil
 ⅓ cup diced onion
 1 anchovy fillet, diced, optional

2 cloves garlic, peeled and minced
1 package fresh spinach (10 ounces), stems trimmed, washed, and coarsely chopped
2 cups cooked, warm long-grain white or brown rice
¼ cup grated Parmesan cheese

Heat the oil in a skillet and add the onion and anchovy. Sauté over medium heat for 3 minutes, stirring occasionally. Add the garlic and sauté for 1 minute. Add the spinach and sauté, stirring frequently until the spinach is wilted, about 2 minutes. Stir in rice and sauté for 1 minute or until rice is heated through. Top each serving with 1 tablespoon of grated Parmesan.

Serves 4

Rice Stuffing with Apples, Apricots, and Toasted Walnuts

Any type of rice may be used for this recipe. A shorter-grain rice will produce a stickier, more solid stuffing. I prefer basmati rice for this dish, although long-grain brown rice is also a good choice. White rice is a bit bland to stand up to this recipe's full-flavored ingredients. To toast the walnuts, place them on a cookie sheet in a 350°F oven for about 8 minutes. Check frequently to make sure they do not burn.

3 tablespoons olive oil
2 tablespoons butter
1½ cups coarsely chopped onions
4 cloves garlic, peeled and minced
1 cup dried apricots, coarsely chopped
1 cup toasted walnuts, coarsely chopped
2 cups peeled, cored, diced apple
6 cups cooked rice, basmati preferred
1 teaspoon grated orange peel
1 teaspoon ground cinnamon
½ teaspoon ground allspice
¼ teaspoon ground nutmeg
2 teaspoons kosher salt
Freshly ground black pepper to taste

1. Heat the oil and butter in a large skillet. Add the onion and sauté over medium heat for 4 minutes. Add the garlic and sauté for 1

minute. Add the apricots and sauté for 3 minutes. Add the remaining ingredients and sauté for 2 minutes.

2. Let stuffing cool completely before using to stuff poultry. To cook it separately, place in a greased baking dish, cover, and bake in a 350° oven for 30–40 minutes.

Serves 6

Stir-Fried Rice with Crispy Peanuts, Ginger, and Orange

Chicken makes a good addition to this recipe. Start by stir-frying bite-size chicken pieces, which takes about 45 seconds (see Chapter 35). Remove chicken, follow rest of recipe, and then add chicken back to the skillet along with the rice. Use ¼ pound of boneless chicken breast. I prefer long-grain brown rice for this recipe.

2 teaspoons grated orange peel
2 tablespoons good-quality soy sauce
1 tablespoon dry sherry
1 tablespoon water or chicken stock
2 tablespoons peanut oil
⅓ cup unsalted peanuts
1 tablespoon minced fresh ginger
3 cups cooked rice, long-grain brown rice preferred
½ teaspoon sugar

1. Combine the orange peel, soy sauce, sherry, and water and set aside.

2. Place a large (at least 12-inch) skillet over high heat for 4 minutes. Add peanut oil and heat for 1 minute or until the oil just starts to smoke. Add the peanuts and stir-fry for about 2 minutes or until crisp but not burned (watch the peanuts carefully — they will turn dark quickly). Clear the center of the pan, add the ginger, and sauté for 10 seconds. Remove pan from heat and stir peanuts and ginger to combine.

3. Place pan back on heat, add the soy sauce mixture, rice, and sugar and cook about 1 minute or until rice is hot.

Serves 4

Lentils and Rice with Smothered Onions

This is one of thousands of variations on the classic beans-and-rice dish served around the world. It is my personal favorite because the flavor of lentils and their size are well suited to rice. Lentils cook up quickly, which makes this a good recipe for last-minute suppers.

½ cup lentils
2 tablespoons butter
1 tablespoon olive oil
1 medium onion, peeled and cut into rings
1 cup long-grain white rice or white basmati rice
1¾ cups homemade chicken stock or 1 cup canned stock plus ¾ cup water
1 teaspoon kosher salt (if using canned stock, reduce the salt to taste)

1. Pick over lentils for stones, rinse well, and boil uncovered in 4 cups water for 12 minutes. Drain.

2. Melt the butter and olive oil in a skillet with a cover. When foam subsides, add onion and cook covered over medium-low heat for 15 minutes, stirring occasionally. Add rice and sauté over medium heat for 1 minute, stirring frequently. Add lentils, chicken stock, and salt and stir to combine. Reduce heat to a simmer, cover, and cook for 15 minutes. Remove from heat and let stand 10 minutes before serving.

Serves 4

Souffléed Rice Pudding

This recipe takes some work, especially compared to the Stovetop Rice Pudding recipe in this chapter. But it's really a rice pudding soufflé and it's elegant enough to serve to guests. This dish has to be served soon after baking — it will not hold well either at room temperature or in the refrigerator. I have tried making this recipe with brown rice — I tried it twice — and both times the results were alarming. This is not a health

recipe — resist the temptation to increase its nutritional value.

6 cups milk
½ cup long-grain white rice
2 eggs, separated
¼ teaspoon kosher salt
½ cup sugar
1 teaspoon vanilla extract
Grated nutmeg and cinnamon for topping

1. Heat oven to 300°F. Combine milk and rice in a large ovenproof saucepan and bring to a simmer, stirring occasionally to prevent sticking. Place saucepan uncovered in oven and bake for 1 hour or until mixture is the consistency of a thick porridge. Do not stir while cooking. Remove from oven, remove "skin," transfer mixture to a large bowl, and let cool to room temperature, at least 1 hour.

2. Beat egg yolks in the bowl of an electric mixer for 1 minute. Add salt and all but 2 tablespoons of the sugar. Beat on high speed until pale yellow and thick, about 4 minutes. Stir in vanilla and then stir mixture into the cooled rice mixture.

3. Beat the egg whites until soft peaks just begin to form. Add the remaining 2 tablespoons of sugar and beat until whites hold a 2-inch peak, just a few seconds more. Stir half the whites into the rice mixture. Fold in the remaining whites with a rubber spatula.

4. Lightly butter the inside of a 2-quart baking dish (a soufflé dish works well). Pour in mixture, sprinkle with nutmeg and cinnamon, and bake in 300° oven for 40–45 minutes or until top is lightly browned and puffed. Let cool for 15 minutes on a wire rack and then serve warm or at room temperature.

Serves 6

Master Recipe for Stovetop Rice Pudding

Rice is full of starch, and that's why rice pudding doesn't need eggs or other thickeners. Just cook short-grain white rice and milk on top of the stove until the mixture thickens (short-grain rice is starchier than long-grain rice). This is my favorite "family" dessert — it's easy to make, and both adults and kids love it. I prefer to serve this dessert warm, not hot. By the way, it's best to use a vegetable peeler or zester, not a grater, for the orange rind — then the peel should be minced. Graters turn orange peel into mush, losing much of the highly flavored oils in the process. For a thicker pudding, let it sit covered on top of the stove after cooking for up to 2 hours. For a creamier pudding, substitute 1 cup half and half for 1 cup milk.

½ cup short-grain white rice
2½ cups water
2 cups milk
½ teaspoon vanilla extract
7 tablespoons sugar
2 teaspoons minced orange peel
¼ cup finely chopped almonds

Combine the rice and water in a large saucepan and bring to a boil. Reduce heat to a simmer and cook for 40 minutes or until most of the water has been absorbed. Add the milk, vanilla, and sugar, bring back to a boil, reduce heat to a simmer, and cook until mixture is the consistency of a thick porridge, about 1 hour, 10 minutes. Add the orange peel and almonds, stir to combine, and serve either hot, warm, or at room temperature.

Serves 4–6

Stovetop Rice Pudding with Rose Water, Pistachios, and Cardamom

Follow recipe above but substitute 1 teaspoon rose water for the orange peel and pistachios for the almonds, and add ½ teaspoon ground cardamom.

Stovetop Rice Pudding with Cinnamon and Nutmeg

Follow recipe above but substitute 1 teaspoon ground cinnamon for the orange peel, eliminate the almonds, and add ¼ teaspoon of freshly grated nutmeg.

Persian Rice with Grated Carrots

This recipe is based on one I found in The Rice Book *by Sri Owen. Persian rice is usually cooked on top of the stove and the bottom becomes wonderfully crusty. In this recipe, the whole dish is cooked in the oven, which simplifies preparation. Departing from the original recipe, however, I use chicken stock and water instead of milk and I sauté the carrots briefly before adding to the rice for extra flavor. This recipe also works well with basmati rice.*

1½ cups short-grain white rice
1 tablespoon olive oil
1 tablespoon butter
1 cup finely chopped onion
3 garlic cloves, peeled and minced
4 cups grated carrots (5–6 medium carrots)
¼ teaspoon ground cardamom
⅛ teaspoon ground nutmeg
1 teaspoon kosher salt
2½ cups homemade chicken stock or 1½ cups low-sodium canned stock plus 1 cup water

1. Soak rice in water to cover for 1 hour. Drain in a colander.

2. Heat oven to 350°F. Oil a large soufflé or other baking dish — the dish should be at least 3-quart capacity. Heat olive oil and butter in a large skillet over medium heat. When foam subsides, add onion and sauté for 3 minutes. Add garlic and sauté for 1 minute. Add grated carrots and sauté for 3 minutes, stirring frequently. Add spices and salt and sauté for 30 seconds, stirring to combine.

3. Combine the drained rice and the carrot mixture and place in prepared baking dish. Pour in chicken stock. Place dish in oven and bake for 1 hour or until there is a golden crust on top.

Serves 4–6

~ 14 ~

What to Do with Dried Beans

Soaking beans overnight is essential to great beans. If you forget to presoak, however, don't use a "quick-soak" method; just cook the beans longer.

~

Many years ago I was exiting a multiplex movie theater and found myself walking behind a family who were having trouble finding their car. I could hear a dispute simmering between the mother and father as to which direction they should take. Finally, the father declared in his best basso profundo, "Everyone who wants a ride home tonight, follow me. Anyone who wants to spend the night in the parking lot, follow your mother!" Of course, his wife and kids picked him up on their way out of the lot.

This brought to mind one of my favorite expressions — "Always wrong but never in doubt" — which, unfortunately, describes many of my deeply held culinary beliefs, which quickly fall by the wayside when tested. One such rule was that quick-soaking dried beans (put them in cold water, bring to a boil, remove from the burner, cover, and let sit for 1 hour) is pretty much as good as soaking them overnight. After testing all sorts of last-minute soaking methods, I found that the overnight soak is vastly preferable. If you forget to do that, however, don't bother with presoaking; just cook the beans longer.

WHAT ARE LEGUMES?

There are three types of dried legumes, or what most Americans call dried beans:

beans, peas, and lentils. They are all referred to as legumes — a confusing term since "legume" is the French word for vegetable — because they are all the dried seeds from plants of the Leguminosae family. Here are the types of dried beans you are most likely to find in your local supermarket:

Black Beans: The black kidney bean (smaller varieties are called turtle beans) keeps it shape when cooked and is often used for bean cakes as well as in salads, soups, and stews. It is native to South America. The outside is black but the inside is cream-colored. Black beans are used in American cooking for black bean soup. In my tests, I found that presoaking black beans made no difference in texture or flavor and shortened total cooking time by only 10 minutes. My conclusion is that black beans do not readily absorb room temperature water during presoaking.

Black-Eyed Peas: When I was a kid, Dorothy O'Gilvie, our cook from the Chesapeake Bay area, used to make black-eyed peas once a week. They are cream-colored, medium-size beans with a distinctive small, dark spot. For my money, their potatolike texture and flavor go well with the punch of boiled and sautéed collard greens and a splash of vinegar. That's how Dorothy prepared them, and that's how I make them for my kids today.

Chickpeas: Chickpeas, also known as garbanzo beans, are usually purchased in cans, although they can also be purchased dried. Chickpeas are used most frequently in hummus (cooked pureed chickpeas with olive oil, garlic, and lemon) and falafel (fried chickpea balls). Chickpea flour is also used in Indian cooking for breads. Don't follow the advice of cookbooks that tell you to add baking soda to the cooking water when preparing chickpeas. Since chickpeas are hard and require a fair amount of cooking, the baking soda is supposed to soften the water, speeding the cooking process. In my opinion, a few minutes one way or the other doesn't make much difference, and I dislike the flavor of baking soda, even when it's dissolved in a large amount of cooking water.

Dried Peas: Dried peas come from field peas, not the usual garden pea. When dried, whole peas are hard and may require soaking before cooking. Split peas, however, cook much faster and do not need soaking. This variety splits naturally when the seed coat falls off during drying — the splitting is not a mechanical process. Split peas are good for a quick soup.

Lentils: There are many varieties of lentil, including the brownish lentil sold in most supermarkets; Le Puy lentils (grown around Le Puy in France), which are smaller and darker and thought to have superior flavor; and yellow or red lentils, also called dal, which are widely used in Indian cooking. Lentils are so small and soft that they do not need to be soaked before cooking.

Pinto Bean: The pinto bean is a speckled bean and can be used in place of the red kidney bean. It is often used in Mexican cooking as the basis for refried beans.

Red Kidney Beans: This is the bean you find in the bean salad at your local salad bar, in chili recipes that call for beans, and in the American version of minestrone soup. It is relatively large and a bright burgundy color.

White Beans: These include the navy bean, which is on the small side and is often used in baked beans or bean soups; Great Northern beans, which are slightly larger; and cannellini beans, which are larger still. All three are interchangeable.

THE PERILS OF INDIGESTION

It's not an old wives' tale that beans are difficult to digest and cause flatulence. That's why some cooks will partially cook beans and then change the cooking water to help remove the hard-to-digest enzyme that causes the problem. I prefer, however, to risk the perils of indigestion in the quest for taste, as the cooking liquid is also full of flavor, and therefore I use the cooking liquid, if possible, in the recipe except when preparing garbanzo beans (the water takes on a strong and unpleasant flavor). I also find it wasteful to discard quarts of boiling water only to have to reheat a new potful all in the name of indigestion. If you are particularly sensitive to beans, try Beano, a product that claims to reduce the digestive difficulties related to beans. I also recommend that you cook beans in lots of water, which will help extract and dilute the offending oligosaccharides, the molecules that cause the digestive difficulties.

COOKING BEANS

HOW TO FLAVOR BEANS

I often add celery tops, fresh herbs, leftover sprigs of parsley — just about anything — to the water when I cook dried beans. Beans can also be cooked in chicken stock (or a mix of stock and water) to add flavor. A few cloves of crushed garlic make another good addition to a boiling pot of beans.

Can Beans Be Cooked Right in the Sauce?

On several occasions I have added partially cooked beans to a tomato sauce or chili recipe and found that even after 2 hours of cooking, they still didn't end up truly cooked inside. I discovered that the answer lies in acidity. That is, an acid environment (tomatoes, for example, have lots of acidity) will make the cell walls of the legume less prone to softening, whereas an alkaline environment will speed up the deterioration.

How Long Should Beans Be Cooked?

Cooking time depends primarily on whether the beans have been soaked overnight, unless you are dealing with lentils or dried lima beans, neither of which needs to be presoaked; age and type of bean are also impor-

tant. A word of caution about the chart of cooking times. Some supermarket beans are very old and dried out and others are relatively fresh. This affects both cooking time and texture, so use these times as a rough guide, not as a precise measurement.

Black-Eyed Peas with Basmati Rice and Spices

Basmati rice is an aromatic rice that is thin and lengthens when cooked rather than swelling in girth. It has a fragrant aroma but can be replaced with any long-grain brown rice. Basmati rice also comes in a "white" rice that has undergone additional milling to remove the layers of bran. If you wish to substitute a long-grain white rice or white basmati rice in this recipe, the cooking time will be about 20 minutes (brown rice takes twice as long to cook as white rice).

Cooking Times for Beans — Presoaked and Not Presoaked

Allow 6 cups of cold water for each cup of dried beans both when soaking and when cooking. After soaking, discard water and replenish before cooking.

Bean Type	Cooking Time When Soaked Overnight	Cooking Time When Not Presoaked	Yield (per Cup of Dried Beans)
Black beans	25 minutes	35 minutes	2 cups
Black-eyed peas	20 minutes	35 minutes	2¼ cups
Chickpeas	25 minutes	90 minutes	2¼ cups
Kidney beans	25 minutes	55 minutes	2½ cups
Large limas	20 minutes	45 minutes	2 cups
Lentils	12 minutes	20 minutes	3½ cups soaked 2½ cups not soaked
Split peas	20 minutes	30 minutes	2½ cups soaked 2 cups not soaked
Great Northern beans	25 minutes	45 minutes	2½ cups
Cannellini beans	25 minutes	60 minutes	2½ cups soaked 2¼ cups not soaked

NOTE: Lentils are not usually soaked, as they cook quickly without soaking and also absorb a great deal of water if soaked overnight (note the large difference in yields). I prefer my lentils toothier, with less water absorption, and therefore do not soak them. Both the kidney beans and the chickpeas will require additional water during the prolonged cooking time.

What If You Forget to Presoak the Beans?

Most beans must be presoaked overnight in water (allow 4–6 cups water for each cup of dried beans) to achieve the best texture when cooked. However, I often forget this step and wanted to test a variety of presoak methods. The result of this test is that I would not bother with the so-called quick-soak method; just cook the beans longer (see cooking times chart on page 151). The beans will not be as creamy or quite as soft as if you had presoaked them overnight, but the quick presoak adds no flavor benefit and for many types of beans actually takes longer overall than simply cooking unsoaked beans until tender.

Presoaking Method	Result When Cooked
Soaked overnight	Best method; creamy, tender beans
Quick-soaked (bring beans to a simmer in lots of water and let sit for 1 hour)	About the same as beans that were unsoaked
Unsoaked	Not as good as overnight soaking, but no worse than quick-soaked beans

2 slices bacon
3 tablespoons olive oil
2 medium onions, peeled and coarsely chopped
4 anchovy fillets, chopped
4 cloves garlic, peeled and minced
1 can (16 ounces) tomatoes, drained and chopped
1 cup brown basmati rice or brown long-grain rice
2 cups chicken stock
1 teaspoon ground allspice
½ teaspoon ground cinnamon
¼ teaspoon ground cardamom
4 cups cooked black-eyed peas
2 ribs celery, diced

1. Cook bacon in a large saucepan, lid off. Remove bacon and all but 1 tablespoon fat. Reserve bacon for another use. Add olive oil, onion, and anchovies and cook with top on for 15 minutes over medium-low heat. Remove top and add garlic. Cook for 5 minutes uncovered over medium heat.

2. Add tomatoes and cook for 5 minutes. Add rice and stir for 1 minute. Add stock and spices, cover, and cook over medium-low heat for 35 minutes, until rice is almost cooked. Add black-eyed peas and celery, stir, and cover. Cook for 5 more minutes, until rice is done.

Serves 6–8

Rice and Beans

This is perhaps the most universal recipe in the world since it's an easy, cheap source of protein and calories. You can cook endless variations of this recipe — for example, using fresh peas instead of cooked dried beans, using Indian spices such as cardamom, or adding other ingredients such as minced vegetables. You can use any type of long-grain rice you prefer.

2 tablespoons olive oil
1 onion, peeled and diced
1 tablespoon minced garlic
4 cups cooked red or black kidney beans
¼ cup white wine vinegar
3 cups cooked long-grain rice, warm
Salt and freshly ground black pepper to taste

1. Heat oil in a pan large enough to hold all ingredients. Add the onion and cook over medium heat for 3 minutes. Add garlic and cook for 1 minute. Add beans and vinegar and cook for 5 minutes.

2. Add rice and mix well. Season to taste with salt and freshly ground black pepper.

Serves 6

Marinated White Beans

Vinegar and cooked beans are a good combination, especially when left overnight to marinate. This dish can be served as a bean salad, as an accompaniment to meat, or even over pasta.

1 cup dried white beans
4 cloves garlic, peeled and lightly crushed
2 bay leaves
1 cup Master Recipe for Vinaigrette (see page 118), made with white wine vinegar
¼ cup chopped flat-leaf parsley
Salt and freshly ground black pepper to taste

Soak beans overnight in 4 cups cold water. Drain and then cook beans in 6 cups of boiling water with bay leaves and garlic for 25 minutes, until just tender. Discard garlic and bay leaves. Drain beans, dress with vinaigrette and chopped parsley, and let marinate in refrigerator overnight. Serve at room temperature.

Serves 4

Lentils and Spinach with Olive Oil and Garlic

This is a quick and easy way to dress up cooked lentils. This dish is excellent with roast chicken or steamed fish.

1 cup dried lentils
¼ cup high-quality olive oil
2 teaspoons minced garlic
1 bag fresh spinach (10 ounces), cleaned, stemmed, and coarsely chopped
2 tablespoons white wine vinegar
Salt and freshly ground black pepper to taste

1. Pick over lentils for stones, rinse well, and cook in 6 cups of boiling water until just cooked, about 20 minutes (check after 15 minutes). Drain.
2. Heat olive oil in a large saucepan or pot and add garlic when hot. Sauté for 1 minute over medium heat. Add spinach and sauté for 2 minutes. Add cooked lentils and cook for 1 minute, stirring frequently to combine. Stir in the vinegar and add plenty of salt and freshly ground black pepper to taste.

Serves 4

Beans with Olive Oil, Bacon, and Rosemary

These beans can also be cooked entirely on top of the stove. Simply simmer covered until cooked. If you are using thick-cut bacon, use only 2 slices. The dish was traditionally prepared in Italy, where the ingredients were placed in a large earthen bottle and cooked overnight by the hearth. You can substitute pancetta for bacon. Be sure to use plenty of salt and pepper.

2 cups dried white beans
4 slices bacon, cut into ½-inch pieces
4 cloves garlic, peeled and minced
¼ cup extra virgin olive oil
4 cups chicken stock
¼ cup minced fresh rosemary
Salt and freshly ground black pepper to taste

1. Soak beans overnight in cold water. Drain and rinse under cold water. Place in a lidded casserole. Heat oven to 375°F.
2. Add bacon, garlic, and olive oil to beans and toss. Add chicken stock and then enough water to cover beans by 1 inch.
3. Bring to a boil over high heat and skim brown scum off the top. Stir in 3 tablespoons rosemary. Cover and bake for about 45 minutes total, checking beans after half an hour. When tender, season with salt and pepper to taste. Use a slotted spoon to serve, and top each serving with a bit of the remaining fresh rosemary.

Serves 8

Black-Eyed Peas and Tomatoes

Be sure to cook the black-eyed peas until they really are tender. Use enough sugar to bring out the flavor of the tomatoes (up to 2 teaspoons). Fresh rosemary needles are easy to mince, as they are still fairly tender. Dried rosemary is brittle and difficult to mince, and therefore I drizzle a little oil on the dried needles before chopping. They can also be pulverized in a mortar and pestle.

1 cup dried black-eyed peas
2 tablespoons olive oil
1 medium onion, peeled and coarsely diced
2 cloves garlic, peeled and minced
1 can (28 ounces) Italian plum tomatoes, drained
¼ teaspoon red pepper flakes
1½ teaspoons finely minced fresh rosemary leaves or ½ teaspoon dried
1 tablespoon white wine vinegar
1 teaspoon sugar (or more)
1 small bunch parsley, tough stems removed, minced
Salt and freshly ground pepper to taste

1. Soak black-eyed peas overnight in 4 cups water. Drain and rinse. Place peas back in stockpot with fresh water to cover, bring back to a boil, add salt to taste, and simmer until beans are just tender, about 20 minutes.

2. Place a large skillet or Dutch oven over medium heat and add oil. When oil is hot, add onion. Cook for 6 minutes. Add garlic and sauté for 1 minute. Add tomatoes, red pepper flakes, rosemary, vinegar, and sugar. Simmer for 15 minutes.

3. Stir in black-eyed peas and simmer for another 10 minutes. Check seasonings (be sure to add plenty of salt to enhance the flavor of the peas). Add chopped parsley, toss, and serve.

Serves 4–6

Vermont Baked Beans

This recipe is based on one found in the July 1992 Yankee *magazine, in an article about George Flanders of Pittsfield, New Hampshire. I have modified it and now use it every year at the Ox Roast, a local covered-dish dinner in the Vermont town where we have a summer home. If you cannot find cider, use either apple juice (unfiltered is best) or chicken stock (in this case, increase molasses by 2 tablespoons). For a more authentic recipe, reduce the maple syrup to ¼ cup. Over time, New England baked beans have become increasingly sweet, to the point that they*

have become more of a confection than a savory side dish. Since baked beans take some time to make and they hold well, I often make a double recipe.

1 pound dried navy beans
3 strips bacon, cut into ½-inch pieces
1 large onion, peeled and diced
2 cloves garlic, peeled and minced
1 tablespoon minced fresh ginger
¼ cup molasses
½ cup maple syrup
1 tablespoon dry mustard
2–3 cups apple cider
½ cup cider vinegar
2 bay leaves
4 sprigs thyme
¼ teaspoon ground cloves
½ teaspoon ground cardamom
½ teaspoon ground allspice
½ teaspoon kosher salt
½ teaspoon freshly ground black pepper
2 additional strips bacon

1. Soak beans overnight in 4 quarts water. Drain.

2. Cook the cut-up bacon for 3 minutes in a 3-quart pot. Add onion, garlic, and ginger and cook over medium heat for an additional 3 minutes. Add drained beans and next 10 ingredients (molasses through allspice). Add salt and pepper and mix well. Cover with remaining bacon strips. Bake in a 300° oven for 5–6 hours, or until beans are very tender. If necessary, add additional cider during cooking to keep beans covered.

3. When beans are cooked, remove thyme sprigs and bay leaves, correct seasonings, and serve.

Serves 8

Black-Eyed Pea Salad

Black-eyed peas are a staple of Southern cooking, usually prepared with greens and vinegar. They are rich and nutty, and nothing reminds me more of American cookery than a big bowl of black-eyed peas. Use your own judgment about the amount of dressing, and be sure to make liberal use of the salt and pepper. An extra splash of vinegar at the last minute won't hurt either.

1½ cups dried black-eyed peas
1 tablespoon kosher salt
2 ribs celery, diced
2 tablespoons minced onion
⅓ cup minced flat-leaf parsley
3 scallions, finely chopped
1 cup All-Purpose Vegetable Salad Dressing (see page 120)
½ teaspoon sugar
2 tablespoons white wine vinegar
  Salt and freshly ground black pepper to taste

Soak the black-eyed peas overnight. Discard water, replenish to cover, and simmer in a large stockpot or saucepan with salt until cooked, about 20 minutes. Drain and rinse with cold water. Combine all ingredients. This salad tastes best when left to marinate for several hours. Check seasonings just before serving. Serve at room temperature.

Serves 6–8

Lentil, Walnut, and Scallion Salad

Be sure to add a sufficient amount of salt and pepper to taste. This salad is best dressed just before serving, as the lentils will quickly absorb the vinaigrette. This results in a dull, less assertive flavor. Taste the salad before serving and add an extra dash of vinegar if necessary.

1 cup dried lentils
6 cups water
½ cup coarsely chopped walnuts
¼ cup extra virgin olive oil
1 teaspoon Dijon mustard
3 tablespoons balsamic vinegar
½ teaspoon kosher salt
¼ teaspoon coarsely ground black pepper
¼ cup finely chopped flat-leaf parsley
¼ cup finely chopped scallions

1. Pick over lentils for stones, rinse well, and bring to a boil with 6 cups water in a covered pot. Simmer for 20 minutes or until tender. Drain and rinse with plenty of cold water. Drain well. Add walnuts to lentils.

2. For dressing, whisk together olive oil, mustard, vinegar, salt, pepper, parsley, and scallions.

3. Just before serving, gently mix dressing with lentils.

Serves 6

Lentil-Rice Salad with Balsamic Vinegar

Rice is an excellent salad ingredient. It absorbs vinaigrette evenly and provides a nice contrast to crisper ingredients such as celery, corn, or greens. Be sure that the salad has enough vinegar and salt — taste it before serving and add a few splashes of vinegar, if necessary, for extra bite.

Salad
1 cup long-grain white rice
1 cup chicken stock
1 cup dried lentils
1 teaspoon kosher salt
1 cup finely diced onion
2 medium carrots, coarsely grated
2 ribs celery, diced
3 tablespoons olive oil
2 cloves garlic, peeled and minced
1 tablespoon minced fresh basil

Dressing
¾ cup good-quality olive oil
4 tablespoons red wine vinegar
1 tablespoon balsamic vinegar
  Salt and freshly ground black pepper to taste

1. Cook rice in 1 cup of chicken stock, using Master Recipe for Long-Grain White Rice (page 142). Allow to cool.

2. Pick over lentils for stones, rinse well, and bring to a boil with 6 cups water in a covered pot. Simmer for 20 minutes or until tender. Drain and rinse with plenty of cold water. Drain well.

3. Combine rice, lentils, and remaining salad ingredients in a large bowl.

4. To prepare the dressing, whisk the olive oil into the vinegars, adding the oil very slowly at first, until the oil and vinegar are well blended and have formed an emulsion. Add to the salad and mix thoroughly. Add salt and freshly ground black pepper to taste.

Serves 6

Chickpea and Pasta Soup

This is a simple Italian soup that requires top-notch ingredients. I wouldn't bother making this soup with store-bought chicken stock; you really need homemade. I prefer canned tomatoes for this recipe (Redpack are quite good), but the rosemary has to be fresh, and the Parmesan cheese better not come in a green cardboard container with a bright yellow top!

- 3 tablespoons good-quality olive oil
- 4 anchovy fillets, chopped
- 4 cloves garlic, peeled and minced
- 1 carrot, finely chopped
- 1 teaspoon sugar
- 2 cups canned tomatoes, drained and chopped
- 1½ cups cooked or canned chickpeas, drained
- 4 cups homemade chicken stock
  Salt to taste
- 2 teaspoons minced fresh rosemary leaves
- ¼ cup minced flat-leaf parsley
- 1½ cups very small uncooked pasta such as ditalini
  Freshly ground black pepper to taste
- ½ cup grated high-quality Parmesan cheese

1. Heat a medium pot of salted water for pasta.

2. Heat the oil over medium heat in a Dutch oven or large saucepan. Add the anchovies and sauté for 1 minute, stirring frequently. Add the garlic, carrot, sugar, and tomatoes and lower heat to medium-low and cook for 3 minutes, stirring frequently. Add the chickpeas and chicken stock and bring back to a simmer. Cook for 10 minutes. Add salt to taste. Add rosemary and parsley. Maintain a simmer while you cook pasta.

3. Cook pasta and drain. Place pasta in individual serving bowls and add soup. Add plenty of freshly ground black pepper and freshly grated Parmesan cheese. If you have leftovers, do not store soup with pasta — the pasta will swell and soak up much of the liquid.

Serves 4

The Best Way to Cook Grains

Most grains can be boiled and then poured into a colander, where they should remain undisturbed for 10 minutes. But the first step is to know whether you have a fine, medium, coarse, or whole-grain grind.

~

I belong to the St. Botolph Club in Boston, where I once met a gentleman who is a minister. At that time, I had been asked to lead a service in our small Methodist church in Vermont and I was anxious for some advice. Instead, he told me a story. One Sunday, he said, he was preaching on the virgin birth, expressing some doubts regarding the veracity of the miracle. After the service, an elderly but upright lady grabbed his hand tightly and looked straight up into his eyes and said, "I am quite sure, Reverend, that we are not better off knowing what you do *not* believe." I admit an equally shaky faith when it comes to the use of grains — I used to find them difficult to prepare — but now, having cooked bulgur, barley, millet, quinoa, and kasha every which way to Sunday, I can honestly admit a renewed devotion to most grains not just for health reasons but for both their taste and their ease of preparation.

FIVE GRAINS FOR HOME COOKING

This chapter is limited to five basic grains with which you should be familiar: barley, bulgur, kasha, millet, and quinoa. They are available at any health food store and in most supermarkets. I have intentionally left out four grains that are often discussed in books about grain but are not sufficiently available to make them practical for the home cook. They are wheat berries (the whole grains of wheat, which are soaked and then used in pilafs, soups, and stews); amaranth (a grain cultivated by the Aztecs, amaranth has a very strong flavor and a tiny seed, which is crunchy even when cooked); teff (a tiny reddish-brown grain that is so small that the germ and bran remain on the grain; it is often used in baking as an accent rather than as a main ingredient); and triticale (a man-made hybrid of wheat and rye, it is shaped like rice and has a chewy outer skin and a starchy interior when cooked).

The first major problem with cooking grains is that many of them come in very different grinds. It's difficult to figure out, for example, whether the bulgur you just bought at the local health food store is whole, coarse, medium, or fine grind. This is of some consequence, as the cooking method for coarse bulgur is quite different than that for a fine or medium grind (coarse bulgur is cooked on top of the stove, the other two are simply soaked in boiling water). I have included information on which grinds are most common for each type of grain in the descriptions below.

Another problem is that most basic grain-cooking instructions are just plain wrong. Most cooks treat grains like rice, cooking them in a covered saucepan until done. But this usually results in sticky or mushy grains. It is far better, for most grains, to boil them in a large quantity of water — a Chinese technique for cooking rice — and then dump them unstirred into a colander. After 10 minutes of draining, the cooked grains can be fluffed and served. This method has another advantage. A grain may require different amounts of water depending on the grind and its age. By boiling in a large amount of water, the home cook has avoided this entire issue — you don't have to get the proportions just right. For example, a fine-grind bulgur might use 2½ cups of liquid per cup of grain, whereas a very coarse bulgur might require 3 cups.

In preparing a variety of grains, I also discovered that I had strong preferences and dislikes. I found kasha, always referred to as "toasty" and "nutty," to be entirely without flavor, although its aroma does live up to its billing. It is also difficult to cook properly — even when sautéed with egg it does not cook up fluffy and separate, although the kasha recipe in this chapter, suggested by Dana Jacobi, an expert in cooking grains, does work well. It is no wonder that most traditional kasha recipes call for lots of onions and garlic! On the plus side, I found millet to be incredibly easy to prepare (even my five-year-old can cook millet so that it is fluffy and light), and it has a wonderful subtle flavor that lends itself to many applications. I eat it regularly for breakfast with milk and make it often as a quick side dish. Barley has a chewy texture, which requires some getting used to, and bulgur is tricky because, as mentioned above, you need to know what type of grind you have to prepare it properly. Quinoa was also a pleasant surprise — it is very easy to

prepare properly, although its light, crunchy texture is a bit limited in application (it's quite good with fish, however). Here's a quick rundown on each grain.

Barley: The most common form of barley is pearl barley, and it cooks in about 30 minutes. Whole hulled barley, available only in some health food stores, must be soaked overnight and then cooked for about an hour. Pearl barley is relatively large and has a split grain that is long, tear-shaped, and light brown. When cooked, it has a chewy texture that is distinctive but not unpleasant. Unhulled barley is very difficult to prepare and is not recommended for cooking at home. You can also purchase barley grits, which is finely ground. This is usually prepared as a hot breakfast cereal. Usually sold pearled or whole, hulled.

Bulgur: This is a derivative of wheat berries, which can derive in turn from either red wheat or white wheat. The berries are parboiled or steamed, dried (some of the bran may be removed), and then crushed into various grinds. Bulgur is available in three different textures: fine and medium can be prepared by soaking in boiling water; the coarse texture has to be simmered in water. The two most common uses for bulgur are in tabbouleh (a bulgur-parsley salad) and as a stuffing for grape leaves in Middle Eastern cooking. Bulgur made from red wheat is small-grained and dark nut brown. When it is made from white wheat, it is pale and golden in color. It looks like birdseed. Usually sold in a medium grind.

Kasha: Buckwheat is actually the fruit of a plant that is a distant relative of rhubarb. Inside the kernel is a seed, referred to as the groat. If this seed is roasted, the result is kasha. If not, it is simply whole, white buckwheat, which is often used for breakfast cereals and is sold as "cream of buckwheat."

Kasha is said to have a nutty flavor, but I find it rather bland compared with bulgur or barley. Kasha is most commonly used as a stuffing (probably because it lacks sufficient flavor and texture to be eaten on its own). It is also the basis for kasha varnishkes, a Jewish dish of kasha and egg noodles. Reddish brown in color, the small, heart-shaped seed (the groat) is soft and therefore must be cooked gingerly, as it will readily turn to mush (see master recipe below). You can also buy kasha in coarse and medium granulations. (The coarse texture looks like a fine birdseed and the medium texture is more powdery, somewhat like finely ground oats. Buckwheat groats — whole kasha — is easy to differentiate from ground because it is light brown all over. The ground varieties are multicolored because the inside of the seed is white.) The medium and fine textures will cook a bit more rapidly than whole or coarse. Usually sold whole.

Millet: Millet is a native of the tropics and has been cultivated for more than six thousand years. It is very high in protein. Millet is ground to make flour for flatbreads and can also be cooked with milk or water to make a porridge. It is not strong-flavored and is a small, yellow grain which cooks up into very small but separate kernels that often retain some crunch even after cooking. Millet benefits considerably from toasting before cooking. Usually sold whole.

Quinoa: Quinoa (pronounced "keen wha") comes from the Andes, in South America, and started appearing in North American cooking in the mid-1980s. It is still grown in South America but now is also cultivated in the United States and Canada. Quinoa, even higher in protein than millet, is very light-textured and delicately crunchy when cooked and may be used in a side dish, a salad, or a porridge. The grains are small and look like tiny, light-colored pearls; there are also yellow and tan varieties, but these are less desirable. If you have a choice, purchase quinoa that is relatively large and light-colored. Be sure to rinse quinoa before cooking, as the kernels contain an outer coating of saponin, a natural insect repellent, which leaves a bitter aftertaste. Usually sold whole.

HOW TO COOK GRAINS

The first step is to wash all grains. This is especially important with quinoa; its natural outer coating, which is usually removed by the processor, is sometimes still present and can leave a bitter, unpleasant flavor. Prior to cooking, you can dry-roast or sauté grains. To dry-roast, simply add the grain to an ungreased frying pan and place over medium heat. Shake or stir the pan continuously for 3–6 minutes (see the chart below). Remove the pan from the heat before the grains turn too dark and start to burn. Now combine with the liquid called for in the basic recipe and proceed with the recipe. Grains can also be sautéed prior to cooking — this is the starting point in making a pilaf, and is an opportunity to add aromatics such as garlic or onion or other vegetables. Use 1 tablespoon

---

Dry-Roasted Grains

Dry-roasting gives a "toasted" flavor to the grain. Place the grain in a nonstick sauté pan and place over medium heat. Shake or stir continuously for 3–6 minutes, until grains are toasted but not burned.

Cooking Times for Dry-Roasting Grains

Barley	5 minutes
Bulgur	4 minutes
Kasha	6 minutes
Millet	3 minutes
Quinoa	4 minutes

of butter or oil per cup of grain and sauté over medium heat for 6–7 minutes or until the grains take on some color.

When cooking these grains, you can substitute chicken, beef, or vegetable stock for some or all of the water called for in the recipe. As a rule, I suggest not replacing more than half the water with stock so that the subtle flavor of the grain is allowed to shine through. I also suggest that you use a low-sodium stock if you buy it canned — the full-strength commercial stocks are extremely salty, especially when used for cooking.

WHY BOILING IS BEST

I started off testing grains by cooking them like rice. One cup of grain was placed in a pot with 2 cups boiling water and ½ teaspoon salt; I reduced the heat to a low simmer, covered the pot, and cooked the grain for 10–20 minutes. I found that the grains did not cook up light and separate; I often ended up with a sticky mass. I then tried an old Chinese method of cooking rice, which is to boil it in a large quantity of water. I used 1 cup of grain in 6 cups of salted, boiling water, reduced the heat to a steady simmer, and cooked uncovered for 10–12 minutes. I then poured the grain and water into a fine colander and let it sit for 10 minutes, finishing by fluffing with a fork. The results were excellent; light, distinct grains with no starchy exterior. (Never stir grains while they are cooking. This will rupture the cells and create a starchy, sticky dish.) My guess is that the extra water helps to dilute the starch that is leached out of the grains while cooking, yielding a less sticky end product. This approach does not work with kasha, which is very delicate and is prepared by a different method (see recipe).

Master Recipe for Grains

This recipe works fine for quinoa, millet, barley, and coarse-grain bulgur. You may substitute chicken stock or vegetable stock for up to half the water.

6 cups water
1 teaspoon kosher salt
1 cup quinoa, millet, barley, or coarse-grain bulgur

Bring the water and salt to a boil. Add grain and reduce heat to a steady simmer. Cook uncovered for the time shown in the chart below. Pour into a sieve or fine colander and let drain for 10 minutes. Fluff with a fork and serve.

Makes 3 cups

Cooking Times for Basic Grains

These cooking times are to be used with the Master Recipe for Grains.

Barley (pearl)	45 minutes
Bulgur (coarse)	12 minutes, remove from heat and let sit for 5 minutes, and then drain
Millet	12 minutes
Quinoa	10 minutes

Master Recipe for Kasha

Kasha has a very soft kernel — it can be chewed raw; the kernels will break apart between your teeth — and therefore cannot stand much cooking. It turns soft and mushy almost immediately. One of the great cooking myths is that kasha should be sautéed with a coating of egg to solve this texture problem. I tried this method a number of times with disappointing results. Dana Jacobi, author of The Natural Health Cookbook, *suggests cooking kasha without the egg — she cooks it like rice but adds olive oil to the water. In a head-to-head taste test, this method was the hands-down winner, producing light, separate grains. I still believe that kasha needs lots of* onion and garlic to make it taste good, but at least this recipe produces the proper texture.

    2 cups water
    ½ teaspoon kosher salt
    1½ teaspoons olive oil
    1 cup kasha

Bring water and salt to a boil. Add olive oil and kasha. Cover and simmer over very low heat for 12 minutes. Remove from heat and let sit covered for 10 minutes. Fluff with a fork.

Makes 3 cups

Master Recipe for Fine- or Medium-Grain Bulgur

Unlike coarse-grain bulgur, fine- and medium-grain bulgur are soaked in either a hot or cold liquid. You can use water, chicken stock, or lemon juice, or a combination. Bulgur prepared in this manner is most often used in tabbouleh, a Middle Eastern salad made from bulgur, parsley, and garlic. The soaking time may vary, depending on the fineness of the bulgur and its condition. Check the texture after 20 minutes and every 5 minutes thereafter.

    1 cup fine- or medium-grain bulgur
    ½ teaspoon kosher salt
    3 cups boiling water or chicken stock or a
      combination

Place bulgur in a medium bowl. Add salt to the boiling water or stock and pour over bulgur. Let sit for about 40 minutes or until tender. Pour into a fine-meshed sieve or colander and let sit for 10 minutes. Fluff with a fork.

Makes 3 cups

Master Recipe for Pilaf

A pilaf begins with grains that have been sautéed in oil or butter before cooking in water or stock. Often garlic, onion, vegetables, and spices are added to the sauté. This recipe works for coarse bulgur, millet, and quinoa.

    1 tablespoon oil or butter
    ¼ cup minced onion
    1 teaspoon minced garlic
    ½ teaspoon dried herb
    1 cup uncooked grain
    2 cups water
    ¼ teaspoon kosher salt

1. Heat the oil or butter in a sauté pan and when hot, add the onion, garlic, and herb. Sauté over medium heat for 2 minutes. Add the grain and cook another 3 minutes, stirring occasionally.

2. Add the water and salt, bring to a simmer, and then cover and cook until almost all of the liquid is absorbed. Uncover and finish cooking (or bake in a 350° oven, covered). Allow 12–20 minutes total simmering time, depending on the grain.

3. Let grain sit uncovered in pan for 10 minutes after cooking and then fluff with a fork.

Makes 3 cups

Master Recipe for Grains with Bitter Greens

This recipe works fine with quinoa, millet, and bulgur. I cook it in the early spring when the first greens sprout. It's easy to make, and the grains benefit from the sharp flavor of the greens. Use kale, collard greens, mustard greens, or broccoli rabe.

    1 pound kale, collard greens, mustard greens,
      or broccoli rabe, stemmed and chopped
    2 tablespoons olive oil
    1 medium onion, peeled and minced
    2 cloves garlic, peeled and minced
    2 tablespoons chicken stock
    2 teaspoons white wine vinegar
    1 cup uncooked quinoa, millet, or bulgur
      prepared according to master recipe (about
      3 cups cooked grain)
    Salt and freshly ground black pepper to taste

1. Cook greens in a large pot of boiling salted water for 5 minutes. Drain.

2. Heat the olive oil in a large saucepan or skillet with a cover. Add the onion and cook over medium heat for 2 minutes. Add the garlic and cook for 2 minutes. Add the drained greens and cook for 2 minutes. Add the chicken stock, cover, and simmer for about 5 minutes or until greens are tender.

3. Stir in the vinegar and prepared grain. Add salt and freshly ground black pepper to taste.

Serves 4–6

Bulgur with Fresh Mint

Next door to the office of Cook's Illustrated, *there is a hole-in-the-wall Middle Eastern deli called King Tut that makes authentic tabbouleh; it is mostly chopped parsley with just a hint of bulgur. Most Americans, however, make tabbouleh with a high proportion of the grain and less parsley. I prefer an even balance; too much parsley produces a sharp, astringent salad, and too much bulgur dulls the light, fresh nature of this dish.*

- 1 cup uncooked medium bulgur, prepared according to master recipe (page 161)
- 3 scallions, minced
- 2 cloves garlic, peeled and minced
- 2 cups flat-leaf parsley, minced
- 3 tablespoons minced fresh mint leaves
- 3 tablespoons fruity olive oil
- 1 cup diced tomato
  Salt to taste

Prepare the bulgur as directed in the master recipe. Combine all ingredients. Add salt to taste. Let sit for 1 hour at room temperature and serve.

Serves 4

Millet with Apples, Pecans, and Currants

Millet has a wonderful nutty flavor and light texture. This simple salad can be served as a side dish or served with romaine as a salad course.

- 1 cup millet, dry-roasted (see box, page 159)
- 1 apple
- 2 tablespoons lemon juice
- ½ cup pecans, toasted and chopped
- ¼ cup dried currants or raisins
- ¼ cup diced scallions
- 5 tablespoons olive oil
  Salt to taste
- 2 teaspoons white wine vinegar

1. Prepare millet according to Master Recipe for Grains.

2. Meanwhile, peel, core, and finely dice the apple. Toss it in 1 tablespoon of the lemon juice.

3. When millet is drained and fluffed, combine it with the diced apple, the remaining tablespoon lemon juice, and all remaining ingredients except white wine vinegar. Let sit for 30 minutes.

4. Add vinegar just before serving and toss salad. Taste for seasoning and add more vinegar and/or salt if necessary.

Serves 4

Barley with Spinach, Parsley, and Chives

Barley is a relatively heavy grain and benefits from a marriage with light, refreshing greens. If you wish to substitute tougher, more bitter greens, add them at the beginning of cooking, after the garlic has been sautéed. Any leftover meat will do just fine in this recipe, although country ham or prosciutto is preferred.

- 1 tablespoon olive oil
- 1 tablespoon unsalted butter
- 1 small onion, peeled and diced
- 2 cloves garlic, peeled and minced
- 1 cup pearl barley
- 2½ cups chicken stock
- ½ cup white wine
- 2 teaspoons balsamic vinegar
- ¼ cup chopped country ham, prosciutto, or leftover meat
- 1 pound spinach, stems removed, coarsely chopped

¼ cup chopped flat-leaf parsley
2 tablespoons chopped chives
Salt and freshly ground black pepper to taste

1. Heat the oil and butter in a large saucepan until foam subsides. Add onion and cook over medium heat for 3 minutes, stirring occasionally. Add garlic and sauté for 1 minute. Add barley and stir to coat.

2. Stir in stock, white wine, vinegar, and meat. Bring to a boil, reduce heat to a simmer, cover, and cook for 30 minutes.

3. Add the spinach, stir to combine, and cook another 10 minutes or until barley is tender. Add parsley and chives and cook for 1 minute. Season with salt and freshly ground black pepper to taste.

Serves 4–6

Kasha with Stir-Fried Asparagus

You can substitute green beans for the asparagus. Be sure to use a large skillet, not a wok, and get the pan very hot before cooking (see Chapter 35 for more information on stir-frying).

⅔ cup kasha
1 tablespoon plus 1 teaspoon canola oil
1 pound fresh asparagus, tough stems removed, cut into bite-size pieces
1 tablespoon minced fresh ginger
1 tablespoon good-quality soy sauce
1 tablespoon chicken stock
2 teaspoons sugar
¼ cup chopped fresh basil
Salt and freshly ground black pepper to taste

1. Cook kasha according to Master Recipe for Kasha (page 160).

2. Heat a large skillet over high heat for 4 minutes. Add 1 tablespoon of the oil, then the asparagus, and stir-fry for 3 minutes or until barely tender. Clear the center of the pan; add the ginger, drizzle 1 teaspoon of oil over it, and mash it down into the pan with

the back of a spatula. Cook for 10 seconds and remove pan from heat. Stir asparagus and ginger to combine.

3. Return pan to heat, add soy sauce, chicken stock, and sugar and toss. Add basil and toss. Remove from heat, add kasha, and stir gently to combine. Season with salt and freshly ground pepper to taste.

Serves 4

Quinoa Salad with Shrimp and Capers

This makes a wonderful salad for lunch and can be served on a bed of lettuce. If you are not partial to capers, try substituting chopped imported olives. Don't hold back on the salt and pepper with this dish; it needs to be fully seasoned.

1 pound shrimp, shelled
⅓ cup high-quality olive oil
2 tablespoons plus 1 teaspoon lemon juice
2 tablespoons capers
1 cup quinoa
¼ cup chopped flat-leaf parsley
Salt and freshly ground black pepper to taste

1. Cook shrimp in boiling water until just cooked, about 1 minute (time will vary depending on size of shrimp). Drain. Do not overcook.

2. Mix together olive oil, 2 tablespoons lemon juice, and capers and add cooked shrimp. Let marinate refrigerated for 1 hour.

3. Meanwhile, cook quinoa according to Master Recipe for Grains.

4. Combine drained and fluffed quinoa with shrimp mixture and toss with parsley. Add salt and freshly ground black pepper to taste and 1 teaspoon lemon juice to boost flavor.

Serves 4–6

Kasha with Bow-Tie Pasta

This is a classic Eastern European dish (kasha varnishkes) that is included in every grain cook-

book published this side of World War II. I prefer to dry-roast the kasha first to enhance its flavor, I don't skimp on the onions, and I have added garlic to boot. Authentic kasha varnishkes recipes use chicken fat instead of oil or butter, which contributes a lot of flavor. Instead, I fry up a slice of bacon and use a bit of the rendered fat, although you may skip this step and just use olive oil and butter. Although I am not a big kasha fan, this grain does have an affinity for pasta, which makes this an unusual but very satisfying dish.

   1 cup whole kasha, dry-roasted (see page 159)
   1 slice bacon, optional
   1 tablespoon butter or olive oil (increase to 1 tablespoon each of butter and oil if not using bacon)
1½ cups chopped onion
   2 cloves garlic, peeled and diced
   2 cups uncooked bow-tie pasta
   1 tablespoon butter
    Salt and freshly ground black pepper to taste

1. Cook toasted kasha according to Master Recipe for Kasha, substituting chicken stock for water.

2. Heat water for cooking pasta. Meanwhile, if using bacon, fry it in a skillet or medium saucepan. Remove when cooked and reserve for another use. Add 1 tablespoon butter or oil to the skillet with the rendered bacon fat and heat. Add the onion and cook over medium heat for 7 minutes, stirring occasionally. Add the garlic and cook for 1 minute, stirring once or twice. Combine contents of skillet with cooked, fluffed kasha, cover and keep warm (place in a 300° oven).

3. Add pasta to salted boiling water and cook until pasta is just tender. Drain and return to cooking pot. Add kasha mixture, 1 tablespoon butter, and salt and freshly ground pepper to taste. Stir to mix.

Serves 6

~ 16 ~

Pasta Sauces

There are two kinds of pasta sauces: cooked and uncooked.
The former are best for colder weather, but raw sauces,
made with fresh, full-flavored ingredients,
are the sauce of choice during warmer months.

~

I once asked James Beard whether it was necessary to salt water when boiling pasta since the sauce itself would be salted. He replied, "Then you would have dull, unsalted pasta topped with sauce. Of course you need to salt the water!" Most home cooks, myself included, are rather timid about salting water, adding perhaps a pinch or two. I finally tested this by cooking pasta in 3 quarts of water three different ways: without salt, with 1 tablespoon of kosher salt, and with 2 tablespoons of kosher salt. The winner was the 1 tablespoon method, which enhanced the flavor of the pasta without overpowering it.

DRAINING AND SAUCING PASTA

The best way to sauce pasta is to drain the pasta and then return it to the warm pot, add the sauce, and then stir. This keeps the pasta from sticking together, keeps it warm for serving, and avoids the use of additional cookware (some cooks combine the sauce and pasta in a preheated bowl). Keep in mind that Americans tend to oversauce their pasta. The pasta should be coated with sauce but not drowning in it.

If you are going to serve the pasta and then top it with sauce, do not completely drain the pasta. Put it back into the pot while it is still a bit wet; this will keep it from sticking together. Or you can fully drain the pasta and then toss it in the pot with a little butter or olive oil. For any sauce with hard cheese in it — Parmesan, for example — the pasta needs to be completely drained, as the water will make the cheese separate from the sauce. Again, you can toss the pasta with butter or oil if you are not adding the sauce right away.

HOW MUCH SHOULD I MAKE, HOW LONG SHOULD IT COOK?

One pound of dried pasta will make 4 dinner-size servings. If you are serving trenchermen, 1 pound will serve only 3 persons. For a first course or side dish, you can serve 6 people from a pound. If you purchase pasta in large multipound containers, use a scale to weigh out the right amount. An electronic scale is well suited to this purpose, as a large bowl can be placed on top of it, the scale can be reset to zero with the push of a button, and then the pasta can be added and weighed.

How long should pasta cook? I am tempted

to say that pasta should be cooked until it is done, which is really the right answer. Simply take a bit out of the pot and taste it. When it is no longer tough and chewy but still has some bite, it is ready. Allow about 7 minutes for dried flat pastas and a good 10 minutes or so for most dried hollow pastas. Fresh pasta cooks almost instantly — allow about 2 minutes. Throwing strands of spaghetti up against the refrigerator door to see if they stick is fun but not very useful.

PASTA SAUCE INGREDIENTS

ANY TIME OF YEAR
Canned tomatoes are almost always better than fresh for a cooked sauce. I use Redpack brand, which are as good as and less expensive than imported plum tomatoes. I also like the ground peeled tomatoes sold under the Muir Glen label. When making an uncooked tomato sauce, it goes without saying that a good, full-flavored, fresh tomato is crucial. You can also toss hot pasta with virtually any steamed vegetable, except root vegetables, and then dress with a simple vinaigrette. Garlic, because it is easily burned and develops a heavy, unpleasant flavor, is often a problem for cooks. I prefer to sauté garlic for no more than a minute prior to adding other ingredients. I sometimes add garlic near the end of cooking instead of at the beginning (using less garlic than called for in the recipe), as this provides a brighter, cleaner flavor.

There are a few ingredients that can be used in a pinch to add depth of flavor to pasta sauces. Anchovies can be minced and then sautéed until they dissolve. Use just one or two anchovies and the sauce will acquire personality without a fishy taste. Unsweetened cocoa is good in a tomato sauce. I use just a half teaspoon with two 28-ounce cans of tomatoes. There is no chocolate flavor, but the sauce is more interesting. Capers, hot red pepper flakes, and a touch of balsamic vine-gar can perk up a dull sauce. Of course, cream can be added to a tomato sauce for depth. I also like to include just a bit — don't overdo it — of sugar to tomatoes to enhance their flavor. Use 1 teaspoon per 28-ounce can of tomatoes.

FRESH SUMMER SAUCES
When my patch of basil grows large enough for trimming, I am all set to make any number of improvised sauces based on a simple pesto. I start with a large amount of fresh basil (if I am cooking for four, I use about 2 cups of packed leaves), which is put into the workbowl of a food processor. Once all the other ingredients have been added, I pulse the machine, adding a thin stream of olive oil through the feed tube until a smooth sauce is formed. By varying the ingredients, I can make a dozen different pasta sauces. I can include a couple cloves of minced fresh garlic and leave it at that. Or I can add some grated Parmesan. I can throw in a few chopped walnuts or, if I want a heartier sauce, throw in a half cup of them. One large seeded tomato can be added for a light sauce which, if you don't mind a touch of fat, can be fortified with a little heavy cream. I can use a bit less basil and then substitute a small amount of mint leaves. I can use a small amount of onion instead of garlic or add a few capers.

The other basic summer sauce is a simple mix of chopped fresh tomatoes with herbs, olive oil, vinegar, garlic, and other flavorings. For more precise directions for summer sauces, start with Pesto, Fresh Tomato Sauce with Balsamic Vinegar, or Cold Tomato Sauce with Basil and Mint and then improvise your own recipes.

Fresh Tomato Sauce with Balsamic Vinegar

You need good tomatoes for this recipe. Do not attempt it with the store-bought variety, unless they are locally grown. This recipe will also not work with canned tomatoes. If fresh marjoram is not available, use ¼ teaspoon dried.

1½ pounds ripe tomatoes, seeded and diced
½ cup minced onion
3 garlic cloves, peeled and minced
¼ cup fresh basil leaves, shredded, or ¼ cup minced flat-leaf parsley
1 teaspoon kosher salt
½ cup olive oil
1 tablespoon fresh marjoram or ¼ teaspoon dried
1 teaspoon dried oregano
1 tablespoon balsamic vinegar
Freshly ground black pepper to taste
Freshly grated Parmesan cheese, optional

Combine all ingredients except black pepper and Parmesan in a large bowl. Let sit at room temperature for at least 1 hour. Before serving, add freshly ground black pepper. Toss with hot, drained pasta and top with freshly grated Parmesan, if using.

Makes enough sauce for 1 pound pasta

Cold Tomato Sauce with Basil and Mint

One culinary wag once defined California cuisine as the art of not mucking up great ingredients. The same is true here. If the tomatoes are earthy and aromatic, and the basil and mint are fresh-picked, you can't go wrong. Be sure to use a high-quality olive oil such as extra virgin. Do not make this recipe with supermarket or canned tomatoes.

2 pounds tomatoes, seeded and chopped into medium dice
½ cup high-quality olive oil
4 cloves garlic, peeled and lightly crushed
2 tablespoons minced fresh basil
2 tablespoons minced fresh mint
1 teaspoon kosher salt
¼ teaspoon sugar
Freshly ground black pepper to taste

1. Place tomatoes in a bowl. Heat olive oil in a small saucepan. When hot, add garlic and simmer for 4 minutes or until garlic is lightly browned. Remove from heat and let steep for 10 minutes and then pour hot oil through a strainer onto tomatoes.

2. Combine all ingredients and let marinate for at least 1 hour.

Makes enough sauce for 1 pound pasta

Pesto

Most pesto recipes call for pine nuts, but I find that walnuts work just fine, though they are more mealy than pine nuts and produce a less creamy pesto. That being said, pine nuts are quite expensive and are apt to sit on a store shelf for some time, resulting in off flavors. I suggest that you make double or quadruple this recipe, as pesto can be frozen and will keep for about 1 year in the freezer. Freeze it in ice cube trays, then remove the frozen cubes and place them in a freezer-proof plastic bag. Pesto is great for a quick pasta dinner and can be quickly thawed in a microwave (use 50% power and cook for about 2 minutes). You can eliminate the parsley and substitute additional basil.

¼ cup pine nuts or walnuts
3 cloves garlic, peeled and lightly crushed
1½ cups basil leaves, tightly packed
½ cup chopped flat-leaf parsley
1 teaspoon kosher salt
Freshly ground black pepper to taste
½ cup olive oil
½ cup grated Parmesan cheese
2 tablespoons softened butter, optional

1. Toast nuts 2–3 minutes in a 450°F oven until lightly browned. Check constantly to prevent burning. Walnuts will take a little more time than pine nuts.

2. Combine all ingredients except oil, cheese, and butter in the bowl of a food processor. Process until combined but still coarse. Add oil very slowly with machine running. Add cheese and optional butter and pulse a few times until blended.

Makes enough sauce for 2 pounds pasta

Tomato Pesto

This is the simplest pasta sauce I know of and is best made in late summer, when vine-ripened tomatoes and plenty of inexpensive fresh basil are available. Just throw everything in a food processor and you are done. Make sure that the pasta is well drained before adding this sauce; otherwise the sauce will thin out, disturbing the balance between basil and cheese. A good sauce can be made with just 1 clove garlic, although I prefer 2 or 3 to pick up the flavor.

    2 cups basil leaves, tightly packed
   ½ teaspoon kosher salt
1–3 cloves garlic, peeled
   1 medium tomato, seeded and coarsely chopped
   2 tablespoons olive oil
   ½ cup grated Parmesan cheese

1. In the bowl of a food processor, combine the basil, salt, and garlic cloves until mixture is finely chopped.

2. Scrape down sides and add the tomato. Start machine and slowly add olive oil through feed tube. Puree until smooth.

3. Remove puree to a bowl and mix in cheese.

Makes enough sauce for 2 pounds pasta

Pasta with Garlic and Parsley

This is a good recipe for a quick midweek pasta dinner. It's easy and fast and has a lot of flavor. The only important variable is the garlic. I suggest using 3 cloves, but you may determine that this is too little or too much. This also depends on the size and freshness of the cloves. Be sure to use the best olive oil you can find.

1 tablespoon kosher salt
¾ cup high-quality olive oil
3 cloves garlic, peeled and minced
¼ cup chopped flat-leaf parsley
1 pound spaghetti
   Salt and freshly ground black pepper to taste

1. Bring 3 quarts of water and the salt to a boil.

2. Meanwhile, heat the oil in a saucepan and when hot but not smoking, add the garlic and parsley. Stir, remove from heat, and let stand.

3. Cook pasta in boiling water until just tender, about 7 minutes. Drain briefly and then return to the warm pot. Toss with olive oil mixture. Add plenty of salt and freshly ground pepper to taste.

Serves 4

Pasta with Olives and Red Peppers

I like to make this pasta recipe during the winter, as it reminds me of the simply marinated, fresh-from-the-garden pasta sauces I make during our summers in the Green Mountains of Vermont.

1 cup imported black olives, pitted and coarsely chopped
2 red bell peppers, seeded and diced
½ cup finely diced red onion
2 cloves garlic, peeled and minced
¼ cup minced flat-leaf parsley
½ cup high-quality olive oil
¼ cup white wine vinegar
   Salt and freshly ground black pepper to taste
1 tablespoon kosher salt
1 pound spaghetti or angel hair pasta

1. Combine the first 7 ingredients (olives through vinegar) and let marinate at room temperature for at least 1 hour. Season with salt and freshly ground black pepper to taste.

2. Bring 3 quarts of water and 1 tablespoon salt to a boil. Cook pasta until just tender, about 7 minutes for spaghetti and 5 minutes for angel hair. Drain briefly and return pasta to warm pot. Toss with sauce.

Serves 4

Master Recipe for Tomato Sauce

This makes enough sauce for 2 pounds of pasta. It's always a good idea to make more sauce than necessary for a particular meal so that you can use the leftovers later in the week. The red pepper flakes are optional. The cocoa powder adds a little depth to the sauce — you won't be able to taste any chocolate flavor.

- 2 tablespoons olive oil
- 1 tablespoon butter
- 2 medium onions, peeled and diced
- 2 ribs celery, diced
- 4 cloves garlic, peeled and minced
- 2 cans (28 ounces) Italian plum tomatoes, drained and chopped
- 2 tablespoons minced flat-leaf parsley
- 1 teaspoon dried oregano or 2 teaspoons fresh
- 1 teaspoon dried basil or 1 tablespoon minced fresh
- ⅛ teaspoon red pepper flakes
- 1 teaspoon sugar or honey
- ½ teaspoon unsweetened cocoa powder
  Salt and freshly ground black pepper to taste

1. Heat the oil and butter over medium-high heat in large sauté pan or pot and when foam subsides add onions. Sauté over medium heat for 6 minutes. Add celery and cook another 5 minutes. Add garlic and cook 1 minute.

2. Add tomatoes to the pan. Bring sauce to a simmer and then add all remaining ingredients except salt and pepper. Simmer an additional 45 minutes. Puree in a food processor if you prefer a smooth consistency.

3. Add salt and freshly ground pepper to taste. Check for acidity — add more honey or sugar if necessary. The proper amount of sweetness is critical to good flavor.

Makes enough sauce for 2 pounds pasta

Anchovy Variation

Eliminate the cocoa powder and add 3–4 minced anchovies along with the onions.

Caper Variation

Eliminate the cocoa powder and add 1½ tablespoons drained capers along with the tomatoes.

Tomato-Ricotta Sauce with Nutmeg

A smooth tomato sauce is best for this recipe. I suggest you quickly puree the sauce in a food processor. Spaghetti is the pasta of choice for this sauce, although any egg pasta is good, too. You can also serve this with a spinach pasta.

- ½ recipe Master Recipe for Tomato Sauce
- ¼ cup grated Parmesan cheese
- ¼ teaspoon freshly ground nutmeg
- 15 ounces room temperature ricotta cheese, forced through a fine strainer
- ½ teaspoon kosher salt
- 1 pound pasta
  Freshly ground black pepper to taste
- 2 tablespoons chopped flat-leaf parsley

1. Puree tomato sauce and keep warm.

2. In a large bowl, whisk together the Parmesan, nutmeg, ricotta, and salt.

3. Cook pasta, drain well, and toss with tomato sauce. Top with ricotta mixture; add freshly ground black pepper and sprinkle with parsley.

Serves 4

Spicy Pink Vodka Sauce

I was first introduced to pink vodka sauce by a good friend who got the recipe from her mother. This is my version, arrived at by trial and error over many years. As with some of the other tomato sauces in this chapter, I find that the cream is a nice balance to the acidity of the tomatoes.

- 2 tablespoons olive oil
- 1 small onion, peeled and diced
- 2 cloves garlic, peeled and minced
- 1 can (28 ounces) crushed tomatoes

½ cup vodka
½ teaspoon red pepper flakes
2 cups heavy cream
½ teaspoon kosher salt or to taste
1 teaspoon sugar or to taste
Freshly ground black pepper to taste

1. Heat the olive oil over medium-high heat in a large skillet. Add the onions and sauté over medium heat for 8 minutes. Add the garlic and cook 1 minute. Add the tomatoes, bring to a simmer, and cook for 10 minutes. Add the vodka and cook another 10 minutes.

2. Add the remaining ingredients except black pepper and simmer another 15 minutes. Check seasonings, especially sugar and salt, and add a few grindings of black pepper.

Makes enough sauce for 1½ pounds pasta

Parmesan Variation

Add ½ cup grated Parmesan cheese about 5 minutes before serving and stir into sauce until blended.

Basic Meat Sauce with Red Wine and Brandy

Dried rosemary can be substituted for fresh, although fresh is better. Use ¼ teaspoon dried instead of the ¾ teaspoon fresh called for in the recipe. I don't bother seeding tomatoes for a cooked sauce. The cream is not necessary but balances the acidity of the tomatoes.

2 strips bacon
1 tablespoon olive oil
1 medium onion, peeled and minced
1 large carrot, minced
2 cloves garlic, peeled and minced
1 pound ground beef or pork
1 can (28 ounces) Italian plum tomatoes, drained, juice reserved
2 tablespoons minced flat-leaf parsley
¾ teaspoon minced fresh rosemary or ¼ teaspoon dried

¼ teaspoon dried oregano
1 teaspoon kosher salt
1 teaspoon sugar
2 tablespoons red wine
1 tablespoon brandy
3 tablespoons heavy cream

1. Sauté the bacon in a large skillet. Remove from pan, drain on paper towel, and reserve for another use. Pour off all but 1½ tablespoons of bacon fat and add olive oil. Over medium heat, sauté the onions for 7 minutes. Add the carrots and cook for 5 more minutes. Add the garlic and cook for 3 minutes. Add the beef or pork and cook another 10 minutes.

2. Place drained tomatoes in the bowl of a food processor and puree for a few moments until smooth, but still a bit coarse in texture. Add to the pan and cook for 10 minutes.

3. Add remaining ingredients except the heavy cream and simmer for about 45 minutes. If sauce becomes too dry, add reserved tomato juice.

4. Add the heavy cream, cook another 2 minutes, and then serve over pasta.

Makes enough sauce for 2 pounds pasta if served Italian-style (lightly sauced); 1 pound if you prefer heavily sauced pasta

Bolognese Meat Sauce

This is a wonderful, rich sauce that requires long, slow simmering to bring out the flavors. I've found that milk or cream has an affinity for tomatoes, reducing the acidity and adding smoothness and body to the sauce. I freeze this sauce in half-recipe-size containers, which is enough for 1 pound of pasta, enough to serve our family of four for a weeknight dinner. This recipe is based on a similar one by Julia della Croce in Pasta Classica.

2 slices bacon
1 tablespoon butter
1 tablespoon olive oil
1 medium onion, peeled and diced

1 rib celery, diced
1 clove garlic, peeled and minced
½ pound ground beef
¼ pound ground pork
½ cup white wine
  Salt to taste
⅔ cup milk
2 teaspoons sugar
¼ teaspoon dried marjoram
  Dash nutmeg
  Dash mace
1 can (28 ounces) Italian plum tomatoes,
  drained and chopped
  Freshly ground black pepper to taste
¼ cup heavy cream, optional

1. Heat the bacon in a large skillet or pot and remove when cooked; reserve bacon for another use. Pour off all but 1 tablespoon of fat. Add the butter and oil and increase the heat to medium-high. When foam subsides, add the onion and celery and reduce heat to medium. Cook for 8 minutes, until onion is very soft but not browned. Add the garlic and cook 1 minute. Reduce the heat to low and add the beef and pork, breaking it up with a wooden spoon. After 3–4 minutes add the wine and salt to taste — the meat should still be pink inside. Simmer for 5 minutes and then add the milk, sugar, marjoram, nutmeg, and mace. Cook for 15 minutes.

2. Add the tomatoes and simmer for 1½ hours. Add freshly ground black pepper to taste and optional heavy cream just before serving.

Makes enough sauce for 2 pounds pasta

How to Make Homemade Ravioli

Homemade ravioli takes only 30 minutes with an inexpensive
hand-cranked pasta machine.

~

Making ravioli is on the outer envelope of what I consider to be the skills necessary for good home cooking. It reminds me of learning Latin. At first, I had a hard time distinguishing between the ablative and dative, but as I grew older, a little bit of Latin came in handy. The same is true of ravioli making. It's not as difficult as it appears, and it is actually quite useful for last-minute dinners and for serving leftovers. Homemade ravioli also tastes infinitely better than the thick, gluey supermarket variety.

There are three ways to make ravioli: by hand, with an electric pasta machine, or with a hand-cranked pasta maker. I tested the hand method and found that rolling out dough to an even thickness is virtually impossible. You can make ravioli but they will be irregular at best. I also spent an afternoon working with an electric pasta machine and found that it is considerably more time-consuming than a hand-cranked machine due to the lengthy kneading and extruding processes. The cleanup is also formidable. Seven separate parts need to be carefully washed, some of them requiring a toothpick to remove tiny bits of hardened dough. By contrast, a hand-cranked pasta machine is easy to use and requires neither cleanup nor

pasta-making skill. The machine is also not particularly expensive, running about $45 retail (I use the Atlas pasta maker).

I have also tested making other types of pasta at home and have found that dried pastas (fettuccine, spaghetti, linguine, and so forth) are best purchased in a store. (Even Italians prefer store-bought for dried pastas.) After using all-purpose flour, I then tried a batch with a special semolina "pasta flour" and found that my homemade pasta was flabby and lacking in tooth. Ronzoni was substantially better. However, filled pastas are best fresh.

THE QUICK METHOD

In the old days, or even in many Italian cooking schools today, ravioli dough was made by mounding flour on a work surface, making a well in the center, and then adding lightly beaten eggs, slowly incorporating them into the flour with a fork. I have tested this method and found that it is both time-consuming and unnecessary. Just add the flour to the bowl of a food processor fitted with the metal blade, start the machine, and then add the whole eggs through the feed chute. In 10 seconds, you're done (when I tested the dough head to head against dough made by the traditional method, I could not tell the difference). Now run the dough through the thickest setting of the pasta machine (the Atlas has 7 settings — setting 1 is the thickest) four times. This kneads the dough by machine rather than having to do it by hand (the old method requires 10 minutes of hand kneading). Once this is done, the dough is run one time through each of the next settings. If you are a beginner, stop at setting 6; the dough will keep its shape better in boiling water. After some experience, you can continue on to setting 7, which produces a considerably thinner dough and also considerably more ravioli.

HOW TO FORM RAVIOLI BY HAND

If you do not have a ravioli form, here's how to make individual ravioli by hand. Once the dough is rolled to the proper thickness by machine, lay out the long sheet of dough on a lightly floured surface. The dough will be about 5½ inches wide. (Most cookbooks tell you to trim the dough so that it is only 4 inches wide. This leaves you with a long strip of dough 1½ inches wide that needs to be combined with other scraps and then rolled out a second time. Instead, use the full width and make larger ravioli.)

Start by squaring off the irregular ends (the ends of the dough will taper off). Beginning 1½ inches from one end, place 1 tablespoon of filling every 2½–3 inches along the length of the dough. The filling should be closer to the near edge of the strip of dough so that the far edge can be folded over it properly. Now fold the far side of the dough over the near side. Crimp the long edge and the two ends with a fork. Cut into individual ravioli and then crimp the sides with either a fork or a ravioli cutter, a small device that looks like a pizza wheel and cuts and crimps the dough at the same time.

HOW TO USE A RAVIOLI FORM

Instead of forming the ravioli by hand, you can use a ravioli form. There are two kinds. The most common is a rectangular metal sheet with round depressions; the form is lightly floured, thin dough is laid over it, filling is added, and then a second layer of dough is placed on top. The sheets of dough are then pressed together with a rolling pin, which also cuts them into individual ravioli. By the way, don't worry if your ravioli don't separate perfectly. Just use a knife, pizza wheel, dough scraper, or ravioli cutter to trim them once they are turned out of the form.

A newer version of ravioli form has holes rather than depressions. The sheet of dough is placed over the form, then a plastic form in the shape of an egg carton is gently pressed on the dough, creating egg-shaped depressions. The filling is added and then the ravioli are finished in the same method as above. I prefer this system. The depressions are slightly deeper and hold more filling.

COOKING RAVIOLI

Unless you cook ravioli immediately (within 30 minutes), they will start to get soggy and turn gray. They will not keep in the refrigerator. Therefore, if you are not cooking them right away, place a lightly floured kitchen towel on a baking sheet, place the ravioli on top, and then freeze. Just throw frozen ravioli into boiling water to cook. Many cookbooks state that as soon as ravioli float they are cooked (most ravioli sink to the bottom of the pot at first). This is nonsense. Ravioli will float before the filling gets hot enough. Once they float, I wait another minute or so, take one out with a slotted spoon, and eat it. If the interior is hot, then they are ready. I also suggest that you serve ravioli with a bit (a teaspoon per serving) of the hot cooking water. This keeps them from becoming sticky.

Master Recipe for Homemade Ravioli

If you use a ravioli form, setting number 6 on the pasta machine will yield 24 small raviolis and setting number 7 will produce 36. If you form them by hand, you will get 12–18 very large raviolis. If you are not cooking the ravioli immediately, place them on a cookie sheet that you have covered with a lightly floured kitchen towel and place in the freezer. Frozen ravioli can go from freezer directly into boiling water. They will take a bit more cooking time than fresh ravioli, but no more than 3 minutes total.

> 2 cups all-purpose flour
> 1 teaspoon olive oil
> 3 large eggs, lightly beaten
> 1½–2 cups filling (see recipes below)

1. In the workbowl of a food processor fitted with the metal blade, pulse flour 3 times. With the machine running, add the oil and beaten eggs until flour forms a dough. If dough is too wet, add more flour 1 tablespoon at a time; if too dry, add water 1 teaspoon at a time. The dough should hold together in a ball but not feel sticky.

2. Place dough on a lightly floured board or work surface. Form into a ball. If you plan to use setting 6 on the Atlas pasta machine, cut the dough in half, press both halves flat, and then wrap one half in plastic wrap to keep it from drying out while you work with the other half. (Cut the dough into thirds if using setting number 7.)

3. Using a hand-cranked pasta machine, feed the dough into the machine on the thickest setting (1). Crank it through. Working on a floured surface, fold the ends toward the middle (the ends will overlap) so the dough is slightly shorter than the width of the machine. Turn over to flour underside of dough. Press either of the unfolded, open edges of the dough together so it is thin enough to fit between the rollers and feed this edge into the machine, cranking the dough all the way through. Repeat the process of folding and feeding through the rollers until

the dough has been run through on setting 1 a total of four times. Notch up the machine one increment (to setting 2) and crank dough through. Lightly flour dough on both sides but do not fold up ends. Turn machine to the next setting and run the dough through once; repeat until the dough has passed once through each setting, ending with the highest setting you intend to use, 6 or 7. Flour dough only if it becomes too sticky to handle easily.

4. Square off ends of sheet of dough and cut it in half crosswise; each piece will measure about 5½ x 14 inches. Work with one piece of dough at a time, reserving the other under a damp kitchen towel. To form ravioli by hand (you can also use a ravioli form — see instructions below), first lay a piece of dough horizontally in front of you on a work surface. Starting about 1½ inches from the end of the piece of dough and 1 inch from the near edge, place 1 level tablespoon of filling every 2–3 inches along the length of the dough (each piece of dough should yield 4–6 ravioli). Now fold the dough lengthwise to cover the filling, and press the tines of a fork along the open edges to seal. Cut into individual ravioli with a fluted pastry wheel, or use a knife or dough scraper, and then crimp the cut edges with the tines of a fork.

5. Place finished ravioli on a cookie sheet that has been covered with a lightly floured dishtowel and put in the freezer. (Ravioli left at room temperature or in the refrigerator will become gluey and unpleasant.) Fill the second half of the sheet of dough in the same way and place the finished ravioli in the freezer.

6. Repeat the rolling and filling process with the remaining portion(s) of dough.

7. Just before serving time, drop ravioli a few at a time into a large pot of salted, boiling water. Cook the ravioli in batches so as not to overcrowd the pot. Cook until they have risen to the top of the water and then cook for an additional 45 seconds (or for about 2½ minutes total). Check 1 ravioli by removing it from the water with a slotted spoon. Cut in half and taste — the filling should be hot. As ravioli are cooked, remove and place in a bowl with some of the hot cooking water to keep them warm until all are done.

8. Serve with just a bit of water from the pot to keep ravioli from sticking together, or toss immediately with a sauce, browned butter, or warm stock. A small amount of cooking liquid is a good way to thin and heat a sauce.

Makes 24–36 small ravioli if made with a ravioli form; 12–18 large ravioli if shaped by hand

If Using a Ravioli Form

Flour form first. Cut each length of dough in half (one half should be about 14 inches long) and place one half over the form. If using the "egg carton" ravioli form, press plastic form onto dough to make depressions for the filling. Now add the filling in heaping teaspoons. Place the second piece of dough over the first. Use a rolling pin to press the two sheets of dough together, placing additional pressure on the raised serrated strips of metal between the ravioli and around the perimeter. Turn over onto a lightly floured surface. Ravioli should fall out of the form. If they do not separate completely into individual ravioli (and they probably won't), use a knife, dough scraper, pizza wheel, or ravioli cutter to separate them.

Spinach-Ricotta Filling

To clean and cook a large amount of spinach leaves or other tender greens for use as a filling, fill your kitchen sink ⅓ full with cold water. If the greens have been purchased in bunches, remove the lower third of the stems with a large knife (don't trim each piece individually). Agitate greens in cold water and remove directly to a large heated pot on top of the stove. Cover and steam (the water from the leaves will turn to steam) for 2 minutes. Now chop greens with a chef's knife and proceed with the recipe.

- 1 pound fresh spinach leaves
- 2 tablespoons butter
- ¼ cup minced onion

- 3 cloves garlic, peeled and minced
- 1 cup ricotta cheese
- ½ cup grated Parmesan cheese
- 1 egg yolk
- ⅛ teaspoon ground nutmeg
- 1 teaspoon kosher salt
  Freshly ground black pepper to taste

1. Wash spinach and, when it is still very wet, place in a large heated skillet, cover, and cook for just a few minutes (the water on the spinach leaves will turn into steam and cook the leaves). Remove from pan and chop fine.

2. Melt butter in a sauté pan over medium heat. Add onions and sauté for 3 minutes. Add garlic and sauté for 1 minute. Add spinach and sauté for 1 minute.

3. Mix together all ingredients in a medium bowl. Refrigerate until ready to use.

Makes enough filling for 24–36 small ravioli

Squash and Sage Filling

Butternut squash is a pale orange color, about 10 inches long, and bulbous at one end. I prefer it to acorn squash because the latter has a stringier, juicier flesh that is less well suited to a filling. However, if you can only find acorn squash, buy two, cut them in half, and then bake at 400°F until the flesh is very soft, about 1 hour. I highly recommend fresh sage leaves for this recipe — use half as much if dried. To peel a butternut squash, trim off the ends and then cut off the bulbous portion. Place the straight section upright on a cutting board and cut off the tough outer layer with a sharp chef's knife. (This is similar to trimming a stalk of broccoli.) Trim the bulbous section in the same manner, scraping out and discarding the seeds.

- 1 butternut squash, 1½–2 pounds
- ¼ pound prosciutto, minced, optional
- 1 egg yolk
- ½ cup grated Parmesan cheese
- 1 teaspoon minced fresh sage leaves or 1 teaspoon dried
- ⅛ teaspoon grated nutmeg
- 1 teaspoon kosher salt
  Freshly ground black pepper to taste

Peel and then cut squash into 1½-inch chunks. Steam or boil until cooked through. Drain. Mash enough of the squash to make 2 cups. Add other ingredients and mix to combine. Refrigerate until ready to use.

Makes enough filling for 24–36 small ravioli

Spinach Ravioli with Walnut Sauce

This recipe is adapted from one Nancy Oakes serves at the restaurant L'Avenue in San Francisco. Instead of spinach, she uses an assortment of wild greens such as nettles, dandelion greens, and so on. In fact, you can substitute any sort of greens you like, including Swiss chard, beet greens, or kale. If you use tougher greens such as kale, cook them in boiling water for 5 minutes before chopping. By the way, walnut sauce is common in the Umbrian province of Italy and is a pleasant change of pace from tomatoes or garlic and oil.

Filling
1 pound fresh spinach
⅔ cup chives
4 cloves garlic, peeled and minced
½ cup ricotta cheese
½ cup toasted fresh breadcrumbs
  Salt and freshly ground black pepper to taste

Sauce
2 cups walnuts
½ cup toasted fresh breadcrumbs

1½ cups grated Parmesan cheese
1 cup heavy cream
½ cup olive oil
  Salt to taste

Dough from Master Recipe for Homemade Ravioli, ready to roll and fill

1. For the filling, wash spinach and, while it is still wet, add to a heated skillet. Steam covered until cooked, about 2 minutes. Chop the spinach with the chives. Add the garlic, ricotta, and ½ cup of toasted breadcrumbs. Mix together and add salt and freshly ground pepper to taste.

2. For the sauce, blanch walnuts in boiling water for 1 minute and drain. Place nuts, toasted breadcrumbs, ¼ cup of Parmesan, cream, and oil in a food processor or blender and process until creamy. Add salt to taste.

3. Make and fill ravioli according to the instructions on pages 174–175. Cook in boiling water for about 2½ minutes. Add 2 tablespoons of pasta water to the sauce to thin (you may add more for a thinner sauce). Place ravioli on serving plates, top with sauce (you will end up with extra sauce; reserve it for a midweek dinner of dried pasta), and sprinkle on remaining Parmesan cheese.

Makes 18 large or 36 small ravioli on setting 7

~ 18 ~

An Illustrated Guide to Shellfish

Why you ought to shuck an oyster with a screwdriver and whether you should kill lobsters before cooking them.

~

If chicken came wrapped in a hard shell, Americans wouldn't eat it. That's the problem with shellfish. You have to work hard just to get at the food. Every time I think about preparing oysters or clams, I hesitate, stalled by visions of work gloves and oyster knives. Soft-shell crabs must have their eyes and mouths snipped off, one of the most appalling recipe directives (if you buy them frozen, this has already been done). Perhaps lobsters present the greatest moral dilemma. Do you kill it first or lower the struggling creature into the pot of boiling water? And who wants to spend 20 minutes at the sink stripping off shrimp shells?

Of course the reason we do all of this is that fried soft-shell crabs in sweet butter or steamed mussels in white wine with chives or a simple boiled lobster dinner is worth the trouble. But it helps to know what you are doing to minimize the mess and bother.

OVER 2,000 VARIETIES OF SHRIMP

Shrimp, crabs, and lobsters are all members of the same family — decapods, which means "ten feet" (decapods have five pairs of walking legs, although the first pair have evolved into pincers, and they have another three pairs of legs that are mandibles, used for feeding). Shrimp are the most prolific, with over 2,000 known species. By the way, there really is no difference between shrimp and prawns; the latter term simply refers to large shrimp, although this nomenclature varies around the world (the English often refer even to smaller shrimp as prawns). In the United States, shrimp are classified by weight. For example, tiger prawns average 2 per pound, jumbo shrimp run up to 15 per pound, extra-large shrimp are 16–20 per pound, large shrimp 21–30 per pound, medium shrimp 31–40 per pound, and ocean shrimp over 150 per pound. It is more convenient to cook with the largest shrimp available, since it is easier to shell 12 shrimp than 30. However, there is a huge difference in per pound price between tiger prawns, for instance, and medium shrimp. The former can go for $16.99 per pound, and medium shrimp are sold for under $9 per pound. That is usually sufficient motivation to spend an extra 5 minutes shelling.

LOBSTER AND CRAB VARIETIES

LOBSTER

Although the Northern lobster (the basic East Coast lobster) is the variety most often sold in the United States, one can also find the spiny lobster, which is found off the coast of Florida and has no claws. The key to a good lobster is freshness. Some experts say that a hard-shell lobster (the shell of a lobster varies in hardness throughout the year — it is hardest in the spring) makes for more tender meat, but I feel that purchasing a freshly caught specimen is most important. A lobster may spend weeks in a tank before being sold and this, in my experience, often leads to loss of flavor. Although the summer may not be the ideal time to purchase lobster (the shell is softer during these months), it is the time of year when they are likely to be freshest.

CRABS

King Crab: Found in the North Pacific, king crabs are caught in winter months by huge trawlers that set out from Alaska. The crabs are caught at a depth of several hundred feet and run 6–10 pounds, although a fully mature male can weigh as much as 25 pounds.

Dungeness Crab: These crabs are found on the West Coast, mostly around San Francisco. They weigh about 2 pounds, although they can grow up to 4 pounds.

Stone Crab: Most of the edible meat is to be found in the large claws. They are found in southern Florida.

Blue Crab: These crabs are native to the East Coast and are the variety used for soft-shell crabs.

HOW TO KILL A LOBSTER, AND OTHER MATTERS

A curious, probably apocryphal, story surfaced in the 1980s about dispatching lobsters. It was said they could be lulled to sleep by standing them on their head with their claws outstretched for balance, then rubbing their tummy until they dropped off. At this point they could be thrown into a pot of boiling water! (I have tried this and was unsuccessful at inducing drowsiness in the subject crustacean.) Although this sounds like a particularly nasty Grimm fairy tale, the stated objective was to calm the lobster before its demise, as a rush of adrenaline was thought to adversely affect the flavor and texture of the meat. I once tested this theory by blind-tasting a lobster that was calm before boiling versus one that was not. (One of my test cooks managed to lull the lobster into a calm state.) I couldn't tell the difference.

For my money, any animal should be quickly and humanely killed before cooking. Killing a lobster, however, will test the outer limits of your endurance as a meat eater. I purchased two small lobsters, keeping them in the refrigerator until just before dinner. I grabbed hold of the first one and it was full of life — its tail curled tightly under the body and its legs were working overtime. I put it on the cutting board, holding it by the body, and then quickly plunged a large chef's knife into the tail section right where it meets the body. This is supposed to sever the spinal cord and kill it instantly. Well, this lobster did a whole lot of moving around for about a minute afterward while my five-year-old daughter peeked her head around the kitchen door (she had been told to stay out of the room during this phase of the preparation) and inquired in horror, "Is it dead yet?" This is not for the squeamish and was not particularly effective. I then tried inserting a

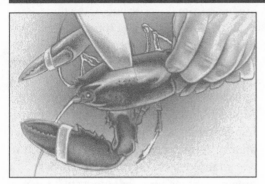

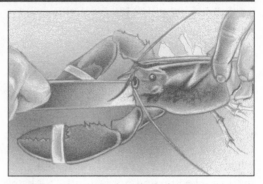

To prepare for grilling or broiling, insert a sharp 10-inch chef's knife into the middle of the body at the point where there is a small indentation.

Cut down through the front half of the body between the eyes.

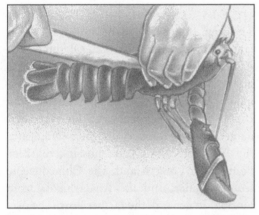

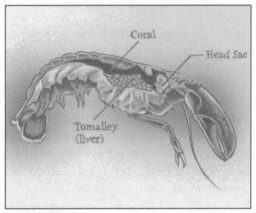

Turn lobster around and cut through the back of the body and the tail.

Crack lobster open and remove the intestinal tract (this is long, thin, and just above the tail meat), roe or coral (if any), tomalley (liver), head sac, and liquid.

chef's knife into the body of a second lobster, right in the middle of the back at the spot where there is a small indentation. At this point the knife is supposed to penetrate the head sac, which should be an effective means of killing the animal. This worked better, but there was still movement, voluntary or otherwise, in the lobster after having been dispatched. In my opinion, a lobster will die more quickly if simply plunged into boiling water, although if you plan on steaming lobster, I would kill it first using the second method. Just be warned that killing a lobster

"instantly" is a misnomer — there is nothing instant about it.

If you are going to remove the cooked meat from the shell before serving, I have some other words of warning. The first part is easy. Twist off the tail from the body and then break off the flipper end of the tail. Now you are supposed to push out the tail meat in one piece (like sliding a push-up Popsicle out of its plastic casing). Sometimes this works, but most often it doesn't. It's easier simply to use kitchen shears to cut through the underside of the tail, split it open, and then remove the meat. Don't forget to make a slit in the top of the tail meat and then remove the intestinal tract.

Getting the meat out of the claw is another matter. Some cookbooks are very delicate, suggesting that you simply crack the claw with the back of a large chef's knife. Have you ever tried to extract claw meat with just a hairline crack in the shell? Forget it. Other books tell you to take a meat pounder and whack away. This sounded more practical until I looked up and noticed bits of lobster meat hanging from my kitchen wall three feet away. Take my advice. Put the lobster claw and other smaller pieces in a plastic bag first and then start pounding. You can also use hinged lobster crackers, which work fine on small claws but are less effective with a large claw with a thick shell.

If you are going to grill a lobster or use it in a soup or stew, you need to split it in half and then clean it. A well-sharpened 10-inch chef's knife is a must here — otherwise it will be difficult to split the lobster properly (it is particularly difficult cutting through the tail without a very large, very sharp knife). Start by inserting the knife into the back at the indentation point and then cutting through the head, between the eyes. Then turn the lobster around and cut through the rest of the body and the tail. There will be a lot of liquid released, so I usually do this on a plastic cutting board placed directly in the sink. Now remove the funny-looking stuff — the stomach, roe (coral), and tomalley (liver). There is also a small sac in the head, which should be discarded. Some cooks enjoy eating the roe and the tomalley, but I simply discard both.

MUSSEL, OYSTER, AND CLAM VARIETIES

Mussels
There is one predominant variety of mussel, and that is the blue mussel (it is actually blue-black). Today, many mussels are farmed, using either the rope method (ropes are hung from floats or buoys; the mussels attach themselves to the ropes) or the pile method (piles are hammered into the seabed). Mussels can also be sown on the seabed itself and then, once they grow to an inch or so, moved to new mussel banks for final growing. Mussels should be scrubbed and the beards removed with scissors or a sharp knife. They are usually steamed, although I have been to restaurants where they are served baked, a preparation method that appears in James Beard's *American Cookery*. Mussels, just like clams, can also be served fried.

Oysters
The four basic varieties of oysters are Atlantic, European, Pacific, and Olympia. The Atlantic oyster (*Crassostrea virginica*) is grown off the East Coast and is the predominant oyster over the eastern half of the United States. Regional varieties take their names from their native growing area, hence the Wellfleet from Massachusetts, the Blue Point from Long Island, the Chincoteague from Virginia, and the Apalachicola from Florida. In general, the farther north the oyster is grown, the colder the water and the better the oyster. For example, oysters grown off Florida tend to be larger than their northern cousins but lack their salty, briny taste. In general, Atlantic oysters are mild flavored, oval, and moderately cupped (the bottom shell is convex). They are also the most difficult oyster to open.

European oysters (*Ostrea edulis*), also known as flats, have a distinctive flat shell (very little cupping) and look like little saucers. They are sometimes erroneously referred to as Belons — Belon is simply one location in Brittany where these oysters happen to be grown. (All Belons are European oysters; not all European oysters are Belons.) They have a metallic, coppery flavor, which some people love and others find unappealing.

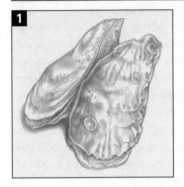

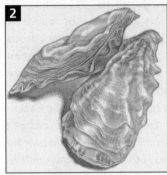

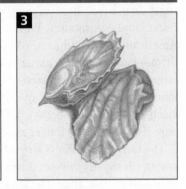

1. **Atlantic oyster**
2. **Pacific oyster**
3. **Kumomato oyster**
4. **Olympia oyster**
5. **European oyster**

Atlantic oysters are harvested from Florida to Maine, and have names that reflect their place of origin, such as Wellfleet (Massachusetts) or Apalachicola (Florida). They are hard to open, oval, moderately cupped, and have a fresh, briny flavor that makes them the favorite of most oyster lovers.

Pacific oysters are found off the West Coast (the best come from the Northwest) and have a well-cupped outer shell that is heavily scalloped. Common names, which reflect their growing areas, include Hog Island, Discovery Bay, Westcot Bay, and Quilcene. Easy to open, they have a strong fruity flavor, reminiscent of melon or cucumber. In my experience, the meat of this oyster is often quite a bit smaller than an Atlantic oyster's, although each growing region is different.

The Kumomato oyster is related to the Pacific variety, although some experts now believe that it is a separate species. I find that they have a milder, cleaner flavor than Pacifics and, in my opinion, are almost as good as Atlantics. They have a heavily ribbed outer shell.

Olympia oysters are tiny; the meat is about the size of a half-dollar. I find the flavor a bit lackluster and the texture quite soft compared to a good Atlantic oyster, and you have to open a whole bunch of them to get 1 serving.

European oysters, also known as flats, have distinctive flat shells and are relatively round. They have a metallic, coppery flavor that you either love or hate. Belons are a type of European oyster, but not all European oysters are Belons.

Pacific and Olympia oysters are predominantly available on the West Coast. The Pacific oyster (*Crassostrea gigas*) is dark, well cupped, and has a heavily scalloped outer shell. The hinge is pronounced, making opening relatively easy. Some Pacific oysters have brown and white stripes. Again, these oysters are named for their growing areas, such as Westcot Bay, Hog Island, or Quilcene. The better Pacific oysters come from

the northwest coast rather than farther south. In terms of flavor, I find that they have a fruity melon or cucumber flavor. If you are used to Atlantic oysters, you may find the Pacific oyster to be an acquired taste.

Usually considered a Pacific oyster, although some experts now believe it is a separate species, the Kumomato (*Crassostrea sikamea*) has a milder, cleaner flavor than other Pacifics, reminiscent of Atlantic oysters. (Kumomato seedlings were exported from their home base in southern Japan to Puget Sound just after World War II. The American oyster industry soon gave up on them—Pacifics were easier to grow and larger—but a few years ago, the Kumomato industry was rebuilt from specimens that survived in old oyster beds off Oregon, since pure Kumomatos no longer existed in Japan.)

The Olympia oyster (*Ostrea lurida*) is only grown off the northwest coast and is the size of a half-dollar. They are always served on the half shell rather than cooked.

Most oysters can be served on the half shell, perhaps with the exception of Atlantic oysters grown off the southeast coast. However, shucking more than a dozen oysters at a time is a lot of work (it will take a good cook about half an hour to handle a dozen oysters). It is best to purchase oysters from a store that will shuck them just before you arrive. Keep them on ice and serve them as quickly as possible. Although oysters can be purchased throughout the year, even in summer months, they taste best when consumed in colder weather — cold water produces tastier oysters. As a general rule, it is best to purchase locally grown varieties. They tend to be freshest.

CLAMS

There are three important types of clams, all of which are quahogs (the term "quahog" comes from the Algonquin word for clam, *quahaug*) and are differentiated by size. Small quahogs are called littlenecks. Medium quahogs are cherrystones, named after Cherrystone Creek in Virginia. These clams measure 2–3 inches in size. The larger quahogs are called steamers and are too big to be eaten raw, while littlenecks and cherrystones are often served on the half shell.

TRICKS FOR SHUCKING OYSTERS, CLAMS, AND MUSSELS

I am amused (irritated might be a better word) by the different designs for knives that are supposed to open clams and oysters easily. Some look like minicleavers. Others are daggerlike. Some resemble small table knives with large wooden handles. Most of these gadgets just don't work. Here's what does work.

Oysters should be opened at the hinge. It's the one point where you can actually see where to insert a knife, for it is often hard to tell where the top and bottom shells meet.

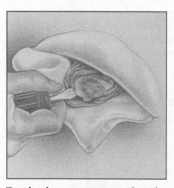 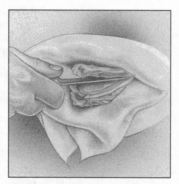 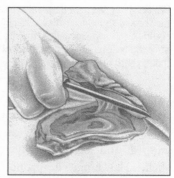

To shuck an oyster, wedge the blade of a stubby screwdriver in at the hinge. This should be relatively easy to do. Now twist to open. Wear a heavy-duty glove or place oyster on a damp dishtowel held in one hand.

Set the screwdriver aside and slide the blade of an oyster knife up under the muscle attached to the top half of the shell.

Lift off the top shell and finish cutting through the muscle.

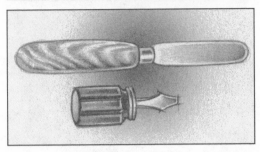

The best oyster shucker in the world is a short, squat screwdriver with a stubby blade. This will open any oyster in seconds. The other tool is an oyster/clam knife, which is relatively sharp on one edge. This is used to separate the oyster or clam from the inside of the top shell.

You need a lot of leverage here to pry the two shells apart. One day when I was struggling with the latest expensive oyster knife and having no success, I paused and started to think about which tool would work best. I went to my toolbox and came across the perfect device — a mini-screwdriver (the kind with the short, stubby handle and the short, stubby blade), which turned out to work like a charm. Just wiggle the blade into the oyster right in the hinge area and then twist, and the top shell pops open. I then turn to a traditional shellfish knife, the one with a long blade that is sharp and narrow on one side and dull and thick on the other, and cut along the inside of the top shell. If you think about it, you really do need two separate tools, because prying open a tightly closed shell requires leverage, whereas cutting the oyster from the top shell simply requires a sharp knife. Be sure to wear a heavy glove or use a thick kitchen towel to hold an oyster while opening.

Clams are more difficult to open because their shell is harder. I start by throwing clams in the freezer for 15 minutes. This does weaken them, giving the cook a slight edge. The lazy man's technique, one that always works, is simply to use a small paring knife (this is terrible for the knife — use an old

one) and insert the sharp edge into the side of the chilled clam opposite the hinge side. It should slide right in. Now cut along the inside of the top shell to detach the clam. At this point you can open the shell and serve the clam as is, on the half shell, or remove it from the shell entirely. This is not the safest method. You are working with a sharp knife, so you should place the clam in a folded-up towel or wear a heavy glove. However, the sharper and thinner the knife blade, the easier it is to insert. By the way, most cookbooks tell you to work the knife in at the side of the clam. I find that at the widest side, opposite the hinge, the line between the top and bottom shells is best defined and therefore it is easier to insert the knife at that point.

Mussels are kid's play by comparison. To test if a mussel is still alive, insert the tip of a paring knife into the open shell and hold it there. If the mussel doesn't close (this may take up to a minute), discard it. To beard a mussel, just trim off that black, seaweed-looking stuff with either scissors or a paring knife. Don't pull it out of the shell, simply cut it off.

Sautéed Soft-Shell Crabs

If you come across fresh crabs that need cleaning, here's how to do it. Rinse the crab in cold water. Snip off its head about ¼ inch behind its eyes (this will kill it instantly). Turn the crab on its back and pull off the triangular apron on the lower part of the shell. Turn over and peel back the points of the top shell and scrape out the spongy gills on both sides. Rinse again and pat dry with paper towels.

It is crucial to use only a thin coating of flour. Otherwise, the cooked crab will have a gummy exterior.

8 soft-shell crabs, cleaned
2 cups buttermilk
1 cup all-purpose flour
⅛ teaspoon cayenne pepper
Salt and freshly ground black pepper to taste

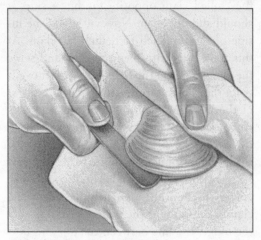

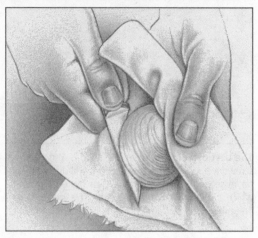

To shuck a clam, slide a clam knife into the edge of the shell. Try placing clams in the freezer 15 minutes before opening to make this step easier.

If this doesn't work, a sharp paring knife will do the trick if it is inserted on the side opposite the hinge. This is dangerous, however, as the knife can slip and cause an accident. Always use a thick dishtowel to hold the clam or use heavy-duty work gloves. This will also damage your knife blade, so it is best to dedicate one paring knife strictly for this purpose.

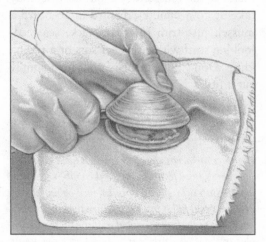

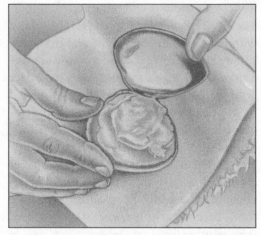

Slide knife up under the muscle attached to the top half of the shell.

Open shell. The clam can now be removed entirely using the clam knife or served as is.

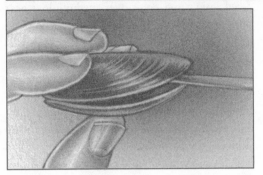

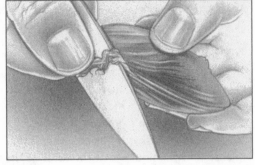

To check if mussels are alive, insert knife tip into open shell. Mussel should close within 1 minute, indicating that it is fresh (otherwise, discard).

Remove beard by cutting it off with a paring knife or scissors.

3 tablespoons butter
1 tablespoon olive oil

1. Soak the crabs in buttermilk (use regular milk in a pinch) for 2 hours in the refrigerator.

2. Combine the flour and cayenne and add salt and pepper to taste. Remove the crabs from the buttermilk, pat dry, and dredge in the flour mixture. Shake off excess flour so only a thin coating remains.

3. Heat the butter and oil in a nonstick skillet until foam subsides. Add crabs 4 at a time (or no more than can be easily accommodated in one layer) and sauté over medium-high heat for about 3 minutes per side. Serve immediately.

Serves 4

Boiled, Poached, and Steamed Lobster

I have tested steamed versus boiled lobster and can't tell the difference. Boiling is my preferred technique, but I have included a recipe for steaming for those who favor this method. Poaching will add some flavor, but it is more work and you need 4 cups of white wine, an added cost. I suggest killing lobster if you plan to steam or poach them — it ain't easy, but it is better than cooking them alive (see instructions at the beginning of this chapter). Experts say that lobster is cooked when an instant-read thermometer inserted into the tail meat reads 140°F. Eight minutes per pound is exact enough

for me. What are you supposed to do? Grab the lobster out of a pot of boiling water and shove an instant-read thermometer through the underside of the shell to get to the meat? Who thinks these things up?

Boiled Lobster

8 quarts water (seawater is best)
2 tablespoons kosher salt
4 whole lobsters

In a large stockpot, bring the salted water to a boil. Add the lobsters to the pot and cook uncovered for about 8 minutes per pound, keeping the water at a simmer (a 1½-pound lobster will take 12 minutes).

Poached Lobster

3 medium onions
4 cups dry white wine
1 bay leaf
6 whole parsley sprigs
8 quarts water
2 tablespoons kosher salt
4 whole lobsters

Cut the onions into quarters and place all ingredients except the lobsters in a large stockpot. Bring to a boil and slowly simmer for 15 minutes. Add the lobsters and simmer uncovered for 8 minutes per pound.

Steamed Lobster

1 cup dry white wine
 Small bunch chives
 Small bunch thyme
4 whole lobsters

Place 1 inch water in a large stockpot, then add 1 cup white wine and the herbs (the exact amounts don't matter very much). Place a steamer basket in the stockpot, making sure that the liquid is at the level of the bottom of the basket. Bring to a boil and simmer covered for 12 minutes. Add the lobsters, cover the pot, and simmer 8 minutes per pound.

Oyster Stew with Dry Vermouth

The best oyster stew I ever tasted was at a luncheon at Julia Child's home in Cambridge, Massachusetts. The oysters were plump and just barely cooked. The milky broth was warm and buttery, a nice contrast to the briny oysters. This is my version of that dish. She served her stew with some grilled peasant bread. I suggest you do the same even if you have to toast the store-bought variety.

24 oysters
 1 tablespoon olive oil
 3 tablespoons butter
 1 medium onion, peeled and diced
 2 cups milk
 2 cups light cream
 1 tablespoon dry vermouth or sherry
 Salt and freshly ground black pepper to taste
 ¼ cup minced flat-leaf parsley
 Hot sauce for table

1. Shuck the oysters (or have them shucked by your fishmonger — they should be cooked soon after shucking) over a bowl. Strain the oyster liquor (using cheesecloth) and reserve.

2. In a pot large enough to comfortably hold all of the ingredients, heat the olive oil and 1 tablespoon of butter over medium-high heat.

When butter has stopped foaming, add the diced onion and cook over medium-low heat until tender, about 12 minutes.

3. Add the milk, cream, vermouth, and strained oyster liquor. Bring to a boil and then reduce heat to a simmer.

4. Meanwhile, heat remaining 2 tablespoons butter in a skillet and sauté oysters until plump and edges curl, about 2 minutes. Add to the simmering milk mixture.

5. Season with salt and pepper to taste. Cook for 4–5 minutes and serve in bowls garnished with parsley. Hot sauce should be placed on the table.

Makes 4 main-course servings or 6 first-course servings

Mussels with Wine and Herbs

You can serve this dish over pasta as a main course. If you use fresh herbs, double the quantities called for in the recipe. The "beards" are the dark, seaweedlike matter that hangs out of the shell. They should be removed. Pieces of shell or other foreign matter can end up in the broth, so you should strain it through cheesecloth or a very fine strainer.

3 shallots, peeled and minced
 ½ cup dry white wine
 4 tablespoons butter
 ⅛ teaspoon dried thyme or ½ teaspoon fresh
 ¼ teaspoon dried summer savory or ¾ teaspoon fresh
 1 bay leaf
 Freshly ground black pepper to taste
24 mussels, scrubbed, beards removed

1. Bring all ingredients except mussels to a boil in a pan large enough to hold mussels. Add the mussels, reduce heat until mixture just simmers, and then cover and cook for 5–10 minutes or until mussels open.

2. Remove mussels and then strain broth. Serve mussels together with strained liquid.

Makes 4 first-course servings

Sautéed Clams with White Wine, Garlic, and Pasta

Most white wine clam sauces are thin and tasteless, having been made with canned clams. This is the real thing and is very easy to make at home. This recipe calls for littleneck clams, the smallest of the quahogs, because they are intensely sweet and flavorful.

¼ cup olive oil
12 small littleneck clams, scrubbed and dried
⅔ pound linguine
1 cup dry white wine
2 tablespoons unsalted butter
½ cup minced flat-leaf parsley
2 cloves garlic, peeled and minced
¼ teaspoon hot red pepper flakes
   Salt and freshly ground black pepper to taste

1. Bring a large pot of salted water to boil. Place a large serving bowl in a warm oven.

2. Heat the olive oil in a large skillet over medium heat. Add the clams 2 at a time. When all the clams are in the skillet, stir, increase heat to medium-high, and cover. Add the pasta to the boiling water.

3. Check the clams every minute or so. When the first clam opens, add the white wine and butter. Continue to cook, shaking the pan from time to time. When most of the clams are open, add the parsley, garlic, red pepper flakes, salt, and freshly ground pepper. Reduce heat to medium.

4. When pasta is done (about 7 minutes for dried pasta), drain and place in preheated bowl. Remove clams from the skillet, pour sauce onto pasta, and toss. Serve pasta with clams on the side of the plate.

Serves 2

Steamed Clams with Butter, Shallots, and Savory

This recipe will also work well with mussels. Be sure that the clams or mussels are tightly shut before cooking, otherwise they may not be alive and are therefore not safe to eat.

18 small littleneck clams, scrubbed and rinsed in two changes of water
½ cup dry white wine
¼ cup shallots or onions, peeled and minced
1 teaspoon minced flat-leaf parsley
1 teaspoon minced chives
½ teaspoon dried savory
1 tablespoon dry vermouth
2 tablespoons butter
   Salt to taste

1. Place clams in a large pot with the white wine, shallots, parsley, chives, savory, and vermouth. Cover and cook over high heat until liquid starts to boil. Reduce heat to maintain a steady simmer, shaking pan occasionally, until the clams open, 5–10 minutes. (If any of the clams are still not open when the others are, leave them in the pot during the next step until they do open).

2. Remove the clams to a bowl and continue cooking the sauce over high heat until reduced about 50 percent. Lower the heat to medium and stir in the butter 1 tablespoon at a time, until melted. Add salt to taste. Pour sauce over clams and serve.

Serves 2 as an appetizer

Seafood Tempura with Cornmeal

This coating can be used with shrimp, soft-shell crabs, or clams. The cornmeal provides a crispy texture, as will the Cream of Wheat, although I prefer cornmeal.

24 large shrimp or 6 soft-shell crabs or 36 clams
¾ cup all-purpose flour
6 tablespoons fine cornmeal or Cream of Wheat
½ teaspoon kosher salt
   Freshly ground black pepper to taste
1 egg
1 teaspoon minced garlic
1 tablespoon minced scallion
6 tablespoons water
½ cup beer
   Canola oil for deep-frying

1. If using shrimp, remove the shells, leaving the tails attached. If using soft-shell crabs, clean according to the instructions for Sautéed Soft-Shell Crabs (page 183). If using clams, shuck them into a colander. Pat dry the shrimp or soft-shell crabs.

2. Whisk together the flour, cornmeal, salt, and pepper. In a separate bowl, whisk together the egg, garlic, scallion, water, and beer, then combine with flour mixture. Let the batter sit for 20 minutes.

3. To deep-fry, use an electric deep-fat fryer or bring 3 inches of oil to 370°F in a large pot. Dip the seafood into the batter and drop into the hot oil. Cook for about 3 minutes. Work in batches and make sure oil comes back up to temperature before adding more seafood.
Serves 3–6

～ 19 ～

How to Cook Fish

There are nine different ways to cook fish: braising, steaming, poaching, pan-frying, sautéing, broiling, grilling, roasting, and marinating.

～

In Peter Matthiessen's book *Men's Lives,* in which he describes the life of fishermen on Long Island's South Fork, a bucket of sea bass had been overlooked in a pile of snow by one fisherman's back door. A month later, after a thaw, the fish was noticed and sent off to the Fulton Market. The fisherman was paid full price for his catch.

BUYING AND STORING FISH

To get a good sense of the problem with purchasing fish in America, it's important to understand where our fish comes from and how it's handled. First of all, most fishing boats don't go out for the day — they may spend five days to two weeks out on the ocean, so by the time the fish is sold at wholesale, it may already have been out of the water for ten days or more. These large trawlers are so expensive to move around that once they get to a fishing ground they need to stay there long enough to fill up the hold. A smart fish buyer (a wholesaler, not a consumer) will ask for the "top of the catch," which means the last fish caught during the voyage. They are physically stored on top of the catch in the hold and are therefore fresher (this reminds me of the old accounting rule "LIFO" — last

in, first out). In addition, the fish are caught in nets, not on individual lines, which means that they are often not in top condition by the time they are gutted and frozen. There has been a movement, started in the 1980s, to train fishermen to avoid the use of nets and to immediately clean and ice the fish, maintaining the proper temperature. However, most fish caught today are not handled as well as they should be. As Mark Bittman notes in *Fish: The Complete Guide to Buying and Cooking,* fish held at 50°F will deteriorate four times faster than fish held at 32°F.

SCIENCE OF COOKING

Why Does Fish Deteriorate More Rapidly Than Meat?

Fish are cold-blooded and therefore have enzymes that work effectively at relatively cold temperatures, even as low as 40°F, the average temperature of the home refrigerator. Cattle or chickens, however, are warm-blooded and their enzymes work very slowly at 40°F. Thus a beef roast will hold for a few days in the refrigerator but a piece of fish is inedible after that same amount of time. This is why I suggest storing fish tightly wrapped in plastic on top of a bed of ice. This lowers the temperature and retards the action of enzymes.

SELECTING FRESH FISH

As a result, it's hard to find a perfectly fresh piece of fish. At *Cook's Magazine,* we tested this theory by asking a well-known promoter of the hook-and-line fishing method from the state of Washington to come to New York for a couple of days and visit the Fulton Fish Market. After touring the market one morning, he indicated that over 80 percent of the fish he saw and checked out was not fresh. A survey done by *Consumer Reports* (February 1992) confirmed this trend and noted that "almost 40 percent of the fish we sampled was past its prime or suffering from improper storage."

However, you can get reasonably, if not perfectly, fresh fish at a supermarket; you just have to be careful. You can still find fish stores that buy from day boats (boats that go out just for the day). The all-natural supermarket where I shop in Boston buys much of its selection from local Gloucester fishermen. The origin of all the fish sold in the store is also posted. The tuna might come from Ecuador, whereas the pollock is caught right off the coast.

Here are some buying tips.

- The best way to determine if fish is fresh is to ask to see your selection and then to stick your finger into it! This is not always possible and is often outlawed by health regulations. If your fishmonger (or supermarket employee) will not let you do it, ask them to do so. If the flesh does not immediately return to its original shape or if the flesh exudes water, you know that this particular fish has been out of the water for some time or was not properly handled at the time it was caught.

- Make sure that the fish is sitting on ice that is still frozen, with no puddling. Melted ice is an indication of bad fish.

- Smelling fish will only tell you if that particular specimen is ready for the compost, it will not tell you if the fish is slightly off.

One reason is that some fish stores use a water solution that contains minute traces of chlorine, which masks low-level odors.

- You should also visually inspect fish. Watch out for opaque white spots or edges (signs of freezing) and eyes that are anything but clear and shiny. The surface of a piece of fish should be bright, almost translucent. Beware of unusual spots of color, which may indicate bruising or spoilage.

- "Fresh" fish, lobster, for example, that has been held in a tank for a week or two may not taste particularly fresh when you get it home. Only purchase energetic specimens.

- Fish markets are often, though not necessarily, better sources for fresh fish than supermarkets are. In New England, for example, some fish such as halibut and haddock are often bought from local fishermen. However, most salmon is now farm raised and swordfish sold on the East Coast comes from the gulf stream of Canada and is therefore not local. In general, however, supermarkets purchase precut fish from wholesalers, which usually means slightly older fish.

WHAT ABOUT FROZEN FISH?

A properly caught, prepared, and flash-frozen fish can in fact taste better than a fresh fish that was mishandled. By and large, denser, less fragile fish (scallops, swordfish steaks) will freeze better than more delicate items (trout, sole, flounder). In many cases, frozen fish is actually superior to "fresh" fish, as the latter must be very carefully prepared and held once it is caught.

If you have to freeze fish at home, use two plastic bags, one inside the other, and then make sure you have a freezer that gets very cold. The temperature should hold at 0°F (the average home freezer, however, runs about 4°–5°F and more when filled — make sure your freezer is not too full and that the cold-air vent is not obstructed). Three weeks is the longest you can reasonably expect to store frozen fish.

STORING FISH IN THE REFRIGERATOR
If you are not going to prepare fish immediately (within 2 hours), you need to store it over ice in the refrigerator or it will deteriorate rapidly. You can place crushed ice in a colander set into a bowl (so the melting ice will drain) and then place the wrapped fish (use a zipper-lock storage bag with all of the air pressed out of it — fish should not be exposed to very much air during storage) on the ice. Or carefully double-wrap fish in plastic and set it directly over ice cubes in a roasting pan. Or place crushed ice in a plastic food storage container and place the fish on top. I sometimes use those blue freezer packs instead of ice, which eliminates the problem of melting ice. Fish stored in this manner should still be prepared within 24 hours.

COOKING NOTES

SUBSTITUTING FISH IN RECIPES
There are three basic types of fish: lean white fish, dark-fleshed fish, and flatfish. Generally speaking, lean white fish are interchangeable within a category. The lean white fish category includes blackfish, cape shark, cod, dogfish, grouper, haddock, ocean perch, pollock, red snapper, rockfish, scrod, sea bass, sea trout, striped bass, tilefish, trout, and whiting. The dark fish are not easily interchangeable since most of these fish have distinctive and often very strong flavors. This list includes bluefish, mackerel, mahimahi, pompano, tuna, salmon, shark, and sturgeon. The flatfish family includes sole, turbot, and flounder. Halibut is an in-between fish, mildly oily with firm texture. Fish steaks are salmon, swordfish, tuna, halibut, mahimahi, shark, sturgeon. If a recipe calls for a salmon steak, you might substitute tuna or swordfish steaks. Monkfish and lobster are usually interchangeable (the textures are quite similar).

A survey of fish stores in the Boston area found that the top seven fish in terms of consumer popularity are scrod, salmon, swordfish, haddock, sole, flounder, and halibut. By the way, scrod is a New England term for a small (2–3 pounds) hake, haddock, cod, or pollock. A 4–8 pound specimen would go by its regular name. Larger fish are sold to restaurants and then cut up into smaller pieces, which sometimes appear on menus as "scrod" even though they come from larger fish. Cod is the blandest fish in this category; haddock has a little more flavor, hake is sweeter, and pollock, which has darker flesh, is more flavorful although not more "fishy."

THE 10-MINUTES-PER-INCH THEORY
James Beard introduced me to this cooking method, which is referred to as the Canadian cooking theory. Simply put, cook fish for 10 minutes per inch of thickness at relatively high heat (450°F or so). This applies to grilling, baking, broiling, even sautéing over a medium-high heat. This method is most commonly used when preparing steaks such as swordfish or salmon steaks, which are thick, and there is some leeway in cooking times. I prefer my fish somewhat less cooked and allow 8–9 minutes per inch. This is a very rough timetable, however, and fish needs to be watched carefully to avoid overcooking. I also prefer to stop cooking fish when the center is not quite cooked. Like a custard, fish will continue cooking on its own.

NINE WAYS TO COOK FISH

There are really nine major ways to cook a piece of fish: braising, steaming, poaching, pan-frying, sautéing, broiling, grilling, roasting, and marinating (seviche).

BRAISING

To braise, sauté the fish (usually a thick steak is called for here) in an ovenproof skillet or Dutch oven with olive oil until lightly browned on both sides. Remove the fish and add onion, garlic, shallots, or other similar ingredients. Sauté for 5 minutes, add about ½ cup of braising liquid (wine, stock, water, vinegar, or a combination) and any additional ingredients (anchovies, capers, et cetera), and bring to a simmer. Add fish, place in a 400°F oven and cook 8–10 minutes per inch of thickness.

Braised Tuna with Ginger and Soy

Toasted (or roasted) sesame oil is not the same as regular sesame oil. The former, used widely in Oriental cooking, has a rich, nutty flavor, and regular sesame oil is not a substitute. If you cannot find it — in the Oriental foods section of your supermarket or at a health food store — simply prepare the recipe without it.

> 5 tablespoons rice wine vinegar
> ⅓ cup dark soy sauce
> ⅓ cup white wine
> ⅛ teaspoon ground cardamom
> ½ teaspoon sugar
> 3 tablespoons peanut oil
> Tuna steaks to serve 4
> 1 small onion, peeled and diced
> 1 tablespoon minced fresh ginger
> 3 cloves garlic, peeled and minced
> 2 teaspoons toasted (Oriental) sesame oil
> 2 scallions, diced
> Salt and freshly ground black pepper to taste

1. Heat oven to 375°F. Combine vinegar, soy sauce, white wine, cardamom, and sugar in a small bowl.

2. Put 2 tablespoons of the peanut oil into a Dutch oven or flameproof casserole over medium-high heat. When oil is hot, add tuna steaks (sauté in batches if pan is crowded) and sauté for about 2 minutes. Turn tuna over and sauté for 1 additional minute. Remove steaks from pan and keep warm.

3. Add remaining tablespoon of peanut oil to pan and sauté onion and ginger for 4 minutes over medium heat. Add garlic and sauté for another 3 minutes. Add the reserved vinegar mixture and bring to a boil.

4. Add the tuna steaks, cover, and bake in preheated oven until done, about 7 minutes for 1-inch-thick steaks (check after 5 minutes; if steaks are closer to ½ inch thick, check after just 4 minutes). Remove steaks from pan and keep warm.

5. Place pan on top of stove and reduce liquid over medium-high heat for 1–2 minutes. Add sesame oil, scallions, and salt and pepper to taste and continue to cook for another minute. Pour liquid over reserved tuna steaks and serve.

Serves 4

Braised Salmon Puttanesca

Puttanesca sauce is made with tomatoes, olives, garlic, and anchovies. Salmon is a rich, oily fish and can easily stand up to this double-barreled sauce. You can drink a light red wine with this dish. If you do serve white wine, make it full-bodied.

> 4 salmon steaks, about 1 inch thick
> 1 can (28 ounces) tomatoes
> 1 tablespoon butter
> 3 tablespoons olive oil
> 1 medium onion, peeled and minced
> 3 cloves garlic, peeled and minced
> ¼ cup dry red wine
> 1 teaspoon minced fresh rosemary or ¼ teaspoon dried
> 2 tablespoons balsamic vinegar
> 12 imported black olives, pitted and chopped
> 4 anchovy fillets, chopped
> 1 tablespoon capers
> Salt and freshly ground black pepper to taste

1. Heat oven to 375°F. Remove pin bones (the small, thin bones that stick straight up) from the salmon with a pair of needlenose pliers. Drain tomatoes in colander, then cut them in half and seed them.

2. In a skillet large enough to hold all 4 steaks in a single layer, heat the butter and 2 tablespoons of the olive oil over medium-high heat. When the butter stops foaming, add the steaks and sauté quickly, about 2 minutes. Turn over and sauté another minute. Transfer salmon to a plate and keep warm.

3. Add the remaining tablespoon of olive oil to the skillet and sauté the onion for 5 minutes. Then add the garlic and sauté for 2 minutes. Add the tomatoes, red wine, rosemary, and vinegar and bring to a boil. Return steaks to pan, cover, and bake in the preheated oven about 10 minutes (check after 7 minutes). Remove steaks and keep warm.

4. On top of the stove, bring sauce in pan to a boil, reduce to a simmer, and cook for 3 minutes. Add olives, anchovies, and capers and simmer for 2 minutes. Add salt and freshly ground pepper to taste.

5. Serve steaks with sauce spooned over each serving.

Serves 4

STOVETOP STEAMING

There are many varieties of steamers (see Chapter 1), but you will need a particularly large one to handle fish. In fact, you can purchase an oval steamer which is perfectly suited for fish cookery. If, however, you do not have a steamer, simply pour about 1 inch of water into a large pot. Next, on the bottom of the pot, arrange 2 or 3 small objects (I use cookie cutters, but you might try thick jar tops or custard cups) upon which to support a metal cake rack above the level of the water (the cake rack will have to be smaller in diameter than the pot). Place the fish on a heatproof plate, then set the plate on the cake rack. Steam until done, not more than 10 minutes per inch. A whole fish will steam in 12–15 minutes. Be sure that the plate is substantially smaller in diameter than the pot, otherwise it will be almost impossible to remove without burning your hand or spilling the fish.

Steamed Halibut with Roast Garlic–Parsley Puree

Roasted garlic has a great deal of flavor that is deep and mellow rather than sharp and biting. Some cooks poach their garlic in milk for 10 minutes before roasting to add moisture — I don't find this necessary or worth the time, especially in a recipe in which the roasted garlic is part of a sauce. Use the leftover garlic as a spread on bread or with salad dressings or pasta sauces.

  1 head garlic
  1 teaspoon olive oil
  ½ cup chicken or fish stock, preferably homemade or low-sodium
  1 cup flat-leaf parsley leaves, stems removed
  2 teaspoons lemon juice
    Salt and freshly ground black pepper to taste
  2 halibut steaks

1. Heat oven to 350°F. With your palm, roll the garlic head back and forth across the counter and remove excess papery skin. Remove about ½ inch from the top of the garlic so that the interiors of most of the cloves are exposed. Place garlic in a square of aluminum foil and drizzle lightly with oil. Gather foil around garlic and twist top together to make a small, well-sealed package. Roast for 1 hour, remove from oven, and open foil carefully.

2. Just before garlic is done, bring stock to a simmer in a medium saucepan. Add the parsley, cover, and steam for 2 minutes. Drain the parsley, reserving the stock.

3. Process steamed parsley leaves in a food processor. Remove 4 large cloves from the roasted head of garlic, squeeze out soft flesh, and add to the bowl of the food processor with the lemon juice. Pulse until combined. With machine on, add reserved stock in a steady stream until sauce is smooth. Add salt and pepper to taste.

4. Wash the halibut and pat dry. Steam until done, about 8 minutes per inch of thickness.

5. While fish is cooking, reheat sauce. Serve the halibut with the sauce spooned over it.

Serves 2

Whole Steamed Fish with Ginger

This is an extraordinarily simple preparation. Simply steam the whole fish on a plate covered with the sauce. This recipe is based on a similar one I found in Bruce Cost's book, Ginger East to West. *Bruce is the restaurateur-chef at Ginger Island, which is located on Fourth Street in Berkeley, California. Instead of a wok, I use a large stainless steel steamer, although any large pot with some sort of rack will do.*

  1½ pounds whole fish, cleaned and rinsed
   1 teaspoon salt
   2 teaspoons light soy sauce
   1 tablespoon dry sherry
   1 tablespoon peanut or vegetable oil
   1 teaspoon toasted (Oriental) sesame oil
  ¼ teaspoon sugar
   1 tablespoon finely diced fresh ginger
   2 scallions, chopped into 1-inch lengths

1. Score fish (make cuts with a knife) at 1-inch intervals and rub salt over entire fish. Combine the soy sauce, sherry, oils, and sugar and set aside.

2. Place a steaming rack in a wok or large pot and add water until the level is 1 inch below the rack (you can also use a steamer). Cover and bring to a boil.

3. Place fish on a heatproof serving platter, pour the sauce over it, and decorate with the ginger and scallion. Place on rack in pot and steam for 12–15 minutes, or until the fish is easily pierced with the tip of a sharp knife.

4. To serve, remove fillets from one side of the fish and serve as one portion. Next, remove the head, bones, and tail in one piece and discard. Serve the remaining fillets to the other diner. Serve fillets with sauce spooned from the serving platter.

Serves 2

POACHING

Instead of following the usual procedure for poaching, which involves bringing the liquid to a boil, adding the fish, and then poaching for 10–15 minutes, I simply combine all ingredients, bring the liquid to a boil, and then turn off the heat. The fish sits in the hot liquid for about half an hour as it gently cooks. The liquid can be water, wine, or stock or a combination, and the flavorings can include lemon zest, bay leaves, parsley, salt, peppercorns, celery, cilantro, or even spices such as crushed cardamom seeds. You may wish to wrap the fish in cheesecloth so that it is easier to remove from the liquid (poached fish is very delicate and can easily break apart).

Salmon Poached in Salt and Pepper

The strong flavor of salmon can stand up to this heavily spiced poaching liquid. Serve with steamed green beans and roasted new potatoes. Leftovers are good served cold for lunch.

  3 pounds salmon (one piece), with skin on
  1 quart chicken or fish stock, homemade preferred
  ¼ cup black peppercorns
  ¼ cup kosher salt

1. Using needlenose pliers, remove the bones sticking up through the center of the fish (see page 63). Cut salmon in half and wrap each piece in cheesecloth. To a large pot add the salmon, stock, and enough cold water (about 3 cups) to cover the fish.

2. Place the peppercorns in a plastic storage bag and crush using a meat pounder or the bottom of a heavy saucepan. Add pepper and salt to liquid.

3. Bring to a boil, remove from heat, and let salmon sit in the water for about 30 minutes.

4. Remove salmon from water, unwrap, and cut into pieces before serving.

Serves 6–8

PAN-FRYING

Pan-frying is a quick, easy way to fry fish that uses only about ½ cup of oil. The oil is heated in a large skillet, the fish is dredged in egg and then in a combination of flour and cornmeal or flour and Cream of Wheat, and then it is fried for just a few minutes per side, depending on thickness.

Pan-Fried Striped Bass with Garlic–Ginger Sauce

You can substitute grouper, bluefish, or mahimahi for striped bass. If you use a thin fillet, make sure that you reduce the cooking time accordingly. Parsley may be used in place of scallions.

 2 eggs
 ½ cup all-purpose flour
 ½ cup fine cornmeal
 ½ cup peanut oil
   Salt and freshly ground black pepper to taste
 1–1½ pounds skinned striped bass fillet, rinsed and patted dry with paper towels
 1 tablespoon olive oil
 1 teaspoon toasted (Oriental) sesame oil
 1 tablespoon finely minced garlic
 1 teaspoon finely minced fresh ginger
 ¼ cup dry white wine
 1 tablespoon soy sauce
 1 tablespoon minced scallions, optional

1. Lightly whisk the eggs in a medium bowl. Stir flour and cornmeal together thoroughly and place on a large plate. Heat a large nonstick skillet over medium-high heat for 3 minutes.

2. Add peanut oil to cover the bottom of the pan by at least ⅛ inch. Heat oil until it shimmers but does not smoke. Lightly salt and pepper fillet and then lightly dredge in the flour mixture, in the beaten egg, and back again in the flour. Shake off excess flour. Place fish in pan and raise heat to high. Reduce heat to medium after 1 minute. Adjust heat so that oil does not smoke.

3. Cook for 4 minutes on one side, turn and cook 3–4 minutes on the other side. Fish is done when a thin knife passes through the fish easily. Remove pan from heat and transfer fish to paper towels to drain.

4. Wipe pan clean and return to stove over high heat. For sauce, add olive and sesame oils, garlic, and ginger and sauté for 30 seconds. Add white wine and cook for 30 seconds. Add soy sauce and stir for 15 seconds, scraping up any bits from the bottom of the pan. Remove from heat and stir in optional scallions. Place fish on serving plates and lightly top with sauce.

Serves 4

SAUTÉING

A simple sauté is best with a thin fillet of fish. I suggest that you use mostly butter here, and not oil, because it will add flavor and result in a crisper outside coating (some oil is necessary to prevent the butter from burning). To sauté, simply dredge the boned fillet in flour, cornmeal, or fine dry breadcrumbs (or a combination) to which you have added salt and pepper. Heat unsalted butter and olive oil in a skillet or frying pan over medium-high heat. Sauté the fillets until brown and crispy on both sides. Do not crowd the pan, and if you have to do more than one batch, let the pan come back up to temperature in between batches. The secret, as in all sautéing, is to make sure that the pan is sufficiently hot to quickly sear the outside coating and create a crispy exterior and a juicy interior but not so hot that the butter burns.

Sautéed Sole with Parsley and Butter

The key to this dish is the cooking temperature. If the pan gets too hot, the butter will burn. If it's too low, the fish will be soggy. You want a nice crisp exterior to complement the tenderness of the fish. You can cook all 4 fillets at once by using two sauté pans. The sole is best served immediately, rather than letting it sit in a pre-heated oven. You can also try this dish with any other thin, delicate fish fillets (these might include flounder, small sea bass, red snapper, or trout).

> ½ cup fine dry breadcrumbs
> 1½ teaspoons kosher salt
> ¼ teaspoon freshly ground black pepper
> 4 fillets of sole, about 1½ pounds in all
> 1 tablespoon olive oil
> 4 tablespoons butter
> 2 tablespoons lemon juice
> 1½ tablespoons minced flat-leaf parsley
> 1 lemon, cut into wedges

1. Put a large ovenproof platter in the oven and then heat to 250°F. Combine the breadcrumbs, salt, and freshly ground pepper in a plastic bag. Wash the fillets and pat dry with paper towels. Add 1 fillet at a time to the bag, shake, remove from bag, and shake off excess breadcrumbs. Dredge only as many fillets as will fit in the pan comfortably (probably 2 fillets).

2. In a large sauté pan, heat the oil and 2 tablespoons of the butter. When butter has stopped foaming, sauté 2 fillets over medium-high heat (be careful not to let the butter brown, but the pan needs to be hot), 1–2 minutes on each side. Remove to the heated platter. Add a little more butter, dredge the remaining fillets, and then sauté. Remove these fillets to the platter.

3. Add the rest of the butter to the pan over high heat and cook for 15 seconds. Remove from heat and stir in lemon juice and parsley.

4. Pour sauce over fillets and serve. Serve fish with lemon wedges.

Serves 4

BROILING

The simplest method for cooking fish is to broil it. Brush fish with a bit of oil or butter. Cook the fish 8–10 minutes per inch. Thin fillets do not have to be turned; thicker steaks do.

Broiled Red Snapper

Broiling is easy, it can be done in the dead of winter, and a great deal of precision can be attained by adjusting the distance from the heat source. A skillet works well for broiling, although a nonstick skillet should not be exposed to excessive heat. Be sure to use a thick oven mitt when handling the skillet after it is removed from the stove. On more than one occasion I have forgotten that a skillet handle is burning hot. These days I always leave the oven mitt sitting on the handle as a reminder.

> 2 red snapper fillets, scaled (about 1½ pounds)
> 1 tablespoon olive oil
> Salt and freshly ground black pepper to taste
> ¼ cup dry white wine
> ¼ cup chicken stock
> ¼ cup minced fresh chives, plus additional chives for garnish
> 1 tablespoon minced fresh tarragon
> 2 tablespoons butter
> 1 cup diced fresh or canned tomatoes
> 1 teaspoon lemon juice

1. Set oven to broil. Brush fish with olive oil and season with salt and pepper. Lightly brush the bottom of a skillet with oil.

2. Place fish skin side up in skillet and set skillet in oven under broiler. Thin fillets should be 2–3 inches from heat source; thicker fillets about 6 inches. Broil until cooked, 8–9 minutes for 1-inch-thick fillets and just a few minutes for thinner pieces of fish. Turn the fillets for the last minute of cooking.

3. Remove fish to a plate, cover with aluminum foil, and place on top of stove to keep warm. Place skillet on a burner over medium heat. Add wine and stock, bring to a simmer, and then cook for 30 seconds. Add herbs and butter and stir until butter melts. Add tomatoes, increase heat to medium-high, and cook another minute. Add salt and pepper to taste and lemon juice. Spoon sauce over fillets and garnish with additional chives.

Serves 4

GRILLING

Grilling is the most difficult method of preparing fish, as the heat is variable and sticking is always a problem. Fish steaks and shellfish can be cooked directly on the grill; use a fish basket for fillets (I only grill fairly thick fillets with the skin on) and whole fish. A good basket has a good long handle and is made of nonstick material. Use moderate heat when grilling fish. The easiest seafoods to grill are shrimp (they cook in under 2 minutes) and thick steaks such as swordfish and tuna. Other shellfish are best cooked through other methods (they will turn out moister), and fillets and whole fish are problematic, hard to judge in terms of cooking time, and will stick unless the basket or grill is carefully prepared. Remove fish steaks from the grill when they are still slightly undercooked. The residual heat in the steak will finish the cooking process. For more information about grilling, see Chapter 33.

Grilled Swordfish Steaks with Capers, Tomatoes, Spinach, and Balsamic Vinegar

Choose steaks that will serve 1 person each. If only larger steaks are available, purchase 2 and then serve half a steak per person. You can also broil the steaks.

¼ cup olive oil
1 tablespoon minced garlic
1 pound spinach, stemmed, washed, and coarsely chopped
2 cups seeded and diced fresh tomatoes or 2 cups chopped canned tomatoes
1 tablespoon capers
2 teaspoons balsamic vinegar
½ teaspoon sugar
 Salt and freshly ground black pepper to taste
4 swordfish steaks, approximately 1 inch thick, or enough fish for 4 people

1. Heat a charcoal or gas grill until very hot.

2. In a skillet or sauté pan, heat olive oil until very hot. Add garlic, reduce heat to low, and cook for 2 minutes, until garlic is light brown. Add spinach and cook, stirring occasionally, for 2 minutes, or until wilted. Add tomatoes, capers, vinegar, and sugar. Cook for 10 minutes over medium heat. Reduce heat to a gentle simmer.

3. Salt and pepper the swordfish and place on the heated grill. Cook for about 4 minutes per side or until a thin knife easily pierces the center of each steak. Remove from heat

4. Place spinach sauce on plates and top with swordfish.

Serves 4

ROASTING

Roasting is the best method for cooking a whole fish. Use a hot oven, 450°F, and baste with oil or melted butter during cooking. I do not suggest roasting shellfish such as mussels and clams; steaming is the preferred method for these.

Roast Whole Fish with Hot and Sour Sauce

You can use this recipe with any whole fish that weighs 3–6 pounds (haddock is an inexpensive choice). The fish is done when the flesh is easily pierced to the bone with the tip of a small sharp knife.

1 whole fish (3–4 pounds), scaled and gutted, with head left on
2 tablespoons olive oil
1 tablespoon minced onion
2 teaspoons minced garlic
1 tablespoon minced fresh ginger
¼ teaspoon cayenne pepper
3 tablespoons soy sauce
3 tablespoons rice wine vinegar
1 teaspoon toasted (Oriental) sesame oil
1 cup low-salt chicken stock
½ cup chopped scallions for garnish

1. Preheat oven to 450°F. Score (make cuts with a knife) each side of the fish two or three times to the bone. Place fish in a lightly oiled baking dish and cook until done, 20–30 minutes.

2. While fish is cooking, place olive oil in a skillet over medium-high heat. When oil is hot, about 3 minutes, add onion. Sauté over medium heat for 3 minutes. Add garlic and ginger and cook for 1 minute. Add cayenne and stir. Add soy sauce, vinegar, and sesame oil and stir. Add stock, bring to a simmer, and then reduce heat to low.

3. Fillet fish (leave skin on) and serve with sauce in heated deep dinner plates or shallow bowls and garnish with scallions.

Serves 4

SEVICHE

This simple method involves no cooking at all. The acid in citrus juice or vinegar transforms the protein in the fish in a manner sim-

ilar to cooking with heat. Seviche (marinated raw fish) does not have to be limited to scallops — you can also try it with flatfish such as sole or flounder or with mackerel — but do not try making it unless the fish is briny fresh.

Seviche of Scallops

Absolutely fresh scallops can be very thinly sliced and marinated for only 15 minutes (the recipe below calls for 2 hours of marinating and thicker slices). To serve, place them directly on serving plates and then drizzle with the vinaigrette in which they were marinated.

¼ cup lemon juice
¼ cup orange juice
¼ cup high-quality olive oil
1 tablespoon scallions, minced
1 tablespoon minced flat-leaf parsley
1 tablespoon minced fresh basil
Salt and freshly ground black pepper to taste
1 pound sea or bay scallops, sliced into ½-inch-thick pieces
Lettuce for serving, optional

Combine all ingredients except scallops and optional lettuce in the workbowl of a food processor or in a blender. Pulse to combine. Place scallops in a glass bowl, pour vinaigrette over them, cover, and refrigerate for 2 hours, turning scallops after 1 hour. May be served on a bed of lettuce.

Serves 4

～ 20 ～

Basic Sauces for Fish and Shellfish

Most sauces for fish are variations on a few simple themes.

～

In Vermont, we have summer season tickets to a small firetrap of a theater with narrow aisles and uncomfortable seats, but with a stellar acting company. They launch the season with an overreaching drama — we tend to skip opening night — but then things take off with the musicals and comedies. I am always amazed at how a small group of people can create the feeling of a crowd by doing double duty; changing roles and costumes in just seconds. It's a bit like the famous Russian military parades, the same circle of tanks endlessly passing the review stand.

I feel the same way about fish sauces. There are only a few master recipes, the rest being variations on a theme. The headliners include an Asian sauce, a tomato-based sauce, a pesto-based sauce, and a sauce based on greens or herbs.

Soy-Ginger Sauce with Scallions

This is the basis for most Asian sauces. Be sure to use Oriental sesame oil, which is nut brown and has a deep, toasted flavor. A high-quality soy sauce is also crucial. Be sure to use a Japanese "shoyu" sauce, which is generally much lighter tasting than the Chinese product. I use Kikkoman, as it is both high in quality and widely

available. This sauce is quite good with grilled fish steaks and can stand up to oilier, stronger-flavored fish such as bluefish or mackerel.

1 tablespoon olive oil
1 teaspoon toasted (Oriental) sesame oil
2 teaspoons minced garlic
1 teaspoon ginger, peeled and minced
¼ cup white wine
1 tablespoon soy sauce
1 tablespoon scallions, minced, optional

Just prior to serving, whisk ingredients together or blend with a food processor or immersion blender.

Makes about ½ cup

Provençal Pesto with Lime

Pesto is a relatively thick sauce made from herbs, pine nuts, Parmesan cheese, and olive oil. This pesto can be made with most any combination of fresh-from-the-garden herbs and is lighter than the classic Italian recipe, which makes it ideal for fish. Be sure to use a high-quality olive oil. I serve this pesto with any lean roundfish, such as bass, grouper, or cod.

1 cup fresh basil leaves
2 tablespoons fresh flat-leaf parsley leaves

2 tablespoons minced fresh herbs such as cilantro, oregano, or tarragon or a combination
2 cloves garlic, peeled and minced
¼ cup freshly grated high-quality Parmesan
¼ cup dry white wine
1 tablespoon lime juice
¾ cup high-quality olive oil
Salt and freshly ground black pepper to taste

Place first 7 ingredients in the bowl of a food processor and pulse until basil and parsley are coarsely chopped. With machine on, pour olive oil in a thin steady stream into mixture. Add salt and pepper to taste.

Makes about 2 cups

Tomato Salsa with Mint

This sauce is best with perfectly ripe, richly perfumed tomatoes. Let ingredients sit at room temperature for at least 1 hour before serving. This is good with any fish.

2 cups diced fresh tomatoes
3 cloves garlic, peeled and minced
2 tablespoons minced fresh basil
2 tablespoons minced fresh mint
½ cup high-quality olive oil
1 tablespoon white wine vinegar
1 teaspoon kosher salt

Combine all ingredients in a medium bowl. Cover and let sit at room temperature for at least 1 hour before serving.

Makes about 3 cups

Tomato Salsa with Olives, Capers, and Anchovies

This is a variation on a classic puttanesca sauce, which is usually served with pasta. Fresh, ripe tomatoes are essential — do not try this recipe with canned tomatoes or winter tomatoes. If you do not have fresh rosemary, use only ½ teaspoon

dried and make sure that it is finally minced. Dried rosemary has tough, hard needles — the easiest way to mince them is in a small spice or coffee grinder. They can also be minced with a knife if a small amount of olive oil is poured over the needles first, or pulverized with a mortar and pestle. This is best served with a full-flavored fish such as swordfish.

2 cups diced plum tomatoes
2 tablespoons capers
¼ cup high-quality olive oil
½ cup imported black olives, pitted and chopped
2 anchovy fillets, rinsed and minced
1 tablespoon balsamic vinegar
2 teaspoons minced fresh rosemary
Salt and freshly ground black pepper to taste

Combine all ingredients in a small bowl. Let marinate at room temperature for at least 1 hour before serving.

Makes about 3 cups

Sauce of Greens, Garlic, and Anchovies

There are hundreds of variations of this sauce, and you can substitute different greens and herbs depending on what is available. Make sure that the greens are tightly packed when you measure them. Serve this with any firm, white-fleshed fish.

2 cups spinach, washed, tough stems removed
2 cups watercress, washed, tough stems removed
¼ cup flat-leaf parsley, washed, tough stems removed
¼ cup fresh basil leaves
1 thick slice of stale country bread, torn into pieces
1 tablespoon capers
3 anchovies
1 clove garlic
1 tablespoon white wine vinegar
Salt and freshly ground black pepper to taste
½ cup olive oil

1. Place wet spinach and watercress in a sauté pan over medium heat and cook for 1 minute covered. Remove from heat.

2. Place all greens, including parsley and basil, in the bowl of a food processor and process until smooth. Add remaining ingredients except olive oil and process until just mixed. With machine on, add olive oil through feed tube in a very thin stream. Process until sauce becomes thick and cohesive.

Makes about 3 cups

Boning, Butchering, and Carving

Once you understand the basic architecture of poultry and lamb,
preparing them for cooking is easy.

~

The best carver I know is an architect. He deconstructs a duck, chicken, or turkey with infinite precision, as if he were pulling down an old farmhouse clapboard by clapboard. He is not fooled by the exterior; he has a keen understanding of the underlying bones and their structure. Even a chicken thigh is exquisitely rendered of its meat and neatly sliced. He understands that cutting up a chicken or carving a leg of lamb is more a matter of bones than meat.

PREPARING A WHOLE CHICKEN FOR ROASTING

Let's start with the chicken you just purchased at the supermarket, which you wish to roast whole. Position it with the legs sticking up, the way most people serve a whole turkey for Thanksgiving. In this position, the bird is really upside down, with the breast side up and the backbone sitting on the work surface (the breastbone separates the two breast halves). Reach inside the body cavity and remove the giblets (the liver, heart, gizzard, and sometimes the kidneys), which are usually packed there, and then look to make sure that the kidneys have been properly removed (see illustration, next page). If not,

scoop them out with your finger. Now wash the bird thoroughly in cold water inside and out, and pat dry with paper towels.

The next step is to remove the wishbone (see page 61), which will facilitate carving the bird after cooking. You may now rush to truss the bird, thinking that the legs should not stick out. I tested this and found that *trussing slows proper cooking of the dark meat,* and therefore it's best to leave the legs splayed. If they are sticking out at odd angles, you may loosely tie the ends of the drumsticks together, but do not tighten! The tips of the wings may be cut off with shears or tucked under the wing itself. The bird is now ready for stuffing or to be seasoned and roasted as is.

CUTTING UP A CHICKEN

I usually purchase whole chickens, not knowing at the time whether I will roast them whole or cut them into parts for frying, stewing, or sautéeing. Parts are also somewhat more expensive, and cutting up a bird takes just 2 minutes if you have a sharp knife and a bit of experience. An added benefit is that I can set aside the wings and backs, which I freeze and use to make stock when I

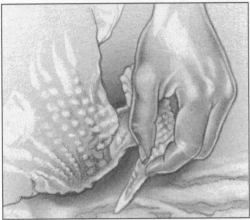

Chicken does not need to be trussed, but you can snip off the last joint of the wing or tuck it underneath the wing as shown here to avoid overcooking. If the legs are badly splayed, however, you can loosely tie them together. Tightly trussing a bird inhibits proper cooking of the thigh meat.

To remove the kidneys, look into the end of the cavity near the tail. If you see small dark red objects the size of marbles, remove them with your thumbs.

have enough on hand. Here's how I cut up a chicken (see illustrations, next page).

Pull a leg away from the body of the bird and use a chef's knife or boning knife to slice through the stretched skin in between. Continue pulling the leg/thigh away from the bird and cut carefully close to the body until the joint where the thigh joins the body is exposed. Bend back the leg until the thighbone starts to pop out of the socket, and use the knife to finish the job of detaching the leg from the body. Don't be afraid to use some pressure bending back the leg. There is a trick to separating the drumstick from the thigh. Place a chef's knife along an imaginary line bisecting the length of the drumstick. Now turn the knife at a 60-degree angle — the knife edge will be above the top of the drumstick. Move the knife about ⅛ inch toward the thigh and cut through the joint. To remove the wings, you need to cut into part of the breast to get at the wing joint. Follow the same procedure as with the leg, bending the wing away from the body and cutting carefully until the joint is exposed and severed. The backbone is removed with either

poultry shears (these are easy to use, very safe, and best for beginners) or a very sharp chef's knife. The breast can simply be cut in half through the breastbone. It's best, however, to remove the breastbone (the white bone separating the two breast halves) first. Using a small paring knife, cut around the breastbone and the white cartilage attached to it, then bend the breast halves backward to separate them from the breastbone. Grab the breastbone by the thickest part and pull it up and away from the breast meat. Now cut the breast halves apart.

BUTTERFLYING A CHICKEN

When a chicken is butterflied, it lies perfectly flat, which makes it easier to both marinate and cook. Place the whole bird on the work surface in front of you, breast side down. With poultry shears or a sharp chef's knife, cut along both sides of the backbone to remove it. (At this point, some cooks suggest that you remove the breastbone, but I prefer to leave it in, as it helps maintain the in-

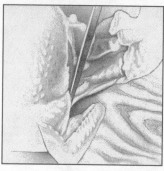

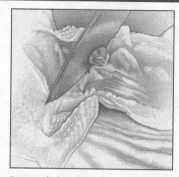

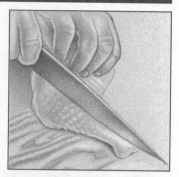

To cut up a chicken for stewing or frying, cut the skin around the leg where it attaches to the body.

Pop each leg out of its socket and then use a chef's knife to cut through the flesh and skin to detach.

To separate the drumstick from the thigh, first place a chef's knife along the length of the drumstick.

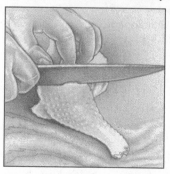

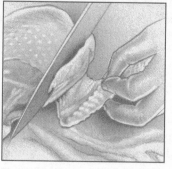

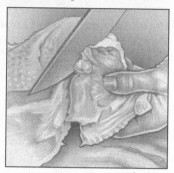

Now turn the knife 60 degrees. Move the knife about ⅛ inch toward the thigh and cut.

To remove the wings, start by cutting into the side of the breast.

Bend the wing backward to pop out the bone. Detach with a knife.

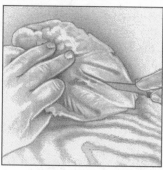

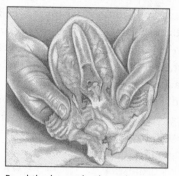

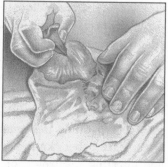

Cut on either side of the breastbone with a small paring knife.

Bend the breast backward to separate it from the breastbone.

Now remove the breastbone with your fingers.

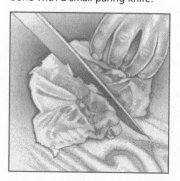

Cut the breast halves apart.

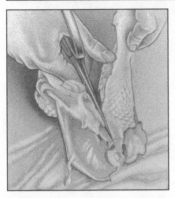

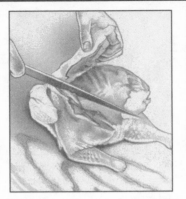

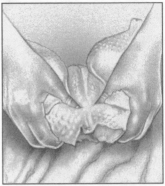

To butterfly a chicken, start by cutting out the backbone with sharp kitchen shears.

You can also use a sharp chef's knife to remove the backbone, but this is more dangerous, as the knife can slip.

Turn the chicken over and bend the breast backward where it attaches to the breastbone. This is done by placing your thumbs on either side of the breastbone and pressing down while pulling up on the outer sides of the breast with your fingers.

tegrity of the bird as it is broiled or grilled.) Flip the bird over, skin side up, and press down firmly on the breastbone to flatten the bird with your hands. The chicken is now ready for marinating or cooking. A butterflied bird, by the way, will cook relatively evenly, the dark and white meat being equally exposed to the heat.

CARVING A CHICKEN OR TURKEY

Before carving, allow the bird to rest 20 minutes. Working on a large cutting board with channels to catch the juices, start with the leg — drumstick and thigh — which should be removed in one piece. Follow the same procedure as when removing the leg before cooking, except use a kitchen towel to grab onto the leg. It should pull away from the carcass fairly easily. Cut into the breast near the wing to expose the wing joint, then cut through the joint to detach the wing. Cut along one side of the breastbone with a boning knife and remove each breast half in one piece. This is facilitated by removal of the wishbone prior to cooking. Now slice the breast at an angle into pieces. This is much easier than trying to slice the breast meat while it is still on the bone. Separate the leg and drumstick as described above. The meat can be removed from the thigh by making two cuts, parallel to and on either side of the bone. The meat of the drumstick can be sliced off easily with a chef's knife by holding the drumstick vertically, the large end resting on the cutting surface. Be sure to carve the bird in the kitchen, not at the table.

PREPARING AND CARVING A LEG OF LAMB

When you purchase a leg of lamb, ask the butcher to do three things. First, have the aitchbone removed. (For years, I thought that it was the H-bone until I saw the name written on a meat chart.) To understand what the aitchbone is, let's start with the leg itself. A leg of lamb is the rear leg up to the hip. (Some butchers will cut the leg at the knee joint and others will make the cut lower down.) The top part of the leg fits into the

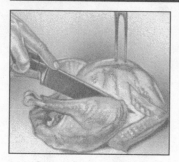

Start by cutting between the leg and the carcass.

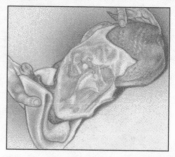

Pull the leg down and away from the carcass until you can see the leg joint.

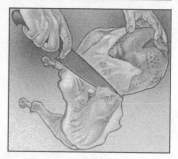

Cut through the leg joint with a chef's knife.

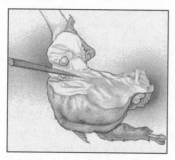

To remove the wing, cut into the breast next to the wing to expose the wing joint. Cut through the joint and detach the wing.

Now make a long cut right next to the breastbone. Run the knife along the rib cage and remove the breast half in one piece.

The breast can be sliced at a slight angle into neat pieces.

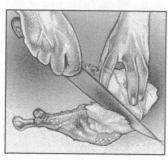

To separate the drumstick from the thigh, first lay the knife blade along the length of the drumstick. Now turn the knife 60 degrees and move it about ⅛ inch toward the thigh. Cut through the joint.

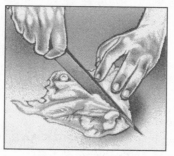

To remove meat from the thigh, cut along either side of the thigh-bone.

The thighbone remains in the middle piece and the two outer portions are all meat.

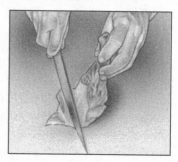

To remove meat from the drumstick, hold it vertically and slice off pieces.

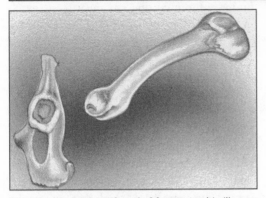

Start by removing the aitchbone. In this illustration, the thighbone is at the right (the extreme right portion fits into the knee joint) and the aitchbone, which is the rear portion of the hip, is at the left. The thighbone fits into the socket in the aitchbone. If the aitchbone is not removed before roasting, carving the leg is very difficult since the aitchbone is at right angles to the thigh.

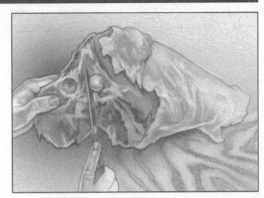

If you feel the aitchbone at the top of the leg (this bone is perpendicular to the length of the leg), use your fingers to find the spot where the legbone fits into it. Now use a boning knife to cut away the meat to expose the joint.

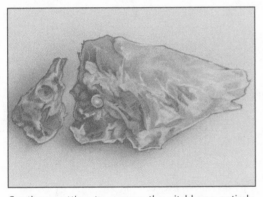

Continue cutting to remove the aitchbone entirely.

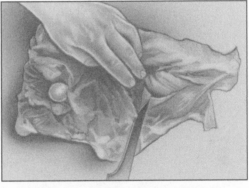

To remove the lymph node, which is strong-tasting, peel back the layers of meat at the midpoint of the leg (in human terms, the lymph node is located in the middle of the thigh). You will find a piece of white "fat" about the size of a peach pit. Either pull it out with your fingers or use a boning knife. This step is not essential but is recommended.

hip, just as in humans, and at the point where it does is the aitchbone. This is often left in a leg of lamb, and because it runs almost perpendicular to the legbone it should be removed to facilitate carving. You can tell whether the aitchbone has been removed by feeling the top of the leg. If there is a bone running across the width of the leg, then the aitchbone is still there. To remove it, first use your fingers to locate the ball joint near the top of the leg. This joint is about 3–4 inches in from the top of the leg. Use a short boning knife and scrape away the meat to expose this joint, then cut through it to cut away the aitchbone. (The actual position of the aitchbone will vary depending on where the butcher made the cut to remove the leg.)

Next, make sure that the silverskin is removed. Also called the fell, this is the shiny translucent skin that covers most of the meat. This is tough and will not render during cooking. To perform this task yourself, use any sharp knife, pulling the silverskin up and away with one hand (it's easier to hold on to if you grip it with a paper towel) and cutting it with the other. Finally, it is best if the lymph node found in the middle of the meat of the leg is removed. It has a very strong, gamy flavor. You can do this yourself. If you were looking at your thigh from the side, this gland would be found about ⅓ of the way up from the knee and in the middle of the muscles behind the legbone. You can find it without cutting any meat. Just search in between the muscles. It is about 1½ inches long and has the appearance and texture of a firm piece of fat. Pull it out with your fingers or cut it out with a boning knife.

To carve a leg of lamb, grasp it at the thin end with a kitchen towel and hold it so that the meaty side is facing up. Now start at the wide end and make a series of vertical cuts at a slight angle down through the meat to the bone. After cutting a few slices, make a horizontal cut parallel to and just above the bone. This will free the slices.

~ 22 ~

How to Sauté Boneless Chicken Breasts

The best sautéed cutlets are marinated and then coated with buttermilk, flour, and cornmeal.

~

A boneless breast of chicken is easy to either undercook or overcook. The outside is readily transformed into a leathery hide, and the coating, when one is used, is often gummy or greasy. To make matters worse, a perfectly cooked boneless breast of chicken is usually a hit-or-miss proposition; fine one evening but mediocre the next. I set out to test each variable to prepare a precision recipe, one that is both foolproof and reliable.

SHOULD CHICKEN CUTLETS BE POUNDED?

In early January 1980, I traveled to Brown Printing in Wisconsin to watch the charter issue of *Cook's Magazine* come off the press. For lunch, the salesman and I traveled to a lakefront eatery where we had a good view of the ice-fishing huts. The cook's specialty was pork cutlets pounded to the size of a 45 rpm record, quickly sautéed, and served on a cheap white hamburger roll. Ever since, I frequently serve chicken or pork this way for lunch, pounded thin and sautéed. I gave it a try with the boneless chicken cutlets but pounded the cutlets only until they were even in thickness and about 50 percent larger in

diameter. (To pound a chicken cutlet, place it between layers of wax paper and smack it with a meat pounder or with the bottom of a heavy 2-quart saucepan.) A cutlet that is uniform ensures that one part will not be over- or undercooked. The chicken cooked in just 6 minutes and also cooked more evenly than cutlets that are not pounded. This version was a winner.

WHAT ABOUT MARINATING?

I have had good success marinating chicken before grilling and decided to give it a shot here. I used the poultry marinade from Chapter 32 and left the skinless cutlets marinating for only 1 hour, about as much time as a home cook might spare for a weeknight supper. The results were fabulous. The flavor was excellent — the lemon juice comes through nicely without being overpowering. Marinating seems well suited to a thin piece of boneless meat, which can dry out quickly during a sauté.

WATER, BUTTERMILK, OR EGG?

I am a bit like the wag who said that before he had children, he had twelve theories about raising them — now he has twelve children and no theories. Over the years I have espoused a large number of definitive theories about which liquid is best for dipping an item being breaded or coated. I am partial to buttermilk for baking and felt that it might work well with chicken, but in previous tests I had found that water was just as good. In this round of tests, however, buttermilk did win out. (My theory is that buttermilk makes a difference with a skinless, boneless cutlet but is less important when dealing with a chicken breast with both skin and bones.) It has more flavor than water, although if you do not like the tart flavor of buttermilk, milk is a fine substitute. The egg made the batter slightly gooey for a simple chicken cutlet, masking the flavor and texture of the meat.

FLOUR OR CORNMEAL?

I tried a batch of cutlets using just flour for the dry coating and found that the taste and texture were without much interest. I then tried all cornmeal, which was a bit much in both texture and appearance — the cutlets were crunchy and looked like they were curried. I then tried a 50-50 combination of flour and cornmeal, which worked the best. By the way, I prefer a fine rather than a coarse-grind cornmeal. The latter is too rough for a simple pounded chicken cutlet. Supermarket brands such as Quaker are well suited to this purpose.

OIL OR BUTTER?

Most sautés use a combination of oil and butter. The butter adds flavor, and the oil keeps the butter from burning. My first test was with all oil, and the cutlets came out fried. I had to turn down the heat, as the oil became quite hot. The all-butter version had by far the best flavor, although this version required

more fat — 4 tablespoons instead of 3 tablespoons. That was a bit much for me, so I decided to compromise by using 2 tablespoons of butter to 1 tablespoon of olive oil instead of 1½ tablespoons of each.

COVERED OR UNCOVERED?

Covering the pan during part or all of the cooking process is supposed to keep the cutlets juicier. In *Cook's Illustrated* we determined that it was best to cover the pan after the first 2 minutes. I tried leaving the pan uncovered for the entire cooking time and found that, in fact, the cutlets were slightly less juicy and tender than the *Cook's* version. Finally, I kept the pan covered throughout the cooking time and found the cutlets marginally more tender and juicy. For my money, keep the pan covered.

THE MASTER RECIPE

It's simple. Be sure to pound the cutlets until they are even in thickness. To cook them, I suggest using a 12-inch nonstick sauté pan or iron skillet; the pounded cutlets will require the extra room. Marinate, use a flour-cornmeal mixture, use more butter than oil, and keep the pan covered. Also be sure to use enough heat. Don't simmer the chicken, sauté it. Adjusting the heat as you go is an important part of success here.

Sautéed Chicken Cutlets

The most important aspect of sautéing perfect chicken cutlets is the pan temperature. Too high and the butter will burn; too low and the meat will stew or poach. When the cutlets are first added, the pan will cool off quickly — this is a good time to keep the heat high. As the pan temperature recovers, reduce the heat until the cutlets are still sizzling but the pan is not smoking.

Keep an eye on the heat throughout the cooking process and adjust accordingly. If you do not have a 12-inch sauté pan, you may have to prepare these cutlets in two batches.

Marinade
½ cup olive oil
4 cloves garlic, peeled and lightly crushed
¼ cup lemon juice
1 tablespoon fresh minced rosemary or thyme
   Freshly ground black pepper to taste

Cutlets
4 boneless chicken breast cutlets (2 whole breasts split in half, boned and skinned, rinsed and dried, and pounded to an even thickness)
½ teaspoon kosher salt
½ teaspoon freshly ground black pepper
¼ cup all-purpose flour
¼ cup fine cornmeal
½ cup buttermilk
2 tablespoons unsalted butter
1 tablespoon olive oil

1. For the marinade: Heat olive oil. Add garlic and let cook for 5 minutes over low heat. Remove from heat and let steep for 10 minutes. Discard garlic cloves and combine oil with remaining marinade ingredients in a large plastic storage bag. Let cool for 10 minutes.

2. Place the pounded cutlets in the plastic bag with the marinade, tie, and shake to cover. Let marinate in refrigerator for at least 1 hour and up to 3 hours.

3. For the cutlets: Place salt, pepper, flour, and cornmeal in a paper bag and shake to mix. Dip the marinated cutlets in buttermilk and then add them to the paper bag. Shake to cover.

4. Heat butter and oil in a heavy 12-inch skillet over medium-high heat. As soon as butter stops foaming and turns a light brown, add cutlets one at a time, tenderloin side down (the tenderloin is the small strip of meat on the underside of the breast). Cover. After about 1 minute, reduce heat slightly, to prevent the oil from smoking while maintaining a sizzling-hot cooking environment. Turn over cutlets after 3 minutes' total cooking time. Cook covered another 2–3 minutes. Chicken is done if firm when pressed and if the juices run clear when it is cut.

Serves 4

The Best Ways to Roast a Chicken

Should chicken be roasted at high heat or low? What's the best
internal temperature for breast and thigh meat? Should you truss
and/or baste? What about cooking in clay or with a vertical roaster?

~

Cooking chicken at first appears to be a simple task. The meat is not tough by nature. The dark meat is relatively forgiving in terms of cooking time. The breast meat is not particularly thick, which means that it should cook evenly. (A thick roast of beef is usually overcooked on the outside by the time it is properly cooked on the inside.)

Yet when I am served a perfectly roasted chicken, the experience is extraordinary. The skin is crisp and well seasoned. The white meat is juicy, tender, but with a hint of chew. The dark meat is fully cooked and succulent and when cut, splashes clear juices onto the plate.

I set out to devise a series of tests — I prepared chickens fourteen different ways by the time I was through — based on a few simple observations. The first is that chicken is made up of two totally different types of meat: white and dark. The white meat is inevitably overcooked and dry by the time the dark meat is less than raw next to the bone. The second is that chicken, unlike beef, has skin, which should be nicely browned and crispy. As I found during the testing, crisp skin is not always consistent with perfectly cooked meat. Finally, chicken is an odd amalgam of meat and bones. The drumsticks and wings stick out, the thigh meat is on the side of the bird,

and the breast meat is on the top (at least when roasted). The cook is dealing with a complex three-dimensional structure when dealing with poultry, quite different from a brisket or a pot roast. This may require a rather complex set of cooking instructions in order to properly cook each part of the bird.

HOW I STRUCTURED THE TESTS

I began my research by rereading an article by Harold McGee in the charter issue of *Cook's Illustrated* entitled "The Way to Roast Chicken." He started his birds at 500°F, reducing the oven temperature to 325°F about halfway through cooking. He found that butter is better for basting than oil; he discouraged tightly trussing a chicken, as that will slow down proper cooking of the thigh and leg meat; he advocated turning the bird once during roasting, finishing with the breast up; and finally, he suggested that the breast be cooked to 150°F internal temperature.

Having prepared a number of chickens according to McGee, I was still left with questions. What about oven temperatures below 325°F? I had had good success with slow-roasting turkeys at 200°F. It might work for chicken. I had found that an internal temperature of 150°F for the breast was underdone to my taste — I'd rather err on the side of overcooking chicken rather than undercooking. Although breast meat cooked to 150°F is juicy, the meat has an unpleasant rawness to it; the texture is loose and fleshy. (I also had some concerns about safety, given that chicken is more prone to bacterial infection than other types of meat. The U.S. Department of Agriculture [USDA] feels that a final internal temperature under 160°F is high risk.) I also wanted to branch out and try some other methods. What about a vertical roaster? Does cooking in a clay roaster make a better chicken? Does one turn really do the trick or are two turns better?

WHAT IS THE BEST ROASTING TEMPERATURE?

I started my tests with an obvious question. What is the best oven temperature for roasting a chicken? My bias for roasting red meat is slow-roasting in a very low oven. I also knew that my Thanksgiving turkey is best slow-cooked in a 200° oven for a nice, juicy, evenly cooked bird (although the bird is started at a much higher temperature for safety reasons). However, a 3-pound chicken is small, so a high-heat roast might work fine, I thought, as the outer layers might not have time to overcook before the inside of the bird was done.

The first bird went into a 450° oven and cooked for 44 minutes. (Each bird was roasted without trussing, and I measured the internal temperature at the thigh, not the breast, because I felt that undercooked dark meat is a more serious culinary error than overcooked breast. The birds were not basted and were roasted breast side up without turning.) The skin was dark and crispy, but I encountered the classic problem with high-heat meat cookery — the outer portion of the white meat was overcooked at the point that the internal thigh temperature registered

160°F. The dark meat was fine, but the white meat was on the tough side.

I then went to the opposite extreme and tested a bird in a 275° oven for 1 hour and 35 minutes and then raised the heat to 425°F for the last 10 minutes to crisp up the skin. The white meat was not quite as juicy as the dark, but it was not dry either. The skin, however, was a light gold, not a rich sienna, and it was chewy and not very tasty, as it had not browned sufficiently.

Finally, I tried a simple, classic approach. The bird was roasted at 375°F for 1 hour. The skin was golden and slightly crispy. At 160°F internal temperature, the juices ran clear, but the dark meat was still not properly cooked near the bone. I continued cooking to an internal temperature of about 170°F (thigh meat), and the white meat was still juicy (the breast meat was close to 180°). This was an interesting discovery. The breast meat of the chicken roasted at 450°F was a bit dry when the thigh registered 160°, yet the bird roasted at 375°F still had juicy breast meat when the thigh registered close to 170°. I also found that "until the juices run clear" is an imprecise measure of doneness — the white meat will be cooked, but the dark meat can still be a little bloody at the bone, a sight that I would prefer to leave to B movies rather than my dinner plate.

I then tried starting the oven out at a higher temperature (450°F), putting in the chicken, and then immediately turning the oven down to 350°F. The bird cooked in 53 minutes and the skin was a pale gold and slightly chewy. Not much difference from the 375° chicken and not quite as good overall. So the winner was the simpler method, a constant 375°F.

SHOULD YOU BASTE THE BIRD? OIL VERSUS BUTTER

Using the 375° method, I set out to determine if basting is a good idea or just another one of those hand-me-down cookbook directions that make no sense. I started with butter and basted every 15 minutes. The results were appalling. Despite a nice brown color, the skin was chewy and greasy. The next bird was basted with oil; this turned out a crispier skin but the color was off — a pale gold. I then brushed a bird before roasting with butter, and shoved it in the oven without any further basting. This was the best method. Great color and great crispy texture. Basting may have made sense when cooking a large piece of meat on a spit over an open fire, which I assume is its culinary origin. The outer layers would get easily overcooked and the basting may have prevented burning or scorching. However, a 3-pound chicken in a 375° oven is a different matter entirely. The skin will not scorch or burn (in fact, if you leave it alone, it will cook rather nicely on its own), and the basting liquid is not going to penetrate the meat, making it more tender. Juiciness has nothing to do with the external application of liquid. Stew meat does not absorb liquid, nor does braised meat. The only reason, therefore, to brush a chicken with butter is to advance the color of the skin. The oven heat turns the milk solids brown and, in the process, also provides added flavor.

I also noted that some cooks suggest placing a piece of cheesecloth soaked in melted butter over the bird during roasting. Just like frequent basting, this will produce lightly colored skin that is not at all crispy. Save your cheesecloth for straining stock.

WHAT'S ALL THIS I HEAR ABOUT TRUSSING?

Have you ever felt a lack of basic motor skills when confronted with those terribly serious step-by-step photos that demonstrate how to truss a chicken or turkey? You start with a long piece of twine, loop it under the tail, cross over, twist around the wings, et cetera. By this time you have figured out that your string is too short and that the photographs weren't taken from the cook's perspective, so you've done the whole thing backward! What if you don't bother trussing at all?

This was easy to test. I trussed a bird according to the best French method and cooked it for what seemed a long time, 1½ hours (this was a good-size bird, weighing in at 3.42 pounds). The white meat was overcooked at the point that the dark meat was just right. It is also interesting to note that the cooking time turned out to be quite a bit longer than for an untrussed bird. My conclusion is that trussing makes it more difficult to properly cook the inner part of the thigh — it is less exposed to heat, and therefore the oven time needs to be longer (McGee came to the same conclusion in "The Way to Roast Chicken"). Voilà! Overcooked white meat. A 3.11-pound bird took only 1 hour at 375°F without trussing, and the white and dark meats were nicely cooked. Those crazy French.

DO YOU REALLY HAVE TO TURN THE BIRD?

I am a great believer in making cooking simple. It always seemed to me that turning a roast in the oven was overdoing it a bit — just leave it alone and enjoy the cocktail hour. However, even cooking is crucial to chicken cookery, so a couple of tests were in order. First, I roasted a bird for 20 minutes on each side and then put it on its back. This was a 3.21-pound chicken and took just 50 minutes total at 375°F. The skin was golden and crunchy, the white and dark meat were perfectly cooked, and the overall presentation was superb. In an effort to make this process a bit easier, I tried roasting another bird breast side down for 20 minutes and then turned it breast side up to finish (the McGee method). This was good, but the skin was less crispy and the dark meat was a bit undercooked at the point the white meat was perfect. Unfortunately, two turns are necessary and are crucial to a properly roasted bird with the 375° method.

WHAT ABOUT THE CLAY AND VERTICAL ROASTERS?

I have heard a lot of good things about clay roasters. I have tried La Cloche, a bell-shaped clay cooker for bread that works well with certain other recipes. I followed the directions and roasted the bird, enclosed in the clay cooker, in a 425° oven. The directions suggested cooking for 90 minutes (they did not specify how large a bird to use), which was absurd — the bird was done in just an hour, and this was a 3.4-pound chicken (at that time, the internal temperature of the thigh registered 168°F). The good news is that the white and dark meat cooked equally and the meat was quite juicy. The bad news is that the skin was pale and although moist, it was chewy rather than crispy. A good method for even cooking, but if you are a skin fanatic, not a first choice.

I had also heard good things about the vertical roaster. There are two models: one consists of a round metal disc with two vertical hoops, and the other, usually a higher-quality roaster, is a cylindrical stainless steel rack that is narrow at the top and spreads broadly at the base for stability. I tested the first model, and a 3-pound bird took about 45 minutes in a 375° oven. The results were pretty good. The white meat was not dry but not real juicy, and the skin was somewhere between crispy and chewy. I also noticed that since the bird was roasted vertically, the portion toward the top of the oven was much darker in appearance than the bottom half.

SLOW-COOKED CHICKEN

Given my tenacious devotion to low-heat roasting, I decided to have a go with a chicken. By low heat, I mean starting the bird at 300°F and then after 30 minutes reducing the heat to 200°F. This notion is not original — I borrowed it from Adelle Davis (*Let's Eat Right to Keep Fit*), the sixties health guru. I started with a 3.2-pound bird and roasted it for a whopping 2 hours, 15 minutes. When it was cooked to an internal temperature of 160°F, I was surprised to find that the juices did not run clear. I also discovered that the dark meat was not cooked at the bone at this temperature. An additional 20 minutes finished the cooking satisfactorily. The white and dark meat were perfectly cooked, very juicy and very tender. The trouble was the skin, which was golden yellow, chewy, and soft. I went back and did it again, this time increasing the oven temperature to 400°F after 2 hours, 15 minutes and cooked the bird an additional 15 minutes. Although the internal temperature was 180°F, which means overcooked, dry meat under normal conditions, both the white and dark meats were still juicy and tender. The skin was also improved, with more crisp and snap. This is a very good and forgiving method overall, although time-consuming.

ARE SLOW-ROASTED CHICKENS SAFE?

If you ask people at the USDA, they will kick and scream and tell you never to cook any meat at 200°F. Of course, they also tell you never to cook a hamburger medium rare, which may be good advice strictly from a safety point of view but does make the meat inedible. However, chicken is particularly prone to bacterial problems because it is sold with the skin on. The skin of an animal is the primary source of contamination, and with beef, pork, lamb, and veal, this is less of a problem, as the skin is separated from the meat during processing. For example, pork sold in a supermarket may carry only a few

Fourteen Ways to Roast a Chicken

Chickens varying in weight from 3 to 3½ pounds were roasted according to different methods and judged on skin color, skin crispness, flavor, juiciness, relative condition of the white and dark meat, and the amount of pan juices left after cooking (the chart below summarizes only the key points). Birds were cooked without trussing (with one exception) or stuffing. Unless otherwise indicated, the birds were brushed with melted butter before cooking and were placed on a rack in an unheated roasting pan. Birds were roasted breast up, unturned, unless noted otherwise.

Method	Skin	White vs. Dark	Comments
Constant 275°F	Chewy, pale	Pretty even	Skin is poor, otherwise a good method for even cooking; not a USDA-approved method
Constant 375°F	Golden	Cooked evenly	Very good skin and moist white and dark meat; one thigh more cooked than the other
Start at 450°F, turn oven to 350°F immediately	Dark golden	White meat overcooked	High heat overcooks white meat as dark meat cooks; great-looking skin with great flavor
Constant 375°F; turn twice (start on side, turn to other side, end breast up)	Crunchy and golden	Cooked evenly	Best presentation and most even cooking of white and dark meats, but sides did not cook evenly
Constant 375°F; preheat pan; turn twice (start on side, turn to other side, end breast up)	Crunchy and golden	Cooked evenly	Both sides cooked evenly; excellent chicken

hundred bacteria per square centimeter, while chicken may have thousands. So chicken does have to be handled carefully.

First of all, very few chickens contain bacteria that are harmful. Although chicken is more problematic than other meats, it is relatively rare to come across a chicken that is contaminated. In addition, the problem, if there is one, is usually on the outside of the chicken, not inside the meat. It is true that the meat can be punctured and therefore contaminated during processing, but for the most part this is an external issue. The problem arises when a contaminated chicken (or any other meat) is subjected to temperatures between 40° and 140°F. I called a microbiologist, Dr. Labbe at the University of Massachusetts, and he indicated that bacteria, if they are present, can multiply rapidly in this zone, especially on the higher end of the range. In fact, bacteria can double every 20 minutes, which can turn 10,000 of those critters into about 40 million in just 4 hours.

My original recipe started the slow-roasted chickens at 300°F. After discussions with USDA hotline experts and a few microbiologists, I decided this was a bit risky, so in order to make this recipe safer, I increased the initial oven temperature to 375°F for 30 minutes, to give the bird enough heat to raise the surface temperature well beyond the 140° mark, the point at which any bacteria are killed. (I tested this theory and found that after 30 minutes, the internal temperature had in fact

Method	Skin	White vs. Dark	Comments
Constant 375°F; turn once (start breast down, end breast up)	Slightly crispy; golden	Dark meat slightly undercooked	Nice appearance, but two turns better than one
300°F for 30 minutes; 200°F for 1 hour, 45 minutes; 400°F for 15 minutes	Golden and crispy	Cooked evenly; both white and dark meat were very juicy	Time-consuming but foolproof; cooking time is not critical; not a USDA-approved cooking method
375°F for 30 minutes; 200°F for 1 hour; 400°F for 15 minutes	Golden and crispy	Cooked evenly; both white and dark meat were very juicy	Much faster and safer than preceding method
Constant 375°F; basted with butter every 15 minutes	Chewy and greasy; very nice color	Cooked evenly	Best appearance of skin, but skin was not crispy
Constant 375°F; basted with oil every 15 minutes	Crispier than with butter, but still not well crisped; pale gold	Cooked evenly	Better than butter for skin texture, but color not as good
Constant 375°F; trussed	Golden and crispy	White meat chewy	In order to cook dark meat properly, white meat must be overcooked
Clay cooker; roast at 425°F	Pale gold; moist and chewy	Cooked evenly	A good method, but skin did not crisp up properly
Vertical roaster; constant 375°F	Slightly chewy; pale gold	Cooked evenly	Oven a mess; skin not evenly cooked
Constant 375°F; buttered cheesecloth on breast	Poor texture; yellow color	White overcooked	Skin was inedible

reached 140°F, so bacterial growth would be stopped.) I also do not truss the bird and do not stuff it, allowing hot air to flow freely inside the cavity.

I then started to wonder about the long cooking time at 200°F, which sometimes exceeded 2 hours for a larger bird (over 3½ pounds). Not only is this inconvenient, but I wanted to get the bird in and out of the oven more quickly for safety reasons. (The USDA claims that even a fully cooked bird should not spend more than 2 hours at room temperature. I felt that 2 hours in an oven at 200°F was pushing the limit of safety.) So I did two last tests, starting both chickens at 375°F for half an hour, then turning the oven down to 200° and cooking one bird for 1

hour and one for ½ hour before ratcheting up the oven to 400°F for the final browning. The bird that cooked for only half an hour at 200°F had chewy breast meat, but the bird that stayed for the full hour was excellent: juicy, tender, and perfectly cooked. Finally, the perfect slow-roasted bird!

Slow-roasting led to one other fascinating discovery. When the bird is roasted at lower temperatures, or given a good rest period at a lower temperature, the temperature differential between the thigh and breast narrows. When a chicken is roasted at a constant 375°F, the breast meat will be 10°–15° higher than the thighs, but when it is slow-roasted, the difference is as little as 5°. My theory is that once meat reaches 150°F in a

200° oven, additional gains in internal temperature are very slow. This gives meat at lower temperatures time to catch up. After 30 minutes at 375°F, the breast meat will run around 140° and the thighs about 130° (this was measured in my testing). I then turn the oven down to 200°F for an hour. During this period, the breast meat rises more slowly in temperature than the thighs because it is already closer to the oven temperature. This theory is supported by a test I did with a 3½-pound chicken. I left it at 200°F for over 3 hours (don't try this at home — this cooking method is not safe) and found that the temperature increased just 2°–3° per hour once the breast reached 150°F, although initially the breast had risen from room temperature to 150°F in under 1 hour.

WHEN IS A CHICKEN PROPERLY COOKED?

As I have discovered when cooking red meat, internal temperatures are relative, not absolute. That is, 160°F means one thing when meat is roasted at 375°F and something quite different when it's roasted at 200°F. It's how you get there that matters. Many experts recommend cooking the dark meat to an internal temperature of 160°F, the premise I used for my testing. Forget it. The dark meat just isn't going to be fully cooked at the bone. The temperature of the dark meat — which is crucial, because the dark meat has to be cooked properly or it is inedible — needs to be between 165° and 170°F (I vote for the latter). However, if you slow-cook a chicken at 200°F, you can cook the dark meat to 175°–180°F without a problem. I also found that when cooking in a clay cooker, the chicken can stand an internal thigh temperature of 175°F.

Why the difference? Because at higher oven temperatures, the outer layers of meat will end up at much higher temperatures than the inner layers. That is, even though the middle of the breast may register 160°F whether slow- or fast-roasted, the outer layer of meat may reach 200°F if roasted at a high temperature but only 170°F if roasted at a low temperature. Although the exact center of the meat may be the same with both methods, a serving of chicken breast will contain some overcooked meat when roasted at high temperatures. Slow roasting guarantees even cooking and more consistent internal temperatures.

I also tested the notion that internal temperature rises after the chicken is removed from the oven, as it does with a beef roast. This simply does not happen. I removed a chicken from the oven and inserted an instant-read thermometer into the breast. It started out at 155°F and immediately began to fall, ending at 140°F after 15 minutes. Although resting for 20 minutes after roasting is important — the meat will be juicier — the bird will not continue to cook.

You should also be aware that measuring the internal temperature of the thigh is difficult. I have found that readings can vary as much as 15°F, depending on where the thermometer is inserted. You want to measure the temperature of the thickest part of the thigh, inserting the thermometer so that the tip rests in the middle of the meat, not next to the bone and not close to the skin. However, it is difficult to place a thermometer horizontally into the thigh, so I suggest that you start by inserting it between the leg and body of the bird and then angle the tip of the thermometer away from the carcass into the thickest part of the thigh. Be sure to get the thermometer well into the meat, otherwise the reading will be inaccurate. It's a good idea to take one or two measurements of the breast as well. As reported above, the breast will register about 10° higher than the thighs when roasted at a constant 375°F and about 5° higher when slow-roasted.

WHY DOES ONE THIGH COOK FASTER THAN THE OTHER?

I also made an odd discovery after roasting a half-dozen birds with the basic 375° method. The thigh that was turned right side up during the second 20 minutes of roasting ended up lower in temperature than the thigh that started off right side up. At first I thought this was just a random measurement, but after four or five birds, it was clear this was a trend. After thinking about it for a few days, I hit on the explanation. The thigh that started off facing the roasting pan was facing a cold pan that reflected little heat. When the other thigh was turned facedown, the pan was now hot and was radiating plenty of heat. So to even things out, you need to preheat the roasting pan. (This is not necessary when slow-roasting).

WHICH IS THE BEST METHOD?

The quickest and easiest method is to roast a chicken at a constant 375°F — this takes about an hour for a 3-pound bird. Start by preheating the roasting pan and then brush the bird with melted butter and sprinkle lib-

How Much Do Roasting Times Vary Based on Weight?

When testing different-size chickens, I found that roasting times did not vary greatly based on weight. In fact, the 4-pound and 4½-pound birds cooked in about the same amount of time. All birds were roasted at a constant 375°F.

Weight	Roasting Time
3 pounds	50–55 minutes
3½ pounds	55–60 minutes
4 pounds	60–65 minutes
4½ pounds	60–65 minutes

erally with salt and freshly ground black pepper. Roast untrussed for 20 minutes on one side, 20 on the other, and then finish with the breast side up. The thigh should register 165°–170°F internal temperature. This method produces evenly cooked meat and golden, crispy skin. It does, however, require two turns and a preheated roasting pan.

Another good method is slow-roasting. The skin is slightly better than that of a quick-roasted bird and the meat is more evenly cooked, the thighs and breast ending up within 5°F of each other. This method has one other advantage: it is very forgiving. You can cook the thigh to 170°, 175°, or 180°F and the chicken will still turn out well. Unlike the basic 375° method, slow-roasting allows the bird to be cooked to much higher internal temperatures without adverse affect. It does take about 45 minutes longer, a disadvantage, but it does not require turning the chicken during roasting.

As for the other methods tested, high-heat roasting (450°–500°F) does produce excellent mahogany-colored skin with great flavor, but some of the meat will be overcooked, especially the breast area around the wings and parts of the legs. You will also need to remove the batteries from your kitchen smoke alarm due to the splattering and smoking. The clay cooker does a nice job of evenly cooking the bird, although the skin does not get very crispy. The vertical roaster did a fine job but no better than either of the recipes in this chapter, which simply use a roasting rack.

READYING A CHICKEN FOR THE OVEN

Be sure to rinse the bird inside and out in cool water (this will remove some surface bacteria and off flavors), then pat it with paper towels until it is absolutely dry. Tuck the tip of the wing back under the wing itself, which avoids overcooking, and remove the wishbone (see page 61), which will greatly facilitate carving. Then brush the bird with melted butter and liberally cover with kosher salt and freshly ground black pepper. The chicken must be placed on a rack in a shallow roasting pan. (A rack is necessary to keep the chicken from sitting in its own juices.) If you don't have a rack, place a few carrots on the bottom of the pan to keep the bird up and away from the pan juices. If you use a V-shaped roasting rack that has sides that press against the sides of the bird, make sure that it is liberally coated with oil, otherwise it will stick. A V-shaped rack will help to keep the chicken positioned on its side if you are going to be turning the bird. If using a cake rack or no rack, use balls of aluminum foil to keep the chicken sitting evenly on its side.

Quick Roast Chicken

The cooking time given here is for a 3-pound bird. For great skin and evenly cooked white and dark meat, the bird needs to be turned twice. Ovens vary as do chickens, so rely on an instant-read thermometer rather than cooking times. I start checking the temperature of the breast meat after 50 minutes. Once the breast registers 155°F, I start measuring the thickest part of the thigh, which ought to read 165°–170°F to ensure a fully cooked bird.

> 1 roasting chicken (3 pounds), giblets removed from cavity, rinsed, and patted dry with paper towels
> 2 tablespoons melted butter
> Salt and freshly ground black pepper to taste

1. Place a shallow roasting pan in oven and heat to 375°F. Make sure that chicken is perfectly dry and then brush with the butter. Sprinkle liberally with salt and freshly ground black pepper.

2. Remove heated pan from oven and

place a roasting rack in it. Place chicken on its side on rack and place in oven. After 20 minutes, turn chicken to its other side. After 20 additional minutes, turn breast side up. Roast another 10 minutes and then check breast meat with an instant-read thermometer. Once the breast reaches 155°F, measure the thigh temperature, which must register between 165° and 170°F (I prefer the latter). When chicken is done, remove from oven and let sit for 20 minutes on a cutting board before carving.

Serves 4

Roast Garlic Variation

Cut 3 heads garlic in half crosswise and toss with olive oil and salt and pepper to taste. Place garlic cut side down on rack next to chicken and then place chicken in oven. When chicken is done, remove garlic and serve half a garlic head per person. The garlic will soften and lose its pungency and may be eaten with the chicken or used as a spread on bread.

Slow-Roasted Chicken

This is similar to the method I use to prepare a Thanksgiving turkey, except that a turkey requires a much longer roasting time and also needs to be covered with aluminum foil. The benefit of low-heat roasting is that the white meat can cook to a higher internal temperature without drying out. When finished at a higher oven temperature, the skin is extraordinary — crispy, light, and golden brown. A slow-roasted chicken should never be stuffed or trussed.

> 1 roasting chicken (3–3½ pounds), giblets removed from cavity, last joint of wing removed, rinsed and patted dry with paper towels
> 2 tablespoons melted butter
> Salt and freshly ground black pepper to taste

1. Heat oven to 375°F. Make sure that chicken is perfectly dry and then brush with the butter. Sprinkle liberally with salt and freshly ground black pepper.

2. Place a rack in a shallow roasting pan. Place chicken breast side up on rack and place in oven. After 30 minutes, reduce heat to 200°F. Roast for 1 hour. Turn oven up to 400°F and roast another 15 minutes. Check thigh meat with an instant-read thermometer. The chicken is done when the thigh registers 170°–175°F (the breast will be 175°–180°F). Remove chicken from oven and let sit for 20 minutes on a cutting board before carving.

Serves 4

~ 24 ~

How to Fry Chicken

*The secret to great fried chicken is to presoak it
for 2 hours in salted water.*

~

In the 1950s, I grew up in a household that had two working parents and a cook, Dorothy O'Gilvie, who was born and raised around Chesapeake Bay. Now, Dorothy could cook just about anything, including soufflés and fancy dinner rolls, but her real love was southern food: black-eyed peas cooked with greens and a dash of vinegar, spoonbread that floated onto your plate from the big-as-your-fist serving spoon, and, of course, the best southern fried chicken I ever ate. There was real crunch to her crust, the meat was tender and juicy, and there was no greasy aftertaste.

When I set out to re-create Dorothy's chicken, I first had to decide whether to deep-fry or pan-fry. I tested both approaches and found that the deep-fry method (the chicken is fully immersed in hot oil) has a major drawback: you can't cook a whole bird at once, since only a few pieces fit in the basket. I also preferred to use less oil and therefore voted for the pan-fry method.

I then wanted to solve the problem of the crust. An all-purpose flour crust just doesn't have enough crunch. I first tested adding cornmeal (1¾ cups flour for ¼ cup cornmeal). This worked very well. It added the necessary texture and bite. However, I had tasted fried shrimp from a chef in Los Angeles

(Michel Ricard at Citrus) who used Cream of Wheat as a coating and decided to give that a try as well. Using the same proportion as with the cornmeal, I found that the Cream of Wheat was good but that the coating speckled when fried. The cornmeal was the clear winner both for flavor and appearance.

I was intrigued by the notion of brining foods before cooking (Pam Anderson, the food editor of *Cook's*, found a recipe for brined and roasted turkey in *The Foods of Portugal*, by Jean Anderson). Brining, or soaking foods in heavily salted water, adds both moisture and flavor. Using a standard brining recipe (½ cup salt per quart of water), the resulting fried chicken was too salty for my taste, although one taster found that it was a nice counterpoint to the fried outer coating. I also tried a buttermilk and a plain water bath. The buttermilk bath was slightly better but the difference in taste and texture was barely perceptible. I found that soaking the chicken in lightly salted water (¼ cup kosher salt per quart of water) was the best method.

Many fried chicken recipes call for large iron skillets. I found it easier to use an electric skillet, which does an excellent job of frying chicken. However, you can also use a large (12-inch) cast iron skillet or Dutch oven. By the way, you might think that the objective is

How Does Frying Work?

Frying is more complicated than it appears. First of all, frying is an excellent technique for cooking foods with uneven surfaces; the hot oil comes into uniform contact with all parts of the food, which promotes even cooking and eliminates sticking. (This is why when sautéing foods, for example, it is important to use enough butter and/or oil, so that all parts of the uneven bottom surface of the food come in contact with the hot liquid.) The most interesting fact about frying is that the outside of the food is cooking at one temperature while the inside is cooking at another. The outside is exposed to oil heated to 360°F or so (at least when the food is first added to the pan), but the inside never gets above the boiling point of water, 212°F. This is why, as I found in my tests, it is a good thing to reduce the temperature of the oil after the initial browning. If the oil were to stay at 360°F, the outside of the chicken would overcook while the inside was still undercooked.

to maintain a constant temperature. In fact, this is not the case. The oil temperature will drop about 100°F as soon as the chicken pieces are added, and they will cook at about 275°F for the rest of the frying time. If you try to raise the temperature back up to 350°F, as I did in one of my tests, you'll find that the chicken burns easily. If you are using an electric skillet, just set it at 350°F. You will never get back up to temperature. If using a regular skillet, I suggest backing off the heat just a bit after the first 5 minutes. Just make sure that the oil continues to bubble and froth or you'll have fried grease, not fried chicken.

I also considered the question of frying medium. Crisco has the advantage of being a refined vegetable shortening and therefore makes an excellent frying medium. However, I do have concerns about eating foods that have been swimming in hydrogenated vegetable shortening (Crisco is very difficult to digest and break down). I vote for canola oil, which is not strongly flavored and is one of the healthiest oils on the market in terms of saturated and polyunsaturated fats. When

testing, I found that canola oil worked almost as well as Crisco, the latter being absorbed somewhat less by the frying chicken.

The final question was whether to cook covered or uncovered. After much testing, I found that it's best to cook chicken covered for the first 5 minutes, then uncover for the next 5. Finally, turn the chicken pieces over and cook uncovered for about 10 minutes more. It is important to start with a covered pan in order to get the chicken fully cooked and then just as important to uncover the pan to produce a crisp skin. A covered pan would produce a steamed, soggy crust.

Dorothy's Best Fried Chicken

Although I know she didn't use canola oil or an electric skillet, this is pretty close to my recollection of Dorothy's peerless fried chicken. It's best served with something light and refreshing, such as cole slaw or a salsa.

If you don't have cornmeal on hand, use Cream of Wheat. It makes a light, crunchy crust, although it will speckle a bit when fried. If you have no health objections, use Crisco — it makes a relatively odorless medium for frying. (Dorothy, however, still swears by lard, which she claims produces the crispiest, tastiest crust.) It's best to find a pan that is large enough to hold an entire cut-up chicken. You will need a good 12 inches in diameter for this to work. Otherwise, the chicken will have to be fried in two batches. (Keep the first batch warm in a low oven while preparing the second batch.)

> ¾ cup kosher salt
> 3 quarts water
> 1 chicken, about 3½ pounds, cut into parts
> 1¾ cups all-purpose flour
> ¼ cup cornmeal
> 2 teaspoons dried thyme or oregano
> ½ teaspoon kosher salt
> ½ teaspoon freshly ground black pepper
> 1 quart canola oil for frying

1. In a large bowl or pot, dissolve ¾ cup salt in 3 quarts water. Rinse chicken pieces and add to bowl. Cover and refrigerate for 2 hours. Remove chicken pieces and rinse under cool water. Place chicken on paper towels.

2. Mix together the next 5 ingredients (flour through pepper) and place in a medium paper bag or a large plastic storage bag. Shake. Add half the chicken pieces, shake to coat, and place on a wire rack. Repeat for remaining pieces.

3. Pour a ½-inch-deep layer of canola oil into an electric skillet set at 350°F or a large iron skillet or Dutch oven (pan should be large enough to accommodate all the pieces). When oil reaches 350°F (measure with a candy thermometer), place chicken pieces into oil, skin side down, and cover the pan. After 5 minutes remove the cover; the pan should remain uncovered for the rest of the cooking. Rearrange pieces if some are browning more quickly than others. After 5 more minutes, turn the pieces over. Cook for 8–10 more minutes or until well browned.

4. While chicken is cooking, rinse off and dry the wire rack. Remove fried chicken to the cleaned rack set over a cookie sheet or jelly roll pan. Let sit for 5 minutes and serve.

Serves 4

Spicy Buttermilk Fried Chicken

This recipe (minus the cornmeal) is served at East Coast Grill, a wonderful neighborhood eatery in Cambridge, Massachusetts. Boneless thighs can be substituted for the breasts. Serve with a green salad and sweet potato fries. The recommended hot sauce is called Inner Beauty and can be purchased from Mo Hotta, Mo Betta, a mail order company specializing in spicy foods. Call 800-462-3220 for a catalog.

> 2 pounds boneless, skinless chicken breasts
> 1 cup buttermilk
> 2 tablespoons hot sauce
> ¾ cup all-purpose flour
> ¼ cup cornmeal
> 2 teaspoons kosher salt
> 2 teaspoons freshly cracked black pepper
> 2 tablespoons fresh mixed herbs such as parsley, oregano, or thyme (or 2 teaspoons dried)
> 1 quart canola oil for frying

1. Clean chicken breasts, removing fat and tendons. Cut into 2-inch-wide strips. Mix buttermilk and hot sauce in a large bowl, add chicken pieces, and marinate overnight in refrigerator.

2. Combine flour, cornmeal, salt, pepper, and herbs in a paper or zipper-lock bag. Remove chicken pieces from marinade and immediately shake in seasoned flour. Fry chicken uncovered for about 4 minutes in oil that has been preheated to 350°F. Turn pieces after 2 minutes.

Serves 4

~ 25 ~

How to Cook a Turkey

For a moist, tender bird, roast it long and slow.

~

Every Thanksgiving, my wife and I take the kids to my mother's farm in Connecticut, where we enjoy a home-grown holiday dinner. The turkey is provided by her neighbors, the Maclarens, who raise organic meats. This is honest New England fare. The vegetables are simply roasted with salt and pepper and the turkey has no fancy under-the-skin herbal stuffings. But it is the best turkey you will ever eat.

The secret? Believe it or not, my mother picked up this recipe from pioneering health guru Adelle Davis and roasts the bird for 1 hour at 300°F (the turkey needs to be placed in a large roasting pan and covered tightly with aluminum foil), then slow-cooks the bird overnight at 200°F. In the morning, she turns off the oven, leaving the bird inside. One hour before the midday feast, she reheats the turkey at 200°F. It's moist, it's tender, and best of all, it's foolproof.

TESTING ROASTING TIMES

I went home after a recent Thanksgiving dinner to try this on my own. I roasted a 20-pound bird all night as my mother did, and at first I was very pleased with the results. I found, however, that since the time the bird has to be held is variable (you might eat Thanksgiving dinner at 1 P.M. or at 6 P.M.), the turkey can easily dry out. I also was not thrilled for health reasons with the notion of holding the turkey for half a day in a cool oven. Plus I wanted a little more snap to the skin and thought that a higher finishing temperature might work well.

For my second test, I cooked the bird breast side down at 350°F, an increase of 50°, for 1 hour and then reduced the heat to 200° and roasted for 3 hours. I then flipped it breast side up for an additional 3 hours, 45 minutes. I removed the bird from the oven and raised the temperature to 400°F. When the oven was ready, I removed the aluminum foil and roasted the turkey for 10 minutes to crisp up the skin. The internal temperature, measured in the breast, was a whopping 180°F, normally a sign of disaster for a roasted turkey, but the meat was tender, evenly cooked, juicy, and delicious. As I discovered when roasting and braising red meat as well as roasting chicken, slow-cooking allows the internal temperature to climb above normal levels while maintaining texture, flavor, and juices.

Since many families only roast a 12–14 pound bird, I roasted a 13.9-pound turkey and found that the 3-hour roasting at 200°F

Is Slow-Roasting Safe?

When I first wrote about slow-roasting in 1994 on the editorial page of *Cook's Illustrated*, I quickly received a letter of great alarm from Susan Conley at the USDA. She pointed out that one should never roast meat at temperatures below 325°F. I responded by changing my recipe for slow-roasted chicken (see Chapter 23 for more information on safety). By starting the oven at 375°F (instead of 200°), I could bring a 3½-pound bird up to an internal temperature of 140° (the point at which bacteria are killed) quickly, thus greatly reducing the opportunity for bacterial growth. After 30 minutes, the oven was reduced to 200°F. With a 12–20 pound turkey, though, it will take much longer for the internal temperature to reach 140°F, and the bird must stay in the oven for about 7 hours. Is this safe? Nobody can answer that definitively, although I am comfortable with this method for my Thanksgiving dinner. If you have safety concerns, however, I suggest that you roast at the USDA-recommended 325°F until the thigh reaches an internal temperature of 170° (the breast will be about 10° higher). To be sure of producing an evenly cooked bird at this temperature, I suggest turning the turkey during roasting. Start the bird on its side, turn to the other side after 1 hour, and then turn breast side up after a second hour to finish.

should be reduced to 2 hours and that the final roasting should also be reduced, to 2 hours, 45 minutes.

OTHER THOUGHTS ABOUT TURKEY

WHAT ABOUT BRINING?

For the November/December 1993 issue of *Cook's Illustrated*, we tested brining a turkey for 4 hours before roasting. The white meat was succulent and flavorful, very similar to the results I achieved with slow-roasting. However, brining (immersing the bird in salty water) requires a very large stockpot and hours of preparation time. (This method is fine for a 3-pound chicken but a 20-pound turkey is a bit awkward.) My mother's slow-roast method is a whole lot easier and yields

similar results. I also found that the brined turkey lacked a bit of tooth. It was moist and flavorful, but it reminded me a bit of the boneless turkey breast sold at a delicatessen. I like turkey with real chew that will stand up to my mother's full-bore root vegetables. It's like serving carpaccio with cole slaw. Slaw needs a half-inch-thick burger, not wimpy slices of raw beef.

GRAVY WITHOUT THE GREASE

The problem with most gravy recipes is that they are made in the roasting pan, using all of the pan drippings. Well, pan drippings are mostly fat, and therefore the resulting gravy is greasy and to my palate inedible. I prefer to make gravy out of stock, using the pan drippings only as a flavoring. Here's how to do it. Just take a 3-quart pot and, at the same time you start cooking your turkey, add the giblets (everything but the liver) and about 2½ quarts cold water. If you like, you can also add a carrot, an onion, a rib of celery, and perhaps some fresh herbs and a bay leaf wrapped in cheesecloth. Place on the stove, bring to a boil, and then simmer for about 3 hours, or until you have reduced the liquid by about ⅔. Strain the stock through cheesecloth and reserve. When the turkey is done, remove 3 tablespoons of drippings from the roasting pan and place in the pot along with the stock. (Try to use the dark, rich portion of the drippings rather than just the clear fat.) Boil rapidly until the liquid is reduced by about ⅓. Whisk in 1 tablespoon of cornstarch mixed with 2 tablespoons of water and you are done. For a thicker sauce, use 2 tablespoons cornstarch mixed with ¼ cup water.

THAWING A TURKEY

It is best not to thaw a frozen turkey at room temperature. Defrost it in the refrigerator, allowing 3–4 hours per pound. A 12-pound bird will take up to 2 days in the refrigerator and a 24-pound bird will take about 3 days.

BASTING

As I discovered when testing roast chicken, it is best to brush with butter only once — before roasting. Basting during cooking will make the skin chewy.

Maw's Thanksgiving Turkey

The recipes that follow are adapted from the one used by my mother, Mary Alice White, who makes the best roast turkey in New England. The first is for a large bird and the second is for a smaller turkey. Both are cooked the day of the meal. When cooking at such low temperatures, I prefer to bake my stuffing separately for safety reasons, although my mother is not one to be put off by warnings from the health department, or from anyone else, for that matter. As for trussing, I sometimes just cut off the last joint of each wing (they tend to burn easily) and leave it at that. Actually, I find that having the legs and thighs standing free from the carcass cooks them more quickly (the dark meat needs more cooking than the breast meat). Be sure not to leave a cooked turkey at room temperature for too long. For safety reasons, it should not be left unrefrigerated for more than 2 hours. You may also serve turkey with one of the brown sauces listed in Chapter 31. If you are concerned about the safety of slow-roasting, roast the bird at a constant 325°F until the thigh registers 170°F, then continue with the recipe (see step 3).

Turkey
 1 turkey, 18–20 pounds, with giblets
 3 tablespoons melted butter
   Salt and freshly ground black pepper

Gravy
   Cut-up carrot, onion, celery rib, plus sprigs of fresh herbs, optional
 2½ quarts water
 1 tablespoon cornstarch
   Salt and freshly ground black pepper to taste

1. Remove giblets from turkey and set aside. Wash turkey with cold water inside and out, and dry thoroughly with paper towels.

2. Heat oven to 350°F. Brush turkey with melted butter, then place bird breast side down on a roasting rack in a shallow roasting pan. Sprinkle with salt and pepper. Cover turkey and pan tightly with aluminum foil and place in oven.

3. Roast for 1 hour. Reduce heat to 200°F. Roast for 3 hours. Turn bird breast side up and roast an additional 3 hours, 45 minutes, or until internal temperature of thighs reaches 160°–170°F. Remove bird from oven and increase temperature to 400°F. When oven is ready, remove foil from bird and roast an additional 10 minutes, or until thigh reaches an internal temperature of 170°–175°F.

4. While bird is roasting (at least 4 hours before serving), place giblets, excluding liver, in a 3-quart saucepan (you may also add a cut-up carrot, onion, celery rib, and fresh herbs wrapped in cheesecloth, if you like). Add about 2½ quarts cold water and bring to a boil. Simmer uncovered for 3 hours, or until you have reduced the liquid by about ⅔. Strain broth through a fine strainer or cheesecloth. Reserve.

5. When turkey is cooked, add 3 tablespoons of pan drippings to a saucepan with the reserved broth. Boil rapidly for about 10 minutes or until the liquid is reduced by about ⅓. Mix 1 tablespoon of cornstarch with 2 tablespoons of water and whisk into sauce. Simmer for 5 minutes. Add salt and pepper to taste.

6. Carve turkey and serve with gravy.

Serves 12 or more

Small Turkey Variation

Smaller birds need between 5½ and 6 hours of roasting at low temperature instead of the 7½ hours required for a 20-pound bird. Using a 12–14 pound turkey with giblets, proceed exactly as instructed in the master recipe with the exception of step 3. Follow instead these roasting times: Roast for 1 hour. Reduce heat to 200°F. Roast for 2 hours. Turn bird breast side up and roast an additional 2 hours, 45 minutes, or until internal temperature of thighs reaches 160°–170°F. Remove bird from oven and increase temperature to 400°F. When oven is hot, remove foil from bird and roast an additional 10 minutes or until the thigh reaches an internal temperature of 170°–175°F. Remove bird from oven and allow to rest on a cutting board for 20 minutes before carving.

A 12–14 pound bird will serve 8–12.

Simple Brown Sauce with Thyme

This is a quick, last-minute sauce that can be served with turkey. An immersion blender can be used to help thicken the sauce, although it is not necessary. This is a good sauce to use with left-overs and on other occasions when making a homemade stock is not practical.

2 tablespoons butter
1 tablespoon olive oil
3 shallots, peeled and minced
1 cup dry white wine
3 tablespoons brandy
1½ cups beef stock, homemade or low-sodium
½ teaspoon dried thyme or 2 teaspoons minced fresh
2 tablespoons cornstarch
Salt and freshly ground black pepper to taste

Place butter and olive oil in a sauté pan over medium-high heat. When hot, add the shallots and sauté for 5 minutes. Add the wine, brandy, stock, and thyme and bring to a boil. Cook until liquid has been reduced by 50 percent. Add cornstarch to ⅓ cup water and stir until dissolved and smooth. Whisk cornstarch mixture into boiling stock. Simmer until thickened. Season with salt and pepper to taste.

Makes about 1¼ cups

～ 26 ～

Improvising Stuffings

Stuffings can be made with breadcrumbs, rice, millet, barley,
bulgur, or kasha and flavored with nuts, fruit, herbs, and aromatics.
Here is a master recipe for all occasions.

I have been told that stuffings were once used simply to soak up the extra juices from a roast bird or joint of meat and were then thrown out. Over the years, however, they've become something special, often rivaling the meat itself in terms of popularity. What most home cooks don't realize is that poultry stuffings can be made not just from breadcrumbs but also from rice or grains and can be flavored with just about anything from fruit to nuts. In fact, a stuffing can be a whole lot more than a sop for juices and when well made, deserves its reputation.

HOW TO MAKE BREADCRUMBS

The single most important ingredient in stuffings is breadcrumbs. Never use the fine dried breadcrumbs sold in supermarkets — these are intended for breading foods for sautéing or frying. You need substantial cubes of bread for a stuffing, and the best way to get these is to cube and dry the bread yourself. You can dry the bread either in an oven or in the open air. I tested the oven method by cutting fresh bread into small cubes (I leave the crust on unless the bread has a tough, thick crust) and putting them in a single layer on a baking sheet. The bread was placed in a 225°

oven. Drying the cubes took 40 minutes for Arnold white bread, although a chewy country bread took just 25–30 minutes and a supermarket Italian loaf was done in 20 minutes. This method works in a pinch, but the inside of the cubes is still a bit soft when the outside is hardened and browned. If you have the time it's best simply to leave the cubed bread on baking sheets on the counter (or, if you don't have enough counter space, place them in large plastic storage bags that are left fully open to the air) according to the times indicated in the chart below.

KITCHEN TEST

How Long Does It Take to Make Dried Bread Cubes from Fresh Bread?

Four different types of bread were cut into ½-inch cubes and placed in a single layer on baking sheets and left to dry.

Bread Type	1 Day	2 Days	3 Days
Arnold white bread	Soft	Soft	Dry
Supermarket Italian bread	Dry		
Chewy country bread	Soft	Dry	
Chewy country bread, sourdough version	Soft	Dry	

I tested all four types of bread listed in the chart in stuffings and found that they were all good with the exception of the sourdough. The sour flavor was too strong for the other ingredients. I also tested and found that extra stuffing should be placed in a buttered baking or soufflé dish and then placed in a 375° oven for about 30 minutes. When cooked without a foil cover, the stuffing dried out. I found that it was best to cover the dish but to remove the foil halfway through the cooking time in order to brown the top.

Master Recipe for Stuffing

This is a simple template for most any poultry stuffing. The fruit and nuts are optional, and there are plenty of variations below. This recipe can be doubled.

   3 tablespoons unsalted butter
   1 tablespoon olive oil
   1½ cups chopped onion
   ½ cup chopped celery
   ¼ cup chopped scallions or chives
   ¼ cup chopped parsley
   4 cups cooked rice, barley, kasha, millet, bulgur, or homemade dried bread cubes
   ½ cup chopped sun-dried tomatoes, canned chestnuts, apples, prunes, or raisins (optional)
   ½ cup walnuts, pecans, or almonds, toasted (optional)
   2 tablespoons minced fresh sage, thyme, or oregano (or 1½ teaspoons dried)
   ⅓ cup white wine or chicken stock
   1 teaspoon kosher salt
   Freshly ground black pepper to taste

Heat the butter and olive oil in a skillet and sauté onion for 5 minutes over medium heat. Add celery and scallions or chives and sauté for 2 minutes. Mix together with all the remaining ingredients in a large bowl. (Prunes and raisins must be soaked in hot water for 5 minutes, then drained and chopped, or they may be soaked in a 50-50 mixture of sherry and water for 2 hours.)

Makes about 8 cups

Roasted Onion Variation

Peel 2 medium onions and cut into thick slices. Toss with olive oil and salt. Place in a roasting pan in a 450° oven for about 60 minutes, turning twice during cooking, or cook over a very hot grill, about 2 minutes per side. Coarsely chop and add to stuffing, omitting the onions and olive oil called for in the master recipe.

Gingered Onion Variation

While cooking the chopped onions add 2 teaspoons ground cumin and 1½ tablespoons grated or minced fresh ginger. Eliminate the herbs.

Mushroom Variation

Add 2 cups of chopped fresh mushrooms (any type will do) to the chopped onions while sautéing, along with an additional 1 tablespoon olive oil. Eliminate the fruit and nut additions.

Sage-Apple Variation

Add 2 apples that have been cored, peeled, and diced to the onion mixture. Use 2 cups of bread cubes instead of 4 and reduce the liquid to ¼ cup chicken stock or ¼ cup apple juice. Use fresh sage for the herb.

Toasted Cornbread-Pecan Stuffing

I always make this stuffing for Thanksgiving. The cornbread has a nice full flavor and texture that goes well with turkey. Use the cornbread recipe found in the Lemon-Buttermilk Corn Muffins on page 351 but eliminate the lemon juice and lemon zest. Spread the batter in a jelly roll pan and bake 10–12 minutes in a 425° oven.

6 cups coarsely crumbled cornbread
¾ cup pecans
¼ pound bacon, cut into ½-inch pieces
2 tablespoons butter
2 tablespoons olive oil
2 cups finely chopped onions
¾ cup finely chopped celery
1 tablespoon fresh thyme leaves or 1 teaspoon dried
1 tablespoon minced fresh sage or 1 teaspoon dried
Salt and freshly ground black pepper to taste
3 tablespoons bourbon
1 cup chicken stock
½ cup minced flat-leaf parsley

1. Heat oven to 350°F. Spread crumbled cornbread onto a baking sheet. Coarsely chop pecans and add to cornbread. Toast in oven for 25–30 minutes or until cornbread is golden, tossing the crumbs once or twice during toasting. Cool and place in a large mixing bowl.

2. Cook bacon over medium-high heat in a sauté pan or skillet. Remove bacon with a slotted spoon to bowl with cornbread and pour off all but 1 tablespoon drippings. Add butter and olive oil to skillet and when butter has melted add onion and sauté for 5 minutes over medium heat. Add celery and sauté another 3 minutes. Stir in thyme and sage and salt and pepper to taste. Add to cornbread mixture.

3. Turn up heat under sauté pan and add bourbon. Stir vigorously for 2 minutes with a wooden spoon, scraping the bottom of the pan. Add chicken stock, cook for 1 minute, and add mixture to bowl. Add parsley to bowl and adjust seasonings.

Makes about 10 cups

Master Recipe for Apple Stuffing

I prefer a Macoun or Northern Spy for cooking. Avoid McIntosh and Red Delicious — they are not firm and crisp enough to bake well — and also Granny Smith, which is somewhat tough and dry.

3 tablespoons butter
1 tablespoon olive oil
½ cup chopped onion
4 cups peeled, cored, and diced apples
1 teaspoon sugar
2 cups dry bread cubes
¼ teaspoon ground nutmeg
¼ teaspoon ground cinnamon
¼ teaspoon ground allspice
¼ cup apple cider or apple juice
1 teaspoon kosher salt
1 tablespoon minced fresh sage

Heat butter and oil in a skillet and sauté onions and apples for 5 minutes over medium heat. Remove from heat and combine with remaining ingredients in a large bowl.

Makes about 7 cups

Prune Variation

Substitute 2 cups of dried pitted prunes for 2 cups of apples. Soak the prunes in hot water for 5 minutes (or soak for 2 hours in a 50-50 mixture of sherry and water), drain, and then chop.

Sausage Variation

Sauté 2 cups (1 pound) sausage meat in a skillet, breaking it up into small pieces as it cooks. When browned, remove from skillet, reserving 1 tablespoon of fat. Replace the olive oil in the master recipe with the sausage fat, reduce apples to 2 cups, increase bread cubes to 4 cups, and proceed with recipe.

~ 27 ~

The Cuts of Meat

What's the difference between country ribs, baby back ribs, barbecue ribs, and spareribs? Where does a sirloin steak come from and why is it different from a T-bone steak? Is a bottom round roast better than a top round roast?

~

In New York in the mid-1970s, I took guitar lessons from Paul Simon's brother, and although I still can't play "Johnny B. Goode," I do remember one piece of advice. He said, "If you stand up in front of an audience and state emphatically that you are going to play 'Greensleeves,' they'll believe you even if you play 'Rock Around the Clock.'" Each time I entered a butcher shop, I kept this advice in mind. I delivered my order confidently, with no hint that I had no clue what I had just ordered. If I asked for a bottom round roast, I would be speechless if the butcher suggested a chuck eye roast instead. Since I had no idea where the cut came from in the first place or what its cooking characteristics were, I had no way of deciding what a reasonable substitute would be. Was the Boston butt cut from the shoulder or the butt end of the animal?

To remedy this situation, I started by visiting two local supermarkets, counting the number of different beef cuts available, and then comparing the two stores to see how many of these cuts were labeled identically. The first store had 38 cuts of beef in its meat section; the other had 34. The shocking statistic, however, was that *only 11 of these cuts were the same*. Although both retailers carried a porterhouse steak, one featured a "top loin clubsteak bone-in" and the other had cuts with names such as "top steak first cut thin sliced" and a "tip roast boneless, oven roast."

The enormity of this problem became clear when I found out that prior to 1976, the year the National Live Stock and Meat Board issued regulations standardizing the cuts of meat, there were over 1,000 cuts. Today there are 314. However, local markets around the country still tend to use local names. A cross rib pot roast is also known as a Boston cut. A top loin steak is also a New York strip steak. Meat wholesalers, on the other hand, have reduced cuts to numbers. Today, the loin without the chine bone (backbone) and the tenderloin is referred to as a 179. This has simplified identification of cuts (although not for the consumer, who is still subject to the whims of local nomenclature) but has taken some of the personality and romance out of the business.

THE GHOSTS OF FOURTEENTH STREET

My introduction to New York's meat district was ten years ago, when I filmed a video on butchering starring Jack Ubaldi, the founder of the Florence Meat Market. At that time, West Fourteenth Street was the center of the universe for meat wholesalers. Walk past the thick plastic flaps at the entrance of any establishment and you were hit by a blast of chilled air with a faint undercurrent of sweet and sour, not unpleasant but always a reminder of the trade. Forequarters and hindquarters hung on giant hooks gliding on overhead rails, moving into line, waiting for the butchers with narrow, well-honed knives held like daggers. The floor was concrete and almost frozen with a sheen of water, fat, and bits of meat. On this slick stage, the butchers moved about with a casual but determined rhythm. The faces of those men were more developed than those you saw uptown — expressive features that had been set hard by time and experience.

I recently returned to Fourteenth Street. Today, the wholesalers are mostly gone, replaced by Kry-O-Vac cuts, boxed and shipped directly from Omaha. The Eastern Meat Market, one of the few survivors, is still breaking down kosher meat with a small crew. Say good-bye to club steaks, Newport steaks, flanken, deckel. They will be forgotten over time, just as we can no longer name the different types of horse-drawn carriages — cabriolets, coupes, phaetons, surreys, and four-in-hands.

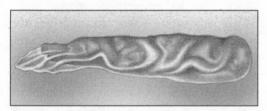

The tenderloin is a long, cylindrical muscle that extends from the bottom of the rib cage to the hip. (The piece shown in the illustration is sealed in Kry-O-Vac, as it is sold at a wholesale market, and is about 2½ feet long.) It is the most expensive piece of beef; both filet mignon and tournedos are cross sections of this cut. It is very tender meat and can stand high-heat cooking.

A Short Course in Animal Architecture

The best way to understand cuts of meat is to start with the dressed carcass of the whole animal and then break it down into its parts as a butcher would. The first step is to split the animal, whether it's beef, lamb, pork, or veal, in half from neck to rump. Looking at each half, we see that all these animals have three major parts: the shoulder, the rib section, and the rump. In a relatively small animal such as a pig, these three areas roughly correspond to the major cuts. A larger animal, however, is divided into more sections because of its size. Each of these sections is referred to as a primal, or basic, cut.

The single most important concept to master is that butchery is the art of dividing up muscles. A butcher can do one of two things when preparing meat. He can "seam out" the muscles (remove them intact, discarding bone and connective tissues) to create cuts of meat that are usually sold as roasts. Or the butcher can leave the muscle attached to the bone and then cut out cross sections, which usually include more than one muscle. A porterhouse steak, for example, is a cross section of a loin of beef and includes both the tenderloin and shell muscles. (The smaller piece of meat is the tenderloin. If the tenderloin were "seamed out" and cut into pieces, it would be sold as filet mignon.) Think of a multilayer birthday cake. Each layer represents a different muscle. You could deconstruct the cake, removing each layer (muscle) intact and then cutting the layer into pieces, or you could slice into the cake so that each piece would have some of each layer plus filling and frosting.

The Grades of Beef

About half of all beef is graded for quality. This is a voluntary procedure paid for by the meat producer. There are three grades: prime, choice, and select. Almost all of the beef available to consumers falls in the choice category. Prime, the best and most costly grade, is generally purchased by restaurants and accounts for less than 5 percent of all beef sales. There is in fact a noticeable difference in flavor between grades of meat. Look for "top choice" when purchasing beef, or "prime" if it's available (the latter is usually sold to restaurants only). The higher the designation, the more flavor and the better the texture. Do not confuse the differences in quality between various cuts of beef with the quality differences from one carcass to another. One animal may have exquisite, well-marbled meat, while the next may be good for nothing more than ground beef. It's the condition of the animal that really counts. Although it is a dying practice, since most meat is now sold prepackaged, the best New York steakhouses and butchers still send buyers down to the wholesale markets to make their selections in person.

MARBLING

Well-marbled beef simply has streaks of fat throughout. As the meat is cooked, this fat melts and adds flavor. Well-marbled cuts usually come from animals that are a bit older, as this type of fat takes time to develop. The secret of leaner cuts was explained to me by a friend who owns a cattle ranch in Wyoming. He said that ranchers who wish to sell "lean" meat simply bring the animal to market at 900–1,000 pounds, before it acquires much fat (most cattle come to market at 1,200 pounds). At the other extreme, good small producers often slaughter their cattle at over 2,000 pounds, producing more flavorful meat. Also take note that many supermarkets will claim "lean" on their packaging when all they have done is trim away some of the exterior fat.

Does Aging Meat Affect Flavor?

A large eye round roast (choice grade) purchased at a supermarket was placed uncovered on a rack in the refrigerator for 5 days to determine if aging affects flavor. Each day, part of the roast was cut off, browned for 5 minutes in 2 tablespoons of olive oil, and then roasted in a 200° oven until the meat reached an internal temperature of 130°F. The results show that aging has a tremendous effect on texture and flavor, but the meat needs to sit for 4 days. One or 2 days in the refrigerator will not make much difference.

Aging Time	Results
1 day	Meat was flavorful but somewhat chewy. Very juicy.
2 days	Slightly less chewy than the 1 day of aging, but same flavor.
3 days	Meat was more tender and still juicy. Flavor was better.
4 days	Very tender, very juicy, terrific melt-in-your-mouth flavor. This was a winner.
5 days	Same as 4 days.

AGING BEEF

Beef is aged to develop the flavor and improve the texture. This process is based on the work of enzymes whose function is to digest proteins while the animal is alive. After slaughter, the cells that contain these enzymes begin to break down, releasing them into the meat. They attack the cell proteins, which start to convert into amino acids, which have more flavor. In addition, the muscles begin to break down as well, and the tissue becomes softer. Proper aging can take from one to several weeks. (To age meat for more than a few days, it must be done under carefully controlled conditions — it cannot be done at home.) To test aging meat at home, I placed a large eye round roast in the refrigerator, uncovered, on a rack above a pan. Each day for 5 days I sliced off a piece and cooked it. The Kitchen Test chart above summarizes what I learned. Clearly, 4 days of aging is best. Most cookbooks tell you to age for 1–2 days. As shown in the test, this is insufficient time to develop flavor and texture. To age a roast of beef at home, start with a fresh specimen that has no odor and is bright red, not dark red or gray. The roast should be placed on a rack over a roasting pan uncovered, to promote good air circulation. This exposure to air will dry out the meat, which concentrates the flavor. Do not age pork, veal, or lamb.

BEEF

CUTS OF BEEF

Looking at a side of beef and starting at the neck and running to the rump, the basic cuts are the chuck, rib, loin, sirloin, and round. The underside of the animal is divided into the brisket, plate, and flank.

Chuck: Let's start with the forequarter of beef, specifically the chuck, which is the area from the neck to the fifth rib. Generally speaking, the chuck is more tender and more flavorful than the rump of the animal, which has less fat and less connective tissue. Why is this so? Well, it's because the chuck, which is really the shoulder, gets a good workout. This results in lots of connective tissues, which melt when heated by cooking, adding both moisture and flavor. There is an old saying — the meat closest to horn or hoof tastes best. The rump, at the top of the leg around the hip, is far away from either horn or hoof and therefore is less well developed.

Within a cross section of the chuck are four major muscles. The eye of the chuck, often sold as a chuck eye roast, is the meat contained within the first five ribs of the animal and is at the center of the chuck. Above this muscle is the shoulder blade, which is home

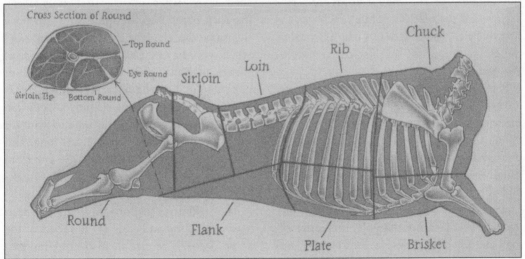

CUTS OF BEEF

Cross Section of Round
Top Round
Eye Round
Sirloin Tip
Bottom Round
Sirloin
Loin
Rib
Chuck
Round
Flank
Plate
Brisket

Beef has six basic cuts, which include the chuck, the rib, the loin, the sirloin, the round, and the brisket/plate/flank. The chuck is an inexpensive and excellent cut for pot roasts, stew, and ground meat for hamburger; the rib is the origin of the rib roast; the loin includes the tenderloin, the most tender and expensive cut of all, and is also home to many classic American steaks, including the T-bone and porter-house; the sirloin is the rear portion of the loin and produces sirloin steaks as well as the top and bottom butt muscles, which are used for both steaks and roasts; the round is very lean and is therefore tough and lacking in flavor, although it is often sold for stew meat and roasts; the brisket/plate/flank is used for a variety of specialty items including flank steaks, brisket, London broil, pastrami, and skirt steaks.

to the remaining three cuts. The underblade meat, often sold as an underblade steak or roast, is in fact directly underneath the shoulder blade. The top blade muscle, often sold as a top blade roast, is above it. The mock tender, an ice cream cone–shaped piece of meat next to the top blade muscle, can also be used for a roast.

One other important muscle that is part of the forequarter is referred to as the shoulder clod. (In human terms, this is the bicep, located in the upper arm.) It is sold as either a shoulder or arm roast and can also be cut crosswise into steaks bearing the same names.

The chuck is also ground, as are most other inexpensive cuts, and sold as ground beef.

Rib: The ribs can be a confusing part of butchery, as they are treated differently with each type of animal. Lamb, veal, and beef have thirteen pairs of ribs and pigs have fourteen. (Humans have twelve pairs of ribs.) Ribs are counted from the front of the animal, so the higher-numbered ribs are toward the rear. The chuck includes the first five ribs, the next seven ribs are part of the rib section, and the last rib is part of the loin.

If you order beef ribs at a restaurant, you are not getting an entire rib from the spine all the way down to the end of the rib, which is about 11 inches. When a steak or a roast is prepared for sale, about 4 inches of the rib is usually trimmed off. This is called a short rib and is often found on menus. However, if a butcher bones out the ribs, making a boneless rib eye roast, for example, the entire rib may be left over. These are often cut into shorter pieces, which are also marketed as "short ribs." Therefore, a short rib simply means any short piece of rib no matter where it came from. (Regardless of length, the ribs you find on a restaurant menu probably come from the front of the animal, where the ribs are particularly meaty.)

The rib section also contains the rib roast and the prime rib. Rib steaks, popular in Europe as entrecôte or bistecca, are cut from the rib. A rib roast comes from the tenth through twelfth ribs (the last ribs in this cut).

Loin and Sirloin: The next cut of beef is the loin, which is between the ribs (the loin does contain the last — the thirteenth — rib, however) and the round. (Think of the loin as the part of your body between your rib cage and your pelvic joint, or hip socket.) This contains the most expensive meat because it is the most tender — but it is far from either hoof or horn, so it is somewhat bland. It is home to two major muscles, the tenderloin and the shell. The tenderloin is a long, cylindrical piece of meat which, if removed intact, may then be cut crosswise into rounds and sold as filet mignon. (This same cut is used for Chateaubriand and tournedos as well, the latter cut on the bias from the small end of the tenderloin.) The shell is a larger muscle that runs along the back parallel to the spine. Humans have this same muscle. It is the one that gets sore when you have a backache. The famous American steaks, including — from the front of the animal to the back — Delmonico, T-bone, porterhouse, and sirloin, all contain both of these muscles, one on each side of the bone. The loin is about 2 feet long, and the number of steaks that can be cut from it depends entirely on how thick the steaks are cut.

The sirloin is the portion of the loin that starts at the hip and ends at the socket of the pelvic bone. The sirloin also contains two muscles — the top butt and bottom butt — which are often sold as steaks (a Newport steak, for example, is cut from the bottom butt) or as roasts (a boneless sirloin is the top butt). The top butt is of higher quality than the bottom butt, although both are relatively inexpensive cuts.

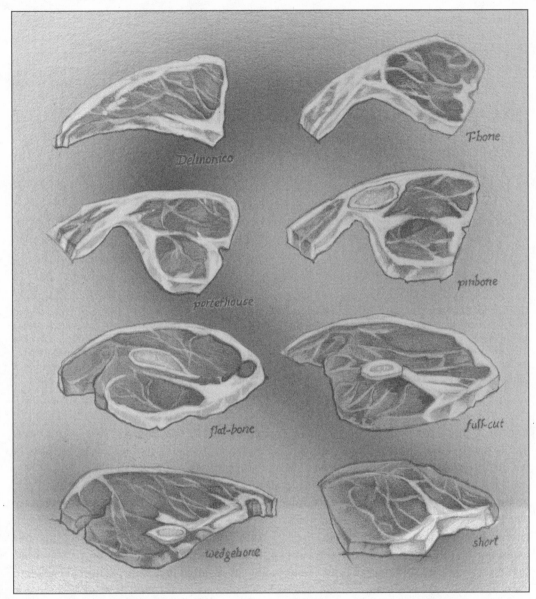

Delmonico

T-bone

porterhouse

pinbone

flat-bone

full-cut

wedgebone

short

Steaks from the Loin and Sirloin: Starting at the rib end (toward the front of the animal) of the loin and ending at the back of the sirloin, the cuts of steak run in the following order: Delmonico, T-bone, porterhouse, pinbone, flat-bone, full-cut, wedgebone, and short. The first three steaks are part of the loin; the last five are part of the sirloin, hence the term sirloin steak. Note that each steak is really a cross section of the loin or sirloin, providing convenient snapshots of the muscles as you move from front to back. If the tenderloin is removed from any of the loin steaks, it is referred to as a shell (or strip) steak. Although the T-bone and porterhouse steaks are usually considered among the best, two sirloin steaks, the flat-bone and wedgebone cuts, are also very good. The pinbone steak is not a superior cut because it contains many nerves, which are tough.

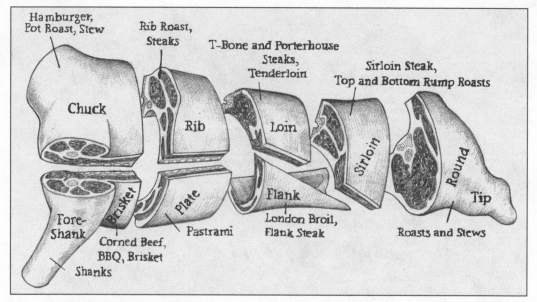

The Cuts of Beef at a Glance: Most cuts of beef are used for more than one purpose. Stew meat and ground meat, for example, can be taken from many different parts of the animal. Steaks can come from the sirloin, the loin, the ribs, or even the chuck. In general, cuts closest to horn or hoof have more flavor, although they must be cooked low and slow to avoid tough, dry meat. That is why many cooks prefer steaks from the rib section to those taken from the loin. The loin is tender but not very flavorful, whereas the ribs, which contain more developed muscles (they are closer to the horns), produce tougher but tastier steaks.

Round: A more complex part of a side of beef is the round, which, in human terms, is the thigh from the knee up to the top of the leg. It contains four separate muscles: the top round, the bottom round, the sirloin tip, and the eye round. Thinking of a human thigh once again, the sirloin tip is the front of the thigh, the top round is the inside, the bottom round is the outside, and the eye round is the back. These cuts are very lean, without much fat and with few tendons, and are therefore difficult to cook well. A bottom round roast, for example, is the worst possible cut for a roast. Unless you slow-roast it (see next chapter), it will be dry and tough. If you are going to roast a cut from the round, buy the top round, which is often roasted and then used in delicatessens for roast beef sandwiches. Restaurants will often roast the entire round, which is then referred to as "steamship" round. However, I cannot recommend purchasing any cut from the round unless it is to be sliced very thin — this cut is tough and lacking in flavor. You are always better off with the chuck.

Brisket/Plate/Flank: These cuts are directly below the chuck, rib, and loin. The brisket, a thin, boneless rectangle of meat, is tough but flavorful and is the basis for corned beef, which is cured in a brine solution. The plate is home to pastrami. The flank is used for skirt steaks and London broil. If you purchase a flank steak, look for a short, thick piece rather than one that is thin and long.

WHICH CUTS TO BUY

Ground Beef: This is usually made from leftovers — ground-up meat from any primal cut. The key in selecting ground beef is fat content, which is measured in percentage of lean, from about 72 percent to 90 percent, the latter often referred to as "diet lean." You want a middle ground here — 80 percent is about right for both flavor and juiciness. The best cuts for ground beef come from the chuck, and I recommend the top blade cut, which either your butcher can grind for you or you can grind at home in a food processor. As discussed above, the chuck has four major muscles, and the top blade is the highest quality. This is the same cut used for the best pot roasts.

London Broil: This comes from a variety of cuts, and is a lower-quality piece of meat that is sold boneless. It is usually broiled and then sliced thin for serving; otherwise, it would be very chewy. London broil comes from both the flank and the shoulder; the shoulder is the preferable cut.

Steaks: This designation can mean just about anything. Steaks come from the chuck, plate, flank, rib, loin, sirloin, and round. The most tender steaks are cut from the tenderloin muscle and are sold as filet mignon. The most popular American steaks (although not necessarily the most flavorful), which all include part of the tenderloin muscle, are found in the loin. They are, from front to back, Delmonico, T-bone, porterhouse, and the sirloin steaks (see illustration, page 237). If the tenderloin muscle is not included in these steaks, they are sold as shell steaks or New York strip steaks. Europeans tend to favor steaks cut from the rib section, usually the fifth through seventh ribs. These are tougher but have more flavor than the loin steaks. You can also purchase steaks from the chuck (e.g., top blade steak boneless), which have a good amount of fat compared to the round but which are not as tender as the loin steaks. Finally, the round can be cut into steaks, including the top round steak, eye round steak, and cube steak. These are very lean, tough steaks.

Roasts and Pot Roasts: The best cut and the most expensive is the rib roast cut from the loin, from the tenth through twelfth ribs. A two-rib roast will serve 4; a three-rib roast will serve 6. Rib roasts can be cut from any other set of ribs, however. You can also purchase less expensive cuts for roasting. Although many roasts (the top round, an eye round roast, or a bottom round roast) are cut from the round, these are relatively lean, tough roasts, even when cooked at low temperatures. Always buy a roast from the chuck, such as a top blade roast or a chuck eye roast, instead of from the round (a supermarket may refer to these chuck roasts as "beef chuck top blade roast boneless" or "top chuck roast").

Be aware that many supermarkets will sell a "chuck eye roast" that is actually the mock tender, the cone-shaped muscle that is next to the top blade roast near the shoulder blade. This is an inferior cut of meat. A real chuck eye roast comes from the first five ribs and is full of marbling and flavor. If the roast is cone-shaped, it is probably the mock tender. If it looks like a rib roast, then you know you have the real thing.

Don't be confused by "pot roasts." These are simply inexpensive boneless roasts that are to be cooked in a pot on top of the stove over low heat with a small amount of liquid. Any boneless roast can be "pot roasted," although chuck roasts will be superior to roasts from the round.

Ribs: If you like meaty beef ribs, purchase ribs from the chuck. These short ribs are called flanken, and they have a good thick (about 1½ inches) layer of meat on top of them (this area of the ribs is meatier due to the muscles in the shoulder area). As you move back toward the rear of the animal, the ribs will have less meat (about half an inch of meat for a typical short rib). The tenth through twelfth ribs will have mostly fat. So if you like meaty ribs, ask for short ribs from the chuck. In general, I suggest that you purchase pork ribs. They have more flavor and fat, and are juicier and more tender when cooked.

Which Is the Best Cut for an Inexpensive Beef Roast?

Three major sections of a side of beef are the home of inexpensive roasts. The chuck is fattier, more tender, and more flavorful than any cut from the round, which is lean and relatively tough. The sirloin is better than the round but not as good as the chuck. Then why is it much easier to find a roast from the round than a chuck roast? Well, having spent some time with a local Boston butcher, I discovered that preparing a chuck roast is time-consuming given the relatively complex construction of the chuck. The round, however, has only one bone and relatively little connective tissue, and the meat is readily sliced off into roast-size chunks.

I roasted ten different cuts: five from the chuck, two from the sirloin, and three from the round. Although I tend to prefer juicier, fattier meat, the top round and the top sirloin were actually quite good. In general, however, the chuck provides more flavor and better texture than either the round or sirloin.

CUTS FROM THE CHUCK

Chuck roasts tend to be fattier, juicier, more tender, and more flavorful than roasts from the round. However, a boneless chuck roast is often not easy to find, since butchers consider it more economical to prepare this cut as steaks or stew meat. Roasts are described in order of preference.

3. Underblade Roast: This is the muscle underneath the shoulder blade. It is quite similar to a blade roast, with lots of connective tissue and lots of flavor.

1. Blade Roast: This was clearly the best roast in the taste test, flavorful, juicy, and tender. It does contain a fair amount of connective tissues, which are relatively unattractive but not unpleasant to eat. A blade roast refers to the "top blade" muscle, which is over the shoulder blade.

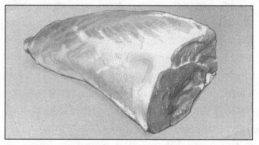

4. Chuck Fillet or Chuck Tender Roast: This roast, made from the "mock tender" muscle, is tougher, stringier, and less flavorful than the chuck eye roast. Many supermarkets mislabel this cut as a chuck eye roast. If the roast is cone-shaped, it is probably the mock tender and therefore an inferior cut.

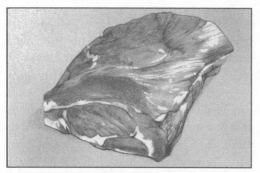

2. Chuck Eye Roast: This is a boneless rib roast cut from the center of the first five ribs. The meat has good marbling throughout, which adds both flavor and moisture. This is an extremely tender, juicy, and fatty piece of meat. It would have won first place in our tasting but was marked down for excessive fat content.

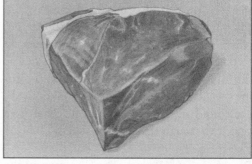

5. Shoulder Roast: This used to be called an arm roast since it is the muscle at the top of the "arm" by the shoulder. It is chewy, grainy, and not very flavorful.

CUTS FROM THE SIRLOIN

There are three important cuts for roasts from the sirloin: the top sirloin, the top rump roast, and the bottom rump roast. I tested two of these. These cuts come from the hip area, between the round and the loin. Roasts are described in order of preference.

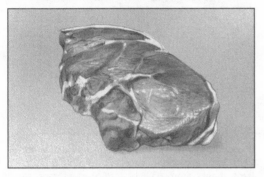

1. Top Sirloin: Relatively juicy, flavorful, and tender. Good coloration on both the outside (dark brown) and inside (bright red). The clear winner among roasts from the rump or round.

2. Bottom Rump Roast: Juicy and with good flavor, but not as tender as either the top sirloin or the top round roast. You can also purchase a top rump roast, which is slightly superior in flavor and texture.

CUTS FROM THE ROUND

Roasts from the round tend to be lean and relatively tough compared to chuck roasts. Generally speaking, they should be sliced very thin for serving. Roasts are described in order of preference. (I did not test the sirloin tip muscle, which is roughly equal to the top round in terms of flavor and texture.)

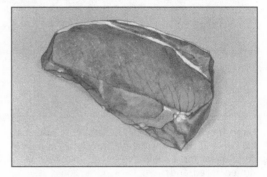

1. Top Round: Not quite as good as the top sirloin, but with good flavor, texture, and juiciness.

2. Eye of the Round: Less juicy and flavorful than the other roasts.

3. Bottom Round: The least tender of all the cuts. Mediocre flavor as well.

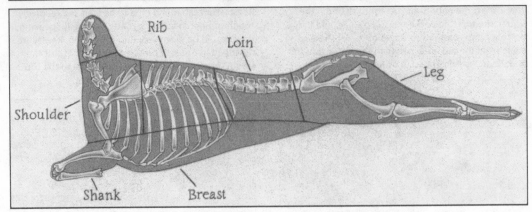

Lamb has five cuts: the shoulder, the rib, the loin, the leg, and the shank/breast. The shoulder is wonderful meat for a stew, and it can also be boned, stuffed, rolled, and roasted; the rib section is used for a rack of lamb or can be cut into chops; the loin is the source of the best lamb chops; the leg is similar to the round in beef and is excellent roasted or braised; lamb shanks are usually braised at low temperature; the breast is stuffed and roasted, or cut into riblets for grilling and braising.

Stew Beef: You want as much fat as possible in stew meat; otherwise, the finished product will be dry. I prefer stew meat cut from the shoulder, although it also comes from just about every other part of the animal.

LAMB

Lamb as we find it in the supermarket comes from animals that are six months to one year old, hopefully on the younger end of the scale. Baby lamb is three to four months old. Lamb over one year old is called mutton. What used to be called spring lamb really doesn't exist anymore. The term used to refer to animals born from March through October. Now that breeding techniques have changed, "spring lamb" is not a term used by the U.S. Department of Agriculture and is currently used only as a marketing tool.

CUTS OF LAMB

Lamb consists of five distinct cuts: the shoulder, the rib, the loin, the leg, and the shank/breast. The first four ribs are included in the shoulder, the next eight are in the rib section, and the last rib is part of the loin. The best lamb is a light red meat, not dark red like beef, the latter indicating an older animal. Lamb is a fatty animal and is best purchased as young as possible. A leg of lamb should weigh under 5 pounds — anything larger is from an older, and therefore undesirable, animal.

Shoulder: This cut is good for stew — it has great flavor but needs to be cooked slow and long due to the muscle development. The shoulder can also be boned, stuffed, rolled, and then roasted. Shoulder chops also come from this cut.

Rib: This is the area of the animal just behind the shoulder and is the source for a rack of lamb. A rack consists of eight ribs on either side still attached to the spine. When cut into individual chops, they are referred to as rib chops. These chops can be formed into an honor guard roast, with crossing frenched ribs (frenching is cleaning the rib ends so that the bones are exposed), or a crown roast, in which the ribs are formed into a circle, or crown.

Loin: The loin and the back legs make up the hindsaddle of the animal. The loin, as with all meat, contains the best and most expensive cuts. It can be cut into top-quality lamb chops. It can be boned out and cut into medallions or noisettes (similar to filet mignon in beef). It can be boned out and formed into an expensive roast called a saddle of lamb. By the way, in lamb the tenderloin is referred to as the eye of the loin.

Leg: A leg of lamb is really the same part of the animal that is referred to as the round in beef. It is the hind leg up to the hip. The leg is sold boneless and tied or with the bone in. A boned leg of lamb can also be butterflied (cut into one even-thickness piece), marinated, and then grilled.

Shank/Breast: The shank, which is cut from the forelegs of the animal, not the rear legs, is cut into crosswise pieces and braised (cooked slowly with some liquid). The breast is the least expensive cut and is not usually sold in supermarkets. It can be cut into riblets or stuffed and roasted.

Which Cuts to Buy

Leg of Lamb: Find the smallest leg you can. Smaller animals are younger and have the best flavor. If you purchase a half leg, ask for the shank end, not the end toward the hip (the sirloin half). The shank end has more flavor and will be more tender when cooked. Be sure to have the aitchbone removed, which will facilitate carving. Also ask your butcher to remove the silverskin (outer membrane) covering the meat and, if he or she is willing, have them remove the lymph node, which contributes to the gamy taste of lamb (for more information, see pages 207–208).

Lamb Chops: The best chops come from the loin, but they are expensive. Thinner chops come from the rib section and are referred to as rib chops. They are less expensive but

not as tender as the loin chops. Shoulder chops are not particularly tender compared to loin chops but have lots of flavor.

Stew Meat: Use pieces cut from the shoulder. They are inexpensive but have plenty of fat and flavor.

VEAL

Bull calves were traditionally slaughtered at birth, as the dairy industry had no use for animals that could not produce milk (one bull per cow was not necessary). The veal industry was born when a dairy-based formula was developed that was fed to the calves until they were slaughtered at 16 weeks. This formula produced tender, white meat even at an age at which the meat should be darker and tougher. Today, however, veal is defined as a young bull calf up to 26 weeks old. Very young calves, only a week or two old, are referred to as bob calves. Their meat is very white and tasteless. The older calves are weaned from milk early and then fed a normal diet. This meat is darker, tougher, and more flavorful. This is the type of veal most often sold in a supermarket.

For many people, the raising and slaughtering of veal is a moral issue. Today there is an alternative to the penned calf, which is the naturally raised bull calf. The animal is allowed some freedom to roam, rather than standing tethered to a stall for its short life. The meat is darker than regular veal and has more flavor than milk-fed. Culinary purists, however, feel that naturally raised veal is really a young calf and represents a tougher, inferior cut of meat. In recipes using milk-fed veal, much of the flavor of the dish comes from other sources — it's the veal's texture, which is much more tender than that of the naturally raised product, that sells it.

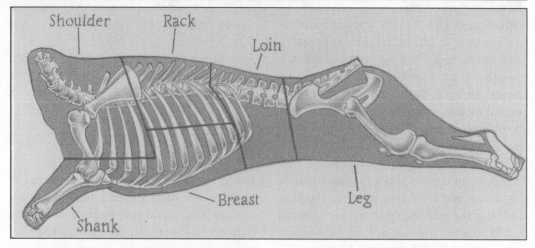

Shoulder Rack Loin

Breast Leg

Shank

Veal has five cuts, including the shoulder, the rack, the loin, the leg, and the breast/shank. The shoulder is used for stew meat or is boned and stuffed; the rack is used for either chops or a rack of veal; the loin is good for chops or the tenderloin, which is very expensive; the leg is used for cutlets, boneless roasts, and the usual bone-in leg; the breast is roasted as is or boned and stuffed; the shank is used for ossobuco.

CUTS OF VEAL

Veal consists of five cuts: the shoulder, the rack, the loin, the leg, and the breast/shank.

Shoulder: As with lamb, the shoulder is often boned and then stuffed. The meat has a good amount of fat and therefore flavor. The shoulder can also be boned and tied into a roast. This muscle is often referred to as the shoulder clod — it is the solid, center muscle of the shoulder. The shoulder also provides good cubes of meat for stews.

Rack: As with lamb, you can purchase a rack of veal consisting of eight ribs, or you can get individual chops (individual ribs that are trimmed).

Loin: The loin is home to the best, most tender chops. The loin can also be boned out into a roast called a saddle roast, a very expensive cut.

Leg: A leg of veal has the same construction as a round of beef. A cross section would show four muscles in order of desirability:

the top sirloin, the top round, the eye round, and the bottom round. Each of these can be boned out and sold as a roast or cut into thin slices for cutlets or scallopini.

Shank: The shank, or the foreleg, when cut into small pieces crosswise, is the basis for the well-known Italian dish ossobuco.

Breast: This can be boned and stuffed and is a relatively economical piece of meat. It can also be roasted with the ribs left in.

WHICH CUTS TO BUY

Veal Chops: Chops come from the shoulder, the ribs, and the loin. Loin chops are the thickest, best, and most expensive. Rib chops are next best, and shoulder chops are the lowest quality.

Veal Roast: Of highest quality is a saddle roast, cut from the loin. Roasts also come from the leg, the top sirloin being the best. After the sirloin roast, I would try a roast from the shoulder, which is inexpensive and very good. A bottom round roast tends to

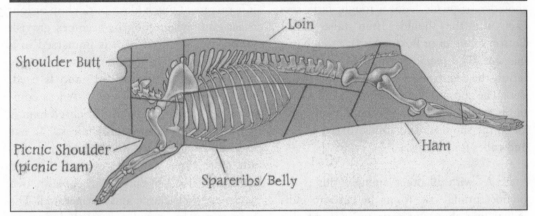

Pork consists of four basic cuts: the shoulder, the loin, the ham, and the spareribs/belly. The shoulder provides the picnic shoulder (as in a picnic ham) and the Boston butt (or Boston shoulder), which is a tougher cut often used for kabobs and roasts; the loin produces center-cut pork chops, the tenderloin, and also Canadian bacon; the ham produces three different cuts, including the pork butt (the top cut), ham (the center cut), and shank (the bottom part of the ham, really the top of the leg); the spareribs/belly produces spareribs and bacon.

cook up tough and dry, just like bottom round in beef.

Stew Meat: Always ask for meat cut from the shoulder for a tender, moist stew.

Scallopini and Cutlets: As this meat will be pounded before serving, you can use a less expensive cut, such as the bottom round or eye round. Cutlets are thicker and should come from a better piece of meat, such as the top round or top sirloin.

PORK

Before World War II, hog fat had many uses, from cooking to being an important ingredient in explosives. In the postwar years, as the only commercial use for pigs became meat, hogs were bred to produce more meat as a percentage of total weight. This meant a decrease in the amount of fat. This trend has been accelerated in the last ten years. Scientists are currently working on schemes to lower fat and cholesterol content, including special injections to increase the muscle-to-fat ratio as a pig develops. Genetic engineer-

ing is also playing its part in creating a leaner pig. However, as it becomes leaner, pork has less flavor and is much less tender.

When cooking pork, keep in mind that most people overcook it due to the fear of trichinosis, caused by a parasitic worm. The USDA recommends that pork be cooked to an internal temperature of 160°F to assure safety. If you do cook pork to this temperature (in a roast, for example) it will continue to rise in temperature after it is removed from the oven and end up being relatively dry and tough. I cook pork to 140°–145°F, remove it from the oven, and let stand for 20 minutes. The roast will rise in temperature another 5° or so. The results will be juicy and flavorful. If, however, you are concerned about killing all parasites (which are less of a problem today than they were many years ago), you may wish to follow the lead of the USDA. It's your choice.

CUTS OF PORK
Pigs are cut into four basic sections: the shoulder, the loin, the ham, and the spareribs/belly (the last is not technically considered a primal cut, however).

Shoulder: This is divided into the picnic shoulder or picnic ham, a tough, fatty section, and the shoulder butt (also called Boston shoulder or Boston butt), a tough primal cut. The picnic shoulder is, in human terms, the arm from the elbow to the shoulder. The Boston butt (or shoulder — the terms are interchangeable) is the large muscle in the shoulder and yields roasts, steaks, and cubes for kabobs.

Loin: As with all other animals, this is the premier primal cut. It can be cut into individual loin chops, or a group of eight ribs can be fashioned into a crown roast. Or it can be cut into a variety of roasts. A roast cut from the rear of the loin is referred to as a rump, or loin, roast. A roast cut from the front (referred to as the rib end) of the loin, is called a rib-end roast. There are two additional roasts in the loin: a center-cut loin roast and a center-cut rib roast. (Center-cut simply means cut from the center.) The tenderloin is also part of the loin; it is a very small piece of meat but excellent for cutlets, medallions, or scallops. Canadian bacon is cut from the back of the animal.

Ham: A ham is the hind leg of a pig. The bony lower part of the ham is the shank, and the center section is used for hams. This is the equivalent of a top or bottom round roast in beef.

Spareribs/Belly: Pork belly is used to make spareribs and bacon. Basic spareribs are taken from the front of the rib cage (underneath the animal) with the sternum (that's the bone in the center of your chest) still attached. Barbecue ribs are the same cut except without the sternum.

WHICH CUTS TO BUY
Ham: There are three types of hams: fresh, wet-cured, and dry-cured. Fresh hams, which are hard to find, are simply the un-

processed, uncured back leg of the animal. It is raw meat much like a pork chop or loin roast and, when cooked, becomes grayish white. A wet-cured ham is immersed in a brine solution. The most common variety is labeled "ham, water added" and is used, for example, by delicatessens. A less common but superior type of wet-cured ham is sold as "ham with natural juices." It has less additional water weight and more flavor. Both types are fully cooked. Canned hams are also wet-cured and come in two varieties: shelf-stable and refrigerated. The former can be stored on a shelf for up to two years, whereas the latter must be refrigerated and will keep for six to nine months. (Both must be stored unopened.) A dry-cured ham, also called a country ham, is packed in salt, which draws out water and slows the growth of bacteria. Other ingredients in cured hams include sugar, which improves texture and offsets saltiness; spices such as pepper; and saltpeter, which not only helps reduce bacteria but contributes to the color of the final cured product. Whether wet- or dry-cured, many hams are then smoked to add flavor and to help preserve the meat. Some hams are smoked for up to two weeks, and a "fully cooked" ham has been smoked to an internal temperature of at least 155°F. Hams are often aged as well. A country ham, for example, is started in the very late fall, cured, smoked, and then hung for about six months through the winter, spring, and summer.

For a ham that is advertised as "ready to eat," simply preheat the oven to 325°F and cook until the internal temperature reaches 140°F. However, country hams, such as Smithfield, usually require soaking and scrubbing before cooking. (A Smithfield ham is, technically speaking, a ham that has been produced within a few miles of Smithfield, Virginia, although the term "Smithfield-style" is used by many producers.) One cook I know from Kentucky, Sarah Fritschner, has a simple method for cooking a country ham. For a 15–20 pound ham, she simmers it in water for 4 hours and then lets it cool in the pot. Some cooks serve country hams without cooking, as one might serve the Italian prosciutto, thinly sliced and in small portions.

In general, a country ham will be salty and strongly flavored. The dry-cure method concentrates flavors and also makes a coarser meat. (A country ham must lose at least 18 percent of its weight during curing and aging.) Wet-cured hams are milder in both taste and texture without the attendant saltiness. Country hams are a bit like single malt scotches — they vary tremendously in flavor and quality and are hard to judge as a group. In a recent blind tasting of country hams, I discovered that the range of tastes and textures is enormous. Some country hams are dark and dry, much like a Westphalian ham. Others are extremely smoky and salty. I found that the best hams have a nice balance between the flavor of pork, the smoke, the salt, and the spices. (My favorite was Father's Country Ham, Gatton Farms, P.O. Box 98, Bremen, KY 42325 [502-525-3437].) If you prefer less salt and less smoke, some producers are now shipping hams that are closer to a delicatessen baked ham than a true country ham, which is, without doubt, an acquired taste. (For the best mild ham, contact Stadler, P.O. Box 397, Elon College, NC 27244 [910-584-1396].)

Although country hams are available in supermarkets, liquor stores, and delicatessens throughout the South, they are mostly mail order items in the rest of the country. Be careful when purchasing a ham labeled as a "portion." The best cuts may have been removed.

A country ham will keep a very long time, but a wet-cured ham will only keep 3–5 days in the refrigerator. (This is also true of canned hams that have been opened.) Don't freeze either type of ham, because its flavor will deteriorate quickly.

Ribs: In addition to the spareribs and barbecue ribs already described, there are two other types of pork ribs: baby back ribs and country ribs. Baby back ribs are the ribs attached to the spine. They are much smaller than beef ribs simply because a pig is so much smaller, and the term "baby back" is simply a marketing term (they are supposed to sound cute). They are usually sold in a strip of ribs containing about ten ribs. Country ribs are usually cut from the three or four ribs closest to the shoulder. They have extra meat because of the muscles in the shoulder area. However, "country" ribs can be made from any of the ribs simply by leaving more meat on the bone, so the term "country," in this context, simply means "with lots of meat." I prefer country ribs because they have more meat and less fat, but many people opt for barbecue ribs because they have more flavor and are more delicate.

Barbecue: The best cut for barbecue is the Boston butt, which comes from the shoulder. It has lots of flavor and fat. It weighs in at around 4–5 pounds.

Pork Chops: The best chops are center-cut loin chops; the others are called end chops. Both come from the loin.

Pork Roasts: Center-cut loin and rib roasts are the most expensive and best cuts for roasts. Boston butt, which I use in barbecue, is a less expensive but excellent cut for roasting.

Stew Meat: Use the Boston butt (Boston shoulder) for stewing. It is tough but flavorful and has plenty of fat, which will keep the stew meat from drying out.

This method is the easier of the two techniques and was shown to me by a butcher in New York's meat district. With a little practice (use a rolling pin as a stand-in for a roast), you can tie this butcher's knot in just a few seconds.

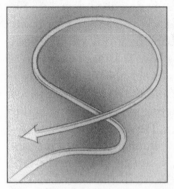

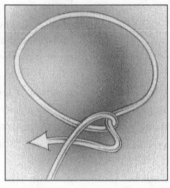

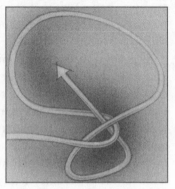

Place the roast flat on the work surface (not standing up) with the long side facing you. Wrap butcher's string around the roast, with the short end (referred to as the "bitter" end) coming up and back over the meat and resting to the left of the long end, which is still attached to the ball of string. You need to use both hands for this process, maintaining light pressure on both ends of the string as you work.

Pull a loop of string from the bitter end to the right underneath the long end.

Using your right hand, twist this loop 180 degrees toward your body, as if you were turning a key.

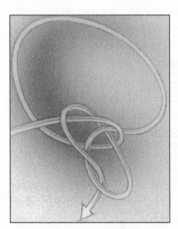

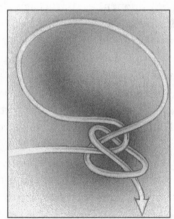

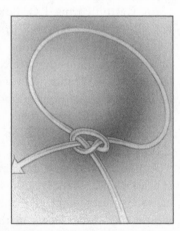

Insert the bitter end (the short end) of the string through the middle of this twisted loop.

Start to pull the knot tight, holding on to both the long and bitter ends.

Pull the bitter end up and away from you, tightening the string against the roast. Trim both ends with scissors or a knife.

This is a more difficult method taught to me by the dean of New York butcher shops, Jack Ubaldi, author of *The Meat Book*. According to Jack, this method provides more control over the tightness of the knot than the first method.

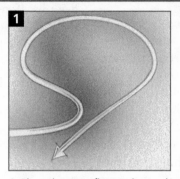

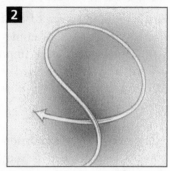

1. Place the roast flat on the work surface (not standing up) with the long side facing you. Wrap butcher's string around the roast, with the short end (the bitter end) coming up and back over the meat and resting to the right side of the long end, which is still attached to the ball of string. You need to use both hands for this process, maintaining light pressure on both ends of the string as you work.

2. Cross the bitter end (the short end) under the long end.

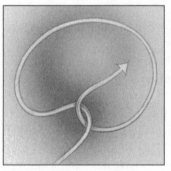

Pull the bitter end up and back to the right.

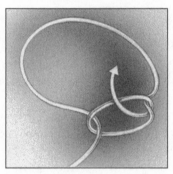

Pull the bitter end over and back under itself, forming a loop.

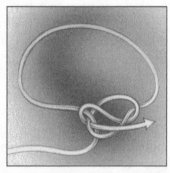

Pass the bitter end over and under the loop as shown in the illustration.

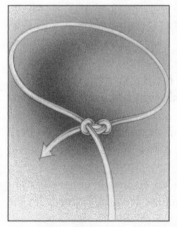

Pull the long end up and away from you to tighten the knot (while also holding on to the bitter end).

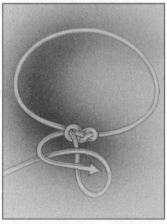

To secure the knot so it will not slip, form a loop with the long end and pass the bitter end through this loop.

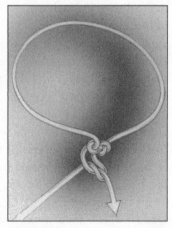

Pull the bitter end through to secure the knot.

A MEAT GLOSSARY

Butchers use all sorts of confusing terms (I suspect they are sometimes confused as well). A few of the most important ones are defined below. I have used terms from human anatomy whenever possible to clarify definitions.

Aitchbone: The rear portion of the pelvic bone. The other end is the hipbone. This should be removed from a leg of lamb prior to cooking to provide a more even, uniform piece of meat. Part of the aitchbone is usually left in a leg of lamb purchased at a market.

Brisket: The top of the beef breast underneath the first five ribs. If you were looking at a steer, this would be the front of the animal between the front legs and underneath the shoulder. Brisket is a tough cut but is flavorful and should be cooked at low temperatures.

Center Cut: The interior portion of a cut of meat after outer edges or sections have been removed. This makes the cut more attractive, desirable, and therefore expensive. Center-cut pork chops, for example, are better than the end chops, which are cut from the ends of the loin.

Chine Bones: Vertebrae. These are sometimes left attached to the ribs and sometimes not, depending on the cut.

Cube Steak: This is a very tough cut made from muscles from several of the major cuts of beef. A machine is used to tenderize the meat. This is a low-grade cut.

Deckel: This is the flap of meat that overlies the shoulder of a steer. If you feel a friend's back, you'll notice muscles from the shoulder that overlie the upper back. This is deckel.

Flanken: The chuck (beef) contains the first five ribs. If eye roast meat is removed from these ribs, the ribs will still contain a wide strip of meat (the meat comes from shoulder muscles that overlie this part of the chuck). These meaty ribs are referred to as flanken.

Ham: The hind leg of a pig from the knee to the pelvic joint.

Hocks: A cut of pork from a bone just above the foot that is connected to the ankle. As in "ham hocks." These are cut like shanks, in small cross-section pieces.

Leg: The thigh of a lamb. The lower leg is the shank.

Mutton: Lamb that is older than one year.

Primal Cuts: Basic major cuts into which a carcass is separated.

Plate: This is the meat underneath the rib section of beef just to the rear of the brisket.

Ribs: Most animals have thirteen or fourteen ribs and they occur in a wide variety of cuts, from rib roasts to chops to a rack. Country ribs have more meat on them and are usually cut from the first few ribs at the front of the animal.

Shell Steak: This is cut from the beef loin with the tenderloin muscle removed. Imagine a porterhouse steak with the filet removed (this is the smaller muscle that is very tender). Also referred to as a New York strip steak.

Shank: The lower portion of either the front or hind leg. Shanks are usually cut from the front leg.

Short Rib: Any short section of rib (less than 7 inches in length) is referred to as a short rib. These can be cut from any part of any beef rib. The best short ribs are taken from the chuck end of the ribs, where the ribs are meatier.

Sirloin: This is the hip region of beef, which is part of the hindquarter of the animal. Other cuts from the hindquarter include the round, the short loin, and the flank. Sirloin steaks are taken from the sirloin.

Standing Rib Roast: The ribs are left attached to the meat and the roast is cooked "standing," with the arched, fatty side up. The meat can also be removed from the bone and rolled before roasting, which is often referred to as a rolled rib roast.

Tenderloin: The long muscle that runs from the rib cage to the pelvis. This cut is available for beef, lamb, veal, and pork and is the most tender, most expensive cut, although without much flavor.

Trotters: The feet of a pig.

How to Roast Meat

Contrary to accepted kitchen wisdom, the final internal temperature of the roast is not the key factor in determining texture, taste, or juiciness. It's how the meat was roasted that really matters.

~

Every August, our small town in Vermont has the annual Ox Roast, a covered-dish supper that attracts everyone from mountain men to weekenders. The before-dinner entertainment is provided by cloggers — they dance on plywood set up on 2-by-4s. After dinner, we all reassemble at the abandoned tennis court, which is lit by half a dozen table lamps, complete with shades, duct-taped to the top of the posts so that we can see to square dance, where we "shuck the oyster" and "dig the clam."

The ox at that picnic is really a good-size heifer, usually the most ornery beast in town, who is chosen by Charlie Bentley, the town's last farmer. The two steamship rounds (the back legs up to the hip) are strapped to a homemade rotisserie, which is kept working by Russell Bain, our 94-year-old expert metalworker. The fire is started the night before and attended by a half-dozen locals stretched out on lawn chairs, drinking coffee, eating spice doughnuts, and trading gossip and well-worn stories. The next morning, at 6 o'-clock, the meat is attached to the rotisserie using a length of sheep fencing and a few springs from an old metal bed. My job is to carve the rounds of beef. Although the rest of the food is quite good, the meat is often tough and dry. Vermonters like their meat *cooked;* not rare, not medium rare, not medium, but *well done.* One year I was asked to decide when the meat should come off the grill and I opted for medium rare. I have not been consulted since.

So what makes meat tough? Is it just the animal? What's wrong with roasting meat over a fire? Why isn't the meat juicier and more tender? At first, roasting seems like a simple process. Throw a piece of meat into a hot oven or over a hot fire and cook it until its internal temperature reaches the proper level. Much like quantum physics, however, the science of roasting is actually quite complex. The more you learn, the less you know.

THE SCIENCE OF ROASTING

Let's begin with texture. When meat is cooked, the muscle proteins are denatured — they become shorter and tighter (over 120°F, muscle proteins will start to shrink in length, expelling juices; under 120°F, they will contract in diameter) — but the connective tissues, the collagen, start to turn soft and jellylike, which acts as a lubricant. So as the meat cooks it is getting both tenderer and tougher at the same time. The maximum benefit in terms of texture occurs when beef, for example, is cooked to a final temperature of 130°–140°F, the temperature at which connective tissues start to gelatinize. After 150°F, the roast begins to lose a great deal of moisture as the water is squeezed from the muscle fibers. In addition, the fat in the meat is rendered (starts to melt). A roast can lose 30–40 percent of its weight by the time it reaches 170°F, the point at which the meat is inedible and no additional liquid will be lost. (Cut into a piece of well-done meat and you'll notice that it will exude no juices.) This process is much like the wringing of a wet towel. The meat proteins get shorter and tighter, expelling water. Since meat is 75 percent water, there is a dramatic change in texture and juiciness during the cooking process from raw all the way to well done.

Other chemical reactions are also taking place. As cell walls break down during cooking, amino acids and proteins start to mix. The Maillard reaction — otherwise known as browning — adds a lot of flavor (that's why cookies and pie pastry taste better when well browned and why you should brown meat for a stew). In addition, the color begins to change due to molecular changes in pigments that are present in beef but less so in pork (that's why pork does not change color as much as beef when roasted).

Most cooks have experienced the effects of these scientific processes. We all know, for example, that a roast of beef cooked to 170°F internal temperature is tough and virtually inedible. As a result, most of us have assumed that the final internal temperature of the roast is the key to success. That is, the oven temperature doesn't matter so much as the final internal temperature of the meat. Based on successful slow-roasting of poultry, however, I thought that lower oven temperatures should be tested. I also wondered if different cuts might require different roasting methods.

ROASTING A TENDERLOIN OF BEEF

The most expensive and tenderest cut of beef is the tenderloin, which comes from the back of the animal between the rib cage and the hip and contains no bones. I began my tests with the loin by trying five different cooking methods, using 2 tenderloins cut into 4-inch pieces. The methods were roasting at 500°F; heating the oven to 500°F and then reducing the oven temperature at the start of cooking to roast at 350°; roasting at 350°F and then increasing the oven to 500° for the last 5 minutes; heavily salting the exterior of the loin, then roasting according to the third method; and roasting at a constant 400°F. (I did not test lower oven temperatures because the tenderloin has little taste and benefits from a maximum amount of browning during the short cooking time. It also is the most tender cut of beef and can handle higher oven temperatures without becoming tough or dry.) The chart below summarizes my

---

KITCHEN TEST

What Is the Best Temperature for Roasting Tenderloin?

Five pieces of beef tenderloin were cooked at different oven temperatures to determine the best method. All roasts were cooked to an internal temperature of 125°F (medium rare).

Method	Comments
Roast at 500°F	Meat slightly tough
Start with oven at 500°F, immediately reduce to 350°F	Slightly less tough than the first
Start at 350°F, increase to 500°F for the last 5 minutes	Very good; juicy, tender, and flavorful
Same method as immediately above, but heavily salt the exterior of the meat	Meat much too salty; not recommended
Roast at constant 400°F	Best and easiest method

findings. The 400° method seemed the winner — it was easy and the meat was wonderful. Heavy salting, which many butchers have suggested, produced an unpleasantly salty piece of meat. One by-product of this testing was the discovery that slight differences in degrees of doneness strongly affected the juiciness and texture of the meat.

Based on my testing, here is the best method of roasting a loin. Heat the oven to 400°F with the roasting pan in the oven. Salt and pepper the outside of the roast (be liberal with the salt — it adds a tremendous amount of flavor to the outer crust). When the oven is hot, take out the roasting pan, place the roast in the pan, and place the pan back in the oven. Cook for 10 minutes. Turn roast in pan and cook for a total of 10 minutes per pound.

It is essential to have an instant-read thermometer on hand. When inserted into the meat, it will register the accurate temperature within 15 seconds. (You can also use a digital, battery-powered instant-read thermometer, which works in only 2–3 seconds.) Always insert the thermometer into the center of the roast so that the tip rests in the middle of the meat. Keep in mind that the outer ends of the roast will be more cooked than the center portion. You'll notice a difference of up to 10°F. A roasted loin should be removed from the oven when the instant-read thermometer, placed in the center of the roast, registers 125°F. Let it sit for 20 minutes after coming from the oven. The juices, which concentrate in the middle of the roast during cooking, need time to drain back into the outer layers. The roast will also continue cooking during this time, rising as much as 8°F in temperature.

UNLOCKING THE SECRETS OF SLOW-ROASTING

Having concluded a series of successful tests, I thought that I understood how to roast meat, but I had some areas of doubt. Perhaps

---

KITCHEN TEST

Bottom Round Roasted in a Dutch Oven at Different Temperatures

Bottom round roasts were browned on top of the stove in a Dutch oven and then transferred to a heated oven and roasted uncovered at five different oven temperatures until the internal temperature reached 130°F. Each roast weighed 2 pounds.

Oven Temperature	Cooking Time	Comments
175°F	2 hours, 10 minutes	Less flavorful than the other roasts. Slightly chewy; pale exterior. After roast sat for a few hours covered, the interior changed from deep red to a pale, pinkish gray. Very evenly cooked, however.
200°F	1 hour, 25 minutes	Juicy, tender, and evenly cooked. Better exterior color than the 175° roast.
250°F	1 hour	Wonderful flavor, very evenly cooked, tender and juicy. A winner.
300°F	45 minutes	A bit tougher than lower-temperature roasts. Good outside crust, but uneven cooking inside. Outer layers were overcooked.
350°F	40 minutes	Exterior well browned. Very uneven cooking, although very good flavor.

Bottom Round Roasted in a Dutch Oven at Changing Oven Temperatures

Bottom round roasts were browned on top of the stove in a Dutch oven and then transferred to a heated oven and roasted uncovered at changing oven temperatures until the internal temperature reached 130°F. Each roast weighed 2 pounds.

Oven Temperature	Comments
Constant 250°F	Evenly cooked, tender and juicy. Exterior still lacking in flavor, however.
250°F until internal temperature reaches 110°F; increase oven to 500°F until done	Excellent flavor, juicy and tender. Wonderful contrast of texture and taste from outside to inside. A winner.
400°F for 15 minutes; reduce oven to 200°F until done	Good texture and flavor inside, and juicy. Outer layers of meat were overcooked, however.
350°F until internal temperature reaches 110°F; remove from oven for 30 minutes; return to oven and cook until done	Absolutely the worst method of all. Very uneven cooking. A large portion of the roast was overcooked by the time internal temperature reached 130°F.

the quality of the meat can affect cooking method. I decided to test a bottom round roast, possibly the toughest, worst cut of beef on the market. Very few people can afford to cook a $25 piece of tenderloin.

I had just returned from Thanksgiving dinner at my mother's, and she had served a wonderful, tender, juicy 20-pound turkey that had been cooked all night at 200°F (see Chapter 25 for more information). This recipe was based on a cooking method proposed by Adelle Davis, author of *Let's Eat Right to Keep Fit*. Simply put, she advocated roasting meat at the temperature you want the interior of the meat to be cooked to. For example, if you want to roast a turkey so that the breast meat is cooked to 165°F, that's the temperature at which you should set your oven.

There were some modifications to this theory. Bacteria reside on the outside of meat (beef is less likely to contain harmful bacteria than poultry), and therefore the external temperature must be raised to 140°F in order to kill them. (It is possible that harmful bacteria may be present within the meat, but this is very rare.) To deal with this, Adelle started off by cooking her turkey at 300°F for 1 hour and then turned down the oven to 200°F. Having spoken to a few food scientists, I decided that browning my beef roasts on top of the stove instead of starting the oven at 300°F would not only kill the bacteria, it would also add flavor and color to the roasts. But before settling on the optimum way to cook a tough roast, I needed to run some tests.

TESTING ROASTING TEMPERATURES

First, I wanted to try the classic method of roasting, which involves no preliminary browning. I cooked five separate roasts at different temperatures, from 300°F to 500°F. Each was cooked in a roasting pan, uncovered, on a rack. The results were disappointing, but I learned two things. First, the lower oven temperature was best. The meat roasted at 500°F became dry — most of the outer layers of the meat were overcooked. The roast cooked at 300°F, however, was fairly tender, juicier, and had better internal flavor. Second, and most important, *the internal temperature of the meat did not necessarily determine the juiciness or texture of the roast.* In other words, a roast cooked at 300°F and cooked to an internal temperature

   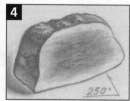

1. When meat is roasted at 500°F, it is medium rare only in the very center when the internal temperature reaches 130°F.
2. When meat is roasted at 400°F, a slightly larger area in the center is medium rare.

3. When meat is roasted at 350°F, the outer layers are still overcooked when the middle reaches 130°F.
4. When meat is roasted at 250°F, most of it is still medium rare when the center reaches 130°F.

of 120°F was tenderer and juicier than meat cooked to the same internal temperature in a 500° oven. Conclusion: It's not just where you are going, but how you get there!

Why is this true? To fully understand what was happening inside the meat, I photographed four different roasts prepared at different temperatures — 250°, 350°, 400°, and 500°F. All were cooked to the same internal temperature — 130°F — and allowed to sit for an additional 10 minutes. The roasts were cut in half. When I compared the photographs, the answer was immediately apparent. The 500° roast was almost entirely overcooked. That is, the center was still red but 70 percent of the remainder was gray and unappealing. By comparison, the 250° roast was light red throughout, with only 10 percent of the outer layer gray and overcooked. It's simply a matter of physics. At higher oven temperatures, the outer layers of a thick piece of meat will overcook before the center comes up to temperature. In a more moderate oven, the meat will cook more slowly and more evenly.

TESTING LOWER OVEN TEMPERATURES
Now that I knew that lower oven temperatures were best, I prepared five different bottom round roasts at temperatures ranging from 175° to 350°F. Once again, I encountered the same remarkable discovery as with the first round of tests. The roast cooked to 140°F in a 175° oven was quite different from the roast cooked to the same internal

temperature in a 350° oven. I also found that 250°F was the ideal oven temperature, turning out a tender, juicy, and flavorful roast when cooked to 130°F.

VARYING OVEN TEMPERATURES
Sometimes with slow-roasting — poultry, for example — changing oven temperatures is the best method. As noted in the chart on page 254, the problem with roasting at low temperatures is the lack of flavor develop-

SCIENCE OF COOKING

The Incredible Shrinking Flank Steak

To demonstrate the fundamental theory proposed by this chapter, that oven temperature is as important as the final internal temperature of the meat, I purchased two flank steaks and cut the first one into five 1-inch-wide pieces. One raw piece was set aside and the remaining four pieces were roasted at 250°F. The four strips were removed from the oven at different internal temperatures, starting at 120°F and increasing to 180°F in 20° increments. The four cooked strips of steak were placed on a cutting board alongside the raw piece and compared. It was quite clear that the strip cooked to 180°F had shrunk about 30 percent compared to the raw strip. However, the strip cooked to 120°F had very modest shrinkage, about 10 percent, as did the other two strips, cooked to 140° and 160° respectively. I repeated this test with the second flank steak but used a higher oven temperature, 375°F. The results were remarkable. Even the piece cooked to 120°F had shrunk a good 25 percent compared to the raw piece. So lower oven temperatures will indeed cause meat to shrink less, even when cooked to the same internal temperature.

ment on the exterior of the meat. The good news is that the outer layers of the roast do not become overcooked while the inside is coming up to temperature. I compared three new oven methods with the winner from the previous testing, a constant 250°F.

Finally, I found the best method. Start the oven at 250°F and cook the browned roast until the internal temperature reaches 110°F. Increase the oven to 500°F and cook another 15 minutes or so, until the roast reaches 130°F internal temperature. This provided the best of both worlds — terrific flavor development on the exterior and an even, juicy, tender roast in the interior.

THE IDEAL INTERNAL TEMPERATURE

Having come this far, I nevertheless wanted to go back and make sure that I was using the proper internal temperature. I then cooked five more roasts (bottom round) to different internal temperatures, starting at 120°F and ending at 160°F. I found that 130°F delivers the most flavor, the best texture, and the most juice. Once I hit 150°F in-

---

KITCHEN TEST

What Is the Best Internal Temperature for a Tough Roast?

Five 1-pound bottom round roasts were browned and then roasted uncovered at 250°F until the internal temperature reached 110°F. The oven was raised to 500°F for the balance of the cooking time.

Final Internal Temperature	Description
120°F	Rare, tender, and juicy; lacking in flavor
130°F	Medium rare, juicy, tender; good flavor
140°F	Medium well, chewier, still juicy; not as much flavor as 130°F
150°F	Overcooked, almost dry, tough
160°F	Dry, tasteless, shriveled, overcooked

---

ternal temperature, the roasts were dry, overcooked, and tough.

COVERED VERSUS UNCOVERED

Adelle Davis also suggested cooking meat in a covered container. This is the same notion as using a browning bag. The theory is that in a relatively closed environment, moisture in the meat will be less likely to turn to steam and exit the meat. This reminded me of high school physics. In a large hot oven, the meat will lose a great deal of moisture in order to create equilibrium. In a much smaller environment, less water is likely to be released. In my first set of tests, I had roasted meat uncovered; when I tested a covered roast, I found a slight loss in flavor — the outer crust did not brown sufficiently. I did not, however, experience any significant improvement in the juiciness or texture of the interior of the roast when roasting covered. (I have found that roasting a large turkey in a covered container does make a big difference, as long cooking times do provide an opportunity for moisture loss.)

WHAT ABOUT A PORK ROAST?

Since pork needs to be cooked to a slightly higher internal temperature than beef, 145°F, I wanted to test it with the slow-roast method. I found that an oven temperature of either 200°F or 250°F works equally well and that higher temperatures were clearly inferior. (The USDA suggests cooking pork to 160°F for safety reasons, although the meat will be relatively dry and tough.)

HOW LONG SHOULD A ROAST SIT AFTER COOKING?

I then wanted to determine the optimum amount of time a roast should sit after coming from the oven. I let a roast sit for 5 minutes on a cutting board on the kitchen counter and then tested it in 5-minute increments up to half an hour. Twenty minutes, the amount of time suggested by most cooks, is in fact the proper waiting period. Additional time is not helpful.

Pork Roasted in a Dutch Oven at Different Temperatures

Pork roasts were browned on top of the stove in a Dutch oven and then transferred to a heated oven and roasted covered at five different oven temperatures. Roasts were cooked to an internal temperature of 145°F.

Oven Temperature	Weight	Cooking Time	Comments
200°F	1.75 pounds	1 hour, 36 minutes	Good flavor, juicy and tender
250°F	1.75 pounds	1 hour, 15 minutes	Good flavor, juicy and tender
300°F	2.25 pounds	1 hour, 5 minutes	Slightly less flavor, juicy, a little chewier
350°F	1.75 pounds	40 minutes	Similar flavor to 300°, still juicy, but not as tender
400°F	1.8 pounds	32 minutes	Not as juicy, rather chewy, lacks flavor

Master Recipe for Tenderloin of Beef

Do not cook this tenderloin to an internal temperature of more than 130°F unless you like medium or well-done meat. Medium is 135°F and well done is 145°F. Use an instant-read thermometer, which when inserted halfway into the middle of the roast will provide the correct temperature within about 15 seconds. Remember to let the roast sit for 20 minutes before carving to allow the juices to spread throughout the meat. During roasting, the juices tend to move to the center of the meat. As the meat cools, they flow back into the outer layers. Ask your butcher to trim the tenderloin of fat and tie it with a butcher's string. To tie a roast yourself, see Chapter 27 for step-by-step instructions.

3 pounds beef tenderloin, trimmed and tied
Salt and freshly ground black pepper to taste

1. Heat oven to 400°F with oven rack in the lowest position. Place a large roasting pan in oven to preheat for 15 minutes.

2. Salt and pepper the outside of the roast and place meat in preheated roasting pan. Roast for 10 minutes, then remove pan from oven and turn meat over. Roast an additional 20 minutes or so (for a total cooking time of 10 minutes per pound), checking internal temperature with an instant-read thermometer.

3. When temperature reaches 125°F in the middle center of the roast, remove from oven. Let stand 20 minutes, slice, and serve. Internal temperature will rise about 5°F after meat is removed from oven.

Serves 8

How Long Should a Roast Sit After Cooking?

I roasted a cut of bottom round at 200°F until the internal temperature reached 130°F and then let it sit for 30 minutes, testing it every 5 minutes. Both the texture and the flavor changed as the roast sat on the counter.

Resting Time	Comments
5 minutes	Very juicy, somewhat chewy, good flavor
10 minutes	Very juicy, less chewy, good flavor
15 minutes	Very juicy, slightly chewy, better flavor
20 minutes	Succulent, tender, and juicy; great flavor
25 minutes	No noticeable change from 20 minutes
30 minutes	No noticeable change from 20 minutes

Beef Tenderloin with Marsala and Balsamic Vinegar

Use a plastic storage bag for marinating, since this requires less marinade to coat the roast.

3 pounds beef tenderloin, trimmed and tied
3 cloves garlic, peeled and cut into slivers
¼ cup Marsala wine
¼ cup olive oil
1 tablespoon balsamic vinegar
½ teaspoon dried thyme
¼ teaspoon kosher salt
   Freshly ground black pepper to taste

1. Make small incisions in the tenderloin and insert garlic slivers.

2. Whisk together remaining ingredients and place in a plastic food storage bag. Add the roast, force out excess air, and twist tie. Rotate bag to cover roast with marinade. Refrigerate for 24 hours, turning occasionally.

3. Follow roasting directions in master recipe.

Serves 8

Slow-Cooked Roast of Beef

For a leaner roast, use either a top sirloin or top round roast. For a juicier, fattier roast, select a blade roast or chuck eye roast. If you have the time, age the meat in your refrigerator before roasting to dramatically improve texture and flavor. If you are using a cut from the round, I suggest you slice the meat thin for serving. Leftovers from a roasted cut of round make excellent roast beef sandwiches. If you prefer your meat less rare, a chuck (but not a round) roast can be cooked to 140°F internal temperature and still be juicy and relatively tender.

1 boneless beef roast, 3–4 pounds, from the chuck or round, tied with string
   Salt and freshly ground black pepper to taste
2 tablespoons olive oil

1. For superior results, place the roast uncovered on a rack in a roasting pan in the refrigerator for 4 days and then proceed with recipe. This step is optional, although aging significantly improves flavor and texture. Trim off any exterior meat that is dried and hard.

2. Heat oven to 250°F. Rinse exterior of meat and pat dry. Sprinkle with salt and freshly ground black pepper. Heat olive oil in a Dutch oven on top of the stove. Add roast and brown thoroughly on all sides. Place uncovered in oven and cook until internal temperature reaches 110°F. Increase oven temperature to 500°F and cook until internal temperature reaches 130°F. Total cooking time will be 60–90 minutes, depending on the size of the roast. Remove from oven, cover loosely with a sheet of aluminum foil, and let sit for 20 minutes before carving.

Serves 8–10

Pork Roast Variation

After browning a 3-pound boneless roast in Dutch oven, sprinkle with salt and pepper and place uncovered in a 250° oven. Roast until pork reaches 115°–120°F internal temperature, about 35–40 minutes. Turn roast over, increase oven temperature to 500°F, and cook until center of roast reaches an internal temperature of 145°F, about 10–15 minutes. (The USDA recommends that pork be cooked to 160°F, but I feel that this produces dry meat. If, however, you are concerned about safety, you should follow the USDA guidelines.)

Serves 8

Roasted Pork Loin with Cumin, Chili, and Cinnamon

The top loin is the premier cut for a pork roast and will run you about $7 per pound (that's $20 for the whole roast). Other cuts include a rib end roast, a center-cut loin roast, and a center-cut rib roast.

2 teaspoons ground cumin
1 tablespoon chili powder
1 tablespoon coriander seeds
1 teaspoon ground cinnamon
1½ teaspoons brown sugar
1 tablespoon kosher salt
1 teaspoon red pepper flakes
2 teaspoons black peppercorns
3 pounds boneless pork loin roast, tied with string
1 tablespoon olive oil

Combine spices (the first 8 ingredients) in a coffee grinder or spice mill and grind. Coat pork loin with ground spices. Follow directions for Pork Roast Variation, above.

Serves 8

Master Recipe for Roast Leg of Lamb

A leg of lamb may vary in weight from 5 pounds up to 10. The recipe below is based on a weight of about 7 pounds, although a smaller leg is always best, indicating a younger animal. For significantly smaller legs, decrease the turning intervals from 20 minutes to 15 and check the temperature of the leg after 60 minutes. Trimming and tying a leg of lamb is best done by a butcher. Ask him to remove the aitchbone (this is a portion of the pelvic bone), the silverskin (or fell), which covers the meat, and also the lymph node (see page 208). Then ask that he or she tie the leg securely with butcher's twine. The objective is to create a package that is as even in thickness as possible. This will result in even cooking. You will note that this recipe starts out with a 450° oven. I discovered

that lamb has an unpleasant texture when roasted at a constant 250°F.

2 teaspoons kosher salt
2 teaspoons freshly ground black pepper
1 teaspoon finely minced fresh rosemary leaves or ½ teaspoon dried
1 whole leg of lamb, prepared per instructions above, about 7 pounds
2 medium cloves garlic, peeled and cut lengthwise into 8 slivers each
2 tablespoons olive oil

1. Mix salt, pepper, and rosemary in a small bowl.

2. Cut 16 slits in roast with point of a paring knife; poke garlic slivers inside. Rub remaining seasonings onto all surfaces of meat, then coat with olive oil. Place leg in roasting pan fitted with a roasting rack. Let stand for 30 minutes.

3. Adjust oven rack to lowest position and heat oven to 450°F. Place roasting pan in oven and roast lamb for 10 minutes. Grasp shank bone with paper towels; flip leg over, and roast 10 minutes longer. Lower oven temperature to 250°F, turn leg top side up, and continue roasting, turning leg every 20 minutes, until instant-read thermometer, when inserted in several locations, registers 130°–135°F (medium rare), about 75 minutes total cooking time. Transfer roast to a carving board; cover loosely with foil and let sit for 20 minutes. (For carving instructions, see page 208.)

Serves 8–10

~ 29 ~

How to Braise Meat

*Braising does not make meat more tender, more flavorful,
or even juicier. It does, however, produce a great sauce.*

~

You probably think that braising — cooking food, usually meat, with a little liquid in a covered pot — makes that food juicier and more tender. At least, that's what I thought until I started working on this book. Then I started asking questions. What makes braising different from stewing? How does a moist cooking environment penetrate a thick piece of meat, thereby changing its texture or juiciness? If tough meat should be cooked at low temperatures (see preceding chapter), wouldn't the braising liquid simply raise the ambient temperature (steam is a better conductor of heat than air), thus toughening at least the outer layer of the meat?

I started by doing some research on braising. According to Madeleine Kamman in *The Making of a Cook,* the term comes from the French *braise,* which means "smoldering coals." Meat was placed in a tightly covered pot called a *braisière,* which was placed on a bed of embers, and then additional coals were placed on the slightly concave lid. Inside, the meat rested on several layers of aromatics (onions, et cetera) and raw ham and veal slices, which were called *fonds de braise.* (This method was developed centuries ago in Europe, before stoves had been invented.)

Madeleine then goes on to explain the science of braising. She says that "the pressure of the steam is such that it bears on the meat fibers and slowly pries them open; the juices now slowly make their way from the center of the piece toward the outside, break through the seared outside layer, and mix with the pan juices." This just didn't sound right to me. Meat fibers release juices when they are heated, not due to pressure from steam. Also, the objective in cooking meat is to stop the fibers from releasing their juices. Otherwise, you end up with dry, overcooked meat.

MY KITCHEN TESTS

As usual, I decided to test braising for myself. I roasted a bottom round roast at 200°F in a covered Dutch oven, and then I cooked a second roast, putting 1 cup of stock in the bottom of the pan. The braised roast, the one with the liquid, turned out about the same as the roasted meat, and the outside of the roast was less flavorful because it did not brown as well. So much for braising as a method for tenderizing meat.

I then called Harold McGee, author of *The Curious Cook* and *On Food and Cooking,* and he confirmed my test results. Ac-

The Effects of Braising on Beef and Chicken

Does cooking with liquid really produce juicier, more tender foods? Items were cooked with and without liquid in a covered pan in the oven; all items were briefly sautéed before cooking in the oven.

Test	Oven Temperature	Cooking Time	Comments
Bottom round roast, 3 pounds; with 1 cup liquid	200°F	2 hours, 45 minutes	On the rare side after 2 hours, 45 minutes; cooked another 45 minutes, but meat was not more tender; nice aroma, and liquid makes a good sauce.
Bottom round roast, 2.7 pounds; no liquid	200°F	3 hours, 15 minutes	Same texture as braised roast, but more flavor since exterior was more deeply browned.
Chicken pieces; with 1 cup liquid	200°F	1 hour, 20 minutes	Great flavor, but meat was chewy; 1¾ cups liquid left in pot, of which ½ cup was fat; liquid unsuitable for a sauce unless excess fat removed.
Chicken pieces; no liquid	200°F	1 hour, 35 minutes	Meat chewy, especially white meat; roasting is a better method.

cording to McGee, braising simply elevates the cooking temperature, because steam conducts heat better than air does. However, he pointed out that the braising liquid can impart flavor. I countered that it seemed unlikely that much flavor would make its way into the interior of a roast, and he agreed. However, fish, a thin cut of meat, or vegetables might benefit.

It also occurred to me that braising does one other thing. As in a stew, the liquid serves as an instant sauce. However, I do not recommend this sauce if braising a fatty food such as chicken with the skin on or a well-fatted roast. You would have to make a sauce using just some of the liquid, adding it to other ingredients such as stock or wine. I find these sauces too rich even when defatted. You can, however, refrigerate the sauce and then remove the congealed layer of fat from the top the next day. But this is not practical if you wish to serve the braised meat soon after cooking.

As a result, I decided that braising might be particularly suited for a thin, lean cut of meat such as brisket. I devised 12 tests with variables including oven temperature, cooking time, internal temperature of the meat, and method of cooking (oven versus stovetop versus crockpot).

As I discovered when roasting meat, lower oven temperatures are best. At higher temperatures, the outer layer of the meat will dry out before the interior is properly cooked. This is especially true when braising, as steam is a better conductor of heat than air. At the same oven temperature, braised foods will cook at a higher temperature than dry-roasted foods. However, it was surprising to me that slow-braised brisket should be cooked to 145°F internally. Thick pieces of meat roasted at higher temperatures are best cooked to 130°F. In all of my slow-roasting tests, including roast chicken and roast turkey, I have found that low-heat roasting not only results in juicier, more evenly

The Effect of Oven Temperature and Cooking Method on Braised Brisket

Three-pound briskets were oven-braised in a covered Dutch oven at four different temperatures, cooked covered on top of the stove, or braised in a crockpot. Each brisket was browned first on top of the stove.

Method	Oven Temperature	Cooking Time	Internal Temperature	Comments
Oven	175°F	3 hours	125°F	Good taste, fairly tender; should be cooked longer.
	200°F	2 hours, 10 minutes	130°F	Meat is rare but not tender enough.
	200°F	3 hours	145°F	Meat is medium and very tender. Good flavor. This is a winner.
	250°F	2½ hours	135°F	Meat not tender.
	250°F	3½ hours	150°F	Meat somewhat tender.
	250°F	4 hours	155°F	Meat is tender. Not as good as 200° method.
	300°F	1 hour, 50 minutes	160°F	Fairly tender, good flavor. Meat starting to dry out.
Stovetop	Low simmer	2 hours	135°F	Meat not tender, and less flavor than oven method.
	Low simmer	3½ hours	155°F	Meat is leatherlike.
Crockpot	Low	2½ hours	135°F	Meat not tender.
	Low	3 hours	140°F	Meat not tender.
	Low	4 hours	155°F	Meat fairly tender. Not much flavor.

cooked foods, it also means that the internal temperature can be higher without a loss of either texture or juiciness.

I was also interested to discover that stovetop cooking is not to be recommended, because it is difficult to control the temperature. Although I tried to maintain a sub-simmer, this is best done in the oven. I had hopes for the crockpot method, but the meat did not seem to tenderize properly nor did it have much flavor.

STEWING VERSUS BRAISING

So why is braising different from stewing? Well, they are really quite similar processes. In fact, Kamman admits that the difference between stewing and braising is that stewing uses little pieces of meat rather than one large piece. I agree that this is the essential difference, as the cooking methods are otherwise the same. A beef roast cooked with some liquid is a braise, whereas cubed pieces of beef cooked with liquid is a stew. Originally, the braising liquid was probably added to prevent foods from scorching as they cooked in a pot over glowing coals. Today, a braised chicken that is cooked with vegetables needs some liquid so that the onions or carrots cook evenly without sticking to the bottom of the pan.

SOME FINAL TESTS

BRAISING IN A TIGHTLY SEALED PAN

I reread Madeleine Kamman's recipes one last time and noted that she was adamant about using the smallest possible pot, using a piece of aluminum foil to cover the top of the meat, then sealing the pot with more aluminum foil and the cover. Her theory is that a larger pot will not produce sufficient pressure and that a loosely covered pot will simply let the steam escape. I also noted that she set the oven to 350°F. I went ahead and performed two additional tests, both with a 3-pound bottom round roast. I also tried braising two pieces of chuck, to see if the cut made any difference.

Although the smaller pot did not make a world of difference, the meat was a bit juicier and there was more liquid left over for gravy. The meat was also cooked to a higher temperature (145°–150°F) than with the larger unsealed pot, yet the meat was still tender and juicy. I also found that it was best to pour the stock over the meat before cooking. This yields a nice glossy look to the finished roast. And I confirmed what I already suspected. The round is a terrible cut for a roast. It's lean and tough. Always select a chuck roast, the top blade roast being the best. The chuck has more fat and connective tissue, which softens and adds flavor during cooking.

BRAISING IN A PRESSURE COOKER

The slight improvement with a sealed pot stirred my interest in using a pressure cooker. I turned to Lorna Sass's *Cooking Under Pressure* for guidance and cooked a 3½-pound chuck roast for 60 minutes under high pressure. The results were remarkable; the beef was juicy and fall-apart tender. However, since most home cooks do not

---

KITCHEN TEST

The Effects of Braising in a Small, Tightly Sealed Roasting Pan

Four roasts were each browned in a small roasting pan — one just large enough to accommodate the roast. Liquid was added, and a sheet of aluminum foil was placed over the meat to protect it from dripping condensation. The pan was then sealed carefully with a second sheet of aluminum foil and a cover. The roasts weighed between 2½ and 3 pounds.

Cut of Meat	Oven Temperature	Cooking Time	Comments
Bottom round	200°F	2 hours, 48 minutes	Meat was cooked to rare at 140°F internal temperature. Meat slightly juicier than basic method in larger pot, and there was more liquid remaining in the pot.
Bottom round	350°F	2 hours, 15 minutes	Internal temperature was 145°F. Meat was chewier than the 200° oven version.
Chuck roast	200°F	3 hours, 40 minutes	Cooked to 150°F internal temperature (medium rare). Tender, flavorful, an excellent roast. Much better than bottom round.
Top blade chuck roast	200°F	3 hours, 5 minutes	Cooked to 150°F internal temperature. Delicious, flavorful, very tender.

have a pressure cooker large enough to handle a roast (you need a 5-quart pot), and since the new pressure cookers are quite expensive (some models cost up to $200), I have included a recipe for this as a variation only (see page 269). It is, however, the best method for preparing an inexpensive roast.

WHAT ABOUT BOILING MEAT?
Although all the experts I spoke to emphasized the importance of maintaining a sub-simmer when braising, there are plenty of recipes that call for boiling meat in lots of liquid. I decided to give it a try with a 4-pound piece of brisket, boiling it in 6 cups of water and 2 cups of beef stock. I also added seasonings and a few vegetables. I maintained a low boil and let the meat cook about 2 hours. The result was virtually inedible — dry, semitough meat without much flavor. This technique might work with a brined piece of meat such as corned beef, but I don't suggest you try it with any other cut.

Braised Chicken, or Chicken in a Pot

Chicken skin is very fatty, and therefore, unless the skin is removed, the braising liquid is too rich for my taste. (Most "chicken in a pot" recipes leave the skin on, which makes the pan sauce indigestible.) Use a 5-quart Dutch oven for this recipe, as the chicken pieces will all fit nicely in one layer. Place the breasts in the pot bone side up to make sure that the meat is thoroughly cooked. Do not use chicken wings. They have too little meat, are hard to skin, and are best used for stock.

3½ pounds skinless chicken parts (breasts, thighs, and legs only)
   Salt and freshly ground black pepper
¼ cup olive oil, approximately
1 tablespoon butter
1 cup chopped onion
2 cups vegetables, cut into ½-inch dice (carrots, potatoes, parsnips, rutabagas, sweet potatoes, turnips, or mushrooms)
¼ cup white wine
1 cup chicken broth

½ teaspoon kosher salt
½ teaspoon dried thyme or 1½ teaspoons fresh
1 teaspoon minced garlic
2 tablespoons minced flat-leaf parsley

1. Heat oven to 200°F. Rinse skinned chicken parts, pat dry, and season liberally with salt and freshly ground black pepper. Preheat a Dutch oven over medium heat and then add 2 tablespoons olive oil and the butter. When hot, brown both sides of the chicken pieces over medium-high heat in two separate batches. (Each batch will take about 10 minutes.) Add more oil if necessary for second batch. Do not overcrowd pan.

2. Reserve browned chicken in a bowl. Add 1 tablespoon olive oil to Dutch oven and sauté onion over medium heat for 3 minutes, stirring occasionally. Add vegetables, turn heat to medium high, and sauté for 3 additional minutes. Remove vegetables to bowl with chicken. Add white wine to pan with heat still on medium high and scrape up browned bits from bottom of pan, about 1 minute.

3. Return chicken to the pan all in one layer, placing the breast pieces meat side down. Scatter the vegetables on top and in between the chicken pieces, and pour in any juices that may have accumulated in the bowl. Add the chicken broth, salt, and thyme (if using dried). Bring broth to a simmer, place a large sheet of aluminum foil over the top of the pan, cover, and place in heated oven. After 30 minutes, add garlic, parsley, and thyme (if using fresh). Stir gently to mix and baste meat. Cook another 15 minutes or until internal temperature of breast meat is 158°–162°F. Taste and add additional salt and freshly ground black pepper if needed. Serve with a small amount of braising liquid.
Serves 4

Master Recipe for Braised Fish

This technique is best for firm steaks or thick fillets that are at least ¾ inch thick. The braising liquid is turned into a quick sauce by reducing it (boiling it down until the volume of the liquid is reduced) over high heat for just a minute or two. The quick cooking time does not require a perfectly sealed pot, and therefore the top does not need to be covered with aluminum foil. Fish can be braised at a much higher temperature than beef or poultry, since it cooks quickly and is not tough to start with.

    3 tablespoons olive oil
    4 fish steaks or thick fillets, rinsed and patted
        dry
    1 small onion, peeled and diced
    3 cloves garlic, peeled and minced
    ¼ cup white wine vinegar or rice wine vinegar
    ⅓ cup chicken stock, fish stock, or high-quality
        soy sauce
    ⅓ cup dry white wine
    2 teaspoons minced fresh tarragon or basil
    2 scallions, diced
    1 tablespoon minced flat-leaf parsley
        Salt and freshly ground black pepper to taste

1. Heat oven to 375°F. Put 2 tablespoons of the olive oil into a Dutch oven or casserole over medium-high heat. When oil is hot, add fish steaks (do this in more than one batch if pan is crowded) and sauté for about 2 minutes. Turn fish over and sauté for 1 additional minute. Remove steaks from pan and keep warm.

2. Add remaining tablespoon of oil to pan and sauté onions for 4 minutes over medium heat. Add garlic and sauté for 1 minute. Add the next three ingredients and bring to a simmer.

3. Add the fish steaks or fillets, cover, and bake in preheated oven until done, about 10 minutes, depending upon the thickness of the steaks. Check after 7 minutes. Remove steaks from pan and keep warm.

4. Place pan on top of stove and reduce liquid over medium-high heat for 1–2 minutes. Add tarragon, scallions, parsley, and salt and pepper to taste and continue to cook for another minute. Pour liquid over reserved fish and serve.

Serves 4

Asian Braised Fish

Add 1 tablespoon of peeled and minced fresh ginger to the onions. Replace the white wine vinegar with rice wine vinegar, the chicken stock with soy sauce, and the tarragon or basil with ⅛ teaspoon ground cardamom and ½ teaspoon sugar. Add 2 teaspoons of toasted (Oriental) sesame oil along with the scallions and eliminate the parsley.

Brisket Braised in White Wine

This is a wonderfully light recipe. The brisket is braised in white wine, chicken stock, and water. Brisket, the cut of meat used to make corned beef, is tough but flavorful, and braising is a good technique for preparing it. Even when braised, however, brisket is not a tender cut. That is why it is sliced thinly and against the grain. Although the juniper berries are optional, they add a lot of flavor, so make sure you use them! They are available in most large supermarkets. To crush them, place them in a small plastic storage bag, place the bag on a cutting surface, and smash with a meat pounder or the bottom of a skillet or saucepan. If you cannot find brisket, use any good chuck roast, such as a top blade roast.

    1 tablespoon olive oil
    2 pounds beef brisket
        Salt and freshly ground black pepper to
        taste
    ½ cup dry white wine
    1 medium onion, peeled and diced
    4 garlic cloves, peeled and minced
    2 medium tomatoes, coarsely chopped
    4 carrots, peeled
    4 medium parsnips, peeled
    ½ cup chicken stock
    ¼ cup water
    1 teaspoon dried thyme
    1 teaspoon dried rosemary
    1 bay leaf
    12 juniper berries, crushed, optional

1. Heat oven to 200°F. Heat oil in large Dutch oven over medium-high heat. Season brisket with salt and pepper and then sear (cook quickly) on both sides in pan. Remove brisket to a platter or bowl, turn heat to high, and add white wine. Scrape bottom of pan with a wooden spoon and reduce wine for 1 minute. Add onion and cook over medium heat for 5 minutes. Add garlic and cook for 1 minute.

2. Return brisket to pan along with any juices that may have accumulated in the platter. Add all remaining ingredients and bring to a simmer.

3. Cover, place in oven, and cook for about 3 hours, or until meat is tender (about 145°F internal temperature). Discard bay leaf.

4. Remove brisket and slice against the grain into thin slices. Arrange on plates with carrots and parsnips, adding broth to each serving.

Serves 4–6

Lamb Shanks with Tomatoes

Shanks are notorious for varying cooking times. The timing depends on the size of the shank. A thick one may take up to 2 hours; a small shank may only require 1–1½ hours. The meat should be very tender, literally falling off the bone. For a less fatty sauce, prepare this dish the day before, refrigerate the sauce separately from the shanks, and remove the congealed layer of fat. Combine the shanks and defatted sauce and reheat gently. Lamb shanks are not always easy to find and are best ordered in advance. Ask the butcher to cut them into sections for you.

- 4 tablespoons olive oil
- 4 pounds lamb shanks, cut into 1½–2 inch sections
- 2 medium onions, peeled and diced
- 5 cloves garlic, peeled and finely minced
- 1 cup dry white wine
- 1 can (14 ounces) Italian plum tomatoes, drained
- ¼ cup orange juice
- 1 cup chicken stock
- 2 teaspoons fresh rosemary or 1 teaspoon dried

- 2 teaspoons fresh thyme or 1 teaspoon dried
- 2 teaspoons fresh marjoram or 1 teaspoon dried
- ¼ teaspoon ground cloves
- 1 bay leaf
- 1 teaspoon balsamic vinegar
- 1 teaspoon sugar
  Salt and freshly ground black pepper to taste
- 4 small waxy potatoes, quartered and in cold water to cover, optional

1. Heat oven to 200°F.

2. Heat 2 tablespoons of the oil in large casserole or Dutch oven over medium-high heat. Brown shanks on all sides in oil in batches — do not overcrowd pan — adding more oil if necessary. Reserve browned shanks in a bowl.

3. Add remaining 2 tablespoons of oil to pan. Reduce heat to medium. Add onions and cook for 5 minutes. Add garlic and cook until softened, about 1 minute. Turn heat to high, add white wine, and cook for 2 minutes, scraping bottom of pan.

4. Stir in all remaining ingredients except lamb, salt and pepper, and optional potatoes. Season with salt and pepper to taste and then return shanks to the pan along with any accumulated juices. Bring to a simmer, cover, and cook in preheated oven for 1 hour. Add the potatoes and cook until shanks are tender and potatoes are done, at least 2 hours more.

5. Remove pan from oven, take out shanks and potatoes and bay leaf, and puree remaining ingredients. Return all ingredients to pot. Check seasonings and serve.

Makes 4 large servings

Braised Veal Shanks with Lemon Zest, Sage, and Olives

This is a very simple preparation, which I prefer to the more robust flavor of a traditional osso-buco, which contains tomatoes and vegetables. Veal is delicate and is easily overwhelmed by sauces more suited to red meat. The perfume of fresh sage works well with this dish, along with the traditional lemon zest, which adds some zip. Be sure to cook the shanks long enough (2–2½ hours) — the meat should be falling off the bone. This dish can be made early in the day and then reheated on top of the stove over low heat (about 15 minutes). Be sure that none of the pith — the white layer just beneath the skin — is attached to the lemon peel. I use a vegetable peeler instead of a knife to remove the zest from a lemon, because it is easier to avoid taking any of the white pith.

> 4 small to medium veal shanks (2½–3 pounds total weight)
> 2 tablespoons unsalted butter
> 2 tablespoons olive oil
>   Salt and freshly ground black pepper
> ½ cup dry white wine
> ½ cup chicken stock
> ¼ cup minced flat-leaf parsley
> ½ cup pitted imported black olives, chopped
> 1½ tablespoons finely minced lemon zest
> 1 tablespoon minced fresh sage or 1 teaspoon dried

1. Heat oven to 200°F. Tie a string around the circumference of each shank (or have the butcher do it for you), so that the meat does not fall off the bone during cooking. Use one of the roast-tying methods on pages 248–249.

2. In a 12-inch-wide Dutch oven or sauté pan with a lid, heat the butter and olive oil over medium-high heat. When the butter foam subsides and the mixture is very hot but not smoking, add the shanks. Sauté for 3 minutes per side, shaking pan occasionally to keep shanks from sticking.

3. Salt and pepper both sides of the shanks. Add the white wine and chicken stock, cover pan, and place in oven.

4. Cook for 2½–3 hours or until the meat is very tender. Add parsley and olives during the last 10 minutes of cooking.

5. Combine zest and sage and sprinkle on top of each serving.

Serves 4

Pot Roast (Braised Roast)

Pot roast is the most common form of braising. Tough, inexpensive meat is cooked for a long time with liquid in a pot on top of the stove. Traditionally, most pot roasts were cooked at too high a temperature and for too long a time, to the point that the meat dried out and easily broke apart into ropy strands. That's why pot roast is braised, to provide gravy to make it palatable. If you like a traditional pot roast, cook until the meat reaches 175°F internal temperature. If, however, you prefer a juicier piece of meat, remove the meat when it hits 145°–150°F.

The secret to good pot roast is the cut of meat. Buy the top blade roast (the top blade is one of four muscles in the chuck), which is often labeled "beef chuck top blade roast boneless" or "top chuck roast." Do not purchase cuts from the round, because these cuts are low in fat and the pot roast will be dry.

You can add vegetables to the pot (carrots, onions, potatoes, parsnips, and so on) at the point you have about 2 hours of cooking time left. If the vegetables are not cooked properly when it is time to serve the meat, simply remove the meat, wrap in foil, and keep warm while you cook the vegetables in the simmering sauce on top of the stove. You can also cook the vegetables separately and then add them to the pot at the last minute, a method that I at first thought troublesome, but now feel is an excellent technique, as the vegetables are perfectly cooked.

Finally, I cook pot roast in the oven, since it is easier to maintain an even heat. Stovetop pot roast cooking is tricky and requires constant checking to make sure that the liquid is not bubbling.

> ½ teaspoon dried thyme
> ¼ teaspoon ground cloves
> ¼ teaspoon ground allspice
> 1 teaspoon ground black pepper
> 1 teaspoon kosher salt
> 1 pot roast (top blade roast or top chuck roast), about 3 pounds
> 2 slices bacon
> 2 tablespoons olive oil
> 1 medium onion, peeled and diced

1 carrot, diced

¼ cup dry white wine

1 teaspoon instant coffee powder mixed with 1 tablespoon hot water

1 cup low-salt beef or chicken broth

1 tablespoon brandy

1 bay leaf

2 teaspoons cornstarch mixed with 1 tablespoon water

1. Heat oven to 200°F. Mix together the first 5 ingredients and rub over meat.

2. Cook bacon in a heavy pot *just large enough* to hold the pot roast. Remove bacon (reserve for another recipe) and all but 1 tablespoon of fat. Add olive oil and brown pot roast on all sides over medium-high heat. Remove meat to a platter or bowl and add onion and carrot and sauté for 10 minutes.

3. Add the next 5 ingredients (wine through bay leaf) and scrape bottom of pot with a wooden spoon. Boil rapidly for 3 minutes, stirring constantly. Add pot roast, along with juices that have accumulated in the bowl, and cook over medium heat until liquid starts to simmer. Ladle liquid over roast and cover top of roast loosely with aluminum foil. Cover top of pot tightly with aluminum foil and then cover with lid. Immediately place in the 200° oven.

4. Cook until interior temperature of the meat reaches 145°–150°F (use an instant-read thermometer), about 3–4 hours. Remove meat from pot and cover with aluminum foil, and then pour braising liquid into the bowl of a food processor. Process for 7 seconds. Return puree to the pot, place over medium heat, and bring to a simmer. Add the cornstarch mixture and whisk until thickened. Serve with sliced pot roast.

Serves 8

Pressure Cooker Variation

This is the best method for cooking a pot roast, but you will need a 5-quart pressure cooker to hold the meat. Follow the directions above, browning the meat in the pressure cooker, and when the pot roast is added back to the pot after browning (middle of step 3), place the roast in the pressure cooker on top of the trivet (most models have round metal trays that allow the roast to sit above the liquid — if yours does not have one, simply place the roast on the bottom of the cooker), secure the top of the cooker, and bring it up to high pressure. Cook under high pressure for 60 minutes. Remove from heat, allow pot to cool on stovetop, and when pressure subsides, remove cover and proceed with step 4.

Braised Romaine with Garlic and White Wine

This is an unusual but delicious way to prepare romaine, but it could be used for any type of green. Braising greens and vegetables is an easy way to boost flavor by way of a seasoned liquid.

2 tablespoons olive oil

2 teaspoons minced garlic

¼ cup dry white wine

1 head romaine (remove wilted outer leaves if necessary), cut into 3-inch pieces
Salt and freshly ground black pepper to taste

Heat oven to 350°F. Heat olive oil in an ovenproof sauté pan. Sauté garlic for 1 minute over medium heat. Add wine and romaine, cover, and cook 25 minutes in preheated oven. Add salt and pepper to taste.

Serves 2

Making a Tender Stew

*The right cut of beef and the proper oven temperature
are the keys to tender, moist stews.*

~

It used to be that when I made a stew, I was never quite sure whether the meat would end up tender or tough, juicy or dry. What was the key to a perfect stew? Was it the cut of meat? The cooking temperature? The amount of liquid? I started to investigate.

IS ALL STEW MEAT THE SAME?

Most stew meat comes from either the chuck (this is the forequarter of the animal, including the shoulder, the neck, and the first five ribs) or the round (the upper hind leg of the animal). I had always been told by butchers that the chuck, rather than the round, is best for stewing, because it has more fat and connective tissues, which add both flavor and tenderness during a long, slow cooking process. I decided to run a test, so I made two stews, one with bottom round and the other with chuck. The stew made with chuck was substantially better: more tender, buttery, really top-notch.

If you have ever been to a meat warehouse or seen pictures of one, you'll know that the chuck is a large piece of meat — it's the size of a riding lawnmower. It can be cut up many ways and includes the top blade, underblade, chuck eye, mock tender, shoulder clod (the large muscle in the shoulder), and short ribs (see Chapter 27 for more detailed information). Although you can ask for any cut from the chuck and do well, I would specify the shoulder or the top blade. You will find, however, that supermarkets typically sell "stew meat," with no other description. This is often cut from the round, usually the bottom round, and is not recommended. If nobody will tell you which part of the animal the meat came from, a common problem since meat is no longer cut up at the store (the butchering and packaging occur out west these days), just take a look at it. If it is solid red, without any streaks of white, it is probably cut from the round and is therefore less desirable. A butcher may also offer you an expensive cut, such as the tenderloin, which is best roasted at high temperature and not suitable for a stew. Stewing is best done with well-muscled meat (actually, stewing was invented to properly cook tough meat). The chuck has lots of muscle, because it is near the head and front legs, areas that get a good workout. The connective tissues melt during prolonged cooking, which adds flavor and moisture to the meat.

DOES OVEN TEMPERATURE MAKE A DIFFERENCE?

I knew from tests with roasts that long, low-heat cooking is the best way to treat an inferior cut of meat. The meat is more apt to retain its moisture, and I find that there is a wider window of time during which the meat is cooked but not overcooked. For large pieces of meat, higher roasting temperatures mean that the outer layers will overcook and dry out while the slower-cooking interior comes up to temperature (a traditional oven cooks from the outside in, unlike a microwave). I wondered if the same theory would apply to the smaller pieces used in a stew. To find out, I cooked three beef stews using top round at three different oven temperatures — 200°, 250°, and 300°F — and for varying times. The clear winner was the 200° oven and the longer cooking time, 3 hours. Although the 300° oven did produce a tender piece of meat, it was dry.

Once it was determined that 200°F was the best cooking temperature, I then tested two different cuts: bottom round and chuck. Both bottom and top round are inferior cuts (the bottom round being the worst) — both are lacking in fat to produce a tender, moist stew. The chuck is fattier and more likely to produce a buttery, tender piece of meat, especially when cooked slowly, and this was confirmed by my test. The stew made from the bottom round was not nearly as tender, flavorful, and juicy as the stew made from the chuck.

HOW TO MAKE A STEW

Most stew recipes call for browning the cubes of meat as a first step. This develops flavor in both the meat and the sauce. Make sure that you use lots of heat for this step and don't crowd the pan. Otherwise, the meat will simply stew in its own juices instead of searing. I have tried flouring the meat before browning — some cooks prefer this method, as the flour helps thicken the sauce later on — but I find that this interferes with the browning process and tends to make the bottom of the pan stickier. To adjust the thickness of the sauce, I simply remove 2–3 cups of liquid from the stewpot to a food processor along with ¼–½ of the potatoes and process; the greater the proportion of pota-

---

KITCHEN TEST

The Effect of Cooking Temperatures on Texture and Moisture of Top Round Beef in a Stew

Cubes of top round were browned in a Dutch oven on top of the stove. Liquid was added and the pan was covered and placed in the oven. The meat was cooked at three different oven temperatures and for different lengths of time.

Cooking Temperature	Cooking Time	Results
200°F	2 hours	Tough
	2½ hours	More tender
	3 hours	Very tender and moist
250°F	2 hours	Somewhat tender
	2½ hours	Tender but a little dry
	3 hours	Meat falling apart but dry
300°F	2 hours	Tough
	2½ hours	Tender but a little dry

The Maillard Reaction

Browning meat develops tremendous flavor because the sugar in the meat begins to caramelize, a process known as the Maillard reaction. This caramelization is the same process that makes a well-browned waffle or pie shell more flavorful than its pale counterpart. With meat, however, there is also a great deal of protein involved, which in effect lowers the temperature at which caramelization occurs. There are, however, no data to suggest that searing meat actually "seals in the juices." Browning or searing meat is for flavor, not juiciness.

1 medium onion, peeled and diced
1 cup hearty red wine
2 large cloves garlic, peeled and minced
2½ cups chicken stock
2 canned tomatoes, seeded and chopped, or 1 tablespoon tomato paste
1 bay leaf
½ teaspoon kosher salt
2 medium onions, peeled and sliced
4 medium carrots, sliced thickly on the bias
2 celery ribs, thickly sliced
4 waxy (Maine or red) potatoes, diced into 2-inch pieces
1 teaspoon dried thyme or 1 tablespoon fresh
Freshly ground black pepper to taste
2 tablespoons minced flat-leaf parsley

toes, the thicker the sauce. Now stir this mixture back into the stew. If you prefer a little sweetness, include a few pieces of carrot when pureeing. I find waxy potatoes preferable to baking potatoes, as they hold their shape better during cooking. Homemade stock is vastly preferable to canned, but if you use the latter, be sure to use a low-sodium variety.

I have also found that it is best not to salt meat for a stew before browning. I performed a head-to-head test and found that when the meat is salted before cooking, it exudes more juices and dries out. Adding the salt to the stew after the meat is browned produces juicier beef or pork.

Master Recipe for Beef Stew

This recipe is designed to work with lean meat from the beef round (the round is at the rear of the animal), which is what most supermarkets use for "stew meat." Top round is preferable to bottom round, and sirloin tip (also from the round) is better yet. By far the best meat for stew, however, is cut from the chuck, including the shoulder, the top blade, and the chuck eye muscles. All cuts should be cooked for the same amount of time.

3 pounds stew beef, cut into 1½-inch cubes
3 tablespoons olive oil

1. Heat oven to 200°F. Pat meat dry with paper towels. Heat 2 tablespoons of the olive oil in a large pot or Dutch oven set over high heat and brown meat in batches on top and bottom. Do not crowd. Remove browned meat to a bowl.

2. Add the remaining tablespoon of olive oil to the pot over medium-high heat. When hot add the diced onion along with ¼ cup of the wine. Sauté for 2 minutes, stirring constantly with a wooden spoon, scraping the bottom of the pan. Add the garlic and sauté for 1 minute, stirring constantly. Add the rest of the wine, the stock, the chopped tomato, the bay leaf, the browned meat with any accumulated juices, and the salt. Cover and bake in preheated oven for 30 minutes. Add sliced onions, carrots, celery, and potatoes and cook another 1½ hours.

3. Add the dried thyme (if using fresh thyme, add it later) and continue cooking for another 30 minutes. Check meat. If tender, add the fresh thyme and cook another 15 minutes. If meat is still tough, continue cooking until tender, adding the fresh thyme for the last 15 minutes of cooking. Check seasonings and add freshly ground black pepper to taste.

4. Remove ¼ of the potatoes and 2 cups of the liquid to a food processor or blender and

puree. Return to the pot and stir to combine. Sprinkle each serving with parsley and serve with large hunks of French or country bread.

Serves 6

Pressure Cooker Variation

As with pot roast, a pressure cooker transforms inexpensive stew meat into a rich, succulent dish. Follow the master recipe through step 2, except add all of the vegetables and the thyme along with the browned stew meat. Then fit the top of the pressure cooker and cook under high pressure for just 12 minutes. Remove from heat and let pressure subside (10–15 minutes). Remove top and serve stew, sprinkling minced parsley and freshly ground black pepper on each serving.

Beef Stew with Cumin, Allspice, and Cocoa

Make sure the potatoes or carrots are cut into moderate-size pieces, no larger than ¼ inch square. You can spice up the stew by adding 1 or 2 small minced chili peppers along with the garlic.

- 2 pounds stew meat, cut into 1½-inch cubes
- 2 tablespoons olive oil
- 1 tablespoon butter
- 1 large onion, peeled and coarsely chopped
- 5 cloves garlic, peeled and minced
- 1 cup full-bodied red wine
- 1 can (28 ounces) Italian plum tomatoes, drained
- 2 teaspoons ground cumin
- ¼ teaspoon ground allspice
- 2 teaspoons unsweetened cocoa powder
- 2 teaspoons paprika
- ¼ teaspoon cayenne
- ½ teaspoon dried oregano
- 1½ cups beef stock
- 1½ cups water
  Salt to taste
- 1 pound potatoes or carrots, cut into bite-size pieces
  Freshly ground black pepper to taste
- 3 scallions, chopped

1. Heat oven to 200°F. Pat meat dry with paper towels. Heat olive oil in a large pot or Dutch oven set over medium-high heat and brown meat in batches on top and bottom. Do not crowd. Remove browned meat to a bowl.

2. Add the butter to the pan and when it has melted, sauté the onions for 5 minutes over medium heat. Add the garlic and sauté for 1 minute. Turn heat up to high and add ⅓ cup of red wine, deglazing (scraping) bottom of pan, about 2 minutes. Return the browned meat to the pan, along with any juices that have accumulated in the bowl. Add the rest of the wine and the next 10 ingredients (tomatoes through salt). Cover pan and place it in the 200° oven and cook for 1 hour.

3. Add potatoes or carrots and cook for an additional 2 hours. Add freshly ground pepper to taste and garnish with scallions. Serve.

Serves 4

Pork Stew with Anchovies and Peppers

Use the pork shoulder for stew meat. It is sold as Boston butt or Boston shoulder. A lean, expensive cut (from the loin, for example) can produce tough, dry meat when stewed. Do not overcook the peppers. They should still have some snap to provide a contrast in texture with the rest of the stew.

- 4 pounds boneless pork shoulder (Boston shoulder or Boston butt), cut into 1½-inch cubes
- 7 tablespoons olive oil, approximately
  Salt and freshly ground black pepper to taste
- 2 large onions, peeled and coarsely chopped
- 5 cloves garlic, peeled and minced
- ¼ cup all-purpose flour
- 1 cup chicken stock
- ½ cup water
- 1 cup dry white wine
- 1 orange, juiced
- 2 tablespoons minced anchovy fillets

1 teaspoon dried thyme or 1 tablespoon
minced fresh
2 teaspoons dried oregano or 2 tablespoons
minced fresh
3 red or yellow bell peppers, seeded and cored
¼ cup imported black olives, pitted and finely
minced

1. Heat oven to 200°F. Pat pork dry with paper towels. In a large Dutch oven, heat 2 tablespoons of the oil over medium-high heat. Brown the pork in batches, being careful not to crowd the pot. Add more oil as needed. Remove each batch with a slotted spoon and reserve in a bowl. Season liberally with salt and freshly ground pepper.

2. Add 2 tablespoons of oil to the pot and heat. When hot, add onions. Stir constantly over high heat, scraping up any accumulated juices from the bottom. After 3 minutes, add the garlic, reduce heat to medium, and cook for about 5 minutes covered, stirring occasionally. Add the flour, and cook for another 3 minutes, stirring constantly.

3. Return browned pork to the pan, along with any juices that may have collected in the bowl. Add chicken stock, water, wine, orange juice, anchovies, and dried herbs (if using fresh herbs, add them during the last half hour of cooking). Cover pan, place it in oven, and cook for 3–3½ hours. Check meat and continue cooking, if necessary, until tender.

4. Meanwhile, in a frying pan, heat 3 tablespoons of oil over medium heat. Sauté the peppers until lightly browned, about 5 minutes. When the stew is done, add the peppers and minced olives and serve.

Serves 8

Master Recipe for Lamb Stew

The best cut of meat for lamb stew is the shoulder, which is about the same as ordering chuck for a beef stew. I have tried this stew with veal and found that the cooking time should be shortened, since veal is more tender and has less fat. I recommend about 1 hour at 200°F before the fi-

nal ingredients are added. If you like a thicker sauce for this stew, remove the solid ingredients after cooking and whisk 3 tablespoons of cornstarch mixed with ¼ cup water into the pan juices. Cook over medium heat, whisking constantly, until mixture thickens slightly, then return solid ingredients to the pan.

3 pounds lamb shoulder, cut into 1½-inch
cubes
3 tablespoons olive oil
1 medium onion, peeled and diced
1 cup good white wine
2 large garlic cloves, peeled and minced
2½ cups chicken stock
1 bay leaf
½ teaspoon kosher salt
2 large onions, peeled and cut lengthwise
into eight wedges
1 cup imported black olives
1½ cups cooked white beans
1 tablespoon minced fresh rosemary
Freshly ground black pepper to taste
3 tablespoons minced flat-leaf parsley

1. Heat oven to 200°F. Pat meat dry with paper towels. Heat 2 tablespoons of the olive oil in a large pot or Dutch oven set over high heat and brown meat in batches on top and bottom. Do not crowd. Remove meat to a bowl.

2. Add the remaining tablespoon of olive oil to the pot over medium-high heat. When hot add the diced onion along with 2 tablespoons of the wine. Sauté for 2 minutes, stirring constantly with a wooden spoon, scraping the bottom of the pan. Add the garlic and sauté for 1 minute, stirring constantly. Add the browned meat, including any juices that have collected in the bowl, the rest of the wine, the stock, the bay leaf, and the salt. Cover pan and bake in preheated oven for 2 hours.

3. Add next 3 ingredients and continue cooking for another 30 minutes. When meat is tender, add rosemary and cook another 15 minutes. Check seasonings and add freshly ground black pepper to taste. Sprinkle each

serving with parsley and serve with large hunks of French or country bread.

Serves 6

Dried Fruit Variation

This sounds like an odd combination, but it makes a wonderful stew. Dried apricots or peaches add an extra dimension to the flavor of the lamb and onions. Substitute 8 ounces dried apricots or peaches for the white beans, and use thyme instead of rosemary.

Rosemary Dumpling Variation

This idea is borrowed from a basic chicken with dumplings. To leaven the dumplings I use buttermilk and baking soda instead of sweet milk and baking powder. I season these dumplings with fresh rosemary, but you can also use sage or thyme. Omit the white beans from the Master Recipe for Lamb Stew. I also suggest that you increase the liquid in the stew to accommodate the dumplings. Increase the white wine by ½ cup and the chicken stock by 1 cup.

Dumplings
2 cups all-purpose flour
1 teaspoon baking soda
1 teaspoon kosher salt
1 tablespoon minced fresh rosemary
3 tablespoons cold butter, cut into pieces
2 tablespoons cold Crisco
¾ cup buttermilk

Place first 4 ingredients in the workbowl of a food processor. Pulse to combine. Add the butter and Crisco and process until mixture resembles coarse meal (about 7 seconds). Remove to a bowl and add buttermilk. Fold ingredients together with a stiff rubber spatula until combined. Dough should hold together in a ball. If too dry, add a bit more buttermilk. If too wet, add a bit more flour. Form tablespoons of dough into balls, pressing them together tightly so they don't break apart in the stew. Drop them into the stew at the point that the meat is tender and cook for 20–30 minutes or until dumplings are cooked through.

Master Recipe for Fish Stew

There is nothing revolutionary about this dish — it is similar to the French bouillabaisse, the Spanish zarzuela, and the bourride of Provence — but it is easy to change around, using whatever fish or shellfish you happen to have available. I prefer a little texture to a fish stew and am therefore partial to shrimp or lobster as a key ingredient, although monkfish also works well. (I list three categories of ingredients below, but you can make this recipe with any one of them or any combination.) You can use many different types of fish, although I find that cod or haddock works fine, and they are relatively inexpensive. Stay clear of mackerel, bluefish, and other strong-flavored fish. Don't bother with this recipe unless you make your own fish stock, which takes only 20 minutes. This is crucial to an aromatic, richly flavored stew.

2 tablespoons olive oil
1 cup diced onion
1 rib celery, diced
1 medium red bell pepper, cored, seeded, and diced
3 cloves garlic, peeled and minced
¼ cup cognac
¼ cup white wine
1 3-inch piece orange zest
2 cups canned tomatoes, drained and chopped
2 bay leaves
2 teaspoons fresh thyme or ½ teaspoon dried
Salt and freshly ground black pepper to taste
2 quarts fish stock (see Master Recipe for Fish Stock, page 281)
⅛ teaspoon cayenne pepper, or more to taste
1 pound shelled shrimp, lobster meat, scallops, or monkfish or a combination, cut into bite-size pieces
½ pound mussels or clams in shell
1 pound cod, haddock, sea bass, or red snapper or a combination, cut into bite-size pieces

⅓ cup Roasted Red Pepper and Garlic Sauce
(page 287)
¼ cup minced flat-leaf parsley

1. Heat oil in a pot large enough to hold all ingredients. Add onion, celery, and red pepper and sauté over medium heat for 8 minutes. Add garlic and sauté for 1 minute. Add cognac and when it starts to bubble, light with a match, standing well clear of the flame. Stir constantly until flame burns out. Add the next 5 ingredients (wine through thyme), bring to a boil, and simmer for 15 minutes. Add salt and pepper to taste.

2. Add fish stock and bring to a simmer. Add cayenne to taste. Now add lobster meat and clams and simmer for 3 minutes; add monkfish and mussels and simmer for 2 minutes; add shrimp, scallops, and fish and simmer for 3 minutes. Remove from heat. Remove fish that is cooked to bowls for serving, letting any uncooked fish remain in hot broth until ready. Remove mussels and clams when they open. Stir roasted red pepper sauce into broth, ladle broth over fish, and top with fresh parsley.

Serves 6–8

~ 31 ~

Stocks and Sauces

Most stocks and sauces are relics of haute cuisine and are therefore of little use to the home cook. Here are lighter, easier-to-prepare recipes that make sense in an American kitchen.

~

There are stocks and glacés, white sauces and brown sauces, fish sauces and meat sauces, egg yolk sauces and mayonnaise sauces, butter sauces and vinaigrettes. The problem is that most of these sauces were developed by chefs, not home cooks, in a place and time that has little bearing on American home cooking. What is one to do with a Chantilly sauce, made from mayonnaise and whipped cream? I suspect very little.

We almost have to start over and ask the basic question, why do we need sauces? One of the original reasons for sauces — to mask the deteriorated state of the underlying meat or fish — is no longer an issue. In addition, food used to be eaten with the fingers, hence a thick sauce was preferred for its clinging power. (A thin sauce would drip onto one's tunic.) It should also be noted that sauces were never cooked by peasants; they were prepared by a small army of chefs. Finally, the current preference for bright, fresh flavors and healthier cooking immediately calls into question virtually all of a French chef's classic repertoire. So a modern sauce must be light, easy to make, healthy, and frugal in construction. That leaves a small circle of stock-based sauces that use herbs, aromatics (onions, garlic), pan drippings, wine, and a thickener.

THE PROBLEM WITH STOCKS

The original sauce used the natural juices of meat or fish exuded during cooking as an ingredient. However, this does not provide a sufficient amount of sauce (according to James Peterson, in *Sauces,* the French often cooked a second roast, a turkey, for example, to provide enough sauce for the first roast), and it is also less convenient to prepare a sauce at the last minute. The chef could not begin making the sauce until after the roast was cooked. As a result, French chefs invented stocks, which could be made ahead of time. Stocks originally were made from meat. (This chapter includes a recipe for chicken broth made from a whole chicken.) This is expensive, although the boiled meat can be used in salads, omelets, ravioli, and other dishes. For the sake of economy, therefore, chefs started preparing stocks with bones, either roasted or not. Although they are more trouble, stocks made with roasted bones — referred to in the trade as brown stocks — have more flavor.

The major issues with stock are flavor and convenience, the latter being of little concern in a restaurant but of paramount concern to the home cook. Chefs often prepare double and triple stocks. That is, they make an extra-strength stock starting with an already prepared stock instead of water. This is time-consuming and expensive, but provides deeper flavor. You have probably enjoyed this enhanced flavor if you have ever ordered roast chicken at a top-notch restaurant, where it is likely that the chef used a double chicken stock to prepare the accompanying sauce. However, this is impractical for the home cook. A simpler approach is to boil down a prepared stock to concentrate its flavors. This technique is borrowed from classic French cuisine. Stocks that have been substantially reduced in volume are referred to as glacés. However, you can overdo this reduction (a reduction is a liquid that has been boiled, thereby reducing its volume and increasing its flavor). Too much boiling makes a stock less aromatic and flatter in taste. You get stronger flavor but less depth.

The problem with most stock recipes is that they have the restaurant chef, not the home cook, in mind. Who has the time to stand by the stove for 3 or 4 hours, skimming the scum off the top every 10 minutes? This is the sort of recipe that drives an enterprising young cook to takeout. So I ran a few tests to figure out how cooking time affects flavor and whether I could discover a quick and easy method.

IN SEARCH OF A NO-WORK STOCK

The initial results were not comforting. It appeared that the traditional method, roasting the bones and then simmering for 3 hours, was the clear winner when tested against shorter cooking times and unroasted bones. I even tried an overnight method. After serving a roast chicken for dinner, I decided to throw the leftover carcass in a pot with a few vegetables, herbs, and water. I covered it and placed it in a 200° oven until the next morning. I thought that I had finally come up with a quick and easy solution. However, when taste-tested against the other methods, the overnight stock was flat, dull, and almost tasteless. All of the complexity had been cooked out of it.

I did have some luck, however, when I prepared a chicken broth instead of a stock. A broth is made by simmering a whole chicken, not just the bones, and takes only 1 hour. The results were very good; less complex than the 3-hour method, but still very aromatic and flavorful. I also found, after some testing, that it is best to use 2 quarts of water per chicken when making stock rather than the 3 quarts called for in many cookbooks. This provides a much more flavorful stock. (For a broth, however, I use 3 quarts of water, since the meat and skin add extra flavor.)

I was also troubled by the problem of bones. It's hard to get bones these days, as most butchers and supermarkets purchase their meat precut and prepackaged. Therefore, I always purchase whole chickens instead of parts, using the leftovers for stock. (This is why it is important to know how to cut up a chicken at home.) I also trim off the wings and freeze them with the neck, making stock when I have a sufficient supply. Finally, I try to make stock the same day I serve a roasted chicken, instead of trying to squeeze the leftover carcass into an already packed freezer.

STOCK-MAKING TIPS

Here are some tips and shortcuts that would deeply offend Escoffier but do turn stock making into a reasonable proposition.

■ Forget the skimming. The theory is that if you don't skim the scum, it will eventually work its way back into the stock, making it cloudy. There is some truth to this; my stock is on the cloudy side. However, the

Making Stock with a Whole Chicken, Chicken Bones, and Roasted Bones

There is no question from these test results that the traditional method — roasting the bones and simmering for 3 hours — produces the best stock. However, the whole chicken method is a good quick alternative. All stocks were made with herbs and vegetables (see recipes in this chapter).

Method	Results
Use whole chicken and simmer for 1 hour.	Very good flavor; excellent for a quick stock.
Use chicken bones and simmer for 3 hours.	Stronger flavor than with the whole chicken.
Use roasted chicken bones and simmer for 1 hour.	Not as good as the whole chicken method.
Use roasted chicken bones and simmer for 3 hours.	Rich, complex flavor; the clear winner.
Simmer chicken carcass overnight.	Dull, tasteless dishwater.

flavor is excellent. Instead of skimming, I simply strain the stock after cooking through a quadruple thickness of cheesecloth, a good but not perfect solution. So, maybe I'll never work at Lutèce.

■ Stocks are not rocket science. They are just water, some meat or bones, a few vegetables, and herbs. You don't really need a recipe. Just throw it all together, higgledy-piggledy, and simmer it. You're done. If you don't have any vegetables or herbs on hand, make it anyway. It will taste fine.

■ Use less water and get more flavor. Many home cooks use too much water and end up with a nice big pot full of warm, slightly fatty H_2O. The best rule of thumb, especially if the stock is to be cooked for only an hour on top of the stove, is to use only enough water to cover three-quarters of the bones — I use about 2 quarts for one chicken.

■ Fennel and red peppers add a lot of flavor to vegetable stocks.

■ Add celery and parsley during the last half hour of cooking. Otherwise, their bright aroma and flavor will become dull.

■ The easiest way to degrease stock is to refrigerate it and then scoop off the chilled fat layer on top. If you are going to use it immediately, let it settle for 10 minutes and then try to spoon off the fat. Then use a triple thickness of paper towel over the top to soak up fat. You can also use a gravy strainer, a plastic container with a spout located near the bottom, that allows you to pour off the stock, leaving the grease layer floating on top (let the stock sit in the strainer for about 10 minutes to allow the fat to rise).

Master Recipe for Chicken Stock

This is more work than the recipe for chicken broth that follows. However, the roasted bones add a great deal of flavor. I usually use a leftover chicken carcass, although you can also start with bones from raw chicken parts and simply roast them longer. You can throw in wings and neck in addition to the basic carcass, and it's good to have some meat still attached to the bones. This recipe must be cooked for 3 hours to produce a deep, rich flavor. Use just enough water to cover the bones. Too much water will thin out the stock, diluting the flavor. This is a concentrated stock and is excellent as a base for sauces. To use it as a soup base, I suggest you dilute it by ⅓ with water.

1 chicken carcass from a roasted or raw chicken
2 quarts cold water, approximately
1 large onion, peeled and coarsely chopped
2 medium carrots, coarsely chopped
1 bay leaf
6 sprigs fresh thyme, oregano, or rosemary
6 whole cloves
2 medium ribs celery, coarsely chopped
¼ cup coarsely chopped flat-leaf parsley
Salt to taste

1. Heat oven to 400°F. Place chicken carcass in a roasting pan and cook for 20 minutes if from a roasted chicken and about 1 hour if from a raw chicken.

2. Place roasting pan on top of stove, remove the bones from the pan, and place in a stockpot. To the roasting pan add 1 quart cold water, and cook over high heat for 2 minutes, scraping any cooked-on juices off the bottom of the pan with a wooden spoon.

3. Place liquid from the roasting pan in the stockpot along with the remaining ingredients except celery, parsley, and salt, using just enough water to cover (up to 1 additional quart). Bring to a boil, reduce heat, and then simmer uncovered for 2½ hours. Add celery and parsley and simmer an additional 30 minutes. Don't bother skimming the foam as it rises to the surface — the stock will be strained after cooking.

4. Remove stockpot from heat. Strain broth, using a quadruple thickness of cheesecloth. Add salt to taste, being careful not to overseason if stock is to be used in a reduction sauce. The broth can now be used or refrigerated. If the latter, remove the congealed fat layer on top of the broth before reheating.

Makes about 3½ cups

Quick-Cook Chicken Stock

This stock requires only 1 hour of cooking, as the meat of the chicken provides a lot of flavor quickly. I suggest you cut up the chicken and vegetables to maximize the flavor during the short cooking time. This stock — it's actually a broth — makes a terrific, fresh-flavored base for soups.

1 chicken, 3½–4 pounds, cut into parts
3 quarts cold water
1 large onion, peeled and coarsely chopped
1 medium carrot, coarsely chopped

COOKING TIP

Refrigerating and Freezing Stock

To prevent the growth of bacteria that can produce toxins, stock — especially chicken stock — should not be left sitting at room temperature. It needs to be cooled down as quickly as possible after cooking. Many chefs throw in a batch of ice cubes to get the temperature down quickly, and then they put the stock in the refrigerator. I find that this dilutes the flavor. Instead, I transfer the hot stock to plastic containers and then set them in a cold-water bath. After a half hour, I transfer them to the refrigerator. (A cold-water bath reduces the temperature of stock faster than the cold air in a refrigerator. Water conducts heat better than air.) You should refrigerate stock for only 2–3 days; otherwise, it should be frozen. Remove the congealed layer of fat from the top of the stock before reheating.

1 bay leaf
6 sprigs fresh thyme, oregano, or rosemary or 1 teaspoon dried
6 whole cloves
2 medium ribs celery, coarsely chopped
4 stems flat-leaf parsley, coarsely chopped
Salt to taste

1. Place ingredients except celery, parsley, and salt in a large pot and bring to a boil. Simmer uncovered for 40 minutes. Don't bother skimming the foam as it rises to the surface — the stock will be strained after cooking. Remove chicken pieces and use with another recipe.

2. Add celery and parsley and simmer for an additional 20 minutes. Remove stockpot from heat. Strain broth, using a quadruple thickness of cheesecloth. Add salt to taste, being careful not to overseason, especially if stock is to be used in a reduction sauce. The broth can now be used or refrigerated. If the latter, remove the congealed fat layer on top of the broth before reheating. Stock can also be frozen.

Makes about 1¼ quarts

Master Recipe for Beef Stock

I call for browning the bones before adding any liquid. Although this is an optional step, I have tested it and found that browning not only helps to color the stock, it adds a great deal of flavor. In my opinion, it is worth the extra work. You can also mix bones — if I have a chicken carcass or a few chicken parts lying around, I'll throw them in the pot, too. However, at least 3 pounds of the bones should be beef. The chicken carcass does not have to be cut up. Ask your butcher to cut up the beef bones for you — if you are using leftover bones and don't have a large cleaver, you can skip this step. I also tested simmering the bones for 1 hour versus 3 hours. The 3-hour stock was dramatically better.

    5 pounds beef bones, cut into 4-inch pieces
    2 carrots, cut into 2-inch pieces (do not peel)
    2 large onions, peeled and quartered
    2 tomatoes, fresh or canned, coarsely chopped
    2 cloves garlic, peeled and lightly crushed
    1 teaspoon black peppercorns
    2 bay leaves
    4 quarts cold water, approximately
    2 ribs celery, coarsely chopped
    ½ cup chopped flat-leaf parsley
      Salt to taste

1. Heat oven to 450°F. Place bones in a roasting pan and add half the carrots. Roast for about 20 minutes, turn the bones over, and then add half the onions. Roast an additional 30 minutes or until bones are well browned but not burned. Watch the onions carefully — they have a tendency to burn if touching the bottom of the roasting pan. Remove bones from pan and place in a large pot. Pour off any excess fat. Place roasting pan on the stovetop over medium-high heat. Add 2 cups of water and bring water to a boil. Cook for 3 minutes, scraping up browned bits from the bottom of the pan.

2. Pour contents of the roasting pan into the stockpot along with the other ingredients except celery, parsley, and salt and cover with remaining cold water (there should be just enough water to cover). Bring to a boil and then reduce heat to a slow simmer. Simmer uncovered for 2½ hours. Don't bother removing the scum as it rises to the surface — it will be strained out after cooking. Add celery and parsley and simmer an additional 30 minutes. Remove pot from heat. Ladle as much stock as possible into a sieve lined with a quadruple thickness of cheesecloth. Remove solids from the pot and let remaining broth settle for 10 minutes. Carefully pour the remaining liquid into the sieve.

3. If stock is too weak, place back in cleaned stockpot and boil until reduced and flavor is increased. Add salt to taste, being careful not to overseason, especially if stock is to be used in a reduction sauce.

Makes about 2¾ quarts

Master Recipe for Fish Stock

The wonderful secret about fish stocks is that they can be made in just 20 minutes of simmering. In tests, I have found that the shorter cooking time is actually preferable. The only rule is to stay away from strong-flavored fish such as mackerel or bluefish. Also, if you use fish heads, the gills should be removed, an unpleasant and surprisingly difficult task. I suggest a good pair of kitchen shears and a pair of rubber gloves to protect your hands (I get a rash from working with the gills that lasts about 3 days — I also get small cuts on my fingers when working with the gills from a large fish such as red snapper). If you are friendly with a local fishmonger or supermarket employee, beg him or her to do this for you. You can also substitute the shells from shrimp or lobster for fish trimmings.

    3 pounds fish bones, cut into pieces (remove
      gills if using fish heads)
    2 ribs celery, coarsely chopped
    1 medium onion, peeled and coarsely chopped
    ½ cup coarsely chopped flat-leaf parsley
    4 cloves garlic, peeled and lightly crushed
    1 tablespoon black peppercorns
    2 bay leaves

2 cups dry white wine
3 quarts cold water

Combine all ingredients in a large stockpot, bring to a boil, and simmer uncovered for 20 minutes. Remove from heat and strain through a sieve lined with a quadruple thickness of cheesecloth. Discard solids. For a stronger stock, use 2 quarts water.

Makes about 3 quarts

Master Recipe for Vegetable Stock

There are three secrets to a good vegetable stock. First, barely cover the vegetables with water for a full-flavored stock. Second, use red bell peppers and fennel, as they add a lot of flavor. Third, add parsley, celery, and fresh herbs during the last half hour of cooking, not at the beginning. You can try adding ¼ cup white wine vinegar along with the water for more flavor. Old, tired vegetables are fine for stock — you don't need perfectly fresh vegetables for this recipe. Roasting the root vegetables first does add flavor but is optional.

- 6 onions, peeled and quartered
- 6 carrots, cut into 2-inch pieces
- 6 parsnips, cut into 2-inch pieces
- 6 white turnips, cut into 2-inch pieces
- ¼ cup olive oil, optional
- 1 bulb fennel, coarsely chopped
- 2 red bell peppers, cored, seeded, and coarsely chopped
- 2 bay leaves
- 1 clove garlic, peeled and lightly crushed
- 6 black peppercorns
- 2 whole cloves
- 1 small chili pepper, seeded and chopped
- 4 quarts cold water
- 2 ribs celery, coarsely chopped
- 1 small bunch flat-leaf parsley, coarsely chopped
- 1 teaspoon fresh thyme leaves
- ¼ cup white wine vinegar, optional
- Salt to taste

1. If you wish to roast the root vegetables (this is optional), heat oven to 450°F. Place onions, carrots, parsnips, and turnips in a large roasting pan and toss with the optional olive oil. Cover and roast for 25 minutes. Uncover and roast an additional 25 minutes, tossing vegetables two or three times.

2. Place vegetables and other ingredients except celery, parsley, thyme, optional vinegar, and salt in a large stockpot. Bring water to a boil, reduce to a simmer, and cook uncovered for 45 minutes. Add celery, parsley, and thyme and cook an additional half hour, adding optional vinegar during last 10 minutes of cooking. Remove pot from heat and strain stock through a sieve lined with a quadruple thickness of cheesecloth. Discard solids. If stock is too weak, place back in cleaned stockpot and boil until reduced and flavor is increased. Add salt to taste.

Makes about 3 quarts

HOW TO THICKEN A SAUCE: POTATOES, RICE, AND BREAD

If you have ever taken a course in classic French cooking, forget almost everything they told you. The French, with great intestinal fortitude, classically thicken sauces with butter, flour, egg yolks, and cream, to name a few of the culprits. They whisk together melted butter and flour to make a roux and then blend in milk (for a béchamel) or stock (for a velouté), which thickens almost immediately. Or they make a paste or little balls of equal parts flour and butter (beurre manié); these are added to sauces or stews as a thickener near the end of cooking. Egg yolks are whisked into a sauce, or reduced cream (cream that has been boiled down to thicken it) is stirred in. Butter can also be a thickener. When it is whisked into a hot liquid, the milk solids and proteins in butter form an emulsion, which suspends the particles of fat in the liquid, creating a thicker, shinier sauce. The problem with this last method, however, is that you need lots of butter to make it work (½ cup butter per cup of liquid — ½ cup butter is an entire stick!). Nobody in their right mind is going to thicken with butter very often these days. Other thickeners include blood, foie gras (goose liver), yogurt, fresh cheese, and bread. And prior to the sixteenth century, coarse bread and ground almonds were the thickeners of choice.

So much for classic French cooking. The quickest and easiest thickener for a home cook is cornstarch. Whisk it with equal parts of water and then add it to a stock or meat juices and you have an instant sauce or gravy. This is how most people thicken gravy for Thanksgiving. But there are three good alternatives. Since most thickeners are starch, the two most obvious thickeners are potatoes and rice. Potatoes are particularly well suited to soups and stews (cook extra potatoes with the dish and then puree them with some of the liquid). I often keep extra cooked rice in the refrigerator as a thickener as well. I puree it with stock and vegetables for a quick, light sauce. I also use stale white bread, which is the traditional thickener for a rouille, a sauce made with roasted red peppers, lots of garlic, and hot peppers.

THE WHITE SAUCE

This classic sauce is based on a roux, which is made by whisking equal volumes of butter and flour together in a saucepan over heat in order to ameliorate the flavor of the flour and to remove lumps. To make a sauce or a base for a soufflé, for example, hot milk, cream, or stock is added to the roux, and in just a few minutes the liquid thickens up nicely. The thickness of the sauce is easily varied by changing the proportion of roux to liquid. For a thin sauce, a French chef uses 1 tablespoon each of butter and flour to 1 cup of liquid; for a medium sauce, 2 tablespoons each; and for a thick sauce, 3 tablespoons

Why Do Flour and Cornstarch Thicken Sauces?

You've probably noticed that neither flour nor cornstarch thickens when stirred into water at room temperature. They just turn into a loose paste. What is missing is the application of heat, which encourages the bonding of starch and water molecules. (Both flour and cornstarch are mostly starch, although flour contains many other ingredients, such as proteins.) The starch granules then start to enlarge (think of blowing up a beach ball), trapping water as they grow. Finally, at temperatures over 150°F and up to a point just below boiling, the rigid structure of the granules breaks up, creating a spidery web of bonded starch and water molecules. This mesh prevents the free movement of water molecules and results in a thick sauce. You probably have also noticed that at this point, the sauce starts to become clearer. That is because the starch molecules are no longer packed tightly together — they are in a looser meshwork after heating — and therefore light is less likely to be deflected. At temperatures above 200°F, however, the large starch granules start to shrink, leaking starch molecules into the sauce. As these swollen granules deflate, the sauce becomes thinner.

Although flour is the traditional thickening agent in French cooking, cornstarch is a more powerful thickener because it is a purer form of starch. It will also create a clearer, shinier sauce. The French clarify their sauces through hours of slow cooking, skimming off the protein as the sauce simmers, and turning them into perfectly clear, shiny liquids, which keep their shine even with the addition of flour. Given the realities of home cooking, this is just not practical, and therefore cornstarch is preferable.

each. Two simple sauces, a béchamel (roux plus milk) and a velouté (roux plus stock), are the basis for classic French white sauces. By adding other ingredients, including cream, cheese, flavored butters, herbs, tomatoes, egg yolks, curry powder, white wine, lemon, onions, peppers, and so forth, the cook can make many different sauces — everything from an Aurore (tomatoes) to a Mornay (cheese). Although these two mother sauces are important as ingredients in recipes, I find them relatively useless for sauces. They are too heavy, too thick, and too high in fat. You do need, however, a béchamel for a soufflé, and a béchamel or velouté is also used in a classic lasagna, along with a basic tomato sauce.

THE BROWN SAUCE

Brown sauces were originally all based on stock. A typical brown sauce started with aromatics (onions, shallots, garlic), which were sautéed in butter. The mixture was then deglazed with wine (wine is added and the mixture is cooked over high heat, stirring constantly). Then stock was added in the form of either a semireduced stock, a demiglacé (a stock that had been reduced and thickened with a roux), or a coulis (a highly reduced stock with no added thickener). To finish the sauce, butter or cream was added along with herbs. Pan drippings could also be added to a brown sauce, a technique that was adapted later by American home cooks. New sauces in the nineteenth century were like new model Chryslers in the 1970s — the same basic construction, just a new name and a slightly different look. Variations were made with white wine, red wine, fortified wine (port, for example), vinegar, cream, and additional stock. Added to the liquids were limitless combinations of flavorings, including herbs, spices, liqueur, citrus juice and peel, truffles, aromatics, mustard, and vegetables.

In developing simple brown sauces for home cooking, I decided on two master recipes. One is based on white wine and the other on red. I have also created a variation on the master recipes using pan drippings. By the way, I find that many brown sauce recipes use all of the drippings, suggesting that the cook spoon off the fat. I find that this is just about impossible to do. I simply pour off all but 1 tablespoon of drippings, then deglaze the roasting pan. The result is a lighter, cleaner-tasting sauce.

These recipes are quite traditional in construction, but they do not use butter or cream to finish them, as a French chef would. It's interesting to note that the gravy served at American tables for at least one hundred years is really based on the French brown sauce. Stock, pan drippings, and some sort of thickener are still with us today.

Master Recipe for Brown Sauce

This is a quick, last-minute sauce that can be served with turkey. This is a good sauce for leftovers and other occasions when making a homemade stock is not practical. I don't find the addition of the cornstarch essential. If you prefer a light, thin sauce, omit this step. If you prefer not to use cornstarch, but do not like a thin sauce, reduce sauce by boiling until desired thickness is reached. If you purchase canned beef stock, make sure that it is a low-sodium brand; otherwise the sauce will be too salty after the reduction. However, I strongly recommend you use homemade stocks for all of the sauces in this chapter. This sauce, which uses red wine, is best served with red meats or game.

1 tablespoon butter
1 tablespoon olive oil
½ cup minced onion
½ cup red wine
3 tablespoons brandy
2 cups beef stock, homemade preferred
½ teaspoon dried thyme or 1 teaspoon fresh
2 tablespoons cornstarch
⅓ cup water
Salt and freshly ground black pepper to taste

1. Warm the butter and olive oil in a sauté pan over medium-high heat. When hot, add the onion and sauté over medium heat for about 5 minutes. Add the wine, brandy, stock, and thyme and bring to a boil. Cook until liquid has been reduced by half, 10–15 minutes.

2. Add cornstarch to ⅓ cup water and stir until dissolved and smooth. Over medium heat, whisk cornstarch mixture into reduced liquid in small portions until you get the desired thickness. Allow mixture to simmer a few seconds. Strain through a sieve and season with salt and pepper.

Makes about 2 cups

Master Recipe for Brown Sauce with White Wine

This is similar to the red wine version but uses carrots, celery, and tomato along with the white wine. If you prefer not to use cornstarch, reduce sauce by boiling until desired thickness is reached. This sauce is good with chicken or turkey.

  1 tablespoon butter
  1 tablespoon olive oil
  ½ cup minced onion
  ¼ cup finely chopped carrot
  1 cup finely chopped celery
  ¼ cup chopped canned tomato
  ½ cup white wine
  3 tablespoons brandy
  2 cups beef stock, homemade preferred
  ½ teaspoon dried thyme
  2 tablespoons cornstarch
  ⅓ cup water
    Salt and freshly ground black pepper to taste

  1. Warm the butter and olive oil in a sauté pan over medium-high heat. When hot, add the onion and sauté for 4 minutes. Add the carrot and celery and sauté for 4 minutes. Add the tomato, wine, brandy, stock, and thyme and bring to a boil. Cook until liquid has been reduced by half, 10–15 minutes. Strain through a double layer of cheesecloth and put back in pan.

  2. Add cornstarch to ⅓ cup water and stir until dissolved and smooth. Over medium heat, whisk cornstarch mixture into reduced liquid in small portions until you achieve the desired thickness. Allow mixture to simmer a few seconds. Strain through a sieve and season with salt and pepper.

Makes about 2½ cups

Brown Sauce with Pan Drippings

After roasting meat or poultry, pour off all but 1 tablespoon of drippings from the roasting pan and place pan over high heat. Add ½ cup of either red or white wine, and scrape the bottom of the pan with a wooden spoon for about 2 minutes or until liquid is reduced by half. Strain contents of pan through cheesecloth and substitute for the wine called for in either master recipe above.

Potato Puree

Potatoes are a good thickener, although they do need to be forced through a sieve to make them smooth enough for a sauce. Use this puree as indicated in the White Sauce for Chicken and Sauce of Raw Parsley, below.

  1 medium russet potato, peeled and cut into
    2-inch pieces
  1 tablespoon butter, softened

  Boil or steam the potato pieces until easily pierced with a sharp knife. While still warm, put potato through a food mill, a potato ricer, or a sieve (do not use a food processor). Whisk together with the butter.

Makes about ¾ cup

Mushroom Puree

You can add a mushroom puree to almost any sauce, especially any of the brown sauces listed in this chapter. To thicken one of the master brown sauce recipes, substitute ½ cup of this puree for the cornstarch. Add more puree for a thicker sauce.

4 cups mushrooms, rinsed and quartered
¼ cup chicken or beef stock, homemade preferred
¼ cup white wine
1 tablespoon butter
1 teaspoon lemon juice
½ teaspoon white wine vinegar

Puree the mushrooms with stock and wine in a blender or food processor. Add all ingredients to a saucepan and simmer until thick.

Makes about 2 cups

Mushroom Sauce

This sauce is best made with mushrooms that have some personality — shiitake, porcini, cepes, morels — rather than the standard, tasteless supermarket variety. Use this sauce in the same manner as you would either version of the brown sauce.

1 tablespoon butter
1 tablespoon olive oil
1 cup sliced mushrooms
1 cup brown sauce (either version)
½ teaspoon red wine vinegar
1 tablespoon minced flat-leaf parsley

Heat the butter and olive oil in a sauté pan over medium-high heat until foam subsides. Add mushrooms and sauté for 2 minutes. Add the brown sauce and vinegar and simmer for 1 minute. Add parsley and serve.

Makes about 1½ cups

White Sauce for Chicken

I use potato to thicken this sauce, which makes it a whole lot better than the greasy white gravy usually served with fried chicken. Be careful if using a canned chicken stock. Since the stock must be reduced by about 60 percent, most canned stocks will become unbearably salty. If you must use store-bought, purchase a low-sodium brand.

4 cups chicken stock, homemade preferred
¼ cup heavy cream
½ cup Potato Puree (page 285), approximately
2 teaspoons minced fresh tarragon or ½ teaspoon dried
Salt and freshly ground black pepper to taste

Place the chicken stock in a saucepan and boil until reduced to 1½ cups. Add the heavy cream and then whisk in the ½ cup of potato a bit at a time. If you prefer a thicker sauce, add more potato. Bring to a simmer over medium-low heat. Add the tarragon and salt and freshly ground black pepper to taste.

Makes a little more than 2 cups

Smothered Onion Sauce

A Soubise is a traditional French sauce made from slow-cooked onions and a béchamel, a thick white sauce. By eliminating the béchamel and adding just a bit of heavy cream, you can make a lighter and more intensely flavored sauce. Be sure to cook the onions low and slow. They must not brown. Serve this with chicken, turkey, or pork.

2 tablespoons olive oil
2 tablespoons butter
5 large onions, peeled and sliced
¼ cup heavy cream
Salt and white pepper to taste

1. Heat the olive oil and butter in a large pot. When foam subsides, add onions and cook covered over low heat for 10 minutes. Uncover and cook another 10 minutes or until onions are soft and have absorbed all liquid. Do not let onions brown. Stir frequently.

2. Place onions and any leftover pan liquids in the bowl of a food processor, add cream, and puree. Add salt and white pepper to taste.

Makes about 2½ cups

Variations

For a little punch, add 2 tablespoons white wine vinegar. You can also add 1 tablespoon tomato paste or ¼ cup of a basic tomato sauce.

Sauce of Raw Parsley

Although the stems of Italian, or flat-leaf, parsley do have flavor, you cannot use them for this recipe, as they will not puree properly. This sauce can be made in less than 5 minutes if you already have a concentrated stock on hand. For a thicker sauce, add a bit of cooked potato, finely mashed and sieved. This sauce is particularly good with fish, especially a firm white fillet.

- ½ cup chicken stock, preferably homemade
- ½ cup heavy cream
- 1 bunch flat-leaf parsley, cleaned and stems removed, yielding about 1 cup packed leaves
- 3–4 tablespoons Potato Puree (page 285)
  Salt and freshly ground black pepper to taste

1. In a small saucepan reduce the chicken stock by half. Add cream and allow to simmer for 1 minute. Place the cream mixture in a blender and add the parsley. Puree until smooth.

2. Pour mixture back into saucepan and whisk in Potato Puree, 1 tablespoon at a time, until you achieve the desired thickness. Season with salt and freshly ground black pepper to taste.

Makes about 1½ cups

Watercress Sauce

This is similar to the parsley sauce but has the sharper flavor of watercress. You could add 2 tablespoons of Potato Puree and reduce the cream

to 1 tablespoon. *Serve this sauce with fish or shellfish.*

- 1½ bunches watercress, washed and trimmed of thick stems
- ½ cup chicken stock, preferably homemade
- ½ cup heavy cream
  Salt and freshly ground black pepper to taste
- ½ teaspoon lemon juice

1. Bring a pot of salted water to a boil. Add the watercress and cook for 1 minute. Drain and refresh under cold water. Drain again, then squeeze the watercress with your hands (you can also place watercress in a dishtowel and wring it dry) to remove as much water as possible.

2. In a small saucepan over medium-high heat, reduce the chicken stock by half. Add the cream and reduce until the sauce is thick and coats the back of a spoon.

3. Put the watercress and the cream mixture in a blender and puree until smooth. Place back on heat to warm slightly and season with salt and freshly ground black pepper to taste. Add lemon juice just prior to serving.

Makes about 1½ cups

Roasted Red Pepper and Garlic Sauce

This is a traditional French sauce, a rouille, which is whisked into a fish stew. I use it with soups and also serve it on toasted bread as an appetizer. The traditional recipe calls for saffron, which is not essential but can be added (add just a pinch — if you have saffron threads, crush them first) if you have some in the house. I also eliminate the egg yolk often called for and use extra bread instead. You can use 1 small hot chili pepper, roasted, peeled, and seeded, instead of the cayenne pepper. If you don't have any stock, use white wine.

- 3 cloves garlic, peeled
- 2 slices (½ inch thick) white country bread, torn into pieces

1 small red bell pepper, roasted, peeled, and seeded
½ teaspoon cayenne pepper
3 tablespoons chicken stock (or fish stock or white wine)
½ cup high-quality olive oil
Salt to taste

Place the garlic in the bowl of a food processor. Process until minced. (If you are using a large food processor, it is best to mince the garlic first with a knife, as a few cloves can easily escape the blade.) Scrape sides of bowl. Add bread and process until finely chopped. Add the red pepper, cayenne, and chicken stock and turn on machine. Drizzle in oil through feed tube and process until thick and smooth. Add salt to taste.

Makes about 1½ cups

~ 32 ~

How to Marinate Meat, Fish, and Poultry

Marinades can break down protein, but they make meat mushy instead of tender. However, they do add flavor if foods are marinated for the proper amount of time.

~

There is no question that marinades can add flavor to meat, chicken, and fish. The issue, however, is whether they really affect texture. To find an answer to that question, I started with a basic review of the foods that were to be marinated.

WHAT REALLY NEEDS TO BE TENDERIZED?

A tough piece of bottom round or flank steak could use some softening up, but a swordfish steak is just fine as is. The same can be said for chicken. I prefer my bird with a little chew — I don't want a soft, mushy hunk of white meat. I decided straight off that tenderizing is only relevant to red meat, although I did want to test the flavoring effects of marinades as well.

The best way to tenderize red meat and add flavor is to age it (see Chapter 27). Food scientists will tell you that acids — vinegar or citric acid — promote tenderizing by breaking down protein. Wine and pureed fruit are not as strong and therefore do not work as well. Some foods contain enzymes that are supposed to break down muscle, pa-

paya being the leading fruit for this purpose, although pineapple is also supposed to be effective. However, I feel that using either of these foods as a tenderizer makes little sense for the home cook — who has a papaya or pineapple sitting around the house when you want to make a marinade? So I ran a series of tests using oil and vinegar or lemon juice to determine the optimum length of time in terms of flavor and texture.

Why Don't Marinades Make Meat More Tender?

Harold McGee, in *On Food and Cooking*, points out that enzymes (many marinades contain enzymes such as papaya or pineapple) do not work effectively at room temperatures and are especially impotent when left at 40°F in a refrigerator. He also points out that marinades that contain wine, vinegar, and/or citrus juices will denature the surface proteins, resulting in drier meat (when protein is denatured it uncoils and loses water). And, as I experienced in my testing, marinades don't get deep down into the meat, causing a change of texture only on the surface. Puncturing meat with a fork, for example, to gain access to the interior, has little effect, although it will enhance the loss of meat juices during cooking, an unintended and adverse effect.

HOW FAR DO MARINADES PENETRATE?

My first discovery was that marinades will not reach deep into a thick cut of meat. Although the outer quarter inch or so will change texture and flavor, the inside remains untouched. This is not unpleasant — it actually makes for an interesting contrast of flavor and texture — but it is superficial. Therefore, the first lesson of marinating thick meat is to make sure that it is cut as thin as possible. If you have a big cut such as a leg of lamb, have your butcher bone and butterfly it to gain the maximum advantage.

I also found that although marinades can change texture, the result is different from the texture one might expect from an expensive piece of tenderloin. That is, a piece of bottom round is never going to take on the buttery, smooth texture of a filet mignon. The meat gets softer, but that doesn't necessarily mean that it's better. In fact, I recommend using marinades to add flavor, not to soften texture. The enzyme action of marinades simply makes meat mushy, not necessarily an improvement. If you want less chewy meat, choose a better cut — don't expect marinades to help out. Or, slice the meat very thin after cooking, as you would for London broil or brisket. Marinades improve flavor, not texture.

HOW LONG SHOULD MEAT, CHICKEN, AND FISH MARINATE?

For this part of the test, I marinated beef, chicken (skin on), and fish (fillets and steaks) for different lengths of time and then cooked them to determine the differences in taste and texture. I was not surprised to find that beef requires 24 hours, whereas chicken needs just 12 hours and a fish fillet was best after only 15 minutes (fish steaks take 30 minutes). Skinless, boneless chicken breast required only 2–3 hours; the marinade penetrates much more quickly without the skin. Foods left to marinate too long will come away with an overpowering, oily flavor. On the other hand, a brisket left just a few hours will derive little benefit. I also found that it is best to reserve a bit of marinade (don't use it to marinate) and serve it with the cooked food. It's an instant sauce.

Use Plastic Storage Bags

Many recipes suggest placing the food to be marinated in a bowl or pan. I found this to be bad advice, as most of the marinade simply sits in the bottom of the bowl, not in contact with the food. It's best to place the food in a plastic storage bag, add the marinade, and then twist the bag tight so that little air is left. Now turn the bag over a few times to completely coat the food. Every few hours (for beef and chicken), it's a good idea to take the bag out of the refrigerator and give it a shake.

Master Recipe for Beef Marinade

You can substitute any red wine vinegar for balsamic vinegar. I prefer rosemary to other herbs, due to its strong flavor, although sage also works well.

- 1 cup olive oil
- 12 cloves garlic, peeled and lightly crushed
- ¼ cup balsamic vinegar
- 2 tablespoons minced fresh rosemary
  Freshly ground black pepper to taste

Heat oil in a small saucepan. Add garlic and simmer for 5 minutes. Remove from heat and let steep for 10 minutes. Strain oil through a sieve. Add vinegar, rosemary, and pepper and stir to mix.

Makes enough marinade for 3 pounds of meat

The Effect of Marinating Time on Beef, Chicken, and Fish

Using the master marinade recipes from this chapter, beef brisket, chicken breasts (on the bone and with skin), fish fillets, and fish steaks were marinated for different lengths of time. In all cases, the marinade did not penetrate into the center of the food being marinated. However, the contrast between the flavor of the outer layer of the food, penetrated by the marinade, and the natural flavor of the food itself, still untouched in the center of the beef, chicken, or fish, was not unwelcome. Meat, fish, and poultry should be refrigerated when marinating. Chicken without the skin, a boneless breast for example, is best marinated for just 2–3 hours.

Item Marinated	Time	Results
Beef	12 hours	Weak flavor
	24 hours	Better flavor, can taste marinade
	36 hours	Marinade slightly overpowering
	48 hours	Oily flavor, less marinade flavor
Chicken (skin on)	2 hours	Not much flavor
	6 hours	Better flavor, but still mild
	12 hours	Excellent flavor
	24 hours	Marinade too strong
	48 hours	Marinade too strong
Fish	15 minutes	Best for thin fillets
	30 minutes	Best for thicker pieces of fish
	1 hour	Marinade too strong
	2 hours	Marinade too strong

Master Recipe for Poultry Marinade

This is similar to the beef marinade but uses lemon juice instead of balsamic vinegar. Chicken is more delicate, so I use less garlic and rosemary.

½ cup olive oil
4 cloves garlic, peeled and lightly crushed
1 tablespoon minced fresh rosemary or thyme
¼ cup lemon juice
Freshly ground black pepper to taste

Heat olive oil in a small saucepan. Add garlic and rosemary and let cook over low heat for 5 minutes. Remove from heat and let steep for 10 minutes. Strain oil through a sieve. Add lemon juice and pepper and stir to mix.

Makes enough marinade for 1 chicken, butterflied or cut into parts

Master Recipe for Fish Marinade

This marinade is particularly good as a sauce for the cooked fish. Set aside some of it before you marinate the fish.

2 teaspoons cumin seeds, toasted
2 tablespoons minced fresh cilantro
1 fresh hot chili pepper, seeded and minced
4 cloves garlic, peeled and minced
1 tablespoon minced fresh ginger
¼ cup lime juice
¼ cup dry white wine
1 teaspoon kosher salt
½ teaspoon sugar
½ cup olive oil

Combine ingredients.

Makes enough marinade for 2 pounds of fish

Yogurt-Mint Marinade

One of my favorite barbecues is a butterflied leg of lamb that is marinated in this mixture. See recipe on page 301.

  6 cloves garlic, peeled and minced
  ½ cup chopped fresh mint
  2 teaspoons grated fresh ginger
16 ounces plain yogurt
  ½ teaspoon ground cardamom
    Freshly ground black pepper to taste

Combine ingredients.

Makes enough marinade for up to 4 pounds of meat

Ginger Marinade

This is a good marinade for red meat such as brisket or flank steak.

2 tablespoons grated fresh ginger
5 cloves garlic, peeled and minced
1 cup red wine
¼ cup olive oil

Combine ingredients.

Makes enough marinade for 4 pounds of meat

～ 33 ～

Grilling and Slow Barbecue

For proper grilling, you need an inferno to quick-cook foods.
For good barbecue, however, you need slow, indirect heat and
plenty of smoke.

～

Grilling and barbecue are everyman's cuisine, and they are uniquely American. Yet most grilled or barbecued foods are virtually inedible. I've had too much charred-on-the-outside, raw-on-the-inside grilled chicken, overcooked Texas brisket, and dry, tough North Carolina pork butt to think that these forms of cooking are easy. In fact, they're among the most difficult cooking techniques to get right and require a lot of knowledge about cuts of meat, marinating, heat sources, and cooking science.

GRILLING VERSUS BARBECUE

These are two very different food preparation techniques. Grilling is done over high heat and is very good for tender foods such as fish or chicken, but it's a lousy way to prepare tough, lower-quality cuts such as brisket. Barbecue, however, is a low-heat method of cooking and is good for inexpensive cuts because the meat is cooked slowly and has time to convert the collagen — the tough connective tissues — into gelatin. The tough muscle fibers do better at low heat as well. With too much heat, the fibers in the outer part of the meat shrink, expelling juices. At a constant low cooking temperature, the exterior and

the interior of the meat cook gently, the outer layers do not get overcooked, and the meat fibers shrink less. That's why a good cook would never grill brisket, skirt steak, or a rump roast but would grill fish, chicken, and the better cuts of beef, such as the tenderloin or sirloin steaks.

To grill, you want plenty of heat — you should be able to hold your palm 5 inches above the grill rack for only a few moments (3 seconds tops). For barbecue, you need low heat (200°F is best), and you also need a closed environment, that is, you need to cover the grill. This is confirmed by my tests with roasting meat in an oven — a low-quality cut such as the bottom round fared best when roasted at 200°F in a covered roasting pan.

WHAT IS SMOKING?

Traditionally, smoking was used as a preservative, not as a cooking method. It was usually done with low heat over a long period of time. Chris Schlesinger, coauthor of *The Thrill of the Grill,* told me that he used to cold-smoke foods in a defunct refrigerator, using a hot plate with a pan of sawdust on top of it. There was very little heat but a whole lot of smoke. There is also the hot-smoke method which, when performed at home, is often barbecue. The difference is in temperature. If the food is being smoked at around 200°F, that's barbecue. If you are smoking at temperatures below 180°F (some foods are smoked at 100°F), that's smoking. Most home smokers are really mini–barbecue pits.

Keep in mind that home cooks should not fool around with any cooking method that leaves meat, poultry, or fish sitting in an environment much cooler than 200°F for any length of time. The bacteria that exist on the outside of the meat thrive in a temperature range of 40°–140°F. If left in this temperature range for a long period of time, around 4 hours, the meat can become contaminated. So don't fool around with low-temperature smoking. Stick to barbecuing or grilling.

EQUIPMENT FOR GRILLING AND BARBECUE

There are all sorts of charcoal grills available, and there isn't much difference between them. After all, a grill is nothing more than a container for hot coals with a wire rack to hold the food. However, you do want a grill with a cover for cooking tougher cuts, and you also want a large grill for grilling, although a small grill is fine for barbecue. Small grills cannot handle two different levels of heat, and they cannot accommodate sufficient food for a crowd. By the way, don't buy a gas grill for barbecue — you'll want to use real briquettes to provide low heat and that authentic smoky flavor.

You will also need a good-size table next to your grill to hold your tools, food, salt, oven mitts, and so forth. Those small wooden leaves that come with some grills are just not big enough. Basic equipment also includes long metal tongs (standard kitchen-length tongs are too short — purchase an extra-long set), a metal spatula with a long handle, a carving fork (with a long handle), a

wire brush for cleaning the grill, metal or wood skewers, and a sharp knife for checking the food and for carving on the spot. You'll also need a platter or roasting pan to place the food in after cooking. A pan with sides is best. For monitoring the temperature of the grill while barbecuing, an oven thermometer is a must. Simply stand it on the grill rack while cooking so that you can quickly check the temperature when you remove the cover to put in additional fuel. A few small disposable aluminum roasting pans are good for drip pans — they are placed under the food to avoid flare-ups from dripping fat and can also be used to hold water, which provides a moist cooking environment.

Weber makes specialty items for barbecue and grilling, including racks for holding ribs and roasts; special steel fuel bins that hold charcoal to the side of the grill (for indirect heating); a steel rack for holding shish kebab skewers; hinged cooking grates, which make adding fuel convenient (the sides of the grill flip open so that briquettes can be added when barbecuing over indirect heat); and a kettle grill with a small gas burner to easily ignite the charcoal.

FUEL AND FIRE STARTERS

Fuel doesn't make much difference for high-heat grilling. I've tried vine cuttings, apple wood, soaked wood chips, charcoal briquettes, and hardwood charcoal and have never been able to tell the difference. The only exception has been the use of mesquite charcoal when grilling fish — the mesquite is strong enough to overpower the delicate taste of fish. When barbecuing, on the other hand, the fuel can make a difference due to the long cooking time. In my opinion, however, this is a worthy discussion topic only among barbecue fanatics who are on their fourth beer. Charcoal briquettes (hardwood

To prepare a covered grill for barbecue, place the coals to the sides of the grill and a drip pan in the center, under the food.

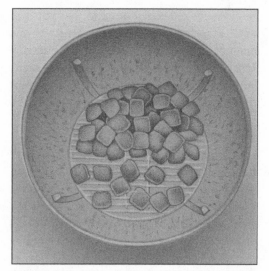

To prepare coals for grilling, cover about ¾ of the grill with a good supply of coals, leaving the balance of the grill with a light covering. Now you have both a cooking surface for foods that require high heat and a spot to place foods that may require slower cooking.

or cedar) are fine for the weekend cook. (Briquettes are as American as the Model T. They were invented by Henry Ford in order to make a buck from the scrap lumber used in manufacturing auto bodies. At first, they were sold only through Ford dealerships.)

When smoking foods, I have found that any soaked wood chips will do fine — cedar and hickory chips being widely available. I dare any barbecue expert to tell the difference between foods smoked with cherry and those smoked using apple chips. That being said, mesquite chips will strongly flavor fish, and to a lesser degree chicken, due to mesquite's unique and strong aroma.

I also don't get too excited about the best method for starting a fire. I used to use an electric starter, which, if you have an electrical outlet nearby, is clean and easy. (Note, however, that an electric starter will not fit comfortably within a small kettle grill, and it requires an extension cord.) I have also used the chimney starter, a small metal flue that uses crumpled newspaper in the bottom and charcoal in the top. Small holes around the bottom perimeter of the flue create a strong

updraft that heats the coals quickly. Odorless starter fluid also works well — I can't taste any chemical residue, as the liquid burns off quickly. I do not like the self-starting briquettes, for they give off an unpleasant chemical odor, although I have not blind-tasted foods cooked in this manner to determine whether flavor is adversely affected. In a pinch, if you are without any of the above, crumple up newspaper and place it under the charcoal grating. The chimney starter is probably the best method overall, as it is economical and works for any sort of charcoal grill.

FIRING UP THE GRILL

For grilling, the most important consideration is that you don't want an even heat throughout the cooking surface. When the coals are hot, spread them out so that about 75 percent of the grill area is well covered and the other 25 percent is more sparsely populated. Now you have a spot to place food that is cooking too quickly and needs to be slow-cooked. Keep in mind that you will need a well-covered area as large as the amount of food you intend to cook at one time. If you are grilling 4 lobsters at once, you may need to have more than 75 percent of the grill area covered with charcoal. If you are doing 2 game hens, you can cover a smaller area.

If you are going to barbecue, that is, cook food over a low heat for a long time, place an aluminum foil drip pan to one side of the grill once the coals are ready, right below the food to be cooked, so that any fat drippings will not cause flaming and so that the meat is not too close to the heat source. Add water to the drip pan. Start by igniting 30 briquettes, let them heat up for 20 minutes (if you have the charcoal holders sold by Weber, place 15 briquettes in each one, putting the holders on opposite sides of the grill), put 6 unheated briquettes on top, and then replenish every hour or so with 6 additional briquettes, jostling the hot briquettes with tongs to knock off the ash. Be sure to use hardwood charcoal that is all natural and has no unpleasant odors. (Some "unnatural" charcoal contains ingredients that give off an unwelcome odor as they are igniting.)

Indirect grilling — placing the food so it is not directly over the hot coals — is not just for slow-cook barbecue. I prefer this method when cooking any foods that are not quick-cooking, including chicken parts (not boneless) and thick cuts of meat (even a tenderloin). Foods that can be cooked in less than 15 minutes can be cooked right over the coals; this includes virtually any fish, vegetables, steaks, thin cuts of meat, fruit, and bread (pizzas). The grill rack should always be hot before cooking.

Whether to grill with the top on or off is also an issue. I always cook with the top on for any food that takes more than a few minutes. This includes all meats, chicken, and thick fish steaks. You get lots of heat but don't have to worry about flames, which can burn the underside of the food. I also find that top-on grilling is really grill-roasting, which means that the food cooks from both direct and indirect heat. This is good for thicker foods where more even cooking is a benefit. If I cook chicken parts, for example, the top-on method will provide a beautiful nut-brown glaze to the skin and a juicy interior — and I don't have to stand around worrying about flare-ups.

FINDING THE RIGHT TEMPERATURE

For barbecue, the experts say that the heat should be kept at a steady 200°F — not 250° or 275°F. In my testing, however, I found that the temperature will jump all over the place, running from 170° up to 230°F. I also found that the temperature at the top of the grill cover (inside) is a good 30°–40° less than the temperature at the surface of the grill rack. I tested this by using two separate thermometers, one an oven thermometer, which was placed on the grill rack, and the other a meat thermometer stuck through one of the vents on top of the lid. Therefore, be aware that if you are measuring at the top of the grill, the reading you get may be 30°–40° lower than the actual temperature where most of the food is being cooked. You will lose a lot of heat when removing the top to add more fuel or soaked chips, so don't expect the thermometer dial to stay within 10°. That needle is going to be traveling! I did not find, however, that this was a big problem. The grill comes back up to temperature in just 2–3 minutes. Many cooks tell you to add 10 minutes to your cooking time each time that the top is removed. I have not found this to be necessary.

On the subject of temperature, I have found a strange anomaly between cooking temperature when barbecuing on a kettle grill and when oven-roasting at low temperature. A 12-pound turkey will take a good 6 hours when oven-roasted at 200°F. However, when I barbecue at 200°F (this is the approximate temperature of the thermometer sitting on the grill surface), the same bird is done in 3½ hours or less. I suspect that this is due to radiant heat. A kettle grill is a very small cooking environment and it is made of metal, which reflects a good deal of heat back to the food. In my experience, therefore, 200°F in a covered grill is more like 250°–300°F or more in a standard oven.

WHAT ABOUT USING A SMOKER?

A smoker is usually a vertical, torpedo-shaped device with a heat source on the bottom (either electric or charcoal), a water pan in the middle, and then racks for the foods to be smoked on top. It produces a nice even heat and for certain foods requires no watching, as the proper amount of fuel is added at the beginning of cooking and when it runs out, the food is cooked. (This is fine for poultry, but when cooking tough meat, you should start with a slow fire and add fuel as you go along.) By the way, most smokers are designed so that you can add soaked chips or charcoal without losing heat. The top ¾ of the "torpedo" sits on a metal pan that holds the fuel. To add more fuel, this top section, including the food racks and the water pan, is removed in one piece, exposing the bottom pan. Since the top cover is still in place, none of the heat is lost.

WHEN IS THE GRILL READY?

Lots of experts say that it takes 30–40 minutes to get a charcoal fire to the point that it is hot enough for grilling. I would forget about any sort of time frame — this is not precision cooking — and use common sense. As for how hot is hot, I am a strong believer in building an inferno. Grilling, like stir-frying, is about heat, and I want plenty of it. The fire should be so hot that you can barely keep your palm 5 inches above the grill rack for 2 seconds and you wouldn't even consider getting it any closer. On a 21-inch kettle grill, I'll use 50–60 briquettes and then, if I am going to be grilling for more than a few minutes, top them off with another 8–10 pieces when the fire is hot. Once you allow your fire to get a bit slow, you've had it — you are better off with plenty of horsepower.

ANATOMY OF A BARBECUE

On my first shot at cooking real barbecue, or at least a backyard grill version of it, I started with pork butt, which comes from the front end (or chuck portion) of the pig and is often sold as Boston butt. Although many recipes call for a 5-pound roast, I found that a 4-pound roast (my piece was 3.79 pounds) is more likely to be available. I started at 7:50 in the morning and finished up at 1:30 with another 20 minutes to let the meat sit wrapped in aluminum foil. I used a 21-inch Weber grill with two metal charcoal bins for indirect cooking. The cooking grill had hinged flaps on two sides so that additional charcoal and water-soaked wood chips could be added during cooking. The Weber comes with a thermometer in the top of the grill, although you can slip a thermometer through one of the air vents in the top. I also used an oven thermometer, which I left standing on the cooking surface. The pork butt had been covered with a half-cup of barbecue rub just prior to cooking. Here is a blow-by-blow account:

7:50 A.M. Started fire with 15 hardwood briquettes on each side.

8:30 Added soaked chips and 5 more briquettes to each side. Placed pork butt on grill and replaced cover.

9:30 Temperature 140°F on top and 150°F on the grill. Opened up the top and bottom vents of the grill wide.

10:00 Temperature now 200°F at the top and 225°F on the grill. Added 3 more briquettes to each side and closed the top vent halfway.

10:30   Temperature is 220°F on top. Completely closed the top vent.

11:00   The meat registered 125°F internal. The temperature was 150°F on top and 190°F at the grill. Added 5 briquettes on left and 3 on the right. Added more soaked chips. Left top vents half open.

11:30   Temperature 200°F on top and 240°F at the grill. Meat registered 132°F. Added chips both sides and 3 briquettes on left and 2 briquettes on the right.

12:10 P.M.   Meat now registers 145°F. Temperature is 155°F on top and 190°F at the grill. Added chips and opened up vents just a bit.

12:30   Meat now registers 140°F internal, a loss of 5°! Must have taken the first measurement in the wrong spot. Temperature is 170°F on top, 200°F at the grill. Vents closed a bit to 25 percent open.

12:55   Meat now back to 145°F internal. Temperature is 170°F on top and 190°F at the grill. Opened top vents to 50 percent.

1:15   Temperature is 180°F on top and 200°F at grill. Meat still at 145°F.

1:30   Meat still at 145°F. Removed meat, wrapped it tightly in aluminum foil, and then placed it in a paper bag.

1:50   Sliced meat into thin strips. Juicy, tender meat with great spice rub on the outside. Best barbecue I've ever eaten!

Although I did end up with great barbecue, I also learned a few things from my first outing. First, I found it best to leave the bottom vents full open and the top vents about 20 percent open. If the top vents are fully closed, there is insufficient draft and the fire will die down. Using this method in subsequent tests, I could maintain a steadier temperature, although this is not a precise art. Be prepared for temperature swings of 50°F. When adding briquettes, I found it best to knock the hot charcoal around a bit to shake off the white ash. This will help start the new briquettes. I also preferred placing the soaked wood chips on top of the new briquettes rather than on top of the hot coals — the wet chips slowed down the fire too much.

GRILLING, BARBECUING, AND SMOKING TIPS

- ■ I have found that hardwood charcoal that comes in irregular pieces cooks faster and hotter than briquettes. I like it for quick jobs such as grilling vegetables or fish.

- ■ Speaking of fish, cook fish until it is not quite done. Otherwise, it will continue to cook off the grill and become overcooked. The center of a fish steak, for example, should still be slightly underdone.

- ■ Large chunks of wood are much better than the bags of fine mulch that are pawned off as "chips" for smoking. These are great around your lilacs but burn off too quickly in a grill. You want your soaked wood to smolder, not burn. I often use hunks of wood the size of baked potatoes, and I soak them at least 20 minutes in water before adding to the fire. When they stop smoking, I take them out of the grill, dunk them in some more water, and then put them back on the coals again.

- ■ Always use more fuel than you think you need. Once the fire cools off, you are in big trouble.

- ■ Grill baskets are great for vegetables and fish fillets; however, they will not fit on most kettle-style grills because the cooking surface is below the outer rim of the kettle.

- ■ A. Cort Sinnes, author of *The Grilling Encyclopedia,* discovered that barbecued ribs should be wrapped in aluminum foil after cooking, placed in a paper bag, and then allowed to sit for 1 hour. This steams the meat a bit, making it more tender. I use this same method for only 30 minutes — I am always too hungry to wait the full hour — after cooking pork butt, beef brisket, or any sort of ribs.

GRILLING VEGETABLES

Grilling should be easy. That's why I avoid vegetables that require any sort of precooking, including cauliflower and butternut squash. I also don't think grilling is the best method for cooking some vegetables, such as broccoli, and I therefore stick to foods that have an affinity for the smoky flavor of the grill, such as yams, sweet potatoes, onions, and red peppers. I prefer the texture of vegetables that have been grilled without precooking. Brushing vegetables with oil is a tedious method, so I prefer to place the vegetables in a large bowl and toss them with olive oil and salt prior to cooking. This does not work, however, with sliced onions, which will fall apart readily; they need to be brushed with the oil. For a more interesting flavor, I make a garlic oil by heating olive oil with crushed garlic cloves and then letting the mixture steep. I toss grilled vegetables with minced fresh herbs and a bit of extra salt.

Vegetables are likely to stick, and therefore the grill surface must be perfectly clean. A hinged grilling basket with long handles makes it easy to turn the vegetables during cooking. This is a problem, however, with kettle grills, since the cooking surface is not even with the perimeter of the kettle, so that a grilling basket with handle will not easily fit. To grill vegetables properly, the fire has to be an inferno. This means that vegetables really cannot be thrown on after the butterflied

COOKING TIMES FOR LOW-HEAT BARBECUE			
Foods were cooked at about 170°F when measured by a thermometer stuck inside one of the top air vents. The actual ambient temperature at grill level was about 200°F. This style of cooking is best for tough meats.			
Cut of Meat	Weight	Cooking Time	Comments
Beef brisket	4 pounds	10 hours	Not worth doing. Too much time, and brisket benefits from sauce or gravy. I prefer to braise it.
Pork ribs	3 pounds	2 hours	Many recipes suggest that ribs need 5 hours of cooking. I found that 2 hours was plenty. I like my spareribs at 150°F internal temperature.
Boneless pork butt	4 pounds	5 hours	I prefer pork cooked to 145°F (the USDA recommends 160°F, for safety). It is very juicy and very tender if cooked properly. If you prefer "real" barbecue, cook it to 165°F, although the meat will be drier.
Small turkey	12 pounds	3 hours, 20 minutes	Breast meat cooked to 165°F.
Duck	5 pounds	3 hours	I prefer to cook duck longer per pound than chicken or turkey. The dark meat needs more cooking to be tender.

The grill has to be super-hot to properly grill most vegetables except potatoes, sweet potatoes, and yams, which are best grilled over a hot but not scorching fire (they take longer to cook and will burn if the fire is too hot). It should be so hot that you cannot get your hand near the cooking surface and can hold it for a bare 2 seconds when it is 5 inches above the grill. Toss prepared vegetables with olive oil and plenty of salt in a large bowl before grilling. Onions, which are prone to separate into rings, should be brushed rather than tossed with oil. All vegetables need to be turned halfway through the grilling time indicated.

Vegetable	Preparation	Grilling Time	Comments
Asparagus	Snap off tough ends	4 minutes	Excellent flavor
Corn	Remove husk and silk	4 minutes	Sweet, rich flavor
Fennel	Cut bulb into 8 wedges	6 minutes	Fennel is tough, but good flavor
Onions	Peel and cut into ½-inch slices	4 minutes	Rich, sweet, delicious
Red peppers	Stem, seed, and cut into eighths	3 minutes	Okay if skin blackens some, but should not char
Potatoes	Cut into ⅜-inch slices	14 minutes	Potatoes are slow to cook; slice thin to quick-grill
Sweet potatoes	Cut into ⅜-inch slices	10 minutes	Sweet, rich, and delicious
Yams	Cut into ⅜-inch slices	9 minutes	Outside will get very dark in order to cook through — excellent flavor
Zucchini, summer squash	Cut into ⅜-inch slices	2½ minutes	Good, easy to prepare

leg of lamb or the chicken breasts unless additional fuel has been added during cooking.

A NEW WAY TO GRILL CORN

I had always thought that silking the ears and then soaking them with the husks still in place was the best method for grilling corn; the water would keep the husks and kernels from burning. To get an update, I called Betty Fussell, author of *Corn,* and she told me that corn is best grilled without any husk at all; the intense heat caramelizes the kernels instead of steaming them inside the wet husk. I tested three ears: one soaked in the husk, one in the husk not soaked, and one husked. Soaking made absolutely no difference. The unsoaked ear burned just a bit at the tip, but the flavor was much like that of boiled corn with a hint of smoke. The fully husked ear, however, was fabulous:

sweeter, smoky, bursting with rich corn flavor. I did find, however, that starchy corn — either low-sugar varieties or corn that has been sitting around a long time — does not fare well when grilled. It dries out and becomes tough. This sort of corn is best boiled or steamed.

HOW TO GRILL LOBSTER

Grilling does add a lot of flavor to lobster, but there are problems. The biggest one is timing. No two fires put out exactly the same amount of heat, resulting in variable cooking time. If you are grilling more than one lobster, each will cook at a different rate, because every fire is uneven. The claws are also problematic, since they often do not lie flat and can be undercooked when the tail meat is done.

I have also found that split lobsters take up a lot of space on the grill. I can accommodate 4 split 1-pound lobsters on my 21-inch Weber, and therefore I use lots of charcoal, about 70 briquettes, so that the entire surface area can be used for cooking. After the first 8 minutes of cooking, it is best to turn the lobsters so that the claws are sitting over the hottest part of the fire. This helps to get them cooked more rapidly. You will also want to make sure that the claws lie flat prior to grilling. If they don't, simply twist them a bit until they do. As you watch them cook, rearrange the lobsters if some are turning red faster than others. All in all, grilling lobsters is a whole lot of work; boiling is faster, easier, and more predictable, although less flavorful.

Grilled Steak with Lemon and Salt

Steak is best cooked in the Tuscan tradition. Use very high heat, cook the steak quickly, and then make liberal use of salt and freshly ground black pepper just before serving. Serve with a sprinkling of lemon juice. The salty char-grilled crust and juicy red interior make a delicious combination.

4 T-bone, porterhouse, or sirloin steaks
Salt and freshly ground black pepper to taste
1 lemon

1. Start the charcoal or wood fire. When the coals are very hot (you should be able to hold your palm 5 inches above the grill for no more than 2 seconds), oil the grill.
2. Cook the steaks for 3–4 minutes per side. Liberally salt and pepper both sides of steak before serving. Cut the lemon into quarters and squeeze a little juice over each steak. Serve.

Makes 4 large or 8 smaller servings

Butterflied and Grilled Leg of Lamb

When grilling, it's important that the food be of even thickness; otherwise, some parts cook faster than others. When a leg of lamb is butterflied, the butcher is supposed to remove the meat from the bone and then cut it to a uniform thickness. I have found over the years, however, that butchers will sell you a boneless leg of lamb but they don't finish the job. The meat is not cut evenly and the silverskin, the thin, tough membrane covering the outside of the leg, is often not removed. This is very tough and difficult to chew. Therefore, check the leg of lamb before cooking, removing any remaining silverskin with a sharp boning or chef's knife and slicing any thicker sections almost in half so that the meat is of uniform thickness.

1 leg of lamb, 3½–4 pounds, boned, butterflied, with silverskin and excess fat removed
1 recipe Yogurt-Mint Marinade (page 292) or Master Recipe for Beef Marinade (page 290)

1. Combine lamb and marinade in a plastic storage bag. Force out excess air, twist-tie, and allow to marinate for 24 hours in the refrigerator.
2. Remove excess marinade from meat, using a brush or damp paper towel. Cook over a very hot fire in a covered grill until internal temperature reaches 130°–135°F (medium rare), about 20 minutes per side for meat that is 2½ inches thick.

Serves 8–10

Rosemary Grilled Chicken

Rosemary is my favorite herb for use with grilled foods because it is highly aromatic and strong enough to stand up to the flavors of the grill.

1 chicken, 3–4 pounds
1 recipe Master Recipe for Poultry Marinade (page 291)
Salt and freshly ground black pepper to taste
1 tablespoon minced fresh rosemary

1. Wash chicken and pat dry. Butterfly it by removing backbone and pressing bird flat (see instructions on page 205). Combine with marinade in a plastic storage bag, force out excess air, and twist-tie. Place in the refrigerator and marinate for 12 hours.

2. Remove chicken from marinade, pat dry, cover with salt, pepper, and minced rosemary, and grill covered over a hot fire until the thigh meat reaches 165°–170°F on an instant-read thermometer, 30–40 minutes.

Serves 4

Gingered Yogurt Chicken with Cumin

Boneless chicken easily sticks to a grill. When cooking rack is hot, clean it with a stiff wire brush and then oil liberally. Chicken thighs are well suited to grilling, because the dark meat does not dry out easily.

> 8 boneless chicken thighs
> Salt and freshly ground black pepper to taste
> 2 lemons, juiced
> 2 cloves garlic, peeled and minced
> 2 teaspoons grated fresh ginger
> 1 cup plain yogurt
> ¼ teaspoon ground cumin

1. Rinse chicken under cool water and pat dry. Lightly salt and pepper.

2. Combine lemon juice and remaining ingredients in a bowl, then place in a plastic storage bag along with the chicken pieces. Force out excess air, twist-tie, and allow thighs to marinate in the refrigerator for 3 hours.

3. Heat grill and then brush it with oil. Remove chicken from marinade and grill over moderate heat until cooked, about 6 minutes per side.

Serves 4

Grilled Game Hens with Citrus, Ginger, and Soy

The cooking time for this recipe can vary a great deal, depending on the heat of the grill. You can

also cook these birds in a smoker. Follow the manufacturer's directions for cooking times.

> *Marinade*
> 1 orange
> 1 lemon
> 3 garlic cloves, peeled
> 1 teaspoon grated fresh ginger
> ½ cup soy sauce
> ¼ cup toasted (Oriental) sesame oil
> ¼ cup sherry or Marsala wine
> 1 tablespoon brown sugar
>
> 3 game hens

1. Grate the outer layer of peel from the orange and the lemon. Juice half the lemon. Place grated peel, lemon juice, garlic, ginger, and remaining marinade ingredients in the workbowl of a food processor and blend until smooth.

2. Have your butcher butterfly the game hens or do this yourself at home by removing backbone and pressing birds flat (see instructions on page 205).

3. Place hens in a plastic bag with the marinade, force out excess air, twist-tie, and leave in the refrigerator overnight.

4. Set up a grill for indirect cooking, placing a drip pan in the middle (pour in 2 cups of water) and the charcoal off to the sides. Remove hens from marinade and grill covered, with bottom vents fully open and top vents about ⅓ open, for about 30 minutes or until breast meat registers 165°–170°F on an instant-read thermometer.

Serves 3–6

Grilled Lobster with Lime and Butter

Lobster must be killed, halved, and then cleaned before either grilling or broiling. Start by killing the lobster by thrusting a large chef's knife into the middle of the body at the point where there is a small indentation. Now bring the knife down, working toward the front of the lobster, and cut through the body between the eyes. Turn the lobster around and, starting at the same point, cut down through the tail. You will need a large and very sharp chef's knife to do this. Then hold each half over the sink and spoon out the intestinal tract, the head sac (this is just behind the eyes and sometimes has to be pulled free), the pale green tomalley, and the dark green roe if it is present. You can also use your fingers to clean out the lobster. (See page 179 for illustrations.)

4 tablespoons unsalted butter
2 tablespoons lime juice
  Salt and freshly ground black pepper to taste
4 live lobsters, 1½–2 pounds each, split in half
1 whole lime, cut into wedges

1. Heat grill. Melt butter in a small saucepan and add lime juice and salt and pepper to taste. Keep warm until ready to cook.

2. When grill is ready, baste the meat with the butter mixture and then grill shell side up for 8 minutes. Reposition the lobsters if necessary so the claws are over the hottest part of the fire and continue to grill for 2–4 minutes. Serve with lime wedges and leftover butter.

Serves 4

Barbecued Shrimp with Ginger, Cilantro, and Vinegar

Shelling shrimp hot from the grill is akin to capital punishment, so I grilled shelled shrimp to see if there was a difference. Unfortunately, shrimp grilled in the shell was much better — juicier and more tender. I have also found that marinating shrimp in the shell is a waste of time, so now I grill unmarinated shrimp in the shell, remove the shells myself, and then toss them with the marinade. To protect your hands while shelling, use rubber gloves.

½ cup olive oil
2 cloves garlic, peeled and lightly crushed
1 teaspoon grated fresh ginger
2 tablespoons minced cilantro or flat-leaf parsley
2 tablespoons lime or lemon juice

1 tablespoon white wine vinegar
⅛ teaspoon Tabasco
1 teaspoon paprika
1 tablespoon dry vermouth
24 jumbo shrimp, unshelled

1. Heat oil in a small saucepan. Add garlic and simmer gently for 5 minutes or until light brown. Remove from heat and let steep for 10 minutes. Combine all ingredients except shrimp in a medium bowl.

2. Heat grill and when hot grill shrimp for about 2 minutes per side, less for smaller shrimp. Shell shrimp and toss with marinade. Serve hot or let marinate for 30 minutes and serve at room temperature.

Serves 6 as an appetizer

Grilled Rosemary Swordfish with Capers

Rosemary has tough leaves. To extract the flavor without serving the tough needles, I simmer the sprigs in oil and then let them steep a few minutes.

½ cup olive oil
2 sprigs fresh rosemary
3 cloves garlic, peeled and lightly crushed
2 tablespoons lemon juice
¼ cup dry white wine
4 swordfish steaks
2 teaspoons capers

1. Heat oil in a small saucepan. Add rosemary and garlic and simmer gently for 5 minutes. Remove from heat and let steep for 10 minutes. Strain oil to remove the garlic and rosemary and combine with lemon juice and white wine in a plastic storage bag. Add swordfish steaks to the bag, squeeze out excess air, twist-tie, and toss to combine thoroughly. Marinate refrigerated for 30 minutes.

2. Heat grill and when coals are ready, remove steaks from marinade and pat dry (reserve marinade). Grill 4–5 minutes per side (about 10 minutes per inch of thickness), removing from grill when just slightly undercooked in the middle—they will finish cooking on their own.

3. While the swordfish is being grilled, heat reserved marinade over low to medium heat, whisking to combine. When swordfish is cooked, strain marinade, add capers, and pour over fish and serve.

Serves 4

Tuna Steaks with Balsamic Vinegar

Many years ago I ate at Le Bernardin in New York City and had an exquisite grouper dish in which vinegar was an important ingredient. I now use vinegar in much of my seafood cookery. It's a good complement to a firm, strong fish. This recipe can be made with any firm fish, such as swordfish, grouper, or pompano. The tuna can also be cooked for the same amount of time in a 450° oven or under the broiler.

  1 tablespoon olive oil
  2 cloves garlic, peeled and lightly crushed
  2 tablespoons balsamic vinegar
  2 tablespoons white wine vinegar
  ¼ cup dry white wine
  4 tuna steaks (enough for 4 servings)
  1 scallion, minced
    Salt and freshly ground black pepper to taste

1. Heat grill. Add olive oil to small saucepan and place over medium-high heat. When oil is hot, simmer garlic gently for 5 minutes or until very light brown — do not allow to burn. Remove garlic and discard. Add vinegars and wine to oil in pan and simmer for 10 minutes or until liquid is reduced by about ⅓.

2. While vinegar mixture is simmering, cook tuna steaks 4–5 minutes per side, allowing 8–10 minutes per inch of thickness.

3. Place fish on preheated serving plates. Add minced scallion to vinegar mixture and drizzle each serving with 2 tablespoons of the sauce. Season with salt and pepper to taste.

Serves 4

Chinese Grilled Duck

I learned this technique from Bruce Cost, author of Asian Ingredients, *and chef-proprietor of Ginger Island, located in Berkeley, California. He boils the duck before grilling. This melts much of the fat, which then soaks into the meat, making it rich and moist. Bruce points out that Chinese cuisine is more sophisticated than Western cooking, in that many foods undergo more than one cooking method. Instead of grilling, you can also finish this duck by roasting it breast side up on a roasting rack in a 500° oven for 20 minutes.*

  1 duck, 4–5 pounds
  3 tablespoons light soy sauce
  1 teaspoon five-spice powder
  4 tablespoons sugar
  ½ teaspoon ground ginger

1. Bring a large pot ⅔ full of water to a boil. Add the duck and simmer for 45 minutes. Remove duck from water, drain, and allow to cool at room temperature.

2. Mix together the remaining ingredients to form a paste. When the duck is cool enough to handle, rub it with the paste, wrap it in foil, and place in refrigerator until ready for grilling (or roasting). This is best done the night before.

3. Heat grill (or an oven to 500°F). Place duck on grill breast side down and sear for 5 minutes. Turn and cook on one side for 10 minutes. Turn duck to the other side and cook an additional 5 minutes. Remove duck from heat and let rest for 5 minutes before cutting into pieces and serving.

Serves 2

Foil-Grilled Vegetables

This is a terrific way to cook vegetables for a barbecue. You do not get a "grilled" flavor, but it is an easy way to create a summer ratatouille on the grill. Don't skimp on the salt and pepper in this recipe. Be sure to use fresh thyme rather than dried. Oregano can be substituted for thyme.

3 potatoes
½ cup olive oil
2 tablespoons balsamic vinegar, plus extra for
  sprinkling
3 cloves garlic, peeled and minced
1 tablespoon minced fresh thyme
  Salt and freshly ground black pepper to taste
2 medium zucchini, cut into ¼-inch slices
3 medium onions, peeled and thinly sliced
6 medium tomatoes, cut into medium slices

1. Wash potatoes and boil for 10 minutes. Cut into ¼-inch slices.

2. Whisk together olive oil, vinegar, garlic, and thyme in a small bowl. Add salt and pepper to taste.

3. Lay out 4 equal sheets of heavy-duty aluminum foil large enough to accommodate the vegetables in 4 secure packages. Brush with olive oil mixture and place equal amount of zucchini on each sheet. Cover with equal amounts of onion, potato, and then tomato. Brush each layer with a bit of the olive oil mixture. Sprinkle with some salt, balsamic vinegar, and a few grinds of fresh pepper.

4. Wrap packages securely and grill about 10 minutes. Turn packages over and grill another 10 minutes or until vegetables are tender.

Serves 8

Grilled Corn

Grilling corn without the husk caramelizes the sugars in the kernels and produces a rich, very sweet flavor. This is by far the best way to prepare supersweet corn; this method is not recommended for low-sugar varieties (these are better boiled or steamed). You can also grill corn and then use it in a chutney, salsa, or salad.

8 ears supersweet corn, husks and silk removed

Over an intensely hot fire, grill ears for 4 minutes, turning frequently. Corn is done when it has plenty of dark brown spots but is not burned.

Grilled Romaine with Garlic Vinaigrette

This recipe was served at a restaurant in Boston near the offices of Cook's Illustrated. *The trick is to quickly grill the romaine so that the exterior wilts while the interior still has some crunch.*

1 head romaine, wilted leaves removed and
  cut in half lengthwise
  Olive oil for brushing
1 Master Recipe for Vinaigrette (page 118),
  made with white wine vinegar

Brush romaine with oil. Grill for 1½ minutes per side. Serve with vinaigrette.

Serves 2–4

Master Recipe for Slow-Cook Barbecue

It's best to have a covered grill with a thermometer built in the top so that you do not have to lift the cover to check the temperature. Be sure to keep the heat low — it should never get above 225°F — and be sure to use indirect heat. Simply place two piles of coals, 15 briquettes each, on either side of the grill, with a drip pan half-filled with water between them, directly underneath the food. Large chunks of wood are better than small chips, which will burn off quickly. Soak chunks or chips in water for 20 minutes. When the coals are hot, add 6 new briquettes to each pile to keep the fire going. I add 3–5 briquettes per hour to each side to maintain the proper heat. Weber makes half-moon-shaped charcoal bins for indirect cooking. They sit on either side of the grill and make slow-cook barbecue easier by keeping the coals in place.

3–10 pounds meat — pork butt, beef brisket,
  ribs, turkey, or duck
1 cup Barbecue Rub for Beef and Pork
  (page 308) per 5 pounds of meat,
  approximately
½ cup Vinegar Moppin' Sauce (page 309) per
  5 pounds of meat, optional
  Hamburger buns or white bread

1. Rub meat with barbecue rub and set aside at room temperature while preparing fire. Start two small piles of charcoal, one on either side of a covered grill, 15 briquettes each. Place a drip pan in the middle half-filled with water, and put an oven thermometer on top of the cooking surface. After 20 minutes, place 6 additional briquettes on each pile of coals, add 2 handfuls of soaked wood chips or chunks on top of the briquettes, and place meat over the drip pan. Cover and cook meat until the internal temperature reaches 145°F and meat is tender, 2–10 hours, depending on the cut (see chart on page 299 for some representative times). Maintain an even 200° cooking temperature by checking every hour or so, adding 3–5 new briquettes to each pile.

2. When meat is done, wrap tightly in aluminum foil, place in a paper bag, and set aside for 30 minutes. If serving the meat chopped, mix it with the sauce and serve on top of fluffy hamburger buns or slices of cheap white bread. If serving slices, offer the moppin' sauce on the side.

Barbecued Pork

Authentic roadside barbecue only uses the fluffiest, cheapest hamburger rolls or white bread available. Each customer is given a half pound of steaming chopped meat in a cardboard container with a huge stack of bread on the side. I prefer hamburger rolls to sliced bread. It's easier to hold a large mess of chopped meat that way — sliced bread is too flimsy. You can serve hot sauce on the side or add a helping of coleslaw on top, as they do in North Carolina. I prefer to serve the pork sliced rather than chopped. I recommend that pork be cooked to 145°F internal temperature, but the USDA states that pork should be cooked to 160°F. If you are concerned about safety, follow the USDA guidelines, although the meat will be dry.

    1 boneless pork butt, 4–5 pounds
    1 cup Barbecue Rub for Beef and Pork (page 308)

    1 cup Vinegar Moppin' Sauce (page 309)
      Hamburger buns or white bread

Follow Master Recipe for Slow-Cook Barbecue and cook about 5 hours or until pork reaches an internal temperature of 145°F and meat is tender. Chop the meat and mix it with the sauce, or slice the meat and serve sauce on the side. Serve with rolls or bread.

Serves 8–10

Barbecued Brisket

Brisket is a very tough cut of meat. It is loaded with fat but needs to be cooked at low heat for a long time to become tender. The fat is melted, the collagen (the connective tissue) is turned into gelatin, and the low heat prevents the muscle fibers from toughening. This recipe will take all day to cook, and the temperature will have to be checked frequently. You want to maintain 200°F if possible throughout the day. In my experience, pork makes a much better barbecue. You may find homemade barbecued brisket a little disappointing given the amount of time it takes to cook.

    1 beef brisket, about 5 pounds
    1½ cups Barbecue Rub for Beef and Pork (page 308)
    1 cup Vinegar Moppin' Sauce (page 309)

Follow Master Recipe for Slow-Cook Barbecue and cook for 8–10 hours or until the internal temperature reaches 145°F. You can cook brisket to a higher internal temperature, but it will dry out.

Serves 10–12

Barbecued Ribs

In Texas, they serve beef ribs. I've eaten them at Rudy's, a barn-red joint off the main strip in Leon Springs, and at Bob's, a run-down shack on the outskirts of San Antonio. But I prefer pork ribs for the extra flavor. There are three types for barbecue. Spareribs have lots of meat, lots of fat, and lots of flavor; these are cut from the belly of the animal. Baby back ribs are smaller and can't stand as much cooking; they are cut from the ribs in the loin section, which is part of the animal's back. Country ribs are usually cut from the first few ribs, near the shoulder; these ribs are meatier than ribs toward the back of the animal. However, "country" simply means that the ribs have plenty of meat on them. I know a Vermont butcher who cuts all fourteen pork ribs country-style by simply leaving a good portion of meat still attached to the bones. (You can also prepare beef short ribs by following this recipe and cooking for about 3 hours.)

2 racks of pork spareribs, baby back ribs, or country ribs
1 cup Barbecue Rub for Beef and Pork (page 308)

Follow Master Recipe for Slow-Cook Barbecue and cook for about 2 hours. The outside of the ribs should have a nice crust and the inside should be hot and juicy.

Serves 4–6

~ 34 ~

The Barbecue Rub and Sauce

The secret to any good rub is plenty of salt and fresh spices. Barbecue sauces can be either tomato- or vinegar-based, but both kinds should be served with cooked foods, not used for basting.

~

My favorite barbecue joint was called Stick to Your Ribs and was located in an abandoned Dairy Queen set in the middle of a desolate parking lot just off Route 95 near New Haven, Connecticut. Their brisket was tender and moist, the pork was succulent, instead of supermarket bread they served scarab-shaped Portuguese rolls, and their sauces were thin, light, and not too sweet. To this day, I don't care much for a thick, tomato-based barbecue sauce. I use a dry rub for barbecued foods and leave it at that or serve a vinegar-based sauce, which is light and punchy and lets the flavor of the meat stand on its own. Grilled foods, which cook quickly, are not usually covered with rubs, and I have also found that it is best not to baste them; the sauce will dry out like ice cream dropped on a hot sidewalk. So simply serve the sauce as an accompaniment to the grilled meat.

Barbecue Rub for Beef and Pork

I always keep a container of this barbecue rub around the house for last-minute barbecue. Although it is hot in its raw state, it loses some of its punch when cooked. Don't be afraid to use it liberally. This rub is best with red meat and pork. If you like a little less heat, back off on the

chili powder and the cayenne. Most cookbooks tell you to let the meat stand 1 hour covered with rub before cooking, but I don't find this to be necessary.

2 tablespoons coarse salt
3 tablespoons brown sugar
1 tablespoon ground cumin
2 teaspoons ground cardamom
2 teaspoons ground allspice
2 tablespoons chili powder
2 tablespoons freshly ground black pepper
2 teaspoons cayenne pepper
3 tablespoons paprika

Mix ingredients. Rub over meat before cooking.

Makes about 1 cup, enough for 5 pounds of meat

Barbecue Rub for Poultry

This low-heat rub is best for chicken, turkey, or duck. I usually double the recipe and store it in a glass container in the pantry.

2 tablespoons whole black peppercorns
5 whole cloves
1 tablespoon ground coriander
2 tablespoons ground ginger
2 tablespoons ground cardamom

1 tablespoon ground cumin
1 tablespoon ground allspice
1 tablespoon kosher salt
½ teaspoon cayenne pepper

Toast the first 3 ingredients over medium heat in a nonstick skillet, about 5 minutes. Shake pan occasionally. Grind in a spice grinder. Mix with remaining ingredients. Rub over chicken before barbecuing.

Makes about ⅔ cup, enough for a chicken or duck. Double the recipe for a turkey.

Vinegar Moppin' Sauce

This is hot stuff and is good with pork or beef. It's a thin, acidic sauce that works well with a heavier, fatty meat.

1½ cups cider vinegar
2 teaspoons hot red pepper flakes
1 tablespoon Worcestershire sauce
2 teaspoons Tabasco sauce
1 tablespoon peanut oil
  Salt and freshly ground black pepper to taste

Mix ingredients in a small saucepan and heat. Serve hot as an accompaniment to grilled or barbecued foods. If you serve barbecued foods chopped, this sauce can be mixed in.

Makes about 1¼ cups

Basic Barbecue Sauce

There are two basic variations on barbecue sauce. One is vinegar-based, like the Vinegar Moppin' Sauce above, and the other is tomato-based, like the one in this recipe. This sauce is served with grilled or barbecued foods after they are cooked, and should not be used for basting. (Basting simply dries out the barbecue sauce.)

1 tablespoon butter
1 tablespoon olive oil
1 large onion, peeled and minced

3 cloves garlic, peeled and minced
3 tablespoons balsamic vinegar
¼ cup peanut oil
1 can (28 ounces) tomato puree
2 tablespoons Worcestershire sauce
1 tablespoon dry mustard
1 tablespoon brown sugar
1 teaspoon dried oregano
  Dash Tabasco sauce

Heat butter and olive oil in a large saucepan over medium-high heat. When foam subsides, add onions. Sauté over medium heat for 5 minutes. Add garlic and cook 1 minute. Add remaining ingredients and bring to a simmer. Cook uncovered for 1½ hours or until thick.

Makes about 1 quart

Peanut Barbecue Sauce

Use this sauce as an accompaniment to grilled chicken. You might try to find all-natural or fresh-ground peanut butter instead of the hydrogenated variety available in most supermarkets. There is a surprising difference in taste and texture. The less processed peanut butters have a richer flavor.

1 cup smooth peanut butter
1½ cups chicken stock
¼ cup sherry
3 cloves garlic, peeled and minced
1 teaspoon soy sauce
2 teaspoons lemon juice
1 teaspoon brown sugar
  Dash Tabasco sauce
  Salt and freshly ground black pepper to taste

In a medium saucepan, combine the peanut butter, chicken stock, and sherry. Add remaining ingredients and blend. Cook over medium heat until mixture reaches a boil. Reduce heat to low and cook for 5 minutes, stirring frequently.

Makes about 3 cups

Sauce for Grilled Poultry

This makes a good sauce for chicken, turkey, or game hens. Brush over grilled or roasted poultry just before serving. Toasted sesame oil has a lot of flavor. It can be found at Asian markets or at health food stores.

2 cloves garlic, peeled and minced
2 shallots, peeled and minced
1 teaspoon grated fresh ginger
1 scallion, chopped
1 tablespoon olive oil
¼ teaspoon dried red pepper flakes
1 tablespoon soy sauce
1 teaspoon red wine vinegar
2 tablespoons brown sugar
2 tablespoons water
2 tablespoons toasted (Oriental) sesame oil or peanut oil

Combine all ingredients except sesame oil in a small saucepan, bring to a boil, and simmer for 5 minutes. Let sit for 10 minutes. Strain into a small bowl. Add sesame or peanut oil.

Makes about ½ cup

Spicy Mint Sauce

This is best with grilled lamb. It's easy to grow a small pot or patch of mint. Just one or two plants will grow like a weed. Mint is handy for summer salads, marinades, and cool drinks.

½ cup chicken stock
½ cup white wine vinegar
2 tablespoons sherry
1 tablespoon sugar
1 cup fresh mint leaves, tightly packed
¼ teaspoon hot red pepper flakes

1. In a medium saucepan, heat the chicken stock, vinegar, sherry, and sugar. Bring to a boil and then simmer for 5 minutes.

2. Reserve 2 tablespoons mint leaves for later use and place the remainder in a bowl. Pour vinegar mixture over leaves and let steep for at least 30 minutes, preferably 1–2 hours.

3. Pour mixture into a strainer, crushing mint with the back of a large wooden spoon. Chop the reserved mint leaves and stir into strained liquid with red pepper flakes. Serve at room temperature.

Makes about 1½ cups

~ 35 ~

How to Stir-Fry

*The most important rule about stir-frying at home is don't use a wok!
Woks are not designed for a flat stovetop and provide less heat
than a large skillet.*

~

The summer before college I spent three months in a Land Rover driving from London to Nairobi, 10,000 miles of potholes and the famous English rock-hard suspension. (The joke was that if you ran over a penny with a Land Rover, you could tell whether it was tails up or down.) The most memorable part of the trip was the drive through the Sahara, especially the 600-mile trek to Agadez. The desert we passed through was devoid of human life except for a military outpost consisting of one small building and half a dozen very hot, unhappy soldiers. On the second day out, we stopped for lunch and a siesta — we never drove during midday — in a canyon where the thermometer registered just over 125°F. I thought that New York City in July was hot, but this was transcendent heat, heat that could make a hyperactive American teenager immobile and speechless for hours.

The difference between what we call a hot day and that day in the canyon in Niger is the difference between home wok cooking and the real thing. To stir-fry properly you need plenty of shimmering, intense heat; enough to caramelize sugars, deepen flavors, and evaporate unnecessary juices. The problem is that a wok married to a home stovetop is a lousy partnership, one that provides, at best, moderate heat.

WHY ARE WOKS SHAPED LIKE WOKS?

Woks are bowl-shaped because in China they traditionally sat on cylindrical pits containing the fire. Food was cut into small pieces to shorten cooking time, therefore conserving fuel. Only one cooking utensil was required for many different methods, including sautéing (stir-frying), steaming, boiling, and deep-frying.

Unfortunately, what is practical in China makes no sense in America. Simply put, woks don't work for American home cooks. A wok was not designed for stovetop cooking, where the heat only comes from the bottom; the bottom of the wok gets very hot and the sides only get very warm. A horizontal heat source requires a horizontal pan. (Some late-model woks have flatter bottoms than older designs, but all woks are essentially bowl-shaped.) Therefore, if you want to stir-fry at home, use a large skillet or Dutch oven (12–14 inches in diameter). Consign your wok to the basement. (In restaurants, woks fit into a special gas-fired burner unit that provides a tremendous amount of heat from all sides — I've seen a wok go from room temperature to the point it will vaporize cooking oil in under 30 seconds.)

The other problem with stir-frying at home is that, even with a skillet, you don't have enough heat to quickly sear and cook either large amounts or large pieces of food. This leaves the home cook with two options. You can blanch (cook briefly in boiling water until barely tender) vegetables ahead of time so they require almost no cooking in the wok. This includes carrots, snow peas, asparagus, green beans, broccoli, and cauliflower (onions, scallions, bell peppers, and mushrooms, on the other hand, do not need precooking). I tested this method and found, not surprisingly, that it was cumbersome. (Restaurant chefs often precook stir-fry ingredients because their woks get so hot and the cooking time is so short that the inside of the vegetable is raw even when the outside is deeply seared.)

I think that stir-frying should be easy last-minute cooking, and that's why I favor the second option: I simply chop the vegetables into smaller pieces so that they will cook quickly. This is the approach I follow in the master recipe below. You also need to cook relatively small amounts of food at one time — too much volume will draw down the heat of the pan and you will end up with stewed meat and vegetables. I also suggest that you add vegetables in batches. Onions, carrots, and cauliflower require a good deal of cooking and should be added first. Fresh herbs, tender greens (such as spinach), scallions, and tomato wedges should be added at the end of cooking. All other vegetables are added in between.

Meat, fish, and tofu should also be cut into bite-size pieces for quick cooking. To make cutting beef or chicken easier, freeze for an hour or two; the slightly frozen texture is perfect for slicing, cubing, or dicing. If the meat is already frozen, transfer it from the freezer to the refrigerator in the morning, and by evening the not-quite-thawed texture should be perfect (this will depend on the size of the cut).

A VISIT WITH A STIR-FRY EXPERT

To test out my own and others' theories about stir-fry cooking, I visited Mindy Schreil in her home in Marin County, just north of San Francisco. Mindy was first hired as a line cook at China Moon, a well-known eatery near Union Square in San Francisco, the brainchild of Barbara Tropp, and then graduated to sous-chef a few years later. Mindy and I set out to cook three different stir-fries: one with beef, one with sea bass, and one with cubes of firm tofu. We started off with a few basic premises. We used a 14-inch skillet instead of a wok, we divided the vegetables into two or three batches depending on the particular recipes, and we cut the vegetables into very small pieces without any precooking.

STIR-FRYING BEEF
The beef stir-fry was first. The meat was cut into small, bite-size pieces and took just under 1 minute to cook — you should only cook meat about three-quarters done and then remove it from the pan (it will go back in the pan later). However, the pan was not sufficiently preheated and the beef did not sear properly. Hence the first and most important rule of stir-frying. The pan needs to be hot, really hot. The food should sizzle, steam, and smoke. (Place the palm of your hand about 1 inch above the pan's surface. If you can hold it there no more than 3 seconds because of the heat, the pan is ready for stir-frying.) I suggest heating the sauté pan for about 4 minutes over high heat, adding a tablespoon of oil, and then adding the meat once the oil just starts to shimmer and smoke. The high heat will sear the meat,

which will add tremendous flavor to the rest of the stir-fry ingredients as you cook. As Mindy pointed out, stir-frying is a delicate balance between cooking and burning; you really have to live on the edge to develop the right textures and flavors.

After removing the beef we added about a teaspoon of oil and then the onions and carrots. These cooked for about 4 minutes. Then we added another teaspoon of oil plus the rest of the vegetables — broccoli and bell peppers. After 3 more minutes, we cleared out a space in the center of the pan and added minced garlic and ginger. We sprinkled a little more oil on top and then mashed the mixture down into the pan, using a metal spatula. After just 10 seconds, we took the pan off the stove, reduced the heat to medium, and then replaced the pan on the burner after about 30 seconds. The timing is important here — you want to cook the garlic and ginger, but you want to avoid burning them. The garlic and ginger were then stirred into the vegetables, the meat was returned to the pan, and the flavoring sauce was added. Everything cooked for another 30 seconds. The resulting stir-fry was good but lacking in flavor because the pan was simply not hot enough when we started out.

FISH AND TOFU STIR-FRIES
With the stir-fry of sea bass, we made sure the pan got good and hot — the oil was just starting to smoke. The bite-size cubes of fish cooked in about 20 seconds. After removing them we let the pan come back up to temperature and then added the onion and cauliflower. They sizzled when they hit the pan. The pan smoked and spattered. A cook once told me that when you can barely see the food through the smoke and steam, that's when you know the pan is hot enough. (Turning off your kitchen smoke alarm before stir-frying is not a bad idea.) We finished up the recipe, using the same method as in the beef stir-fry, and the results were much

better. The dish had twice the flavor (the tiny cauliflower florets were browned, which imparted a nutty flavor), all of it due to the right amount of heat. We finally tried the tofu stir-fry, which was also very good. Keep in mind that tofu needs about 2 tablespoons of oil to start; otherwise, it will stick to the pan. It also requires about 2 minutes of initial cooking, about twice as long as meat.

LESSONS LEARNED
This testing not only demonstrated the fundamental need for sufficient heat, it also led me to some other interesting conclusions. First, most American home cooks use too much meat or seafood. A good stir-fry should be heavy on the vegetables and light on the meat. This is both more authentic — meat was a luxury and was used sparingly in China — and, to my mind, preferable. The vegetables should be at least double the meat or seafood by weight. A second interesting conclusion is that there is absolutely no reason to use cornstarch or other thickeners in the flavoring sauce. This makes a sauce that is close to my childhood memories of bad suburban Chinese restaurants. Why thicken? The stir-fry is much brighter and cleaner in taste with a purer, thinner sauce. The cornstarch simply gunks it up, muddying the texture and flavor. Finally, be wary of sugar. A stir-fry should not be sweet. We are used to overly sweet Chinese restaurant food, but this is neither desirable nor authentic. Would you add a tablespoon of sugar to a bowl of fresh steamed peas? Then why add it to a vegetable stir-fry? A small amount of sweetness can enhance flavor, but I have used a minimal amount in the sauces in this chapter.

During this and other testing, I learned a few other valuable lessons:

- Proper vegetable preparation is crucial. Most vegetables should be cut into pieces no bigger than a quarter. (Onion and cabbage can be larger.)

How to Prepare Vegetables for a Stir-Fry

In order to get the maximum heat out of your pan, it is best to try to divide your vegetables into two or even three batches depending on the required length of cooking. If you place 1½ pounds of vegetables in the pan all at once, the heat will drop radically and you will no longer be stir-frying. This is not a rigid system — these vegetables are simply listed in the approximate order in which they should be added to the pan. Be sure to take relative cooking times into account when selecting vegetables so that they end up properly cooked when divided into batches.

When to Add	Vegetable	Preparation
First	Carrots	Cut in half lengthwise and then into thin slices or on bias
	Cauliflower	Cut into tiny florets
	Onions	Cut into slices and quartered
	Peppers	Large dice
Second	Asparagus	½-inch pieces
	Green beans	½-inch pieces
	Broccoli	Tiny florets
	Butternut squash	Small cubes
Third	Cabbage	Medium strips
	Celery	Thin slices
	Chard	Thick strips
	Fennel	Thin slices
	Mushrooms	Halved and sliced
	Peas	Shelled
	Sugar snaps	Ends trimmed
	Summer squash	Halved lengthwise and sliced
	Zucchini	Cut into slices and then half-moons or quarters
Last	Fresh herbs (basil, mint)	Whole leaves
	Scallions	Chopped
	Tender greens	Whole stemmed leaves
	Tomatoes	Small wedges

■ Tofu, eggplant, and mushrooms tend to soak up oil. Therefore you'll have to use about twice as much oil as usual when using large quantities of these ingredients. I also find that fish has a tendency to stick to the pan, so I add an extra 2 teaspoons of oil at the outset of cooking.

■ If you prefer a spicy stir-fry, add ½ teaspoon red pepper flakes or 1 teaspoon minced hot peppers along with the garlic and ginger.

■ A great last-minute addition to a stir-fry is a small handful of fresh basil or mint leaves. Just add them whole, without the stems, after the other vegetables and stir-fry for 20 seconds or until the leaves are wilted.

■ Many home cooks feel compelled to confine themselves to "Chinese" vegetables — broccoli, green beans, water chestnuts, sugar snap peas, scallions, et cetera. There is no reason you cannot stir-fry virtually anything found in an American supermarket. Tomato wedges, added to the vegetables for the last 30 seconds, are great with beef. Spinach leaves are wonderful added whole (stemmed first) and then cooked until wilted. Peas, fennel, cabbage, and chard are just a few other items that can be successfully stir-fried.

- You can use leftover cooked meats such as chicken. Just add them to the end of the stir-fry. You can also use ground meats — beef or pork — cooking them as you would the cubed meat.

- I call for equal amounts of garlic and ginger. However, beef can stand more garlic and fish can stand more ginger. If you like, increase one ingredient by ½ teaspoon and lower the other by the same amount.

- I have found that aromatics (garlic, chives, ginger) should be added toward the end of cooking rather than at the beginning. Otherwise, these delicate ingredients will burn, ruining your dish. However, onions are always added first so that they have a chance to develop flavor.

- Finally, I have tested many different combinations of foods and offer the following suggestions. Beef — flank steak is a good choice — has an affinity with asparagus, mushrooms, chard, and broccoli. Chicken does well with celery and summer squash. Fish — use a firm fish such as swordfish, tuna, sea bass, salmon, or halibut — is great with greens, fennel, celery, peas, and corn, and also works nicely with a curry sauce.

Master Recipe for Stir-Fry

To compensate for the low heat of a home wok, make sure that you cut the foods, especially the vegetables, into small pieces. In fact, I strongly suggest that you not use a wok; use a large (12–14 inch) sauté pan instead. The secret to a good stir-fry is lots of heat, and therefore preheating the pan is crucial. Heat it for about 4 minutes over high heat, add the oil, and then add the meat or seafood once the oil starts to shimmer and smoke. In a good stir-fry, there is lots of smoke, lots of steam, and lots of sizzle. Otherwise, you are braising the food and will not develop the proper texture or flavor. This recipe can be halved to serve 2 — if you halve the recipe, the cooking times will decrease — but it
should not be increased, as a home stovetop has insufficient heat to cook greater quantities of vegetables. (I don't suggest using two pans at once for larger quantities, since stir-frying requires perfect timing and attention to detail. If you must, make two stir-fries, holding the first in a warm oven. Stir-fries are best served hot from the pan, however, so I really do not recommend this.)

Meat, Seafood, or Tofu
 ¾ pound of meat, poultry, shellfish (shrimp, lobster, scallops), firm-fleshed fish, or firm tofu, cut into small, even-size pieces
 1 tablespoon soy sauce or tamari sauce
 1 tablespoon dry sherry

Sauce
 1 recipe flavoring sauce (see following recipes)

2–3 tablespoons canola or peanut oil

Vegetables
 1½ pounds vegetables, cut into small pieces and divided into two or three batches (see chart at left)
 1 tablespoon minced garlic
 1 tablespoon minced fresh ginger
 2 tablespoons chopped scallions

1. Toss meat, poultry, seafood, or tofu with soy sauce and sherry in a medium bowl; set aside.

2. Prepare flavoring sauce.

3. Heat a 12–14 inch skillet over high heat for 4 minutes (the pan should be so hot that you can hold your outstretched palm 1 inch above its surface for no more than 3 seconds). Add 1 tablespoon oil (add 2 tablespoons for tofu and fish) and rotate skillet so that the bottom is evenly coated. Let oil heat for about 1 minute or until it just starts to shimmer and smoke. Drain meat, poultry, seafood, or tofu, add to the pan, and stir-fry until seared and about ¾ cooked (about 20 seconds for seafood, 60 seconds for meat, 2 minutes for tofu, 2½–3 minutes for chicken). Spoon cooked food into serving dish. Cover and keep warm.

4. Let pan come back up to temperature, about 1 minute. When hot, drizzle in 2 teaspoons of oil and when oil just starts to smoke, add the first batch of vegetables. Stir-fry until vegetables are just tender-crisp, about 4 minutes. Leaving first batch in the pan, repeat with remaining vegetables, stirring them all together. Add about a teaspoon of oil for each batch (the amount of oil will depend on the pan you are using — nonstick pans require about a teaspoon, other pans may require 2 teaspoons).

5. Once all the vegetables have been added, clear the center of the pan and add the garlic, ginger, and scallions. Drizzle with ½ teaspoon oil. Mash into pan with back of a spatula. Cook for 10 seconds. Remove pan from heat, reduce heat to medium, and with pan still off heat stir garlic-ginger mixture into vegetables for 20 seconds.

6. Return pan to heat, add the cooked meat, poultry, seafood, or tofu to skillet, stir in flavoring sauce, and stir-fry to coat all ingredients, about 1 minute. Serve immediately with rice.

Serves 4

Flavoring Sauces

For the sauces below, simply combine all ingredients and use in the master recipe above as indicated.

Ginger Sauce

A mini–food processor is good for dicing ginger. If you don't have one, start by trimming the root so that the sides are even, peel with a vegetable peeler, cut the root into thin strips lengthwise, stack the strips and cut into thin matchsticks, and then cut across the width into small dice (see page 68). A very sharp knife is essential. This sauce works with almost any ingredient, but it is particularly good with fish or shrimp.

3 tablespoons light soy sauce
½ teaspoon sugar
1 tablespoon dry sherry
¼ cup minced fresh ginger
¼ cup diced scallions
2 tablespoons chicken stock

Orange Sauce

Orange peel (zest) is best removed with a vegetable peeler, avoiding any of the white pith, and then finely minced. I find that grated orange peel has less flavor, perhaps because some of the aromatic oils are left behind. I like to use this sauce with chicken or beef.

2 teaspoons minced orange zest
¼ cup orange juice
½ teaspoon sugar
2 tablespoons chicken stock
1 tablespoon light soy sauce
¼ teaspoon kosher salt

Oyster Sauce

This is a full-bodied sauce best with beef.

3 tablespoons oyster sauce
¼ cup dry sherry
2 teaspoons toasted (Oriental) sesame oil
½ teaspoon sugar
¼ teaspoon freshly ground black pepper

Lemon Sauce

I like lemon sauce with chicken and as an all-purpose sauce for vegetarian stir-fries.

2 teaspoons finely minced lemon zest
3 tablespoons lemon juice
1 teaspoon sugar
2 tablespoons chicken stock
1 tablespoon light soy sauce
¼ teaspoon kosher salt

Curry Sauce

Curry sauce is good with both chicken and fish.

3 tablespoons light soy sauce
½ teaspoon sugar
1 tablespoon dry sherry
2 teaspoons curry powder
¼ cup diced scallions
2 tablespoons chicken stock

Peanut Sauce

I had to try half a dozen times before I came up with the right texture for this sauce. I prefer a light sauce, and most peanut sauces are thick and overpowering.

2 tablespoons peanut butter
½ teaspoon sugar
1 tablespoon soy sauce

2 tablespoons minced flat-leaf parsley
2 tablespoons sherry
2 tablespoons chicken stock
2 teaspoons toasted (Oriental) sesame oil

Hot and Sour Sauce

Before mincing a chili, slice it in half lengthwise and scoop out the seeds and white pith with a ½-teaspoon metal measuring spoon.

2 tablespoons cider vinegar
2 teaspoons minced hot chilis
2 teaspoons sugar
2 tablespoons chicken stock
1 tablespoon light soy sauce
¼ teaspoon kosher salt

～ 36 ～

Quick and Easy Homemade Pizza

How do you get pizza on the table in 75 minutes start to finish?
Use rapid-rise yeast and turn your oven into a proofing box.

～

A friend of mine is a food writer and the quintessential perfectionist. He recently went to Naples to research pizza, and I went to visit him soon after he returned. Behind his house was a large hole with some rocks dumped in it. I asked, "Neapolitan pizza oven, right?" He grinned sheepishly and admitted that was what he had in mind. Never mind that he lives in northern Vermont and that his pizza oven would be encased in either ice, snow, or mud for most of the year. If he ever gets it built, I am anxious to blind taste-test my 75-minute pizza against one he makes in his oven, on the off chance that my pizza will win. Now *that* would be satisfying!

This chapter is not about making the world's best pizza. It's about a good, practical recipe that will get the pizza on the table in less than 90 minutes, so that you can serve it during the week. After all, pizza is not haute cuisine, it's everyman's food, a staple of the American diet. It should be quick and simple, well made but not fussy.

PIZZA DOUGH SHORTCUTS

To come up with a recipe for from-scratch pizza that could be made any night of the week, I knew I'd have to depart from traditional methods. Making the yeast dough is the most time-consuming part of the job, so I started there. Since a food processor makes short work of mixing and kneading, I focused on the problem of rising time. I tested making the dough in the morning before leaving for work and storing it in a covered bowl in the refrigerator. When I got home, I removed the bowl and placed it on top of a warm stove. This was not a success — the refrigerator is so cold that the yeast had no chance to develop. It still took 2 hours for the dough to rise once I got home. So next I tried using only ½ teaspoon of yeast (instead of 2 teaspoons) and leaving the dough in a cool place, not in the refrigerator. This seemed to do the trick. When I returned home, the dough had risen and was ready to shape. However, I found this technique to be problematic — it depended entirely on the temperature of the room, and the dough could easily overrise, something that happened to me on more than one occasion. I also found it difficult to remember to start the pizza dough before leaving for work.

I then tried rapid-rise yeast as a means of cutting rising time. This worked well, but I still wanted to turbocharge the process — I wanted the dough to pop up even faster so I could get it into the oven. I ran across a copy of *The Pizza Book*, by Evelyne Slomon. She recommends turning your oven into a proofing box by preheating it for 10 minutes at 200°F, turning it off, and the placing the dough in the oven for the first rise. I also decided to start with very warm water (about 125°F — it will cool a bit when it comes in contact with the bowl of the food processor). These three factors — rapid-rise yeast, extra-warm water, and proofing in a warm oven — allowed me to reduce the initial rising time to only 40 minutes, a major breakthrough (many recipes call for 2 hours). Mixing the warm water with the sugar and the yeast first, before adding the other ingredients, helps to jump-start the rising. I also cut short the second rise to only 10 minutes, after which the dough is shaped and baked. You are done in about 75 minutes from start to finish. When I tasted my pizza head to head with a more traditional recipe from *Cook's Illustrated*, I found that the *Cook's* recipe was a bit better, but mine was clearly in the ballpark and could be made in about half the time.

OTHER PIZZA DOUGH RECIPES

Once I had discovered the secrets of a rapid-rise recipe, I tinkered with the ingredients to see if the flavor and texture of the dough could be improved. I tried a combination of milk and water. This created a soft, breadlike dough that had no chew. I also tried using bread flour, which I find makes a finer, less chewy pizza. So I stick to all-purpose flour. I also tried using a starter of flour, water, and yeast, which I placed on the kitchen counter overnight and then combined with the rest of the ingredients the next day. This was done to increase the flavor of the dough (a longer rising time should in theory allow the growth of more flavor), but since pizza has toppings, this did not matter much and was clearly not worth the extra effort.

THE NO-COOK TOMATO SAUCE

The next problem was the tomato sauce. First, I find that cooked tomato sauces taste dull and stale on pizza because they are cooked twice, once on the stove and once in the oven. Also, cooking a tomato sauce in addition to making the dough just complicates pizza making to the point that it becomes a special-occasion recipe. The recipe I developed, the No-Cook Tomato Sauce later in this chapter, solves both these problems, and I think it tastes better than a cooked sauce. It's no more than canned chopped tomatoes with olive oil, minced garlic, salt, and a dash of sugar. You can also use canned whole tomatoes (which need to be drained, chopped, and then drained again) or crushed tomatoes.

SHAPING THE DOUGH

The final impediment to making pizza a regular part of my cooking repertoire was shaping the dough. Over the years I had tried just about every technique, including smearing the dough over a Crisco-greased baking pan (the crust was very tough), using a rolling pin (impossible to get the dough thin enough), and stretching the dough over my fists, a

---

COOKING TIP

Stretching Pizza Dough the Easy Way

There is a product called Dough Easy, which contains whey and L-cysteine, an amino acid. This product, a white powder, was developed by commercial pizza makers and is used as a flour additive (1 teaspoon per cup). When the dough is stretched and pulled to form a pizza, the addition of Dough Easy makes it less likely to shrink back on itself, a major problem for home cooks as well. Call The Kitchen Supply Company, Forest Park, Illinois, 708-383-5990. You can also use Lora Brody's Dough Relaxer. For more information, call 617-964-0016.

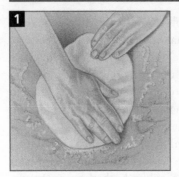
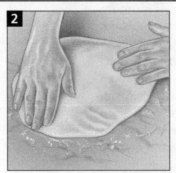
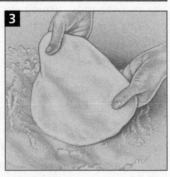

1. Start by pressing the ball of dough gently into a 7-inch round with the flat of your hands. Hold one corner of the dough with your left hand and place your right hand at a spot about 25 percent farther along the circumference of the dough. Stretch the dough by moving your right hand away from your left hand (this is done gently). Imagine stretching the sides of a square. Rotate the dough a quarter-turn and stretch again; repeat until you have stretched all four sides.

2. Now stretch the dough across its diameter, using the same method used in the last step, stretching and rotating until the pizza is about 11 inches in diameter.

If the center of the dough becomes dangerously thin, stretch only the sides.

3. Pick up one edge of the dough with both hands, holding it between your thumb and fingers. Leave most of the dough resting on the work surface. Now gently stretch the perimeter of the dough (your hands should end up about 7 inches apart). Try not to stretch the very edge — you want a thicker edge for a good crust. Work your way around the circumference of the circle, lifting and stretching, until you have gone around the pizza twice. The dough should now be shaped into a 12-inch round.

technique shown in every pizza book, which I find to be quite difficult — the dough always breaks. Cookbooks that suggest throwing the dough into the air should be taken from the shelf and burned — nobody can do this at home.

After months of trials, however, I developed a simple method that combines techniques from a variety of cooks and is so easy that anyone can do it, even a beginner. This method leaves the dough on the work surface as much as possible. You need to handle the dough gently. Once the dough becomes overworked, it will pull back after stretching, which makes it difficult to achieve the proper diameter.

Start by gently pressing one of the balls of dough into a 7-inch round. Now, lightly stretch the sides of the circle in increments, holding an edge of the circle with one hand and then pushing away with the other hand. One quarter of the circumference of the dough is stretched at a time. Now stretch the

dough across its diameter, turning the round a quarter-turn after each stretch. These stretching steps are repeated until the pizza dough is about 11 inches in diameter. Finally, one edge of the dough is picked up with both hands, leaving most of the dough still on the counter. Gently gripping the dough between thumb and fingers (your hands should be turned palms up, with the thumb on top), slowly stretch the dough by pulling your hands apart. Go around the perimeter of the dough twice. You should now have a 12-inch round.

ASSEMBLING THE PIZZA

Once the dough is stretched into shape, I transfer it to a pizza peel — a long-handled paddle — that has been lightly dusted with cornmeal. I brush the dough with a mixture of olive oil, garlic, and a fresh herb such as rosemary. I also find that a good sprinkling of salt at this point enhances the flavor of the baked crust. I then add the topping, although I have found that some toppings are best when added only for the last few minutes of baking. If you are using a tomato sauce as a base, place this on the crust first. Next, add toppings such as freshly shucked littleneck clams, pancetta, goat cheese, uncooked sausage, caramelized onions, pepperoni, imported black olives, or roasted tomatoes. I have found from kitchen testing that if mozzarella is added at the outset, the crust becomes soggy as the steam is trapped by the top layer of cheese. However, when added for the last 3 minutes of baking only, the mozzarella has time to melt and the crust turns out crispier. Pesto is also added for the last 3 minutes only, to maintain its fresh, lively flavor. I sprinkle on Parmesan cheese after baking, to preserve its pungent, nutty bite.

BAKING THE PIZZA

In pizza making, as in other kinds of cooking, a major issue is oven heat. All sorts of pizza experts go on and on about professional brick ovens, making the point that without 800°F of wood-fired heat, you just can't make good pizza. Well, I eat at plenty of "authentic" pizza places and almost never get a good pizza. It's not the oven, it's the cook. First of all, heat your oven to the highest possible temperature (usually 500°F) for at least half an hour before baking. Second, baking tiles really are worth the trouble. A pizza pan goes into the oven cold, whereas the tiles are nice and hot when the pizza slides onto them in the oven. I place my tiles on a rack set at the lowest position. Some cooks suggest placing the tiles directly on the bottom of the stove (only if you have a gas oven). This does not work for me because the heat is very uneven — half of the pizza burns while the other half is undercooked. It is true that pizza stones are a bit expensive (Williams-Sonoma sells one for about $30), but I prefer them to individual tiles (if you do purchase tiles, the unglazed Mexican Saltillo tiles are a good choice) because the latter slide around too much in the oven, separating and no longer providing a flat, even surface.

To move pizza in and out of the oven I use a peel. I have both a metal and wooden peel and find no difference between them. I have found through testing that fine cornmeal is better than flour for sprinkling the peel. There is no need to sprinkle the baking stone with cornmeal, however, since a fair amount will stick to the bottom of the pizza as it is transferred from the peel. If too much cornmeal ends up on the hot baking surface, smoking may result, and the bottom of the crust will become black and burned.

Master Recipe for Pizza Dough

This recipe is adapted from The Pizza Book, *by Evelyne Slomon. By using hot water, rapid-rise yeast, and a preheated oven for rising, this recipe will let you put pizza on the table in only 75 minutes, start to finish. If you have the time, use regular yeast and let the dough rise outside of a preheated oven until doubled, about 90 minutes (time will vary depending on the ambient temperature). The crust will be slightly improved.*

> 1 cup warm water (about 125°F)
> 1 package rapid-rise yeast
> 1 tablespoon sugar
> 1½ teaspoons kosher salt
> 3 cups all-purpose flour
>
> 2–3 tablespoons olive oil or brushing mixture (see below), for brushing dough
> Cornmeal for dusting

1. Place tiles or pizza stone (if using) on bottom rack of oven and heat oven to 200°F. Turn oven off after 10 minutes of heating.

2. Put the warm water in the bowl of a food processor fitted with either the metal or plastic blade and sprinkle in the yeast and sugar. Pulse twice to dissolve the yeast. Add the salt and flour and process until the mixture forms a cohesive mass. The dough should not be sticky (if it is, add 2 tablespoons of flour and pulse briefly), nor should it be dry and crumbly (add 1 tablespoon of water and pulse). Let rest for 2 minutes. Process for another 30 seconds.

3. Remove dough from food processor and knead by hand on a floured work surface for 1 minute or until dough is smooth and satiny (the dough will feel a bit tough at this point). Form into a ball.

4. Very lightly oil a large bowl with vegetable oil and place dough inside (do not coat dough with oil). Cover bowl with plastic wrap and place in the heated oven (which has been turned off). Let dough rise for 40 minutes or until doubled in size. Remove risen dough from oven and punch down to deflate. Remove dough from bowl, divide in half, and shape into two balls. Let dough rest on the counter for 10 minutes under a damp dishtowel.

5. While dough is resting, start preheating the oven to 500°F.

6. At the end of the resting time, place one of the balls of dough on a lightly floured surface and shape according to the instructions in this chapter. Lightly dust a baker's peel with fine cornmeal and transfer the dough to the peel. Brush with olive oil or a brushing mixture. The dough is now ready for topping (see suggestions below) and baking. While first pizza is baking, repeat with remaining ball of dough.

Note: Baking times will vary depending on your oven. The total cooking time can be as long as 15 minutes if you are using a pizza pan or as little as 10 minutes if you are using a pizza stone.

Makes dough for 2 thin-crust 12-inch pizzas

Grilled Pizza

Divide the dough into four balls to make four smaller pizzas (it is difficult to handle a 12-inch pizza on a charcoal grill). Grill over high heat about 2 minutes on one side. Flip the dough and add a precooked topping and grill another 1–2 minutes. You can grill pizza dough and serve it with just a brushing mixture (see below) and no topping — a quick and easy focaccia. You can also grill pizza dough and then add an uncooked topping after it comes off the grill. Try the Cold Tomato Sauce with Basil and Mint on page 167.

No-Cook Tomato Sauce for Pizza

Tomatoes do not benefit much from cooking. In fact, I prefer the flavor of a no-cook tomato sauce. Of course, a no-cook sauce is also a timesaver — you don't want to have to make the dough and the sauce and also prepare a topping. Pizza making should be more of a last-minute affair. This recipe does make a garlicky sauce (since the garlic is not cooked, it is pungent). Reduce the garlic to 1 teaspoon for a milder version. I suggest you use canned crushed tomatoes for this recipe. This makes just enough sauce for two 12-inch pizzas. If you like a lot of sauce, increase quantities by 50 percent.

1 can (28 ounces) whole skinned, chopped, or crushed tomatoes
2 teaspoons finely minced garlic
1 tablespoon olive oil
¼ teaspoon kosher salt
½ teaspoon sugar
  Freshly ground black pepper to taste

If using whole canned tomatoes, drain and coarsely chop, then place in a colander and let drain for 5 minutes. Place tomatoes in the workbowl of a food processor and add the remaining ingredients. Pulse until blended. Taste and adjust salt, sugar, and pepper.

Makes just enough sauce for two 12-inch pizzas.

Brushing Mixtures

To add flavor to any pizza, regardless of topping, I use a mixture made from olive oil, garlic, and a fresh herb. This is brushed on the dough before topping. For enough mixture for one recipe, combine 2 tablespoons olive oil with 1 teaspoon each minced garlic and minced fresh rosemary or other herb (if you don't have a fresh herb, omit it entirely). I also suggest that you add a generous sprinkling of salt after brushing the dough and before adding the topping.

Toppings

You can use virtually anything as a topping as long as it has lots of flavor. Vegetables don't work very well; imported black olives, sausage, and pepperoni do. Cooking times will not be affected by the amount or type of topping, since the crust is sitting on preheated tiles. Note that most ingredients are added before baking, while others, such as mozzarella, Parmesan, and pesto, are added later. All pizza dough should be brushed first with a brushing mixture or with a good-quality olive oil. A sprinkling of salt on the dough before adding the topping is also recommended. Also note that I have not listed quantities for some of the topping recipes, as this is strictly a matter of individual taste.

Unless otherwise noted, these recipes are for one 12-inch pizza.

Clams and Garlic

Shuck 16 littleneck clams. Brush pizza dough with garlic and rosemary brushing mixture and add 8 clams per pizza. Sprinkle with salt.

Plain Tomato

Spread dough with No-Cook Tomato Sauce. If you want, sprinkle on grated Parmesan — add it *after* the pie is baked. You can also top with Pesto (see recipe, page 167) or fresh basil leaves for the last 3 minutes of baking.

Basic Cheese

Use the No-Cook Tomato Sauce, bake approximately 7 minutes, and then top with ⅓ pound coarsely grated mozzarella for the last 3 minutes of cooking or until just melted.

Sweet Italian Sausage

Spread pizza dough with No-Cook Tomato Sauce and top with ⅓ pound uncooked, crumbled sausage meat.

Caramelized Onions

Peel and thinly slice 3 large onions. Peel and lightly crush 3 garlic cloves. Put 3 tablespoons of olive oil in a large sauté pan and heat. Add the onions, the garlic, and 1 tablespoon of minced fresh herbs (rosemary, thyme, or oregano) or 1 teaspoon dried. Cook over low heat until onions turn golden and lose their moisture, about 30 minutes. Remove and discard garlic. Add salt and freshly ground black pepper to taste. Coat pizza with an herb-and-garlic brushing mixture, top with onions, then bake.

Pesto

Add Pesto before the last 3 minutes of cooking. Sprinkle with Parmesan once pizza is cooked (optional).

Roasted Tomatoes

Top pizza dough with roasted tomatoes (see Roasted Eggplant Sandwiches with Onions and Tomatoes, step 2, page 87). Sprinkle with Parmesan after baking, or add ¼ pound coarsely grated mozzarella 3 minutes before removing pie from oven.

37

The Secrets of Yeast Breads

Don't proof yeast, use a food processor for kneading,
and use your oven as a preheated proofing box.

~

I have been attending the same church in Vermont since 1955. Built in 1877, it stands on the edge of a cornfield by the Green River, and if I sit in the right pew, I can look out over the pasture where we still harvest corn with a team of mules hitched to a mechanical corn binder.

Inside the church, things haven't changed much either. Hymns are played on an Estey pump organ made in the 1880s, and the carpet covering the foot pedals is now threadbare. The chandelier is Victorian but simple — gray metal scrollwork capped by large tulip globes. The pews themselves are original, made of oak that has turned dark over the years. It's a modest church — practical and spare — but it serves its purpose in the Yankee tradition of economy and function.

Since our town is without a restaurant or store, one of the church's functions is to serve as a meeting place. After the service, the congregation heads for the back room for coffee and gossip. Following a recent service, I was working on my second biscuit when the town's last farmer came up and asked, "What do you hear about those electric bread machines?"

Well, that was quite a question coming from a man whose toolbox contains a ham-

mer, a pair of pliers, a grease gun, and a few yards of baling twine. He owns three vintage Farmall tractors (one of which he bought new in 1949); he knows how to keep them running and uses each for a specific purpose. Like a good cook, he prefers his equipment simple and well made — he doesn't pay for extras. Yet here he was, asking about a $250 piece of kitchen gadgetry that is supposed to replace the best tools any farmer can have: his hands.

Now, I have kneaded bread by hand, in a food processor, and in a standing mixer. I have used a microwave oven to quick-rise the dough. I have made dozens of loaves of bread in bread machines. I recently spent six months of weekends figuring out how to make a rustic, chewy loaf at home. And I have found that the secret to bread is that it is easy to make and endlessly forgiving. I have also found that the process of bread making is full of conventional wisdom, much of which is dead wrong.

BREAD-MAKING BASICS

DO YOU REALLY NEED TO PROOF YEAST? If you are like most home cooks, you still believe that it is necessary to let yeast and wa-

So-called active dry yeast has dead cells encapsulating live cells. The dead cells need to dissolve in order for the live cells to start working. However, this will happen in short order in the dough mixture during kneading, and so proofing is unnecessary.

ter react with each other for 5–10 minutes before mixing a dough, to make sure the yeast is live. What if you just skip this step? Well, I stopped proofing yeast years ago with no ill effect. I simply dissolve the yeast in water and then mix it in with the flour. I followed up with phone calls to the King Arthur flour company and to Fleischmann's yeast to find out why proofing is still recommended. They agreed that proofing yeast is no longer necessary. I suppose that many years ago either the yeast was not a sure thing — you might end up with a bowl full of flour, water, and dead yeast — or that the yeast needed more time in contact with water in order to get it started. Modern yeasts, however, have no such problem, so don't bother proofing.

Which Is the Best Yeast?

I taste-tested several yeasts, including Fleischmann's Rapid Rise Yeast, Fleischmann's Active Yeast, Fleischmann's Cake Yeast, Red Star Quick Rise, King Arthur Instant Yeast, Fleischmann's Instant Yeast, and Red Star Instant Yeast. (Many of these yeasts are recommended for breads different from the all-purpose American loaf I used for the testing; the results might be quite different with another recipe.) The surprising winner was Fleischmann's Instant Yeast, with Fleischmann's Cake Yeast and Fleischmann's Rapid Rise Yeast close seconds. (I retested the cake yeast due to an overly yeasty flavor with the first batch. The results were excellent, putting it at the top of the list with the instant yeast. It dissolves well, without clumping, and is

slightly less expensive than packets of dry yeast. It does have a shorter shelf life, however.) The instant yeast is a mail-order yeast, not always sold in supermarkets, and cake yeast is not always available; therefore I recommend the Fleischmann's Rapid Rise as an excellent all-purpose yeast.

The most startling result from this taste test, however, was that while Fleischmann's Rapid Rise came out third, the regular Fleischmann's Active Yeast placed dead last. It should be noted that the rising methods were also different — the doughs made with rapid-rise yeasts were placed in a warmed oven for just 40 minutes, whereas breads made with the regular active yeast took about 2 hours when left to rise on top of the stove. The faster rise also gave rise to more flavor and produced a noticeably sweeter bread. One theory is that a rapid rising provides less time for the creation of acidic byproducts of fermentation, hence a sweeter loaf.

All of this prompts the question, "How can rapid-rise yeast outperform regular active yeast?" It seems logical that a longer, gentler rise would allow the dough more time to produce complex flavors. This may be true for a European-style loaf, but an American bread contains both fat (milk) and sugar (honey), and thus the complexity of flavors evident in a plainer loaf is easily missed. But more to the point, quick-rise yeast is by no means an inferior product. First of all, yeast is a plant, not bacteria, and is similar in construct to the single-cell mushroom. Different varieties have quite different qualities, similar to the differences among roses. Rapid-rise yeast was genetically engineered to reproduce the best characteristics of yeasts from around the world. So, in many ways, rapid-rise yeast is in fact a superior product.

As for its working faster, there are two reasons for this. First, it has an open, porous structure, which means that it absorbs liquid instantly. Second, its superior enzyme structure converts starches to sugar at a brisker pace than regular-rise yeasts. When rapid-rise varieties were first introduced, consumers had difficulties because, contrary to the manufacturer's directions, they would proof the yeast, which, due to its efficiency, rapidly ran out of food (starch) and died during the proofing process. (The yeast was supposed to be mixed directly into the flour.) To correct this problem, scientists added more starch to the mix, providing enough food for the yeast to survive proofing.

However, to make the rustic country loaf in this chapter, I did not use a rapid-rise yeast because I wanted a long, slow proofing process, to develop more complex flavors. For this sort of loaf, which does not rely on milk or butter for flavor, I preferred to create a starter of flour, yeast, and water and then allow it to sit out overnight.

IS KNEADING BY HAND ESSENTIAL?

No. Kneading by hand is pleasurable, and many people like to do it. But you can knead a basic bread dough in a food processor (use the metal blade) in *only 40 seconds!* (Although I discovered that additional kneading by hand does make a better loaf, you can let the food processor do all the work and still turn out a decent loaf.) You can also knead it in the bowl of a standing mixer, using the dough hook. You can underknead and overknead and still get good bread. I have tested kneading in a KitchenAid mixer for 10 minutes, 15 minutes, and 20 minutes and I couldn't tell the difference in the baked loaf. Contrary to what many bread books tell you, this is not a delicate operation with a thin margin between success and failure. I also found that a machine will generally produce a better loaf of bread than one that is hand kneaded because the home cook usually adds too much extra flour during kneading. If you have a choice, use a standing mixer rather than a food processor. Dough mixed in the latter benefits from being

Is It Possible to Overknead Bread Dough?

Well, yes and no. A harder, high-gluten flour such as bread flour will maintain its strength and elasticity longer than an all-purpose flour, which is weaker. That is one reason commercial bakers use hard flour — it stands up well to the action of commercial machines. At home, it is almost impossible to overknead dough, especially when using bread flour. It is possible to overdo it in a food processor, however, but you should have no trouble with a dough hook in a standing mixer. By the way, a commercial baker will measure the temperature of the dough to determine when it is properly kneaded. Dough that gets too hot is an indication of overworking. At home, the easiest method of determining if dough has been sufficiently kneaded is to pull it apart. It should be elastic and easily stretched without breaking. The exterior of the dough may be sticky or not, depending on the amount of water used in a particular recipe.

kneaded for 4 minutes by hand after machine processing; the standing mixer requires just a few seconds of hand kneading.

WHAT'S THE DIFFERENCE BETWEEN BREAD FLOUR AND ALL-PURPOSE FLOUR?

The difference is the wheat that the flour is made from. A bread flour is made from a "harder" wheat, which simply means that the kernel of wheat is physically harder. It also means that the wheat has a higher percentage of protein. Bread flour usually contains 12–14 percent protein, all-purpose flour is in the 10–12 percent range, and pastry and cake flours run under 10 percent.

In breadmaking, the gluten (protein in the flour) is developed through kneading. This creates an elastic structure that is adept at trapping the gases caused by the fermenting yeast. This in turn results in a light, fine-textured bread. With less protein or gluten, the structure does not develop as well, and you end up with a denser, coarser loaf. However, the difference between all-purpose and bread flours is modest at best, and you can substitute all-purpose for bread flour without major problems. In my testing, I did find, however, that bread flour will absorb more water than all-purpose (so will whole wheat and rye flours). As a general rule for any bread recipe, I suggest that if you do substitute all-purpose for bread flour, you reduce the liquid by 10 percent.

WHAT ABOUT USING A MICROWAVE OVEN AS A PROOFING BOX?

Forget it. In *Bread in Half the Time,* the authors make the case that rising time can be cut in half by using a microwave oven. The authors are correct — rising time is reduced. What they don't tell you up front is that you will spend the better part of an hour moving dough in and out of a microwave oven in a series of carefully timed exercises. It's a whole lot easier to put the kneaded dough in a bowl, cover with a damp towel or plastic wrap, and walk away, even if it does take more time. It's like a waiter informing you that your dinner will be prepared in just half the time if you would be so kind as to go into the kitchen and cook it yourself! I'd rather sit back and have a second gin and tonic.

SHOULD I PURCHASE A BREAD MACHINE?

The short answer is that bread machines are lousy ovens. The crust is pitiful and the interior is mediocre at best. They are, however, great kneaders and, to a lesser extent, proofing boxes. Just don't bake bread in one. See page 35 for more information.

DON'T FORGET THE SALT

I once made a loaf of bread and forgot to add the salt. It was inedible. Tasteless, flat, empty — completely lacking in appeal. In bread baking, salt is king. Although the amount of salt for a specific bread recipe will vary depending on what else is with the flour, I use about 1 level tablespoon of kosher salt (2 teaspoons of table salt — kosher salt is not as salty as an equal volume of table salt) with 3 cups of flour for a typical American-style loaf. Don't forget that a little sugar or honey is also helpful. It will brighten the flavor of the flour and also help to brown the crust.

MILK VERSUS WATER

Lots of bread recipes use milk, eggs, or melted butter. These ingredients add fat, which yields a softer, more cakelike texture. A Parker House roll, for example, is a simple bread recipe with fat in it. It is very soft and pliable, not dense and chewy. So if you like bread with some tooth in it, don't add fat. If you like a nice soft sandwich or tea loaf, go ahead and add dairy products.

THE AWFUL TRUTH ABOUT STARTERS

Many bakers tell you to make a sponge (this is a combination of flour, water, and yeast that is allowed to sit around and develop) and then use a part of it as a starter for baking bread. You keep the rest in a refrigerator and have to feed it every week. If you don't, the bacteria will run out of food and become dormant. Bakeries and restaurants have starters that they have kept going for years, the theory being that each starter has a unique flavor that is difficult to replicate. This is great for professionals who bake bread daily or at least once per week, but it is nonsense for most home cooks. Although some bakers now claim that starters can be kept for up to 6 months in a closed container in the refrigerator without feeding, they do have to be revived, which takes 2–3 days. In addition, breads made with starters are slower to rise than loaves made with commercial yeast. So if you make bread every week and if rising time is not a factor, use a starter if you want to experiment with more complex flavors. Otherwise, stick to commercial yeast.

BREAD-BAKING EQUIPMENT

Home cooks have four basic choices when it comes to bread pans: aluminum, nonstick aluminum, glass, and the heavy-duty commercial-grade pans available at most kitchen supply stores. The aluminum pan turns out good bread, but the bottom is soft and the pan needs to be thoroughly greased; otherwise, the loaf can be difficult to remove. The nonstick pan has the same baking characteristics but solves the problem of the sticky pan. A glass loaf pan reduces baking time by at least 5 minutes, and the bottom of the loaf is crustier. Finally, the commercial-grade pan turns out the best loaf of all, with a great crust, top and bottom. I have discovered, however, that the inside of the loaves is not affected at all by the choice of pan.

If bread is not baked in a loaf pan, it should be baked on tiles that remain in the oven all the time on the lowest rack (see Chapter 36 for more information). There are wooden peels and metal peels (peels are the large, long-handled spatulas used by bread and pizza bakers) to get bread in and out of the oven. I have both and don't have a preference, although the metal peels are slightly thinner and easier to slide under the loaf. Do not flour the peel, use cornmeal. A sticky dough will not slide off a flour-dusted peel but will glide right off a peel sprinkled with lots of cornmeal.

A dough scraper—a stiff, wide metal blade with a wooden or plastic handle—is a must for scraping dough off a work surface or moving it around. Larger models are big enough to slide under a full 6 cups of bread dough. I also suggest that you purchase a heavy-duty electric mixer such as a KitchenAid for kneading dough. There is no benefit to hand-kneading other than the sheer pleasure of it.

An instant-read thermometer is essential. Stick it into the bottom of the loaf to tell when it is properly cooked. A dough that feels wet and sticky before baking, such as the Rustic Country Bread in this chapter, needs to be cooked to 208°F. A more traditional loaf, such as the No-Knead American

Bread, which feels smooth and satiny after the final rise, is done at around 195°F. If you are not sure what type of dough you are working with, use 195°F as the proper temperature. Properly baked bread has a moist but not sticky interior. (Most books tell you to thump the bottom of the loaf until it sounds hollow, which is akin to predicting winter weather based on the furriness of the woolly caterpillar. Use the thermometer unless you are a pro.) You can purchase a very expensive digital thermometer or get a cheap instant-read with a dial. I'd go for the latter.

After bread dough has risen once, it needs to rise a second time. Loaf breads do the second rise directly in the baking pan. Small loaves and rolls rise directly on a baking sheet. But large round loaves need to rise in some sort of basket. These baskets are referred to as bannetons, and in a professional Parisian bakery they are lined with muslin. The muslin is coated with flour that has been rubbed in by hand. Even a sticky dough will not adhere to this surface, and the basket provides shape to the dough as it rises. The problem with bannetons is that they are incredibly expensive. I bought one to test it and the bill was over $70! However, like a good Yankee, I found a great and cheap substitute. Just purchase a pastry cloth (they cost about $4 and are used as a surface for rolling out pie dough), rub in as much flour as possible by hand, and lay it in a colander.

SHORTCUTS, TIPS, AND ADVICE

- A wetter dough always produces a thicker, chewier crust and more air holes. A drier dough is easier to handle but also gives you a thinner crust and a more refined texture. To achieve the degree of moistness you prefer, try adding or subtracting ¼ cup flour from any bread recipe that uses at least 4 cups of flour.

- Rising times vary a great deal, depending on temperature and other factors, including the amount of yeast spores in the air. A professional bakery is always humid and is crawling with yeast, so the bread will rise far more quickly there than in a home kitchen.

- For denser bread, let the dough rise only about 75 percent during the second rise (not double).

- A serrated knife works well for slashing the top of a large loaf of bread before baking.

- Use a very quick backward jerk to slide a bread loaf off the peel and onto the baking sheet or stone.

- Inevitably, bread crust will start to lose its crunch, especially in humid weather. Just pop the loaf into a 400° oven for up to 10 minutes to restore it.

HOW TO MAKE A RUSTIC COUNTRY LOAF

I set out to discover a reliable home recipe for a crusty, rough-textured country bread. I was looking for the kind of bread that is a main course all by itself; the kind where the first bite hits you with a heady burst of crackle and chew, an inspired whiff of yeast, and a hint of sourness. I didn't want a tea party sandwich loaf; I wanted some peasant cooking, the kind of bread that, when sliced and stuffed into a basket at a white-tablecloth restaurant, looks like Hercules in a skirt.

My first task was to determine which of four types of country bread to test. The four different types result from four different methods of leavening the bread: with a natural starter (a mixture of flour and water left out for 24 hours, during which time the mixture attracts yeast spores from the air); a mixed starter (a piece of dough reserved from a previously made batch added to fresh ingredients); a standard yeast starter (packaged yeast mixed into the dough at the beginning); or a sponge starter (a "sponge" of flour, water, and yeast, left to ferment and then combined with additional flour, water, and other ingredients).

The first and second methods are inconvenient for home cooks. The third method lacks the flavor I was looking for, because there's no time for the flavor-producing bacteria to develop. The last method promised to be a good compromise.

FINDING THE SECRET TO A GREAT CHEW
In *Chez Panisse Cooking,* Paul Bertolli suggests making a sponge, covering it, and letting it sit out overnight before making the dough. I decided to follow this method. In his recipe, however, Bertolli uses only ¼ of the sponge as a starter, reserving the rest for use in future loaves. Since most home cooks don't have the patience to keep a starter going in the refrigerator, I decided to deviate from his recipe by using the entire sponge in a single loaf.

It worked well. As I had expected, there was more flavor than with a quick rise using a greater amount of packaged yeast. In fact, I only used ½ teaspoon dry yeast (most recipes call for up to a tablespoon) for 6 cups of flour. I also varied Bertolli's sponge recipe by increasing the amount of whole wheat flour to 50 percent for added flavor and texture.

Having figured out my sponge recipe, the next step was a trip to California, where I visited Steve Sullivan at the Acme Bakery in Berkeley. Steve, formerly the bread baker for Chez Panisse, is no French-cuff yuppie. I was immediately struck by his total focus on the very *idea* of bread, to the exclusion of his physical surroundings, which consisted of a disheveled room above the bakery, stuffed with an industrial-size washer and dryer, empty detergent bottles, and a garage-sale-quality sofa and chair.

Steve echoed what many experts had told me: bread with a high water content produces a chewier texture. However, like most bread professionals, Steve threw around water percentages like softballs.

Ed Behr, editor and publisher of the newsletter *The Art of Eating,* finally sat me down and explained it. To figure out the amount of water as a percentage of the flour (by weight), simply calculate the weight in grams of the water in the recipe (each cup of water weighs 237.5 grams) and divide that by the weight of the flour (a cup of flour weighs 130 grams), then multiply by 100.

From this conversation and from a seminar I attended in San Francisco led by Joe Ortiz, author of *The Village Baker,* and David Leider, author of *Bread Alone,* I concluded that a water content of 68 percent would be about right. The theory was that the higher percentage of water — most bread recipes run around 60 percent — would make the bread chewier. I tried it, but with mediocre results. It was good bread, but it lacked the big-league chewiness I was seeking.

About this time, my wife came across Iggy's Bakery, just outside Boston. Their bread was perfect: very chewy, very crusty, and very flavorful. I rushed out to meet Igor, the chief baker, who reinforced my ideas about a wet dough. When I stuck my hand into his vats of dough, I found a sticky mass that would just about pour. Eureka! My idea of bread dough had always been a nonstick, satiny ball, easy to handle and more solid than liquid. But this stuff puddled and pulled; it shimmied and shook. Igor also told me that he used a mixture of three flours — high-protein, whole wheat, and rye — for reasons having to do with both flavor and texture. I hurried home to duplicate what I had seen.

First, I increased the water to near-dangerous levels, using 2½ cups of water to 6 cups of flour, which brought the percentage of water to flour up to a whopping 76 per-

cent, a percentage so high it borders on heresy. However, this high water content was slightly counteracted by the fact that 25 percent of the flour was whole wheat and rye. I had chosen them for flavor and sourness, but both of them also absorb more water than white flour does. The other 75 percent of the flour was a high-protein white flour given to me by Igor.

Professional bakers use giant mixers and special shaping machines, which can easily handle very moist dough. At home, the dough stuck to my hands, to the wooden counter, to the bowl, to the damp dishtowel, and even to the heavily floured peel. I tried to knead the dough by hand, but it was almost impossible. But at the end of the day, the bread was a big advance on my previous efforts. Although the texture was a bit sticky, it had cavernous air holes and was wonderfully chewy. This was an inside-the-park home run, but it still needed a few refinements.

HIGH-PROTEIN FLOUR VERSUS ALL-PURPOSE

I now turned my attention to the flour. Previously I had been using a high-protein flour (13.8 percent protein) obtained from a professional baker. Now I decided to try loaves made with all-purpose flour and with regular bread flour to see if the protein content had a noticeable effect on the finished product.

The results were fascinating. The dough made with regular bread flour, while wetter than that made with Iggy's high-protein flour, was workable; the all-purpose flour yielded a dough so wet it couldn't be handled at all. After additional testing, it became clear that the higher-protein flour could absorb more water, so the recipe had to be adjusted for the different flours. When I reduced the amount of water from 1½ cups to 1⅓ cups for the bread flour and from 1½ cups to 1¼ cups for the all-purpose flour, the results were fine. (An additional 1 cup water had already been used to make the

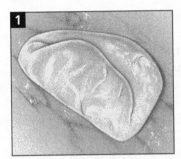 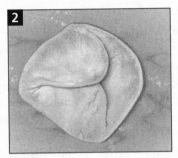 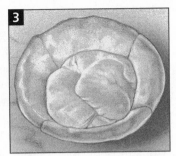

1. To shape a round loaf for the second rise, flatten the dough gently into a round. Fold in one edge toward the middle.
2. Repeat with the other three sides, always folding toward the middle.
3. Let loaf rise, folded side up, in a colander lined with a floured kitchen towel or pie pastry cloth and covered loosely with aluminum foil. You can also use a banneton, which is a basket lined with muslin. They are available through the King Arthur Flour baking catalog.

starter.) In fact, the regular bread flour was better, yielding a good chewy crumb.

How to Knead and Handle a "Stickum" Dough

While it can be done, kneading by hand was not my first choice. To get around it, I first tried using a food processor with the metal blade. This worked fine, except that my $250 machine sounded like a lawnmower in a dense patch of weeds; all that was missing was the curl of blue smoke and the smell of burning rubber. The machine simply could not handle 8½ cups of quicksand. So I divided the recipe into two batches and tried again. This worked pretty well. I found that leaving the metal blade in the processor between batches is best (although you won't get all of the first batch of dough out of the processor bowl). Otherwise, your hands will get sticky and dough may ooze out around the center core of the bowl during the second batch. Also, I found that the machine worked fine for the first 25–30 seconds and then started to slow down. My processor can *just* handle the load (although it seemed compelled to walk across the counter like a dog off its leash). I recommend you process for 30–40 seconds, which is enough time to knead the dough. And I only recommend this method if you have a good-quality, heavy-duty processor.

The best way to knead the dough was in a heavy-duty standing mixer with a dough hook. Using this, I simply threw in the ingredients, mixed them briefly with a large, stiff rubber spatula, and then turned the machine on at its lowest setting for 15 minutes. (As mentioned earlier in this chapter, mixing times are not precise. Fifteen minutes is a good "safe" amount of time — the bread will be neither over- nor underkneaded — but I have run the mixer for as little as 10 minutes and still turned out a good loaf.) When the kneading was done, I transferred the dough to an oiled bowl, covered it with plastic wrap, and let it rise for about 2 hours, until it tripled in volume. Allowing the dough to triple in volume improved its rustic flavor and helped it develop more "muscle" so that it would maintain its shape.

Even after the dough was mixed and kneaded, it was a problem to handle. For the first rise, you can use a rubber spatula to transfer the wet dough to an oiled bowl or plastic tub. After letting the dough rise, use the same spatula to transfer the dough onto a lightly floured surface. Flour both the dough and your hands (the former lightly), then press the dough very gently into a disk and fold the edges in toward the middle (see illustrations). Note that you should handle the dough as little as possible at this point, both because it is still sticky (you'll be tempted to add extra flour) and because excessive handling is bad for rustic bread — you want an irregular texture with lots of air holes.

Incidentally, from here on out, the best way to move the dough is to use a large dough scraper, two metal spatulas, or a thin, flat-edged floured cookie sheet.

Transfer the dough, smooth side down, into a colander or basket that has been lined with a piece of cloth (muslin, linen, or a cotton pastry cloth) into which plenty of flour has been rubbed to prevent sticking.

The dough needs to be covered during the second rise. I tried using a damp dishtowel as a cover, but it stuck to the dough, and unwrapping it was like unwrapping a piece of salt-water taffy on a hot day. Aluminum foil works best because the dough is less likely to stick to it, and because, since it does not form a tight seal like plastic wrap, it allows the dough to breathe. This in turn causes the dough to rise less, which is important, because allowing the dough to rise too much at this point will produce a dough with fluffy texture that will lose its shape when transferred to the peel.

Salt and Honey

I also wanted to experiment with varying the amount of salt as well as testing the impact of other ingredients. Most recipes with 6 cups of flour use 2 teaspoons of salt. I found this amount of salt insufficient and boosted it to a generous tablespoon. (These quantities are for kosher salt. If you use regular table salt, use 2 teaspoons.)

Next, I decided to try a little sweetness to boost flavor and promote browning. I added 2 tablespoons of barley malt (which I subsequently changed to honey for the sake of convenience). The flavor was better with the sweetener, and the crust was a rich nut-brown.

Does Steam Make a Better Crust?

The major issue with a country bread is the texture of the crust. The key to a great crust,

according to most of the experts, is steam. To test this theory, I baked one loaf with no steam at all. The crust was thin and unappealing. The truth is that bread *does* need steam, but there are many ways to provide it. Some bakers throw ice cubes on the floor of the oven. Others pour hot water into a pan at the beginning of baking. Some use a spritzer and mist the outside of the dough every few minutes.

My tests showed that the pan of hot water is the best option. This was confirmed by Steve Sullivan, who noted that it takes 225 calories (calories are a measurement of heat expended — the more calories used, the more the oven will drop in temperature) to turn a gram of ice into steam, and only 120 calories to turn an equal amount of tap water into steam. So why throw ice into an oven where you want lots of heat? My tests confirmed that ice cubes lower oven temperature much more than hot water. A head-to-head test also proved that you get a better crust with hot water versus ice cubes. As a side note, if you count yourself among the ice cube flingers, be aware that you could blow out the heating element in an electric oven if you don't throw the ice cubes into a container (this also goes for throwing tap water onto the floor of the oven).

And speaking of containers, I put my water for steaming in a small *preheated* pan placed on a separate rack in the oven. The theory among bread pros is that you want steam immediately, in the first few minutes of baking. A cold pan will not do the trick — the hot water will just sit there. By using 2 cups of boiling water, you get both instant steam and enough residual water to keep a nice steamy environment throughout the cooking process. A preheated pan, however, will vaporize some of the hot water the second it is poured in, which leads me to the issue of safety. Wear thick oven mitts and a long-sleeved shirt when pouring the hot water into the pan — a long-spouted watering can works well. Finally, I tested spritzing the bread every few minutes. The results were poor — a thin, pliable crust. So use hot water, preheat the pan, and most of all, no peeking! If you open the door in the first 20 minutes of baking, you'll let out the steam.

OVEN TEMPERATURE AND BAKING TIME

Most bread recipes say that bread should be baked to an internal temperature of 190°F. This produces undercooked bread, at least with my very wet recipe. This bread needs to reach 208°F. You can measure this by pushing an instant-read thermometer halfway into the loaf from the bottom. When the bread reaches this temperature, it should also have a very dark brown crust. If you do not have an instant-read thermometer, just bake the bread until the crust starts to turn brownish black in spots.

I tried starting the bread off in a 500° oven and then immediately turning the oven down to 400°F, on the theory that the higher temperature offsets the drop in temperature caused by opening the oven door (the dough absorbs a great deal of heat quickly). The resulting crust was thin and disappointing. So I tried starting the bread off at 500°F for 15 minutes and then reducing the temperature to 400°F. This time the crust was scorched — it cooked so fast that the interior did not have time to cook properly. The best baking temperature turned out to be a constant 450°F.

Rustic Country Bread

Whole wheat and rye flours contribute to this bread's full flavor, and extra oven time gives the bread its thick crust. Because of its high water content, the bread will be gummy if it is undercooked. To check doneness, make sure its internal temperature has reached 208°F by inserting an instant-read thermometer halfway through the loaf from the bottom. Also look at the crust — it should be very dark brown, almost black. Because the dough is so sticky, a heavy-duty standing mixer is best for kneading, but food processor and hand-kneading instructions follow this recipe. Keep in mind that rising times vary, and the times listed below are minimums. You can vary the bread's texture by increasing or decreasing the amount of flour. For bread with a finer crumb and a less chewy texture, experiment with increasing the flour in ¼ cup increments. For coarser, chewier bread, decrease the flour ¼ cup each time you bake it, till you get the texture you like. Your oven will give a much more even heat if you lay out a baking platform of quarry tiles on the rack before preheating. If you decide to do this, preheating will take longer.

Sponge
½ teaspoon active dry yeast (not rapid-rise)
1 cup cool water
1 cup bread flour
1 cup whole wheat flour

Dough
3½ cups bread flour
½ cup rye flour
1⅓ cups warm water
2 tablespoons honey
1 generous tablespoon kosher salt or 2 teaspoons table salt

Coarse cornmeal for sprinkling on peel

1. For the sponge, dissolve yeast into water in medium-size bowl. With rubber spatula, mix in flours to create a stiff, wet dough. Cover tightly with plastic wrap; let sit at room temperature for at least 5 hours, preferably overnight.

2. For the dough, use rubber spatula to mix flours, water, honey, and sponge in bowl of an electric standing mixer. Knead, using dough hook attachment, on lowest speed until dough is smooth, about 15 minutes, adding salt during final 3 minutes. Transfer dough to large, lightly oiled bowl. Cover with plastic wrap; let rise until tripled in size, at least 2 hours.

3. Turn dough onto lightly floured surface. Lightly dust hands and top of dough with

flour. Lightly press dough into a disk. Fold edges toward center, overlapping them slightly (see illustrations, page 331). Transfer dough, smooth side down, to colander or basket lined with heavily floured muslin. Cover loosely with large sheet of aluminum foil; let rise until almost doubled in size, at least 45 minutes.

4. As soon as dough begins to rise, adjust oven rack to low-center position and arrange quarry tiles to form 18 x 12-inch surface (or larger). On lowest oven rack, place small baking pan or cast iron skillet to hold water. Heat oven to 450°F.

5. Liberally sprinkle coarse cornmeal over entire surface of a baker's peel. Invert dough onto peel and remove muslin. Use scissors or serrated knife to cut 3 slashes on top of dough.

6. Slide dough, with a quick jerk, from peel onto preheated tiles. Carefully add 2 cups hot water to pan or cast iron skillet. Bake until instant-read thermometer, when inserted halfway into bottom of loaf, registers 208°F and crust is very dark brown, 35–40 minutes, turning bread around after 25 minutes if not browning evenly. Turn

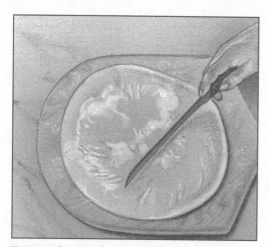

To score the top of a loaf before baking, use a serrated knife. A razor blade or scissors also work, but I find a serrated knife easiest. If the bread is not scored, the dough may erupt as it bakes, creating a misshapen loaf.

oven off, open door completely, and let bread remain in oven 10 minutes longer. Remove from oven, then let cool on a cake rack to room temperature before slicing, about 2 hours. To crisp the crust, bake in a 400°F oven for 10 minutes.

Makes 1 round loaf

Note: Regular supermarket bread flour has a protein content of 12–13 percent, whereas the flour I prefer to use is closer to 14 percent. (This type of flour is available from the King Arthur Company. Call them at 800-827-6836 or write to Baker's Catalogue, Box 876, Norwich, VT 05055). If you wish to use this high-protein flour, increase the water in the dough from 1⅓ cups to 1½ cups. You might also try making this recipe with King Arthur all-purpose flour, decreasing the water from 1⅓ cups to 1¼ cups. The results are good, although I find the bread to be a bit tougher in texture than I like.

Food Processor Variation

To knead the dough, mix half of sponge, half of flours, and half of honey in food processor fitted with metal blade. Pulse until roughly blended, 3–4 one-second pulses. With machine running, slowly add ⅔ cup water through the feed tube; process until dough forms a ball. Let sit for 3 minutes, then add half the salt, and process to form smooth dough, about 30 seconds longer. Transfer dough to large, lightly oiled bowl, leaving the metal blade in the processor (some dough will remain under blade). Repeat process with remaining half of ingredients. Proceed with recipe.

Hand-Kneaded Variation

To knead by hand, place sponge and all dough ingredients except 2 cups of bread flour in large bowl. Stir mixture with a wooden spoon, about 5 minutes. Work in reserved flour and turn dough out onto floured board. Knead by hand 5 minutes, incorporating no more than ¼ cup additional flour. Dough will be *very* wet and sticky. Proceed with recipe.

AMERICAN LOAF BREADS

American loaf breads are quite different from their European cousins; they contain fat, in the form of milk and melted butter. This produces a more tender crumb, a softer loaf that is best for sandwiches, for which a less assertive slab of bread is best suited (notwithstanding the current ill-conceived trend of using focaccia and other industrial-strength loaves for this purpose). The greatest impediment to the whole process is, of course, the notion of kneading bread dough by hand. So I tested hand-kneaded bread against bread kneaded by machine, both in a standing mixer and in a food processor, since most home kitchens have one or the other of these appliances but not both. The recipe contained 3½ cups unbleached all-purpose flour, 1 heaping teaspoon salt, 2 tablespoons honey, 1 package rapid-rise yeast, 1 cup warm milk, ⅓ cup warm water, and 2 tablespoons melted butter. The results were eye-opening. *The hand-kneaded loaf was not as good as the two loaves made by machine!* It was denser and did not rise as well, and the flavor was lacking the pleasant yeastiness found in the other loaves. After some additional testing and discussion, I hit on a reasonable explanation. When kneading by hand, most home cooks cannot resist the temptation of adding too much additional flour, because bread dough is notoriously sticky. In a machine, however, no additional flour is added and the resulting bread has the correct proportions of liquid to flour.

DOUGH HOOK VERSUS PADDLE ATTACHMENT

Now that I knew that machine-made bread was actually preferable to the hand method, I set out to refine the techniques. Starting with the standing mixer, I tested the dough hook versus the paddle attachment. The hook is vastly preferable, as the dough quickly gets caught in the paddle, which requires frequent starting and stopping to free it. However, even with the dough hook, the machine must be stopped two or three times to release the dough from the hook. Keep in mind that the dough will stay adhered to the hook for most of the kneading process, which is fine unless it creeps too far toward the top (at which point the dough must be released). I also found that a medium-speed setting (number 4 on the KitchenAid mixer) is better than a slow setting. Although the hook appears to move at an alarming rate, the resulting centrifugal force throws the dough off the hook, resulting in a more thorough kneading.

BREAD FLOUR VERSUS ALL-PURPOSE FLOUR

I discovered that bread flour is preferable to all-purpose when using a standing mixer (although all-purpose was best in the food processor). This is because bread flour has a higher gluten content, which improves the bread's capacity for expansion during rising, which in turn yields a lighter, more delicate bread appropriate for an American loaf. With a food processor, a bit of hand kneading turned out to be recommended after kneading in the machine. Four minutes of kneading on a floured surface improved both the rise and the flavor. However, this required additional flour for the hand kneading (so that the dough did not get too sticky).

This anomaly is consistent with the experience of commercial bakers. They use very high-protein flours in their machines rather than a lower-protein variety such as all-purpose, which seems to be better suited for kneading methods that produce loaves with lower moisture content.

HOW MUCH SALT? HOW MUCH HONEY?

The master recipe I was trying to develop was short on flavor so I tested adding more salt, more honey, and more melted butter; tried canola oil instead of butter; and tried sugar instead of honey. The extra salt (1 tablespoon kosher, up from half that amount) and honey (3 tablespoons, up from 2) were a big improvement. Extra butter made the bread too rich and dense, the canola oil turned out a very dull-tasting loaf, and the honey won out over the sugar.

What About Oven Temperature and Baking Times?

Testing oven temperatures at 350°, 375°, and 400°F, I found that the higher temperatures overcooked the crust by the time the inside of the loaf was done. Unlike most European breads, this American loaf — because it contains milk, butter, and honey — is prone to quick browning. (Fats and sugars enhance the browning process.) Most cookbooks tell you to tap the bottom of a loaf to see if it is done. This is, at best, an inexact method. It is much better to use an instant-read thermometer, inserting it halfway into the loaf in the middle of the bottom. When bread was tested at 190°, 195°, and 200°F internal temperature, the 195° reading was clearly the winner. (This is in contrast to the Rustic Country Bread, which is a wetter dough and requires cooking to a higher temperature.) The lower temperature produced dense bread, and at the higher temperature the bread was dry and overcooked. It should be noted that how long you bake bread has a tremendous effect on texture and quality, and therefore the judicious use of an instant-read thermometer is critical.

How to Shape a Loaf

I tried four different shaping methods and found that the simplest methods were best. First, risen dough was pressed into a rectangle 1 inch thick and no wider than the length of the pan. It was then rolled into a cylinder and turned seam side up, and the seam was pinched closed. The loaf was then placed into the pan seam side down. The rise

was excellent, although the side of the top of the loaf can crack during baking, an effect I find pleasing. Instead of making a rectangle, you can roughly shape the dough into a loaf, patting it and turning the edges underneath and pinching the bottom seam together. Turn the ends under and pinch those to seal as well, then plump the loaf with your hands and place seam side down in the pan. Either of these methods works fine and results in a good rise.

A number of other bread books suggest the following methods, which I found to be inferior due to a lower rise. (It is my opinion that bread dough should be handled gently between rises, with no kneading and a minimum of handling. Overworking the dough at this point will make a squatter, denser loaf.) For the first method, the dough was flattened into a rectangle about 12 inches long and 10 inches wide. It was then folded like a business letter, turned seam side down, and pinched along the seam to seal. The ends were turned under and pinched. The finished loaf was squat in appearance, without the soaring, high-cap rise that I like from a loaf-pan bread. The last method was similar — the rectangle was folded in half, not thirds, and then the dough was rolled toward the baker until the seam side was up. Then, a deep crease was formed along the seam line with the fingertips, the dough was folded in half along this line to shape a cylinder, and the edges were pinched to seal. This loaf also suffered from a lack of rise, and the top of the baked bread had unsightly "stretch marks."

THE BEST AMERICAN LOAF

At the end of two months of testing, I had produced a terrific loaf of bread in just 2 hours start to finish. Using rapid-rise yeast, the dough is kneaded in a standing mixer for 10 minutes and then by hand for a mere 15 seconds. It is proofed in a warmed oven for only 40 minutes, at which point it is gently shaped and placed in a loaf pan. The second rising takes 20 minutes, and then the dough is baked at a moderate 350°F for 30–40 minutes or until the internal temperature reaches 195°F. This recipe can also be made in a food processor or by hand, methods requiring more hands-on kneading. I've also added six variations on the master recipe, for oatmeal bread, whole wheat bread, and the like.

Master Recipe for No-Knead American Bread

This recipe uses a standing electric mixer, but a food processor variation also follows. You can make this recipe by hand, but I found during testing that too much flour will be added, resulting in a somewhat inferior loaf. (Sticky dough is difficult to knead, and most home cooks will overcompensate by adding too much extra flour.) If you do not have bread flour, you can substitute all-purpose (the bread flour will make slightly better bread). If you have buttermilk, I suggest you make the Buttermilk Variation that follows the master recipe. It won my taste test hands down.

- 3½ cups bread flour
- 2 teaspoons table salt or 1 tablespoon kosher salt
- 3 tablespoons honey
- 1 cup warm milk (110°F) or, preferably, buttermilk (see variation below)
- ⅓ cup warm water (110°F)
- 2 tablespoons butter, melted
- 1 package rapid-rise yeast

1. Heat oven to 200°F for 10 minutes and turn off. Place flour, salt, and honey in the bowl of a standing mixer fitted with a dough hook. In a separate bowl, combine the milk, water, and butter and add yeast, stirring to dissolve. Turn mixer on to low and slowly add the yeast mixture. When dough comes together, increase speed to medium (setting number 4 on a KitchenAid mixer) and mix

for 10 minutes. The dough will be sticky and adhere to the hook. Stop the machine two or three times and scrape the dough from the hook with a rubber spatula. If dough is too wet, add more flour 1 tablespoon at a time.

2. Turn dough onto lightly floured work surface. Knead by hand for 15 seconds.

3. Form dough into a round and place, top side down, in a *very lightly* oiled bowl. Rub dough top around bowl to lightly coat with oil. Turn dough right side up. Cover bowl with plastic wrap and place in warm oven until dough doubles in size, about 40 minutes. When dough has risen sufficiently, remove bowl from oven and heat oven to 350°F, placing an empty loaf pan on the bottom rack. Grease a 9 x 5 x 3-inch loaf pan.

4. Turn dough out onto a lightly floured surface and gently press into a rectangle 1 inch thick and no wider than the length of the loaf pan. Roll it firmly into a cylinder, pressing gently with your fingers with each turn to make sure the dough sticks to itself. Turn seam side up and pinch seam closed. Place dough in pan seam side down and press gently so that dough touches all four sides of pan.

5. Cover pan with plastic wrap and set aside in a warm spot for 20 minutes or until dough doubles in size. Bring 2 cups of water to boil.

6. When loaf has risen sufficiently, remove plastic wrap. Place pan in oven and immediately pour heated water into the preheated empty loaf pan. Close oven door and bake until an instant-read thermometer inserted halfway into the bottom of the loaf reads 195°F, about 30–40 minutes. Remove bread from pan and cool on a rack.

Makes 1 loaf

Food Processor Method

Substitute all-purpose flour for bread flour in the master recipe, using all of the other ingredients as listed. Heat oven to 200°F for 10 minutes and turn off. Place flour and salt in the bowl of a food processor fitted with a steel blade and pulse to combine. Add honey. In a separate bowl, combine the milk, water, and butter and add yeast, stirring to dissolve. With the machine running, pour this liquid through the feed tube and process until a rough ball forms. (Check feed tube to make sure that no clumps of yeast or thickened butter are left behind.) If dough is too wet, add flour, 1 tablespoon at a time, and process until dough forms into a rough but solid mass. Let dough rest 2 minutes. Process for 35 seconds. Turn dough onto a lightly floured work surface and knead by hand for 4–5 minutes. Dough will be sticky, but avoid adding too much extra flour. Follow directions in master recipe beginning with step 3.

Slow-Rise Variation

If you do not have rapid-rise yeast on hand, use cake yeast (1 small cake) or regular active dry yeast (1 envelope), and do not do the first rise in a preheated oven. (Cake yeast produces superior-tasting bread, although it can be difficult to find.) The first rise will take about 2 hours, and the second rise will take 45–60 minutes. Times will vary depending on the ambient temperature and how many yeast spores are floating around your kitchen. (Home cooks who bake bread frequently find that their rising times diminish, since the kitchen is full of active yeast spores, which provide extra lift to the rising dough.) Keep in mind that our taste tests revealed that rapid-rise yeast produces excellent bread, somewhat sweeter in flavor then regular yeast, and therefore you are not sacrificing quality when you use the rapid-rise variety.

Buttermilk Variation

Substitute buttermilk for milk but don't heat it. Increase the first rise to 50 minutes. Buttermilk makes a substantially better bread than regular milk.

Whole Wheat Variation

Replace 1⅓ cups of flour with whole wheat flour. Increase the first rise to 50 minutes and the second rise to 40 minutes.

Oatmeal Variation

Cook ¾ cup rolled oats in ¾ cup boiling water for 90 seconds. Reduce flour to 2¾ cups. Add ¾ cups of the cooked oatmeal to flour and eliminate the water. Bake for 45 minutes or until internal temperature reaches 195°F.

Oatmeal-Raisin Variation

Follow the Oatmeal Variation and add ¾ cup of raisins tossed with 1 tablespoon of flour to the dough after it comes out of either the mixer or food processor. Knead the dough briefly to work in the raisins. Bake for 45 minutes or until internal temperature reaches 195°F.

Cornmeal Variation

Bring ½ cup water to a boil. Slowly whisk in ¼ cup cornmeal. Cook for 1 minute, stirring constantly. The mixture will be very thick. Replace honey with dark brown sugar. Reduce milk to ¾ cup. Add cornmeal mixture to the flour and mix briefly before incorporating the liquids.

Anadama Bread Variation

Follow the recipe for Cornmeal Variation, but use molasses instead of brown sugar.

Master Recipe for 2-Hour European White Bread

This recipe is a variation on the No-Knead American Bread above. I call this European bread because it uses water not milk and is a sturdier, toothier loaf than the softer American loaves. You can double this recipe, but a food processor cannot handle a double amount of dough at one time. If you wish to use this kneading method (instructions follow the master recipe), process the dough in two batches. This dough can also be kneaded entirely by hand for about 10 minutes. The master recipe uses a loaf pan for baking the bread, but you can also shape the dough into a round free-form loaf or a long, slender French bread loaf (see the variations below).

3½ cups unbleached bread flour
1 tablespoon kosher salt or 2 teaspoons table salt
2 tablespoons honey
1⅓ cups hot water (125°F)
1 package rapid-rise yeast

1. Heat oven to 200°F for 10 minutes and turn off. Place flour, salt, and honey in the bowl of a standing mixer fitted with a dough hook. In a separate bowl, combine the water and yeast, stirring to dissolve. Turn machine to low and slowly add the liquid to the flour. When dough comes together, increase speed to medium (setting number 4 on a Kitchen-Aid mixer) and mix for 10 minutes. The dough will be sticky and adhere to the hook. Stop the machine two or three times and scrape the dough from the hook with a rubber spatula. If dough is too wet, add extra flour 1 tablespoon at a time.

2. Turn dough onto lightly floured work surface. Knead by hand for 15 seconds.

3. Form dough into a round and place, top side down, in a *very lightly* oiled bowl. Rub dough top around bowl to lightly coat with oil. Turn dough right side up. Cover bowl with plastic wrap and place in warm oven until dough doubles in size, about 40 minutes. When dough has risen sufficiently, remove bowl from oven and heat oven to 350°F, placing an empty loaf pan on the bottom rack. Grease a 9 x 5 x 3-inch loaf pan.

4. Turn dough out onto a lightly floured surface and gently press into a rectangle 1 inch thick and no wider than the length of the loaf pan. Roll it firmly into a cylinder, pressing gently with your fingers with each

turn to make sure the dough sticks to itself. Turn seam side up and pinch seam closed. Place dough in pan seam side down and press gently so that dough touches all four sides of pan.

5. Cover pan with plastic wrap and set aside in a warm spot for 20 minutes. Bring 2 cups of water to a boil.

6. When loaf has risen sufficiently, remove plastic wrap. Place pan in oven and immediately pour heated water into the preheated empty loaf pan. Close oven door and bake until an instant-read thermometer inserted halfway into the bottom of the loaf reads 195°F, about 30–40 minutes. Remove bread from pan and cool on a rack.

Makes 1 loaf

Food Processor Method

Substitute all-purpose flour for bread flour in the master recipe, using all of the other ingredients as listed. Heat oven to 200°F for 10 minutes and turn off. Place flour and salt in the bowl of a food processor fitted with a steel blade and pulse to combine. Add honey. In a separate bowl, combine the water and yeast, stirring to dissolve. With the machine running, pour this liquid through the feed tube and process until a rough ball forms. (Check feed tube to make sure that no clumps of yeast are left behind.) If dough is too wet, add flour, 1 tablespoon at a time, and process until dough forms into a rough but solid mass. Let dough rest 2 minutes. Process for 35 seconds. Turn dough onto a lightly floured work surface and knead by hand for 4–5 minutes. Dough will be sticky, but avoid adding too much extra flour. Follow directions in master recipe beginning with step 3.

Free-Form Variation

After the first rise, flatten dough gently into a round. Fold the top edge in toward the middle. Repeat with the other three sides, always folding toward the middle. Place dough folded side up in a colander lined with a well-floured kitchen towel or pie pastry cloth (preferable) and cover loosely with aluminum foil. Let rise 35 minutes. Turn over onto a baker's peel liberally coated with cornmeal. Score the top of the loaf in 3 or 4 places with either a serrated knife, a razor blade, or a pair of scissors (open them wide and then make a shallow cut in the top of the loaf). Bread should be baked in a preheated 350° oven on baking tiles or a pizza stone.

French Bread Variation

After the first rise, halve the dough and set aside one half. Working on a well-floured surface, press the first piece into a rectangle about 7 inches long. Fold in thirds like a business letter and then, using the side of your hand, make a trough down the center of the dough. Now fold the dough along the trough and pinch to seal. Use your palms to roll the length of dough back and forth on the work surface, working from the center toward the ends, until you have shaped a loaf that is about 16 inches long. Place the dough in a French bread pan, seam side down. Repeat with second half of dough. When both loaves have been shaped and placed in pans, let rise 35 minutes in a warm spot, covered with a damp dishtowel. If you do not have French bread pans, place the loaves on a well-floured pastry cloth and cover with a damp dishtowel (the dishtowel should not actually touch the dough and needs to be propped up like a flat-topped tent). After the second rise, slide the baguettes seam side down onto a baker's peel or a baking sheet well coated with cornmeal. Slide the loaves from the peel or baking sheet onto preheated baking tiles, pizza stone, or baking sheet. Although the peel method is more difficult, I find that it makes superior bread, because the dough is sitting on a very hot surface rather than on a room-tempera-ture bread pan. French bread takes 20–25 minutes to bake.

Slow-Rise Variation

If you cannot find rapid-rise yeast, use regular active dry yeast (1 packet) or cake yeast (1 small cake) and do not do the first rise in a preheated oven. The first rise will take about 2 hours, and the second rise will take 45–60 minutes. Times will vary depending on the ambient temperature and how many yeast spores are floating around your kitchen. (Home cooks who bake bread frequently find that their rising times diminish, since the kitchen is full of active yeast spores, which provide extra lift to the rising dough.)

BREAD MACHINE BREAD

Bread baked in a bread machine just isn't very good. In my tests, I found that these loaves have a spongy texture, almost cake-like, with less chew and a more open, flimsier structure. I used a recipe for basic bread machine white bread and then tried a half-dozen variations, including the basic recipe that came with the machine. The crust was brown but almost crunchy, more like the crust of a slightly overcooked angel food cake (the interior of the loaf also felt a bit like angel food cake). I then decided to do a test, baking a loaf of bread in a bread machine and then, using the same recipe, using the bread machine to proof the dough through the first rise, then removing it, shaping it, letting it rise a second time in a basket, and baking it in a conventional oven. The oven-baked loaf was vastly better, with good crust and quite a different interior texture, more like a regular loaf of bread. The bread machine is a great kneading and proofing box but useless for baking. Leave that to your oven.

I then discovered that as long as the bread machine is not used as an oven, special recipes are unnecessary, other than adjusting for the size of the machine. Bread machines are finicky, and a specific machine often needs a customized recipe that suits its particular characteristics. When the machine is used simply for kneading and proofing dough, however, you can use any of the master recipes above. But you will have to reduce the quantities used in order to accommodate the particular model you are working with. Just look at the recipe book that comes with the machine as a guide to quantities.

38

How to Make Dinner Rolls

The best dinner rolls use bread flour (not all-purpose), half water and half milk, and a whopping ¼ cup sugar.

~

In 1959 my family moved into a new house, a big box of a place with a long, winding staircase, a wonderful old pantry with a deep soapstone sink, and a dining room with a fireplace and a pair of elegant French doors leading to the main hall. What I remember most about that house, however, is dinnertime. It was quite formal, served exactly at 7 o'clock, and my sister and I were expected to be nicely dressed (a tie and a jacket were mandatory for males), nails clipped and hair brushed. And, of course, we were expected to be on time. Dinnertime was not a quick feed; both the food and the conversation were taken seriously. And so were the dinner rolls. This was not some sort of thrown-together al fresco supper with baskets of thick, coarse country bread. This was refined suburban food with homemade crescent rolls one night and Parker House rolls the next. Even the rolls had to dress for dinner.

Since then, I've used all sorts of recipes for dinner rolls, from a mother-in-law recipe cut out of a 1960s *Ladies Home Journal* to a basic American white bread recipe shaped into crescents and fans. Over the years, I had devised a hybrid formula, taking the best features of each of these recipes. It contained 2 teaspoons vegetable oil, 2 eggs, 4 tablespoons butter, 2 cups hot milk, 6 cups all-purpose flour, 2 tablespoons sugar, and 1 package dry yeast. The dough was mixed in a standing mixer with a dough hook or paddle, allowed to rise for about 90 minutes, shaped, and then set aside for a second rise.

When it came time to write this book, I decided to take a new look at this old standby. I also wanted to test a number of variations, including using a whisk instead of a dough hook with the mixer, using the food processor to knead, a quick version using rapid-rise yeast and a warm oven for proofing, and a slow version using an overnight starter for flavor.

TESTING THE BASIC INGREDIENTS

I started by increasing the butter to 6 tablespoons; this resulted in no change in either texture or flavor. I then replaced half the milk with water, which gave the rolls a bit more body. Bread flour instead of all-purpose made a finer roll, with a softer texture (I had to use an additional 2 tablespoons of water, as bread flour has more gluten, which absorbs liquid readily). Two packages of yeast instead of 1 gave the rolls some kick; they were fluffier and

Shouldn't Bread Flour, with More Gluten, Produce a Chewier, Rougher Dinner Roll?

The simple answer is no. Bread flour has a lot of gluten, a protein substance, which, when subjected to kneading and the presence of water, will form a cohesive, elastic structure. (Cake flour is "soft" and has little gluten; all-purpose flour has a moderate amount.) Before kneading begins, the gluten molecules are coiled chains of amino acids, which fold back onto themselves in mutual attraction. Kneading unfolds and aligns these chains to form a structure that becomes more regular. However, the gluten molecules still have kinks in them capable of expanding and also contracting, which is the essence of elasticity. Flour with a lot of gluten molecules, therefore, makes for a more elastic dough. This structure, when in the presence of active yeast, will do a good job of containing the resulting carbon dioxide gas. This makes for a better rise, which in turn results in a lighter, finer loaf of bread. Think of a balloon. Bread flour, with lots of gluten, is quite good at making balloons that expand readily. All-purpose flour, on the other hand, isn't quite as good at trapping gases and results in a slightly less inflated "balloon." So if you want more chew, don't use bread flour, use all-purpose.

livelier. I also increased the sugar from 2 tablespoons to ¼ cup, which boosted the flavor. I tried adding another teaspoon of salt, which was a failure — the rolls were unpleasantly salty.

VARIATIONS IN METHODS

There are many ways to knead bread dough. You can do it by hand, which requires no special equipment. However, I usually rely on a large standing electric mixer, using either the dough hook or paddle attachment. Many cooks don't have either of these attachments and must use the basic whisk or beaters that come with the machine. With my master dinner roll recipe, I have included a simple variation for the whisk, which involves a combination of electric mixing and hand kneading.

A food processor, which I have found successful for kneading both regular bread doughs and pizza doughs, can also be used for dinner rolls. The problem is that a food processor can handle only half the master recipe at one time. Half the dry ingredients are added to the workbowl and pulsed. Then half the liquid ingredients are added through the feed tube with the machine running. When the dough forms into a cohesive ball, the machine is shut off and the dough rests for 2 minutes. Finally, the machine is run for an additional 35 seconds, the dough is removed and hand-kneaded for a minute, and then the whole process is repeated a second time with the remaining ingredients. All things considered, I feel that the food processor method is by far the best for a half recipe, but a standing mixer is a lot easier for the full amount.

I was also interested in using an overnight starter, the method I had developed for my recipe for Rustic Country Bread (see Chapter 37). One cup each of water and flour are mixed together, along with ½ teaspoon active dry yeast. The mixture is left on the counter overnight, where it bubbles and develops flavor. This is used the next day as the starter for the dough. In a blind tasting, I could not tell the difference between this variation and the master recipe. The reason is that this dough has plenty of milk and sugar and subtle variations in flavor are easily missed. This was clearly a case of taking a simple recipe and making it unnecessarily complicated.

Finally, I tried out my superfast pizza dough method on dinner rolls and it worked just fine. The liquids are added hot, not warm, to the flour and yeast, a preheated oven is used as a proofing box, and the recipe calls for rapid-rise yeast. I was able to make dinner rolls in about 90 minutes start to finish. This was a winner.

How to Make the Best Dinner Roll

Kitchen testing was based on a recipe I had been using for several years, which contained 2 teaspoons vegetable oil, 2 eggs, 4 tablespoons butter, 2 cups hot milk, 6 cups all-purpose flour, 2 tablespoons sugar, and 1 package active dry yeast. These are some of the ingredient variations I tested en route to developing the Master Recipe for Dinner Rolls.

Variation	Results
Increase butter to 6 tablespoons	No change in flavor or texture
Use half water and half milk	A little better texture; slightly better chew
Use bread flour and increase water by 2 tablespoons	Finer and softer texture
Use 2 packages yeast instead of 1	Fluffier, livelier rolls
Use buttermilk instead of sweet milk	Much greater rise, which does not work well with most dinner roll shapes; rolls look bloated
Increase sugar by 1 tablespoon	Better flavor but not sweet
Increase salt by 1 teaspoon	Too salty

Master Recipe for Dinner Rolls

This is a simple master recipe for dinner rolls, which then can be shaped into Parker House rolls, crescents, or any other shape desired.

- 2 eggs
- 2 teaspoons vegetable oil
- 6 cups bread flour or all-purpose flour (bread flour is preferred although only slightly better for this recipe)
- ¼ cup sugar
- 1 tablespoon kosher salt
- 2 packages active dry yeast
- 4 tablespoons butter, softened
- 1 cup hot milk (125°F)
- 1 cup hot water (125°F)
- 6–8 tablespoons butter, melted, for brushing on shaped rolls

1. Whisk together 2 eggs. Grease a large bowl with 2 teaspoons oil and set aside.

2. Combine flour, sugar, salt, yeast, and softened butter in the bowl of a standing mixer fitted with either the paddle attachment or dough hook. Turn speed to low. Gradually pour in hot milk and water while mixing. Add beaten eggs. Beat on low for a total of 12 minutes.

3. Remove dough from mixer and knead by hand for 1 minute or until smooth and elastic. Shape into a ball and place into greased bowl. Turn dough upside down in bowl so that the top is now greased. Cover bowl with a damp kitchen towel or plastic wrap. Place in a warm, draft-free environment and allow dough to rise until doubled in size, approximately 1½ hours.

4. Punch dough down gently and turn onto a lightly floured surface. Form into a smooth ball. Let rest for 15 minutes covered with inverted bowl used for rising. Proceed with specific shaping instructions below.

Parker House Rolls: Place 8 tablespoons (1 stick) melted butter in a large roasting pan, making sure that bottom of pan is covered. Set aside. On a lightly floured surface, roll out dough to a ½-inch thickness. Cut circles using a 2¾-inch floured biscuit cutter. Working with one piece of dough at a time, shake off excess flour, fold piece in half, and dredge in the butter. Place rolls in the pan, flat side down and in rows, each roll slightly overlapping the last. *Makes 36 rolls.*

Crescent Rolls: On a lightly floured surface, roll ¼ of the dough into a 12-inch circle and cut into 8 wedges, like a pie. Roll up each wedge from the perimeter to the tip. Curve ends to make a crescent. Place roll on ungreased baking sheet, with central tip underneath, and brush with melted butter. Repeat with remaining dough, placing rolls 1½ inches apart. *Makes 32 rolls.*

Cloverleaf Rolls: Pinch off small amounts of dough and gently roll between the palms of your hands into 1-inch balls. Grease muf-

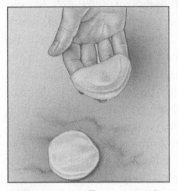

Parker House rolls are cut with a 2¾-inch biscuit cutter and folded in half. They are then dipped in butter and placed slightly overlapping in a roasting pan.

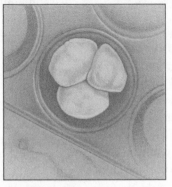

Cloverleaf rolls are made by dropping three 1-inch balls of dough into a muffin tin.

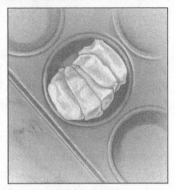

Fan rolls are fashioned from 5 stacked strips of dough, which are cut into squares and then placed end up in a muffin tin.

Crescent rolls are shaped by starting with a 12-inch-diameter circle of dough, which is cut into 8 wedges.

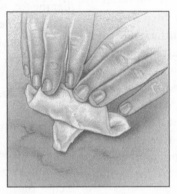

Each wedge is rolled up, starting at the widest end.

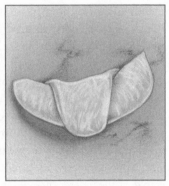

The ends are then slightly curved to shape a crescent.

fin tins and drop 3 balls into each cup. Brush with melted butter. *Makes 36 rolls.*

Fan Rolls: Roll the dough into a ⅜-inch sheet and then cut into long 1¾-inch strips. Make stacks of 5 strips each and then cut the stacks into squares. Place squares on edge in greased muffin tins. Brush with melted butter. *Makes 30 rolls.*

Round Dinner Rolls: Divide dough into 4 equal balls and cover with a damp cloth. Let rest for 10 minutes. Press the first ball flat and cut in half, then cut each half into thirds. Form a smooth ball out of each piece. Place finished balls into greased muffin tin. Repeat for remaining dough. Brush with melted butter. *Makes 24 rolls.*

5. Once the rolls have been shaped, cover loosely with a damp towel, wax paper, or aluminum foil (the covering should not touch dough — it may have to be "tented" over the rolls) and place in a warm, draft-free environment until rolls double in size, about 40 minutes. Heat oven to 400°F. Bake rolls for 18–20 minutes. Turn pan halfway through baking. Tops should be golden brown.

Whisk Attachment Variation

If you don't have a dough hook or paddle attachment, or if your standing mixer is not a heavy-duty model, follow the master recipe with these modifications. Step 2: Start with 2½ cups of flour instead of the full amount. Use the whisk attachment of an electric mixer on low speed to mix together the dry ingredients plus the softened butter, and then gradually pour in the hot milk and water while mixing. Add beaten eggs. Increase mixer speed to medium and beat for 2 minutes. Add about ¾ cup flour to thicken the dough. Continue beating for 2 minutes, adding 1 cup of flour at a time until dough forms a cohesive ball and is no longer sticky (you will use approximately 6 cups of flour in total). Step 3: Turn dough onto a lightly floured surface. Knead by hand until smooth and elastic, about 5 minutes. Shape into a ball and place into greased bowl. Turn dough upside down in bowl so that the top is now greased. Cover bowl with a damp kitchen towel or plastic wrap. Place in a warm, draft-free environment and allow dough to rise until doubled in size, approximately 1½ hours. Proceed with step 4 of the master recipe.

Food Processor Variation

This recipe can be made in a food processor fitted with the metal blade. Begin by dividing the liquid and the dry ingredients each into two equal batches, then mixing together the dry and liquid ingredients separately (do not mix in the 2 teaspoons vegetable oil, which are used to grease the bowl the dough will rise in). Place half of the dry ingredients in the workbowl of the food processor and turn on. Pour half of the liquid ingredients through feed tube until dough forms a cohesive ball. Add more flour if too wet, more liquid if too dry. Let rest for 2 minutes. Process for 35 seconds. Remove from bowl and knead by hand for 1 minute on a floured work surface. Repeat for other half of ingredients. Knead the two batches of dough together into one large ball of dough. Place dough into a greased bowl. Turn dough upside down in bowl so that the top is now greased. Cover bowl with a damp kitchen towel or plastic wrap. Place in a warm, draft-free environment and allow dough to rise until doubled in size, approximately 1½ hours. Proceed with step 4 of the master recipe.

2-Hour Dinner Roll Variation

Use rapid-rise yeast. Heat oven to 200°F for 10 minutes and turn off. Follow the master recipe or one of the variations (the food processor method is faster) and place bowl of dough in warm oven for the first rising (end of step 3). Let rise 40 minutes. Shape dough and proceed with step 5, letting dough rise the second time for 20 minutes instead of 40 minutes. Bake.

39

Pancakes, Waffles, Muffins, and Biscuits

A gentle touch and buttermilk are the secrets to successful breakfast baking.

~

Why is it that there is no common standard for a good American waffle? Some are thin, others are thick; some are soft and cakelike, others are flabby; some are rich with melted butter, others are drab, flavored with pedestrian corn oil. Some cooks beat the batter mercilessly with an electric mixer and others barely touch the batter, treating it like a potential explosive. Lots of folks use a mix and others do it all from scratch. But nobody seems to care very much about the outcome. They are "just" waffles! Well, for me, that's like saying "Have a Little Talk with Jesus" is just an old Baptist hymn. If you've ever attended a Southern Baptist church, you know that there is nothing ordinary about a fired-up congregation singing that traditional favorite. There is also nothing ordinary about a perfectly prepared waffle, rich and buttery, crisp on the outside, light and steamy on the interior.

IN SEARCH OF THE PERFECT WAFFLE

What is the perfect waffle? My ideal waffle has a crisp, well-browned exterior — browning develops flavor — and a moist, fluffy in-

terior. It should be like a just-cooked soufflé encased in a flavorful crust. After testing more than fifteen variations on a basic recipe and speaking with a trio of food scientists, I found that the basic waffle described in most cookbooks sheds little light on the inner workings of a recipe that requires a delicate balance of imperfectly understood chemical reactions. Two things became clear during my work: my ideal requires a thick batter, so the outside can become crisp while the inside remains custardy; and it takes quick cooking, because slow cooking overcooks the center.

I began my quest for the perfect waffle with the batter. The proportion found in most recipes is 1 cup milk to 1 cup flour. This makes a rather thin batter, which results in a gummy waffle with a dry, unappealing interior. I found that ⅞ cup buttermilk (or ¾ cup sweet milk) to 1 cup flour is a far better proportion.

Most recipes omit buttermilk entirely, or at best list it as an option. Yet I found that buttermilk is absolutely crucial. Why? Because buttermilk and baking soda create a much thicker batter than the alternative, which is sweet milk and baking powder, and a thick batter is key. If you do not have buttermilk on hand, follow my sweet milk recipe; it not only has a reduced proportion of milk to flour, but contains a simple homemade baking powder, which creates a much thicker batter than can be made with sweet milk and store-bought baking powder.

What Is the Difference Between Baking Powder and Baking Soda?

Baking powder is made from an acid, such as cream of tartar, and baking soda. When baking soda comes in contact with a moist, acidic environment, it forms carbon dioxide gas, creating "rise." This chemical reaction is quite pronounced in a buttermilk batter, because the large amount of lactic acid in buttermilk reacts with the soda, generating a thick, spongy batter in seconds. The air bubbles (carbon dioxide gas) are trapped by the structure of the batter, much the way whipping cream thickens when aerated through beating.

Baking powder is useful in doughs or batters that don't contain other acidic ingredients, that is, those in which sweet milk is used rather than buttermilk. But the combination of sweet milk and baking powder is not as powerful as that of buttermilk and baking soda; the batter remains thin. This is partially because most baking powder is "double-acting" — it contains two different acid ingredients (different baking powders use different acids, including a few — how about sodium acid phyophosphate? — that sound distinctly unappetizing), one of which creates carbon dioxide at room temperature, the other at temperatures of 120°F or higher.

Double-acting baking powder is designed to create gas slowly and over a longer period of time, so that a cake, for example, has time to bake and set before all of the bubbles dissipate. I have found that the rise from baking powder occurs mostly at oven temperatures (over 120°F). But with waffles (and pancakes), which cook quickly, you want the rise to take place at room temperature. Store-bought baking powder doesn't do this.

It's best, then, when using regular milk, to make your own baking powder right in the bowl, adding cream of tartar to the baking soda. And if you have a favorite waffle recipe containing both buttermilk and baking powder, try substituting the same amount of baking soda; you'll probably see an improvement.

WHY USE BAKING POWDER AND BAKING SODA TOGETHER?

Although you need not add baking powder when using a buttermilk–baking soda combination, many recipes call for it. This makes no sense to me, since baking powder's two main ingredients are already present in such a recipe. The first, cream of tartar, is an acid, and buttermilk is loaded with lactic acid. The second, baking soda, is also present in abundance. So when I eliminated the baking powder from my buttermilk waffle recipe and increased the amount of baking soda, the batter improved and my waffle was crisper. Out of curiosity, I also tried to make a waffle with buttermilk and baking powder, eliminating baking soda as a separate ingredient. This was inedible by any standard, since there was too much acid and not enough baking soda.

TESTING OTHER INGREDIENTS

Because crispness is so important in waffles, I tried substituting cornmeal for a bit of the flour and found that 1 tablespoon per cup of flour adds extra crackle to the waffle. I also experimented with cake flour, whose lower gluten content produces a finer crumb and a more tender product. I started by replacing ⅓ of the all-purpose flour with cake flour, and was disappointed. The waffle was indeed tender, but it lacked sufficient contrast between crisp exterior and creamy interior. When I reduced the amount to 2 tablespoons, the results were better but still not worth the trade-off; I want as much crispness as I can get.

Although I am not a fan of low-fat recipes, I felt obliged to attempt to create a lower-fat waffle by removing the melted butter from the recipe. This created a bland, tasteless waffle, with a limp exterior. Why? Well, when butter or oil is added, the outside of the waffle will cook at a higher temperature. Oil is a better conductor of heat than the water, egg, flour, and other ingredients in the waffle batter. The oil also improves the heat transfer from the waffle iron to the batter itself. Inside the waffle, however, the batter is being steamed (even with the addition of butter) and the interior will reach no more than 212°F as long as it is still moist (an instant-read thermometer inserted into the middle of a just-cooked waffle will read 200°F). That is why the exterior of a waffle is crisper than the interior — two different cooking processes are at work. Vegetable oil will produce the same outside crispness as butter, although with a loss of flavor. I recommend this substitution only if you are desperate to reduce the saturated fat in your diet; the caloric content is the same.

PUTTING THE INGREDIENTS TOGETHER

Once I had the ingredients sorted out, I had to find the best way to put them together. The first question was whether the egg should be separated and the whites beaten and folded in. It turned out that this was an improvement over using a whole egg. The batter was glossier and the waffle fluffier. If you cut through a cooked waffle made with beaten egg whites, you can actually see pockets of air trapped inside. Cutting through a waffle made with whole egg reveals a flatter, more consistent texture.

Look at a number of waffle recipes and you'll see a wide range of recommendations as to how to combine the ingredients. One author carefully mixes with a whisk until the liquid and dry ingredients are *just* combined; another throws everything into the bowl of an electric mixer and cranks up the horsepower. But most have this in common: they add all of the liquid at once. This practice necessitates overmixing and usually results in clumps of unmoistened flour.

The objective in all of this is to moisten the flour thoroughly, not to create a smooth batter, and for this there is no question that a gentle hand is crucial. This is the technique I have found works best: Whisk together the dry ingredients, whisk together the liquid ingredients, and then slowly pour the liquid ingredients into the dry, mixing gently with a rubber spatula. Use a thin, steady stream, as you would when adding oil to vinegar to form an emulsion for salad dressing, and be careful not to let the addition of the liquid get ahead of mixing. When most of the liquid has been added, the batter becomes thicker; switch to a folding motion, similar to the folding of egg whites, to finally combine and moisten the batter. At this point, the batter should still be only partially mixed, with large streaks of dry flour still evident. The last step is to fold in the beaten egg white.

There is also debate about resting the batter before baking. I let two different batters rest in the refrigerator for about an hour: a whole egg recipe and one in which the egg white was separated and beaten. In both cases, the results were disappointing. The theory of resting waffle or pancake batter is based on the notion that the gluten (protein) in all-purpose flour has a chance to relax, producing a more tender product. But the quick development of carbon dioxide in a buttermilk-based batter, which makes the batter thick and puffy, mandates a quick move to the hot waffle iron (or griddle for pancakes). Letting the batter sit only allows the gas to escape, deflating the batter and the final waffle. In a pinch, the batter can sit for up to 15 minutes at room temperature without ill effect.

BAKING A WAFFLE

When you bake waffles, remember that darker waffles are better than lighter ones. In scientific terms, this is due to the Maillard reaction, which refers to the reaction and subsequent transformation of sugars at temperatures in excess of 300°F. The sugar breaks down, throwing off hydrogen and oxygen, leaving a higher concentration of carbon compounds, which are sweet and flavorful. This is why well-browned cookies have more flavor than light ones, why dark beers have more flavor than regular brews, and why nuts are roasted before use in pesto and desserts. This chemical reaction, which is evidenced by browning (and *not* by "tanning"), creates a lot of flavor. Waffles should therefore be cooked to a medium brown, not a light brown. Empirically, I also found that light brown waffles become soggy more quickly than darker counterparts. It's as if the waffle has to "set" properly, much like a cake or soufflé. Just don't overdo it — the perfect waffle is still moist and creamy inside.

Usually, you must check each waffle visually; the conventional wisdom about a waffle being properly cooked when the iron stops steaming is useless (the waffle will be overcooked if you wait this long). The best waffle iron (the Vitantonio) has a green light that really works — it goes on when the iron is back up to temperature, which coincides with the exact moment when the waffle is perfectly cooked. For most models, however, you must check the waffle after 3 minutes of cooking time. Again, the exterior should be a toasty brown; manila-colored waffles turn soggy in seconds.

It's surprising how quickly even properly cooked waffles begin to deteriorate. A minute after you remove them from the iron, the crispy exterior starts to absorb moisture from the softer interior; all too soon, the result is a limp, soggy square or circle. This problem is compounded if the waffle is left on a plate; the bottom quickly turns soggy as the moisture from the interior of the waffle cannot escape into the air. To combat this problem, make sure that you thoroughly cook the waffle as described above; a crisp exterior holds its texture better. You can also hold waffles on a cake rack in a 200° oven for up to 5 minutes. Unfortunately, this causes the interior to start to become dry, dense, and tough: that fluffy, moist texture does not hold up for long. My advice is to eat each waffle immediately. Like a soufflé or a morsel of fried food, the ultimate waffle is a passing delicacy.

IN SEARCH OF THE PERFECT PANCAKE

The problems with pancake recipes are the same as with waffles: too much liquid, the use of baking powder instead of baking soda, and overmixing of the batter. On my tenth batch of batter, it began to dawn on me that I was dealing with almost the same recipe as with waffles. All the same rules applied and other than the cooking method, perhaps the same recipe would work for both. It did. In fact, pancakes and waffles are the same animal, just served up differently.

Master Recipe for Buttermilk Waffles and Pancakes

The secret to great waffles and pancakes is a thick batter, so don't expect to pour this one. Reduce the buttermilk by 1 tablespoon if not using cornmeal. For pancakes, which require a slightly thinner batter, increase the buttermilk by 2 tablespoons, to 1⅛ cups from 1¼ cups, and don't use the optional cornmeal; the extra-thick batter is okay for waffles. It's best to use an electric griddle for pancakes — set it to 350°F, not 375° or 400° as suggested by many manufacturers. (These are very thick pancakes and require a lower temperature for thorough cooking.) For both waffles and pancakes, be sure not to overbeat the egg whites — they should just hold a 2-inch peak.

If you have leftover waffle batter, make toaster waffles — undercook the waffles a bit, cool them on a wire rack, wrap them in plastic wrap, and freeze. Pop them in the toaster for a quick breakfast.

  2 cups all-purpose flour
  2 tablespoons cornmeal, optional
  1 teaspoon kosher salt

½ teaspoon baking soda
2 eggs, separated
1¾–1⅞ cups buttermilk
4 tablespoons unsalted butter, melted

1. Heat waffle iron or griddle. Whisk dry ingredients together in a medium bowl. Whisk egg yolks with buttermilk and melted butter.

2. Beat egg whites until they just hold a 2-inch peak. *Do not overbeat.*

3. Add liquid ingredients to dry ingredients in a thin, steady stream while gently mixing with a rubber spatula; be careful not to add liquid faster than you can incorporate it. At this point the batter should still be very rough, with large spots of unincorporated flour. Gently fold in the egg whites, using a light touch. Batter should just be mixed. *It is better to undermix than overmix.*

4. Cook in either a waffle iron or on a griddle. Waffles should be a deep brown. Pancakes should just be cooked through. Turn pancakes when small air holes appear on the surface. Serve immediately.

Serves 4

Sweet-Milk Waffles and Pancakes

If you are out of buttermilk, try this sweet-milk variation. Add 4 teaspoons of cream of tartar to the dry ingredients and in place of buttermilk substitute a scant 1½ cups milk for waffles and 1⅜ cups milk for pancakes.

THE BEST BREAKFAST MUFFINS

I prefer an honest, sturdy muffin to an overly sweet bakery version that is dressed up with streusel toppings and a long set of recipe directions. A good muffin should be tender but firm, a solid carrier of melted butter and apricot jam or a twirl of honey. I started by testing cake flour in place of all-purpose (cake flour is a "softer" flour — it has less protein — and therefore produces a finer crumb), but I found that though the muffins were softer, they lacked the chew and texture I prefer. I also varied the amount of fat in the recipe and found that too much butter or shortening made the muffin too soft.

As I had found with other breakfast breads, buttermilk worked better than milk and baking soda was required, although in this case baking powder was also necessary, because the muffins needed that extra boost in a hot oven. (Double-acting baking powder, remember, has two leaveners, one of which kicks in at higher temperatures.) It was also crucial to handle the batter as gingerly as possible.

A few tricks. If you like big caps on your muffins, just fill the muffin cups all the way to the top (be sure to grease the top surface of the muffin tin first). Also, some recipes say that you only need to grease the bottoms of the muffin cups. I find that it's best to grease the whole inside area, even when working with nonstick bakeware. Use a small ice cream scoop for placing batter in the muffin tin — one full scoop should be just right for one muffin.

Lemon-Buttermilk Corn Muffins

You can substitute 2 teaspoons of bacon fat for 2 teaspoons of oil for more flavor. If you tire of grating lemon zest as a flavoring, the King Arthur Flour company has a direct-mail catalog that offers lemon and orange baking extracts. Be sure to combine the dry and liquid ingredients gently with a rubber spatula.

1 egg
1 tablespoon grated lemon zest
1 tablespoon lemon juice
4 tablespoons melted butter
2 tablespoons canola oil or corn oil
1 cup buttermilk
1 cup all-purpose flour
1 cup yellow cornmeal
1½ teaspoons baking powder

½ teaspoon baking soda
¼ cup sugar
½ teaspoon kosher salt

1. Heat oven to 400°F and grease cups of muffin tin with soft butter or a vegetable spray.

2. Whisk together the egg, lemon zest, lemon juice, melted butter, and oil in a large bowl. Whisk in the buttermilk. Mix the flour, cornmeal, baking powder, baking soda, sugar, and salt in another bowl. Add the flour mixture to the buttermilk mixture and stir gently with a rubber spatula until just blended.

3. Spoon batter into muffin tin (fill cups ¾ full — you can fill to the top if you grease the top of the muffin tin first). Bake for about 15 minutes or until done (until edges start to pull away from the sides of the cups). Remove from tin and serve hot with butter and jam or honey.

Makes 10 muffins

The Best Bran Muffins

This recipe is adapted from a recipe that appeared in the September/October 1993 issue of Cook's Illustrated. I cut back on the sugar, simplified the ingredients list, and added grated carrots for a moister muffin. I prepare the batter and let it rest in the refrigerator overnight, which is great for quick breakfasts.

    2¾ cups all-purpose flour
    3 teaspoons baking soda
    1 teaspoon baking powder
    ½ teaspoon kosher salt
    4 tablespoons melted butter
    ¼ cup vegetable oil
    ¼ cup molasses
    ¾ cup light brown sugar
    1 teaspoon vanilla extract
    3 large eggs, lightly beaten
    2 cups buttermilk
    1 cup wheat germ
    1¼ cups natural bran

    1½ cups dark raisins
    ¾ cup grated carrots

1. Whisk first 4 ingredients together in a bowl and set aside.

2. In a large bowl, whisk together the next 7 ingredients (butter through buttermilk). Fold in wheat germ and bran. Add dry ingredients and mix gently with a rubber spatula. Fold in raisins and carrots.

3. Cover bowl with plastic wrap and let sit in refrigerator for 1 hour or overnight. (If the batter is not allowed to rest, the bran will not hydrate properly, producing a thin batter and a weak muffin.)

4. Preheat oven to 400°F. Lightly grease muffin tins, including the top. Fill cups full. Bake for 10 minutes, turn muffin tins around in oven, then bake another 10 minutes. Remove from oven, and let cool for 5 minutes in tins. Using a dull table knife, transfer muffins to a wire rack to cool. Serve after 10 minutes.

Makes 18 muffins

BAKING POWDER BISCUITS

Biscuit dough is very similar to pie pastry, though there is much less fat (about half as much) and of course the dough includes a leavener. I have found that 7 tablespoons of fat per 2 cups of flour is the right ratio in making biscuits. I have also found that 4 tablespoons of butter to 3 tablespoons of Crisco provides both flavor and good texture. (The combination of butter and Crisco also tested best when I made some thirty different piecrusts while developing a master recipe for Chapter 41.) If you prefer a tougher biscuit, you can reduce the amount of fat, although I would not suggest that you increase it — the biscuit will become too soft and crumbly. James Beard went so far as to publish a recipe for cream biscuits, which used no shortening, just substituted cream for water when mixing the dough. This yields a very toothy biscuit, but one that is both easy and satisfying.

Having spent a lot of time in both Baltimore and Washington, D.C., as a kid, I am very familiar with beaten biscuits, which are indigenous to the Maryland area. These are, to my mind, flat, sad little biscuits that never seemed to take off. The reason for their lack of stature is that the dough is whacked, usually with a rolling pin, which makes absolutely no sense to me. It's more work and makes a tough, short biscuit. My rule is the exact opposite. After making thousands of biscuits, I have found that barely touching the dough, using not much more than the weight of the rolling pin to roll it out, is the easiest route to a light, fluffy product. I also like my biscuits tall, so I cut the dough when it's about ½ inch thick, no thinner. Many recipes also suggest that the dough be kneaded five or six times after it is removed from the bowl and before rolling, but I have found this to be a mistake. In fact, I just press the dough together into a ball, place it on a floured surface, lightly flour the top of the dough, and then roll it out. If you don't have a biscuit cutter, use the mouth of a thin-walled drinking glass or the screw top from a jar. Don't twist the cutter when you cut biscuits — just press down straight and decisively. In Nika Hazelton's *American Home Cooking,* she suggests letting the biscuits sit on the counter for 10 minutes before baking. I find that when you are using buttermilk and baking soda, as I do below, this adds a bit of rise to the dough (the buttermilk and baking soda are busy creating carbon dioxide gas).

Baking Powder Biscuits

There are two basic types of biscuits: a fluffy biscuit and a beaten biscuit. The latter variety is worked over pretty good and baked into fairly thin, flaky but tough rounds. I prefer my biscuits light, fluffy, and high. If you do not have buttermilk, you can substitute regular sweet milk as indicated in the variation below. If you leave the cut biscuits sitting on the baking sheet for 10 minutes prior to baking, they will rise higher when baked.

    2 cups flour
    ½ teaspoon kosher salt
    2 teaspoons baking powder
    ½ teaspoon baking soda
    4 tablespoons chilled butter
    3 tablespoons chilled vegetable shortening
    ⅔–¾ cup buttermilk

1. Heat oven to 425°F. Combine the flour, salt, baking powder, and baking soda in the bowl of a food processor fitted with the metal blade. Process for 2 seconds to mix.

2. Add the butter, cut into 1-tablespoon pieces, to the flour and pulse 7 times for 1 second each. Add shortening in 1-tablespoon dollops and pulse another 6 times or until mixture looks like coarse meal (the flour will take on a slightly yellowish hue from the butter).

3. Place mixture in a large bowl. Using a rubber spatula, fold mixture together while adding buttermilk in a very thin stream. When mixture starts to hold together, use the flat side of the spatula to form the dough into a cohesive mass (your fingers will stick to the dough). Note that you may use a little more or less than the ⅔ cup buttermilk called for.

4. Turn dough onto a floured surface and roll out very gently to a thickness of ½ inch. Use a biscuit cutter to cut, and then place biscuits on an ungreased cookie sheet and bake in the preheated oven for about 10 minutes, turning sheet after 5 minutes.

Makes ten thick 2¾-inch biscuits or sixteen 2-inch biscuits

Sweet-Milk Variation

Substitute milk for buttermilk, add 3 teaspoons cream of tartar, and reduce baking powder to 1 teaspoon.

～ 40 ～

How to Cook an Egg

Easy does it is the rule for most egg cookery.

～

My culinary mentor, Malvina Kinard, started her career at the age of fifty-nine, when she took a six-month tour of Europe to learn the art of cooking. When she returned, she opened a cookware store–cooking school in Greenwich, Connecticut. During one of her classes, which catered to the rich, powerful, but not necessarily competent, she asked one of the students to separate 7 eggs. She came back a few minutes later to find 3 eggs in one bowl and 4 in the other!

THE CHEMISTRY OF EGGS

Eggs are the most complex and most important ingredient in cooking. They are high in protein, which consists of complex, coiled molecules similar to mattress springs. Heat or whipping causes these coils to unwind. They then attach to one another, creating a three-dimensional mesh that traps air or liquid. This action is most obvious in custards and beaten egg whites. The trapped air or liquid is then set permanently in this mesh when the mixture is heated and the egg protein turns to a solid.

As the temperature differential between thickened eggs and scrambled eggs is only about 10°F, it's important to cook custards, for example, over low heat. This will extend the time between success and failure. Over high heat, the margin for error is slim, a matter of seconds rather than minutes. Cooks often take a shortcut when making a custard. They use either cornstarch or flour to aid in the thickening process. This enhances the creation of a protein "mesh" and minimizes the possibility of curdled eggs.

In baking, eggs also provide moisture, which results in steam that leavens popovers, for example. They also act as emulsifiers; one

---

SCIENCE OF COOKING

Why Do the Yolks in Hard-Boiled Eggs Turn Funny Colors?

Egg yolks contain iron and the whites contain sulfur. When heated, some eggs (especially less than fresh eggs) create hydrogen sulfide gas, which, when it comes in contact with iron in the yolk, creates a harmless compound, ferrous oxide. This can be seen as that odd greenish-gray discoloration on the outside of the yolk of a hard-boiled egg. To minimize this problem, don't overcook eggs, and plunge them into plenty of cold water as soon as they are done. This decreases the pressure within the egg, which will prevent the hydrogen sulfide gas from leaking into the yolk, where the ferrous oxide is created.

How to Boil an Egg

Unshelled eggs were boiled in water to cover for different times. In one series of tests the eggs were started in cold water; timing began when the water came to a boil. In the other series of tests, eggs were dropped into boiling water.

Although cooking schools tell students to start eggs in cold water, there was no discernible difference between the two methods. Also, timing is more precise when starting in boiling water, as it is difficult to pinpoint the exact moment that water starts to boil.

Method	Time	Results
Started in cold water (timing begun when water came to a boil)	2 minutes	Runny yolk and soft-cooked white
	3 minutes	Slightly solidified yolk; center is dark yellow
	4 minutes	Yolk is solid
	5 minutes	Hard-cooked
	6 minutes	Hard-cooked; yolk still dark yellow
	10 minutes	Overcooked; outside of yolk has a gray edge
	15 minutes	Same as 10 minutes
Started in boiling water	2 minutes	Not cooked; white is cooked on outside only
	3 minutes	White undercooked slightly
	4 minutes	Good soft-boiled egg
	5 minutes	Outside edge of yolk is beginning to solidify
	6 minutes	Yolk is soft-cooked, not runny
	10 minutes	Nice hard-boiled egg
	15 minutes	Overcooked

end of the molecule attracts water and the other attracts oil. That's why some salad dressings call for egg yolks and why they are used in mayonnaise.

HOW TO BOIL AN EGG

Cooking schools will tell you to start an egg in cold water and then begin timing once the water comes to a boil. In theory, this makes a lot of sense, since this is a slower, more gentle means of cooking. With any sort of protein, a gentle heat is preferable. However, when testing this approach head to head against the "drop it in boiling water" method, I found no difference. In addition, it may be difficult to determine exactly when simmering ends and boiling begins, so for timing purposes the boiling water method is preferable. Other cooks tell you to cook eggs in water that is at a bare simmer, but I find

that this method also presents timing difficulties.

To test timing, I cooked eggs in boiling water, removing 1 egg every minute starting at 2 minutes. At 4 minutes, the white was just cooked; at 5 minutes, the outside edge of the yolk began to solidify; at 6 minutes, the yolk was soft-cooked; and 10 minutes was the proper time for a hard-boiled egg. Conventional wisdom also says that fresh eggs are not ideal for hard-boiling, as they will be more difficult to peel. (If the pH of the egg white is below 8.9, it is likely to adhere to the inner membrane of the shell, making it more difficult to peel. Fresh eggs tend to have a pH of 8.0; a 3-day-old egg is a little over 9.0). The conventional wisdom may be true, but it really makes little difference, since most of us purchase eggs from a supermarket, where we have no idea whether the eggs are 1 day or 10 days old. If you were sufficiently organized, you could set aside eggs in the refrigerator, but this seems to me to be beyond the pale of reasonable expectations. So what if the eggs are slightly harder to peel?

HOW TO POACH AN EGG

I tested two methods for creating a nicely shaped poached egg, starting in both cases with a pan of boiling water. One method involved swirling the water vigorously, dropping the egg into the center of the "whirlpool"; the other method consisted of adding vinegar to the cooking water to achieve the same result. The swirling method is difficult to master and will not yield a perfectly shaped poached egg — there will always be loose ends of the white trailing away from the egg. The vinegar method requires no practice and yields a nice solid white. I found that 1 tablespoon of vinegar per 6 cups of water works fine; additional vinegar is unnecessary.

HOW TO FRY AN EGG

Most fried eggs are tough because the skillet is too hot. I prefer to heat the skillet, then turn heat to low, adding the butter and then

---

KITCHEN TEST

How to Poach an Egg

Vinegar is necessary for a nicely shaped poached egg, since it speeds the coagulation of the surface of the albumen (the white). Use 1 tablespoon vinegar per 6 cups of water.

Method	Results
Swirled water; no vinegar	Hit-or-miss proposition; water must be swirled vigorously; some loose ends of cooked egg white
1 tablespoon vinegar per 6 cups of water	Egg white is a solid shape; no vinegar taste
2 tablespoons vinegar per 6 cups of water	Not better than 1 tablespoon test

---

the eggs. I also add water and then cover the pan so that the top of the egg steams. This avoids having to flip the egg to make sure the white on top of the yolk is properly cooked. I ran tests to determine the proper amount of butter and water. For both sets of tests, I fried 2 eggs in butter in a covered 9-inch nonstick skillet. Water was added to the pan to create steam to cook the tops of the eggs. I tested three quantities of butter and found that 1 tablespoon was best both for flavor and for stopping the eggs from sticking. (You will need additional butter if your pan isn't nonstick.) I also tested three quantities of water for creating steam and again found that 1 tablespoon was best. Lesser amounts did not generate sufficient steam to properly cook the upper surface of the eggs.

HOW TO SCRAMBLE AN EGG

Many years ago, *Cook's Magazine* ran a story on James Villas, the food editor of *Town & Country* magazine. He shared a breakfast menu, which included his slow-cooked scrambled eggs, prepared in a double boiler. My scrambled egg recipe shares many of the same features — very slow heat, butter, and cream — but I find a double boiler unnecessary. Just use a nonstick pan and stir eggs slowly with a wooden spoon. I also add 1 tablespoon of water to make the eggs moist. Since I did not want to dilute the texture or flavor of the eggs, I varied the amount of heavy cream and found that 3 tablespoons was just right for 2 eggs. Two tablespoons of cream was insufficient — the eggs were a bit "eggy" — and a full ¼ cup of cream created a mushy texture and washed-out flavor.

HOW TO BAKE AN EGG

I have found shirred eggs — eggs baked in ramekins — to be quite difficult to prepare. The whites overcook by the time the yolks cook at all, the outer perimeter of the whites becomes rubbery and pockmarked with small holes, and the timing is never accurate. That sort of result calls for a water bath to moderate heat around the perimeter of the baking dish, so I started my tests using a water bath and baking the eggs at 250°, 300°, 350°, and 400°F. It was no surprise that the lowest oven setting, 250°F, was the winner. What was surprising, almost shocking, was that when baked without a water bath, the winner was the egg cooked at the highest temperature, 400°F, for just 12 minutes. The egg dry-baked at 250°F, for example, took 30 minutes and the white was a bit rubbery. If you have the time, go for the slow water-bath method. If you can't wait 40 minutes for breakfast, forget the water bath and bake at 400°F. Keep in mind, however, that the water-bath method makes a vastly superior shirred egg.

HOW TO MAKE AN OMELET

For years I had trouble with omelets. I started out with an omelet pan, which when properly seasoned worked like a charm. After the pan was scoured a few times with soap, it lost its finish and the eggs started sticking. In disgust, I moved on to other pans, including enameled cast iron, which was a complete disaster. (I find that enameled cast iron has hot spots, and for some reason, this surface has an affinity for eggs — it's like Velcro.) Then I stopped making omelets altogether.

A few years ago, I started playing around with the new nonstick skillets, which were not low-stick (the basic Calphalon anodized aluminum pans are low-stick) but really nonstick. An additional nonstick coating is bonded to the anodized aluminum surface. After testing six leading pans, I preferred the Calphalon skillet for its weight and finish. I even cooked a small omelet without any butter at all, and it didn't stick a bit. Today, I make omelets frequently, both for breakfast and as a light supper. They can be filled with everything from apricot jam to smoked salmon, sour cream, and caviar. They're fast and easy.

Start by whisking in salt, pepper, fresh herbs (tarragon works well with eggs), and 1

KITCHEN TEST

How to Shirr an Egg

Eggs were baked in individual buttered ramekins with and without a surrounding water bath at different oven temperatures. The water-bath method was determined to be vastly preferable, although the ideal oven temperature was 250°F, which takes a whopping 40 minutes. The dry oven, by contrast, was best heated to 400°F, to avoid overcooking the whites.

Method	Oven Temperature	Cooking Time	Result
Water bath	250°F	40 minutes	Very good texture; best method
	300°F	23 minutes	Nicely cooked; not quite as good as 250°F
	350°F	17 minutes	A little soft but cooked
	400°F	15 minutes	White is a little mushy
Dry baking	250°F	30 minutes	White a bit rubbery
	300°F	23 minutes	Yolk slightly overcooked; white is just cooked through
	350°F	16 minutes	White cooked, but a little rubbery near bottom of cup
	400°F	12 minutes	Cooked nicely with good texture, but not nearly as good as the water-bath method

teaspoon of water per egg. The water lightens the texture. Melt the butter in a nonstick skillet over medium-high heat, add the beaten egg mixture, reduce the heat to medium-low, and wait about 10 seconds. Using a pancake turner, pull in on the edges of the omelet, tipping the pan slightly so that the uncooked eggs run off to the side of the pan and underneath the cooked portion. Do this around the perimeter of the omelet until most of the uncooked egg has disappeared. If you don't do this, the bottom of the omelet will overcook, since the top will take too long to set. If you wish to fill the omelet, add the filling now, spreading it to within an inch of the perimeter. (Although some cookbooks tell you to place filling just in the center of the omelet — both sides are eventually folded over it — I have found it best to spread the filling over the entire omelet, leaving an inch-wide perimeter uncovered. This way the filling heats up more quickly. This is especially important when using cheese fillings, which have just seconds to melt before the omelet is folded and served.) Cook for 10 seconds. Now fold the omelet as you would a business letter: first fold the bottom third over the middle third, and then either make the last fold in the pan or slide the unfolded third onto a plate and then flip the folded portion on top of it (this is easier than it sounds).

Poached Eggs

The rule for poaching eggs is 1 tablespoon of vinegar per 6 cups of water. You can poach eggs without vinegar, but as I found when I tested this method, you are likely to end up with ropy strands of white floating in the water. Vinegar speeds up the coagulation of the albumen (the white).

    6 cups water
    1 tablespoon vinegar
    2 eggs

Bring water and vinegar to a quiet simmer. Add the 2 eggs, carefully pouring them from the shell. Cook until whites are just set, about 3 minutes.
Serves 1–2

Boiled Eggs

Place unshelled eggs in boiling water. At 3 minutes, the whites will almost be cooked but not quite. At 4 minutes, the eggs will be soft-boiled: cooked whites and runny yolks. At 5 minutes, the perimeter of the yolks will start to set up. At 6 minutes, the yolks will be cooked but still moist. At 10 minutes, the eggs will be hard-boiled but not overcooked. To make peeling hard-boiled eggs easier, place them in cold water immediately after cooking.

Scrambled Eggs

Do not add more cream than called for in the recipe. The eggs will lose their flavor and the texture will suffer. The eggs may be cooked in the top of a double boiler, though I prefer a nonstick pan.

    2 eggs
    3 tablespoons cream
    1 tablespoon water
       Salt and freshly ground black pepper to
       taste
    ¼ teaspoon dried tarragon or ½ teaspoon
       minced fresh
    2 tablespoons grated cheese, optional
    1 tablespoon butter

1. Crack eggs into a bowl, add cream and water, and whisk together with a fork. Add salt and freshly ground pepper to taste. Add the tarragon and cheese and whisk to incorporate.

2. Melt the butter in a small saucepan over very low heat. When the butter has melted, add the egg mixture and stir the bottom of the pan slowly with a wooden spoon over very low heat. Continue cooking and stirring until eggs just reach desired consistency.

Serves 1

Fried Eggs

The secret to tender fried eggs is low heat and steam. Once you add the eggs, reduce the heat to very low. Add a bit of water and then cover the pan, allowing the steam to gently and thoroughly cook the whites. These fried eggs are tender, with fully cooked whites and runny yolks. For extra flavor, cook some bacon in the pan first, pour off all but 2 teaspoons of grease, and then proceed with the recipe.

1 tablespoon unsalted butter
2 eggs
   Salt and freshly ground black pepper to taste
1 tablespoon water

Heat the butter in a skillet over medium-high heat. When foam subsides, reduce heat to low and break eggs into the skillet. Sprinkle on salt and pepper and then add water to pan (don't put water on top of eggs). Cover pan and cook slowly until done. These eggs will not need to be turned, as the steam will cook the whites over and around the yolks.

Serves 1–2

Shirred Eggs with Bacon

There are two ways to bake an egg. The water-bath method, used here, is considerably better but takes 40 minutes. If you are in a rush, bake the eggs without the water bath in a 400° oven for 12 minutes.

2 slices bacon
⅓ cup grated mild cheese
4 eggs
8 drops Tabasco sauce

Salt and freshly ground black pepper to taste

1. Preheat oven to 250°F. Bring 6 cups of water to a boil. Butter 4 small custard cups or ramekins. Fry bacon and remove to paper towels.

2. Crumble half a slice of bacon into each prepared cup. Divide cheese evenly among cups and then break 1 egg into each cup. Top with 2 drops Tabasco and season with salt

---

Should You Consume Raw Eggs?

Salmonella enteripibis is the strain of bacteria found in contaminated eggs. It is thought that this strain is present when the shell is formed and is not introduced at a later date through outside sources. Improper handling, storage, and cooking can create a favorable environment for multiplication of these bacteria, should they be present. If you consume a contaminated egg, the effects can be serious, with all of the symptoms of a severe stomach flu, and can lead to dehydration and even death.

That being said, what if you want to make a chocolate mousse, ice cream, or homemade mayonnaise? Well, you are certainly taking a risk, although, statistically speaking, a small one. (Specifically, 9,000 people died in 1995 in this country from all food-related illnesses, salmonella being just one cause. This includes incidents in restaurants as well as home kitchens.) You can lower, although not eliminate, this risk by storing eggs and products containing raw eggs at temperatures no greater than 40°F and by not using eggs with a cracked shell. Generally, uncooked egg whites may be safer than the yolks, since the former have a high pH level — whites are alkaline — which is less favorable to the growth of salmonella. Nonetheless, the meringue on a lemon meringue pie, if not heated to 160°F (the temperature at which this strain of salmonella is killed), could still be a problem if made with contaminated egg whites.

Personally, I occasionally use raw eggs in cooking, but I purchase eggs from a small, high-quality supplier and keep them and any raw-egg products well refrigerated to lower the risk. However, both the United States Department of Agriculture and the Centers for Disease Control strongly recommend that eggs be properly cooked before eating.

and pepper. Place ramekins in a small roasting or baking pan and pour boiling water around them to create a water bath (the water level should be about even with the top of the eggs in the ramekins).

3. Bake for 40 minutes or until whites are set. Yolks should still be soft.

Serves 4

Omelet with Variations

An omelet can be folded in half or can be folded as you would a letter, in thirds. The best omelets are still wet and creamy inside, not dry and overcooked. It's better to undercook than overcook.

Omelet
2 eggs
2 teaspoons cold water
  Salt and freshly ground black pepper to
  taste
1 tablespoon butter

Filling
¼ cup grated cheese, chopped meat, or cooked
  vegetable mixture (see below)

1. Crack the eggs into a bowl and whisk together until blended. Add the cold water and salt and pepper to taste, and whisk another 5 seconds.

2. In an 8-inch nonstick frying pan or skillet, melt the butter over medium-high heat. When foam subsides, reduce heat to low and pour in the egg mixture. When the eggs have just set, about 10 seconds, use a pancake turner to pull in the edges of the omelet, tipping the pan slightly so that the uncooked eggs run off to that side of the pan, under the cooked portion. Do this around the perimeter of the omelet until most of the uncooked egg has disappeared.

3. If you wish to fill the omelet, add the filling now, leaving about an inch of uncovered area around the perimeter of the omelet, and cook another 10 seconds. Now fold the omelet as you would a letter, beginning by folding the bottom third over the middle

third. Make the final fold as you slide the omelet out of the pan, flipping the folded section of the omelet over onto the unfolded section.

Serves 1

Omelet Fillings

Cheddar Cheese Omelet: ¼ cup grated cheddar
Parmesan Omelet: ¼ cup grated Parmesan
Jam Omelet: 3 tablespoons jam or jelly
Bacon Omelet: ¼ cup crumbled cooked bacon
Sour Cream–Salmon Omelet: 2 tablespoons sour cream and 1 ounce smoked salmon cut into thin strips

Parmesan-Spinach Omelet

This is an unusual recipe because it consists mostly of egg whites. You can use onion instead of shallots. Be sure to use enough salt and pepper. For more flavor, cook 3 pieces of bacon and drain off all but 2 teaspoons of bacon fat. Proceed with step 2. Crumble the bacon and add it to the spinach mixture along with the 3 whole eggs.

10 ounces fresh spinach or 5 ounces frozen
2 shallots
9 eggs
1 tablespoon olive oil
¼ teaspoon ground nutmeg
  Salt and freshly ground black pepper to
  taste
2 tablespoons butter
3 tablespoons Parmesan cheese

1. If using fresh spinach, rinse and then blanch (cook briefly) in salted boiling water for 45 seconds. Drain, rinse with cold water, and drain again. Squeeze spinach to remove excess water (or place spinach in a kitchen towel and wring tight). If using frozen spinach, thaw and remove excess water. Peel and mince the shallots. Separate 6 eggs, reserving the yolks for another recipe.

2. In a small sauté pan, heat 1 tablespoon olive oil and add minced shallots. Sauté for 3–4 minutes over medium heat, until soft and translucent. Place the spinach, shallots, nutmeg, and salt and pepper to taste in the workbowl of a food processor and puree. Whisk 3 whole eggs together and add to the spinach mixture. Pulse to combine, or stir together in a separate bowl.

3. Beat 6 egg whites until they just hold a 2-inch peak. Fold in the spinach mixture.

4. In a 9- or 10-inch skillet, melt 1 tablespoon of butter, completely coating the bottom and sides. Add half the mixture to the pan and gently stir until whites begin to set, about 1 minute. Sprinkle 1½ tablespoons Parmesan over omelet, fold omelet in half, and cook for another 15–30 seconds, removing the omelet from the pan when the inside is still quite moist. Repeat for second half of mixture. Serve each omelet in three portions (or two for larger servings).

Serves 4–6

Maple Soufflé Omelets

I got the idea for this recipe from remembering large Sunday morning breakfasts that started with pancakes and ended with 2 fried eggs on the same plate. I always liked the combination of egg and syrup. A well-seasoned iron skillet is best for this recipe. Lower-grade maple syrup (dark or amber) has more flavor than the fancy, more expensive varieties.

3 eggs
¼ teaspoon kosher salt
   Freshly ground black pepper to taste
1 tablespoon maple syrup
2 tablespoons butter

1. Heat oven to 400°F. Separate the eggs.

2. Whisk together the egg yolks, salt, pepper, and maple syrup in a medium bowl. Beat the whites until soft peaks form. Fold into the yolk mixture.

3. Melt 2 tablespoons butter in a medium-size ovenproof skillet over high heat (a seasoned iron skillet is recommended). When the foam subsides, add the egg mixture and immediately reduce heat to medium-low. Cook for about 2 minutes, until the bottom of the mixture is brown and firm.

4. Place skillet in preheated oven. Mixture will rise like a soufflé. Remove when just cooked, about 3–4 minutes. If the omelet bakes too long, it will fall when served.

5. Cut omelet in half and serve.

Makes 2 large servings

～ 41 ～

Perfect Piecrust

*A good piecrust is the most difficult test for the home cook.
Here are step-by-step instructions for making a foolproof crust
that is tender and easy to roll out.*

～

Making piecrust can be a home cook's worst nightmare. Despite your best efforts, the crust can turn out hard, soggy, flavorless, oversalted, underbaked, too short, or totally unworkable. One expert tells you butter is the secret to perfect crust, another swears by vegetable shortening, still others, for health reasons, use only canola oil. Some cooks work the dough by hand, others do everything in a food processor.

After hundreds of piecrusts and twenty years of mixed results, I felt like an addicted gambler at the racetrack, seeking out that magical piece of information that would make me a winner. If only I could discover the right system. To get some real answers, I tried thirty-three variations on a basic pie dough to devise the perfect crust.

CHOOSING FAT, FLOUR, AND LIQUID

The most controversial ingredient in pastry is fat. For years, I believed that Crisco was the answer to flaky, easy piecrusts. Then a few years ago, I read Jim Dodge's *The American Baker,* in which he cast his lot with the all-butter crowd, saying that he found no dif-ference in flakiness between butter and vegetable shortening. In my tests, however, I found that while an all-butter crust has the best taste, it isn't as flaky as one made with shortening. On the other hand, an all-Crisco crust has a wonderful texture but is lacking in flavor. The crust made with lard is a little heavy and too strongly flavored. After testing a variety of combinations, I found that 6 tablespoons butter to 4 tablespoons Crisco was the optimum mixture for flavor and texture.

SCIENCE OF COOKING

What Is Crisco?

Crisco is a vegetable oil that is hydrogenated in order to incorporate air (hydrogen gas) and to raise its melting point above room temperature. (Hydrogenation is a process by which hydrogen gas is forced into a substance at high temperature and pressure. According to Harold McGee, author of *On Food and Cooking,* a small amount of nickel is also introduced to the vegetable oil to assist in the hydrogenation process. The nickel is subsequently filtered out.) This is much the same process as "creaming" butter and sugar, in which the sharp sugar crystals cut into the fat and create pockets of air. This is why regular vegetable oils, which hold no more air than does water, make a lousy pie dough, whereas Crisco, which is about 10 percent gas, does a good job of lightening and tenderizing.

With the fat question settled, I tested salt and sugar. A full teaspoon of salt was clearly too much for pie pastry, yet ¼ teaspoon was too little; ½ teaspoon is just right. However, ½ teaspoon of sugar is insufficient; a full tablespoon greatly enhances flavor.

I then tested different flours. The protein content of flour is important in any sort of baking. Bread flours are very high in protein, since bread needs a strong, elastic dough. Pastry flour (similar to cake flour, pastry flour is used mostly by professional bakers) is low in protein, to produce a soft, tender product. To find the best flour for piecrust, I tried substituting cornstarch for part of the all-purpose flour (a cookie-baking trick that increases tenderness), adding ¼ teaspoon baking powder to increase rise, and mixing cake flour with the all-purpose flour (again to increase tenderness). But none of these variations was an improvement on plain all-purpose flour.

I was also intrigued with the notion of adding liquid ingredients that contain lactic acid, such as buttermilk or sour cream, because of the dramatic effects these ingredients have on batter for waffles, pancakes, and biscuits. I also tested the addition of apple cider vinegar, an ingredient found in many old American cookbooks. None of these variations was an improvement on the original recipe, and some, such as the vinegar version, were substantially worse.

MIXING TECHNIQUES

I have converted to the food processor after years of using a hand-held pastry blender or just my hands. Pulse the butter and flour for five 1-second pulses, then add the Crisco and pulse four additional times. To see how much difference the proper mixing makes, I also made one piecrust using only three and then two pulses, and one using five and then four pulses followed by 20 seconds of continued processing. The undermixed crust shrank when baked and was hard and crackled and not consistent in texture, remarkably similar to the first piecrusts I made twenty years ago. The overprocessed crust was very short and cookielike. I concluded that overprocessing is better than underprocessing, but neither is as good as a perfectly textured crust.

Using a fork to mix in the water required an additional tablespoon of water (for a total of 4 tablespoons), and the result was too soft and not as flaky as the master recipe I eventually developed. The whisk proved to be entirely the wrong tool for the job — the dough clumped together and became overworked. A rubber spatula turned out to be the ideal tool. The water is mixed into the dough with a folding motion, and then the mixture is pressed together with the broad side of the spatula. The folding action exposes all of the dough to moisture without overworking it, thus minimizing the water used (and the less water used, the tenderer the dough), as well as reducing the likelihood that the dough will be overworked. Also, a spatula is larger and therefore easier on the dough than a fork. This technique is by far the best, especially for a novice baker.

RESTING, ROLLING, AND PREBAKING

Once the dough is mixed and formed into a ball, it should be flattened into a disk, placed in a plastic storage bag or covered with plastic wrap, and refrigerated for at least 30 minutes and up to 1 hour (an hour is best when working in hot weather). If the dough rests for more than 1 hour in the refrigerator, let it warm up a bit at room temperature before rolling (allow 45 minutes if the dough has rested overnight).

When rolling out dough, don't use too much flour on the work surface. Use a flour

Why Does Pie Dough Need to Rest?

Pie dough needs to rest in the refrigerator for two reasons. First, a rest period allows for even hydration, the absorption of water. When a pie dough is first mixed, the water is not evenly distributed throughout the dough. Second, a cool environment will stop the butter in the dough from further liquefaction. As dough is worked, it heats up and the butter starts to melt. (Some of the butter should remain intact in order to provide a flaky piecrust. If the butter melts, the crust will be mealy, a little bit like a soft shortbread.) Contrary to popular belief, the gluten (protein) in the dough is not really resting during this time. In fact, gluten is activated in the presence of water and some gluten development will occur during the rest period. Generally speaking, gluten development leads to a tougher pastry.

sifter (a canister with small holes in the top) to lightly dust the surface, or throw 2 tablespoons or so across it. Be frugal. Excess flour will be incorporated into the dough and cause it to become tough. To use a rolling pin, work from the center of the dough outward, to avoid rolling over the same area more than necessary. Apply only light pressure to the dough. If the dough becomes sticky and unworkable, put it back into the refrigerator for 15 minutes.

To get the dough into the pie pan, use a dough scraper (a six-inch-wide dull metal blade with a wooden handle) to get under the dough and then lift it onto a rolling pin. With the dough draped over the pin, move the dough and lay it into the pan. You can also fold the circle of dough in half and then in half again, and then lift it from the work surface with your hands. Place the folded point of dough in the center of the pan and then unfold.

SINGLE-CRUST PIES AND TARTS

For single-crust pies or tarts, push the dough down into the sides of the pan. This greatly reduces shrinkage of the sides of the tart or pie shell. If the sides of a prebaked crust shrink too much, it will not be able to hold a sufficient amount of filling. Once the excess dough has been trimmed, you can push up the sides of the tart a little bit so that they have more height, which will compensate for any shrinkage.

For a tart pan, use a rolling pin along the top edges of the pan to trim the excess dough. For a pie plate, use scissors to trim the dough to ½ inch from the rim of the plate. Now fold the edge of the dough under itself and then form a design around the rim, using either your fingers or a fork.

DOUBLE-CRUST PIES

For a double-crust pie, press the bottom layer of dough into the pie plate and trim so that it is even with the rim of the plate. Roll out the top crust so that it is at least 2 inches wider in diameter than the rim of the pie plate, fill the pie, and then drape the circle of dough over the rolling pin and lay it on top of the filling. (I start at one side of the pie, leaving 1 inch of overlap beyond the rim, and then slowly unroll the dough onto the pie.) Now trim the top layer of dough, leaving ½ inch of overlap beyond the rim of the pie plate. (If you find spots where the top crust is not wide enough, roll out a bit of dough, cut out a filler piece that is slightly bigger than the hole you are trying to fill, moisten the edges of the area that needs filling with water — a pastry brush works well — and then press the extra piece of dough into place. This technique also works well for filling holes in the bottom crust.) Fold that extra ½ inch of dough back under the edge of the bottom crust. Now shape the edge of the crust either by pressing with a fork or using your fingers to make a fluted edge. Make a few slits in the top crust with a paring knife so that steam can escape easily during baking. There is no need to brush the crust with cream, milk, egg yolk, or a combination. It will brown nicely on its own. Some

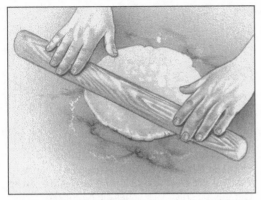

When rolling out dough, always start in the middle and work outward, to avoid overworking the dough.

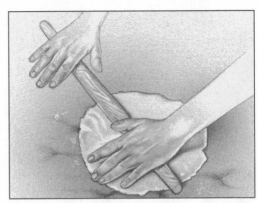

To use a tapered rolling pin, the pin I favor for pies, work the middle of the pin around the perimeter of the dough.

To measure the diameter of the dough, place the pie plate directly onto it. There should be sufficient overlap to form the sides and edge of the crust. This will depend on the depth and shape of the pie pan.

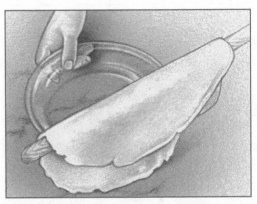

To move dough into a pie plate, drape it over the rolling pin using a dough scraper.

To move dough, you can also fold it in half twice, place it in the pie plate, and then unfold.

To fit pie pastry into a pie plate, always push the sides of the dough well down into the plate. This helps to avoid shrinkage when baking, especially important when prebaking.

For a two-crust pie, trim the bottom layer even with the edge of the pie plate. Scissors work well. For a single-crust pie, leave ½ inch of dough beyond the rim of the plate; this will be used to form the edging.

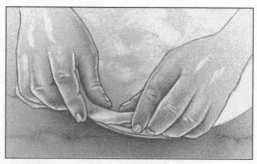

To shape the edging, fold the dough back under itself. Use this same method for a 2-crust pie, except fold the top crust back under the bottom crust.

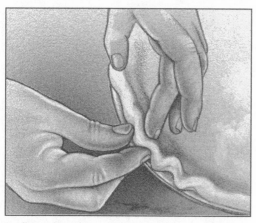

To flute the edge, place the thumb and forefinger of one hand on the outside edge and push gently with a finger of your other hand.

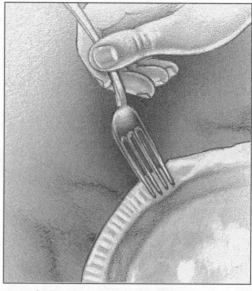

Use a fork to create a simpler edge by simply pressing the tines into the dough.

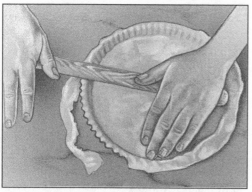

To fit pie dough into a tart pan, push the sides of the dough down into the pan and then use a rolling pin to trim off the excess.

bakers also sprinkle the top crust with a bit of sugar, which I find unnecessary — I don't like a sugary crust paired with a sweet filling. The pastry crust should be more on the savory side to offset the sweeter filling.

PREBAKING PIECRUSTS

To prebake a crust, freeze the dough in the pie plate for 10 minutes. Prick the firmed dough with a fork at ½-inch intervals. Use a double thickness of aluminum foil (an extra-wide roll is recommended), and place it gently into the chilled pie shell, pressing the foil into the corners of the pan. Prick foil and dough with a fork 10–15 times. Place in freezer for another 20 minutes or refrigerate for 1 hour. Bake in a preheated 400° oven for 15 minutes or until the dough just sets. Remove the foil and bake another 10 minutes, checking regularly after 5 minutes. Any areas that start to bubble can be pricked carefully with a fork. This is done to allow steam, which is caused by the heating of the moisture in the shortening, to escape. If the steam is allowed to build up, it will cause the baking dough to puff up. One last trick. Save a bit of dough at room temperature so that it is soft. It can be rolled out and placed over any trouble spots after prebaking. It will melt into the shell, which is still hot from the oven, to seal up any holes. (More detailed prebaking instructions are given in Chapter 43.)

THE MASTER RECIPE

This recipe uses a high proportion of fat to flour (about 1:2, whereas some recipes use as little as 1:5), which is crucial to a tender dough. In fact, the amount of shortening is the crucial factor in tenderness. I have also discovered that browning is critical to good flavor. In one of my tastings, there was one crust that was a bit overbaked (it was a very dark brown) but had a wonderful flavor —

buttery, rich, complex, and mature. By comparison, the others tasted young and undeveloped. A good piecrust is solid nut brown, not light brown. In addition to cooking time, fat, sugar, and acidity will also contribute to browning. That's why a sweet, high-fat crust will brown much better than the low-fat version.

Master Recipe for American Pie Dough

To cut the butter into small bits, halve the stick of butter lengthwise with a large knife, rotate the stick 90 degrees, and halve lengthwise again. Then cut the stick crosswise into ¼-inch pieces. Leave butter in the refrigerator until you need it. Otherwise, it will soften while sitting on the counter. Dough should be rolled about ⅛ inch thick (about the thickness of two quarters).

For a single-crust 8- or 9-inch pie
- 1¼ cups all-purpose flour
- ½ teaspoon kosher salt
- 1 tablespoon sugar
- 6 tablespoons chilled unsalted butter, cut into ¼-inch pieces
- 4 tablespoons chilled all-vegetable shortening (e.g., Crisco)
- 3–4 tablespoons ice water

1. Mix flour, salt, and sugar in a food processor fitted with the steel blade. Scatter butter pieces over the flour mixture, tossing to coat butter with a little of the flour. Cut butter into flour with five 1-second pulses. Add shortening and continue cutting in until flour is pale yellow and resembles coarse cornmeal, with butter bits no larger than small peas, about four more 1-second pulses. Turn mixture into a medium bowl.

2. Sprinkle 3 tablespoons of water over the mixture. With blade of a rubber spatula, use a folding motion to mix, then press down on dough with the broad side of the spatula until dough sticks together, adding up to 1 tablespoon more water if dough will not come together. Shape dough into a ball with your

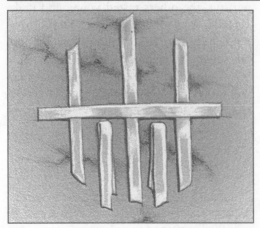

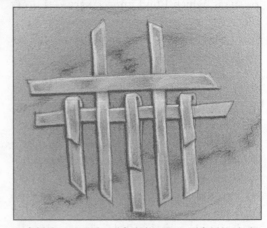

For a lattice-top pie, place 5 strips of dough across the top of a pie that has been fitted with a bottom crust cut so there is ½ inch of excess dough beyond the rim. Fold the second and fourth strips in half and place a long strip of dough across the center of the pie, at a right angle to the other strips.

Unfold the second and fourth strips and fold back the other three strips. Add a second crossing strip of dough and unfold the folded strips.

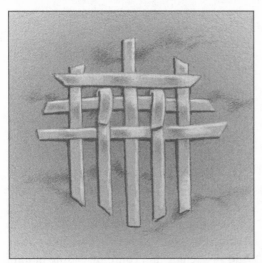

Fold back the second and fourth strips for a second time and add a third crossing strip of dough. Unfold the strips.

Repeat this process on the other half of the pie, alternating folds, and adding two more cross-strips of dough (you will have a total of ten strips of dough, five running in each direction). Trim off the excess lattice ends, then fold the surplus edge of the bottom crust up over the lattice strips and crimp.

hands, then flatten into a 4-inch-wide disk. Dust lightly with flour, wrap in plastic, and refrigerate for 30 minutes before rolling.

Single-Crust Variation for 10-Inch Regular or 9-Inch Deep-Dish Pie

These ingredients are for oversize single-crust pies.

  1½ cups all-purpose flour
  ½ teaspoon kosher salt
  1 tablespoon sugar
  8 tablespoons chilled unsalted butter, cut into ¼-inch pieces
  4 tablespoons chilled all-vegetable shortening (e.g., Crisco)
  4 tablespoons ice water

Double-Crust Variation for 8- or 9-Inch Pie

The dough should be divided into 2 balls, one slightly larger than the other. The larger ball is used for the bottom crust, the smaller one for the top.

  2¼ cups all-purpose flour
  1 teaspoon kosher salt
  2 tablespoons sugar
  11 tablespoons chilled unsalted butter, cut into ¼-inch pieces
  7 tablespoons chilled all-vegetable shortening (e.g., Crisco)
  4–5 tablespoons ice water

Double-Crust Variation for 10-Inch Regular or 9-Inch Deep-Dish Pie

With these larger quantities, make sure that the butter and Crisco are sufficiently processed into the flour. Otherwise, the crust will be very tough and will shrink if pre-baked.

  2½ cups all-purpose flour
  1 teaspoon kosher salt
  2 tablespoons sugar
  12 tablespoons chilled unsalted butter, cut into ¼-inch bits
  8 tablespoons chilled all-vegetable shortening (e.g., Crisco)
  5 tablespoons ice water

～ 42 ～

How to Thicken Fruit Pies

The chemistry of starches holds the key to which thickener — flour,
arrowroot, cornstarch, or tapioca — is best for fruit pies.

～

For many years I tried flour and cornstarch to thicken a fresh blueberry or strawberry-rhubarb pie, with poor results. As I cut into the cooled pie, the filling slid out onto the pie plate like melted cheese off the end of a slice of pizza; or I had to use so much thickener that the bright, fresh flavor of the fruit was adulterated. Nothing worked.

So I decided to do a kitchen test to determine the best thickener. I baked 3 cups blueberries with 1 teaspoon lemon juice, ½ cup sugar, and then 2 tablespoons of one of several different thickeners: tapioca, cornstarch, arrowroot, and all-purpose flour. I also tested one batch with 4 tablespoons of flour, because flour is not a strong thickening agent. The flour and cornstarch tests both yielded dull fruit, lacking in bright flavor and noticeably less acid. As a result, the mixture tasted sweeter and heavier. Both the arrowroot and the tapioca were clear winners, the tapioca showing a bit more thickening power. The all-purpose flour test with 2 tablespoons did not firm up sufficiently, and the 4-tablespoon pie was very gummy and almost inedible.

THE SCIENCE OF STARCHES

Next, I contacted Shirley Corriher, the *Cook's Illustrated* consulting food scientist, and also the folks at Kraft Foods to explain the test results. I found that there are two basic types of starchy molecules used for thickening: amylose starch and amylopectin. Cornstarch and flour both contain amylose, which forms a long chainlike bar that bonds with itself and other ingredients. A cherry pie thickened with cornstarch, for example, will be very thick and gluey the next day due to the superior bonding properties of amylose. This is the same chemical action that is responsible for the hard, clumpy texture of day-old rice. The downside of amylose is that the mixture will be cloudy (the bonding of the amylose is responsible for this as well), and I personally find that the resulting texture is a bit gluey, especially for a fruit pie (this was confirmed by the test results). Unlike tapioca, which has no flavor, both cornstarch and flour have considerable flavor. Flour, by the way, does have a lot of amylose in it, but it also has a number of other things. As a result, flour is a less pure form of starch and you need at least twice as much of it by volume to end up with the same thickening properties as, say, cornstarch. This amount of flour will also adversely affect your cherry or blueberry pie — you can taste it.

The second type of starch is amylopectin, which has branches that inhibit bonding with itself and other ingredients. This more delicate bonding agent may not be as strong a thickener as cornstarch, but it provides a crystal-clear pie and one with a more delicate texture. Arrowroot and tapioca fall into this category. Keep in mind, however, that all thickeners contain both types of molecules; some have a higher percentage of one over the other (cornstarch, for example, has 28 percent amylose, and tapioca has about 17 percent). Amylopectin is also preferred by commercial bakers because it freezes well. Pies made with cornstarch or flour (amylose) will lose water from the bonded structure when frozen and thawed.

In evaluating the various thickeners, I had to consider that both sugar and acidity may adversely affect the thickening process. It is true that sugar robs the thickener of water, necessary to the thickening process. (Sugar is also absorbed into the cells of the fruit and helps it keep its shape during baking.) A thickener can absorb up to 100 times its weight in water, but sugar will compete for the water, bonding water around its molecules. In a fruit pie, however, the proportion of sugar is low enough that there is sufficient free water for the thickening agent to do its work. In addition, acidity is said to have an adverse effect because it reduces the molecular weight of the starch, thus inhibiting thickening. In a lemon meringue pie, for example, this can be a problem, so the lemon juice is usually added after thickening occurs. However, in a fruit pie with only 2 teaspoons of lemon juice per 6 cups of fruit, the home cook need not worry.

TAPIOCA, THE THICKENER OF CHOICE

When developing recipes for berry pies, I decided to choose Minute Tapioca as the thickening agent. Based on the initial testing, flour and cornstarch robbed the fruit of its bright, fresh flavor, and tapioca performed much

Where Do Thickeners Come From?

Arrowroot comes from arrowroot roots (*Maranta arundinacea*), tapioca comes from the root of the cassava plant (also called the tapioca plant or manioc), cornstarch is made from corn, rice starch from rice, sago starch comes from the pith of palm trees, and wheat starch from wheat.

The tapioca plant is grown in much of the world and is harvested when its roots are 6–12 inches long. The root itself can be boiled and eaten. It is a substitute in many countries for rice or potatoes. When the starch is removed from the plant, it is separated from the plant and cellulose material. The starch molecules are contained in granules. These granules are, in their natural state, insoluble and only begin to absorb water with the introduction of energy in the form of heat. An unrefined starch will absorb water to the granule-bursting point, letting the starch molecules escape from the granules. This results in a less pleasant, slimier texture to the cooked product. That is one reason manufacturers further process starches, such as Minute Tapioca, to avoid bursting granules, preserving a creamier, more pleasant texture during thickening. The processing also makes starches less likely to have their thickening properties impaired by acids such as lemon juice. For example, you may have noticed bags of tapioca starch in Chinese grocery stores. This is a very inexpensive starch refined for thickening, but it is apt to hydrate more quickly, resulting in starch granules that burst more readily than will a further processed starch.

Raw materials used in manufacturing commercial starches are inexpensive, ranging from 2 cents per pound for cornstarch to 8 cents per pound for tapioca. Cornstarch is relatively inexpensive because it is a domestic product and because manufacturers sell off the processing by-products, including corn oil and animal food, whereas tapioca is imported from Thailand and incurs extra shipping costs.

Pearl tapioca is made from tapioca starch, which is heated into pearls. To create Minute Tapioca, the starch is partially gelatinized and then pressed into pellets to improve its thickening powers. For example, a processed starch, as compared to a raw starch, is less likely to lose its viscosity when in the presence of an acid such as lemon juice. The starch granules are also less likely to burst, which detracts from the texture and mouth feel of the thickened food.

better in a subsequent head-to-head test with arrowroot. (I baked two blueberry pies using 6 cups of fruit and 4 tablespoons of thickener — one with tapioca and the other with arrowroot — and the tapioca pie turned out considerably thicker.) Tapioca is also cheaper than arrowroot (an 8-ounce box costs about $2.49, whereas a 1.87-ounce jar of McCormick's arrowroot costs $3.89). During additional testing, I found that the amount of tapioca should be varied depending on the juiciness of the berries. If you like a juicy pie, you might try 3 tablespoons of tapioca with 6 cups of fresh blueberries. If you like a really firm pie with no juices, increase the quantity to 5 tablespoons. When the test kitchen staff at Kraft were queried about their tapioca-heavy back-of-the-box recipe (they suggest about 1 tablespoon of tapioca per cup of fruit), they explained that they like to operate with a large margin of safety — that is, they suggest using a larger amount of tapioca to be absolutely sure that the pie firms up properly. I like some juice and therefore opt for the lower quantity recommended in the master recipe below.

When I made a lattice-top pie, I ran into trouble. At the time, I was testing pearl tapioca (these are the large, fish-eye rounds that become translucent when cooked), and I found that the tapioca on top of the fruit baked into hard bits that made me feel like I was eating Tic-Tacs. For an open or lattice pie, therefore, I suggest mixing the tapioca with ¾ of the fruit, filling the pie, and then adding the balance of the fruit on top. This is less of a problem with Minute Tapioca, which is processed into smaller bits, but I recommend that you follow the same procedure anyway. By the way, if you find only pearl tapioca in your pantry, just place the tapioca in a spice grinder, blender, or food processor and grind away. Now you have "instant" Minute Tapioca. The other solution, suggested by one manufacturer, is to allow pearl tapioca to soak in water before

using. However, upon testing, I found that the thickening powers were greatly diminished because the thickener had already sucked in about as much water as it could handle before baking. However, high heat does increase the ability of a thickener to absorb water, so it did thicken somewhat, albeit at a greatly reduced rate. As a result, I don't recommend presoaking.

I also found that it is important to let fruit pies sit and cool, as this allows the juices to thicken. A fresh fruit pie will not completely set until it comes to room temperature (allow at least 1 hour).

Master Recipe for Fruit Pie

The quantities of both the sugar and the tapioca are variable in this recipe, depending on the sweetness and juiciness of the fruit. Tart blueberries, for example, can take a full cup of sugar. Very sweet berries, however, can do with ¾ cup or even a bit less. The tapioca will also depend on the fruit and the cook's preference for juiciness in the sliced pie. If you want perfect individual pieces, with no juice running out onto the pie plate, go with 4–5 tablespoons. Less juicy fruit will firm up nicely with 3–4 tablespoons. Although it is not essential, I let the tapioca-fruit mixture stand for 15 minutes before filling the pie to give the tapioca extra time to hydrate.

1	Master Recipe for American Pie Dough, Double-Crust Variation for 8- or 9-Inch Pie (page 369)
6	cups fruit, prepared (cored, peeled, sliced)
1	teaspoon grated orange or lemon zest
2	teaspoons lemon juice
¾–1	cup sugar
3–4	tablespoons Minute Tapioca
2	tablespoons butter (optional)

1. Make the pie dough and refrigerate for at least 30 minutes (let warm up for 10 minutes at room temperature if refrigerated for more than an hour).

2. Heat oven to 400°F. Toss the fruit with the other ingredients except the butter and let sit for 15 minutes. (If you are making a lattice-top pie, toss the fruit with all ingredients except the butter and the tapioca. Set aside ¼ of the fruit mixture and toss the balance with the tapioca. When filling the pie shell, add the larger amount of fruit first and then top with the quarter without tapioca.)

3. Roll out half of the chilled pastry dough so that it fits an 8- or 9-inch pie dish with at least a 1-inch overlap. Push dough down into edges of plate and then cut with scissors so it is even with the rim of the pie plate. (Dough should overlap by ½ inch if making a lattice-top pie.) Add fruit mixture and dot with optional butter. Place in freezer while working with top crust. Roll out remaining dough, place over pie, and trim, leaving ½ inch of overlap. (If you are making a lattice top, follow the instructions on page 368.) Fold edge of top crust under bottom crust and crimp with a fork or your fingers. Make three 3-inch-long slits in the top crust with a paring knife. If pie dough is very soft, chill in freezer for 10 minutes before baking.

4. Set pie on a baking sheet, place in preheated oven, turn oven down to 350°F, and bake for 1 hour. Check after 35 minutes and rotate if not browning evenly. Juices should bubble before pie is removed from oven.

5. Let pie sit and cool to room temperature before serving so that juices thicken (allow at least 1 hour).

Makes one 8- or 9-inch double-crust pie

Strawberry-Rhubarb Variation

Use 3 cups hulled and sliced strawberries and 3 cups rhubarb cut into 1-inch pieces. Use 1 tablespoon orange zest (instead of 1 teaspoon). Add ¼ teaspoon vanilla extract to the fruit mixture and use 1 full cup of sugar.

Peach Variation

Use 6 cups peeled, pitted, and sliced peaches. Add ½ cup brown sugar, reduce white sugar to ¼ cup, and add 1 tablespoon crystallized ginger diced into small pieces, ¼ teaspoon ground nutmeg, ¼ teaspoon ground allspice, and ¼ teaspoon salt to the peach mixture.

Blueberry Variation

Use 6 cups fresh blueberries. Omit the orange zest. Add ¼ teaspoon ground allspice and a pinch of nutmeg to blueberry mixture. Use ¾ cup sugar if blueberries are sweet. I do not recommend frozen blueberries — in a taste test against fresh, they were deemed virtually inedible.

Cherry Variation

Use 4 cups of pitted, canned sour cherries packed in water (drain the cherries), 1 cup sugar, ⅛ teaspoon ground allspice, ⅛ teaspoon ground cinnamon, ⅛ teaspoon almond extract, 1 tablespoon brandy, and ¼ cup quick-cooking tapioca. Eliminate the orange zest but use the lemon juice. If cherries have been canned in a syrup, drain and rinse with water, then drain again. Use 3 tablespoons of tapioca.

Custard Pies, Chiffon Pies, and Holiday Pies

Tenderness is the key to a good custard-based pie. The number of eggs, the proper ratio of heavy cream to milk, and knowing just when to remove the pie from the oven are all crucial to success.

~

Crissier is a tiny Swiss town just outside Lausanne, and its claim to fame is Fredy Girardet's restaurant. Unlike many celebrity-hungry chefs, Girardet has only one establishment, does his own shopping at 5:30 A.M., and has no known plans for opening an eatery in Disney World or Santa Monica. Many years ago, my wife and I spent a week cross-country skiing in Switzerland. Due to exceptionally warm weather, we cut the trip short, rented a car, and headed down to Crissier for what would be the most exceptional meal of our lives.

Before lunch, Girardet showed us around his kitchen. The jars of tangerine-size truffles were impressive, but I was most taken with the pastry chef, who managed to roll out paper-thin sheets of dough for the dessert tarts. (The most famous of these confections is his Tarte Vaudoise, which consists of nothing more than an ⅛-inch layer of sugar, heavy cream, and cinnamon on top of a tart shell, stirred together with the fingers and then baked.) Although a French tart and an American pie are different animals, the pastry chef did demonstrate an essential step in prebaking piecrusts, a crucial step in making the perfect American custard-based pie.

HOW TO PREBAKE A PIE SHELL

MINIMIZING SHRINKAGE

The first and most important step in prebaking a piecrust is using the correct recipe for the dough. The flour requires sufficient fat (butter and/or Crisco) to coat it properly. Otherwise, you will end up adding too much water before the dough will form into a cohesive ball. Then, as the dough prebakes, the pastry will shrink. Also be sure to use a butter such as Land O'Lakes, which has a very low moisture content. You want fat, not water. The master recipe in Chapter 41 is designed for this purpose. I have tried prebaking recipes using less fat and found that they shrink more readily.

The next trick, the technique I picked up at Fredy Girardet's, is to push the dough well down the sides of the pie plate before you trim and crimp the edges. Since the sides of the pie shell are no longer stretched — in fact, they are somewhat compressed — they are less likely to shrink. At Girardet's, the pastry chef pushed the dough down the sides of the pan, trimmed it with a rolling pin (the excess dough falls off around the outside of the pan), and then pushed the sides of the tart back up so that they were higher than the pan itself. The dough will shrink a bit during baking, ending up even with the sides of the tart pan when it is done. I use this technique today when baking tarts.

After a good deal of testing, I also found that freezing the pie shell for 10 minutes before pricking the bottom and then for 20 minutes afterward helps to both relax the gluten in the flour and resist shrinking. Although this is conjecture, I also feel that with freezing, the shell is more apt to set before the butter and vegetable shortening melt and the dough loses its shape. I have found, by the way, that freezing is better than refrigeration. You want the dough really cold.

PRICKING, FOIL, AND WEIGHTS

I used to prick the dough a few times before freezing it, figuring that a few holes would be sufficient to let the steam escape and prevent bubbling of the shell during prebaking. Over the years, however, I have found that you want to prick the bottom *and* sides every ½ inch. This really does cut down on bubbles in the pastry.

I have tested prebaking shells with and without an aluminum foil lining and have found that although foil is not essential, using it is safer. You don't need to butter the bottom of the foil — I have never had a problem with the foil sticking to the dough — and it is best to use a double thickness of heavy-duty foil (the extra-wide rolls are best). This is especially important for the sides of the pie shell, which need all the support they can get. I have also tested prebaking with and without weights sprinkled in the bottom and have found that it is best to use them. You will get less puffing of the bottom crust, although two layers of heavy-duty foil will help to mitigate this problem. You can purchase a can of pie weights or use dried beans.

I have also tested many different prebaking temperatures, from 350° to 450°F and

prefer the middle road, 400°F. The lower temperatures take too long to set the dough, and the higher temperatures will not provide enough time to set the structure. It is important to leave the foil on the pie shell long enough to set the shell. This is about 15 minutes, but make sure that the sides of the shell are dry and hard enough to stand up on their own. Bake another 10 minutes or so if the shell is to be baked a second time with filling. If the filling requires no baking, *be sure to continue baking until the shell is a nice nut brown.* This is necessary to develop sufficient flavor.

THE SECRET OF TENDER CUSTARDS

In all baking, food will continue to cook after it is removed from the oven. This is true of roast meats (they will rise in temperature a good 5°F while standing), fish (a fish steak cooked perfectly in the oven will be overdone by the time it is served), and, most important, custards. The center of a custard should still be wobbly when you remove it from the oven. For an 8- or 9-inch pie, this means that the middle 2 inches should be a bit loose (jiggle the pan to see if the center moves), although the perimeter of the pie will be set. Most cooks cook a custard or custard pie until it is completely set, which produces an overcooked, tough dessert.

THE BEST CUSTARD PIE

I started with a master recipe that used 4 eggs, ⅔ cup sugar, 2 cups milk, 1 cup heavy cream, plus salt and flavorings. This was an excellent recipe, the custard was light and delicate, but I wondered if I could use egg yolks for some or all of the whole eggs. I tried substituting 1 yolk for a whole egg (no difference) and using 4 egg yolks (a disaster — the custard curdled). When I used only 3 eggs, the custard had trouble setting, and therefore the cooking time had to be extended to the point that the top was over-browned.

I also wondered about the proportion of cream to milk, trying all milk (this lacked flavor and the pie collapsed in the middle during baking) and 2 cups cream to 1 cup milk (the texture was heavy, with a filmy aftertaste). I also fiddled with the proportion of sugar and settled on the original ⅔ cup. Finally, I thought that a lower baking temperature made sense — eggs should cook low and slow. But when baked at 350°F, which took 55 minutes, the custard had toughened by the time the pie had set. It reminded me of an overcooked custard pie you might find at a third-rate diner. The hotter oven, 400°F, was the winner. (I encountered the same phenomenon when baking eggs — the hotter oven temperature produced a more delicate egg.) So, all in all, the master recipe needed no changes.

IN SEARCH OF THE PERFECT CHIFFON PIE

Chiffon pies consist of a simple stovetop custard, thickened with cornstarch and then gelatin, which is folded into whipped cream and then poured into a prebaked pie shell. (A cream pie, on the other hand, is a custard pie thickened with cornstarch and then topped with whipped cream.) Some recipes don't set up properly; you can't get a nice clean slice. Others are too tough — the cream mixture loses that light, silky quality and becomes heavy on the palate. I was searching for a moist, rich pie with plenty of flavor but still delicate, and with a firm but pleasant texture.

I started with a basic recipe that used 2 whole eggs, 2 egg yolks, 2 cups milk, 1¾ cups heavy cream, ¾ cup sugar, 2 tablespoons cornstarch, and 1 packet of unflavored gelatin, plus salt, a bit of butter, and flavorings. My first test was an odd one. I had experimented with adding gelatin to whipping cream when perfecting a recipe for whipped cream frosting and thought that this might be a good technique for chiffon pies. Having made lots of chiffon pies, I knew that adding the gelatin to the custard created a problem — you had to fold in the whipped cream at just the right moment; otherwise, the custard would have set too much and it would be hard to incorporate the cream. However, upon testing, I found that adding the gelatin to the cream is also problematic. If you are not careful, the gelatin will start to rope when it comes into contact with the beaters. I solved this by slowly incorporating the dis-

---

KITCHEN TEST

In Search of the Perfect Custard Pie

Eight variations were tested on a basic custard pie recipe using 4 eggs, ⅔ cup sugar, 2 cups milk, 1 cup heavy cream, salt, and flavorings. The master recipe came through with flying colors, needing no changes.

Test	Results
Use all milk	Custard much too bland; collapsed in middle
Use 2 cups cream, 1 cup milk	Custard too heavy; deadens flavor
Use 3 whole eggs plus 1 yolk	About the same as 4 whole eggs
Use 3 whole eggs	Not enough thickening power; baking time had to be increased, which overcooked the top of the pie
Use 4 yolks only	A disaster; would not set up; curdled
Use ½ cup sugar	Custard lacked flavor
Use ¾ cup sugar	Custard a bit too sweet
Bake at 350°F, not 400°	Took 55 minutes; custard overcooked by the time it had set

Why Do Custards Thicken?

Eggs, the thickening agent in most custards, contain albumen proteins. These consist of long chains of amino acids that are coiled up like sleeping snakes. These chains retain this shape because of the bonding properties of different parts of the chain, yet the chains themselves will not bond to each other because each of them has a net negative charge, which causes repulsion (only opposites attract in chemistry). With the application of heat, however, these coiled chains start to unwind. As this happens, the chains themselves become more attracted to each other and start bonding. Eventually, a web of chains is created, which traps water molecules. Now the custard starts to thicken. Problems occur with overcooking because this encourages the proteins, the chains of amino acids, to bond more tightly, which squeezes out the water held between them. As a result, the custard becomes tougher and starts to "weep," or exude water. So for a delicate but firm custard, it is crucial to provide just enough cooking to trap the water molecules but not so much that the custard begins to weep. That is why I recommend removing a custard pie from the oven when the center is still not set. If the pie remains in the oven until it is completely set, it will overcook as it stands on the counter cooling (custards continue cooking after removal from the oven).

solved gelatin into the cream before cranking up the electric mixer, but then I came across a second problem. With this method, the custard did not stabilize properly. So I went back to the traditional approach, adding the dissolved gelatin to the custard after it had been cooked and strained. To solve the problem of folding in the whipped cream, I decided to whip the cream until firm *but not stiff*. A stiff whipped cream is very hard to fold into a rapidly thickening custard base. This method worked fine.

I then wondered if more cornstarch would be an improvement. I made a pie with 3 tablespoons and it was slightly thicker, although the master recipe was also fine. I like a chiffon pie that sets up but is still a little wobbly and very moist, so I stayed with the lesser amount. I tried making the custard with all milk instead of 2 cups milk and 1 cup heavy cream, and the result was unappealing: not as creamy and definitely lacking in substance. When I tried using 4 egg yolks instead of 2 whole eggs and 2 yolks, however, the pie was silky smooth, with just the texture I was looking for. (In the Master Recipe for Custard Pie, the 4 egg yolk variation did not work because the mixture was baked until it thickened. With a chiffon pie, the mixture is cooked less, depending on gelatin and cornstarch for most of its thickening power.)

I also found that using an ice water bath for the custard once it comes off the stove dramatically shortens preparation time (place the custard in a metal bowl that has been set in a large bowl containing cold water and ice cubes). The vanilla and butter are whisked in and then the gelatin is dissolved in ⅓ cup milk, which is then stirred in as well. Now it takes just 10 minutes for the gelatin to kick in, thickening the custard (without a water bath, this step takes a good half hour). It's important to stir the custard frequently as it sets; otherwise, it may thicken too much for folding.

Master Recipe for Prebaked Pie Shell

Use the master recipe for pie dough in Chapter 41. Be sure to follow these directions precisely and you should have no trouble prebaking.

1 Master Recipe for American Pie Dough (page 367)

1. Make master recipe and refrigerate dough for at least 30 minutes. If dough has spent more than 1 hour in the refrigerator, let it warm up a few minutes on the counter before proceeding.

2. Roll out dough and place into an 8- or 9-inch pie plate (see illustrations, page 365). Push dough gently down the sides of the pan.

Trim dough around edge of pan, leaving a ½-inch border. Fold excess dough under and shape edge of crust using a fork or fingers (see illustrations, page 366). Place in freezer for 10 minutes.

3. Remove pie pan from freezer and prick bottom and sides of shell with a fork every ½ inch. Fit a double thickness of heavy-duty aluminum foil (the extra-wide rolls are best) over shell, pressing foil carefully into bottom of pie plate and against the sides. Prick bottom of foil 8–10 times with a fork. Place in freezer for 20 minutes. Heat oven to 400°F.

4. Remove from freezer and add pie weights or dried beans, enough to generously cover bottom of pie plate. Bake on lower rack of preheated oven for 15 minutes or until sides of pie shell are set. Remove foil. Bake another 8–10 minutes if shell is to be baked a second time with filling; if not, bake until shell is a rich nut-brown, 35–40 minutes in total. Remove from oven and cool on a rack.

Master Recipe for Custard Pie

Although custard pies look simple, they require the perfect combination of ingredients to produce a light, delicate custard with good body and flavor. Be sure to remove this pie from the oven when the center 2 inches is still very wobbly (the rest of the pie will have set). The custard will continue cooking after it is removed from the oven. Don't replace the heavy cream with milk to make a "lighter" pie — the custard will not set up properly. For variations, try using fresh or softened dried fruit in the pie shell along with the custard.

   1 hot prebaked 8- or 9-inch pie shell

Custard
   4 large eggs
  ⅔ cup sugar
   1 teaspoon vanilla extract
  ½ teaspoon freshly grated nutmeg
  ¼ teaspoon kosher salt
   2 cups milk
   1 cup heavy cream

1. Heat oven to 400°F. Gently whisk together the first 5 ingredients of the custard. Heat the milk and heavy cream in a saucepan until mixture starts to steam. Pour into a 4-cup glass measuring cup and let cool for 30 seconds. Pour into egg mixture, whisking gently.

2. Place pan with pie shell on a baking sheet on the middle rack of the oven. With the oven rack pulled halfway out, pour in the custard mixture. Slide rack into oven, close door, and bake for 25–30 minutes. Remove pie from oven when perimeter of custard is set but center 2 inches is still wobbly. Cool on a wire rack for at least 2 hours before serving.

Makes one 8- or 9-inch pie

Orange Custard Variation

The addition of orange juice will make a custard that is a little bit looser than the master recipe. However, it will still set up properly, and the flavor is excellent. Add 1 tablespoon of minced (not grated) orange zest, ¼ cup orange juice, and 1 extra egg yolk. Reduce vanilla to ½ teaspoon. Increase sugar to ¾ cup. Eliminate nutmeg.

Coconut Custard Variation

I find that opening and grating fresh coconut is not worth the trouble. Health food stores carry unsweetened dried coconut that is just fine. I would, however, avoid the bags of shredded coconut sold in most supermarkets. I prefer dried coconut on the coarse side; the finely grated variety doesn't provide enough texture. The coconut will float to the top of the custard during baking.

   3 large eggs
  ⅔ cup sugar
  ¾ teaspoon vanilla extract
  ½ teaspoon freshly grated nutmeg
  ¼ teaspoon kosher salt
 1½ cups milk
  ¾ cup heavy cream
   1 cup shredded dried coconut

Follow directions for master recipe and add coconut along with milk and heavy cream. If you prefer toasted coconut, place shredded coconut on a baking sheet in a 375° oven for about 8 minutes.

Master Recipe for Chiffon Pie

There are two secrets to a really good chiffon pie. Use all egg yolks instead of a combination of whole eggs and yolks. This produces a silky, rich texture. Second, don't whip the cream until stiff. A firm but still moist whipped cream will fold easily into the setting custard base. This recipe has endless variations.

1 prebaked 9-inch pie shell (shell should be baked for 35–40 minutes or until a rich nut-brown)

Filling
4 egg yolks
2 tablespoons cornstarch
¾ cup sugar
¼ teaspoon kosher salt
1 tablespoon dark rum or cognac
2 cups milk
1¾ cups heavy cream
2 teaspoons vanilla extract
1 tablespoon unsalted butter
1 packet (2 teaspoons) unflavored gelatin
½ teaspoon freshly grated nutmeg
2 tablespoons superfine sugar

1. Whisk together the first 5 ingredients in a medium bowl. Heat 1⅔ cups of the milk (reserving ⅓ cup for gelatin) and 1 cup of the cream (reserving ¾ cup) in a large saucepan until bubbling around the edges. Remove from heat and whisk into egg mixture slowly.

2. Place custard back into saucepan and heat, stirring constantly, until mixture thickens, 3 or 4 minutes. Do not let mixture boil (if mixture starts to steam heavily, remove from heat and whisk rapidly to cool down). Strain custard into a metal bowl to remove lumps and whisk in vanilla and butter.

3. In a small saucepan, sprinkle the gelatin over reserved ⅓ cup milk and when softened, place over very low heat and heat until dissolved. Stir into warm custard.

4. Place metal bowl of custard in a larger bowl half filled with cold water and ice cubes. Stir custard mixture every minute until it starts to set (about 10 minutes). Meanwhile, in a separate bowl, whip reserved ¾ cup cream until it starts to thicken. Add nutmeg and sugar and continue beating until firm *but not stiff*. Stir ⅓ of the whipped cream into the custard. Fold custard and remaining whipped cream together. Pour into fully prebaked shell and chill for 2 hours before serving.

Makes one 9-inch pie

Banana Chiffon Variation

Cut 2 ripe bananas in half lengthwise and then into ¼-inch slices. Fold them into the custard just before adding the whipped cream (step 4).

Chocolate Chiffon Variation

Melt 8 ounces of semisweet chocolate in a small saucepan in a 250° oven (about 15 minutes), or use a microwave oven (50 percent power for 3–4 minutes; stir after 2 minutes). Add chocolate to custard just before straining (step 2).

Coconut Chiffon Variation

Add 1 cup of grated dried coconut to the whipped cream just before folding into the custard (step 4). After filling pie shell, top pie with ⅓ cup toasted dried coconut (toast coconut on a baking sheet in a 375° oven for about 8 minutes — check frequently to avoid burning).

Pumpkin Pie

This is a basic custard pie that uses pumpkin puree in place of the milk. If the crust starts to overcook during baking, cover with aluminum foil, leaving the filling still exposed. For a "souf-fléd" version of this recipe, separate 2 of the 3 eggs called for in the recipe; use the yolks in the filling and whip the whites. Fold the whites into the filling just before placing in the pie shell. Follow all other instructions. It is best to place the hot filling into a hot prebaked pie shell, as this will ensure a crisp crust.

1 hot prebaked 9-inch pie shell

Filling
2 cups pumpkin or squash puree
¾ cup brown sugar
3 tablespoons molasses
½ teaspoon kosher salt
¼ teaspoon ground nutmeg
¼ teaspoon ground ginger
½ teaspoon ground cinnamon
⅛ teaspoon ground cloves
1 cup heavy cream
3 tablespoons bourbon
3 eggs

1. Heat oven to 425°F. Whisk together all filling ingredients except the eggs in a medium saucepan. Place over low heat and cook, stirring occasionally, until bubbling. Remove saucepan from heat and whisk in eggs one at a time.

2. Pour filling into still hot prebaked pie shell and place on a baking sheet in the oven. Bake for 10 minutes and then lower heat to 350°F. Turn pie around so that filling bakes evenly.

3. Bake 13–15 minutes longer, but start checking the pie after 10 minutes and every minute thereafter. A custard pie will set up quickly. Check by jiggling pie slightly. Mixture should be puffed up and set around the perimeter but still wobbly in the very center (about a 2-inch-diameter circle in the middle of the pie should not be set — it will continue to cook and firm up after the pie is removed from the oven). Remove from oven and let cool on a rack for at least 1 hour before serving.

Makes one 9-inch pie

Creamy Pecan Pie

It seems like every cook in America has his or her own recipe for pecan pie, which is really a variation on a basic custard pie. For my version, I've added heavy cream, which makes the filling softer and creamier. The first version below is the quick and easy method. For a superior pecan pie, try the Crisp-Crust Variation, which involves prebaking the crust and preheating the filling. For a more elegant presentation, bake your pecan pie in a tart pan.

1 Master Recipe for American Pie Dough (8- or 9-inch crust) (page 367)

Filling
1½ cups pecans
3 eggs
1 cup dark corn syrup
½ cup dark brown sugar
½ teaspoon vanilla extract
1 tablespoon bourbon or dark rum
½ cup heavy cream
¼ teaspoon kosher salt
2 tablespoons melted butter

1. Spread out the pecans on a baking sheet and toast in a 375° oven, about 7 minutes. Check frequently to avoid burning. Chop coarsely. Heat oven to 425°F.

2. Beat the eggs with a whisk until blended. Whisk in the corn syrup, sugar, vanilla, bourbon, heavy cream, salt, and melted butter.

3. Roll out the pastry dough and fit into a 9-inch pie pan. Trim, leaving a ½-inch overlap. Fold the excess dough under and crimp with a fork or fingers.

4. Fold pecans into filling, pour filling into pie shell, and bake for 10 minutes. Reduce heat to 375°F and bake for another 20 minutes or so, or until knife inserted in the center comes out clean. Be careful not to overbake, as filling will become tough and hard. Cool on a rack to room temperature before serving.

Makes one 8- or 9-inch pie

Crisp-Crust Variation

Although it is a bit more difficult, it is best to prebake the crust and also heat the filling. This shortens the oven time and results in a crispy crust. Follow the directions for pre-baking on page 377. Prepare filling and heat in a medium saucepan until hot but not bubbling. Pour into hot prebaked crust and bake 12–14 minutes in a 425° oven.

Graham Cracker Crust

I use the bottom of a drinking glass to press the graham cracker crumbs into the pie plate. You can also use a slightly smaller pie plate. Try to make the crust as even as possible — sometimes it's hard to gauge the thickness of the bottom crust. The crust will harden as it cools — don't worry if it still appears a little dry and loose when it first comes from the oven. This type of crust works well with a chiffon pie and it's also a lot easier than prebaking a pie shell.

1 cup crumbled graham crackers
2 tablespoons brown sugar
4 tablespoons butter

1. Heat oven to 350°F. Process graham crackers to fine crumbs in the bowl of a food processor. Add sugar and process a few seconds to mix. Melt butter. Add butter and process until well blended.

2. Press mixture into a pie plate (this recipe is enough for an 8- or 9-inch pie plate).

3. Chill in refrigerator for 20 minutes. Bake in preheated oven for about 15 minutes, and remove from oven just before crust starts to brown.

Makes one 8- or 9-inch piecrust.

~ 44 ~

The Best Chocolate Cake

Use cocoa not chocolate, buttermilk not sweet milk, add 1 extra egg white and 2 teaspoons of instant coffee for a light, moist, intensely flavored chocolate cake.

~

My first culinary outing was at age nine, when I grabbed a banged-up copy of the *Fannie Farmer Cookbook* and set out to make a chocolate cake from scratch for my dad's birthday dinner. I am quite certain that my short-term goal was to create a bowl that needed licking, but the cake itself turned out pretty well, although the boiled icing ended up as a thin, transparent gruel. Since that time, I have made dozens of cakes and discovered that the relationship between ingredients and result is at best random and sometimes inverse. You can't theorize about cake baking, you just have to do it.

THE BASIC RECIPE

Thirty-six years after that first foray, I had learned a few things about cake baking. I knew that cocoa powder is better than chocolate itself. The cake will have a deeper, more chocolaty flavor. I knew that the butter and sugar had to be creamed to get a nice light texture. I also thought that cake flour was probably best, although I intended to do a blind taste test with all-purpose flour as well. I know many cooks and many cake recipes that call for the latter.

I started with a master recipe that I had developed over many years and thought was quite good. I use cake flour, sweet milk, 2 eggs, and Dutch process cocoa. I made it again but with all-purpose flour and, to my surprise, the difference was noticeable but not substantial. The cake was still light but a bit more compact. Although I call for cake flour in the final recipe, all-purpose flour can easily be substituted. I also tried self-rising flour, which, when I left out the salt, baking powder, and baking soda, worked just fine.

I then replaced the milk with buttermilk, my favorite baking ingredient, and was not surprised to find that the cake had a richer chocolate flavor and was also moister. This was a clear winner. When I tried sour cream, however, I was disappointed to find that the texture was a bit too airy for my taste.

Marion Cunningham, who authored the most recent edition of the *Fannie Farmer Cookbook*, told me that adding water to a cake batter can make a difference. I tried it, adding 2 tablespoons, and was disappointed. The cake had lost some of its rich chocolate flavor, the texture was a bit more compact, and it was not noticeably moister. An extra egg didn't help much either, resulting in a looser, less fine-textured cake. I did, however, make a fascinating discovery when I added 2 additional egg whites; the extra whites completely changed the "mouth feel." The cake coated the inside of my mouth with a rich, chocolaty flavor. But the texture was too light, almost like a sponge cake. I cut back to 1 additional egg white and the texture came into line nicely.

THE MASTER RECIPE

So my new master recipe uses buttermilk, 1 extra egg white, and cake flour. I went on to also add 2 teaspoons of instant espresso to give the cake a little extra depth. Use 8-inch cake pans for this recipe, as there is not enough batter to fill 9-inch pans. You can use two single-layer pans or one deeper pan, cutting the cake in two after baking for filling.

Master Recipe for Chocolate Cake

Dutch process cocoa is treated to remove some of its natural acidity; this creates a darker, more mellow-flavored cocoa. Droste and Van Houten are two well-known brands. Buttermilk produces a much deeper chocolate flavor and a moister texture. If you don't have cocoa, melt 3 squares of unsweetened chocolate with 2 tablespoons of water (in a 275° oven for 15 minutes or over very low heat, stirring frequently) and set aside. Add to the batter after the eggs have been incorporated.

1½ cups cake flour
½ cup unsweetened Dutch process cocoa
2 teaspoons instant espresso or instant coffee powder
¼ teaspoon baking powder
½ teaspoon baking soda
½ teaspoon kosher salt
12 tablespoons (1½ sticks) unsalted butter, softened
1¼ cups sugar
2 whole eggs, room temperature
1 egg white, room temperature
1½ teaspoons vanilla extract
1 cup buttermilk

1. Grease the bottom of two 8-inch round baking pans. Line with parchment or wax paper. Grease paper and lightly flour pans; turn pans upside down and lightly tap to remove excess flour. Preheat oven to 350°F. Adjust oven rack to middle position.

2. Sift the flour, cocoa, instant coffee, baking powder, baking soda, and salt onto a sheet of waxed paper. Add butter to the bowl of an electric mixer and beat for 1 minute or until light-colored. Add sugar gradually and beat on medium-high speed for 3 minutes until mixture is very light-colored and fluffy (scrape down 2 or 3 times). Add whole eggs and egg white one at a time, beating for 20 seconds after each addition. Add the vanilla and beat for 10 seconds.

3. Add the flour mixture in three parts alternately with the buttermilk. Beat on low speed after each addition and scrape down the sides of the bowl with a rubber spatula. Do not overbeat.

4. Pour batter into pan(s) and bake 25–30 minutes (about 10 minutes longer if using only one pan). Cool for 15 minutes and then

---

COOKING TIP

How to Cut a Round of Parchment Paper

While I was watching Marcus Farbinger, head of pastry instruction at the Culinary Institute of America, demonstrate cake making during a taping of Julia Child's television baking series, I picked up a great way to quickly and easily cut a round of parchment paper for the bottom of a cake pan. Turn the pan upside down and place a sheet of parchment paper over it. Run the back (the dull, upper part of the blade) of a large chef's knife around the outside of the bottom of the pan. This will cut through the parchment paper, producing a perfectly-sized round. You may have to go over the same section more than once until the parchment paper separates. Don't worry if the edge of the round tears a little — this will not affect the cake at all.

The Perfect Chocolate Cake

My original master recipe was baked with many variations. Buttermilk and 1 additional egg white increased the depth of flavor and dramatically improved the "mouth feel" of the cake. The addition of 2 teaspoons of instant espresso or coffee also punches up the flavor.

Test	Result
Original master recipe	Very fine crumb, tender, very light
Substitute self-rising flour	Same as above
Substitute buttermilk for milk	Very good; moister and richer chocolate flavor
Substitute sour cream for part of the milk	Very soufflélike, loose, a bit too light
Add 2 tablespoons water	Chocolate flavor diluted, compact texture, cake not moister
Add 1 whole egg	Looser, less fine-textured, good flavor
Add 2 egg whites	Excellent flavor and mouth feel, but too much like a sponge cake
Substitute all-purpose flour	Light, but more compact texture than with cake flour, although a minor difference
Use buttermilk plus 1 extra egg white	Excellent; great mouth feel
Use buttermilk, 1 extra egg white, and all-purpose flour	Slightly less airy; not quite as good
Add 2 teaspoons instant espresso powder	Deeper, richer flavor

remove cake from pan onto wire rack. Let cool fully before frosting.

Makes two 8-inch rounds

Mocha Variation

Substitute ½ cup of strong coffee for ½ cup buttermilk.

Creamy Chocolate Glaze

This is a simple glaze that is poured over the cake when it has been placed on a wire rack. It's easier to use than a frosting and provides an elegant, glossy look. Determining when the glaze is ready to be poured over the cake is the only crucial step. To test this, drizzle a spoonful of the glaze back into the pan. When the glaze is ready, it should mound up a little as it touches the glaze in the pan. It's like drizzling honey into honey, although the glaze won't be quite that thick.

8 ounces semisweet chocolate
1 cup heavy cream
¼ cup light corn syrup
½ teaspoon vanilla extract

1. Chop the chocolate in the bowl of a heavy-duty food processor (an inexpensive processor may not be able to handle this task). You can also chop it by hand with a large chef's knife.

2. Combine cream and corn syrup in a saucepan. Bring to a simmer. Remove from heat and add chocolate. Let stand for 8 minutes.

3. Add vanilla. Stir mixture very gently over low heat until chocolate melts completely and mixture is smooth.

4. Allow glaze to cool until tepid. Drizzle a spoonful of glaze back into the pan. When it mounds a little, the glaze is ready for pouring over the cake.

5. Place cake to be frosted on a wire rack set over a roasting or jelly roll pan to catch the drippings. Pour contents of saucepan over middle of cake. Use a metal spatula if necessary to completely cover cake. Use a small needle to puncture air bubbles. Let sit about 1 hour or until glaze fully sets.

Makes enough glaze for a single-layer 8- or 9-inch cake.

Creamy Chocolate Frosting

This recipe is almost identical to the one above, but the frosting is allowed to harden a bit more, creating a thick frosting rather than a thin glaze. If your refrigerator is not cold enough, this frosting could take 2–3 hours to become stiff. If that happens, place frosting in the freezer and check and stir every 10 minutes.

12 ounces semisweet chocolate
 1 teaspoon instant espresso or instant coffee powder
1⅔ cups heavy cream
 ¼ cup light corn syrup
 ¼ teaspoon vanilla extract

1. Place chocolate and instant espresso in the bowl of a food processor and chop fine. Heat the heavy cream in a small saucepan until bubbles start to form around the edge. With the food processor running, add the cream, then the corn syrup and vanilla extract. Process until the chocolate has melted and the mixture is smooth.

2. Remove to a bowl, cover, and refrigerate until mixture is the texture of a thick frosting. Check frequently, stirring to check the consistency.

Makes enough frosting for a 2-layer 8- or 9-inch cake.

Magic Whipped Cream Frosting

Most whipped cream frostings don't hold up well, so I have developed this version, which uses a bit of dissolved unflavored gelatin to give the whipped cream some stiffness and staying power.

1 teaspoon unflavored gelatin
2 cups heavy cream
¼ cup confectioner's sugar
½ teaspoon vanilla extract

1. Chill bowl and beaters of an electric mixer in the freezer for at least 10 minutes.

2. Sprinkle gelatin over 2 tablespoons water in a small saucepan. Let dissolve for 4 minutes. Over very low heat, melt gelatin mixture, about 3 minutes.

3. Place heavy cream and melted gelatin in the chilled bowl. Beat on low speed for 30 seconds until dissolved gelatin is thoroughly mixed into cream. Increase speed to high and beat until cream just starts to take shape. Add sugar and vanilla and beat until stiff.

Makes enough to frost the top and sides of an 8- or 9-inch cake.

Almond, Orange, and Lemon Variations

Use ½ teaspoon of almond extract, orange extract, or lemon extract in place of the vanilla.

~ 45 ~

Angel, Sponge, and Chiffon Cakes

These three cakes are all based on beaten egg whites, yet their textures are remarkably different.

~

Angel food, sponge, and chiffon cakes are really quite different, although all three depend on beaten egg whites for their structure. Angel food, the purest of the three, uses no egg yolks and is nothing more than a mixture of cake flour, beaten egg whites, and flavorings. A sponge cake is a bit heartier, as it incorporates egg yolks as well as whites, making it slightly more cakelike. The chiffon cake, which was invented by a Los Angeles insurance salesman and then sold to Betty Crocker (General Mills) in 1947, uses ½ cup vegetable oil, which makes it a cross between an angel food cake and a butter cake. It has a rich, moist texture and keeps well. The vegetable oil also helps to tenderize the egg whites, and therefore less sugar, as a percentage of the total ingredients, is required (sugar also tenderizes the protein in egg whites).

TESTING CAKE STRUCTURE

Since all three cakes are rather similar, I made up a list of basic tests to perform before working with individual recipes (I used a basic angel food recipe as a control). I wanted to test all-purpose flour versus cake flour, the amount of flour and sugar in rela-tion to the egg whites, the oven temperature, and also whether cream of tartar is really an essential ingredient. With breads, I have found that all-purpose is often interchangeable with bread flour; with muffins and many cakes, I have found cake flour and all-purpose to be almost identical. However, my testing showed that an angel food cake made with all-purpose flour is very coarse and unpleasant. This is one category of recipes for which cake flour is a must.

I then started wondering about the amount of flour. I decreased the flour from 1 cup to ¾ cup and discovered that the cake collapsed during cooling. I had inadvertently made a soufflé, not a cake! There just wasn't enough flour to create a lasting structure. I then reduced the quantity of sugar and the cake became tough and tasteless. Although an angel food cake is quite sweet, it depends heavily on the sugar content for both tenderizing and flavor. When I bumped the oven temperature to 375°F, I found that the outside of the cake took on a darker, more golden texture, which added a good deal of flavor. Finally, the most interesting test was the cake made without cream of tartar. It was tough and lacked structure, exhibiting a very uneven texture.

So I had discovered that cake flour was

best, a 375° oven was better than lower temperatures, that cream of tartar was essential, and that both sugar and flour must be present in large enough quantities to create structure, tenderize, and to add flavor. Now I went on to test specific recipes.

TESTING THE RECIPES

IN SEARCH OF PERFECT ANGEL FOOD

How many egg whites is the right amount? Most recipes call for 10 whites, which is what was in my initial master recipe. However, when I increased the amount to 12, the cake was slightly better; a bit fluffier, a bit lighter, and a winner. I also tested 8 egg whites and found that the cake was a good deal shorter and denser — not at all what I expect from a sky-high angel food recipe.

I had also been told that water is a good addition for many cakes. Rose Beranbaum, author of *The Cake Bible*, was once having trouble with a meringue cake — the texture was tough and unpleasant — and Shirley Corriher, a well-known food scientist, told her to add water to the recipe. It was a success, moister and more tender. However, when I tried adding 1 tablespoon of water to

my angel food recipe, it didn't improve the cake at all; in fact, I thought that the texture was a little less substantial, a bit like cotton candy. I then tried adding ½ cup water and the cake was a disaster; it fell during baking and was a wet mess of a cake. The egg whites just couldn't hold that much liquid. (I did add water successfully to the other two cakes, sponge and chiffon, however.)

THE SECRETS OF SPONGE CAKES

My master recipe, one I had been using for years, was quite similar to an angel food recipe except that it called for the addition of 6 egg yolks and 2 tablespoons of cold water. I was curious about the egg yolks, so I tried two different cakes, one made with 5 yolks and the other with 4. I could not tell the difference. They looked and tasted exactly the same, so I went with the 4-yolk version and saved on fat. I then tried one version with no water at all — it was slightly tougher and drier. The big surprise was the version with ¼ cup water; it was a lot moister. It was clear that the egg yolks provided enough structure so that the cake could absorb the water and keep it bonded by the proteins. The water in effect dilutes the proteins, making the cake more tender.

THE CHIFFON CAKE

A chiffon cake is much more of a traditional cake than either a sponge cake or an angel food cake. It has double the amount of flour, ½ cup vegetable oil, and a bit of baking powder for lift (it needs a chemical lift due to the weight of the extra ingredients). I started off by decreasing the amount of sugar and found, as I had with the angel food cake, that the full amount (in this case, 1½ cups) was necessary for good flavor. I also tested the amount of water and found that ½ cup worked well, double what I used with the sponge cake. This illustrates once again that the strength of the cake structure determines how much water can be added. An angel

---

SCIENCE OF COOKING

Why Is Cream of Tartar an Essential Ingredient?

Cream of tartar is an acid and it is particularly good at denaturing (unwinding) the strands of protein in egg whites. This enhances their bonding properties — that is, the proteins start to bond with each other, forming a spiderweb structure — which results in a more stable, more structured cake. Until the protein strands unwind, it is more difficult for them to join together (when the proteins are coiled like a snake, many of the molecules are hidden and are not available for bonding). Acid has the same effect when a custard that contains fruit (an acid) is baked. The fruit will make the custard set faster.

food cake is the most delicate of the three recipes and can't handle extra water. The sponge cake has egg yolks and could carry ¼ cup, whereas a chiffon cake, with double the flour and vegetable oil, can handle a full ½ cup.

I also tried a version with only ¼ cup oil and the cake was a bit drier, not as rich and moist. And I made one cake with melted butter instead of oil and found that the flavor was wonderful — you could really taste the butter — but that the texture was about the same. If you want to boost the flavor of this cake and don't mind the extra cholesterol, go with the butter.

BAKING THE CAKES

All three cakes are baked in ungreased 10-inch tube pans. Why ungreased? As the egg whites expand in the oven, they need to "climb" up the sides of the pan, which would be impossible if they were greased. After baking an angel food cake, the tube pan is turned upside down, which prevents the delicate cake structure from collapsing during cooling (the cake hangs upside down while the protein structure is setting). However, this is not necessary for either a sponge or chiffon cake because the added ingredients create sufficient structure to avoid collapsing. In fact, when I tried this technique with a sponge cake, the cake simply fell out of the pan onto the counter.

The Best Angel Food Cake

Angel food cake is a bit like cotton candy; it's all air and sugar. I like to serve angel food with slightly sweetened berries; peaches and strawberries are my favorites since they produce so much juice, which goes well with the cake. The lemon juice in this recipe is an acid, which helps to create structure for the cake; it also whitens the crumb.

1 cup cake flour
1¼ cups sugar
¼ teaspoon kosher salt
12 egg whites
1 teaspoon cream of tartar
1 teaspoon vanilla extract
1½ teaspoons lemon juice

1. Heat oven to 375°F. Place the flour, ½ cup of sugar, and the salt in a sifter and sift onto a large piece of wax paper.

2. Beat the egg whites in the bowl of an electric mixer at medium speed for 1 minute or until whites begin to foam and bubble. Add cream of tartar. Turn mixer to high and beat until whites start to form very soft peaks and have increased three or four times in volume. Slowly add remaining ¾ cup sugar and continue beating until whites hold soft peaks. Add vanilla and lemon juice and beat until whites can just hold a 2-inch peak.

3. Placing sifter over egg whites, sift ⅓ of flour mixture over whites at a time. After each sifting, fold flour into egg whites using a rubber spatula. Work quickly but smoothly — this step should take about 2 minutes in total.

4. Turn batter into an ungreased 10-inch tube pan (although a springform pan can be used as well). An ungreased pan allows the batter to cling to the sides as it rises. Bake for 20–30 minutes but check after 20. The top should be a rich gold and should spring back when touched lightly. If the top of the cake does not spring back, bake an additional 5–10 minutes (check every 5 minutes).

5. Remove pan from oven and turn upside down (if pan has feet) or balance pan on top of three or four solid mugs or glasses turned upside down. After 30 minutes, run a thin knife or spatula around the inside of the pan, as this cake is sticky and will adhere easily to the sides. Remove from pan and cool completely on a wire rack, bottom side up.

Makes one 10-inch cake

Angel Food, Sponge, and Chiffon Cakes

A few basic tests were performed to determine basic proportions, and then specific tests were performed for each type of cake.

	Test	Results
Basic Tests	All-purpose flour instead of cake flour	Very coarse
	Baked at 375°F	Nicely browned; rich golden crust adds flavor
	Baked at 350°F	Good, but crust not as flavorful as at 375°F
	Baked at 325°F	Too wet and sticky
	Less flour (¾ cup instead of 1 cup)	Cake collapsed when cooling
	Less sugar (1 cup instead of 1¼ cups)	Very tough and not much flavor
	No cream of tartar	Tougher; thin, uneven texture
Angel Food Tests	12 egg whites instead of 10	Excellent; light and fluffy
	8 egg whites instead of 10	Short — not as high and fluffy
	Added 1 tablespoon water	Texture suffers; drier and like cotton candy
	Added ½ cup water	Disaster; cake collapsed and was wet and soggy
Sponge Cake Tests	6 egg yolks	Very good texture
	5 egg yolks	Same as 6 yolks
	4 egg yolks	Same as 6 yolks
	No water	Slightly tougher and drier
	Water increased to ¼ cup	Definitely moister; slightly more tender
Chiffon Cake Tests	Less sugar (1¼ cups instead of 1½ cups)	Flavor not as bright
	Added ¼ cup water	Good texture
	Added ½ cup water	Definitely moister; excellent cake
	Substituted melted butter for oil	Terrific flavor; no change in texture

Master Recipe for Sponge Cake

A sponge cake is almost identical to an angel food cake, except that it has a few egg yolks thrown into the mix. I prefer sponge to angel food, as the cake has a more robust, less cottony texture and flavor.

1 cup cake flour
4 egg yolks
1½ teaspoons vanilla extract
¼ cup cold water
1¼ cups sugar
8 egg whites
½ teaspoon kosher salt
1½ teaspoons cream of tartar

1. Heat oven to 375°F. Sift flour onto a sheet of wax paper.

2. Place egg yolks in the bowl of an electric mixer and beat until thick and pale yellow, about 3 minutes. Add the vanilla and slowly add the water as you continue to beat. Slowly add the sugar (reserve 2 tablespoons) and beat until thick and very pale.

3. Place a 10-inch tube pan in the oven to heat. Sprinkle ⅓ of the flour over the beaten yolks and fold in with a rubber spatula. Repeat twice with remaining flour.

4. Beat egg whites with an electric mixer for 45 seconds on high speed. Add the salt and cream of tartar. Beat until the whites just start to hold a peak. Sprinkle in the remaining 2 tablespoons sugar and continue to beat until whites can hold a 2-inch peak but are still moist.

5. Stir ¼ of the beaten whites into the yolks

to lighten them, then fold in the rest gently with a rubber spatula or with your hand.

6. Pour mixture into preheated tube pan. Bake 25–35 minutes or until top is golden brown and springs back when lightly pressed with a fork. If the top of the cake does not spring back, bake for an additional 5–10 minutes (check every 5 minutes). Let cool in pan for 1 hour. Remove from pan.

Makes one 10-inch cake

Citrus Sponge Cake

Add 1 tablespoon grated lemon zest and ¼ cup orange juice to the beaten egg yolks. Increase flour to 1¼ cups.

Master Recipe for Chiffon Cake

A chiffon cake is quite similar to an angel food or sponge cake with one major difference. Chiffon cakes use oil and therefore less sugar is called for (in proportion to the other ingredients), providing a tender but not overly sweet cake. In an angel food cake, for example, the excessive amount of sugar is required to tenderize the protein in the egg whites. Due to the added flour and vegetable oil, however, a chiffon cake does need a chemical leavener to raise the structure. You can substitute melted butter for the vegetable oil if you like a strong butter flavor. This cake will keep better than the other two due to the added amount of fat.

  2¼ cups cake flour
  1½ cups sugar
   2 teaspoons baking powder
   ½ teaspoon kosher salt

  ½ cup vegetable oil or melted butter
  6 egg yolks
  ½ cup water
  2 teaspoons vanilla extract
  9 egg whites
  1 teaspoon cream of tartar

1. Heat oven to 375°F. Sift together the flour, 1 cup of sugar (reserving ½ cup), the baking powder, and the salt into a large bowl. Whisk together to blend.

2. In a separate bowl, whisk together the oil (or butter), egg yolks, water, and vanilla. Pour the liquid ingredients into the flour mixture and beat until smooth (this can be done by hand with a whisk or wooden spoon).

3. Whip the egg whites until frothy and then add the cream of tartar. Beat until soft peaks just begin to form. Add the remaining ½ cup sugar and beat until whites hold a 2-inch peak. Do not overbeat; whites should be billowy and glossy.

4. Fold the beaten whites into the batter and pour into an ungreased 10-inch tube pan. Bake for 35–45 minutes. Press lightly with a fork. If the top of the cake does not spring back, bake for an additional 5–10 minutes (check every 5 minutes).

5. Remove cake from oven and let cool in pan for at least 1 hour. Remove from pan.

Makes one 10-inch cake

Citrus Chiffon Cake

Replace ½ cup water with ½ cup orange juice. Add 1 tablespoon of grated lemon zest. Reduce vanilla extract to 1 teaspoon.

Baking a Cookie

What could be simpler than a chocolate chip cookie? The fact is that cookies are just as complex, variable, and difficult to perfect as any cake.

~

Until I began testing cookie recipes, I thought that they were rather simple combinations of flour, eggs, and fat. I quickly found out that those "simple" recipes were actually rather complex, rarely obeying what I consider to be the established culinary rules of cause and effect. In essence, cookies are little cakes, with all of the attendant difficulties.

THE UNIVERSAL COOKIE

I started with a master recipe for refrigerator cookies, dough that can be held for some time and used when needed. The recipe provides a simple canvas on which you can paint just about any flavor, so the master recipe is endlessly variable. These are straight-up sugar cookies: sturdy, good for a lunch box or a picnic, and as American as pot roast. Here's the universal recipe used by almost every baker:

1½ cups all-purpose flour
1 egg
½ cup sugar (brown or white)
½ cup shortening (butter or Crisco)
¼ teaspoon baking soda or baking powder
¼ teaspoon kosher salt

Flavorings (chocolate, vanilla, citrus, spices, almond, etc.)
½ cup nuts, optional

Once you look at this recipe on the page, it's easy to see how to make quick and simple variations. Want a chocolate cookie? Just add chocolate flavoring (unsweetened cocoa plus additional sugar, or melted semisweet chocolate). Want a spice cookie? Add spices (and use dark brown sugar for more flavor). Want a lemon or orange cookie? Simply add grated zest plus some citrus flavoring.

For a shortbread, simply increase the proportion of shortening to flour (use 12 tablespoons instead of 8) and eliminate the leavening so the cookie is denser. Want a soft, rich chocolate chip cookie? Increase the proportion of sugar and shortening and add chocolate chips. Want a thinner cookie? Take out the baking soda or baking powder. Want a nut cookie? Just add nuts (and maybe some nut flavoring, such as almond extract).

The master recipe below is my version of the universal cookie recipe. I have tried using different flours, including cake flour, and have tried substituting cornstarch for part of the all-purpose flour. Both techniques are designed to create a softer cookie. However, I have found that the dough is very difficult to work, plus the resulting cookie is simply too soft. I like some bite in my food, not a dainty fall-apart confection. I have also cut back on the sugar just a bit and have used 1 egg plus 1 egg yolk instead of 2 eggs. I find this provides a bit more body and texture.

There are many ways to shape these cookies. The three techniques I like the best are simply dropping spoonfuls of batter on a cookie sheet, rolling the dough in a log in wax paper and chilling it until needed (these are the original "refrigerator" cookies and are quickly sliced and put onto the cookie sheet), or rolling out the dough and cutting out cookies with a cookie cutter, biscuit cutter, or drinking glass.

This is a good recipe for improvisation. Don't be afraid to change and juggle the ingredients list, as long as you keep the basic proportions about the same. Try more butter. Add some chocolate chunks. See what happens!

THE BEST OATMEAL COOKIE

The search for the perfect oatmeal cookie turned out to be akin to finding the Holy Grail. I started with a master recipe that was very heavy on shortening and set out to try a few variations. (The recipe included 2 sticks of butter, 1 cup sugar, ½ cup light brown sugar, 2 large eggs, ½ teaspoon vanilla extract, 1 cup all-purpose flour, 2½ cups oats, 1 teaspoon baking soda, ½ teaspoon salt, 1 cup raisins, and a few spices.) However, when tested, the cookies were flat and greasy, a far cry from my ideal, which has good height, lots of chew, and lots of flavor.

KITCHEN TESTS, ROUND ONE
I tested refrigerating the dough to create a thicker cookie, a technique that works well with chocolate cookies, and found that the dough had to chill for a good 45 minutes before baking. I decided that the slight im-

provement in thickness was not worth the wait. Adding an extra egg white just made the cookie stickier. Melting the butter instead of creaming it made the cookie thinner and a little greasier. I also tried molasses, which was bitter, as well as adding an extra egg yolk, reducing the sugar, and reducing the butter, all with disappointing results.

FANNIE FARMER AND QUAKER OATS
I put aside the master recipe and went through my 1914 edition of Fannie Farmer's *Boston Cooking School Cookbook*. That recipe used a much lower proportion of shortening. The good news was that the cookie finally had some height; the bad news was that it had no taste and was very dry. In desperation, I followed the recipe on the back of the Quaker Oats container, and this worked fairly well, although the flavor was still rather pedestrian and the texture was a bit dense. I then came across the *Red Lion Inn Cookbook* and found an oatmeal cookie recipe that used 2 teaspoons of baking powder. I tried this addition and the cookies were much lighter, but the texture suffered a bit, producing a less chewy cookie.

After all this testing, however, I still had two problems. First, these cookies did not taste much like oatmeal. They tasted like spice cookies with a slight hint of oats. Second, the texture was all wrong, more cakey than chewy. To solve these problems, I called the baker at the Claremont Café in Boston, where I had just eaten the world's best oatmeal cookie, and she shared with me her recipe. Compared with my original master recipe, hers used an additional ½ cup each of oats, flour, and sugar. I baked a batch and found that these were terrific cookies with a slightly crispy exterior and great chew. But they were a bit too sweet, so I dropped the white sugar by ¼ cup. I also omitted her additions of ginger and cinnamon and doubled the amount of nutmeg. Too many spices masks the clean, fresh flavor of oats.

In Search of the Perfect Oatmeal Cookie

The initial master recipe used 1 cup of butter to 3½ cups of flour/oats, all white sugar, and no baking powder, just baking soda.

Test	Results
Refrigerate dough for 2 hours	Thicker cookie, but not worth the wait
Add 1 egg white	Stickier cookie
Melt butter, don't cream it	Slightly thinner cookie, somewhat greasier
Add extra egg yolk	Slightly stickier cookie
Reduce white sugar to ¾ cup	Not quite as sweet; shape and texture unchanged
Increase oats to 3 cups	Terrific oatmeal flavor
Use molasses	Bitter, unpleasant flavor
Use all dark brown sugar	Overpowered taste of oatmeal
Add baking powder	Thicker cookie; less chewy
Increase flour to 1½ cups	Sturdier, thicker cookie with great chew

As a final variation, I tried putting ½ cup of the oats through a food processor, creating a do-it-yourself oat flour, but this batch of cookies turned out slightly denser and more refined (although slightly thicker). All in all, I preferred the coarser, cracklier version, without this final variation.

THE BEST CHOCOLATE COOKIE

I have searched for years for the best recipe for a chocolate cookie. Until recently, my favorite recipe came from Malvina Kinard, my kitchen mentor and a native of Birmingham, Alabama. As Malvina would say, "These cookies taste so good that it's like I died and went to heaven." For this cookbook, however, I set out to test a number of recipes from all over the country. The clear winner was from Al Ducci's Italian Pantry in Manchester, Vermont, whose recipe for "Chocolate Chubbies" was even more chocolaty and more heavenly than Malvina's recipe. I like a chocolate cookie to be lightly crisp on the outside

and chewy on the inside. The texture should be somewhere in between cakey and fudgy, moist but not wet, rich but not candylike. The recipe below uses semisweet baking chocolate, melted and combined with the beaten sugar and eggs, as well as chocolate chips, which are blended into the cookie dough.

In testing, I found that a bit more flour than called for in the original recipe gave these cookies a little extra body, which I preferred. I also found, as recommended by John the baker at Al Ducci's, that the secret to these thick, chewy cookies was letting the dough cool in the refrigerator for 2 hours. This recipe uses a tremendous amount of chocolate, which helps to make a very thick dough when chilled. When the dough is used at room temperature, the cookies flatten out readily and are less moist and chewy.

THE BEST CHOCOLATE CHIP COOKIE

Cook's Illustrated once received an article on how to make the best chocolate chip cookie.

The author had written a compelling and detailed account of how she had perfected a master recipe after working through 40 variations. We baked a batch and found that they were good but not great. Two hours after baking, they became crispy, losing the chewiness that I think is essential to a great chocolate chip cookie. The manuscript was sent back, and two months and another 10 variations later, we had her new recipe, which was very good, a real gourmet store cookie. But I still wasn't completely satisfied, though I was somewhat daunted by the difficulties involved. It was clear that developing a chocolate chip cookie is hard work, a little like doing a watercolor in the dark. You never know how it is going to turn out.

REFRIGERATING DOUGH AND THE RIGHT MIX OF EGGS

I started with a few obvious tests. Refrigerating the dough, a trick I use for chocolate and oatmeal cookies, didn't affect the texture much. I varied the eggs, using 2 whole eggs instead of 1 egg plus 1 yolk. The batter was thin and spread quickly when baked, and the interior was still cakelike, a big problem with the master recipe. However, I then tried using 1 whole egg plus 1 egg white, and this made a much better cookie with more chew. I also tried using 2 whole eggs and 1 white, and the batter was much too thin.

COOKIE DOUGH SHOULD BE MIXED BY HAND

Although I had found that mixing oatmeal cookie dough by hand made some difference, I was surprised to find that an electric mixer will turn chocolate chip cookie dough to soup. This dough must be mixed with a wooden spoon. I also decided to cream the butter instead of melting it, and this was a big improvement. The cookies were much chewier. I was surprised by the results when I substituted ¼ cup Crisco for the same amount of butter. This made a puffier,

chewier cookie than the all-butter version. There was still plenty of butter in the recipe, so there was no lack of flavor. I increased the baking soda from ½ to 1 teaspoon, resulting in more lift. I also tested reducing the flour to 2 cups (a reduction of 2 tablespoons), and the cookies were too thin. I then increased the flour to 2½ cups and produced a nice, thick cookie with good texture. I also tried bread flour, which produced a very stiff cookie.

A CONVERSATION WITH A FOOD SCIENTIST

I had now found 3 variations that made a difference. Substituting ¼ cup Crisco for butter gave the cookies a lighter texture; increasing the flour to 2½ cups gave the cookies more body; and using 1 whole egg plus 1 egg white added a bit of chew. But I still wasn't totally satisfied. I wanted more structure to the cookie, more contrast between a crisp exterior and a chewy interior.

I called Shirley Corriher, the *Cook's Illustrated* consulting scientist, and she let me in on one of the secrets of cookie making. She pointed out that if I wanted a thicker cookie, the dough needed to set quickly in the oven. For that to happen, she said, it needed more acidity. Shirley listed a few items that are acidic, including brown sugar and an ingredient in baking powder. Since I already was using 1 cup of brown sugar, I decided to substitute baking powder for baking soda (baking soda is alkaline, whereas baking powder contains both acidic and alkaline ingredients). This produced a great batch of cookies; thick, crispy at the edges, and chewy on the inside. They also kept well, maintaining a good moist chewiness for 2–3 days.

In my testing I also found that good-quality bittersweet or semisweet chunks are preferable to the usual chocolate chips. (One brand is made by Guitard.) I also tested a variety of baking temperatures and found that 350°F is best. Since I had found over the years that 375° is ideal for the standard Toll House recipe, I tried it; but I was disappointed. These are thick, chewy cookies, and the higher temperature overcooks the exterior before the center has time to bake properly.

Master Cookie Recipe

This is American cooking at its best, simple, adaptable, and good for last-minute company. You don't need fancy imported equipment, and anybody can make these cookies. This is a real draft horse of a recipe — over the years, it will pull more than its weight.

    3 cups all-purpose flour
    ½ teaspoon baking soda
    1 teaspoon cream of tartar
    1 teaspoon kosher salt
    1 cup (2 sticks) butter, softened

Cookie-Making Tricks

I use parchment paper to bake cookies on, which reduces the need for lots of cookie sheets, lets the dough spread more evenly, and prevents the bottoms from burning. Place the shaped dough onto a sheet of the parchment, which has been set on a cookie sheet. When the cookies have baked, remove the parchment paper with the cookies still on it to a cooling rack, cover the baking pan with a fresh sheet of parchment, and load on more dough. This also saves on cleanup. I also found in testing that parchment paper makes a better cookie, chewier and with more body.

For thicker cookies, make sure that your dough is chilled properly. (The one exception is chocolate chip cookies, which do not benefit from chilled dough.) I also found that cookie doughs mixed by hand, without an electric mixer, were definitely better. One of the editors at *Cook's Illustrated* discovered this trick at cooking school. Three groups of students were making the same cookie recipe, and one of them used just a wooden spoon for mixing. The manual method won hands down. This result is consistent with my tests with muffins, pancakes, waffles, and the like. The more gently you handle a dough, the better the texture.

Ice cream scoops (these come in many different sizes) are good for scooping dough and placing it on cookie sheets.

    ⅞ cup sugar
    1 egg
    1 egg yolk
    1 teaspoon vanilla extract

1. Sift together the first 4 ingredients onto a sheet of wax paper.

2. Place butter in the bowl of an electric mixer and beat on high speed for 2 minutes or until pale yellow and fluffy. Add the sugar and beat on medium-high speed until mixture is very pale and very light. Do not overbeat (mixture will start to lose volume). Scrape down sides of bowl and add the last three ingredients. Beat for 30 seconds. Add the flour mixture and beat at medium-low speed for about 20 seconds or until mixture forms a rough dough. Scrape down the bowl (and remove dough from beaters) and mix for an additional 5 seconds.

3. Shape cookies as directed below and bake on parchment-lined baking sheets in a 375° oven. To toast nuts for variations, place them on a cookie sheet in a 450° oven for 6–8 minutes. Check after 4 minutes, tossing frequently.

Makes 60 drop cookies or 100 refrigerator cookies

Drop Cookies: Place dough in a bowl, cover with plastic wrap, and let rest in refrigerator for at least 1 hour. Place heaping teaspoons of batter onto a parchment-lined cookie sheet, 2 inches apart. Bake for 8–10 minutes or until lightly browned.

Refrigerator Cookies: Divide the dough into four pieces. Shape each piece into a log 1½ inches in diameter and 8 inches long. Wrap with wax paper or plastic wrap and refrigerate for at least 1 hour (or up to 3 days). Unwrap and cut into ¼-inch-thick cookies with a thin knife. Bake about 9 minutes or until lightly browned. (Note that the yield will vary dramatically, depending on the diameter of the cookies. A 2-inch-wide log, for example, will yield only 45 cookies, compared to over 100 cookies if they are 1½ inches wide.)

Rolled Cookies: Refrigerate dough in a bowl covered with plastic wrap for 1½ hours. On a lightly floured surface, roll dough out until ⅛–¼ inch thick depending on the thickness desired. (This is a very stiff, very short dough and is hard to roll out.) Cut into shapes with a cookie cutter. A ⅛-inch cookie will take 6–7 minutes to bake. (Yield will vary, depending on thickness and on size of cookie shapes.)

Chocolate Variation

Add ½ cup unsweetened cocoa to the dry ingredients and increase sugar by ⅓ cup. You can also add, for extra flavor, 1 tablespoon of very strong coffee (or you can use instant coffee mixed with hot water).

Pecan or Walnut Variation

Add ¼ teaspoon ground allspice and ¼ teaspoon ground nutmeg to the dry ingredients. Add 1 cup of toasted then finely chopped walnuts or pecans to the dough mixture before the last 5 seconds of mixing.

Almond Variation

Add ½ teaspoon almond extract to the butter-sugar mixture along with the eggs. Add 1 cup toasted, finely chopped, slivered almonds to the dough mixture before the last 5 seconds of mixing.

Orange and Lemon Variations

Add ½ teaspoon orange extract and 2 tablespoons grated orange zest with the liquid ingredients. For lemon cookies, use lemon extract and lemon zest.

Spice Variation

Substitute dark brown sugar for the white sugar called for in the recipe. Add ½ teaspoon each ground cinnamon and ground allspice, ¼ teaspoon each ground ginger and ground cloves, and ⅛ teaspoon mace to the dry ingredients.

The Best Chocolate Cookie

These are extra-large cookies; use an ice cream scoop to move the dough from the bowl to the cookie sheet. When they are baked, there will be a very thin crispy outer layer and a rich, fudgy center. These cookies do not hold well and should be eaten within 48 hours.

1 pound semisweet chocolate, coarsely chopped
1 stick plus 2 tablespoons butter
6 large eggs
2 cups sugar
¾ cup all-purpose flour
1 teaspoon baking powder
12 ounces coarsely chopped walnuts or pecans (about 3½ cups)
12 ounces chocolate chips (about 2 cups)

1. Melt chocolate and butter in a saucepan until smooth (I often do this by placing the saucepan in a 250° oven for about 15 minutes), or melt in a glass bowl in a microwave oven at 50 percent power for 3 minutes, stirring after 2 minutes. Whip eggs and sugar together until thick and pale yellow, about 5 minutes on high speed. Using a rubber spatula, combine melted chocolate with egg mixture until well blended. Whisk together the flour and baking powder and then fold into egg-chocolate mixture until fully incorporated. Add nuts and chocolate chips and blend.

2. Cover bowl with plastic wrap and refrigerate dough for 2 hours. Heat oven to 350°F. Cover a baking sheet with parchment paper. Place mounds of dough 3 inches apart using an ice cream scoop. Bake for 18 minutes, turning the pan once halfway through baking. Remove parchment paper with cookies and cool on a cake rack. Repeat with a new sheet of parchment paper until all the dough is baked.

Makes 18 cookies (about 4 inches in diameter)

The Best Oatmeal Cookie

The problem with most oatmeal cookies is that they don't taste like oatmeal and they don't have enough chew to them. By using a full 3 cups of rolled oats and plenty of butter, and no spices other than nutmeg, this recipe has plenty of oat flavor and a crispy exterior with good chew. This recipe is similar to one used by the baker at the Claremont Café in Boston.

 2 sticks butter, softened
 1 cup light brown sugar
 ¾ cup white sugar
 2 eggs
 1½ cups all-purpose flour
 1½ teaspoons kosher salt
 1 teaspoon baking powder
 ¼ teaspoon freshly ground nutmeg
 3 cups rolled oats
 1½ cups raisins, optional

1. Heat oven to 350°F. In the bowl of an electric mixer or by hand, beat the butter until creamy, then add sugars and beat until fluffy, about 3 minutes with an electric mixer. Beat in eggs one at a time.

2. Sift together the flour, salt, baking powder, and nutmeg. Add to the butter mixture and stir to blend with a wooden spoon or large rubber spatula. Stir in oats and optional raisins.

3. Form dough into balls about 2 inches in diameter and place on a baking sheet covered with parchment paper. (The parchment paper is optional.) Bake 15–17 minutes, until the bottom edges turn brown. (The cookies will still be soft and feel a bit undercooked at this point.) If using parchment paper, slide off onto a cooling rack. Otherwise, allow

cookies to cool for 2 minutes on the baking sheet and then remove to the rack. Allow cookies to cool for at least 30 minutes before serving.

Makes about 24 large cookies

The Best Chocolate Chip Cookie

As a true Vermonter might say, this is a "pretty good" cookie. The texture is good — not too cakey — and it also has some chew to it, not as soft as the famous Toll House recipe. The condition of the butter is crucial to success. Too soft, and the dough will not have the proper consistency. It should be just soft enough to beat with a wooden spoon.

 ¼ cup Crisco
 ½ cup unsalted butter, softened but still firm
 1 cup lightly packed dark brown sugar
 ½ cup white sugar
 1 whole egg
 1 egg white
 2 teaspoons vanilla extract
 2½ cups all-purpose flour
 1 teaspoon baking powder
 ¼ teaspoon kosher salt
 10 ounces chocolate chips or chunks (about 1¾ cups)

1. Heat oven to 350°F. Beat the Crisco and butter in a medium bowl with the back of a wooden spoon until pretty smooth but with a few harder pieces still left (about 1 minute). Add the sugars and beat until well blended. Add the egg, egg white, and vanilla and beat until smooth. In a separate bowl, whisk together the flour, baking powder, and salt. Add to the batter and mix together until smooth. Add the chocolate chips and fold in.

2. Line two large cookie sheets with parchment paper. For each cookie, shape 2 tablespoons of dough into a ball with your fingers and place on the paper with 1½ inches between it and the next ball of dough.

3. Bake for about 14 minutes or until tops are well browned.

4. Slide parchment paper onto wire racks to cool. Repeat with remaining dough and fresh sheets of parchment paper.

Makes about 20 large cookies

Nut Variation

Add 1½ cups of roughly chopped pecans or walnuts to the batter along with the chocolate chips.

Molasses Cookies

This recipe was developed by Rosemarie Brophy, the mother of one of the employees at the New England Soup Factory, located in Brookline, Massachusetts, next door to the offices of Cook's Illustrated. *She makes these cookies each Christmas, and they are now a bestseller at the store. These are best when made as large as possible so the interior is plenty chewy.*

  12 tablespoons (1½ sticks) butter, softened
   1 cup sugar
   1 egg
   ¼ cup molasses
  2¼ cups all-purpose flour
   2 teaspoons baking soda
   ¼ teaspoon kosher salt
   ½ teaspoon cloves
   1 teaspoon cinnamon
   1 teaspoon ground ginger
      Extra sugar for dipping

1. Beat the butter and sugar with a wooden spoon until creamy and smooth. Add the egg and molasses and beat until fully incorporated. In a separate bowl, whisk together the remaining ingredients (except sugar for dipping) and then stir into the butter-sugar-molasses mixture. Cover bowl with plastic wrap and refrigerate dough for 1 hour. Heat oven to 350°F. Line two cookie sheets with parchment paper.

2. Shape dough into walnut-size balls (about 1½ inches in diameter). Dip tops in sugar. Place 3 inches apart on lined baking sheet. Sprinkle each ball with 2–3 drops water to create a crinkled surface. Bake for 10–12 minutes. Do not overbake.

Makes 34 cookies

~ 47 ~

The Perfect Brownie

The texture of a brownie can be changed dramatically depending on whether you cream the butter or simply melt it, creating either a light, moist texture or a dense, chewy confection.

~

The one recipe that every home cook from San Diego to Bar Harbor, Maine, has in his or her repertoire, and the one most often submitted in recipe contests, is for brownies. Some taste like little chocolate cakes. Others are nothing more than fudge. Some have nuts, others don't. Some are moist, some gooey, some dry, some chewy.

My objective was to create two quite different recipes: one that was chewy, dense, and fudgy and another that was lighter, with a more subtle flavor and a moist but delicate texture. I began by searching for a chewy brownie.

SOME LIKE THEM CHEWY

My starting point in the quest for a chewy brownie was a hybrid recipe that used 1 stick butter, 2 ounces unsweetened chocolate, ⅔ cup cake flour, 1 cup sugar, 1 teaspoon vanilla extract, 2 eggs, ¼ teaspoon salt, ½ teaspoon baking powder, and ½ cup chopped walnuts. The result was very cakelike, not at all what I had in mind. I then tried refrigerating the batter for 1 hour before baking and the results were not dramatically different; perhaps a bit moister in the center but still a

cakey brownie. Adding 1 egg white to the batter did not help at all, but adding 1 whole egg did seem to produce a moister brownie, although it was not chewier. All-purpose flour instead of cake flour did add a bit of chew to the batter, a definite improvement. Bread flour, however, did not make much difference.

MORE TESTING, NO ANSWERS
I knew that cocoa worked well in chocolate cakes, so I tried it here. The brownies were more granular tasting, as if the sugar had not dissolved properly. An additional square of chocolate did make a fudgier product, but the taste was not as good as the 2-square version — the recipe seemed out of balance. A 300° oven was a disaster — the brownies baked up into a sticky mess. I also tried light brown sugar instead of white sugar, which lent an unpleasant earthy flavor. Adding a bit more flour (I was using all-purpose flour at this point) did not seem to help either.

FANNIE FARMER TO THE RESCUE
I finally made up a batch of Chewy Fudge Brownies from *The Fannie Farmer Baking Book* (Knopf, 1984) and, to my distress, found that they were the best so far! They were rich, moist, and fudgy, but not really

chewy. The secret was a whopping 4 ounces of chocolate (I was using only 2 ounces), ¼ cup more sugar (I was using just 1 cup) to make up for the additional unsweetened chocolate, and melting the butter with the chocolate rather than creaming it with the sugar. There was also no baking powder. I felt that the amount of chocolate needed to be reduced slightly, since the chocolate was overpowering, making the flavor a bit less pleasant. I also thought there was insufficient batter for the 8 x 8-inch baking pan. Perhaps if there were more batter, I thought, I could cook the outside until it was chewier, while the inside remained moist and fudgy. I tried increasing the batter by 50 percent and the brownies took a good hour and a half to bake. They were chewy but also greasy, and the baking time was just too long. I then tried increasing the ingredient quantities by about 25 percent, although I left the chocolate, sugar, and eggs the same, and still found that the brownies were a bit greasy — the butter was actually bubbling in the pan during baking. So I went back one last time and fiddled with the original recipe. I reduced the chocolate from 4 ounces to 3 for better flavor, increased the flour from ½ cup to ¾ cup, increased the nuts from 1 cup to 1¼ cups, increased the salt and vanilla, and then left the butter at 8 tablespoons and the sugar at 1¼ cups. These were excellent. They had a good chew on the top and around the edges, but the inside was still moist and fudgy. I also found that they were even better the next day — they took on a bit more chew overnight.

IN SEARCH OF A MOIST, LIGHT BROWNIE

Brownies are clearly a matter of personal preference — some folks like them gooey and chewy, others like a simpler, lighter version — so I felt obliged to satisfy those in the latter camp. Since I was now asking everyone I knew for their favorite brownie recipe, Mark Bittman, author of *Fish*, suggested the recipe from *The Settlement Cookbook*, which was his personal favorite. He faxed it over, and it was quite good. Light but with great flavor, well balanced and very moist. In this recipe, the butter and sugar need to be creamed before the eggs are beaten in and then the other ingredients added. I made two batches: the first was good, but made thin brownies; the second was much higher, with better texture. It turned out that I had made the second batch with eggs and butter that were close to room temperature, while the first brownies used eggs right out of the refrigerator and butter that was still rather cold.

THE SCIENCE OF CREAMING BUTTER

To understand the difference, I called my food science expert, Shirley Corriher, and she explained the problem. It turns out that to cream butter successfully, it needs to be at just the right temperature. Butter melts between 67° and 68°F, yet the ideal temperature of butter for creaming is 65°F. It needs to be firm yet warm enough to successfully incorporate air. Since the temperature in most refrigerators is between 35° and 40°F, a stick of butter just taken out of the fridge will be too cold. It needs to sit on the counter until the stick is malleable — it should give when pressed — but still firm and unmelted. The amount of time this takes will depend on the starting temperature of the butter and the temperature of your kitchen. I would allow a good hour in a kitchen that is 72°F. Be warned, however, that butter that is too soft will simply melt when beaten and will not incorporate much air. (You can tell this is happening if the mixture appears very slick and shiny.)

Beating butter (the sugar is usually beaten with the butter, although some chefs add the sugar later) aerates it, which makes it light and fluffy. Many home cooks do not beat the butter sufficiently for proper volume. You should allow 4–5 minutes with a heavy-duty mixer and 6–7 minutes when beating by hand or with a less powerful hand-held mixer.

If you did not remember to soften the butter before starting a recipe that calls for creaming butter, cut it into tablespoon-size pieces and place it in the mixing bowl. If your butter started out at 50°F, it will take about 40 minutes to reach 65°F, the proper temperature for creaming. If you want to be precise about it, use an instant-read thermometer and stick it through three or four pieces to get a good reading. Simply leave it there until the dial reads 65°F.

THE PROBLEM OF COLD EGGS

My next problem was cold eggs. As soon as the eggs were added to the creamed butter, the mixture often separated and looked gritty. This same problem was discussed by Stephen Schmidt in an article on pound cake for *Cook's Illustrated*. The problem is that cold eggs added to creamed butter will not incorporate properly — the difference in temperature is simply too great. His solution was to warm up the eggs in a hot-water bath before adding to the creamed butter and sugar. I found that it was easier to simply leave the eggs at room temperature for a couple of hours. As the eggs are added, the butter mixture should be dull, thick, and smooth, not at all shiny or grainy. I also decided to add the hot, melted chocolate directly to the butter-sugar-egg mixture, which also helped bring the batter up to the proper temperature.

OTHER SOLUTIONS TO A COLD BATTER

I have seen professional chefs deal with this problem in other ways. Some will actually put a blowtorch to the side of the bowl (for just a few seconds) to warm up the batter. Others will heat the bowl over a gas stovetop. If the mixing bowl feels cold and the mixture looks grainy, a home cook without the benefit of a handy blowtorch can run the side of the bowl under hot water or run the bowl briefly over a gas flame. Now continue beating at high speed and the batter should take on a dull, smooth appearance.

THE FINAL RECIPE

With the techniques for creaming well in hand, I then reviewed the recipe from *The Settlement Cookbook* and decided to add an extra egg, a technique that seemed to work well in my original testing. These were terrific brownies; great flavor, moist and light, but not crumbly, and with good "mouth feel" — the texture coated the tongue nicely with a very pleasant aftertaste.

So if you like a chewy brownie with a deep, chocolate flavor and a really fudgy center, try the recipe for Chewy, Fudgy Brownies. By melting the butter and using more chocolate, these brownies have chew and goo. If you like a lighter, more delicate brownie, something more appropriate for a "ladies luncheon," try the second recipe, which uses the lift from creamed butter to produce an airier, more refined confection.

Chewy, Fudgy Brownies

The secret to these brownies is that they use more chocolate than most recipes. This gives them more chew when they cool. The butter is simply melted, not creamed with the sugar, which also results in a less cakelike texture. If you like really chewy brownies, bake them 50–55 minutes.

3 ounces unsweetened chocolate
8 tablespoons unsalted butter
2 large eggs
1½ teaspoons vanilla extract
1¼ cups sugar
½ teaspoon kosher salt
¾ cup all-purpose flour
1¼ cups walnuts, in pieces

1. Heat oven to 350°F. Grease an 8-inch-square baking pan.

2. Melt the chocolate and butter together over low heat, stirring frequently. Whisk the eggs and vanilla together in a medium bowl. Add the melted chocolate mixture and whisk to combine (mixture will thicken considerably). Add all other ingredients and mix together with a rubber spatula or wooden spoon.

3. Pour batter into baking pan and level out top. Bake about 45 minutes or until a cake tester comes out clean when inserted into center. Allow to cool at least 2 hours before cutting and serving. (The brownies will continue cooking and become chewier as they cool.)

Makes 16 brownies

Moist, Light Brownies

Unlike the chewy brownie recipe, this one calls for creaming the butter with the sugar, which gives these brownies a lighter texture. With less chocolate (2 squares instead of 3) and less sugar, these brownies also have a more balanced, delicate flavor. The trick with this sort of batter is to make sure that the ingredients are at room temperature. If they are too cold, the batter will become grainy and separate. I leave the eggs for 2 hours at room temperature and the butter for an hour before starting this recipe. You can also try warming the mixing bowl in the preheating oven for just a minute or two until it is warm but not hot. The batter should be dull, thick, and smooth-looking.

Do not try to make these brownies with butter directly from the refrigerator.

8 tablespoons unsalted butter, room temperature
1 cup sugar
3 large eggs, room temperature
2 ounces unsweetened chocolate, melted and hot
1 teaspoon vanilla extract
½ teaspoon kosher salt
½ cup all-purpose flour
1 cup walnuts, coarsely chopped

1. Heat oven to 350°F. Grease an 8-inch-square baking pan.

2. Cream the butter and sugar together in a metal bowl with an electric mixer for 3 minutes on high speed. Scrape down the sides of the bowl every minute. Add the eggs one at a time, scraping down after each addition. Add the hot melted chocolate and continue beating for 1 minute on high speed. If the mixture looks separated or grainy, heat the bowl over a gas flame or run hot water over the bottom. Continue beating until the mixture looks smooth and dull.

3. Add the remaining ingredients and fold in gently with a rubber spatula or a wooden spoon.

4. Pour batter into baking pan and level out top. Bake 30–35 minutes or until a cake tester comes out clean when inserted into center. Allow to cool at least 2 hours before cutting and serving.

Makes 16 brownies

48

Mastering the Soufflé

Oven temperature and the ratio of egg whites to yolks are crucial for a high-rise, moist soufflé.

~

The perfect soufflé has a crusty exterior packed with flavor, a dramatic rise above the rim, an airy but substantial outer layer, and a loose, rich center that is not completely set. More important, a great soufflé has enough fat and substance to convey a mouthful of flavor, bursting with the bright, clear taste of the main ingredient, be it chocolate or carrots, apricots or cranberries. This balancing act between taste and texture is the essence of this relatively simple but impressive dish.

It turns out, however, that the perfect soufflé is elusive. Julia Child once told me that she had to make 20 separate raspberry soufflés trying to get just the right texture and flavor. At the time, that sounded excessive, even compulsive, but I now realize that she was right; soufflés require a delicate balance between fat and foam. After much testing, I determined that there are five basic types of soufflés, distinguished by what is used for the base: a béchamel, a pastry cream, a bouille, a fruit puree, or a vegetable puree.

GETTING STARTED

Soufflés are a combination of a "base" and whipped egg whites. The base provides sub-stance and flavor, and the whites provide lift. The cook can use any one of five bases: a béchamel (a classic French sauce made with equal amounts of butter and flour whisked with milk over heat), a pastry cream (egg yolks beaten with sugar and then heated with milk), a bouille (milk and flour cooked until thickened, to which butter is added), a puree of fruit, or a puree of cooked vegetables. To this base are added egg yolks if none have already been incorporated. The base is cooled briefly and then whipped egg whites are gently folded in. The mixture is placed in a soufflé dish (a baking dish with perfectly straight sides) and then baked in a moderate oven for about half an hour. So far so good.

To determine which bases I preferred, I performed a simple blind taste test using *Cook's Illustrated* staff members as tasters. Using a standardized ratio of 8 egg whites to 4 yolks, we made three chocolate soufflés: one with a béchamel, one with a pastry cream, and one with a bouille. The béchamel came out on top with all tasters, providing the soufflé with good chocolate flavor and a light, airy texture. By contrast, both the pastry cream and bouille versions were too dense and puddinglike for our tasters' palates. In additional taste tests, I discovered that I preferred a simple fruit puree base for fruit soufflés, although a combination of a vegetable puree and a béchamel worked best for vegetable soufflés. I decided to drop the pastry cream and bouille and concentrate further tests on the three remaining bases.

I next went on to determine exactly what consistency of béchamel made the best soufflé. A light béchamel uses 1 tablespoon of butter and 1 tablespoon of flour to 1 cup of milk (the butter is melted, the flour is whisked in to create a roux, and then the milk is whisked in to create a thick sauce), the medium uses 2 tablespoons each of butter and flour, and a thick béchamel uses 3 tablespoons each. I always use a thick béchamel with good results, but I decided to test a medium recipe as well as a superthick béchamel using 5 tablespoons each of butter and flour. The medium béchamel produced a soufflé with substantially less flavor. (A medium béchamel contains less fat than a thick béchamel, and fat contributes flavor.) The superthick béchamel was a test to see if the soufflé would hold its shape longer after baking. (A little extra flour added to a soufflé to prevent a quick collapse is an old French restaurant trick.) The result was uninspiring. It never truly collapsed, reminding me more of a cake than a soufflé. The bad news was that the soufflé had a mediocre rise and a flat, floury taste. The classic thick béchamel was the clear winner.

How Many Whites, How Many Yolks?

Some cookbooks call for 4 yolks and 4 whites, while others tell you to use 8 whites with 4 yolks. It turns out that there is no right answer for all soufflés. To determine the proper proportion for each of my three basic soufflé varieties, I started by making four different variations of the basic béchamel soufflé, always using 4 egg yolks but varying the amount of egg whites from 5 to 8. The clear winner was the 8 egg white to 4 egg yolk version. When only 6 whites were used, for example, the soufflé was custardy and too

eggy-tasting. I then tested soufflés that used pureed vegetables and found that 6 egg whites to 4 egg yolks was best. The versions with more egg whites produced a texture that was too airy, and the crust was on the chewy side. I also tested the pureed fruit–base soufflé. Although it was quite similar to the pureed vegetable recipe, I thought that the amount of sugar might require a different proportion of whites to yolks. In fact, it didn't. The 6-to-4 ratio was also the winner.

What About Oven Temperature?

For most recipes, a 25° variance in oven temperature is not critical. I was therefore surprised to find that such a minor variation dramatically changed the results. My control temperature was 375°F, and I tested both 350° and 400°F as well. The lower temperature produced less flavor, and the interior texture was too even. I was looking for a loose center at the same time that the exterior was nicely cooked. The higher oven temperature resulted in an overcooked exterior and an undercooked interior.

What About a Water Bath?

For certain desserts, a cheesecake, for example, a water bath dramatically improves the final texture. (The baking dish is placed in a roasting pan surrounded by hot water. This moderates the heat around the baking dish, creating a moister, more delicate baked product.) For a soufflé, however, the water bath was a truly awful idea. When tried with all three types of soufflés, the outer crust was wet, with a gelatinlike appearance, and it did not rise well, although the taste was not adversely affected.

RICH CHOCOLATE SOUFFLÉ

After a week of refining my recipe for the chocolate soufflé, I sent it off to our test kitchen for a final check. Our food editor, Pam Anderson, noted that the chocolate flavor was muted by the milk used in the béchamel. (We had noticed this problem over the years in other recipes. Milk dulls the taste of chocolate, as is evident in the difference between milk chocolate and dark chocolate candy bars.) She had recently spoken to Stephen Schmidt, a frequent contributor to *Cook's Illustrated*, who had made an interesting discovery during a cooking class. He was preparing a chocolate truffle cake but forgot the flour, and the resulting dessert was soufflélike with an intense chocolate flavor. Starting with his recipe, Pam removed the flour, separated the eggs, whipping the whites separately, and reduced the amount of butter. The result was excellent—this was the most intense chocolate dessert I had ever tasted. In this version, the soufflé base is made with egg yolks beaten with sugar until thick. This gives the soufflé plenty of volume but eliminates the milk, the ingredient that was holding back the chocolate. I went on to refine this recipe by adding 2 more egg whites to lighten the texture. I have included both the original béchamel chocolate soufflé and this more intense variation in this chapter.

BEATING EGG WHITES

Beating egg whites to the proper consistency is considered both crucial to a good soufflé and extremely demanding in terms of split-second timing. To test this notion, I made three soufflés and used the "raw egg method" to determine how much the whites had been beaten. For the first soufflé, the whites did not hold peaks, and a raw egg in the shell placed on top of them quickly fell to the bottom of the bowl. For the second test, the whites were beaten to soft peaks and the egg sank just a bit, with the top 25 percent or so still showing. The last soufflé was made with whites that were beaten to firm (but still glossy) peaks—the raw egg was completely supported by the whites. The results when the three soufflés were baked were completely unexpected. The underbeaten whites did rise more than those beaten to firm peaks, *but the initial volume was substantially less, and therefore the firm whites resulted in a higher soufflé.* When the first soufflé was poured into the dish, the top of the mixture was 1½ inches below the rim. After baking, the soufflé had risen 2 inches, ending up ½ inch above the rim. The third soufflé, however, started out at just ¼ inch below the rim and then rose to 1¼ inches above the rim after baking. In addition, the firm whites provided a slightly lighter, more ethereal texture; the other two soufflés were a bit wet and soggy. But perhaps the most interesting finding was that *no matter how much you beat the egg whites, you still end up with a good soufflé!*

BAKING TIPS

■ Use a 1½-quart dish for most of the recipes below. A 2-quart baking dish is generally too large; you don't get that nice high rise and creamy, moist center. I tried using a Corning Ware casserole dish for one of the tests, and the soufflé rose right out of the dish into the oven! The problem was that the Corning dish did not have perfectly straight sides. Make sure that you are using a real soufflé dish.

What Is the Best Proportion of Egg Whites to Egg Yolks and What Is the Best Baking Temperature?

Two different types of soufflés were tested, using different proportions of egg whites to egg yolks. A 1½-quart soufflé dish was used for all testing, and the soufflés were baked for 30 minutes in a 375° oven unless otherwise noted. All béchamel-base soufflés were made with a thick béchamel except as noted otherwise.

Method	Ratio of Whites to Yolks	Results
Vegetable and Fruit Puree–Base Soufflés		
Baked at 375°F (the 6 whites, 4 yolks ratio was the winner)	5 whites, 4 yolks	Dark golden exterior with a flavor that resembles bread crust; inside very breadlike and tastes like a light, airy quiche. Barely rose to the top of a 1½-quart soufflé dish. Good flavor.
	6 whites, 4 yolks	Light and airy; slight crusting around top and edges; nice light brown. Best in consistency and texture.
	7 whites, 4 yolks	Rose to 1 inch above rim; nice texture, light and airy. Not quite as good in texture as with 6 egg whites.
	8 whites, 4 yolks	Slightly chewy exterior crust; very fluffy texture; outer crust a little chewy. Required slightly longer cooking time.
Baked at 350°F	6 whites, 4 yolks	Not as light as the version baked at 375°F; the lower temperature adversely affects texture.
Baked at 400°F	6 whites, 4 yolks	Edges were either overcooked or burned; the middle was undercooked.
Baked with water bath	6 whites, 4 yolks	Outside texture of soufflé was wet with a gelatinlike appearance; taste was fine although it looked unappealing. Did not rise well.
Béchamel-Base Soufflés		
Citrus Soufflé		
Baked at 375°F (the 8 whites, 4 yolks ratio was the winner)	6 whites, 4 yolks	A cross between a custard and a soufflé; inside not runny enough. Good flavor.

■ When folding egg whites into the flavored base, the mixture doesn't have to be perfectly homogenous. It's best to leave a few streaks of beaten egg whites in the mixture. Otherwise, the egg whites will deflate and you will lose height during baking. Use a large flexible rubber spatula or, in a pinch, use your hands, which are actually well suited to the task.

■ After the baking dish is filled, run a table knife around the mixture, about 1 inch in from the perimeter. This will give the risen soufflé a nice flat top. (This step is not necessary when preparing individual soufflés.)

■ Be sure to bake soufflés on the middle rack of the oven. On the lowest rack, the bottom of the soufflé will burn. On the top rack, it will rise into the top of the stove or the heating elements.

■ Finally, and most important of all, never overcook a soufflé. It should be very wet in the middle and firm around the outside,

Method	Ratio of Whites to Yolks	Results
	Béchamel-Base Soufflés (cont.)	
Citrus Soufflé (cont.)		
	7 whites, 4 yolks	Much lighter and soufflélike than the 6-whites version. A little too eggy-tasting.
	8 whites, 4 yolks	Light golden on top; rose nicely. Needs to cook an additional 5 minutes. The best ratio for a citrus soufflé.
Baked at 350°F	8 whites, 4 yolks	Soufflé cooked too evenly; middle not loose enough. Flavor not quite as good as 375° version.
Baked at 400°F	8 whites, 4 yolks	Middle undercooked and edges overcooked.
Baked with water bath	8 whites, 4 yolks	Soufflé collapsed quickly after baking. The outside texture was wet and congealed; texture was heavy throughout.
Made with medium béchamel (2 tablespoons flour, 2 tablespoons butter)	8 whites, 4 yolks	Spongier in texture; flavor not as strong. Did not rise as high as the other tests.
Chocolate Soufflé		
Baked at 375°F (the 8 whites, 4 yolks ratio was the winner)	6 whites, 4 yolks	Nice chocolate flavor; subtle orange flavor; tasted like a very light brownie. Did not rise very high; a little too heavy for a soufflé.
	7 whites, 4 yolks	Better than with 6 whites; rose a little higher, but still not light enough.
	8 whites, 4 yolks	Light and airy; good flavor; rose higher, with cracks on the sides. Enough body to give this soufflé both great texture and substance. Clear winner.
Baked at 350°F	8 whites, 4 yolks	Heavier texture, brownielike flavor.
Baked at 400°F	8 whites, 4 yolks	Outside edges overcooked and middle too loose. Bottom spongy and wet.
Baked with water bath	8 whites, 4 yolks	Outside was wet and congealed; did not rise as high as without the water bath. Not recommended.
Made with medium béchamel (2 tablespoons flour, 2 tablespoons butter)	8 whites, 4 yolks	Loss of flavor; orange flavoring in the chocolate did not come through very well.

almost like a pudding cake. The center should not be liquid but still quite loose and very moist. I find that once you can smell a soufflé baking in the oven, it is about ready to come out.

Master Recipe for Dessert Soufflé (Béchamel Base)

To prepare this recipe in individual ramekins, bake 16–18 minutes. When test-baked on the bottom oven rack, this soufflé was a disaster. The

bottom was ruined and the outside was burned. It is best to bake a soufflé on the middle rack (the upper position is often too close to either the top of the oven or the electric coils in an electric oven). I have two methods for determining when a soufflé is properly cooked other than oven time. When a soufflé stops rising or when you can detect the rich aroma of the main flavoring ingredient, it is usually ready to serve.

Butter and sugar for coating dish
3 tablespoons unsalted butter
3 tablespoons flour

1 cup milk
¼ teaspoon kosher salt
8 eggs, separated
1 flavoring recipe (see below)
¼ teaspoon cream of tartar

1. Heat the oven to 375°F. Butter the inside of a 1½-quart soufflé dish and add a few tablespoons of granulated sugar to coat inside of dish evenly. Knock out excess sugar.

2. Melt the 3 tablespoons butter in a medium-size heavy saucepan. Add the flour and whisk for 2 minutes over medium-low heat. Add milk and salt, increase heat to medium, and cook, whisking constantly, until mixture thickens, about 2 minutes (mixture will start to thicken after about 30 seconds). Remove from heat and transfer to a large bowl.

3. Beat 4 egg yolks into the mixture, one at a time. (Reserve the other yolks for another recipe.)

4. Stir the flavoring ingredients (see below) into the yolk mixture.

5. Beat 8 egg whites with the cream of tartar in a separate bowl until soft peaks are formed. Stir about ¼ of the whites into the yolk mixture to lighten it and then fold in the remaining whites as gently as possible, using a rubber spatula.

6. Turn mixture into soufflé dish and bake 25–30 minutes. Do not overbake. The center of the soufflé should be wet and a bit loose. Serve immediately.

Serves 6

Citrus Flavoring

6 tablespoons sugar
1 tablespoon juice (lemon or orange)
2 teaspoons grated zest (lemon or orange)
2 tablespoons citrus liqueur

Chocolate Flavoring

2 ounces unsweetened chocolate
½ cup plus 1 tablespoon sugar

3 tablespoons strong coffee or espresso
½ teaspoon vanilla extract
1 teaspoon grated orange zest

Melt the chocolate in a microwave oven (use 50 percent power for 3 minutes, stirring after 2 minutes), or in a 250° oven (about 12 minutes, stirring every few minutes), or in the top of a double boiler. Stir in remaining ingredients.

Note: This recipe yields a bittersweet soufflé. Try using semisweet chocolate if you prefer sweeter desserts. If you follow the recipe as is, serve with a sweetened whipped cream.

Rich Chocolate Soufflé

To prepare this recipe in individual 8-ounce ramekins, fill each to the top, clean off the rim with a wet paper towel, and bake 16–18 minutes.

Softened butter and sugar for coating dish
8 ounces semisweet chocolate
4 tablespoons butter
1 tablespoon instant coffee or espresso powder
1 tablespoon hot water
⅛ teaspoon salt
½ teaspoon vanilla extract
1 teaspoon grated orange zest
6 egg yolks
⅓ cup sugar
8 egg whites
¼ teaspoon cream of tartar

1. Heat oven to 375°F. Butter the inside of a 2-quart soufflé dish and add a few tablespoons of granulated sugar to coat inside of dish evenly. Knock out excess sugar. Place dish in the refrigerator. Either melt the chocolate in a microwave oven (use 50 percent power for 3 minutes—stir after 2 minutes and add the butter) or chop coarsely and melt with butter over low heat in a heavy-duty saucepan or double boiler. Stir instant coffee into hot water and add along with the salt, vanilla, and orange zest to the melted chocolate mixture.

2. Whisk together yolks and sugar for 3 minutes until mixture becomes pale and yellow. Add to the melted chocolate mixture and fold together until well mixed.

3. Beat the whites with cream of tartar until stiff peaks have been formed and mixture can just hold the weight of a raw egg. The whites should still be glossy. Do not overbeat.

4. Vigorously stir ¼ of the whipped whites into the chocolate mixture to lighten. Gently fold together the remaining whites and chocolate mixture, spoon into soufflé dish, and bake for about 25 minutes or until the outside of the soufflé is set but the interior is still a bit loose and creamy.

Serves 6

Make-Ahead Chocolate Soufflé

This recipe only works with chocolate soufflés, since the chocolate provides a great deal of structure as it cools. This mixture can be frozen and held for up to 2 days.

Follow the directions for Rich Chocolate Soufflé except use individual ramekins (they do not need to be refrigerated) and reduce the amount of sugar to 5 tablespoons. Instead of beating the yolks with the sugar, melt the sugar with 2 tablespoons water and bring to a boil. Slowly add the water-sugar mixture to the egg yolks and beat until mixture triples in volume, about 3 minutes. When whipping the whites, add 2 tablespoons of confectioner's sugar when the whites just start to thicken and continue whipping. Fill individual ramekins to the top and clean off edges with a wet paper towel. Freeze for up to 2 days. Bake in a preheated 425° oven for 16–18 minutes. Do not overbake.

Serves 6

How Can You Tell When a Soufflé Is Done?

I have three tricks. A soufflé is done when you can smell the main flavoring ingredient, when it stops rising, and when only the very center of the top jiggles when gently shaken. Of course, these are all imprecise methods. If you are not sure if your soufflé is done, take two large spoons, pull open the top of the soufflé, and peek inside. If the center is still soupy, *simply put the dish back in the oven!* Although most cookbooks tell you that it will collapse immediately, most soufflés will hold their shape and continue to cook without adverse effects (this works especially well with chocolate soufflés).

Master Recipe for Dessert Soufflé (*Fruit Puree Base*)

Unlike a béchamel-base dessert soufflé, this variety uses only 6 egg whites instead of 8. Note that more sugar is required for this recipe since there is less fat to help carry the flavor.

    Butter and sugar for coating soufflé dish
1 recipe fruit flavoring base (see below)
6 eggs, separated
¼ teaspoon cream of tartar

1. Heat oven to 375°F. Butter the inside of a 1½-quart soufflé dish and add a few tablespoons of granulated sugar to coat the inside of the dish evenly. Knock out excess sugar.

2. Warm pureed fruit flavoring base over low heat in a heavy saucepan. Remove from heat and whisk in 4 yolks, one at a time. (Reserve the other yolks for another use.) Transfer mixture to a large bowl.

3. Beat the egg whites with the cream of tartar in a separate bowl until soft peaks are formed. Stir about ¼ of the whites into the yolk mixture to lighten it and then fold in the remaining whites as gently as possible, using a rubber spatula.

4. Turn mixture into soufflé dish and bake 25–30 minutes. Do not overbake. The center of the soufflé should be wet and a bit loose. Serve immediately.

Serves 6

Apricot Flavoring Base

¾ pound dried apricots
¾ cup water
1 cup sugar

Simmer apricots in water and sugar until apricots are plump. Puree apricots and liquid in a food mill or a food processor, being careful not to overprocess.

Cranberry-Raspberry Flavoring Base

2 cups cranberries, frozen or fresh
1 cup frozen raspberries
1¼ cups sugar
5 small strips orange peel
3 tablespoons water

Cook all ingredients uncovered for 30 minutes or until cranberries start to pop. Remove orange peel. Puree in a food mill or food processor. Do not overprocess.

Master Recipe for Savory Soufflé (*Pureed Vegetable Base*)

This recipe requires fewer egg whites than the dessert master recipe because a savory soufflé should be heartier than the dessert variety. Carrots work especially well in this recipe. Be sure to season the vegetables well with plenty of salt and pepper plus spices and/or herbs if you like additional flavorings.

Butter and flour for coating soufflé dish
1 cup cooked, well-seasoned, pureed vegetable (see below)
2 tablespoons grated Parmesan cheese
3 tablespoons butter
3 tablespoons flour
1 cup milk
½ teaspoon kosher salt
6 eggs, separated
¼ teaspoon cream of tartar

1. Heat the oven to 375°F. Butter and lightly flour the inside of a 1½-quart soufflé dish. Combine cooked vegetable base with cheese and set aside.

2. Melt the 3 tablespoons butter in a medium-size heavy saucepan. Add the flour and whisk for 2 minutes over medium heat. Add milk and salt and cook, whisking constantly, until mixture thickens, not more than 2 minutes (mixture will start to thicken after about 30 seconds). Remove from heat.

3. Beat 4 egg yolks into the flour mixture, one at a time. (Reserve the other yolks for another recipe.) Place all of the whites in a large mixing bowl.

4. Stir vegetable-cheese mixture into the yolk mixture. Let cool for 10 minutes.

5. Beat the egg whites with the cream of tartar until soft peaks are formed. Stir about ¼ of the whites into the yolk mixture to lighten and then fold in the remaining whites as gently as possible, using a rubber spatula.

6. Turn mixture into soufflé dish and bake about 30 minutes. Do not overbake. The center of the soufflé should be wet and a bit loose. Serve immediately.

Serves 6

Carrot Soufflé Base

Boil or steam 8 ounces of carrots. Puree with ½ teaspoon dried oregano or 1 teaspoon fresh, 1 tablespoon of butter, and plenty of salt and freshly ground black pepper to taste. Makes 1 cup of pureed vegetable for the master recipe above.

Spinach Soufflé Base

Steam 1 pound of spinach and purée with 1 tablespoon butter, ⅛ teaspoon ground nutmeg, and plenty of salt and freshly ground black pepper to taste. Makes 1 cup of pureed vegetable for the master recipe above.

49

How to Poach Fruit

The secret to good poached fruit is to go easy on the sugar and use uncommon flavoring ingredients such as peppercorns and bay leaves.

~

In 1983 I was shopping for a home in Connecticut and stumbled across an 1850 colonial that stood empty, the former owner having just passed away. When I first entered the library, I was struck by an odd coincidence. The shelves contained only one book, all the others having been sold at auction. It was in poor shape, a deep yellowish brown, and the cover was badly stained. It was a copy of the 1914 edition of Fannie Farmer's *Boston Cooking School Cookbook*! I took this as a good omen and submitted a successful bid for the house that day.

Over the years, I have consulted that book many times. Although it has proved quite useful, I have found that the amount of sugar called for in most of the dessert recipes is at least ⅓ higher than what most cooks would consider reasonable today. This is especially true when it comes to syrups for poaching. I find that virtually all recipes, especially the classic French versions, are so sweet that the natural flavors of the fruit get lost. Even the "light" syrups are beyond the pale. So when I set out to devise the best recipe for poaching fruit, I focused on sweetness as the first important variable.

HOW SWEET IS SWEET?

In my research I was amazed to find that a heavy poaching syrup often called for 1½ cups sugar to 2 cups liquid! This might be a good formula for doing in your wealthy, diabetic grandmother but would be a culinary disaster. The lightest syrup I found used ½ cup sugar to 2 cups liquid. After much testing, I discovered that ½ cup sugar per 3 cups liquid suited me about right for most recipes, although I sometimes use ½ cup to 2 cups. This ratio has enough sweetness to enhance the flavor of the fruit without masking it. Heavy syrups are dull and not refreshing.

OTHER FLAVORINGS

A few years ago, my wife and I left the kids at home and took off for a weekend in New York City to catch up on theater and city dining. We had lunch on the upper east side at a small French bistro that served poached pears for dessert. The syrup was light and complex, with a hint of spice. I correctly guessed that it was whole peppercorns that made the difference, an ingredient that I now include in many of my poaching syrups (use 20 peppercorns per 3 cups of liquid). Two years later I was having dinner at Grey Kunz's Lespinasse, also in New York, and he served poached plums, using herbs such as mint, bay leaves, and thyme as the main flavoring ingredient. I liked his recipe so much that I have included 1 bay leaf in my master recipe, although you might wish to try out other herbs or spices. Fresh mint is an obvious choice, although a hint of rosemary works with pears and anise works well with orange slices. For a more complex flavor, try toasted cardamom seeds (be warned that cardamom seeds without the pods are hard to find and expensive). Of course liqueurs are an obvious variation — use ¼ cup per 3 cups of liquid.

SELECTING FRUIT AND TESTING POACHING TIMES

Fruit should be very firm and just ripe. Overly ripe fruit will become too soft and unappealing in a hot poaching syrup. Unripe fruit will have little flavor and still be hard after poaching (you can simmer unripe fruit in a poaching syrup to soften texture, but the flavor will be bland).

To test the notion of poaching times, I used just-ripe peaches and poached them in four separate batches: one batch was placed in the simmering liquid and then the pan was immediately removed from the heat; the other batches were simmered for 3 minutes, for 6 minutes, and for a full 10 minutes. The first batch, the one that was immediately removed from the heat, had the firmest texture. However, it also became apparent that there were only small differences between the batches. That is, the fruit poaches and softens considerably even when sitting in a hot liquid off the heat.

I also tested orange slices and found that

they should not be simmered at all. In fact, the syrup should be cooled first and then poured over the slices. Otherwise, the oranges will lose their bright flavor and the texture will suffer.

Master Recipe for Poached Fruit

This recipe yields a very light syrup. If you prefer a sweeter, thicker syrup, use ¾ cup sugar. If you have fresh herbs available, don't be afraid to throw a few sprigs of rosemary, thyme, or mint into the poaching syrup. Rosemary is particularly good with pears.

Basic Poaching Syrup
2 cups water
1 cup white wine
½ cup sugar
1 bay leaf
1 strip (3 inches) orange rind
½ stick cinnamon
1 piece vanilla bean (2 inches), split in half lengthwise, or ¼ teaspoon vanilla extract

Fruit
1 quart (about 3 pounds) peaches, berries, or apricots, or a mixture

1. Combine ingredients for poaching syrup in a large saucepan (large enough to also hold the fruit), bring to a boil, and simmer for 5 minutes.

2. Prepare the fruit (berries should be washed, peaches should be peeled, pitted, and quartered, apricots should be halved and pitted, not peeled). Add fruit to the syrup and remove from heat and cover. Let sit until syrup reaches room temperature.

3. Place fruit with syrup in refrigerator. Serve chilled.

Serves 6

Poached Pear Variation

Peel, core, and halve 3 pounds pears. Omit cinnamon and add 20 crushed black peppercorns and ¼ cup sweet dessert wine.

Poached Plum Variation

Halve and pit 3 pounds plums. Use red wine instead of white wine. Omit cinnamon and add ⅛ teaspoon ground allspice.

Poached Oranges

To peel an orange for this recipe, use a large, very sharp chef's knife. Cut off the top and bottom. Place the orange on its now flat bottom. Cut off the peel in vertical strips, being sure to remove all of the white pith. At this point, you can either cut the orange into rounds or segment the orange, the latter technique yielding pieces without pithy membranes. However, rounds are more attractive for serving. See illustrations on pages 59 and 62.

  4 large seedless oranges
  ¾ cup water
  ¼ cup white wine
  ¼ cup sugar
  1 teaspoon anise seed

1. Juice 1 of the oranges and put ½ cup of the juice in a heavy saucepan. Peel the remaining oranges and slice into thin rounds.

2. Add the water, wine, and sugar to the saucepan with the orange juice and bring to a boil. Add anise and simmer gently for 2

minutes. Let liquid cool for 1 hour. Pour room-temperature liquid over sliced oranges.

3. Refrigerate for at least 1 hour. Serve.

Serves 4

Peaches with Ginger

This recipe requires perfectly ripe peaches, as they are not really poached; the flavoring syrup is cooled before it is added to the fruit. If your peaches are underripe, I suggest pouring the hot syrup over them and then chilling. To peel the peaches, place them in boiling water for 30 seconds and then immerse them in ice water to stop the cooking. The skins will now peel off easily if the peaches are ripe. Crystallized ginger is usually found in bottles in the spice section of supermarkets. This dessert can be served with ice cream, a dense cake, or a cookie such as the Italian biscotti or English shortbread.

  1 lime
  ½ cup sugar
  1 cup water
  1 cup white wine
  ¼ cup diced crystallized ginger
  4 ripe peaches

1. Juice the lime. Combine the sugar, water, wine, and ginger in a saucepan. Bring to a boil, reduce to a simmer, cover, and cook for 7 minutes. Remove from heat and add 1 tablespoon lime juice. Chill for 1 hour.

2. Peel, pit, and slice the peaches, toss with remaining lime juice, and reserve in a nonreactive bowl.

3. Pour syrup over peaches, toss peaches, and refrigerate for 1 hour.

4. Serve slightly chilled but not cold from the refrigerator.

Serves 4

Pears Poached in Sherry with Ginger

Instead of a sweet dessert wine or sherry, you can use a drier, slightly sweet wine such as a Sancerre or Tokay. That being said, any decent white wine will do in a pinch. *The ripeness of the pears is crucial to this recipe. Too hard and the pears will have no flavor. Too soft, and they will be mushy. A good ripe pear will give just a smidge when pressed, but is still firm.*

  1 cup water
  ¼ cup honey
  6 slices (¼ inch thick) peeled fresh ginger
  1 piece (2 inches) cinnamon stick
12 whole cloves
  4 ripe but firm pears
  2 tablespoons lemon juice
  ½ cup sweet dessert wine or dry sherry

1. Combine the first 5 ingredients in a saucepan and bring to a simmer.

2. While the poaching liquid is heating, peel, quarter, core, and stem the pears and place in a bowl and toss with lemon juice.

3. Add the pears and the wine to the poaching liquid and bring liquid back to a simmer. Immediately remove from heat and let pears cool in the liquid. Serve with plenty of poaching syrup.

Serves 4

~ 50 ~

Baked Fruit Desserts

*Cobblers, shortcakes, crisps, betties, and buckles are workhorse
recipes that are simple variations on established themes.*

~

Back in the fifties and sixties in Vermont, fruit desserts were a matter of what grew near the house. There were plenty of wild raspberries in July and blackberries in August — they grew up over the top of the ridge in an old sheep pasture. Crabapples and wild pears were plentiful but used only for jelly or, for some old-timers, homemade wines. I didn't know anyone who grew peaches, plums, or cherries, so we just didn't eat them. Of course, apples were king, the mainstay of any fruit recipe. They kept well in root cellars and were good for pies, cobblers, and cakes, as well as for baking or eating out-of-hand out in the barn or while perched on the metal seat behind a pair of draft horses, mowing a field or pulling a stone sled.

So it wasn't until much later that I became accustomed to the wide variety of baked fruit desserts, from cobblers to crisps, from betties to buckles. It slowly became clear to me, however, that baked fruit desserts are variations on other themes. A shortcake is really just baking powder biscuits with sweetened fruit (the dough recipe is often varied slightly but is in essence the same), a buckle is nothing more than fresh fruit baked with yellow cake batter, and crisps and betties are baked fruit with a simple topping of sweetened oats, nuts, or breadcrumbs.

SHORTCAKES AND COBBLERS

After reviewing a dozen shortcake recipes, it was clear that they all were essentially just biscuits with fruit. Since I had already created my version of the perfect baking powder biscuit, there wasn't that much to test. I did note, however, that some recipes called for adding an egg or egg yolk to the dough. Most recipes also added some sugar. I tested the egg version and found that it was really a matter of taste. The biscuit is a bit more substantial, but I prefer my fluffy buttermilk biscuits as they are. Two tablespoons of sugar picked up the flavor nicely. Some cookbooks suggest that the biscuits be topped with a sugar-nut mixture before baking (an almond topping is the most common variation), and although this is not a pure shortcake, it is an easy embellishment. There are also endless fruit topping variations, and I have included two following my master recipe.

A cobbler is virtually the same thing as a shortcake except that the biscuit dough is placed on top of the fruit and then they are baked together. If you like your fruit very juicy, as I do, you don't need any thickener at all for the fruit (I like extra juice with the fluffy biscuits). If you prefer a slightly less juicy cobbler, use 1 tablespoon of Minute

Tapioca. I did extensive testing with fruit pies and determined that tapioca was much better than flour, cornstarch, or arrowroot for thickening sweetened fruit desserts. The flavor is better, and the resulting mixture is lighter and less glutinous (see Chapter 42 for more information).

CRISPS AND BETTIES

Crisps are baked fruit with a simple topping of streusel, a combination of flour (or oats), sugar, and spices. A betty is the same thing except that the streusel is made of buttered breadcrumbs, some of which are actually tossed with the fruit. Besides using topping variations such as nuts or oats (my master recipe for the crisp includes oats), you can also try various flavoring ingredients such as grated or minced fresh ginger and spices; and I find that a bit of lemon or orange zest, minced not grated, picks up the fruit flavor. The trick with these recipes is to properly judge the amount of sugar. You want to extend and enhance the flavor of the fruit, not bury it. I prefer ½–¾ cup of sugar for 6–8 cups of fruit. This depends, however, on the fruit. Rhubarb will need more sugar, as will tart blueberries or apples. Use only ½ cup if making a crisp that has additional sugar in the streusel topping.

BUCKLES AND FOOLS

What's a buckle? Nothing more than fresh fruit (about half as much as is used in a betty or crisp) mixed with a cake batter and then topped with a streusel. If I have perfectly fresh, full-flavored fruit, I prefer a cobbler, shortcake, betty, or crisp because the fruit stands out better. But a buckle is a nice compromise between a cake and a fruit dessert. However, don't be fooled by the plain sound of this recipe. A blueberry buckle is one of summer's grandest recipes, simple but teeming with juicy berries, moist cake, and a touch of sweet in the topping.

To make a fool, simply cook fruit with sugar and flavorings and then layer it with whipped cream. In extensive testing, I found that a bit of unflavored gelatin added to the fruit halfway through cooking gave the final product more texture. Otherwise, the fruit is very loose. Adding the gelatin directly to the simmering fruit avoids having to sprinkle the gelatin over water to soften and then heating the mixture to dissolve. Many fool recipes call for layering the whipped cream and fruit. I prefer simply to top the fruit with the cream. It's easier, and I like a higher proportion of fruit to fat.

Master Recipe for Shortcake

A shortcake consists of baking powder biscuits served with fresh sweetened fruit and whipped cream. Handle the biscuit dough gently when you are rolling it out for maximum height and tenderness.

Fruit
   4 cups fresh berries (blueberries, strawberries, blackberries, raspberries), hulled and washed
   ¼–⅓ cup superfine sugar
   ½ teaspoon minced lemon zest, optional

Biscuits
   2 cups all-purpose flour
   ½ teaspoon kosher salt
   2 teaspoons baking powder
   ½ teaspoon baking soda
   2 tablespoons sugar
   ½ teaspoon vanilla extract
   4 tablespoons chilled butter
   3 tablespoons chilled vegetable shortening
   ⅔–¾ cup buttermilk

Whipped Cream
   1½ cups heavy cream
   2 tablespoons superfine sugar
   1 teaspoon vanilla extract

1. For the fruit, mix berries, sugar, and optional lemon zest and let stand at room temperature for 45 minutes. Chill. Meanwhile, place the bowl of an electric mixer or any metal bowl in the freezer or refrigerator along with a whisk or beaters from an electric mixer.

2. Heat oven to 425°F for the biscuits. Combine the flour, salt, baking powder, baking soda, sugar, and vanilla extract in the bowl of a food processor. Process for 2 seconds to mix.

3. Add the butter, cut into 1-tablespoon bits, and pulse 7 times for 1 second each. Add shortening and pulse another 6 times or until mixture looks like coarse meal (the flour should take on a slightly yellowish hue from the butter).

4. Place mixture in a large bowl. Using a rubber spatula, fold mixture together while adding buttermilk in a very thin stream. When mixture starts to hold together, press the dough with the side of the spatula to form a rough ball. Note that you may use a little more or less than the ⅔ cup buttermilk called for in this recipe.

5. Turn dough onto a floured surface and roll out very gently to a thickness of ½ inch. Use a biscuit cutter (I use a 2½-inch cutter, and serve 2 biscuits per person) to cut, and then place on an ungreased cookie sheet 1½ inches apart and bake in the preheated oven for about 10 minutes, turning sheet after 5 minutes in oven. Remove from oven.

6. For the whipped cream, whip cream with the sugar and vanilla using chilled bowl and beaters.

7. Serve the fruit with 2 biscuits per person and top with whipped cream. Traditionally, the biscuits are cut in half for serving, but I prefer them whole, as they do not get as soggy from the fruit syrup.

Serves 6

Almond Variation

Add ½ teaspoon almond extract to the dough. Moisten tops of cut biscuit dough with milk and sprinkle a few sliced almonds on each (about ½ cup in all). Top with a sprinkling of sugar, bake as directed, and then serve with fruit.

Blueberry-Peach Variation

Use 2 cups each of blueberries and peeled, sliced peaches in the fruit topping.

Ginger-Peach Variation

Use 4 cups peeled, sliced peaches instead of the berries and mix them with 1 tablespoon of minced crystallized ginger, along with the sugar and optional lemon zest.

Buttermilk Fruit Cobbler

A cobbler is made from sweetened biscuit dough (a similar dough is used for authentic strawberry shortcake) rolled out and placed on top of sweetened fruits. You may use berries, peaches, or nectarines or a combination, although to my mind blueberries are best, since they yield such concentrated flavor and abundant juice. This recipe is unusual since the fruit is first baked for 15–20 minutes without the cobbler topping. I have found this is a better method than topping the fruit immediately, as the dough cooks in about 15 minutes (the average biscuit takes just 10–12 minutes in a hot oven), which leaves you with either undercooked fruit or overcooked dough. This way the fruit is juicy and the dough is still light and tender. Pan size is also critical. I use an 8-inch-square pan for 6 cups of fruit and a 9 x 11 pan for 8 cups.

Fruit Mixture
6–8 cups fruit (berries, peaches, nectarines, or a combination)
     Juice of half a lemon
½–¾ cup sugar, superfine preferred
  ½ teaspoon minced lemon zest
  ½ teaspoon grated fresh ginger
  1 tablespoon Minute Tapioca

Cobbler Dough
  2 cups all-purpose flour
  ½ teaspoon kosher salt
  2 teaspoons baking powder
  ½ teaspoon baking soda

2 tablespoons sugar
3 tablespoons butter, chilled
2 tablespoons vegetable shortening, chilled
¾ cup buttermilk
  Sugar for sprinkling

1. Preheat oven to 350°F. Prepare fruit (wash, peel, hull, core, slice, etc.) and cut into bite-size pieces if necessary. Make sure fruit is well drained. Toss it with lemon juice, sugar, lemon zest, ginger, and tapioca. Pour fruit into a baking pan.

2. In the bowl of a food processor, combine the first 5 ingredients of the cobbler dough and pulse for 2 seconds to mix. Then add the cold butter cut into small pieces. Process in five 1-second bursts. Add shortening and process another 5–7 bursts until flour is slightly yellow in color and the texture of coarse meal.

3. Transfer flour-butter mixture to a large bowl and gradually add the buttermilk, mixing with a rubber spatula. Add only enough buttermilk to make mixture just hold together in a ball. This may be as little as ½ cup. Now form dough into a ball, lightly dust with flour, and place in a plastic bag and refrigerate.

4. Place pan with fruit mixture in oven. When fruit has cooked for 15 minutes, remove dough from refrigerator and roll out until it is slightly smaller than the baking dish. Cut dough into rounds with a biscuit cutter. Remove fruit from oven when it has baked 20 minutes and place dough closely spaced on top of fruit. Sprinkle dough with sugar.

5. Raise oven temperature to 425°F. Return baking pan to oven for an additional 15 minutes or until dough is browned and fruit is bubbly and tender. Allow cobbler to cool for 30 minutes before serving with heavy cream or vanilla ice cream.

Serves 8

Sweet-Milk Variation

In making the dough, substitute regular milk for buttermilk, add 3 teaspoons cream of tartar, and reduce baking powder to 1 teaspoon.

Blueberry Variation

Use 6–8 cups blueberries, adding ¼ teaspoon allspice to fruit mixture. Since blueberries range from very sweet to quite tart, the amount of sugar required will vary.

Strawberry-Rhubarb Variation

Use 3 cups rhubarb and 3 cups strawberries. Substitute 1 teaspoon of orange zest for lemon zest. Add ¼ teaspoon of vanilla extract to the fruit mixture, and use ¾ cup sugar.

Blueberry-Peach Variation

Use 3 cups of blueberries and 3 cups of peaches. Add ¼ teaspoon freshly ground nutmeg, and ½ teaspoon lemon juice.

Peach-Raspberry Variation

Use 4 cups peaches and 2 cups raspberries. Add ¼ teaspoon nutmeg, ¼ teaspoon allspice, and ¼ teaspoon salt. Increase tapioca to 3 tablespoons — raspberries give off a lot of juice during baking.

Ginger-Peach Variation

Replace superfine sugar with ½ cup brown sugar and ¼ cup granulated white sugar. Add 1 tablespoon crystallized ginger diced into small pieces and ¼ teaspoon freshly grated nutmeg. Omit the lemon zest.

Master Recipe for Fruit Crisp

A crisp is a casual cobbler. A simple streusel is tossed over a dish of fruit and baked. This streusel — a combination of oats, flour, sugar, salt, and spices — is made in seconds in the bowl of a food processor.

  Fruit Mixture
  6–8 cups fruit
    Juice of 1 lemon

½ cup sugar, superfine preferred
½ teaspoon minced lemon zest
½ teaspoon grated fresh ginger
1 tablespoon Minute Tapioca, optional

Topping
½ cup all-purpose flour
½ cup rolled oats
¼ cup light brown sugar
1 tablespoon sugar
¼ teaspoon ground cinnamon
¼ teaspoon freshly ground nutmeg
¼ teaspoon kosher salt
4 tablespoons unsalted butter, cut into pieces

1. Preheat oven to 375°F. Prepare fruit (wash, peel, hull, core, slice, etc.) and cut into bite-size pieces if necessary. Make sure fruit is well drained. Toss it with lemon juice, just enough sugar to sweeten, lemon zest, ginger, and tapioca. Pour fruit into a 2-quart baking dish.

2. In the bowl of a food processor, combine the topping ingredients except the butter and pulse for 2 seconds to mix. Add the cold butter and process in ten 1-second bursts or until butter is incorporated.

3. Sprinkle topping over fruit and bake 30–35 minutes or until fruit bubbles.

Serves 8

Fruit Variations

See suggestions for fruit cobbler, above.

Nut Topping Variation

Reduce flour to ¼ cup and substitute ⅔ cup chopped pecans or walnuts for oats.

Master Recipe for Fruit Betty

A betty is much like a crisp but uses buttered breadcrumbs instead of nuts or oats in the topping. Do not use store-bought bread-crumbs, as the betty will taste like warm sand.

To make fresh breadcrumbs, place slices of firm white bread — a chewy country loaf is best — in the bowl of a food processor and pulse until the texture of granola. This dessert does not hold well — it must be served warm. When cold, the breadcrumbs turn soggy and unappealing.

Fruit Mixture
6–8 cups fruit
      Juice of a half lemon
½–¾ cup sugar, superfine preferred
½ teaspoon minced lemon zest
½ teaspoon grated fresh ginger, optional

Topping
2½ cups *fresh* breadcrumbs, lightly packed (see recipe introduction)
6 tablespoons unsalted butter, melted
¼ teaspoon kosher salt
3 tablespoons sugar

1. Heat oven to 375°F. Prepare fruit (wash, peel, hull, core, slice, etc.) and cut into bite-size pieces if necessary. Make sure fruit is well drained. Toss it with lemon juice, just enough sugar to sweeten, lemon zest, and ginger.

2. Mix together topping ingredients and mix ½ cup topping with the fruit.

3. Place 1 cup of topping in the bottom of a 2-quart glass baking dish. Pour in the fruit. Top with remaining 1 cup topping. Cover pan with aluminum foil and bake for 25 minutes. Remove foil and bake another 15 minutes or until breadcrumbs are brown and the fruit bubbles. Serve warm.

Serves 8

Master Recipe for Fruit Buckle

This is really a simple cake with fruit added and a crumb topping. In a taste test of five cobblers, a betty, a crisp, and a blueberry buckle, the buckle won a surprising first place from our neighbors. The combination of cake, topping, and fruit makes this recipe a winner. Blueberries are the fruit of choice.

3 cups fruit (blueberries, raspberries, blackberries, or peaches)
2 tablespoons all-purpose flour

Cake Batter
   1 cup all-purpose flour
   1½ teaspoons baking powder
   ¼ teaspoon kosher salt
   10 tablespoons unsalted butter, softened
   ½ cup sugar
   1 teaspoon vanilla extract
   3 large eggs
   1 egg white
   ½ teaspoon minced lemon zest

Topping
   4 tablespoons unsalted butter, in small
      pieces
   ¼ cup lightly packed light brown sugar
   2 tablespoons sugar
   ¼ cup pecans or walnuts, toasted
   2 tablespoons all-purpose flour
   ¼ teaspoon ground cinnamon
   ¼ teaspoon freshly grated nutmeg
   ½ teaspoon minced orange zest

1. Heat oven to 375°F. Prepare fruit
(wash, peel, hull, core, etc.) and cut into bite-
size pieces if necessary. Make sure fruit is
well drained. Toss it with 2 tablespoons of
flour. Butter an 8-inch-square baking dish.
Whisk together the 1 cup flour, baking powder, and salt in a small bowl.

2. Whip the butter, sugar, and vanilla on
high speed in an electric mixer until light,
3–4 minutes. Beat in the eggs, one egg at a
time, and the egg white until incorporated.
Add lemon zest. Gently mix flour mixture
into the batter and fold in fruit. Pour into
prepared dish and spread evenly.

3. Place all ingredients for topping in the
workbowl of a food processor. Pulse until
mixture is coarsely combined. Scatter over
cake batter.

4. Bake 45–55 minutes or until cake is set
in the middle. Cool on a wire rack. Serve
warm with heavy cream (whipped or liquid)
or ice cream.

Serves 8

Master Recipe for Fruit Fool

*A fool is cooked fruit layered or folded together
with whipped cream. After testing many different
recipes, I found it best to add a teaspoon of
gelatin to the hot berries in order to thicken them
slightly when they cooled. Otherwise, the mixture is a bit too loose. I prefer not to layer the
fruit with whipped cream. It is easier and I think
more appealing to simply top the fruit with the
cream. The rhubarb version of this recipe is out-
standing. It makes a tart and refreshing dessert.*

Fruit Mixture
   4 cups berries or rhubarb cut into 1-inch
      lengths
   ½ cup unfiltered apple juice
   ½ cup sugar
   ½ teaspoon vanilla extract
   1 teaspoon unflavored gelatin
   ½ teaspoon minced lemon zest

Whipped Cream
   1 cup heavy cream
   2 tablespoons superfine sugar
   ¼ teaspoon vanilla extract

1. Combine berries or rhubarb with apple
juice, sugar, and vanilla in a saucepan and
bring to a boil. Simmer for 5 minutes, stirring
occasionally. Sprinkle the gelatin over the fruit
and cook another 5 minutes. Mash about ⅓ of
the berries or rhubarb into the syrup. Remove
from heat, add lemon zest, and chill.

2. Chill bowl and beaters of an electric
mixer in the freezer for at least 10 minutes.
Place heavy cream in the chilled bowl. Beat
with chilled beaters until cream just starts to
take shape. Add sugar and vanilla and beat
until stiff.

3. Place chilled fruit into goblets or large
wineglasses. Top with whipped cream. Chill.

Serves 6

Orange Variation

Substitute orange extract for vanilla in both
the fruit and the whipped cream and use orange zest instead of lemon zest.

Yogurt Variation

Use plain yogurt (you can also try flavored yogurts, although I prefer the simple, somewhat tart flavor of plain yogurt) in place of the whipped cream and sweeten with superfine sugar to taste.

Master Recipe for Baked Apples

A good baked apple has everything to do with the apple and little to do with anything else. My favorite baking apple is Macoun, followed by Northern Spy. Don't even think about making this recipe with McIntosh, Red Delicious, or Granny Smith apples — these varieties are not well suited to baking. I tested baking apples both covered and uncovered and find it best to cover them. They are juicier and plumper.

⅓ cup sugar
½ teaspoon ground cinnamon
¼ teaspoon freshly grated nutmeg
1½ cups apple cider or unfiltered apple juice
¼ teaspoon vanilla extract
½ teaspoon minced lemon zest
4 apples such as Northern Spy, Macoun, or Cortland, washed and dried

1. Heat oven to 350°F. Mix together the sugar, cinnamon, and nutmeg. Mix together the cider, vanilla, and lemon zest. Core apples *without cutting through the bottom,* using either an apple corer or a melon baller. Peel top of apple, leaving a 1-inch-wide band. Place apples in a baking dish and fill cores with sugar mixture. Pour cider mixture into baking dish. Cover dish with aluminum foil.

2. Bake apples for 30 minutes, basting with cider once or twice. Pierce the largest apple with a small paring knife to see if it is tender. Continue baking until done (baking time can vary a great deal depending on the type and size of apple, from 40 to 60 minutes). Serve warm.

Serves 4

Walnut-Raisin Variation

Toss sugar-spice mixture with ¼ cup each of chopped walnuts and raisins and use to fill apples.

Index

~

rib steak, 236
Ricard, Michel, 222
rice, 138–48
  with Aromatic Spices, 145
  Baked, 142
  basmati, 140, 142; Almond Salad,
    129; Black-Eyed Peas with
    Spices and, 151–52
  and Beans, 152
  Brown, Master Recipe for,
    144–45
  with Chives and Sesame Oil, 145
  "converted," 139
  cooking methods for, 140–42
  determinant of stickiness in, 139
  facts about, 138–39
  with Hot Pepper, 145
  Lentil Salad with Balsamic Vine-
    gar, 155–56
  and Lentils with Smothered
    Onions, 147
  long-grain vs. short-grain, 139
  Long-Grain White, Master Recipe
    for, 142
  newer varieties of, 140
  with Parmesan, 145
  Persian, with Grated Carrots, 148
  pilaf: cooking in microwave, 52;
    Master Recipe for, 143–44;
    Oriental, 144
  reheating in microwave, 48, 52
  Rice Cooker, Master Recipe for,
    142
  rinsing, 142
  risotto, 52–53; Master Recipe for,
    144
  in salads, 125
  Short-Grain White, Master Recipe
    for, 143
  Skillet, Master Recipe for, 142
  with Spinach and Onion, 145–46
  Stir-Fried, with Crispy Peanuts,
    Ginger, and Orange, 146
  Stuffing with Apples, Apricots,
    and Toasted Walnuts, 146
  thickening sauces with, 283
  with Toasted Cumin, 145
  with Toasted Nuts, 145
  white vs. brown, 139
  see also wild rice
rice cookers, electric, 33, 34, 34–35,
    142–43
  makers and models, 35
  Master Recipe for, 142
  "right" amount of water for,
    142
  steaming vegetables in, 35
rice pudding:
  with Cinnamon and Nutmeg, 148
  with Rose Water, Pistachios, and
    Cardamom, 148
  Souffléed, 147
  Stovetop, Master Recipe for,
    147–48
rice starch, 371
rice wine vinegar, 114, 115, 116

ricotta:
  Spinach Filling for Ravioli, 175
  Tomato Sauce with Nutmeg, 169
risotto, 52–53
  Master Recipe for, 144
Rival, 19, 21, 22, 26, 28, 29, 32, 35
roast(ed), roasting:
  beef, see beef, roast
  Beets, 78
  Carrots, 105
  Charcoal-, Potatoes, 95–96
  chicken, 212–21; see also chicken,
    roast
  Corn Relish, 85–86
  Eggplant, 87; Caviar, 87; Sand-
    wiches with Onions and Toma-
    toes, 87
  fish, 197; Whole, with Hot and
    Sour Sauce, 197–98
  garlic, 193; recipe for, 105–6
  Gingered Beets with Orange, 78
  Leg of Lamb, 260
  meat, 252–60; see also meat,
    roasting
  New Potatoes with Rosemary and
    Garlic, 106
  Onion Stuffing, 230
  pork, 257, 258; best cuts for, 247;
    Loin with Cumin, Chili, and
    Cinnamon, 259–60; Slow-
    Cooked, 259
  Red Pepper and Garlic Sauce,
    287–88
  root vegetables, 98; recipe for,
    105
  turkey, 225–28; see also turkey,
    roast
  tying methods for, 248–49
  vegetables, 104–6
roasting pans, 38
roasting racks, 38, 39, 220
rockfish, 191
Rockwell scale, 14
Rolled Cookies, 396
rolling pins, 41
  using, 364, 365
rolls, see dinner rolls
romaine, 124
  Braised, with Garlic and White
    Wine, 269
  Grilled, with Garlic Vinaigrette,
    305
Ronzoni, 172
root vegetables:
  roasted, 74, 98, 104–6; recipe for,
    105
  Steamed, Puree of, 100
  in vegetable soups, 134
  see also specific vegetables
Roquefort, 125
rosemary:
  Beans with Olive Oil, Bacon and,
    153
  dried, mincing or pulverizing,
    153–54
  Dumplings, Lamb Stew with, 275

flavoring oil with, 303
  Grilled Chicken, 301–2
  New Potatoes with Garlic and,
    106
  Roasted Potato Fans with, 94–95
  Swordfish with Capers, Grilled,
    303–4
Rose Water, Rice Pudding with Pis-
  tachio, Cardamom and, 148
round (beef), 235, 238, 238, 239,
    240
  aging, 234–35
  eye, 238, 239, 241
  roasts, 238, 239, 241; braising,
    261–62, 264, 268; roasting,
    254, 255–57
  as stew meat, 270, 271, 272
Round Dinner Rolls, 345, 345
roux, 282, 283
rubs, see barbecue rubs
rump roast (beef), 241, 293
rump roast (pork), 246
rustic country loaf, 329–35
  finding secret to great chew in,
    329–30
  Food Processor Variation, 334
  four types of, 329
  getting great crust on, 332–33
  Hand-Kneaded Variation, 334–35
  high-protein vs. all-purpose flour
    in, 330–31
  kneading and handling dough for,
    330, 331, 331–32
  mixture of flours in, 330
  oven temperature and baking time
    for, 333
  recipe for, 333–35
  salt and honey in, 332
rutabagas, peeling, 59

Sabatier, 15, 17
saddle (lamb), 243
sage:
  Apple Stuffing, 230
  Braised Veal Shanks with Lemon
    Zest, Olives and, 267–68
  and Squash Filling for Ravioli,
    175–76
sago starch, 371
salad dressings, 113–22
  All-Purpose Vegetable, 120–21
  best ratios for, 115–16, 119
  Creamy Avocado, with Tofu,
    121–22
  dressing salad with, 124
  flavored oils or vinegars in, 115,
    117
  Ginger-Carrot, 121
  lite, 117; recipe for, 119
  making emulsion for, 115,
    116–17
  Master Recipe for Vinaigrette,
    118–19
  Olive Vinaigrette, 122
  other ingredients for, 117
  science of, 116